D0421395

WATER POWER
IN SCOTLAND
1550-1870

PROPERTY OF
CURRIE
DISTRICT
HISTORY
SOCIETY

WATER POWER
IN SCOTLAND
1550-1870

JOHN SHAW

National Museum of Antiquities
of Scotland

JOHN DONALD PUBLISHERS LTD
EDINBURGH

© John Shaw 1984

All rights reserved. No part of this publication may be reproduced in any form or by any means without the prior permission of the publishers, John Donald Publishers Ltd., 138 St Stephen Street, Edinburgh, Scotland.

ISBN 0 85976 072 3

Exclusive distribution in the United States of America and Canada by Humanities Press Inc., Atlantic Highlands, NJ 07716, USA.

The publisher acknowledges the financial assistance of the Scottish Arts Council in the publication of this volume.

Phototypeset by Burns & Harris Limited, Dundee.
Printed in Great Britain by Bell & Bain Ltd., Glasgow.

Acknowledgements

Were I to thank individually all those who, in one way or another, have helped in the writing of this book, the list would run to several pages. In the interests of brevity I must offer them merely a general thanks.

However, there are those whose perseverance deserves particular mention. At the Department of Geography, University of Edinburgh, I would like to thank Dr Ian Adams who, from as far away as Oregon, acted as supervisor for the PhD on which this book is based, Dr Ian Morrison, who took over during Dr Adams' absence, and my fellow historical geographers during that period for their advice and encouragement. My thanks also go to the staffs of the Technology Department, Glasgow Museums, and the Country Life Section, National Museum of Antiquities of Scotland, for their indulgence in allowing me to continue work on the thesis and the book.

Special commendations for patience must go to the staffs of the Scottish Record Office and the National Library Map Room, and to my mother, Eileen Shaw, who typed the original 900-page draft. Lastly, I must record my thanks to Liz Lambie, Cate Brown and Pam Swan for keeping my mind on and, where necessary, taking my mind off the subject of mills over the last ten years.

John Shaw.

Abbreviations

AAC	Ayrshire Collections/Ayrshire Archaeological Collections
AgHR	Agricultural History Review
AHS	Abertay Historical Society
APS	Acts of the Parliaments of Scotland
BOEC	Book of the Old Edinburgh Club
EcHR	Economic History Review
IA	Industrial Archaeology
IRA	Inquisitionum ad Cappellam Domini Regis Retornatum Abreviato
NLS	National Library of Scotland
NSA	New Statistical Account
OS	Ordnance Survey
OSA	(Old) Statistical Account
OSP	Old Court of Session Papers, Signet Library
PP	Parliamentary Papers
PSAS	Proceedings of the Society of Antiquaries of Scotland
RCAHMS	Royal Commission on the Ancient & Historical Monuments of Scotland
RMSRS	Registrum Magni Sigilli Regnum Scotorum (Register of the Great Seal)
RSSRS	Registrum Secreti Sigilli Regnum Scotorum (Register of the Privy Seal)
SBRS	Scottish Burgh Record Society
SGM	Scottish Geographical Magazine
SHR	Scottish Historical Review
SHS	Scottish History Society Publications
SPAB	Society for the Preservation of Ancient Buildings
SRO	Scottish Record Office
SRS	Scottish Record Society
SSIA	Scottish Society for Industrial Archaeology
TELA & FNS	Transactions of the East Lothian Antiquarian & Field Naturalist Society
TGAS	Transactions of the Glasgow Archaeological Society
THAS	Transactions of the Hawick Archaeological Society
TH & AS	Transactions/Prize Essays of the Highland and Agricultural Society

Contents

Introduction

The use of water power in grain milling, and its contribution to the early stages of the Industrial Revolution, particularly in textile manufacture and iron-working, are widely acknowledged. However, a view of the Industrial Revolution as a relatively late, primarily urban phenomenon, has tended to overstress the importance of steam power while minimising, or even writing off, that of water power. Musson, among others, has emphasised the need to redress the balance, but has had to base his case on mostly English data. In Scotland, where the case for revision might be expected to be even stronger, little work has been carried out beyond local or thematic studies by Jespersen, Turner, Butt, Hume and Donnachie.

The aim of this work is to establish the spatial and chronological development of the water mill in Scotland and to relate this to innovations in technology, impact on the landscape, the rise of steam power and the overall evolution of the Scottish economy. The period covered extends from 1550 to 1870; particular attention is given to the century 1730-1830, when the use of water power was at its height.

In an exploratory work of this nature, covering so broad a subject over so long a period, the space available does not allow each application to be covered in great depth. Nevertheless, by examining the utilisation of water power industry by industry, it can be determined how many mills of each type were being used where, when and by whom. The pattern which emerges confirms, and emphasises further, the crucial role of water power in grain-processing industries and in wool, linen and cotton textile manufacture, besides indicating just how much the early stages of the Industrial Revolution owed to the utilisation of water power. Furthermore, it lends support to the view that, in Scotland, water power was of greater significance *vis-a-vis* steam power, for longer and in a wider range of industries, than some earlier inter-pretations of power in the Industrial Revolution, based largely on English evidence, would suggest.

1

On Water Wheels

Before considering the processes to which the power of water was applied, something should be said of the means whereby it was harnessed. The most significant point to be considered concerns the dichotomy between horizontal and vertical types of mill, both of which occurred in Scotland.

Mills with horizontal wheels

Water mills having horizontal water wheels, set on the same vertical shaft as the millstones themselves, are known to have had a very wide distribution. A Greek epigram, written in the 1st century BC by Antipater, is generally accepted as being the first reference to such a mill, and Asia Minor as the area in which it was first used.[1] In a northern European context there is archaeological evidence for its early use in Denmark and Ireland. At Bolle, North Jutland, excavations by Axel Steensberg revealed what appeared to be a horizontal water mill and dam of the 1st century BC,[2] though not all scholars accept this dating. More widespread archaeological investigation may confirm a far wider, possibly earlier distribution than a reliance solely on documentary sources would have indicated.

In Ireland the evidence is both archaeological and documentary. In 1956 E. M. Fahy produced a summary of excavations.[3] The extensive use of oak timbering in the watercourses of mills suggests dates prior to the climatic deterioration of 1200-1300 AD. Here the skills of radio-carbon dating and pollen analysis could be usefully combined. Dendrochronology has been used to date at least one Irish mill to the 8th century.[4]

The written evidence has been examined by A. T. Lucas and others.[5] Various manuscript sources — the Brehan Laws, the Annals of the Four Masters, the Annals of Ulster, the Annals of Tigherneach and an 11th-century poem by Cuan O'Lochain — suggest possible dates for Irish horizontal mills as far back as the 3rd century AD.

The problem of how horizontal water mills came to be used in Asia Minor, in Denmark and in Ireland, at such an early date, is one which still awaits a solution.

Turning to more recent times, there is an ever growing record of their past and current use over a very wide area, from China to Portugal and from North

Africa to Finland.[6] With so much information coming to light, there is a need to draw together these diverse publications, notwithstanding problems of language. Were such a difficult task to be completed, there would surely be evidence enough in terms of dating, technological details, socio-economic and topographic contexts for affinities, if not lines of diffusion, to be identified. Such an enquiry lies well outwith the scope of this work, and we must now turn to the horizontal mill in Scotland.

The early evidence for horizontal mills in Ireland has been referred to already. Similar mills are known to have been common on the Isle of Man,[7] but with the exception of one unsubstantiated site in Cumbria,[8] the only evidence of their use in Great Britain comes from Scotland.

Cuan O'Lochlain's 11th-century poem (page 1) relates how a 3rd-century King, Cormac Mac Art, brought a millwright from across the sea to set up a mill on the stream of Nith, near Tara, so that a beautiful slave girl might be saved the trouble of grinding corn in a quern. Some writers have taken the country across the sea to mean Scotland.[9] Be that as it may, we have very little archaeological evidence to support such an assertion. A piece of oak, found in a bog at Dalswinton, Dumfriesshire, has been identified as a vane from a horizontal mill, and its curved shape has affinities with vanes excavated in Ireland, but as yet no date has been ascribed to it.[10] On other occasions it has been suggested that socket stones, mostly from Highland counties, may have been used as bearings for the spindles of horizontal mills. Here, too, further clarification is needed, in this case through examination of wear marks to eliminate other possible uses.

By way of contrast, the Northern and Western Isles, and the North-West mainland, offer irrefutable documentary and material evidence (Figure 1). Goudie[11] summarises published accounts of Shetland mills. The earliest (Low, 1774) describes the mill as follows:

> It consists of a very simple set of machinery; a small horizontal wheel for the water to play on, the top of its axis runs thro' the lower and supports the upper stone as in other water mills; a hopper and shoe with a lever to level the upper stone, completes the apparatus.[12]

Low's account is accompanied by a diagram which, for all its inaccuracies, shows flat water wheel vanes, a feature referred to again and again by later writers, and corroborated by evidence from surviving mills in the field. Flat vanes are also found in Faroese and Norwegian mills, a feature which sets them apart from the curved vane tradition of Irish mills which has, in turn, affinities with the horizontal mills of Iberia. The validity of this distinction will be discussed further at a later stage.

Much has been made of the Norse connection, to the extent of applying the term 'Norse Mill' to horizontal mills in Shetland. Perhaps the strongest argument in its favour comes from the terminology of Shetland mills, noted by Goudie and analysed more recently by Fenton. Goudie pointed to the close similarity in Shetlandic and Norwegian terms as evidence of a common origin:

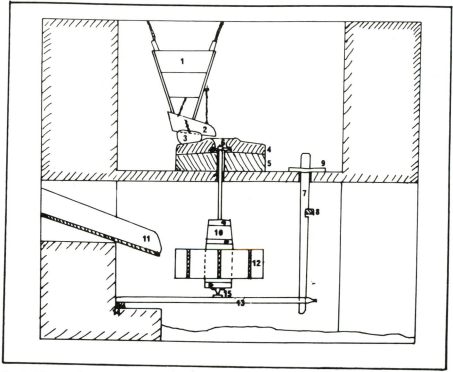

Fig 1. The machinery of a Shetland horizontal mill. 1: hopper. 2: shoe. 3: clapper. 4: upper stone. 5: nether stone. 6: sile (rind). 7: lightening tree. 8: cross tree. 9: sword. 10: tirl. 11: trough. 12: feathers. 13: sole tree. 14: bolster head. 15: ground sile. After *Goudie*

    . . . if not introduced into Shetland direct from Norway, it was in existence in both countries at an early period when one language was common to both.[13]

Recently, however, Fenton has established that 'the terminology shows links with Scandinavia only in relation to those parts that are the same as in hand-mills'.[14] In other words, terminology alone cannot be advanced as evidence of a common, localised ancestry.

During a visit to Shetland in 1814 Sir Walter Scott estimated the number of horizontal mills as 500.[15] Although this can only have been a guess, it tallies well with the 500 or so mills marked on the first Edition 6″/mile Ordnance Survey maps, surveyed in 1878 (Figure 2). As many as nine mills might occupy one short water course.[16] Prior to Scott's time, we have no estimates. Fenton states that 'in the late eighteenth and nineteenth centuries, horizontal mills *became* (my italics) very common in Shetland' and, drawing on evidence from the Faroes, suggests that they 'may not have been so common before the eighteenth century'.[17] A few complete mills, mostly restorations, can be seen to this day.

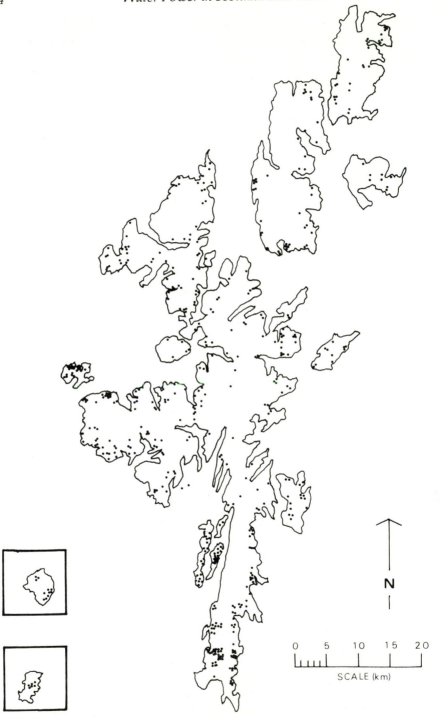

Fig 2. Horizontal mill sites in Shetland, 1878. *Ordnance Survey, First Edition, 6 inches/mile*

From Orkney we have no indication of their ever having been common. J. Storer Clouston[18] indicates that, in Orkney, mills, presumably of the vertical type, 'enjoyed a monopoly practically equivalent to the feudal "sucken"', to which he ascribes a Danish origin.[19] Under such circumstances the scope for horizontal mills would be limited, to say the least. The Old Statistical Account for Orphir parish refers to two mills, 'which go under the name of Dub-mills. These are of no use in the summer season'.[20] It is tempting to see this as a reference to horizontal mills, but the reference is tantalisingly inconclusive. Clouston sees evidence for horizontal mills in a 15th-century dispute over water rights on the Burn of Corrigall in Harray.[21] Elsewhere he notes that a horizontal mill had been built at Skelbister, Orphir in the early 1800s and another, at Jenadane in the Harray hills, had worked within living memory. In the hillside district of Birsay two horizontal mills had worked 'not so very long ago'; one of these, dating from the 19th century, was repaired by the Orkney Archaeological Society and offered to the then Office of Works in 1932. Since that time it has been a Guardianship Monument.[22]

Besides the restrictions imposed by law, other reasons can be found for the scarcity of horizontal mills in Orkney. Its gentle rolling landscape, with few streams, was ill-suited to horizontal mills which fared best on small, steeply falling watercourses. Likewise the topography of Orkney fitted it well, from at least the Middle Ages, for cereal production. Clouston, among others, has made a convincing case for the number of mills being far too small to meet requirements, had they been of the horizontal type.[23]

Outwith the Northern Isles, the only other known concentration of horizontal mills was in the Hebrides and notably in Lewis. Martin Martin (1695) states that the number of mills was then on the increase.[24] The first Ordnance Survey maps (Lewis, surveyed 1849-53, Harris 1871-76) show about 150 mills (Figure 3). By the end of the 19th century only a very few were still in working order.[25]

In most respects the Lewis mills were similar to those of Shetland, though early photographs and surviving remains today show differences in building construction. Shetland mills were gable-ended and stone-built throughout, whereas those in Lewis were hip-roofed with low stone walls, topped by courses of turf.[26] Goudie mentions horizontal mills in Taransay and Mull, where they were known as *blackmills*.[27] MacCulloch's early 19th-century account is especially interesting, for whereas later writers describe the wheel vanes as flat boards (as in Shetland mills), he speaks of them as 'sixteen or eighteen rude sticks, scooped at their outer end like a spoon'.[28] This ties in the Lewis mills with those in Ireland and suggests that a similar, if not quite so late, changeover from scooped to flat vanes may have taken place in Shetland. What better construction material than sawn deals from Norwegian saw mills? Were this the case, then the argument for a common and independent Shetland/Norway mill type would be weakened further.[29]

MacCulloch's description is of interest on another count, for instead of speaking of a 'clickmill', 'Norse mill' or even 'Lewis mill', he uses the term

Fig 3. Horizontal mill sites in Lewis, 1849-53. *Ordnance Survey, First Edition, 6 inches/mile*

'Highland Mill'. Paradoxically, the Statistical Account for North Yell and Fetlar, Shetland also speaks of horizontal mills as being 'on the same construction as the mills used formerly in the Highlands of Scotland'.[30]

If we turn to the Highlands of mainland Scotland, what evidence of horizontal mills do we find? In Reay, Caithness and Sutherland, in 1793, each half of the parish had 'a highland mill, having but one horizontal wheel immediately under the mill stones'.[31]

In his researches Gilbert Goudie came across a Mr. Alexander Mackay who

Fig 4. Place names in *mhuilinn* on the Scottish mainland. *Ordnance Survey, First Edition, 6 inches/mile*

remembered from his youth a working 'Highland mill' at Kirkomy, near Swordby, Farr, Sutherland. This mill also had curved vanes, and was noticed, with another at Kinlochbervie, by Dr. Arthur Mitchell in 1864.[32] However, there is no reason to assume that the mills referred to by William Young, factor to the Sutherland estate, were horizontal mills, as has been implied recently.[33] At the far end of the Western Highlands, in Kintyre, a horizontal mill was

discovered at Balmavicar township in 1965.[34] The township had been un-
inhabited since at least the late 1770s, and little survived of the mill above
stone floor level.

Throughout the Western Highlands *mhuilinn* (Gaelic, mill) appears widely
as a topographical term on the first Ordnance Survey maps, often in localities
devoid of settlement (Figure 4). Were more fieldwork to be carried out, as is
now being done by the Highland Folk Museum, many more horizontal mill
sites might come to light.

In the Central Highlands evidence remains thin. Following the analogy of
the term used in Mull (blackmill, Gaelic — mhuilinn dubh), the 'Black Mill of
Clocheran' which appears in a 1687 rental of Lochtayside, but not in later
ones, could be interpreted as a horizontal mill, but more conclusive evidence is
required.[35]

Surprisingly, some of the strongest evidence for horizontal mills in the
Highlands comes from that part furthest removed from the north-west, the
Grampian glens of Angus and Aberdeenshire. A legend relating to Glen-
quoich, Deeside, and quoted by Dick Lauder, centres on a horizontal mill,
though its being managed by a lowlander seems somewhat anachronistic.[36] We
come closer to our prey in the New Statistical Account for Aboyne and Glentanner, Aberdeenshire (1842). Writing of his parish as it had been fifty years
previously, the minister recalls that 'though the *laddle mill* had disappeared, it
had been only superseded by the *cog and rung*'.[37] 'Cog and rung' refers to the
type of gearing once used in vertical mills. 'Laddle mill' is a term used in
Ireland[38] and elsewhere to signify a horizontal mill. The use of the term 'laddle
mill' without explanation implies that, at least in that part of Aberdeenshire,
the meaning was still clear in the 1840s. The *Scottish National Dictionary*
defines *laddle* as a paddle on a water wheel, without making the definition
specific to horizontal mills. The *Dictionary of the Older Scottish Tongue* gives
no definition for laddle in this sense but, like the *SND*, does give the generally
understood meaning of the word, that is to say a large, cupped utensil for
liquids. Without wishing to carry deduction beyond reason, could there be
here a clue to the shape of the horizontal mill's vanes? Certainly there could be
few better analogies for curved, slightly cupped mill-wheel vanes than the
familiar domestic utensil. Were this to be accepted, then the flat vanes of later
times would appear even more likely to be a comparatively recent innovation.
It is in Glenprosen, Angus that we finally come face to face with the beast in a
1684 document headed 'Ane nott of the aprysing of the Miln of Ednaughtie,
which is a laidle miln'.[39] The note details the machinery and deserves to be
quoted at length:

> The said mill hes a litle bedston brokin in two lying on the stoole having therin a
> little iron spindle fastened on a piece timber [w]hic]h piece timber is girded with
> thrie iron girds [w]her]in the awes or laidles ar fastened. The bedston is very thin,
> the stoole consists in aught pieces of timber old and worn with the water. The hapr
> is made up of sivin pieces of dailes and fur pieces of other timber /rotin/.

Without question this is a description of a horizontal mill in which the 'laidles' are the vanes of the wheel.

Besides extending the known range of horizontal mills, the document raises an interesting question. If, as we are led to believe, horizontal mills were privately owned, why was this mill being surveyed and valued on behalf of the estate? The tenants in Ednaughtie testified 'that the said miln did not grind any these two years bygon'; surely, had the mill been in their own hands they would have put it to rights long before. Overall, the picture that emerges is quite contrary to that of independent-minded men happily grinding their corn at their own little mill. Rather it is one of tenants having to make do with a run-down estate-owned mill, of second-rate design, because their limited custom would not justify the building of an improved, vertical mill.

Just over the Perthshire border, on the Banff Estate, Alyth parish, there was an earlier 'laidle mill'. A paper dated 1534 refers to an already defunct mill as 'ane mylne of Foyell callit the Scottismanis mylne, alias the ladill myll'.[40] It is worth noting that this predates, by many years, the first authenticated record of horizontal mills in Lewis, Shetland or the Western Highlands. Two mills in Aberdeenshire bear the name Scotsmill, as does a third, in Banffshire, the Scotsmill of Boyne.[41] In the Banff document 'Scottismanis mylne' might be seen as a synonym for 'ladill myll'. Extending the speculation further, 'Scottismanis mylne' as opposed to what? Perchance a vertical mill, introduced from England? The concept of changing terms — Scotsman's mill, Highland Mill, Norse mill — paralleling the northward and westward retreat of horizontal mills, is a neat and attractive proposition, but one which is, perhaps, too pat to equate very closely with reality. On the basis of established knowledge, 'Highland mill' is a term quite appropriate to that area; 'Scotsman's mill' can only be a matter for conjecture.

Undeterred by the hazards of speculation, several writers have made claims for horizontal mills where no clear evidence exists. Goudie[42] enters into a prolonged speculation on click, clack and clock mills, with particular reference to Clock Mill, Edinburgh. Inspired, or perhaps misdirected by Goudie, Jardine[43] confidently asserts that mills in the Hawick area were formerly of the horizontal kind, citing millstones of $2\frac{1}{2}$ to 3 feet in diameter and stone sockets in the Hawick Museum as evidence.[44] Jardine does not discuss the possibility that the millstones might have come from large querns or small vertical mills and does not entertain any uses for the socket stones other than as bearings for horizontal mill shafts.

The most recent work on Scottish mills is also guilty of speculation. It is Enid Gauldie's *The Scottish Country Miller*.[45] Mrs. Gauldie writes of how horizontal mills were replaced, at varying periods up to the early 19th century, by superior landlord-built mills. She also claims that horizontal mills

remained in use after that time on farms which, having freed themselves from the restrictions of thirlage, were able at last to abandon their easily hidden hand querns and house mills and apply their own water resources to the more efficient production of their own grain and in such areas as had never known landlords' mills.[46]

Further on, a paragraph which starts with Scott's enumeration of Shetland mills concludes with a reference to 'no fewer than a hundred' 'small mills' in Berwickshire. The context suggests that these were horizontal mills, but this is not made clear. A similar statement appears on page 37. This is followed by a quotation concerning the once bad state of kilns and mills in Ayrshire,[47] which the writer cites as a criticism of horizontal mills. The writer then states that horizontal mills were commonly constructed 'entirely of wood rough-hewn in the vicinity'.[48]

More startling is the revelation that 'in the Lothians and in the hinterland of Glasgow the little mills [i.e. horizontal mills] . . . had disappeared *almost completely* (my italics) by the beginning of the nineteenth century',[49] though these last survivors were said to co-exist with the baronial mills.

It is alleged that some Scottish tenants built the small Highland mills at their own initiative and at their own expense,[50] but it is hardly likely that improving landowners found, 'very often', that the mill of the thirl had 'crumbled into desuetude while the tenants resorted to the primitive mills of their own construction'.[51] If so, no examples are given.

Mrs Gauldie also considers that 'while in some parts of Scotland the quern was only slowly being replaced by the horizontal water mill, the Scots engineer John Rennie had already been called from his Lothian workshop to build the Albion Mills'.[52] There are absolutely no grounds for thinking that the horizontal mill was the successor to the quern, and at so late a period.

For all the confidence with which these statements are made, no evidence is advanced to back them up. Until such a time as evidence is presented, they cannot be entertained as fact.

To summarise, from documentary and archaeological evidence horizontal mills are known to have existed two thousand years ago in Asia Minor and possibly in Denmark; evidence of both types indicates that they were used in Ireland perhaps as early as the 3rd century AD and certainly by the 8th. In more recent times horizontal mills were to be found over a wide area from the Far East to Iberia and from Finland to North Africa. The areas where they were used tended to be those where terrain, climate or agricultural practices were not conducive to large-scale cereal production and where farmers were not obliged to make use of landowners' larger, vertical mills.

In a Scottish context, the strongest and most recent evidence for their use comes from the Northern and Western Isles and from the adjacent mainland areas. From the terminology, it cannot be assumed that during the Viking occupation anything more sophisticated than the quern was in use. Scandinavian links suggested by the use of flat instead of scooped vanes may be merely a reflection of a common late survival in Lewis, Shetland and Norway. The use of the term 'Highland Mill' suggests that they were once common north of the Highland line; topographic names point towards this possibility and, were fieldwork to be carried out, more positive evidence might come to light. Horizontal mills were certainly being used in the south-east Grampians during the late 17th century.

There is no firm evidence for the use of horizontal mills in the central Lowlands or the Southern Uplands. In every instance where adequate evidence is given, the indications are that more complex mills, with gearing and vertical water wheels, were in use.

Mills with Vertical Wheels

Vertical mills have a documented history as long as that of mills with horizontal wheels. They were first described, between 20 and 11 BC, by the Roman engineer, Vitruvius,[53] and, if we are to believe Curwen, may have been his own invention. Their early history has been closely identified with the Roman Empire, though the abundance of slave labour restricted their use, at least until the coming of Christianity. Latterly they extended their range northwards across mainland Europe. Curwen suggests the 7th or 8th centuries as the time when they reached Britain. No fewer than 5,624 mills are listed in Domesday. Curwen, perhaps rashly, takes the absence of references to changing technology to mean that English mills have always been of the vertical type, though the earliest unambiguous indication of their use does not come until the 14th century.[54]

Vertical water mills could have reached Scotland through the Anglo-Saxon or Norman occupations, but no proof can be offered. Several mills are mentioned in 12th-century charters, some on streams too large to suit horizontal mills. However, it is the use of mills for purposes other than grain milling that confirms the presence of vertical mills. The first of these, cloth fulling, is first recorded in Scotland during the 14th century (see p.45). The significance of the vertical mill for subsequent developments lies in its ability to power, through cams or through gearing, an endless range of mechanical contrivances which, until the coming of the turbine in the 19th century, could not be driven by the simple horizontal mill. In all likelihood vertical grain mills were already being used in Scotland; the first fulling mill, probably driven by cams on a horizontal axle, provides confirmation. During the late 16th and early 17th centuries axles and cam machines found uses in pulping rags for paper, forging iron, crushing ore and working bellows for smelting hearths. Even simpler devices, consisting of vertical water wheels and horizontal axles, were applied to draining water and hauling coal from mines. A crank mounted on the end of an axle could drive a frame saw.

None of these new applications had to use gearing, though there are ample grounds for believing that it was widely, if not generally, used in corn mills by the late 16th and 17th centuries. If we are to believe that all horizontal mills were privately owned by tenants (though it has been shown that this is not necessarily the case), all references to mills in charters to lands must relate, by implication, to vertical mills. In the few cases where the extent of a mill's *thirl* is known, the extent is too great to be served by a horizontal mill. If there were not many more than 100 mills in the rich arable county of Berwickshire,[55] but 500 horizontal mills in the poorer, smaller county of Shetland, then the former must have been of the larger, vertical kind.

Above all else, there are occasional records of mill machinery which make it quite clear that geared vertical machinery was in use. In 1598 Robert Lindsay broke the mill, millstones, and wheels of the Mill of Dunrod, Renfrewshire, and took away the spindle rynd and 'trymmil brodis' (*trundle boards*).[56] In 1624 an inspection of the Peebles burgh mills revealed that the 'Rind Mylne' had an 'inner quheill of new aik' and an 'utter quheill new of asch' whilst the 'Auld Mylne' also had adequate inner and outer wheels.[57]

In 1656 there is a reference to 'the trouble and expenses of cogge, rung, awes, great timber and stones' at Haychesters Mill, Roxburghshire.[58] In 1680 the Mill of Banff had 'tua wheills on ane extrie', 'ane uther extrie with ane wheill and ane pair of lying trindills'.[59] In 1704 the Mill of Rotwall, Angus had an outer wheel, inner wheel, axletree, and trundle and spindle — in other words all the basic gearing for a grain mill.[60]

By the late 16th and 17th centuries, therefore, vertical water-wheels with gearing were already being used to drive corn mills, and the possibilities opened up by vertical wheels were being utilised in a number of other processes.

The vertical water-wheel could be modified to take advantage of differing sizes of fall. Thus, where the waterfall was a small one, an undershot or breast-shot wheel could derive its power from the impact of the water, but where a greater fall was available naturally, or made available artificially, an overshot wheel, fitted with buckets, could utilise not only the impact of the water but also its weight (Figure 5). While undershot or breast-shot wheels fitted with *starts* and *awes* were by far the most common in Scotland, more efficient over-shot wheels were also in use during the period 1550-1730, notably in draining the mines where large, powerful wheels were employed (Figure 17).

If a mill were to function, some provision had to be made for a water supply. In the days before land drainage the landscape was peppered with marshes and lochans, which helped regulate stream flow. Normally an artificial water-course or *lade* was drawn off from a stream and, having been applied to the water-wheel, returned thereto. Under the simplest arrangement, part of a stream was diverted to a mill without the use of a dam. Such mills were known as *burn mills*. Where several springs and small streams lay within the catch-ment area, simple *gather-dams* might be constructed, while on larger streams a *dam-dyke* of peats, divots, or loosely piled boulders was usually built.[61] The most spectacular examples, involving damheads several hundred feet long and lades several miles long, were to be found in relation to the coal industry (see p. 69).

More detailed consideration is given to the technology of vertical mills in the chapters which follow.

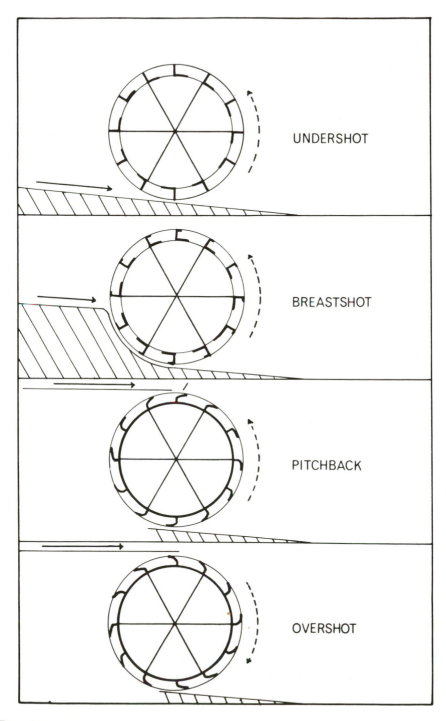

Fig 5. Types of vertical water wheel

Tide Mills

In populated coastal districts, where conventional water power was not available, tidal variations could be exploited to drive mills. The earliest record of a tide mill in Britain concerns one at Dover, which appears in Domesday Book (1086).[62] Recently Minchinton has summarised the evidence for tide mills in England and Wales.[63] Out of a total of 168 sites, no fewer than 59 are known to date from before 1500, with a further 30 datable to the 16th century. While their distribution might reflect no more than the intensity of fieldwork in certain areas, sites have been identified from the Solway Firth in the north to Cornwall and Kent in the south, with mills on most estuaries throughout the country.

In Scotland, tide mills (known there as sea mills) were uncommon, not so much on account of the shortage of good estuary sites but rather on account of the general availability of conventional water power (Figure 6). The earliest reference to *sea mills* is to a pair of mills at Inverdivot, Fife which are listed in a charter under the Great Seal, dated 10th September 1526; the description given, 'molendini maritum vulgariter nuncupat seymyllis', is almost certainly a reference to tide mills.[64] References to the mills continue until the early 19th century, by which time a third mill had been added. No other details are known.[65] In 1526, the first year in which the Inverdivot mills come to light, licence was granted to Alexander Acheson to build a harbour near Preston-pans, East Lothian.[66] In the confirmation to the charter, permission is given to build tide mills inside the harbour,[67] an option which appears to have been taken up by 1587, when the Register of the Great Seal mentions two sea mills there, both employed in grinding meal.[68] The mills had a long and useful life and in the 1790s were grinding flint for local potteries.[69] Another pair of sea mills, for grinding meal, were built on the green at Blackness, West Lothian by Alexander, Earl of Linlithgow, c. 1608.[70] These mills are referred to in 1629 and again in 1632 and 1642,[71] but thereafter no more is heard of them until 1722, by which time they were said to be in ruins.[72]

In 1621 a pair of tidal meal mills was projected and built at great expense near the quayside of Aberdeen,[73] but although they appeared in the Register of the Great Seal some seventeen years later,[74] the venture seems to have failed and the mills left to decay.[75]

More successful than either Blackness or Aberdeen were the sea mills of Burntisland. Young, in his *History of Burntisland*, infers that they dated from the late 16th century and that one was used for sawing timber, but he fails to quote his source on either point.[76] The earliest reference to the mills in the Register of the Great Seal does not occur until 1638, and even then there is no indication of what purpose the mills served.[77] It is certain, however, that at least one of the mills was a grain mill, to which the inhabitants of the burgh were thirled, and that the other either started out as, or was later converted to, a saw-mill. According to Young, the astriction also extended to the saw-mill, but here again no documentation is produced to support the assertion.[78] One

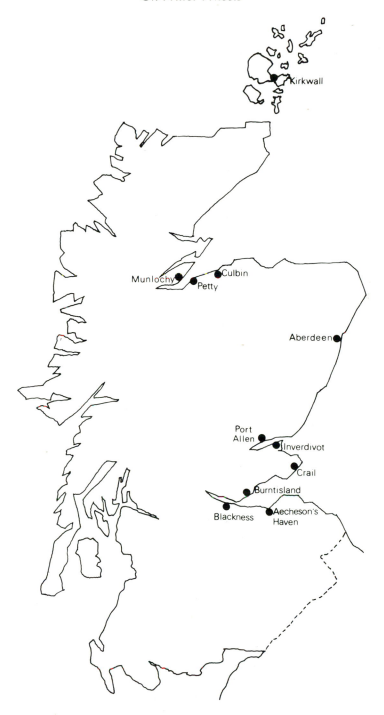

Fig 6. Distribution of tide mills

of the mills is indeed identified as a saw-mill on a map dated 1843.[79] Despite efforts by the burgh council to buy the mills in 1655, to establish a horse mill in 1670 and a windmill in 1683, thirlage of the burgh to the mills continued to stand, even after 1712 when, by Act of Parliament, the maltmen and brewers were thirled to the burgh's steel malt mills.[80] The meal mill apparently still stood in 1961, though the mill wheel had been removed some four years previously.[81] According to the New Statistical Account, the mill was capable of grinding for fourteen hours per day.[82]

Sea mill occurs as a place name in Ayrshire (NS 2047), but from the position of the mill it is clear that it was not a tide mill. One such mill was certainly operating in Crail parish, Fife during the 1790s,[83] and another in Orkney in the 1890s,[84] but by far the best documented site is the sea mill of Petty, Inverness-shire. The earliest reference to this mill is in 1682, when the millers were accused of 'sabbath grinding'. A valuation of machinery,[85] taken in 1754, is particularly informative, and runs as follows:

	£	s.	d.
To the utter wheels and axle trees	5	12	0
To the inner wheel	4	16	0
To the 4 bolstors		16	0
To the four miln stones	30	6	0
To the crubs and happers	2	16	0
To the two bridges, two clos two breast trees and the two bands	3	4	0
To the two cradles	1	4	0
To all the iron work	17	6	0
	£66	0	0

The two outer-wheels and the four millstones provide a likely explanation as to why so many Scottish tide mills are referred to as being in pairs: later evidence confirms that both incoming and outgoing tides were employed at Petty,[86] and this was very probably the system used elsewhere. The upkeep of the dam-dyke at Petty was the joint responsibility of the Earl of Moray's tenants, each being assigned a section to keep in repair.[87] The mill ceased to work c. 1825 and was allowed to fall into decay.[88] Overall, the contribution which sea mills made to water-powered industry as a whole was small, despite the widespread interest shown in them in the 17th century. Locally, however, they could provide a source of motive power in areas otherwise poorly served, notably the eastern coastal burghs. At Aberdeen, the burgh's milling requirements had led to the erection of a windmill prior to 1621,[89] while in Dundee the inadequacy of the burgh's Castle Mills and windmills was such that under a charter of 1641 the corporation was granted liberty to erect sea mills. Most striking, however, was the need for power in the Prestonpans area, where, besides the sea mills at Morrison's Haven, windmills and water-mills driven by mine adits were in use by the 17th century.

The Emergence of the Millwright

In contradistinction to the traditional meal and fulling mills, the new commercially orientated users of water power who appeared during the period 1550-1730 had no suckeners to draw upon when a breakdown occurred. In the absence of such a tied labour force, a demand was created for craftsmen such as masons, joiners and millwrights who could be called upon to build and repair mills as and when required. By the end of the period, the practice of employing wage labour had extended back to grain mills (p. 27). James Meikle, a wright in East Lothian, had shown his skill as a millwright by applying the new grain-mill technology which he had found in Holland, while two younger members of the family, Andrew and Robert Meikle, were receiving the training in millwrighting which was to make them the greatest millwrights that Scotland has ever produced. Elsewhere in Scotland, the skills accumulated by millwrights were to stand the country in good stead when, in the following century, developments in technology provided many new opportunities and a well-trained class of Scottish millwright was able to make full use of them and contribute new ideas of its own.

NOTES

1. Curwen, E. C., 'The Problem of Early Water-mills', *Antiquity*, XVIII (1944), 134-5. The issue is complicated by Curwen's use of the term 'vertical mill' to signify a horizontal mill's vertical plane of drive.

2. Steensberg, A., 'The Horizontal Water Mill. A Contribution to its Early History', *Prace I Materialy Muzeum Archaeologicznego I Ethnograficznego W Lodzi. Seria Archaeologiczna* Nr. 25 (1978), 345-356.

3. Fahy, E. M., 'A Horizontal Mill at Mashanaglass', *Journal of the Cork Historical and Archaeological Society* LXI (1956), 15-57.

4. Baillie, M. G. L., 'A Horizontal Mill of the Eighth Century AD at Drumard, Co. Derry', *Ulster Journal of Archaeology* XXXVIII (1975), 25-32.

5. Lucas, A. T., 'The Horizontal Mill in Ireland', *Journal of the Royal Society of Archaeology of Ireland* LXXXIII (1953), 1-36.

6. For some indication of the breadth of its distribution see Curwen, *op. cit.*, 144-5; Avitsur, S., *Water Power in Eretz-Israel and Abroad*, Tel Aviv, 1969; Dias, J., 'Moulins Portugais', *Etnografia* VI, Museu de Etnografia e Historia (N.D.); Budis, M., 'Citrva cu Ciutura diu Zona "Port ilor de Fier"', *Revista Muzeelor* L, 451-6 (1968); Ponomarev, N. A., *Istoria Techniki Mukomolnogo i Krujanogo Proizvodstva*, Moscow, 1955; Tucker, D. G., 'Windmills and Watermills in Iceland', *IA* IX/3, 278-284 (1972).

7. Megaw, B. R. S., 'Mwyllin Beg', *Journal of the Manx Museum* IV (1940), 199 *et seq*; Megaw, B. R. S., 'More about the Little Watermills', *Journal of the Manx Museum* V (1944), 147-8.

8. Size, N., 'Click Mill at Buttermere', *Transactions of the Cumberland & Westmorland Antiquarian and Archaeological Society* XXXVI (1936), 192 *et seq.*

9. See, for example, Gribbon, H. D., *The History of Water Power in Ulster*, Newton Abbot, 1969, 12.

10. Maxwell, S., 'A Horizontal Water Mill Paddle from Dalswinton', *Transactions of the Dumfries and Galloway Natural History and Archaeological Society* XXXIII, 185-196.

11. Goudie, G., 'The Horizontal Water Mills of Shetland', *PSAS* XX (1885-6), 257-297.

12. *Ibid.*, 259.

13. *Ibid.*, 295.

14. Fenton, A., *The Northern Isles: Orkney and Shetland*, Edinburgh, 1978, 410.

15. Scott, W., *Diary*, 4th August 1814, quoted by Goudie, *op. cit.*, 261.

16. Fenton, *op. cit.*, 406, figure 199.

17. *Ibid.*, 408.

18. Clouston, J. S., 'The Old Orkney Mills', *Proceedings of the Orkney Antiquarian Society* III (1924-5), 49-54, 65-71.

19. *Ibid.*, 53-54, 65.

20. *OSA* XIX, 397, Orphir, Orkney.

21. Clouston, *op. cit.*, 52-53.

22. Cruden, S., 'The Horizontal Mill at Dounby', *PSAS* LXXXI (1946-7), 43-47; Fenton, *op. cit.*, 400-401.

23. Clouston, *op. cit.*, 50.

24. Martin, M., *Description of the Western Isles of Scotland* (1695), 204-5, quoted by Fenton, A., *Scottish Country Life*, Edinburgh, 1976, 105.

25. Goudie, *op. cit.*, 285.

26. Fieldwork and photographs in the Country Life Archive, National Museum of Antiquities of Scotland.

27. Goudie, *op. cit.*, 285.

28. MacCulloch, J., *A Description of the Western Isles of Scotland* (3 vols.), London, 1819, II, 30.

29. For one possible instance of a curved Shetland vane, see Maxwell, S., 'Paddles from Horizontal Mills', *PSAS* LXXXVIII (1954-5), 232.

30. *OSA* XIII, 286, North Yell and Fetlar, Shetland.

31. *OSA* VII, 576, Reay, Caithness and Sutherland.

32. Goudie, *op. cit.*, 283.

33. Gauldie, E., *The Scottish Country Miller*, Edinburgh, 1981, 117.

34. RCAHMS *Argyll* Volume I, Kintyre, Edinburgh, 1971, 192-6, fig. 183.

35. SRO GD112/9/33.

36. Dick-Lauder, Sir T., *An Account of the Great Floods of August 1829, in the Province of Moray and Adjoining Districts*, Edinburgh, 1830, 365.

37. *NSA* XII, 1068, Aboyne and Glentanner, Aberdeenshire.

38. MacAdam, R., 'Ancient Water Mills', *Ulster Journal of Archaeology* IV (1856), 6.

39. SRO GD205/23/126.

40. SRO GD83/45.

41. OS 6"/mile 1st Edition, Grid references NJ563186, NJ829138, NJ608653.

42. Goudie, *op. cit.*, 286-287.

43. Jardine, J., 'Weensland: Past & Present', *THAS* (1909), 97-103.

44. *Ibid.*, 99.

45. Gauldie, *op. cit.*

46. *Ibid.*, 115.

47. *Ibid.*, 117. Further confusion arises from the transposition of 'mills' and 'kilns'.

48. *Ibid.*, 117.

49. *Ibid.*, 38.

50. *Ibid.*, 44.

51. *Ibid.*, 45.

52. *Ibid.*, 120.

53. Curwen, *op. cit.*, 130.

54. *Ibid.*, 133.

55. Macfarlane, W., *Geographical Collections* III, SHS (1908), 184.

56. *RMSRS* V, 495.

57. 'Charters and Documents Relating to the Burgh of Peebles (1165-1710)', *SBRS*, Edinburgh, 1872, 365.

58. SRO GD157/1001.

59. SRO GD16/29/120.

60. SRO GD16/27/164.

61. SRO GD110/740 (peats and divots); SRO GD45/18/162 (stone).

62. Bennett, R. & Elton, J., *The History of Corn Milling* (1898-9), 4 vols., New York, N.D., II, 218.

63. Minchinton, W. E., 'Tidemills of England and Wales', *Transactions of the International Symposium of Molinology* IV, 339-353. I am grateful to Professor Minchinton for providing a copy of this article.

64. SRO GD1/128/2.

65. *IRA* Fife, 42 (1560); SRO GD1/128/9 (1594); *RMSRS* XI, 619 (1664); SRO GD1/128/44 (1791), /47 (1802), /48 (1803).

66. Graham, A., 'Morrison's Haven', *PSAS* XCV (1961-2), 300.

67. *RMSRS* III, 2362 (1541).

68. *RMSRS* V, 1307 (1587); *IRA* Haddington, 50 (1609), 136 (1632), 352 (1684).

69. *OSA* XVII, 74, Prestonpans, East Lothian; Forrest, W. (Map of) *Haddington-shire*, 1799.

70. *RMSRS* VI, 2195 (1608).

71. Dalyell, Sir J. & Beveridge, J. (eds.), 'Binns Papers 1320-1864', *SRS* LXX (1938), No. 125; *RMSRS* VIII, 1977 (1632); *NSA* II, 76, Carriden, West Lothian.

72. Dalyell & Beveridge, *op. cit.*, No. 550.

73. Kennedy, W., *Annals of Aberdeen*, 2 vols., London, 1818, I, 142.

74. *RMSRS* IX, 860 (1638).

75. Kennedy, *op. cit.*, I, 410.

76. Young, A., *A History of Burntisland*, Kirkcaldy, 1913, 30-31.

77. *RMSRS* IX, 795 (1638).

78. Young, *op. cit.*, 31.

79. *Ibid.*, 31.

80. *Ibid.*, 32-33.

81. Pencilled footnote in Edinburgh Central Library's copy of Young, *op. cit.*, 31.

82. *NSA* IX, 416, Burntisland, Fife.

83. *OSA* IX, 439, Crail, Fife.

84. Bennett & Elton, *op. cit.*, II, 222-223.

85. SRO GD23/4/173.

86. *NSA* XIV, 401, Petty, Inverness-shire. The sea mill at Petty also made use of the accumulated waters of a small burn.

87. *Ibid.*, 401.
88. *Ibid.*
89. Kennedy, *op. cit.*, I, 410-411.

Part One

Early Industries, 1550-1730

2

Grain Mills

Rural Meal Mills

Technology

Without any doubt, it was to the grinding of oats and bere that water power was first applied in Scotland: several such mills appear in Scottish charters of the 12th century,[1] at least two hundred years before the earliest references to cloth fulling mills.[2] The machinery used in grain milling, or at least the water wheel and gearing, formed the basis for all subsequent types of water mill and therefore deserves to be covered in depth.

A wooden *water* or *outer wheel*, generally low breast-shot, was fitted with *starts* and *awes*, set at an angle to each other (Figure 7). A wooden axle-tree, supported by *inner-* and *outer-headstocks*, and banded at each end with iron, passed through the centre of the wheel; a clasp-arm frame held it in position. Near to the inner end of the axle-tree was fixed, in a similar frame, the *inner* or *cog wheel*, around the inside edge of which were set a ring of pegs which meshed with the spars of a lantern pinion or *trundle*. The trundle was fitted around a short wooden *spindle* or stone pinion, supported at its lower end by a *bridge-tree*, and carrying at its top end a projection, in iron or steel, referred to as the *rind*. This fitted into a socket in the eye of the *upper-* or *runner-stone*, while the *lying-* or *bed-stone*, through which the spindle passed, was held stationary by a heavy wooden framework. Often the stones were encased in wooden *hoops* or *rings*, which prevented the grist, be it *shillin* or *meal*, from spilling out onto the *stool*, or platform, on which the stones were supported. Since most rural mills had only one pair of stones, the space between them had to be altered for the differing requirements of shilling and mealing; such an alteration was performed by means of a sword, a lever which passed down through the stool and which was hinged to one end of the bridge-tree. Grain and shillin were fed to the eye of the runner-stone from a *happer* (hopper) via a *shoe*, the latter being activated by a primitive form of damsel known as a *clapper*; a wooden frame, the *crub*, supported the happer, although in some cases it was simply hung from the roof.

Just as the machinery of the corn mill showed, for the most part, a dependence upon locally available raw materials, so also did the building itself. Roofs, carried on a framework of branches, were normally of straw thatch, heather or *divots*,[3] while rubble and divots were the customary materials for

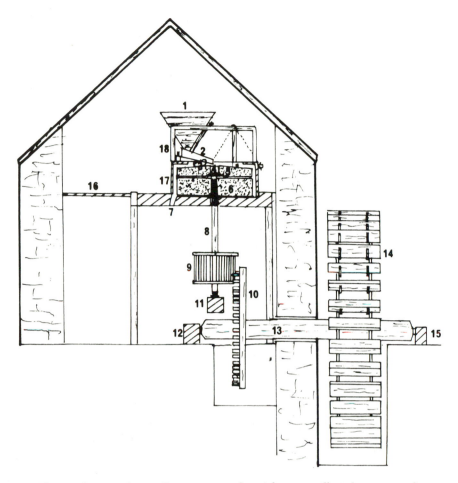

Fig 7. The machinery of a pre-Improvement Scottish corn mill. 1: hopper. 2: shoe. 3: clapper. 4: rind. 5: upper stone. 6: nether stone. 7: mill eye. 8: spindle. 9: trindle. 10: inner wheel. 11: bridge tree. 12: inner headstock. 13: axletree. 14: outer wheel. 15: outer headstock. 16: mill stool. 17: hoops. 18: crub.

walling; by the early 18th century slate was being used in roofing,[4] and lime with stones in walling, with skilled masons and wrights supervising mill construction. However, over much of the country mill construction, including damwork, was achieved through the reluctant labour of the *suckeners*. In urban areas, where the need to keep the mills operational was particularly great, and the performance of services by the *suckeners* unknown, much greater care was taken in building dams.[5] By the early 18th century outside labour was being employed in dam construction in rural areas, as at Kinnaird Mill, Angus, where in 1719 a £100 (Scots) contract was signed for such a project.[6]

Distribution

During mediaeval times the success of the meal mill, or corn mill, as it is commonly known in Scotland, was such that by the period under consideration something like 4,000 of them were in active use, with examples in all but the most isolated or sparsely populated parts of the country. Even in Highland Scotland, contrary to popular belief, the water-mill was well established by the late 16th century. With the exception of those areas too lightly cultivated or populated to support a mill, the only areas from which they were largely absent were those above 750 feet, presumably the upper limit of cultivation.

In water-mills the landowner possessed, for the first time, a means whereby an income, over and above that accruing from the land itself, could be obtained from a manufacturing process. First, however, a local monopoly had to be established.

Competition from the Quern

Before the monopoly could be established, a certain amount of groundwork had to be done. Long before the water-mill had reached Scotland, the quern had come into use; throughout the period under consideration it continued to offer a cheap, if laborious, alternative to the water corn mill, especially where only small quantities were to be ground. The breaking of querns, under orders from Barony or other courts, was a common measure. Such was the action taken at Mid Calder in 1598, when a fine of 40 shillings Scots (about 17p) was imposed on anyone found in possession.[7]

Nevertheless, circumstances did not always permit such sweeping measures: at the Mill of Fearn, Easter Ross the water supply was so precarious that as late as 1720 it was found necessary to permit the use of querns during July, August and September, they being handed in during early October, to protect the mill's thirlage until the following summer.[8]

Establishing a Thirlage

Once a mill had been built, it became necessary to guarantee its use, and for this a *thirl* or astriction had to be established over a certain area, normally the estate of the mill proprietor. In most circumstances the area thus thirled would yield sufficient *multures*, or dues, to justify the building or leasing of a mill; occasionally, however, the income from a mill was too small ever to yield an adequate return, on account of the limited extent of an estate or because of existing thirlages to other mills. The thirl of Old Cambus mill, Berwickshire was restricted to three *husbandlands* in Old Cambus itself,[9] while the rent of Mill of Inverdunning, Perthshire had to be reduced from twelve *bolls* of victual to four, for so small was the thirl that the dues paid for grinding came to less than the former rent.[10] At Cransmill, Aberdeenshire the thirl was of sufficient extent, but the rent still had to be reduced, from 80 to 70 Merks Scots, 'upon certain consideration that the s(ai)d sucken of the s(ai)d miln, at least meikell of it, is oft tymes waist and cannot bear the rent th(e)r(e) of'.[11] Not surprisingly, and contrary to Court of Session rulings,[12] thirlages were sometimes amalgamated, although the opposite process, whereby new thirlages were created within existing ones, was still taking place in the late 17th century.[13]

Where a thirl included lands belonging to another landowner, it was not unusual for the latter to encourage those of his tenants within the thirl to use his own mill instead, even to the extent of building one specifically for their use. Once such a step had been taken, the Court of Session, a slow and costly arbiter at the best of times, could do little to help, even going so far as to rule that a mill, once built and set a-going for forty-eight hours, could not be demolished.[14] Hardly less consoling was their judgement in the case of McDougal v. McCulloch. During the 1680s McCulloch of Moole built a mill at Slock, within the thirl of McDougal of Logan's Clonyard Mill, Wigtownshire. McDougall took the case to the Lords of Session, who, finding McCulloch thirled to the mill of Clonyard, ruled that Slock Mill be demolished. However, on examination the former mill was found to be unfit to serve, and its successor, a windmill, was not recognised as holding the thirl. Far from being demolished, the Mill of Slock was still going strong at the time of General Roy's survey , some sixty years later.[15]

Types of Thirlage

Depending on the location of a mill, and the nature of the lands which it served, one of three different types of thirlage could be established. Unique to burgh lands was thirlage of *invecta et illata*, under which corn consumed within the thirl had to be manufactured at the burgh mill, regardless of where it was grown. In Royal Burghs control of the mill lay with the Incorporation, but in Burghs of Barony it generally remained in the hands of the feudal superior. Burgh mills will be considered in greater detail later in this chapter.

In rural areas, two types of thirlage obtained. Under the lighter of the two, known as the *thirlage of grindable grain*, the astriction was limited to oats and barley grown within the thirl for household use. Since such a thirlage did not prevent suckeners from buying in meal from outside, they could, in theory at least, evade the thirlage altogether by depending solely on this source for their own needs.[16] More onerous was the thirlage of *omnia grana crescentia*, under which all grain grown within the thirl, excepting only seed corn and horse corn, was liable to astriction. In 1565 the Court of Session made allowances whereby grain could be sold on the open market to raise funds for such payments as teinds; grain enough to pay for threshing and plough repairs was also exempted. However, their rulings generally failed to be implemented, and on subsequent occasions even the Court itself failed to take account of these allowances.[17]

Multures

While the creation of a thirlage established a monopoly, it did not, in itself, create a source of income for the mill owner. Only the imposition of a duty, over and above the real expense of grinding, could do that. In Scotland such a duty was known as multure, an imposition which frequently led to confrontations between miller and mill owner on the one hand and suckeners on the other. All the grain brought to the mill carried a multure, normally at a rate of 1/24th to 1/13th of the total. In addition to this sum small, supposedly voluntary, payments were made to the miller (*bannock*) and to his servant or knave (*knaveship*). Where only the miller himself served the mill, the latter term was often used for his payment. These two payments together represented about half that deducted as multure.

Much of our knowledge of multure comes from the writings of the late 18th century, and by the same token so do our attitudes to them. However, evidence from the period 1550-1730 does not altogether tally with such views; indeed, there is reason to believe that neither were multures such an oppressive and universally exacted tax, nor was the miller such an arch-demon as later writers would have us believe. It would appear that the practice of abstracting grain was fairly widespread, and that grain so abstracted was manufactured at other, though not necessarily more accessible, mills, at the lower *outentown* multure rate. This view is corroborated by the fact that most mills offered this rate to those from outwith their thirl; were outentown rates not aimed at those thirled elsewhere, then one can only assume that they were paid by those not thirled to any mill.

The practice of *abstracting* could seriously detract from the value of a mill, and if, as was generally the case, the mill was set in tack, this would cut into the income from which the miller paid his rent. At the end of his tack, the miller could find himself unable to make the necessary repairs, and the mill, its value impaired by abstractions, would have to be let at a lower rate.[18] Through the medium of the Barony Court, efforts could be made to recoup the losses caused by abstractions and to prevent further losses, but the success of such measures depended on the co-operation of the accused. Should he confess, or fail to appear, a fine or *unlaw* of £2 to £10 Scots was imposed, plus a volume of corn equal to double that which would have been paid in multures. On the other hand, anyone who appeared at Court and denied the charges stood a good chance of being absolved. In 1712, when the tenant of the Mill of Guthrie, Angus raised a complaint against certain suckeners, they denied all charges, forcing the miller to waive all past abstractions and settle for a strongly worded, but basically ineffectual, re-enactment of the Act of thirlage, requesting them to keep to the mill in future.[19]

Maintaining the Mill

Besides paying multure and knaveship, suckeners were expected to perform certain duties in connection with the mill's upkeep. Many different tasks might be asked of them: carrying home millstones,[20] repairing damheads, [21] clearing lades,[22] thatching the mill roof,[23] leading building materials[24] and carrying timbers such as axle-trees[25] were all performed by the suckeners of one mill or another. In 1621 the Court of Session ruled that the duty to perform such tasks was implicit in every form of thirlage.[26] The Barony Court could call upon suckeners to perform services, but only those which were 'used and wont'.

Services as outlined above have been viewed as particularly onerous but this is, again, the view of a later age. The bringing home of millstones, though time-consuming, united the whole community, and involved the consumption of large quantities of free bread and ale before the millstones could be brought to rest at the mill. Nor was the journey so arduous as it might have been: a millstone , with a bough or *wand* slotted through the eye, could be trundled along the roughest of tracks without much effort. Here again, the miller was dependent on the active co-operation of the suckeners, a co-operation which was not always forthcoming. In 1627 the Barony Court of Colstoun, East Lothian had ruled that, should the millers require new stones, they 'sall bringe theme hame yearlie befor August, otherwayis na persoun to be astrictit or oblist to helpe thame with the saidis mylstanes . . . in tyme cuming'.[27] In 1688 the suckeners of Kevock Mill, Midlothian refused to carry millstones or pay a commutation.[28] Not surprisingly, millers changed their stones as infrequently as possible, often working them down to an inch or two's thickness.[29] After tenants in Stitchill Barony, Roxburghshire had refused to provide thatch for the estate's mill, a temporary arrangement had to be made, under which the miller and tenants were each to cast and lead half the quantity needed. When eventually a more permanent agreement was reached, it required the tenants to provide and lead straw for the mill, proportional to the extent of their lands. While they were also asked to make available divots, casting and leading had to be at the miller's own expense.[30]

As for the provision of timbers, this was usually the joint responsibility of miller and mill owner, the former supplying small timbers and the latter the large ones.[31] Where such arrangements did not exist, responsibility lay with the owner alone.[32] Occasionally, a sort of insurance was paid along with the rent, the proceeds of which could be used to pay for repairs to the mill.[33] In only a few cases did the suckeners need to provide help, and even these were confined to occasions when the amount of work to be carried out was above the capacity of the miller himself.

Generally, it would seem that mill services were performed only grudgingly, and were so ill-executed that, by the end of the period, a money commutation was obtained wherever possible, with hired labour and skilled craftsmen taking the place of the reluctant suckeners.[34]

The Miller's Obligations

It has already been suggested that so long as so many mills continued to serve so few people, the creation of thirlages and the imposition of multures were necessary evils, especially if the mill were to be set in tack. The need to prevent or at least restrict, abstractions was a real one, but the rulings of the Barony Court were not always effective, nor did they indiscriminately favour the miller at the expense of the tenantry. On the contrary, the miller had very definite obligations towards the thirl, as is attested by both mill tacks and court records.

As often as not, the miller was expected to collect corn for grinding.[35] Despite the confusion which reigned with respect to measures,[36] efforts were made to standardise those used in any one area, and to prevent fraud. The miller at Shaws Mill, Fife had to 'accept and imbrace his lo(rdshi)p's owine *metts* and measures for metting of the cornes and maill',[37] while at Colstoun, in 1643, 'ane trew visite and sicht' was taken of the *firlots, pecks* and dishes used at the nearby mills of Bothans and Bolton, measures which served as standards for those used at the Over and Nether mills of Colstoun.[38] Clauses in successive tacks of Shaws Mill give a particularly detailed account of what might be expected of a miller. Besides the standardisation of measure already referred to, the miller was to 'grind, mill and kill (*Anglice*—kiln) the haill grindable cornes' grown in the Barony of Raith, taking as much care with the tenants' corn as with the master's. The meal produced was to be as good as that from any other mill within a four-mile radius. Should the corn be in any way 'spoylt or damnified' by him, he was to provide compensation, 'at the sight of . . . the Noble Earle or his Chalmerlane'.[39] The runner-millstone was to be provided with an iron girth, the water-wheel kept free of *backwater*, and the mill kept locked at night.[40] Anyone appointed as an under-miller had first to meet with the approval of the mill owner, and was expected to work at a wage rate set by him. Once notified by a suckener, the miller was expected, the following day, to collect grain for milling from anywhere within the barony, and to return it once ground. Malt for the Earl was to be ground free of charge.[41]

At another of the Earl of Melville's mills, Monimail, malt could be taken elsewhere if the miller was unable to grind it at twenty-four hours' notice.[42] At Quarryford Mill, East Lothian two men had to be kept for serving the mill and kiln,[43] while at most mills each client had to 'stand his roume' or wait his turn, those from within the thirl having preference over those from outwith, even if the latter had arrived at the mill first.[44] All in all, the lot of the suckeners was much better than is commonly assumed.

Occupational Hazards

Besides the obligations outlined above, the miller faced other impediments. A miller whose work failed to please might be subjected to physical violence,[45] or brought up before the Barony Court,[46] the members of which, it should be remembered, were chosen from within the ranks of the tenantry, and were also, therefore, suckeners of the mill.[47] In court, the inadequacy of a mill could be sufficient grounds for abstraction.[48]

Nor was it just the suckeners whom the miller had to fear. The 16th, 17th and 18th centuries were violent times in Scotland, and it was often the mill, a necessary element in the manufacture of food and an important source of income for the laird, that bore the brunt of the violence.[49] One common practice was to remove the sluice gate or break down the dam head, but other parts of the mill, both structural and mechanical, might be broken or carried off. In 1611 one John Forrest came by night to the Mill of Crawfordjohn, Lanarkshire, broke the 'utter and inner quheillis, axtrie, spindle, happer, trouch . . . rinnand and lyand stanes' and finally demolished the building. The mill was subsequently rebuilt, only to be burnt down by the same person.[50] While the destruction or disablement of a mill might be a source of inconvenience to the suckeners,[51] it was a disaster for the miller, who could no longer obtain the dues which provided his livelihood and paid his rent.

The periods during which a mill could operate were limited by other factors too. The Church frowned upon Sunday working, a practice which was particularly common in dry areas with limited water catchment,[52] and although its views were embodied in an Act of Parliament,[53] the practice remained sufficiently common to require a re-enactment some twenty years later.[54]

Much more serious an 'Act of God' was the scarcity or superabundance of water, a problem which could be especially harmful for 'burn mills' which had no storage capacity. It has already been shown that the inadequacy of a mill's water supply could be used in defence of abstractions (p. 25); the only group to whom this line of defence was closed were those who were already abstracting when the supply had dried up.[55] Despite the Court of Session's ruling to the contrary, exemption from thirlage during drought was a widespread practice,[56] as illustrated by the following clause, written into a thirlage agreement by the feuers of Maybole, Ayrshire:

> 'And gif the milne shall happine not to be in capacitie threw drouth and want of water, to grind all the corn and malt that shall be brought be ws to grund th(e)rat, then, and in that caice, it shall be leisuin to ws to take als much of our cornes and malt as the said milne shall not be able to worke, to any uthr milne, to be grund th(e)rat.[57]

Storm damage, frost and backwater in winter could be just as disabling as drought in summer, offering equally legitimate grounds for abstraction. In Angus, the suckeners of the Mill of Guthrie were free, in such circumstances, to go elsewhere to grind corn for household use, or to borrow an equal quantity of meal from the miller, until such time as the mill was once more capable of grinding.[58]

If, for any of these reasons, the mill was out of action for any length of time, the miller could face substantial losses.

The Miller as Tenant

It is all too easy to forget that the miller, like the suckeners, was usually a

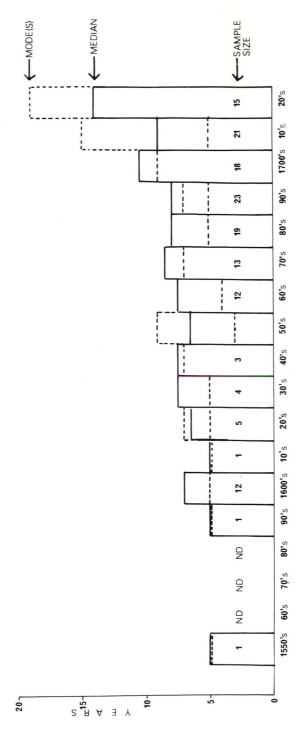

Fig 8. Duration of mill tacks, 1550-1729

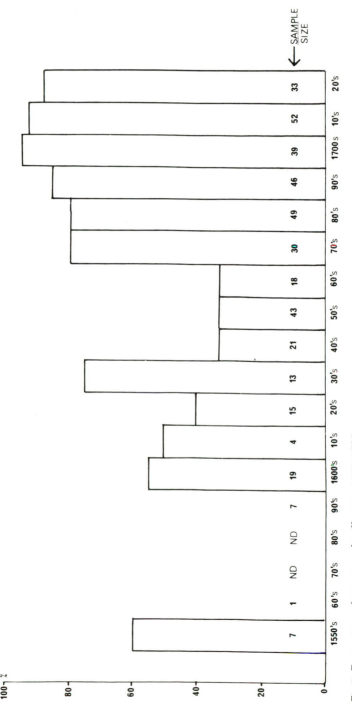

Fig 9. Percentage of commuted mill rents, 1550-1729

tenant, and bore the same responsibilities to the landowners as did the rest of the tenantry. Mill tacks generally ran for three, five, seven or nine years, although feuing, liferenting, and long leases of up to thirty-one years were not unknown (Figure 8). By the early 1700s longer leases were appearing, with nineteen-year terms common by the 1720s. In payment of his rent, the miller was expected to find a wide range of produce: a typical rent might comprise twenty bolls of oatmeal, ten bolls of bere, a mill swine, twelve capons and twenty poultry. Among the additional items which might be expected were geese,[59] eggs,[60] linen cloth and yarn,[61] lambs,[62] wedders,[63] butter,[64] malt,[65] tallow,[66] wheat,[67] bran[68] and salmon.[69] Besides providing these, the miller had to carry out services such as arrage (ploughing),[70] provide a horse and sled or a sickle during harvest[71] and carry a variety of commodities such as crops,[72] coal,[73] peat,[74] heather[75] and turfs.[76] Besides his rent in kind, many a miller paid cash sum or silver mail; from the 1670s onwards there was a rapid increase in the number of mills paying a cash rent, as commutation of rents in kind spread (Figure 9). For example, at Oakwood Mill, Selkirkshire a rent comprising sixteen bolls of malt, sixteen of meal, thirty-two kain fowls and a mill swine had been commuted to a cash sum of £269 6s 8d Scots by 1693.[77]

As for comparisons between mill rents at different times and in different places, the presence of so many unknown variables makes for enormous difficulties. The amount of land let with a mill, the size of the thirl, prevailing multure rates, conditions of let and responsibility for repairs varied from mill to mill, whilst all could affect the rate at which a mill was let. Furthermore, one is faced with the inconvertibility of items making up mill rent. How, for example, does one convert twenty bolls of meal, twenty bolls of bere, a mill swine, twelve capons and three loads of peat to a cash equivalent? And were it possible to do so, how does one go on to establish their real money value? Obviously there is scope for much more research on this topic, but unfortunately it cannot be dealt with in any greater depth in the present context. All that can be said is that the rent from a mill and mill croft was likely to be much greater than that of a purely agricultural holding of a similar size.

By building a mill on his estate, and by monopolising the manufacture of grain, a landowner might hope to generate more income, especially in cash form. If such a monopoly were to operate successfully, it was in his interest to have a serviceable mill and a fair miller. Traditionally the suckeners have been portrayed as being oppressed by landowners and miller alike, and forced to pay exorbitant sums for badly executed grinding at inconveniently situated mills. True, multures did force them to pay more than the real cost for milling, but very high multure rates of 1/13th or 1/11th so often cited by later writers were not so common as were rates of 1/16th or 1/24th.[78] Furthermore, the widespread practice of offering outentown multure rates suggests that many paid much lower rates. Allowances should also be made for the inherently biased nature of the evidence available, notably Barony and Session Court records, which emphasise those cases in which abstractions were detected while ignoring those which went unnoticed. What is more, by paying a *dry multure*[79] to compensate the miller for loss of income, a suckener under thirl-age of *grana crescentia* could sell his corn on the open market, or even take it to another mill to be ground at outentown rates. And for all the criticism of in-conveniently sited mill, the establishment of thirls tended to minimise the distance from a mill in an age of chronically poor transport facilities, although there may have been cases where another mill was more accessible. Certainly the number of mills was much greater than could have been supported by a 'free' clientele, and when, during the century after 1730, a move away from grain monoculture and the development of more sophisticated technologies brought an end to thirlage, the number of working grain mills fell sharply.

Burgh Mills

Burgh mills operated in circumstances rather different from those of their rural counterparts: little grain was grown within the bounds of the thirl, and most of that needed by bakers, brewers and other persons was brought in from outwith it. *Invecta et illata*, that particular type of thirlage which developed in burghs, has already been referred to in a general context. In this section it will be examined in more detail.

As centres of population, burghs could be expected to yield much more sub-stantial profits from the imposition of thirlage than could rural areas. Throughout the period the magistrates of royal and ecclesiastical burghs sought to turn this fact to some advantage, by obtaining control of those burgh mills which were not already theirs, creating or strengthening thirlage to them, and setting them in tack for cash rents.

Acquiring Mills

Mills came into the hands of burgh authorities through various agencies: in 1641 the burgh of Dundee was granted, by royal charter, the two Castle Mills plus a windmill in the burgh, as well as multures and sequels;[80] in 1670 Jedburgh bought the East, Town and Abbey Mills of that town from Lord Lothian,[81] while in 1617 the town council of Edinburgh added Bonnington to its existing mills, paying Robert and George Logan 1230 Merks for it.[82] By imposing a 2d per pint duty on ale and beer, the same corporation was able, in 1722, to buy *inter alia*, Leith Mills.[83] Linlithgow was granted its burgh mills by the Prioress of Manuel Convent in 1586 for a mere 20 Merks.[84]

Establishing a Thirl

In burghs of Barony control of the mills usually rested with the feudal superior; multures were payable either to him or his tacksman, and it was by him, or his predecessors, that the thirlage was established. In many ways these burgh mills resembled those of rural areas. However, such thirlages did not necessarily exist in royal and ecclesiastical burghs, and when it came to acquiring a mill on the burgh's behalf, it was sometimes necessary to create a thirlage from scratch, as did Jedburgh in 1670.[85] In 1576 the burgh council of Glasgow attempted to establish a thirl over the town, and to let the mills on a year by year basis.[86] The town's common mill (Figure 10) was rebuilt at a cost of £98 18s 10d Scots,[87] and while these alterations were being made, another mill, which was to stay in the burgh's hands, was leased from Alexander Lyon.[88] However, the scheme was looked upon with disfavour, and by 1581 it was being claimed that, on account of the mills' inadequacy, the thirlage should be abolished:

> . . . nane of the saidis mylnis at na seasoun of the yeir wilbe able to mak continewall and daylie seruice to this tounschip, being populus and haifing hour-elie victuale of gritt quantitie to grind, and becaus the said mylnis are situat on burnis quhilk will stand the haill symmer seasoun dry without watter, nocht withstanding thair wer sufficiensie of watter yit ar thei nocht able to grind nor mak seruive to the haill inhabitantis of this toun.[89]

Under such pressures, thirlage had to be abandoned, though the mills continued to be set in tack for a small sum;[90] in 1608, the idea was resurrected, with a view to clearing the town's debts.[91]

Common Good

In an age when burghs had very limited funds, and many uses for them, the income derived from the burgh mills must have represented a vitally important item of revenue. In 1569 the Burgh of Peebles allocated the next thirteen years' profits from its waulk mill and two corn mills to the building of town walls.[92] By feuing out its mills c. 1575, Aberdeen was able to clear a debt of 600 Merks, and still have an annual income of 18 Merks from them; any profit which might have been made was lost, however, when in 1596 the burgh decided to repossess the mills prematurely, at a cost of 5000 Merks. From that time onwards they yielded a steady 10,000 Merks per annum on three-year tacks.[93] By the early 18th century Edinburgh's mills were yielding some 10-12,000 Merks per annum in rent,[94] and those of a much smaller burgh, Dumfries, nearly 2500 Merks.[95] Brechin used the income from its Meikle Mill, let in 1580 to 'defray the great expense of law and taxation'.[96] A one Merk per boll duty imposed by the Burgh of Ayr on malt ground at its mills was expected to raise enough money over ten years to carry out repairs on the harbour there.[97] An agreement dated 1616 shows the sorts of uses to which the people of Stirling expected to put the proceeds of the Common Good fund:

> because the toun hes lytill commoun gude or meinis ather to intertenye thair ministerie, thair Kirk, tolbuyth, brig, schoir, calseyis, schole, or uther commoun warkis and effaires, quhilk cannot be susteinit without the rents and commoditie of mylnes as utheris tounes hes, thairfoir how soone the toun may have occasioun to acquyre and gett mylnes able to serve the toun, we . . . sall consent and grant, with the remanent inhabitantis of this burgh, to thirle our selffis to the saidis mylnes for siclyik servyce and deutis paying as the burrowis of Lynlithgow or Glasgow payis and gevis.[98]

Malt Milling

If urban thirlages were to be effective, then the co-operation of brewers and maltmen was essential, for while their contribution was of only minor importance in most rural areas, it was malt, as much as grain, which provided grist to a burgh's mills. Although Edinburgh's mills (seven in 1573,[99] twelve by 1599[100]) relied partly on the thirlage of the baxter's wheat , the abstraction of malt was serious enough to cause 'grete hurt' to the common mills as early as 1556,[101] while by 1710 it could be claimed that, without the brewers, the town's mills would not have been worth maintaining,[102] a claim which might have been made of most Scottish burghs, but especially of those such as Dundee[103] or Pittenweem,[104] where mills had been erected solely for the grinding of malt.

Glasgow's Burgh Mills

At Glasgow the same dependence was in evidence, for although some grain was taken to the burgh's mills, the baxters had their own mill on the River Kelvin since 1578;[105] when, in 1608, thirlage was re-imposed on Glasgow, they were specifically given exemption for wheat and rye.[106] The brewers, on the other hand, had to agree to 'brew na manir of malt in tyme cuming bot that malt that beis ground at the townis milns'. Those failing to comply were to pay double multure, plus an unlaw of £5 Scots.[107]

With the revival of thirlage in Glasgow, it was necessary to ensure that the town had an adequate milling capacity, and with this in mind the council leased the Old Mill of Partick from the Bishop of Glasgow,[108] and Subdean Mills (comprising two water mills and a man mill) from the Laird of Minto.[109] These, with Archibald Lyon's mill (alias New Mill), and the town's mill (Auldtoun Mill), were set in tack to George Anderson of Woodside, and James Lightbody, visitor of the maltmen and mealmen, for a period of five years, at a rent of 4400 Merks per annum.[110]

The re-establishment of thirlage had required the active co-operation of the guilds, but even assuming that it was forthcoming in the first place, it was short-lived. On 2nd July 1608, less than two months after the mills had been let, there were complaints of malt being abstracted,[111] and by the following September, in a desperate effort to uphold the value of its mills, the burgh was threatening that abstracters 'sall never heireftir bruik office in kirk or commoun weill of this burgh', and that their freedoms would be 'dischairgit and cryd doun'. As a further measure, the unlaw of £5 Scots was quadrupled.[112] These measures, while drastic, seem to have been effective, for at the expiry of the mill lease in 1613, confidence in the strength of the astriction was such that the lease was rouped for a further five-year term at a rent of 6466 Merks per annum.[113] Trouble threatened to erupt again in 1625, after one miller had given a customer's unground malt to his horse,[114] but the establishment of a biannual mill court, at which grievances could be heard, prevented further troubles. At the court's first sitting the millers' duties were

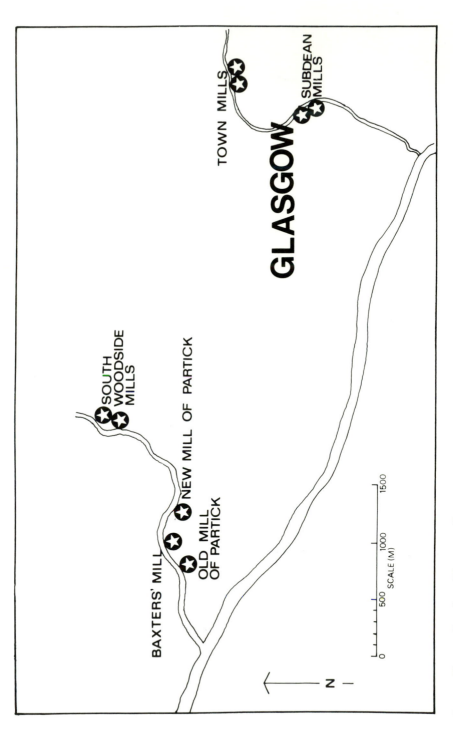

Fig 10. Glasgow Burgh and Baxter mills

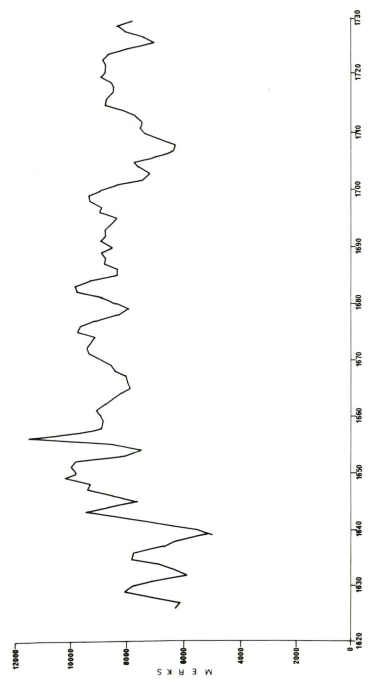

Fig 11. Rate of Glasgow Burgh mill tacks, 1626-1730. *SBRS Glasgow Burgh Records, I-IV*

restated, and Tuesdays and Thursdays reserved for grinding malt.[115]

From 1626 onwards the mills were rouped annually, yielding 6060 Merks in the first year, and continuing to bring in a revenue of between 5000 and 11550 Merks per annum throughout the rest of the period (Figure 11). Only when plague visited the city,[116] or when exceptionally cold winters froze the mills tight,[117] was it found necessary to partially refund the rent. Over the years, the proceeds of letting the mills came to represent a considerable sum of money, which was applied to several major projects; by 1655 the council could claim that the townsfolk had been able to 'repair thair kirkis, brigs, build thair tolboothe, commoune *caseys* paying thair ministers stipends, and many mae commoune workis, to the great guid, commodatioune, and decorment of the citie'.[118] Two years later the unlaw for abstraction was raised from £20 to £100, presumably with a view to guaranteeing the continued prosperity of the burgh.[119]

The Introduction of Roller Mills

The peace with the maltmen was never an easy one. In 1667, to pay for additional taxation, an extra 15s per mask was put onto existing malt duties,[120] and in 1689 the council was forced to refund 600 Merks to the tacksmen of the mills to compensate for a refusal by the maltmen to pay this, or another, imposition.[121] Another source of discord, not only in Glasgow, but all over Scotland, was the phrase 'tholling fire and water', which appeared in many articles of thirlage. While it was accepted that the phrase referred to malt, there was a singular lack of agreement as to whether the term included malt brewed within the thirl, or just signified that malted there. In 1680 the Court of Session found the former to be the case,[122] but in 1682 the same body found the brewing of malt to be outwith the scope of the term.[123] Not infrequently, malt bypassed the mill altogether; the brewers of Edinburgh were certainly guilty of this and in 1660 it was ordered that all hand-mills be destroyed, in an attempt to keep them to the burgh's mills.[124] Efforts to prevent abstractions by brewers were further hampered by the appearance of steel roller mills in Scotland in the late 17th century,[125] for whilst the preparation of meal required a grinding motion, that of malt involved only a bruising, which could be carried out more effectively with a hand-operated roller mill. In 1699 it was reported that 'a new custom of grinding malt by hand (i.e. steel) milnes hes creepit in amongst the brewers burgesses of Edinburgh',[126] a custom which continued despite efforts to eliminate such mills.[127] The confrontation with the brewers culminated in 1710 in a prolonged legal case in which the thirlage was found to stand,[128] but for the Magistrates of Edinburgh it was a hollow victory, and in 1711 it was decided to commute the thirlage and multure of malt for 12d Scots per barrel of beer sold.[129] In 1728, 'those concerned with breweries' in Glasgow asked that the thirlage of malt be commuted, and that they be allowed to grind it with steel mills on their own premises.[130]

Some counter-measures had already been taken: when, in 1725, a thirlage had been established over Port Glasgow, with a view to financing harbour repairs, the precaution had been taken of installing two steel mills in the port's mills,[131] while in 1727 the burgh of Glasgow bought a tack of Sir James Hamilton's mill at Newark for the 'benefit' of its steel mills at Port Glasgow.[132]

During the course of the next hundred years or so, many a Scottish burgh was to add steel mills to its existing mills, but so great were the incentives for brewers to install them in their own premises that such effort did little to stem the tide of abstractions. Although burgh mills were to find other lucrative sources of income, it was malt which represented the most important input to urban grain mills in the period 1550-1730. By creating astrictions to include malt, burghs could let their mills at high rents, the proceeds from which could be channeled into a great variety of projects, or used to pay debts and taxes.

Even when, as at Edinburgh, spending far outran income from burgh mills, they could be used as security on loans.[133] With few other sources of income available, it would appear that however detrimental it may have been in rural areas, thirlage was 'to the great guid' of the Scottish burgh.

Flour Mills

While the diet of the great bulk of Scotland's population continued to be based on oats and bere, rather than on wheat, it was unlikely that flour mills should be built anywhere other than the largest urban centres. None of the burgh mills of Glasgow had the requisite milling and boulting machinery, but the baxters are known to have had a wheat mill.[134] At Edinburgh, wheat and rye were ground on the town's common mills, and the implication is that here, as in other burghs known to have had incorporations of baxters, ordinary corn mills were used and boulting, if carried out at all, was performed by hand.

Pot Barley Mills

Something should also be said of Scotland's first pot barley mill, built at Saltoun, East Lothian in 1712. On 17th April 1710, Andrew Fletcher of Saltoun entered into an agreement through his brother, Henry, with James Meikle, wright at Wester Keith, under which Meikle was to visit Holland and investigate Dutch methods of making pot barley.[135] Returning to Scotland, Meikle built for Fletcher a mill which incorporated an edge-running millstone, and Dutch fanners previously unknown in Scotland. During the 18th century Saltoun barley mill, and the later bleachfield which bore its name, came to enjoy a widespread reputation.

NOTES

1. Roxburgh Mill and Ednam Mill both appear in charters dated 1128, Chalmers, G., *Caledonia* 4 vols., London, 1810, I, 135; Burleigh, J., *Ednam and its Indwellers*, Glasgow, 1912. Mills at Crailing, Jedburgh and Selkirk are all referred to in charters of David I (1124-53), Chalmers, *op. cit.*, I, 136, 997.

2. The earliest known reference to cloth fulling mills concerns one at Innerleithen during the time of David II (1329-71), Chalmers, *op. cit.*, I, 935.

3. SRO GD110/740/1; SRO GD62/275.

4. SRO GD44/17/8. Mitchell, Sir A. (ed.), 'Macfarlane's Geographical Collections', *SHS* LI (1906), LII (1907), LIII (1908), LI 105.

5. *SBRS*, 'Extracts from the Records of the Burgh of Edinburgh', IV, 1573-89, Edinburgh 1882. A new damhead for the Wester Mills of Edinburgh, built in 1584, used ashlar stone.

6. SRO GD90/2/196.

7. McCall, H. B., *The History and Antiquities of the Parish of Mid-Calder*, Edinburgh, 1894, 40.

8. McGill, W., *Old Ross-shire and Scotland*, Inverness, 1909.

9. Morison, W. M., *Dictionary of Decisions of the Court of Session*, 36 vols., Edinburgh, 1811, XI, 8895.

10. SRO GD121/408/1/38.

11. SRO GD44/19/10/H.

12. Morison, *op. cit.*, XIV, 15965.

13. *Ibid.*, III, 1818. In 1695 a new corn mill was built at Camserney, Perthshire, to which the suckeners of the Mill of Aberfeldy on the north side of the Tay became thirled. SRO GD 50/133/35.

14. Morison, *op. cit.*, XI, 8897-8.

15. SRO GD141/265.

16. Morison, *op. cit.*, XXXV, 15988.

17. *Ibid.*, XXXV, 15959, 15971, 15972, 15974, 15979.

18. For an example see Gunn, C. B. (ed.), 'Records of the Baron Court of Stitchill, 1655-1807', *SHS* L (1905), 22.

19. SRO GD188/3/4.

20. Barron, D. G. (ed.), 'The Court Book of the Barony of Urie in Kincardineshire, 1604-1747', *SHS* XII (1892), 90; Gunn, *op. cit.*, 88, 112; Broun-Lindsay, Lady (ed.), 'The Barony Court of Colstoun: Extracts from its Records', *TELA&FNS* II (1930-31), 125-6; SRO GD18/695; SRO GD50/159; SRO GD245/7/4.

21. SRO GD50/159.

22. Barron, *op. cit.*, 38; SRO GD50/159; SRO GD245/7/4.

23. Gunn, *op. cit.*, 152; Barron, *op. cit.*, 94-5.

24. SRO GD25/1/776; SRO GD50/159; SRO GD205/24/154; SRO GD225/1033.

25. Barron, *op. cit.*, 94-5; Gunn, *op. cit.*, 122; SRO GD245/7/4.

26. Morison, *op. cit.*, XXXV, 16968-9.

27. Broun-Lindsay, *op. cit.*, 125-6.

28. SRO GD18/695.

29. *SBRS*, 'Extracts from the Records of the Burgh of Glasgow', I, 1573-1642, Glasgow, 1876, 136. When the town's mill on the Kelvin was inspected in 1589, it was found to have a runner of only two inches thickness. SRO GD26/5/650. An appraisal of Shawsmill, Fife, taken in 1693, includes a runner stone only one inch thick.

30. Gunn, *op. cit.*, 169-70.

31. SRO GD73/1/32(b).

32. SRO GD10/1214; SRO GD86/726.

33. SRO GD109/3120; SRO GD157/1001.

34. SRO GD90/195-6; agreements on payment for the construction of a 'mill stool' and 'mill wall' at Powmill (NO634557) and a mill-dam at Kinnaird (NO632578), both in 1719.

35. SRO GD16/27/102; SRO GD26/2/1; SRO GD26/5/74; SRO GD27/2075.

36. Cochran-Patrick, R. W., *Mediaeval Scotland*, Glasgow, 1892, 163-8.

37. SRO GD26/5/74.

38. Broun-Lindsay, *op. cit.*, 147.

39. SRO GD26/5/87.

40. *Ibid*.

41. SRO GD26/5/74. For similar obligations see Gunn, *op. cit.*, 113.

42. SRO GD26/2/1.

43. SRO GD28/2075.

44. SRO GD137/3546.

45. SRO GD225/1033, 11 May 1727: The miller at the Upper Mill of Rathven, Banffshire was set upon by one Jean Wilson and her three sons and suffered the humiliation of having to be rescued by his wife.

46. SRO GD52/313; SRO GD62/266.

47. Smout, T. C., *A History of the Scottish People, 1560-1830*, London, 1969.

48. Morison, *op. cit.*, XXXV, 15975.

49. *RSSRS* 1st Series V, 193 (1594); VI 423 (1602); VI 504 (1602); XI 51-2 (1616); *RSSRS* 2nd Series II 596 (1628); III 14-15 (1629); V 640-1 (1634); *RSSRS* 3rd Series I 399 (1662); II 650 (1669); III 133 (1669); VII 567 (1682); X 198 (1685). The same practice was extended to other types of mill with even more damaging results. *RSSRS* 3rd Series I 399 (1663).

50. *RSSRS* 1st Series X 180 (1613).

51. McGill, *op. cit.*, Tain No. 420 (1678). When the Laird of Calrossie's Ross-shire mill was destroyed, its suckeners were faced with 'all the toyell and trouble . . . of going over the sands to the Milns of Morvie and Milntown'.

52. *Synod of Fife 1611-87*, Abbotsford Club (1937), 29.

53. *APS* V 269 1640 c.15.

54. *APS* VII 262 1661 c.281. For an example of similarly directed local legislation see SRO GD50/136/1 vol. 1, 11/12 July 1660.

55. Morison, *op. cit.*, XXXV, 15969.

56. SRO GD137/3546 (1631) (Balmerino, Fife); SRO GD50/136/1 (1683) (Menzies, Perthshire); SRO GD25/6/233a (1678) (Maybole, Ayrshire); SRO GD26/2/1 (1666) (Monymail, Fife). A limited form of exemption.

57. SRO GD25/6/233a. The mill in question was Deansmill.

58. SRO GD188/3/4.

59. SRO GD44/51/747; SRO GD45/18/385; SRO GD52/250; SRO GD52/387; SRO GD124/17/175.

60. SRO GD25/6/39; SRO GD25/9/47; SRO GD25/9/76; SRO GD109/2973, 3120, 3276, 3388, 3616.

61. SRO GD45/18/177, 385, 1497; SRO GD45/21/6; SRO GD124/17/175; SRO GD188/3/4; SRO GD248/1384.

62. SRO GD44/51/747; SRO GD52/250, 387; SRO GD121/224/15.

63. SRO GD1/447/26; SRO GD16/28/307; SRO GD44/51/747; SRO GD45/18/1497; SRO GD45/20/102; SRO GD52/387; SRO GD121/224/33.

64. SRO GD52/387.

65. SRO GD52/387; SRO RH15/25/93.

66. SRO GD18/734, 736; SRO GD28/2075; SRO GD52/250, 387; SRO GD110/840; SRO GD121/223/44; SRO GD157/990, 1001; SRO GD203/11/4; SRO GD/237/202.

67. SRO GD128/47/8; SRO RH15/25/93.

68. SRO GD121/224/15.

69. *RMSRS* V, 754 (1584).

70. SRO GD26/5/123; SRO GD121/224/15; SRO GD203/11/44.

71. SRO GD1/413/12, Garvald, p.33.

72. SRO GD26/5/119, 123.

73. SRO GD26/5/84, 86, 93, 107, 147, 148; SRO GD28/2161.

74. SRO GD1/447/26; SRO GD16/28/307; SRO GD121/224/15; SRO GD124/17/175.

75. SRO GD121/224/15.

76. SRO GD121/224/15.

77. SRO GD157/990. For further comments on income from mills see Sanderson, M. H. B., *Scottish Rural Society in the Sixteenth Century*, Edinburgh, 1982, 17, 31-2, 42; Whyte, I., *Agriculture and Society in Seventeenth Century Scotland*, Edinburgh, 1979, 32-33, 35.

78. Of the thirty mills for which multure rates were available, four had rates of 1/25th, nine of 1/24th, two of 1/21st, two of 1/20th, one of 1/17th, six of 1/16th, and six of 1/13th. Sources — various.

79. See Glossary.

80. SRO GD205/2 (Cond. 2).

81. Bennett, R. & Elton, J., *The History of Corn Milling*, 2 vols., Liverpool, 1898-9 and 4 vols., New York, N.D., II, 218.

82. Irons, J. C., *Leith and its Antiquities*, 2 vols., Edinburgh N.D., II, 98.

83. *Ibid.*, II, 151-2.

84. *OSA* XIV, 557, Linlithgow, West Lothian.

85. Bennett & Elton, *op. cit.*, IV, 214.

86. *SBRS*, Glasgow, I, 56.

87. *Ibid.*, I, 463.

88. *Ibid.*, I, 57.

89. *Ibid.*, I, 86-7.

90. *Ibid.*, I, 136.

91. *Ibid.*, I, 277.

92. *SBRS*, 'Charters and Documents Relating to the Burgh of Peebles, 1165-1710', Edinburgh, 1872.

93. Kennedy, W., *Annals of Aberdeen*, 2 vols., London, 1818, I, 410.

94. Morison, *op. cit.*, 8899-8901.

95. McDowall, W., *History of Dumfries*, Edinburgh, 1867, 544-5.

96. Black, D. D., *The History of Brechin to 1864*, 2nd Edition, Edinburgh, 1867, 45.

97. *APS* IX, 456.

98. *SBRS*, 'Extracts from the Records of the Royal Burgh of Stirling 1519-1666', Glasgow, 1887, 143.

99. *SBRS*, 'Extracts from the Records of the Burgh of Edinburgh', II 1528-1557,

Edinburgh, 1871, 6.

100. *SBRS*, Edinburgh V 1589-1603, 258.

101. *SBRS*, Edinburgh II, 233.

102. Morison, *op. cit.*, XI, 8899-8901.

103. *RMSRS* XI, 883 (1666).

104. SRO GD62/263.

105. Cleland, J., *Annals of Glasgow*, 2 vols., Glasgow, 1816, II 512-3.

106. *SBRS*, Glasgow I, 278.

107. *Ibid.*, I 280-1.

108. *Ibid.*, I 278.

109. *Ibid.*, I 279.

110. *Ibid.*, I 280. This sum included the 'ladles' or market dues.

111. *Ibid.*, I 284-5.

112. *Ibid.*, I 289.

113. *Ibid.*, I 337.

114. *SBRS*, 'Extracts from the Records of the Burgh of Glasgow', II 1630-1662, Glasgow, 1881, 562-3.

115. *Ibid.*, 564.

116. *Ibid.*, II 127 (1647); 371 (1657).

117. *Ibid.*, II 27 (1635).

118. *Ibid.*, II 309.

119. *Ibid.*, 360.

120. *SBRS*, 'Extracts from the Records of the Burgh of Glasgow', III 1663-1690, Glasgow, 1905, 90.

121. *Ibid.*, III 421-2.

122. Morison, *op. cit.*, XXXV, 15984.

123. *Ibid.*, XXXV, 15987.

124. *Ibid.*, XI, 8903.

125. SRO RH15/102/1. In 1694 one was bought in London for the corn mill at New-mills Manufactory, East Lothian.

126. *SBRS*, 'Extracts from the Records of the Burgh of Edinburgh', XII, 1689-1701, Edinburgh, 1962, 247.

127. *Ibid.*, XII 247, 279.

128. Morison, *op. cit.*, XI, 8899-8901.

129. *SBRS*, 'Extracts from the Records of the Burgh of Edinburgh', XIII, 1701-18, Edinburgh, 1967, 212.

130. *SBRS*, 'Extracts from the Records of the Burgh of Glasgow', V, 1718-38, Glasgow, 1909, 266. For a contemporary rural example of steel mills, see SRO GD6/1028.

131. *SBRS*, Glasgow, IV, 208-10, 222.

132. *Ibid.*, 290.

133. *SBRS*, 'Extracts from the Records of the Burgh of Edinburgh', X, 1665-80, Edinburgh, 1950, xxxiii.

134. *RSSRS*, 3rd Series, I, 1661-4.

135. East Lothian County Council, *East Lothian Water Mills*, Haddington, 1970, 12. The contract is reproduced on the same page.

3

Water Power in the Textile Industry

From mediaeval times onwards the growth, manufacture and export of wool assumed an important place in the economy of Scotland, and by the late 16th century textile production as a whole had become, by Scottish standards, 'ane industry of considerable stature'.[1] Wool, being a plentiful natural resource, and a ready source of foreign revenue, was exported raw throughout the period: in a table of Scottish exports for the period 1611-1614 *wool fells*, valued at £143,000 Scots, represented the largest single item, while wool, valued at £52,000 Scots, ranked fifth out of seventeen commodities with a total value of £736,000 Scots.[2]

There was, however, an awareness that by exporting wool as cloth Scotland could obtain more foreign revenue than by exporting only raw wool; as Sir Thomas Craig pointed out in 1605:

> In future our people must pay very particular attention to the manufacture of cloth, for thence will proceed our ability to import wines, merchandise, and those things on which men set store. Otherwise, we shall find it hard to raise the money to pay for our imports.[3]

What Sir Thomas Craig's appeal fails to bring out is that Scotland already had a significant domestic wool manufacture which provided for the needs of the majority of Scots and which had been using water power in one process for several centuries.

Origins, Introduction and Technology of Fulling

From its earliest application to the textile industry in the 12th century,[4] water power was confined to fulling, a finishing process whereby warp and weft fibres were matted together. The machinery employed consisted of a lying shaft, fitted with cams, which alternately depressed and released a hinged arm, at the far end of which was fixed a wooden block which rose and fell in a trough of water (Figure 12). The movement of the block on a piece of cloth immersed in the trough imitated the action of feet, the use of which had given the name walking or waulking to the fulling process. When the process was mechanised, the name stuck, and in Scotland fulling mills were known as waulk mills.

Although teasing, carding, spinning and weaving continued to be performed

Fig 12. The machinery of a 17th-century fulling mill. *Strada, 1617*

by hand, the application of water power to the laborious process of fulling was sufficiently important a breakthrough to be considered as an 'Industrial Revolution' in its own right.[5] The fulling mill soon found its way to Scotland, the earliest known being one mentioned during the reign of David II (1329-1371) at Innerleithen, Peeblesshire.[6]

A waulk mill could be readily built using resources gathered from a small area. The construction of a particularly fine mill at Gifford, East Lothian exemplifies this well. Sandstone, cut from quarries at Garvald and Quarryford Mill, was carried by cart to the site: two pairs of men carted over a hundred loads of lime which, together with the stone, was used by two masons (both from Gifford) to build the mill. Of the timber required, nine oaks were cut in the Cersell Wood, one in the Deer Park, and two pieces were taken from the wood yard; two elms were cut in the Briken Gett and one birch tree from the end of Lamintien's Walk. The eight thousand nails used were provided by the local smith, who also made locks, hinges and other items of ironwork. Two wrights, working at different periods, put in one hundred and three days' work, at 20d per day. They and their five assistants installed floor boards, wooden beams, seventeen windows, six doors and a staircase. A gang of ten day-labourers helped the craftsmen, excavated lades, and carried the one hundred and forty-seven loads of stone needed for the damhead. The waulk-miller himself had lived in the next parish and took part in the construction of the mill. The total expenditure of £115 18s 9d represents a sum well above what might be laid out on building a more typical waulk mill.[7]

Distribution

According to Gulvin, fulling mills were still scarce in the 17th century, only a few Lowland centres having one.[8] Unfortunately, no complete list exists, but research has revealed that they were by no means scarce at that time, there being at least three hundred fulling mills in Scotland, from Orkney to Galloway and from Berwickshire to Islay (Figure 13). As one might expect, their distribution coincides with those areas most associated with woollen cloth manufacture during the period. Aberdeenshire, Strathmore, Perth-Dundee, the Fife Leven, the Stirling area, North Ayrshire, Galloway, Edinburgh, the Esk Valley, Haddington and the Borders all show concentrations of mills; Galashiels and Huntingtower, Perth each had three fulling mills.[9] Also apparent, however, is the widespead dispersal of mills throughout much of Lowland Scotland, for besides the cloth which found its way onto the market, great quantities were woven for domestic use wherever wool could be obtained.

Operation

For a landlord with the capital to spare, the establishment of a waulk mill could provide a steady income in the form of rent, generally in cash rather than kind. Sums varied from £4 Scots (plus twelve capons) in 16th-century Aberdeenshire, to £60 Scots in 18th-century Wigtonshire.[10] A survey of certain parishes, carried out in 1626, cites the absence of waulk mills as one reason for the low valuation of Newton parish, Midlothian, and their presence as the reason for the augmented value of Logie parish, Stirlingshire.[11]

Although no multure could be exacted, a thirlage similar to that of corn

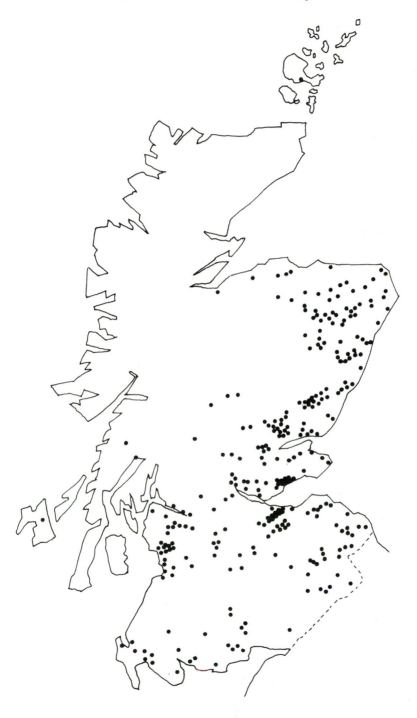

Fig 13. Distribution of fulling mills, 1550-1730

could be established over the tenants of the mill owner. At Stitchill, Roxburghshire in 1698, all those living within the barony were thirled to Stitchill waulk
mill during their residency, with a £5 Scots fine for each abstraction. In
exchange for this, the suckeners were offered safeguards similar to those which
applied to grain mills:

> . . . if any . . . persons have ground of complaint for insufficient work, either
> litting or waking, or for ther wakers detayning ther cloath longer than the dew
> reasonable tym, the waker shall be obleidged to repair the complainer in all
> damnage that they have therby suffered. And lykewyse shall be fynned in the
> soum of 5lib Scots for each failzie, the one halfe to be given to the complainer
> besyd his reparation of damnage for said. Lykewyse declairing that if it can be suf-
> ficiently instructed by any of the saids persons that the waker refused ther work at
> reasonable pryce (which is heirby declared to be the ordinar pryce of other
> workmen in the country) they shall have liberty to imply uther and cary the work
> to uther mylnes. The waker is ordayned to go through the parioch and cary away
> the cloath and bring it back again.[12]

Besides the rural waulk mills, there were those associated with burgh crafts,
such as weavers, bonnetmakers and skinners. (Skinners used waulk mills to
soften hides.) In Edinburgh, an agreement (later found to be unlawful) was
made between the deacons of the bonnetmakers and the walkers of Edinburgh,
involving mills at Roslin, Colinton, Silver Mills, Bells Mill, Wester Woodmill,
Baldony Mill and elsewhere.[13] Between Woodhall, in Colinton parish, and the
sea, there were at least ten waulk mills operating on the Water of Leith during
the period 1550-1730, all largely dependent upon work supplied by Edinburgh
guilds. In smaller burghs, one or other of the guilds often owned, or at least
rented, a mill of their own: the bonnetmakers of Dundee had their own mill at
Balmossie Mill[14] while at Kilmarnock the bonnetmakers had a waulk mill
which still bore their name in the 19th century.[15]

Although new mills might be built and others converted from corn mills,
there was nothing inherently new in the organisation of either rural or urban
waulk mills: seldom, if ever, were they anything other than isolated units in
the manufacturing process, taking in cloth which had been woven elsewhere,
and spun in yet another place. In the mid-17th century, however, a new type of
unit began to appear, in which the various stages in manufacture were spatially
integrated. These new 'protofactories', if one might call them that, also
departed from tradition in the type of cloth produced, for, instead of the usual
coarse cloth, they were primarily concerned with producing high quality
products.

For some time the Government had sought to improve the woollen industry.
In 1582, legislation was passed enabling a group of Flemings to come to
Scotland to instruct apprentices, and a second group were later brought over
for similar purposes. In both cases, little benefit was derived, although in 1609
the few members of the latter group still resident in Scotland were said to be
giving 'grite licht and knawledg to the country-people'.[16] A Standing Committee for Manufactures, set up in 1623, failed to make any lasting impression,

and it was not until the passing of Acts aimed at helping the fine woollen sector, in 1641 and 1645, that even limited success was achieved. Under the Acts manufacturers were permitted to import, duty-free, wool, oil and dye-stuffs; the cloth made was also free of all duties, and the manufacturers and their workmen were granted exemption from military service.[17] As a result of the two Acts, woollen manufactories were set up at Edinburgh (Bonnington), Ayr and Newmills, near Haddington. Those at Bonnington and Newmills were said to have had some success, but the latter failed to survive General Monk's occupation of Haddington in 1651.[18] The Newmills operation definitely included a fulling mill: in the early 17th century a fulling mill there had been converted into two grain mills, but by 1649 one had been converted back again, probably to serve the manufactory.[19]

The Glasgow Manufactory

Not so well known, but probably better documented, was a manufactory set up in Glasgow in 1650. On 2nd March that year, the burgh council decided to engage Simon Pickersgill, an English clothier, to build and manage a cloth manufactory;[20] for his services, Pickersgill was to receive £45 Sterling per annum, an indication of the importance attached to his skills.[21] Events moved with a speed uncharacteristic of 17th-century Scotland: by the end of March, Simon Pickersgill and one John Carse had been promised 40s to cover their expenses in visiting waulk mills in the 'east country' (presumably the Edinburgh area), and by the end of April sufficient progress had been made for work to begin on cutting the lade to serve a new waulk mill at Partick.[22] The design of the mill was probably based, therefore, on the best to be found in Scotland. For their looms they looked further afield, and on 4th May 1650 Peter and John Johnstoun were instructed to go to Holland, where they were to buy £500 worth of equipment for the manufactory.[23]

Within the year of Pickersgill being taken on, the manufactory was well established, buying its own wool and dyestuffs from abroad, spinning yarn, weaving cloth, and fulling and dyeing it. Without hesitation the council engaged Pickersgill for a second year, at a slightly augmented salary.[24] Revolutionary as this degree of integration may have been for its time, the next step taken was even more so. In May 1651 the sale of cloth, and the profit accruing therefrom, was brought under the control of the manufactory. Edward Robiesoun, the man responsible for marketing, was to collect dressed (i.e. fulled) cloth from the manufactory, sell it and return the proceeds for re-investment in raw materials such as wool and dyestuffs. Prior to being sold, each piece was to be inspected and valued.[25]

Whether on account of poor results, or just lack of interest, the burgh council's direct involvement with their ambitious and far-sighted project was short-lived. In July 1652, the manufactory was set in tack to Pickersgill,[26] and thereafter no more is heard of the manufactory, or of its waulk mill until 1660, by which time the original integrated organisation had ceased to exist. The weavers offered to take the 'hous of manufactorie' for a period of seven years, at £60 Scots per annum, while the waulk mill was leased to the litsters, for the same duration, at £100 Scots per annum; in effect, control had reverted to the guilds, and in that respect the mill had come to be no different from any other urban waulk mill. Although the litsters' tack incorporated the provision that they should vacate the mill were it needed for any other purpose,[27] they continued in possession for five years, took a second term in 1665 and were offered a third in 1671.[28] Despite repairs in 1689, the mill had fallen into ruin by 1695, and the tacksman had sunk deep into debt. In the latter year, a litster, Thomas Brown, took over the mill with promises to rebuild it; the following year he obtained a nineteen-year tack of the restored mill at 100 Merks (£66 13s 8d Scots) per annum, and was offered a further eleven years on the expiry of the first term.[29] By 1717 the mill was once again in ruins, with the water wheel broken to pieces and the watercourse running through the mill itself.[30] Once again the mill was restored, and although flax-scutching equipment was installed in 1735 (see p. 187), it was only on condition that part of the mill be kept always as a waulk mill.[31] As for Simon Pickersgill, he seems to have held his interest in the manufactory long after the weavers had taken over, and not until 1675 was his imminent departure noted.[32] For all the capital invested and effort expended in establishing the manufacture of fine woollen cloth, very little was achieved, and even when, in 1661, the Act of 1641 was re-enacted, it was to little effect in the absence of a well-protected home market.[33] Not until 1681, with the passing of the Act for Encouraging Trade and Manufactures, was a positive move made towards providing such protection.

Besides banning the importation and wearing of certain luxury items, the Act prohibited the importation of many different types of fine cloth. Foreigners possessed of either capital or technical skills were to receive naturalisation on setting up manufactures of cloth, linen, stockings or soap and on teaching the trade to Scots. Any raw materials required for a manufactory qualifying under the Act were to be admitted free of custom and all other public duties in perpetuity. Any manufactured products exported were to be exempted from duties for a period of nineteen years. The capital invested was declared not to be subject to public or local taxes; soldiers were not to be quartered in manufactories, and workers were to have seven years' exemption from military service. Lastly, the Act prohibited the export of home-produced raw materials such as lint or yarn.[34]

The favourable industrial climate created by the Act led to the establishment of fine-cloth manufactories in Edinburgh, Glasgow, Musselburgh and at Gordon Mills (Aberdeen), Harcarse (Berwickshire) and Gardin (Angus),[35] but the first, and the most successful, was the resuscitated Newmills manufactory, near Haddington.

Newmills Manufactory

The buildings and lands of the earlier manufactory had come into the hands of Sir James Stampfield, and it was he, with Robert Blackwood, a prominent Edinburgh merchant, who held most of the shares in the Newmills company of 1681. Stampfield agreed to let to the company 'that great manufactory stone house on the south side of the village of Newmylnes, being 101 foot in length, 21 foot in breadth within the walls and three storie high', dimensions not untypical of the cotton mills of a hundred years later (p. 319); the waulk mill was also included in the lease.[36] With favourable government policies and the prestige of royal patronage, there was little difficulty in raising capital; indeed, in its early years finance was the least of the company's problems. Initially, there was difficulty in recruiting weavers from England and when, in October 1681, production did start, it was with only two looms which produced not fine but coarse cloth. For some time after the prohibition of fine cloth imports, demand for fine woollen cloth outstripped production at Newmills. By 1683 the number of looms had increased to twenty-seven and, this not being sufficient to meet demand, a further ten looms were ordered.[37] The company now felt in a position to submit tenders for the military uniforms which the Privy Council had recently approved, but in the event it was found that they could provide only part of the cloth needed, and this at a price well above that of English cloth. In the interests of economy, but much to the company's disappointment, a special licence was granted under which cloth for this purpose was imported from England. The granting of licences ceased in 1685, but despite this, and the granting to the company of further privileges, complaints about the importation of fine cloth and the export of wool were still being made in 1696. Only with the passing of a further Act in 1701 were these imports and exports banned, and even then the legislation proved to be ineffectual; in 1704 the full resumption of wool exports received official consent.[38] For all its difficulties, the company managed to survive in one form or another for a period of thirty years. Employment had been found for 700 people at a time when the provision of work was considered of paramount importance; to accommodate workers a 'considerable village' had been built.[39] Besides a fulling mill, which Defoe later described as 'very good',[40] the company installed a gig-mill for raising the surface of cloth.[41] Such mills first appeared in Europe during the late 15th century, and had been used in England since at least 1640. That at Newmills was imported from England. As for frizzing mills, which by a circular rubbing motion gave the cloth a granular effect, none are recorded at Newmills, though two had been installed at Restalrig paper mill by 1690. In 1673 the owner of the paper mill, James Hamilton of Little Earnock, received ratification from Parliament of the privileges of a manufactory for frizzing cloth.[42]

The application of power to fulling and probably to cloth raising helped to remove a major bottleneck in production, but a continued dependence upon skilled manual labour for every other process ensured that production remained inflexible and incapable of fulfilling large orders or benefiting from any potential economies of scale. In this vital respect the manufactories of the late 17th century differed from the mechanised textile mills of the late 18th century. Furthermore, the Newmills company had to pay higher wages to attract English workers; according to Gulvin, wage rates for immigrant workers were fifty per cent higher than those paid in England and nearly twice those paid to Scots. Fine wool, unobtainable from Scottish sources, had to be imported from England and Spain, and to buy these the Scots had to bid against the better-established Dutch and English industries.

The Scottish fine cloth industry had never achieved a state of good health. Government policy had failed to help, and even before 1707 the industry was mortally ill; the Union did little more than administer the death-blow, most of the manufactories being given up soon after. By 1711 preparations were being made to wind up the Newmills works, and on 20th March 1713 the machinery was sold off.[43] Whatever the benefits of the Union may have been for other industries, there were few obvious ones for the Scottish woollen industry. Exports of raw wool were banned and Scottish manufactories were exposed to open competition from England.

But however little hope there was for the fine woollen industry, the traditional manufacture of coarse woollens survived unscathed: low quality also meant low price and, for the great majority of Scots, clothing needs continued to be met by the household manufacture of wool from local sheep, employing the services of nearby litsters, waulkers and custom weavers. The home market continued to offer an outlet for surplus production, while markets for cheap cloth in the English colonies, now legitimate customers for Scottish traders, helped to compensate for any lost in Europe.[44] When, eventually, power was applied to other processes in the manufacture of wool, it was, significantly, not large joint-stock companies but the owners and lessees of waulk mills who were able to seize the opportunity and put production on a true factory basis.

NOTES

1. Lythe, S. G. E., *The Economy of Scotland in its European Setting 1550-1625*, Edinburgh, 1960, 39.

2. Pryde, G. S., *Scotland from 1603 to the Present Day*, Edinburgh, 1962, 28.

3. Quoted in Pryde, *op. cit.*, 28.

4. See Scott, E. K., 'Early Cloth Fulling and its Machinery', *TNS* XII, 1931-2, 30-52.

5. Carus-Wilson, E. M., 'An Industrial Revolution in the Thirteenth Century', *EcHR* XI-XII (1941-3).

6. Chalmers, G., *Caledonia*, 4 vols., London, 1810, II, 935.

7. *NLS* Acc. 4862, Box 46 f. 1.

8. Gulvin, C., *The Tweedmakers*, Newton Abbot, 1973, 20.

9. *RMSRS* X 139 (1653).

10. *RMSRS* VI 1902 (1607).

11. *Reports on the State of Certain Parishes in Scotland 1627*, Maitland Club XXXIV, Edinburgh, 1835.

12. Gunn, C. B. (ed.), 'Records of the Baron Court of Stitchill, 1655-1807', *SHS* L (1905), 139.

13. *RMSRS* 1st Series X 589 (1616).

14. SRO GD45/18/444.

15. OS 6"/mile 1st edition Ayrshire (1856) (GR NS437392).

16. Gulvin, *op. cit.*, 22-23.

17. *Ibid.*, 23.

18. Scott, W. R., *Joint Stock Companies to 1700*, 3 vols., Cambridge, 1910-12, III, 138 *et seq.*

19. *RMSRS* VII 1595 (1617); *RMSRS* VIII 1547 (1630); *RMSRS* IX 2039 (1649). The manufactory had certainly started by 1644, in which year Sir Adam Hepburn of Humbie and Sir James Riddell, an Edinburgh merchant, took in William Sykes, an English clothier, as partner.

20. *SBRS* Glasgow II, 185.

21. *Ibid.*, 185.

22. *Ibid.*, 186. An earlier waulk mill at Partick is referred to in *RMSRS* V 1406 (1587).

23. *SBRS* Glasgow II, 207.

24. *Ibid.*, 199, 200.

25. *Ibid.*, 207.

26. *Ibid.*, 234.

27. *Ibid.*, 435.

28. *SBRS* Glasgow III, 64, 158.

29. *SBRS* Glasgow IV, 161, 178, 204, 534.

30. *Ibid.*, 618.

31. *SBRS* Glasgow V, 434.

32. *SBRS* Glasgow III, 199.

33. *APS* VII, 261-2.

34. Scott, W. R. (ed.), 'New Mills Cloth Manufactory, 1681-1703', *SHS* XLVI (1905), xxxvii-xxxviii; *APS* VIII, 348-9.

35. Gulvin, *op. cit.*, 24.

36. Scott, *op. cit.* (1905), lvi.

37. *Ibid.*, lxiii.

38. Gulvin, *op. cit.*, 25-6.

39. Scott, *op. cit.* (1905), lxv; Mitchell, Sir A. (ed.), 'Macfarlane's Geographical Collections', *SHS* LI (1906), LII (1907), LIII (1908).

40. Defoe, D., *A Tour thro' the Whole Island of Great Britain*, 2 vols., London, 1727, II, 701.

41. SRO RH15/102/1.

42. *RSSRS* 3rd Series XV, 1690; *APS* IX, 340, 1693 c.83.

43. Scott, *op. cit.* (1905), lxxxiv.

44. Gulvin, C., 'The Union and the Scottish Woollen Industry 1707-1760', *SHR* L (1971).

4

Paper Mills

The art of paper making seems to have originated in China, and to have reached Europe via Spain, through the agency of the Arabs. As early as the 12th century, the stamping mill had been applied to the industry at Xatava in Spain,[1] where it was often used to soften and pulp rags, a natural development from the fulling mill; during the course of the next few centuries paper-making, incorporating the use of water-powered stamping mills (Figure 14), became well established in France, Switzerland, Germany and the Low Countries, the processes involved being the object of much secrecy. About the year 1495, one John Tate built England's first paper mill in Hertfordshire. Two additional mills were founded in the 1550s, but not until 1585, with the establishment of a mill at Dartford by a German, Hans Spielman, did a commercially successful mill appear.[2] Only five years later, in 1590, Scotland had her first paper mill. In 1588 James IV had granted privileges, then a monopoly, to 'Pietter Gryther and Michaell Kysar, almanis paper makeris'. In paper, as in metallurgy, the technically advanced Germans were, by the late 16th century, seeking opportunities to exploit their knowledge in countries other than their own. Furthermore the favourable attitude of the crown towards industrial development offered an incentive for such people to settle in Scotland.

Dalry Paper Mill

By 1590, a paper mill with a nine-year monopoly was in operation at the Wester Mill of Dalry, on the Water of Leith near Edinburgh.[3] By a contract of 3rd May 1594 the Russells, owners of Dalry Mills, agreed to provide further accommodation by raising the mill walls by eight feet and installing a loft for paper drying in the space thus made available; Mungo Russell and his son, Gideon, had taken a share in the enterprise, which by this time was apparently thriving.[4] In exchange for an eleven-year tack, Michael Keysar and another German, John Seillar, were to pay £200 Scots per annum, and to undertake to instruct apprentices as chosen by Gideon Russell.[5] Any suggestion that this might have been a public-spirited move to disseminate this useful knowledge is contradicted by another clause, which prohibited the Germans from giving assistance in the building of other paper mills.

The mill is mentioned in 1605, but in the absence of any subsequent refer-

Fig 14. The machinery of a 17th-century paper mill. *Strada, 1617*

ences, both Waterston and Thomson were led to postulate that the mill was
given up, and that not until 1673 was paper making at Dalry resumed. A paper
mill at Dalry appears in the Register of the Great Seal in 1642, but the
document concerned is apparently based on that of 1605.[6] What is certain is
that in 1673 a mill at Dalry was leased by a copartnery of six Edinburgh
merchant burgesses, and that they had obtained manufactory status by 1675.[7]

French craftsmen were introduced including one Nicholas de Champ, who was to figure prominently in the early Scottish paper industry.

After a fire in 1675 the mill was rebuilt for 'making gray and blue paper much finer than ever this country previously offered'.[8] After a second fire in 1679, Alexander Daes, the merchant burgess who had run the mill, was reduced to becoming the showman of an elephant. Although Daes later returned to paper making at Dalry, no more is heard of the mill; Daes died in 1684, and by 1699 the mill had reverted to corn grinding.[9]

Other Coarse Paper Mills

Long before the final demise of the Dalry Mill, paper mills had been established elsewhere in Scotland. At Canonmills, on the Water of Leith, one had been founded c.1652; in 1659 it was held in tack by John Paterson who, in 1681, sublet it to Peter Bruce, a German (Flemish) Engineer.[10] Bruce spent £1,000 on the mill, and successfully petitioned for a monopoly in the manufacture and sale of playing cards. The patent was to have taken effect as from April 1st 1682, but in March of that year the mill suffered malicious damage which put it out of action: water was diverted away from the mill and Bruce's wife was thrown into the mill dam. To keep going Bruce built a small mill nearby, but in the following year, after obtaining recompense for the damage to his first mill, he left Canonmills, and moved to Woodside, near Glasgow, where John Campbell of Woodside was to have a new mill ready for him by 1st May 1683. Here too there were difficulties. On returning from a recruiting drive in Holland, Bruce found that Campbell and James Peddie, the third member of the partnership, had been interfering with the mill and its workers, apparently with a view to preventing Bruce from fulfilling an agreement to buy Peddie out. Bruce brought an action before the Privy Council, and was awarded 1,000 Merks damages. Despite the success of this action, he left Glasgow and returned to Edinburgh where, in 1686, he established a mill at Restalrig, with James Home, one of the Dalry co-partners. In 1690 the mill and the playing-card monopoly were transferred to James Hamilton of Little Earnock; thereafter no more is heard of Bruce.[11]

In 1661 the Register of the Great Seal refers to a paper mill at Spylaw, on the Water of Leith.[12] According to Thomson, the Upper Spylaw mill dates only from 1681, in which year Sir James Lithgow started paper making there with help from Nicholas de Champ, who had left Dalry after the second fire.[13] It must be assumed, therefore, that either the 1661 mill occupied a different site and was short-lived or that it was, in fact, the same mill as that referred to in 1681. In either case, there was almost certainly a mill in the Spylaw area earlier than was previously thought. Apparently the mill was still in Lithgow's possession in 1700, and after his death in 1703, his widow held it in tack until at least 1704.[14] De Champ seems to have left Lithgow's employment in the early 1680s: in 1686 he was working for Bruce, and in the same or the following year he moved to Glasgow and established his own mill at Cathcart on the White Cart Water. The mill prospered, and was still in operation in the early 19th century.[15] Another mill was started at Ayton, Berwickshire in 1693 by William Home. Little is known of the mill other than the fact that it made grey paper; Thomson assumes that the mill was short-lived.[16] In 1696 Patrick Sandilands of Coton established paper making on the River Don at Gordon's Mills, near Aberdeen.[17] Despite the establishment of these mills, imports of paper were still running at 6,000 reams per annum during the period 1685-1696,[18] probably because home production was confined to blue, grey and pressing papers, while writing and printing papers still had to come from outside. The production within Scotland of these latter classes of paper was to be the object of the most ambitious paper-making project of the era.

The Scots White Paper Company

In 1694 a company was floated, under the title of the Society of the White Writing and Printing Paper Manufactory of Scotland, the principal partners in which were Nicholas Dupin and Denis Manes. Dupin, a French Protestant of considerable ability, had already succeeded in floating six companies in England, Scotland and Ireland.[19] Under an agreement dated 27th November, 1694, Dupin and Manes on the one part and the subscribers on the other part agreed to establish a joint-stock company with a capital of £4,200 Sterling. Seven hundred £3 shares were to be subscribed for in Scotland and an equal number in England; all were to be paid up in three six-monthly instalments, commencing 1st May 1695. To assist in the administration of the company's business, thirteen people were to be employed at Edinburgh and a like number at London. Samples of paper sent from the company's London Office would be circulated in Scotland with a view to discovering 'which shall prove most markittable and profitable', and whether it would be more economic to export paper to London or sell it within Scotland. Dupin and Manes were to pay £60 towards the cost of obtaining a patent in Scotland,[20] £60 towards the construction of the company's first paper mill at Gifford, and £30 for recruiting skilled workmen. John, Earl of Tweeddale and High Chancellor of Scotland, had leased the Gifford site to the company for a forty-year period and, with twenty shares, equalled Dupin, Manes, John Learmond (an Edinburgh merchant), and his own son, Lord Yester, as the largest share-holder. Among the smaller Scottish shareholders were to be found a book-seller, an advocate, a customs officer, an apothecary, a smith, a stocking manufacturer and a brewer; although dominated by landed and mercantile interests, the company seems to have attracted a wide range of small investors, drawn from the middle classes.[21] Dupin contributed not only his entre-preneurial skill, but also his knowledge of technology: by a contract dated 16th August 1695, certain alterations were made to the original financial arrangements, and Dupin and Manes undertook to 'oversee the building of two paper-milnes for makeing of white wryting and printing paper for the use of the said company and the buying and furnishing of all material necessaries for the said milnes, which milnes·are to be built and materials furnished thairto upon the companeys charges, the one thairof at Yester and the other near Edinburgh[22] whair the aire and water shall be found most agreeable for the makeing of good and sufficient whyte wryting and printing paper'. Besides these duties, they were to train a vatman, a coucher, a leveer, a beaterman and a finisher for each of the two mills.[23] From inventories compiled in 1704, it is apparent that the mills were built on similar lines. Besides 'kooves' (vats) and presses, both had eight timber or stone mortars, each one holding three iron-shod hammers, worked by water power. Paper, both white and grey, was made in imperial, crown and pot sizes.[24]

As far as the functioning of the company was concerned, little is known; according to Scott,[25] the venture ended in difficult circumstances after a short period. From the little information we have, this would seem to have been the case. Dupin and Manes seem to have got into financial difficulties, and in 1703 the mill, with a backlog of unpaid rent, was leased to a group representing the company. In the same year the company's clerk was imprisoned for embezzle-ment.[26] Despite the great number of subscribers, interest was so low that, during 1704, four successive meetings failed to raise a quorum; in 1707, produc-tion was threatened by shortage of rags.[27] For all its difficulties, the Company managed to stumble on until 1715; in 1714 the Braid Mill had been given up, and in the following year the untimely death of the tacksmen to whom they had leased the Yester Mill forced the Company to write off the backlog of tack duty due to them and resign the feu held from the Marquis of Tweeddale, along with the mill which they had built at their own expense.[28] In their representations to the Marquis, the partners of the paper company found no lack of reasons for their demise. It was claimed that they

> were imposed upon by Nicholas Dupine, a foreigner his luxuriant skems, and with a reasonable show of probabilitie of success, to venture in the prosecution of severall manufactories in company and, amongst the rest, your petitioners were involved in this of the paper manufactory, wherein wee advanced a considerable stock, in hope to have made it effectuall not only for the generall good of the nation, but likewayes to our own privat advantage and profite. But this our society and company as well as oth'r societies & companys hes had a ruineing con-sequence of the loss of our stock and interest of it, tho really the design and project of the success of the manufactory hes taken place, in so far as there is a demon-stration that paper can be made here tollerably good and serviceable for severall uses as is known yet our being a company & the concern so . . . divided in so many hands occasioning thereby not only a neglect of many things [that] might have been of advantage to the work, but the multitude of persons concerned brought on a great expences and charges.
>
> It is also certain that the said Dupine, a foreigner, made very inadvertant bargains in the first settlement giving rent for so much ground as might have made a purchase of so much land. And your lo[rdshi]p for will be pleased to consider that the company payes a considerable few duty to your lo[rdshi]p for a very small piece of ground and upon which they have been at vast expences in erecting and building a paper miln and other necessaries about it and have lykeways for

several years been throwing out money in hope att length to overcome all deficulties and bring the manufactory to a bearing. But after all, throw the unsteadieness of a society and their uncertain attendance assistance and advances, each trusting to and depending upon another, all at once failed.[29]

This did not, however, mark the end of paper making at Yester: since at least 1700, and probably earlier, both Yester and Braid had been making banknotes for the Bank of Scotland. By 1721 the Yester Mill, still carrying the Bank of Scotland contract, was in the hands of the Watkins family, Edinburgh printers and papermakers, of English extraction. In that year, and again in 1723 and 1729, the mill was visited by bank officials,[30] and from various other sources it can be shown that the mill continued to operate until the 1770s.[31]

The Early 18th Century

The Watkins, printers first of the *Edinburgh Gazette* then of the *Courant*, were not the only example of a link between Edinburgh printers and local paper mills. On the death of her husband Andrew Anderson, Agnes Campbell had succeeded to his title of King's Printer, and had staunchly defended it throughout the last years of the 17th century.[32] In 1708, at the age of seventy-one, she concluded an agreement with Sir John Clerk of Penicuik whereby, in exchange for the tack of 'a convenient stance', and the use of the River North Esk, she was to build a paper mill, pay £60 or so entry money, and provide one ream of the finest white paper, and one of coarse, by way of tack duty.[33] In 1709 a tack was entered into to run for a period of 9 x 19 years from Martinmas 1708 at the higher tack duty of £86 Scots plus two reams of finest white paper and two of coarser white.[34] The mill, later known as Valleyfield Mill, went into production in the late 1700s, making paper which generally seems to have met with Clerk's approval, with the exception of one batch in 1713 which he described as 'sinking paper' — 'can make no use except to give to my wife for recepts for kane fouls.'[35] In 1716, the year of her death, Agnes Campbell sold the mill to her grandson, William Hamilton of Little Earnock, the son of James Hamilton who had taken over Restalrig Mill from Peter Bruce.[36] In 1727 the mill came into the hands of the Watkins family.[37] It was another Edinburgh printer, John Reid, who established Scotland's next paper mill; in 1714 he leased Jinkabout Mill, presumably to supply paper for the *Edinburgh Gazette*, which he had acquired in 1699.[38] In 1717, the nearby Bogs or Vernour's Mill was converted from a corn mill to produce paper, by Nicol Lithgow, and in the same year Redhall Mill, a few hundred yards upstream, on the opposite bank, started making paper under William Hamilton of Little Earnock.[39]

The establishment of these three mills near Edinburgh, and a fourth, founded in 1716 at Cathcart, near Glasgow, is difficult to reconcile with the drop in Scottish paper production which took place in the early post-Union years: between 1712 and 1722 output fell from over 100,000 lbs to 40,000 lbs, possibly in response to the removal of trade barriers.[40] Although production had returned to its former level by 1730, it was not until the mid-1740s that it

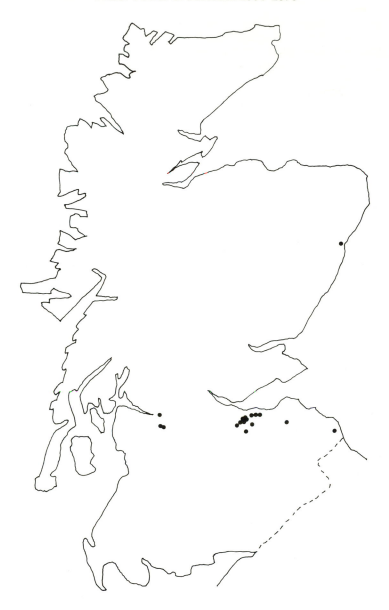

Fig 15. Distribution of paper mills, 1550-1730

began to show signs of vigorous growth and a new era of mill building began. When that did happen, the technology and skills were already established in Scotland and could be put to good use immediately. The distribution of paper mills for this period is shown in Figure 15.

NOTES

1. Overton, J., *in* Singer, C., Holmyard, E. J., Hall, A. R. & Williams, T. I. (eds.), *A History of Technology*, 5 vols., Oxford, 1956-59, III, 412.

2. Thomson, A. G., *The Paper Industry in Scotland 1590-1861*, Edinburgh, 1974, 3.

3. Cochran-Patrick, R. W., *Early Records Relating to Mining in Scotland*, Edinburgh, 1878, 81; Waterston, R., 'Early Paper Making near Edinburgh', *BOEC* XXV (1945), 56.

4. Waterston, *op. cit.*, 56-7.

5. *Ibid.*, 57.

6. *RMSRS* IX, 1061.

7. Thomson, *op. cit.*, 13.

8. *Ibid.*, 13.

9. *Ibid.*, 14.

10. *Ibid.*, 10-11. Bruce's exploits had included supplying Edinburgh with piped water from springs at Comiston (1674) and both designing and building a harbour at Cockenzie for the Earl of Winton (1678). In 1680 he obtained patents for a water pump to drain mines and quarries, and an engine for cutting iron (slitting mill?), mainly for nail-makers.

11. Thomson, *op. cit.*, 11-12.

12. *RMSRS* XI, 93.

13. Thomson, *op. cit.*, 14.

14. *Ibid.*, 15.

15. *Ibid.*, 16.

16. *Ibid.*, 17.

17. *Ibid.*, 18.

18. *Ibid.*, 17.

19. Shorter, A. H., *Paper-Making in the British Isles*, Newton Abbot, 1971, 16.

20. Waterston, *op. cit.*, 65.

21. NLS MS 1913.

22. At Braid (GR NT247703).

23. Waterston, *op. cit.*, 62-3.

24. NLS MS 1913.

25. Scott, W. R., *Joint-Stock Companies to 1720*, 3 vols., Cambridge, 1910-12.

26. Thomson, *op. cit.*, 18.

27. NLS MS 1913.

28. Thomson, *op. cit.*, 18.

29. NLS Acc. 4862/15/f.1.

30. Waterston, R., 'Further Notes on Early Paper Making near Edinburgh', *BOEC* XXVII (1949), 46-7; Shorter, *op. cit.*, 193.

31. NLS Acc. 4862/151/f.1; *Caledonian Mercury*, Saturday, 4 June 1774.

32. Waterston, *op. cit.* (1949), 49-50.

33. SRO GD18/1317/B.

34. SRO GD18/889.

35. SRO GD18/1317/B.

36. Waterston, *op. cit.* (1949), 50.

37. Waterston, *op. cit.* (1945), 70; (1949), 50.

38. Waterston, *op. cit.* (1949), 49.

39. Thomson, *op. cit.*, 119; Waterston, *op. cit.*, (1945), 70.

40. Thomson, *op. cit.*, 74, Fig. 8; Shorter, *op. cit.*, 193.

5

Coal Mining

Between 1550 and 1700 Scottish coal production underwent an expansion which Nef has described as 'revolutionary',[1] and while his figures represent only an estimate, it is probable that something like this suggested expansion, from 40,000 to 500,000 tons per annum, did take place.[2] Several factors favoured this growth. Much of the coal lay in church lands and, as such, had not yet been subject to large-scale commercial exploitation. With the Reformation and the emergence of a prosperous and commercially orientated landed class, the possibilities of coal as an export commodity, especially as an earner of Dutch riks-dollars, began to be appreciated. A well-established Dutch merchant fleet could carry Scottish coal to wherever it could find a sale and, unlike the tiny Scottish fleet, could pay cash on receipt. In the face of such powerful vested interests, the successive attempts which the crown made to restrict, or at least benefit from, coal exports were doomed to failure.[3]

Within Scotland, the use of coal for domestic heating in Edinburgh and elsewhere kept several pits at work, while industrial development, notably in salt and iron, offered a ready market for otherwise unsaleable small coal. After the Regal Union of 1603, trade with London also developed.

Before coal reserves could be exploited on a large-scale commercial basis, drainage techniques had to be improved. Illustrations in Agricola's *De Re Metallica*[4] indicate that by 1550 the use of water-powered mine drainage was common in Europe (Figure 16); by the 1590s several such pumps had been installed by both English and Italian engineers, to provide a water supply for London.[5] One of their number, Bevis Bulmer, was to figure largely in Scottish ore mining during the early 17th century.[6] The first water-powered pumps in Scotland appear in 1595, not providing an urban water supply, but draining flooded coal workings. In 1575, Sir George Bruce of Carnock obtained a lease of Culross Colliery, on the north shore of the Firth of Forth.[7] According to the preamble, he possessed 'great knowledge and skill in machinery', and was considered to be the person best able to re-open the then abandoned mines.[8] From a complaint made in 1607, it would appear that by 1595 Bruce had built a dam on the Muir of Culross, with a view to storing water to drive the mill at his coalworks.[9] In addition to the water mill or 'engine', a horse-mill or 'gin' was installed, and while it may have been the latter machine which drained the famous undersea workings, the water engine must have made a useful contribution towards drying flooded seams.[10] As far as later developments were

Fig 16. A 16th-century rag and chain pump. *Agricola, 1556*

concerned, the water engine was certainly the more important. In 1598, Gavin Smith and James Aitchison (Goldsmith to King James) were granted a patent on a mine draining device, to be powered by wind, water, horse or men.[11]

Development and Control

With expanding markets, and landowners eager to exploit new reserves of coal, it is hardly surprising that the use of water power in mining spread, particularly on the northern side of the Firth of Forth, where geological conditions made drainage necessary, and topography made water catchment feasible. When from time to time the crown tried to intervene in the industry, the coal owners were always quick to stress the great expense of establishing 'water coilheuchis', and the need for foreign sales to pay for their maintenance. Typical was their reaction to restrictions imposed on coal exports in 1609:

> And first, thay [the coal owners] afferme constantlie and we heir it by credible report of utheris, that the watter coilheuchis hes bene wynne, and ar still intertenued and upholdin, upoun very grite chargeis and expenssis, some of thame having alreddy coist the awnair above fiftie thousand merkis, and the poorest of thame surmounting every oulk, in ordinarie chargeis for intertenying of thair watter ingynis, three hundreth merkis, and utheris of thame, as namely Airth, Alloway, Carribdin and Sawchie, five or sex hundreth merkis.

Home demand, it was claimed, could not even pay for half the colliers' wages; coupled with this was the threat that without foreign sales, 'all men wilbe skarrit fra unirtaking ony suche worke . . . heireafter'.[12] In 1625, having conceded that point, the crown attempted to control the shipping in which coal was exported by imposing a tax of 48 shillings on each foreign ship loading coal, in the hope that this might stimulate Scottish merchant shipping. The coal owners, in turn, argued that the Scottish fleet was hopelessly inadequate in size, and that home sales would not support their 'watter workis' for one month. Needless to say, the tax had to be dropped.[13]

When, in 1631, it was proposed that English salt imports from Scotland be limited, the coal owners were quick to point out that 'without the benefit of salt these sumptous (sic) water workes and mynes required for maintenance and wining the coale cannot be upholding'. By this time an estimated 10,000 people were employed in the Scottish coal and salt industries, and any threat to coal owners was seen as endangering their mine drainage systems, the working of which was vitally important if employment was to be maintained.[14] In 1634,[15] and again in 1641,[16] pressure from the economically powerful mine owners led to the abandonment of legislation.

Construction and Maintenance

It would be tempting to see as exaggerated the claims made as to the expense of 'water coalheughs', were it not for other contemporary evidence. In 1661, at Cameron, Fife, the Earl of Wemyss was empowered to 'set doun sinks, coal piteyes, levelles, and to erect windmills and watermills and other things necessary for winning and transporting . . . coal'.[17]

During the course of the next seventeen years he spent no less than £100,000 Scots (over £8,300 Sterling) on improving his collieries and building a new harbour at Methil.[18] A wheel which was to be installed on a 44-fathom sink at Clackmannan, in the 1690s, was reckoned to cost 57,000 Merks (£3,166

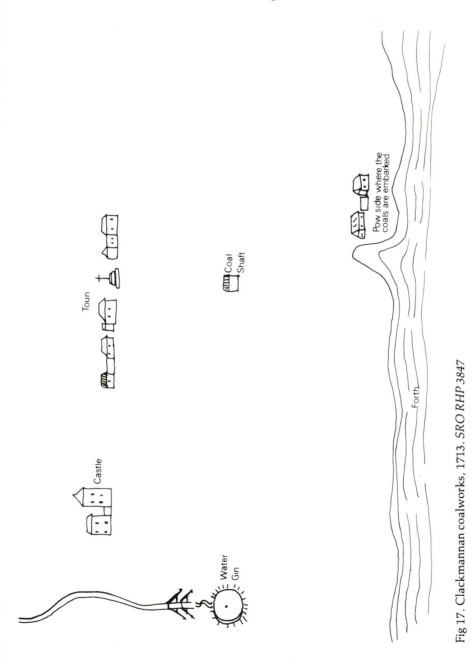

Fig 17. Clackmannan coalworks, 1713. *SRO RHP 3847*

Sterling).[19] Large overshot wheels, with elaborate lade systems and sometimes extensive dams, appear to have been typical of Scottish water engines (Figure 17). With such substantial works to undertake, it is hardly surprising that a heavy capital investment was required.

The problems of maintenance àre perhaps best exemplified by the wheel at Thornton, East Lothian. At some date prior to 1678, 392 deals and 82 couples had been used to build the elaborate system of dams and elevated wooden troughs which served the overshot wheel on Thornton Coalworks. The iron chain, 23 fathoms long, had thirty buckets attached to its length, each with three iron hoops.[20] For all this investment, it was not long before difficulties arose, and by October 1681 the working of the system had run into serious problems:

> To speak shortly and in generall of the conditione of these works, they are so ruinous and decayed that (if not prevented) in a very short tyme they will either totally ruine and decay or else come into such a conditione as they cannot easily be recovered without great charges and expenss, ffor the aquaduct from the head therof all along (where it is artificial) is for the most pairt furred and shott together. The dammheads with there slouces broken doun and decayed. The short trowes fixed upon Innerwick bridge for carrieing the water over Innerwick burn are totally overturned and lying upon the ground, and the timber belonging thereto all if not the most part stollen and miscarried. The long trowes which carries the water from the aquaduct to the wheill are in so chattered and ruinous a conditione that if not speidily helped they will altogether perish and decay. The water wheill in so defective a conditione that shoe will not weill be able to move without reparatione. The great iron chaine so weakened and bouked . . . that it hardly can be of any use till it be laid in a forge. The buckets being 28 or 30 are all wanting except 8 or 10 which are in no good conditioune. The materialls and instruments belonging to the work . . . are embezeled and wanting. The old bearing sinck in such a conditione that (if not guarded against) will be lost and clapt together to the very great prejudice of the work. The iron-work of the axeltrie such as gudges, chainie bands and other iron work belonging thereto all of them defective.[21]

Distribution

However great the cost might have been, water 'engines' continued to be built. George Sinclair, writing in the 1670s, speaks of them as being common, and identified two types. The first involved the use of a continuous chain with detachable buckets which scooped up water and emptied it into a trough as the buckets turned over an axle-tree at the top. The second system also used chains, but fixed with plates instead of buckets. As the plates passed upwards through hollow pipes, they lifted water to the surface, where it was discharged into a trough.[22] When it comes to identifying individual sites, however, evidence is fragmentary. What little information there is has been used to compile Figure 18. On the basis of this, it would seem that during the 17th and early 18th centuries water engines were installed at many collieries on the north side of the Firth of Forth, but few on the south side. With the exception of some on the Ayrshire coast, collieries in the west of Scotland were hemmed in by land, and could not therefore expand to the extent that those in the eastern coalfields could. In the Lothians most mines could be drained by levels,

Fig 18. Distribution of coal mine water engines, 1550-1730

△ Probable
▲ Confirmed

and where this proved impracticable horse gins were usually adequate for drainage requirements; large sums were invested in both methods. The Mid- and East Lothian coalfield, with its proximity to Edinburgh, and its limited coastal exposure, was orientated towards land sales, though some exporting mines were created during the period.

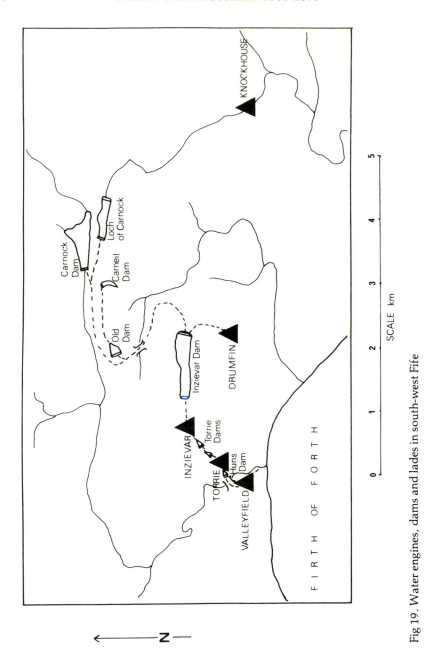

Fig 19. Water engines, dams and lades in south-west Fife

Water Engines in South-West Fife

Despite the lack of information for Scotland as a whole, developments in one small area, to the east of Culross, are well documented, and can therefore serve as an illustration.[23] At some date in the late 16th or early 17th century, a reservoir by the name of Inzievar dam (NT0387) was constructed in Torryburn parish, Fife, probably to drive water engines on the Torry coal, but possibly for those on the Valleyfield coal (Figure 19). Two smaller dams, the over and nether dams of Torrie, may date from the same period. In 1612 Preston of Valleyfield was granted the right to mine the coal of Valleyfield, and during the years that followed, extended the workings under the Firth of Forth, in much the same way that Sir George Bruce had at Culross. To drain these workings, Preston installed a water engine which was linked to the existing lade system on the opposite side of a deep ravine by an elevated wooden trough supported on posts. The coal of Inzievar was, in 1619, held in tack by Roger Duncanson, an Edinburgh merchant burgess. He too installed water engines to drain his coals, but had to lay on additional water supplies to Inzievar dam before he was permitted to use its waters to drive them. The available volume of water was further augmented when, in 1629, Alexander Bruce of Inzievar was granted permission to build a dam and sluice on his brother George's lands of Carnock, for the use of his 'coalwork ingynes of Inziewar'.[24] The marriage of John Preston's daughter, Mary, to George Bruce probably helped to ensure that Preston's access to Inzievar dam would continue unimpeded for some time.

The additions made to Inzievar dam in 1619 and 1629 had involved the construction of a second reservoir (probably at NT0489) and water courses from it to that at Inzievar. Immediately to the south of this new dam lay the Loch of Carnock, a natural body of water straddling the boundary between the lands of the Earl of Kincardine,[25] and those of Halkett of Pitfirrane. In 1642 Halkett had been granted permission to build dams on the Loch for his 'coal and water works' of Knockhouse[26] (NT0686), but by the mid-1650s the situation had changed. Halkett of Pitfirrane's coalworks had apparently been given up, or had at least ceased to need water, while the Earl of Kincardine's new coal works at Drumfin (NT0386) needed it to drive water engines. Inzievar dam was the obvious source, but the needs of those collieries at Inzievar, Torrie and Valleyfield were already putting a strain on its limited capacity. The problem was solved by linking the Loch of Carnock to the system of lades which fed Inzievar, thus extending the latter's catchment area. In 1654 Alexander Bruce, brother of Edward, Earl of Kincardine, was granted permission to build dams at Halkett of Pitfirrane's end of the Loch of Carnock, by which means its level could be raised to a height sufficient to divert the water into the lades serving Inzievar dam. In the event of Halkett's needing water for his coal works, the dams were to be lowered again, and the agreement to be annulled.[27] To accommodate the additional volume of water, Inzievar dam was extended to cover 60 Scots acres, and the turf damhead enlarged to give a total length of 500 feet, a height of 10 feet and a thickness at the base of 30 feet. A cutting in the opposite (i.e. eastern) end of the dam released the water which drove the Drumfin engine. The turf damhead at Carnock Loch was 400 feet long, 46 feet thick and 5 feet high. Together, these two reservoirs covered about 40 Scots acres. A compensation reservoir at Carneil had a stone damhead 12 feet high and 22 feet thick.

The Torrie coal was given up in 1633, and that at Drumfin in 1673, but Valleyfield continued to use the waters of Inzievar dam until the 18th century. With such 'sumptous water works' to construct and maintain, it was hardly surprising that overseas sales were so vital.

The Early 18th Century: Alloa Colliery

By the early 18th century the search for more efficient water engines was 'the great object in view with all coal-masters'.[28] One such man was John, Earl of Mar, owner of the coal works of Alloa. In 1709 he sent his colliery manager to Newcastle, at that time the most advanced area in Britain in the technology of mining. As a result of the visit, the Earl obtained drawings of machinery in use there and, wishing to apply such machinery to his own mines, he engaged George Sorocold of Derby[29] to prepare plans. Sorocold duly visited the mines, stayed for several days and received £50 for his services. The most significant innovation which he recommended was the substitution of pumps, worked by cranks on a water wheel, for the traditional chain and bucket engine. Unfortunately, no millwright capable of constructing such a machine could be found in Scotland, and in the event the new wheel was built with chain and buckets.[30]

The Earl of Mar had the misfortune to be on the losing side in the 1715 rebellion, and as a result of forfeitures the Alloa collieries deteriorated. When, in 1723, the situation was finally taken in hand, it was found that two powerful engines would be required, and that in the absence of sufficient water supplies one would have to be driven by steam.[31] This expensive and unpopular measure was avoided, however, by the construction of Gartmorn Dam, an extensive reservoir fed by a 3 km long lade taken from the River Black Devon. Damages of £36 Scots were paid to the owners of the land which it occupied.[32] In the 19th century water from the dam was still powering coal engines, besides several other mills.

By investing so much capital and effort in deep mining, the commercially orientated landowners of the period were able to increase output many times over, while sales to overseas markets, either directly or in the products of the closely linked salt industry, enabled them to accumulate the capital necessary for the maintenance of and further investment in the expensive plant needed for such mining. Both in Scotland and England the increasing need for fuel in the salt, lime-burning, iron-working and glass-making industries further stimulated production. The domestic use of coal, already well established in Scotland, became increasingly popular in London as timber became scarcer and scarcer. Many mines could be worked successfully with levels or horse gins; in some places, however, the absence of water engines was enough to close a mine: the Harperhill Coal on the Alloa estate was wrought for a while, and sold well, but by 1714 it had been given up as unprofitable for, as was said at the time, 'water cannot be brought to it for making a machine serviceable to drain it'.[33] It should be noted too that when the steam engine first appears in Scotland it is as a means of lifting water to drive water wheels for mine drainage. In 1701 James Smith of Whitehill, near Edinburgh, obtained the Scottish rights for Thomas Savory's engine.[34] Smith may not have sold any steam engines, but he is known to have advised at least one potential customer to use one to pump water for a 20-foot overshot wheel, at a point only 10 feet above high tide level.[35] Only four Newcomen engines have been identified in Scotland for the period up to 1730;[36] had water power been available, it is unlikely that steam engines would even have been contemplated, and for another hundred years or so water engines were to continue to offer a viable alternative to steam.

NOTES

1. Nef, J. U., *The Rise of the British Coal Industry*, 2 vols., London, 1932.

2. *Ibid.*, I, 19.

3. *APS* II, 543, No. 22 (1563); III, 147, No. 28 (1579).

4. Agricola (Hoover, H. C. & Hoover, L. H. (eds)), *De Re Metallica*, 1556 (New York, 1950).

5. Armytage, W. H. G., *A Social History of Engineering*, London, 1961, 72.

6. Bulmer was also responsible for a slitting mill, patented in 1588; see also page *et seq.* Gale, W. K. V., *The British Iron and Steel Industry*, Newton Abbot, 1967, 28.

7. Bowman, A. I., 'Culross Colliery: A Sixteenth Century Mine', *IA* VII (1970), 355.

8. Cochrane, A., *A Description of the Estate of Culross*, Edinburgh, 1793, 9-11.

9. *RSSRS* 1st Series, VII, 314. *RSSRS* 2nd Series, VIII, 267.

10. Bowman, *op. cit.*, 353-372.

11. National Coal Board, *A Short History of the Scottish Coal-mining Industry*, 1958, 42.

12. *RSSRS* 1st Series, VII, 568-9.

13. *RSSRS* 2nd Series, I, 169-70.

14. *RSSRS* 2nd Series, IV, 255-7.

15. *RSSRS* 2nd Series, V, 341.

16. *RSSRS* 2nd Series, VII, 160.

17. *RMSRS* XI, 111 (1681).

18. Pryde, G. S., *Scotland from 1603 to the Present Day*, Edinburgh, 1962, 29.

19. SRO GD76/358.

20. SRO GD6/1256.

21. SRO GD6/1254.

22. Sinclair, G., *The Hydrostaticks*, Edinburgh, 1672, 298-300.

23. Much of the information on Inzievar dam comes from a Court of Session case, Erskine of Carnock v. Preston of Valleyfield, OSP 4:87, 80:1.

24. SRO GD15/897.

25. I.e. Edward Bruce, son of George Bruce the younger.

26. Webster, J. M., *History of Carnock*, Dunfermline, 1912, 224.

27. SRO GD15/900.

28. Bald, R., *A General View of the Coal Trade of Scotland*, Edinburgh, 1808, 10.

29. The same George Sorocold designed the great water wheel for Britain's first factory, the Derby silk mills. Armytage, *op. cit.*, 79-80.

30. *NSA* VIII, 27.

31. SRO GD124/17/532.

32. SRO GD124/17/539.

33. SRO GD124/17/532.

34. Dickinson, H. W., in Singer, C., Holmyard, E. J., Hall, A. R. & Willis, T. I. (eds), *A History of Technology*, 5 vols., Oxford, 1956-59, IV, 172.

35. SRO GD246/63/4.

36. Duckham, B. F., *A History of the Scottish Coal Industry*, I (1700-1815), Newton Abbot, 1970, 365-8.

6

The Mining and Manufacture of Non-Ferrous Metals

Technology

Just as European drainage technology was applied to the Scottish coal industry in the late 16th and early 17th centuries, so also was the technology of crushing and smelting applied to the refining of non-ferrous metals. Crushing plant, first referred to in the early 1600s (p. 77), probably consisted of vertical, water-powered stampers, of a kind already in use in Cornwall and still known as 'Cornish Stamps' (Figure 20). Finer particles might be broken down by grindstones.

Carew's *Survey of Cornwall*, published in 1602, provides a good description:

> Three, and in some places six great logges of timber bounded at the ends with yron, and lifted up and downe be a wheele, driven with the water, doe break it [the ore] smaller. If the stones be over-moyst they are dryed by the fire in an yron cradle or grate. From the stamping mill it passes to the crazing mill, which betweene two grinding stones, turned also with a water wheel, bruseth the same to find a sand; howbeit, of late times they mostly use wet stampers, and so have no need of crazing mills for their best stuffe.[1]

The use of water power in smelting mills was confined to operating bellows employing the same axle and cam system which drove stamps (Figure 21). As far as can be discerned, the earliest smelting mill in Scotland was that of Thomas Foullis, established c. 1592 (p. 76). Although water power was extensively used at a later date in the drainage of lead mines, those of the period under consideration were probably drained by levels or, possibly, horse gins: only one reference to pumps (not necessarily water-powered) has been found for the 17th century, and not until the 1720s, with the advent of improved bob engines, was water power definitely brought into use (p. 80).

Foreign Exploitation of Mines

While the exploitation of coal reserves was primarily in the hands of estate owners, the skills and capital required to mine and manufacture lead, silver and gold were beyond most Scots. In order to exploit these minerals as a means of increasing revenue, the crown initially granted rights to foreigners,

Fig 20. A 16th-century ore-stamping mill. A: crushing platform. B,C: frame for stampers. D,E: stampers. F: axle. G: cams. *Agricola, 1556*

notably Germans and Flemings: Cornelius de Vos and Abraham Petersen in 1567,[2] Arnold von Bronchorst in 1572, and Abraham Petersen once more in 1576.[3] A few Scots, notably the Duke of Atholl and George Douglas of Parkhead, figured in this early period of exploitation,[4] but in 1583, with the transfer of all mines and mineral rights to a Fleming, Eustacius Roche, for twenty-one years, all existing rights were annulled.[5] However, under pressure from such parties as the Lindsays of Glenesk and in the face of suspected non-payment of dues, Roche's rights were, in turn, annulled by Act of Parliament in 1592.

The Act Anent Mines, 1592

The removal of Roche no more than cleared the ground for the Act's other,

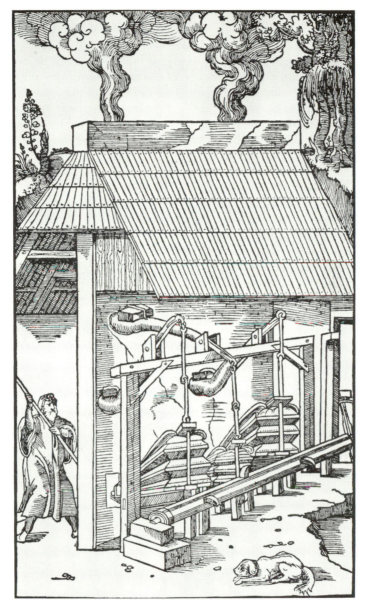

Fig 21. A 16th-century smelting mill. Note the water wheel at the far right. *Agricola*, 1556

more extensive, provisions. At a time when private capital was beginning to be channelled into the development of other industries, such as paper-making (p. 54) and coal mining (p. 62), it is interesting to note the importance which the crown attached to ensuring control of gold, silver and lead mining and, significantly, the refining of these metals in Scotland, a process which had previously taken place abroad, much to the detriment of the Scottish economy. Predictably, the Act Anent Mines starts by recounting the shortcomings of licensing aliens 'quha nather haid substance to caus labour and wirk the hundreth pairt of ony ane of the saidis mynis nor yit instructed vtheris liegis of this realme in the knawlege thairof'.[6] In place of this system, mineral rights were to be feued to the proprietors of ore-bearing lands, and a new office, that of Master of Metals, was to be created to co-ordinate mining operations and to supervise the collection of duties. Without his consent no mineral-working contract was considered to be legal; he was empowered to set up markets for foodstuffs, construct roads to provide access to mines, and to hire both Scottish and foreign workmen. In pursuit of his duties, he could take 'places for all maner of houssis mylnes mylne landis fornaceis and fyre out of the nixt adjacent mossis and woddis necessar for thar workis'. To attract labour and to compensate for dangerous working conditions, workers in the industry were exempt from taxation and from other duties such as military service and quartering troops (cf. p. 50). Special courts were to be established in each shire which could bypass the cumbersome legal system and resolve disputes more readily.[7] The post of Master of the Metals was to be occupied by John Lindsay, the parson of Menmuir, Angus, who had been instrumental in bringing down Roche; besides being a prospector of great renown in his own country, Lindsay had visited England, Germany and Denmark, where he had built up a good knowledge of mining techniques.

Perhaps the most significant advance, however, was in the refining of metals within Scotland. Previously, ore had been exported to Flanders where it was refined and sometimes re-imported into Scotland. While the crown derived a little income from export duties, most of the benefit accrued to the country in which refining took place. The Act Anent Mines sought to remedy this situation by establishing refining plant in Scotland. Apparently such plant already existed. In the early months of 1592, Thomas Foullis had been sent to London to consult Sir William Bowis; back in Scotland, he was to build 'ane strang and large house' in which the reduction of metals for coins could take place under Bowis's direction.[8] As an Edinburgh goldsmith Foullis had amassed great wealth and, having lent to the crown, he was well favoured by the king. It may well have been in connection with the above activities that his smelting mill, mentioned in the Act, was set up:

> . . . Thomas foullis gouldsmyth hes found out the Ingine and moyane [means or way] to caus melt and fyne the vris of mettallis within this cuntrie and hes brocht in strangearis and beiggit houssis and mylnis for this effect to his grit coist and expenss and to the grit and evident weilfair of the haill cuntrie within the quhilk no vre in grit wes never meltit of befoir and fynit: bot the same wes evir transportit out of the cuntrie vnmeltit and refynit.

The smelting mill was to refine all the metal ores won and wrought in Scotland,[9] and the officials of burghs and free ports were asked to ensure that no metals were exported unrefined.[10] As to the location of the mill, it was almost certainly at one of the two places on the Water of Leith that bear the name Silvermills,[11] that at Leith being the more likely.

Conflicting Authorisations

However clear and ambitious the provisions of the Act may have been, the decade or so which followed saw much confusion in the industry, with conflicting claims to minerals in the Lowther Hills and in West Lothian. In the year which saw the passing of the Act, Thomas Foullis took over the Glengonnar mines at an annual rent of 500 Merks and, in the following year, the mines on Friarmuir, Lanarkshire, at 1,000 Merks. To assist him in his searches Foullis engaged Bevis Bulmer, an English prospector and engineer, who had been associated with ore mining in Scotland since the late 1560s.[12] Among his more original ideas was the creation of 'Golden Knights' who, in exchange for a knighthood, were to give £300 towards mining operations. Bulmer was to take overall charge of the mines, it being proposed that 'clouses, dammes and water-courses be made fitting to the . . . gold workes and washing of gold etc., and that all sorts of water-mills, stamping-mills and plash-mills' be erected.[13] Despite the failure of this particular scheme, Bulmer received financial help from the crown between 1603 and 1606, and in the latter year he was granted a tack of all the precious minerals in Scotland.[14] Up to three hundred men were employed in various operations, and at Long Cleuch Head, where a small vein of auriferous quartz had been found,[15] Bulmer built a stamping mill. Although he succeeded in obtaining some 'small mealy gold',[16] serious damage was done to the mills in 1607, when various persons 'reft the haill trows, stamparis, burdeis, wheillis, extreis and uther furntoure'.[17]

During the same period, George Bowes, working in the Lowther Hills, was also in receipt of financial help from the crown.[18] Bowes had built houses for his skilled English miners near his workings along Wanlock Water, but had been consistently hampered by bad weather, outbreaks of scurvy and harassment by Thomas Foullis, on whose behalf Bulmer was working in the area. Workmen were bribed away and operations interfered with; by the end of 1604, Bowes had given up.[19]

Unlike the unfortunate Bowes, Bulmer continued to go from strength to strength. In 1606 a collier, Sandy Mauld, stumbled across a piece of 'red metal' at Hilderstone, near Linlithgow. A sample was sent to Bulmer who, on testing it in his assay furnace, found it to be rich in silver. Before long, Bulmer was engaged in mining the metal.[20]

Bulmer's original role at Hilderstone is difficult to assess: the property belonged to Sir Thomas Hamilton who, in 1607, took on the post of Master of the Metals, and until the end of 1607 he and Bulmer had conflicting royal authorisations.[21] By the spring of 1608, however, the position had been clarified, and in exchange for generous compensation Hamilton yielded his interest in the mine to the crown.[22]

Under the new Mines Royal, Bulmer became governor, George Bruce of
Carnock (the coal owner) was appointed treasurer, and Archibald Primrose[23]
was made secretary.[24] To refine the silver ores, the smelting mill at Leith
(probably that built by Foullis) was repaired,[25] and in 1609 new stamping and
smelting mills were built on the Loch Burn, Linlithgow.[26] Between 3rd July
1608 and 7th May 1609 no less than £20,135 10s 10d Scots was spent on
building and running the silver mills, an indication of the importance attached
to silver production. The mines themselves were on a large scale, employing
over sixty men;[27] pumps, probably designed by Bulmer and possibly using
water power, were used to keep the workings dry.[28] For all the capital sunk in
the exploitation of the silver deposits, the mines failed to live up to expectations, and in 1613 mines, 'fyre workis' and stamping-mills were handed over to
a group headed by Thomas Foullis, though the crown continued to maintain a
monopoly of its product.[29] Foullis continued to use the crushing and smelting
plant,[30] but on the whole the group seems to have had little success in mining,
and by 1652 only a few stones remained of the ruined mills.[31]

For all the hopes which it had held out, the Act Anent Mines seems to have
been a failure. Scottish involvement in mining had increased, but so also had
that of the English who were taking over where the Germans and Flemings had
left off. Twenty years after it had first appeared, the Act had still not been
implemented,[32] while over the period 1611-1614 the average annual value of
'leid urris' leaving the country was almost as great as that of coal and nearly
twice that of linen cloth.[33] On the other hand, the initiative behind it and the
fact that a Scot had gone so far as to build a smelting mill in Scotland, both
show a desire to improve the state of the Scottish economy and an attempt to
move away from exporting basic, unrefined commodities. Furthermore, the
change of policy as to who should search for and exploit the mines produced
so enthusiastic a response that by 1649 there was some alarm over the extent to
which ground had been broken, woods and orchards destroyed and property
damaged, all in the course of over-zealous mineral prospecting.[34]

Leadhills and Wanlockhead, 1615-1730

Despite widespread prospecting, only Leadhills and Wanlockhead provided
ore in any quantity and, while other deposits came to light after 1730, lead
mining in Scotland from 1615 up to the 1720s was largely confined to these
two adjacent localities. It is therefore worth considering their development in
detail, not least because both furnish examples of the use of water power.

Bevis Bulmer died in 1615, and in the same year his friend and assistant,
Stephen Atkinson, was granted permission for life to search for and exploit the
mines on Crawford Moor. Atkinson's stay does not seem to have lasted long,
however, for in 1621 the same mines, with others, were leased to a physician,
John Hendlie, for a period of twenty-one years.[35] Throughout this period,
overall control remained with the Foullis family: Thomas was succeeded by his
brother Robert, and in 1637, on the latter's death, Anne, his only surviving

child, inherited the mines.[36] Throughout her marriage to Sir James Hope of Hopetoun, the Foullis mines in the Leadhills area passed to the family which became the Earls of Hopetoun.[37] On his first visit to the mines on 29th May 1638, Sir James found two smelting mills with water-powered bellows, one in poor condition and the other perpetually out of use. By the time of his second visit on 7th October 1639, one mill had been rebuilt but the other, for double bellows, was in no better condition than it had been the previous year.[38] Under the family the mines seem to have prospered, and by the mid-century the Lead-hills mines, then the only ones in Scotland, had been wrought to a depth of twenty-four fathoms, and were producing three to four hundred tons of ore per annum, giving employment to fifty workers.[39] Notwithstanding the existence of smelting furnaces in the late 1630s, much of the output from the mines was sent, according to Smout, to Holland as unrefined galena.[40] However, there were certainly facilities in Scotland by the early 1690s, when a new slaghearth was incorporated into an existing smelting mill,[41] and in the same decade the Earls of Hopetoun established a wind-powered crushing and smelting mill at Leith.[42] The family still owned the mines in 1730 and continued to do so for long afterwards.

In 1675 there were favourable reports on deserted workings at Wanlock-head, on land belonging to the Duke of Queensberry.[43] In 1680 Sir James Stampfield took a lease of the mines, during which he built a smelting mill and houses for workers. In 1691 a new lease was made out to Arthur Wall and Matthew Wilson, both of County Durham, for a period of nineteen years. The terms of the lease granted them permission to make shafts and levels, 'with liberty also of watergates and other ingines necessary for carrying of the water from the said mines'. This latter clause is almost certainly a reference to water-powered drainage. Wilson and Wall were either to build new houses and a 'lead miln for melting the lead oar', or to repair the existing ones; the making of watercourses was also specifically mentioned.[44] From this time onwards smelting was to be concentrated at the place of extraction, a move facilitated by the substitution of peat for charcoal in refining.[45]

Meanwhile, in England, further developments were taking place. In 1692, William and Mary granted to Constantine Vernatty a charter incorporating 'The Governor and Company for Smelting down Lead with Pitt Coale and Sea Cole'.[46] By 1704 Quakers with mining interests in North Wales and Northumberland had taken over control of the company[47] and when, in 1709, Wilson and Wall gave up the Wanlockhead mines, the 'Governor and Company' obtained a lease of them from the Duke of Queensberry. Under the lease, the Company was to pay a rent one-seventh of the dressed ore produced, and to smelt it if asked to. The Duke was to take a twenty-five per cent stake in their profits and working costs.[48] Despite initially poor results, the discovery and working of the New Glencrieve vein gave much better yields.[49] In England the Company were using the newly invented reverberatory furnace, but it is doubtful whether they introduced it to Wanlockhead, an area with adequate water power but with relatively poor access to coal. Furthermore, it is unlikely that the Company did, in fact, use coal to smelt at their Scottish mines. In 1721 the 'Friendly Mining Society', with partners in Edinburgh, Newcastle and London, joined forces with the Smelting Company, and together they worked the mines until 1727, when the partnership split and the two companies took on separate sectors of the field.[50] The new, improved pumps which were being applied to the coal industry in the early 18th century also found their way into lead mining: according to Smout,[51] a bob gin was installed at Wanlockhead in the 1720s, while Brown[52] refers to water wheels installed by the Smelting Company, though probably after 1730.

By the 1720s, lead mining and smelting in Scotland were well-established, if still financially risky, activities. The use of water power, firstly to provide the blast for smelting-mills, later, where 'levels' proved inadequate, to drain mines, had contributed to the wealth of Scotland and to the strength of her economy: as Smout points out, a ton of smelted lead brought twice the price of a ton of ore. The construction of a road from Leith to the Wanlockhead/Leadhills area had gone some way towards easing the problem of transporting ore for export; a much greater improvement, however, could be achieved by smelting ore at the mines, thereby reducing its bulk by nearly two thirds.[53] Furthermore, once Scotland had her own lead-smelting capacity, there was no need to export lead ore and re-import it as lead; what lead she needed could be procured from within Scotland, and a surplus, if any, could be exported as a much more valuable commodity than lead ore.

On the other hand, results were, in some respects, disappointing. The capital needed to open up and exploit mines was great, and the risk of failure high. Even the Leadhills/Wanlockhead area, which consistently dominates Scottish lead production from this period onwards, was small by English standards and minuscule by those of continental Europe; despite several new finds in the century after 1730, it remained true that Scotland's lead ore deposits were small, dislocated and inaccessible. Of the precious metals gold, again from the Leadhills/Wanlockhead area, failed to appear in anything but the smallest quantities. The El Dorado which had always been hoped for never quite materialised. Silver contributed little more, but its occurrence in the Forth Basin, the heartland of Scotland's economy, made its exploitation easier, as did the proximity of the royal palace to the crushing and smelting mills at Linlithgow. Even these mines were, however, short-lived, and an attempt to re-establish the Linlithgow smelter in 1718 seems to have come to nothing.[54]

More significant in the long term, though not in itself, was the discovery of a rich pocket of silver at Alva, near Stirling, which in the more hospitable political climate of Scotland after 1707, triggered off a new wave of mineral prospecting which was to bring to light hitherto unknown reserves.

Fig 22. Distribution of lead and silver mills, 1550-1730

NOTES

1. Carew, R., *Survey of Cornwall*, London, 1602, 12.
2. Cochran-Patrick, R. W., *Early Records Relating to Mining in Scotland*, Edinburgh, 1878, xvi; Lythe, S. G. E., *The Economy of Scotland in its European Setting, 1550-1625*, Edinburgh, 1960, 53.

3. Cochran-Patrick, *op. cit.*, xxxv.

4. *Ibid.*, xxxv.

5. *Ibid.*, xviii.

6. *Ibid.*, 40.

7. *Ibid.*, 40-43.

8. *RSSRS* 1st Series, V, 730-733.

9. Cochran-Patrick, *op. cit.*, 45-47.

10. *Ibid.*, 40-43.

11. GR's NT247747, NT264761.

12. Lythe, *op. cit.*, 53.

13. Atkinson, S., *The Discoverie and Historie of the Gold Mynes of Scotland* (1619).

14. *RSSRS* 1st Series, VII, 306.

15. Wilson, G., *Special Report on the Mineral Resources of Great Britain* Vol. XVII, *Lead, Zinc, Copper & Nickel Ores of Scotland*, Edinburgh, 1921, 15.

16. Atkinson, *op. cit.*, 39.

17. *RSSRS* 1st Series, VII, 346-7.

18. Lythe, *op. cit.*, 54.

19. Cochran-Patrick, *op. cit.*, xix.

20. *Ibid.*, xxxviii.

21. *RSSRS* 1st Series, VII, 306, 358.

22. Lythe, *op. cit.*, 55-6.

23. In 1610 Primrose was licensed to make iron in Perthshire (Cochran-Patrick, lviii); in 1616 he was granted a monopoly of copper and lead mining on Islay, Mull, Skye and Lewis.

24. Cochran-Patrick, *op. cit.*, xli; Wilson, *op. cit.*, 66.

25. Chambers, R., *Domestic Annals of Scotland from the Reformation to the Rebellion, 1745,* Third Edition, 2 vols., Edinburgh 1874, I 412.

26. GR NS998778; SRO GD215/1825; Cochran-Patrick, *op. cit.*, 142.

27. Lythe, *op. cit.*, 56.

28. Cochran-Patrick, *op. cit.*, 142, 148.

29. *Ibid.*, xlii.

30. NLS Acc. 5381/46/f.3.

31. SRO GD215/1825.

32. Cochran-Patrick, *op. cit.*, lxiv.

33. Lythe, *op. cit.*, 55.

34. Cochran-Patrick, *op. cit.*, lxiv.

35. *Ibid.*, xix.

36. Wilson, *op. cit.*, 11.

37. Cochran-Patrick, *op. cit.*, lv.

38. Hopetoun Lead Mining Papers No. 5 Class 1, 2/1, 2/2.

39. Smout, T. C., in Payne, P. L., (ed.), *Studies in Scottish Business History,* London, 1967, 104.

40. *Ibid.*, 107.

41. Hopetoun Lead Mining Papers No. 5 Class 2, 22/8 (30th August 1694).

42. Donnachie, I. L., 'Scottish Windmills: an Outline and Inventory', *PSAS* XCVIII (1964-6), 295.

43. Wilson, *op. cit.*, 11.

44. SRO GD45/26/132.

45. Smout, *op. cit.*, 105.

46. Raistrick, A., & Jennings, B., *A History of Lead Mining in the Pennines*, London, 1965, 117.

47. *Ibid.*, 119.

48. SRO GD45/26/143.

49. Brown, J., *The History of Sanquhar*, Dumfries, Edinburgh & Glasgow, 1891, 424.

50. Because of the complexity of company organisation, there is a distinct possibility that the two were part of the same company.

51. Smout, *op. cit.*, 106.

52. Brown, *op. cit.*, 427-8. The wheel was installed on the Straitstep vein, on the north side of Wanlock Burn.

53. Smout, *op. cit.*, 107.

54. NLS Acc. 5381/46/f.3.

7

Water Power in the Iron Industry

All too often the history of the Scottish iron industry is seen as having begun with the Highland iron smelters of the 18th century, or even later, with the establishment of the Carron Iron Works in 1759. Prior to 1730, however, several developments had taken place, including the application of water power, and the industry had been established in both Highlands and Lowlands.

Technology

By 1730, two types of water-powered machinery had found their way into the Scottish iron industry: the blast furnace and the forge. The blast furnace was similar to the smelter used in the lead industry, employing an axle, fitted with cams or a crank to alternately raise and lower bellows, thereby increasing the available draught. The forge, or trip hammer, used a principle similar to that employed by waulk mills and ore crushers, with a horizontally mounted lever or 'hammer' fitted with a metal head, which was raised and dropped by cams on an axle (Figure 23). Neither had achieved very widespread use in Scotland by 1730. (Figure 24).

Background

Scattered across the Highlands were the small 'bloomeries' which, using local bog ore and charcoal, produced poor quality iron. Sited on exposed hills or in narrow valleys, they could utilise natural air movements, and thereby achieve higher temperatures than would otherwise be available. Many sites have been located[1] but dating is difficult, and in the present context they are of only marginal concern. Suffice it to say that they were well enough established in north-west Stirlingshire by the late 15th century for rents there to be paid in iron and for an iron market to be held at Aberfoyle, at which locally produced iron could be exchanged for salt and other commodities.[2] The second area in which the industry took root was around the Firth of Forth, but here activities were limited to the smithing, or forging, of iron. By the second quarter of the 16th century, mineral coal was being used to 'resolve and melt' iron, 'which was therefore very useful and profitable for smiths'.[3] The proximity of coal was to be of great importance in the continuing presence of the industry in the

Fig 23. A 16th-century tilt hammer. A: hearth. B: bellows. C: tongs. D: hammer. E: cooling water. *Agricola, 1556*

area, as was the availability of charcoal wood for the Highland smelting industry.

One use to which coal, exported to the Low Countries, was applied was the smithing of scrap iron, a commodity so abundant there that by the mid-16th

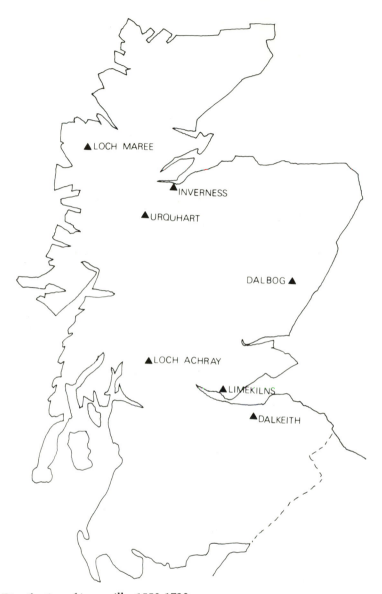

Fig 24. Distribution of iron mills, 1550-1730

century it was being carried as ballast on ships coming to Scotland to load coal and salt. The development of iron-working industries, such as the manufacture of girdles at Culross and nails at Dysart and St. Ninians, was closely linked, therefore, to other industrial developments in the area, notably the export-orientated coal industry. So successful was the industry at Culross that in 1549 the smiths of that place signed a mutual document restricting the erection of additional forges, and in 1599 they obtained a monopoly in girdle making; in 1663 the privilege was extended to cover smiths working on the Preston of Valleyfield estate (see p. 69), a favour possibly obtained through that family's links with the Bruce family.[4]

Another industry which had benefited from the growth of the coal industry was salt. Partly with a view to using up unsaleable small coals, salt pans were erected along the shores of the Forth estuary, from Thorntonloch in the south-east to Alloa in the north-west. At the same time, however, the salt industry was also a consumer of iron, in the form of the iron plates with which salt pans were constructed. By 1573 there were thirty-eight salt pans between Preston-pans and Musselburgh, whilst Kirkcaldy had twenty-three;[5] such was the growth of the industry and so inadequate the supply of metal plates that by 1574 the owners of salt pans were complaining of the dearth of iron.[6] It is hardly surprising, therefore, that it was from the Forth basin that a new initiative was taken in the iron industry.

The Loch Maree Ironworks

In 1598 a group bearing the title 'the Fife Adventurers' obtained from the crown the right to colonise the Isle of Lewis but, through the combined efforts of the island's feuding chieftains, Mackenzie of Kintail and McLeod of the Lews, their attempts at settlement were defeated. In 1607 a further grant was made to one of the Adventurers, Sir James Spens of Wormistoun, and to Lord Balmerino and Sir George Hay; they too failed but, in exchange for the group's rights in Lewis, Hay and Spens accepted from Mackenzie of Kintail a cash payment plus the woods of Letterewe, which were to be used for iron smelting.[7] This was in 1610; it is possible, however, that Hay had been involved in ironmaking since 1607 at a site near Letterewe on the Lewis road.[8] The works which Hay founded were the first in Scotland to use the blast furnace and therefore the first to use water power to provide an artificial draught. Trip hammers, also driven by water power, may also have been used. To understand the origin of the works, however, it is necessary to look at contemporary developments in England.

By the late 16th century the Weald, traditionally the centre of the English iron industry, was experiencing severe problems. One Ralph Hogge had been granted a patent for the casting of cannon there, but by 1573 it was apparent that many others, including the Queen herself, were ignoring it. In response to a complaint made by Hogge, the English Privy Council ordained that licences should be obtained from the crown before anyone could make cannon; once a licence was obtained, a record was to be kept of every piece cast and of each customer to whom they were delivered. In 1576 the casting of ordnance in the Weald was prohibited; similar measures were taken in 1579. In 1588 and 1589 production was again suppressed. Two years later, in an effort to stop exportation, bonds were taken from all furnace owners in the Weald and, in 1602, the Privy Council once more prohibited further casting. Whether or not they were effective, these measures, coupled with an already bad and worsening fuel situation, seem to have turned attention towards alternative sites.[9] Pressures appear to have been brought to bear on the Furness district of Lancashire, and protective legislation had to be enacted for that area too.[10]

At the time when Sir George Hay was setting up his Loch Maree iron works, several Englishmen, skilled in ironworking, were in Scotland at the request of King James. Hay was on sufficiently close terms with the king to be allowed access to whatever knowledge these Englishmen might have brought with them. Some suggestion of this can be seen in the presence of two Lancashire surnames, Kemp and Cross, in the Loch Maree area as late as the 19th century, for it is probably from the Furness district that Hay recruited his skilled labour. Some English capital may also have been employed: export of English cannon to Spain, by far the largest market, was either strictly controlled, or altogether prohibited. South Wales was well placed for illegally exporting cannon 'because from that place very easilie they may be caried into Spayne';[11] how much better situated was Loch Maree, in an area outwith the jurisdiction of England and practically outwith that of Scotland too. Furthermore, English investment in Scotland was favoured by the relatively open financial and commercial relations between the two countries in the years immediately after the Union of 1603. In the absence of positive proof, however, the presence of English capital must remain a matter for conjecture.

Three iron furnaces, at Letterewe, Talladale and the Red Smithy, have been identified in connection with Sir George Hay. Quasi-archaeological examinations of these sites have revealed that the iron ore used was of three types: a locally obtained bog iron, red haematite (almost certainly from Cumbria), and clayband ironstone, probably from southern Scotland.[12] The use of Cumbrian haematite ties in with the conjectured presence of English capital and identifies the Loch Maree group as precursor of various other charcoal ironworks erected in the Highlands to smelt English ores in the 18th century. The presence of clayband ironstone links these works with Hay's Fife interests.

The prospect of the further depletion of Scotland's limited timber reserves seems to have caused some concern in official quarters. The Act anent the making of Yrne with Wode, of 1609, in speaking of the Highlands, states that 'some personis, vpoun advantage of the present generall obedience in those partis wald erect yrne milnis in the same pairtis, to the vtter waisting and consumeing of the saidis wodis'. Under the Act, the making of iron with wood was prohibited, any iron thus produced being subject to confiscation. The working of the Act, if it was in fact implemented, had little effect on Hay's activities, and in 1610 he obtained a gift of 'the privilege of making of yron and glas workis within the Kingdome of Scotland'.[13] By 1613 it would seem that there was little that Hay could do wrong; according to a proclamation of that year, certain subjects had 'interprysit the practise and making of yrne' and had at great expense 'brought that work to ane ressonable good perfectioun of purpois and resolutioun'. By this time Hay was shipping ore to his works from the Fife coast[14] and, to protect this trade, it was ordered that no iron ore was to be exported from Scotland.[15] In 1620 Hay's works was still using Fife ores shipped via St. Monance.[16]

Besides producing cannon and other cast-iron goods for export, Hay's works seem to have made bar iron, as is testified by the remains of water-powered forges.[17] It is probable that some found its way to the Firth of Forth, and it was almost certainly with this area in mind that, in 1621, contrary to existing laws, Hay was granted permission to transport his manufactured iron to any port or harbour of any burgh.[18]

The Limekilns Iron Mill

In 1622 Hay became High Chancellor of Scotland; his ironmaking monopoly still had many years to run, and in his absence the works probably continued to operate under a manager or factor.[19] Despite his retirement from smelting, Hay may still have been involved with the iron industry. The need for iron, already substantial in 1574 (p. 87 above), must have been much greater by the 1620s, and it is not surprising to find that by the early 1630s an 'iron mill' or forge had been established on the Fife coast, near Limekilns. Although it has been claimed that the mill was the creation of the Bruce family,[20] Sibbald, writing in the 1700s when the mill was still working, states that it was, in fact, George Hay who had built it.[21] Two surviving papers relating to the mill throw a little light on its activities. According to Turner,[22] iron was extracted from local ore; the accounts for the period 1635-40 do not, however, bear this out, for although the mill was using both Scots and Swedish iron, the difference between the quantity of 'gad iron' received and ironwork delivered (9,146 st. 3 lb. and 8,025 st. 10 lb. respectively) is not sufficiently great to be that between iron ore and pig or bar iron. Almost certainly the iron mill was a forge. During the period 1635-40 ironwork was being delivered at the rate of 15-20,000 stones per annum, and although destinations are seldom noted, those that are, such as Kirkcaldy and Prestonpans, suggest that the salt industry with its great demand for iron plates was an important customer.[23] Lythe points out that the Dutch were substantial buyers of Scottish salt and that, especially after 1622, direct exports to the Baltic were rising fast; were this the case, Swedish iron would furnish a useful return cargo. The scale and technical achievement of the salt industry in the mid-1630s is indicated by the observations of Sir William Brereton: at one saltworks near Edinburgh, he saw iron evaporating pans eighteen feet long by nine feet broad — larger, he claimed, than the famous ones at Shields in England; and in expressing the number of pans along the Forth estuary, he spoke in terms of 'infinite' and 'innumerable'.[24]

Besides the salt industry, the many small users of iron, such as nail and griddle making, would offer a ready market for the iron mill's products. It is tempting to suggest that some of the iron used at the mill came from Hay's Loch Maree works, but in the absence of more positive proof, it must remain no more than a suggestion.

Later Furnaces and Forges

Little else is heard of water power in the iron industry prior to the 1720s. In 1634 there are references to a proposed ironworks in Urquhart, Inverness-shire, including the right to make dams and water-courses. According to Mackay,[25] iron was worked there, the ore being brought in from the south and the finished iron returned by the same route; apart from this, there is no indication that the works was ever built. In 1631 Sir John Grant of Grant agreed to enter into partnership with the purchaser of woods in Strathspey if ironstone was discovered and to share the cost of building an ironworks.[26] McNair, in his *County of Angus in 1678,* speaks of an iron smelter in the Wood of Dalbog, Edzell,[27] and in the late 17th century Cameron of Locheil was said to be building an iron mill.[28] In the absence of any other information, all these projects must be assumed to have been failures. Only in the early 18th century is anything heard of such ventures proving to be successful.

In April 1718 two Irishmen, John Smith and John Irvine, bought the woods of Inchcailloch on Loch Lomond-side and a division of the Menteith woods, to be cut in four and seven years respectively. The two partners were at liberty to make charcoal and to mine ore in Menteith and Buchanan, and were allowed to erect an iron mill with outbuildings, dams and lades.[29] Whether or not they built an iron mill, the contract had been transferred to local interests by 1723 and an iron mill had been established at Achray in Aberfoyle parish, Perth-shire. The mill appears to have used both scrap and ore, the former being imported via Port Glasgow and carried to the works on pack horses, while the latter came from the Fintry district. Charcoal was made with timber cut from the extensive local birch woods. Besides its isolation, the mill faced other problems. In August 1723 when the manager, John Wilson, wrote to the partners, the payment of wages was so far behind that his life was endangered:

> I am very hopeful that you will relieve me out of this thraldome by speedy sending up of some mo(ne)y, for this unhappy crew are like to tear me in pieces.[30]

Work was frequently retarded by broken trip hammers, but despite the mill's isolation, labour troubles and mechanical failures, it was still operating in 1738, by which time it had gained a good reputation.[31] Although it is known that both bar and plate iron were produced, little is known as to where these products were sent. One isolated reference speaks of plates being sent to Saltcoats in 1723, and it is tempting to see them as being used in salt pan con-struction there, but there is, yet again, no proof.[32]

With the exception of the works erected in the Highlands during the late 1720s, which will be considered in Chapter 25, only one other site, a forge at Dalkeith, Midlothian, can be identified as existing before 1730.[33] Few as these early sites may be, they represent the beginnings of an organised iron industry on a scale too great for bloomeries or smithing by hand; only by applying mechanical power could such a change be effected. The link had been estab-lished between Highland charcoal and Cumbrian ores, a link which was to last into the 19th century, with water-powered ironworks situated close to fuel supplies. Closer to home markets, water power had also been applied to forging bar iron in response to the growing needs of coal, salt and other industries. Sales of coal and salt, particularly to overseas markets, benefited the Scottish iron industry in more ways than one. The income which accrued from such sales, re-invested in these and other industries, tended to increase the demand for iron, while the ships that carried coal and salt from Scotland could bring back iron from the Baltic or scrap iron from the Low Countries. It is no coincidence that between the 1560s and the 1630s Scottish imports of Baltic iron increased nearly fivefold.[34] While Scotland had come nowhere near to achieving the status of England in the production of iron, a start had been made, so that with further growth in the century which followed, Scotland was able to surpass England in the technology, if not in the scale, of iron making.

NOTES

1. Macadam, W. I., 'Notes on the Ancient Iron Industry in Scotland', *PSAS* XXI (1886-7).

2. Turner, G., 'The Ancient Iron Industry of Stirlingshire and Neighbourhood', Paper read to the Stirlingshire Natural History and Archaeological Society, 20th November, 1910, 9-10.

3. *Ibid.,* 10.

4. *Ibid.,* 10-11.

5. *RSSRS,* 1st Series, II, 263, 296.

6. *APS* III, 93b. The salt masters also complained of the shortage of coal and horse-meat.

7. Macadam, *op. cit.,* 110; Dixon, J. H., *Gairloch,* Glasgow, 1886, 77.

8. Dixon, *op. cit.,* 78.

9. Ashton, T. S., *Iron and Steel in the Industrial Revolution,* Manchester, 1924, 5-9.

10. *Ibid.,* 9.

11. *Ibid.,* 8.

12. Dixon, *op. cit.,* 89; Macadam, *op. cit.,* 109-123.

13. Macadam, *op. cit.,* 111.

14. Turner, *op. cit.,* 11.

15. Cochran-Patrick, R. N., *Early Records relating to Mining in Scotland,* Edinburgh, 1878, 162.

16. *RSSRS* 1st Series, XII, 187.

17. Macadam, *op. cit.,* 122-123.

18. *Ibid.,* 89.

19. Dixon, *op. cit.,* 82.

20. Turner, *op. cit.,* 13.

21. Sibbald, R., *History of Fife and Kinross* (1710), Edinburgh, 1803, 299.

22. Turner, *op. cit.,* 13.

23. SRO GD15/898/1-2.

24. Lythe, S. G. E., *The Economy of Scotland in its European Setting 1550-1625*, Edinburgh, 1960, 51.

25. Mackay, W., *Urquhart & Glenmoriston*, Inverness, 1893, 451.

26. Lindsay, J. M., 'The Use of Woodland in Argyllshire and Perthshire between 1650 and 1850', Edinburgh PhD Thesis, 1974.

27. McNair, J., *County of Angus in 1678* (1883). Cited by Lindsay, *op. cit.*, 565.

28. Mitchell, Sir A. (ed.), *Macfarlane's Geographical Collections, SHS* LI (1906), LII (1907), LIII (1908), LI, 51-5.

29. Lindsay, *op. cit.*, 567.

30. SRO RH15/120/91.

31. Taylor, *op. cit.*, 15.

32. SRO RH15/120/91.

33. SRO GD 224/282/1 1720.

34. Lythe, *op. cit.*, 62.

8

Sawmills

By the mid-16th century most of the great Caledonian Forest had been cleared from the Lowlands of Scotland, and while a few remnants such as Presmennan Wood, East Lothian still survived, the scarcity of good stands of timber close to centres of population was such that most of Scotland's timber requirements were met from Norway. By making use of water-powered sawmills Norway had been able to exploit its substantial forests to produce much greater quantities of squared timber than could be prepared by handsaw and axe:[1] by 1688 there were about 650 such mills in Southern Norway, each turning out about 7,500 deals per annum.[2] In the Scottish Highlands there was still much timber as yet unexploited, but one person speaking of Angus in 1678 pointed out that the dependence on Norwegian timber was due not so much to the lack of timber in Scotland, but rather to the 'rugged and impassable rocks which prevent its being transported from the places where it grows'.[3] The transportation of Norwegian timber to Scotland's east coast presented relatively few problems.

Technology

From contemporary European illustrations and from Scottish examples of the later 18th century, it would appear that the sawmills established in Scotland during this period used heavy frame saws. Figure 25 shows a sawmill built at Fochabers, Moray, c.1750, but probably similar enough to earlier examples to serve as an illustration. The frame which carried the saw is mounted vertically between two runners which guide its movement. The frame is connected to a rod and thence to a crank attached to a small water wheel. While the use of a small wheel may have reduced the amount of power available, it had the advantage of giving relatively rapid motion to the saw, without the necessity of putting a strain on intermediate gearing. Timbers for sawing into slabs or deals were placed on a moveable carriage which passed through the frame of the saw.

The Introduction and Development of Sawmilling

From the 16th century there are scattered references to sawmills exploiting Scottish forests and producing commodities similar to those turned out by

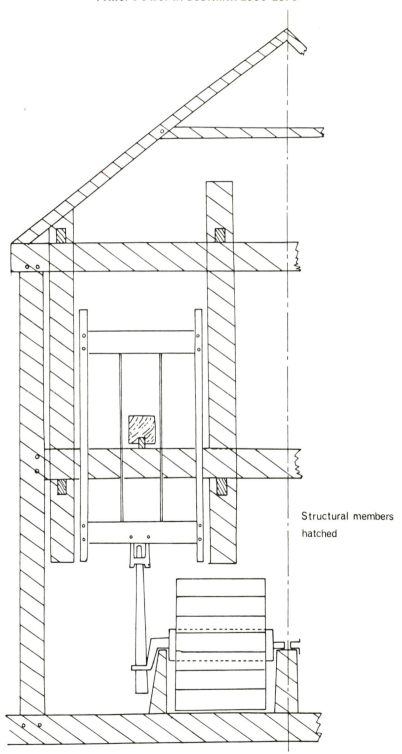

Structural members
hatched

Norwegian mills. As early as 1502 sawmills are mentioned in a list of pertinents in Badenoch and, while there is no indication that they actually existed, the suggestion is that such mills were known of and could be expected to be operating in that area.[4] By 1564 the widespread exploitation of timber and bark in the counties of Aberdeen, Banff, Moray, Nairn and Inverness led the Privy Council to express concern lest the 'hail polecie' should perish,[5] but it is not until 1630 that the first definite reference to sawmills occurs. In that year the Laird of Grant let his woods of Abernethy, Kincardine and Glencarnie to Captain John Mason, an Englishman acting on behalf of the Earl of Tullibardine, for a period of forty-four years. The grant included water mills and water courses, with power to build and uphold new mills and the right to float timber, free of tolls, down the River Spey to the sea. For these privileges and the use of the woods, Mason paid £20,000 Scots.[6] A mill at Nether Inver, Glenmoriston is referred to in 1643,[7] one at Rothiemurchus in 1650[8] and one at Invercharon, Ross-shire in 1652.[9] By the 1680s sawmills are also known to have existed in Glenmore[10] and at Rothiemurchus,[11] both in Badenoch.

It is hardly surprising to find that it was the woods of the eastern Highlands which saw the first use of sawmills, for while the area was not as yet totally subjugated by the crown, it was at least more stable than the west and more open to outside influences; once landowners became aware of and interested in the commercial potential of their woods, safe working conditions were all the more likely to exist. Furthermore, access to the sea and then to east-coast markets could be obtained either by river or loch, as in the case of the Badenoch or Glenmoriston sawmills, or directly, as at Invercharon.

Similar developments took place on Deeside, Aberdeenshire. A charter dated 1638 reserves the liberty to build 'an saw water miln or a saw windmiln'.[12] From the mention of wind-powered sawmills it would appear that this still relatively new piece of Dutch technology had already reached Scotland by the 1630s.[13] At the mouth of Glenquaich, also on Deeside, a sawmill was built in 1695. Figure 26 shows the distribution of water-powered sawmills in Scotland between 1550 and 1730.

Two Perthshire Examples

The best documented mills and those which best illustrate the problems of exploiting Highland timber are those which were set up in Rannoch and Glenlyon, on the upper tributaries of the Tay. At some time prior to 1661, Alexander Robertson of Strowan had constructed corn, saw and waulk mills, all under the same roof, at Kinlochrannoch. Unfortunately, the damhead on the mouth of Loch Rannoch held back the loch's waters to such an extent that they overflowed onto the lands of the Laird of Wemyss.[14] This particular problem was solved with relative ease and without bloodshed: on the

Fig 25. Sectional view of a frame saw mill. The right-hand side of the mill had a similar frame with a single saw and its own water wheel. *SRO GD44/10/19/17*

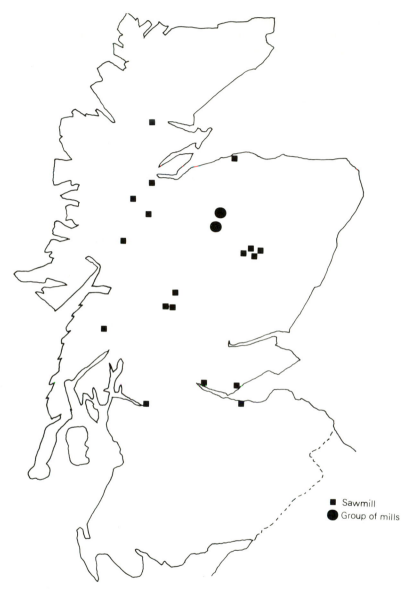

Fig 26. Distribution of saw mills, 1550-1730

judgement of a mutually chosen arbiter Robertson agreed to pay damages.

Much more serious were the problems which arose in 1675 and 1676. In a petition to the Privy Council Robertson stated that, having a considerable wood on Loch Rannoch, he had built a sawmill which had been making deals at the rate of seven to eight thousand per annum, thereby converting the otherwise useless woods into a transportable and saleable product. Robertson also stressed the employment which he had created, a cause persistently close to the heart of 17th-century Scottish administration. Having made out a case in favour of his sawmill, he went on to relate his problems to the Privy Council: the stands of timber stood twelve miles up Loch Rannoch from his sawmill and, in making the journey, floats were often broken up by storms and the timbers swept ashore, or right over the top of the mill dam; by the time that Robertson could make any moves to retrieve them, the logs had fallen prey to the country people, who regarded them as fair game. Even if timber did reach and pass through the mill, there was a possibility that the deals cut from it would disappear during the night.[15] The following year Robertson's problems came to a head. The mill had been built on his own land but, being surrounded by the lands of the Marquis of Atholl, it was only with the latter's grudging consent that Robertson had been able to build a damhead. The Marquis's enthusiasm for the mill apparently continued to cool, and in 1676 he sent his factor and a band of four hundred armed men to demolish the dam. Robertson's appeals to the Privy Council brought only confirmation of Atholl's right to do so.[16]

As a result of this incident the sawmill was moved to Carrie, on the south side of Loch Rannoch where a mill could be powered by Allt na Bogair. By 1683, by his own estimates, Robertson had made 176,000 deals there and in the same year, by obtaining the right to oversee the highways from Carrie to Apnadull (Appin of Dull) and from his sawmills to St John's Town (Perth), he was able to ease the awkward problem of transporting them to lowland markets.[17] Robertson's woods seem to have been more than adequate for the demands of his sawmill, and extraction continued into the 18th century: in 1720 the mill was being let at £125 Sterling per annum,[18] and by 1750 two mills were in use.[19]

The Glenlyon sawmills also had their problems. Like Robertson of Strowan, Campbell of Glenlyon, the owner of the woods being exploited, was losing quantities of floated timber to the local inhabitants, and in 1672 he too turned to the Privy Council for help.[20] Although there is no conclusive evidence of there having been a sawmill at this stage, the inclusion of deals among the items being floated certainly points to there being one. In 1675 or thereabouts, Campbell entered into a contract with Captain John Crawford, setting to him for twenty-one years the whole fir woods (probably Scots pine) on the Glenlyon estate with power to use the existing sawmill,[21] or to build new mills. Crawford was free to use whatever ground he needed for workmen's houses and to dam up the River Lyon at any point for the purposes of the mill. For the first three years the agreement worked well; Crawford paid the yearly tack duty and started to cut a lade through rock to serve a new mill, probably on the River Lyon.[22] Work on the lade was nearing completion when, it was claimed, a band of men led by Campbell himself appeared on the site, stole tools and threatened the workers, who eventually fled. Either before, or shortly after, this time the original lessee died and the lease was taken over by Patrick Stewart of Ballachen. In a complaint to the Privy Council he claimed that Campbell, accompanied by the usual band of armed men, had turned up again on 1st August 1678 and carried off the saw, various tools, three hundred deals and a thousand great trees ready for market. A year later to the day Campbell appeared yet again, this time to occupy the sawmill. From the defence which he gave, it would appear that Campbell was more than a little perturbed by the rate at which Stewart was extracting timber: between April and July 1678 he was said to have cut down no less than eight thousand fir trees, a very large number considering the already small extent of the woods. Furthermore, whether or not Campbell had foreseen it at the time of granting licence, the damming of the River Lyon had damaged his salmon fisheries, a valuable asset on a Highland estate. The Privy Council found that Stewart had been wrongfully dispossessed, but in view of the difficulties of occupying such a tenancy in the Highlands against the will of the landowner, it is unlikely that Stewart returned for long, if at all.[23]

The Early 18th Century

Despite the rebellion of 1715 the early post-Union years seem to have provided an environment more conducive to the exploitation of the Highland forests than that of the 17th century. The English navy needed large quantities of timber and other naval stores, and it was with a view to obtaining these from British territories that, during the reign of Queen Anne, Acts were passed encouraging the importation of naval stores from America and from Scotland. According to the Scottish Act there was, in Scotland, a great store of pine and fir trees fit for masts and for making pitch and tar, but mostly in remote, mountainous places, away from navigable rivers. To encourage the proprietors of such woods to make roads by which timber might be extracted, premiums were offered for tar, pitch and turpentine, masts, yards and bowsprits, on condition that these products were transported from Scotland to England, and in British ships.[24]

Significantly, a copy of the Act is to be found among the papers of the Duke of Gordon, who owned the Woods of Glenmore, Inverness-shire. There had been a sawmill in Glenmore in the late 17th century, and in 1712 the Duke engaged John Brander, a millwright. Brander, who had already built sawmills above Loch Morlich in Glenmore and at Fochabers, was to oversee the Glenmore sawmill operations for a three-year period. To facilitate the floating of timber down the water of Luineag to the Spey, a dam and sluice were constructed on Loch Morlich under the supervision of John Smith from Leith. The following year the burn was cleared to facilitate floating operations. John Brander also seems to have been responsible for a short-lived mill which the Duke of Gordon operated on Rothiemurchus lands, at Slianaman or Struahamain; after the mill was abandoned the lands were resumed by Grant of Rothiemurchus. A third mill was built below Loch Morlich, apparently at Ardru, which also lay on Rothiemurchus lands. This mill, on the Water of Luineag, was the work of Mr. Gage, an Englishman who had a lease of the woods from the Duke of Gordon, some time before 1715. By that year Mr. Gage had completed one sawmill and was contemplating another, but having joined in the '15 on the losing side, he had to give up his sawmilling activities, and one by one his twelve or so workers also left. Between 1715 and 1718 the Duke took direct control of the sawmill; a wagon road from the woods to Torgarve, on Speyside, dates from this period if not before. In 1718 the woods were again let, this time to Smith and Francis, two Englishmen, who worked them for a further three years. At the termination of their lease the Duke once again took personal charge, but gave up the sawmill as unprofitable in 1725.[25]

The interest shown in the woods by both English speculators and Scottish landowners indicates an attempt to benefit from the Scottish Timber Act by exploiting these isolated woods. The woods on Deeside were also attracting attention: in the early 18th century sawmills operated at Invercauld, Prony and Glenlui.[26] In 1725 the Wood of Derry was estimated to contain enough timber to keep a sawmill going for five or six years, or enough for a ten-year bargain if put up for sale. The eleven thousand trees in the wood were each valued at 10s. Scots; a sawmill could be erected for 400 Merks (£266 13s 6d Scots) exclusive of the digging of lades, which could be done by the laird's own tenants. Once built, the mill could be expected to manufacture between seven and eight thousand deals per annum.[27] The Glenlui mill, built about that time, may well have been the one in question. Production figures for 1728 show that in that year three thousand and fifty-one broad deals, nine hundred and seventy-four narrow deals and one thousand three hundred and forty-four backs were sold, mostly in small batches of six to twenty-four, though occasionally sixty or a hundred and twenty were sold at a time. Although the Glenlui mill, unlike those of Badenoch, depended on local markets, the profits made were adequate, rising from £323 16s 8d Scots in 1725 and 1726 to £1076 18s 6d Scots in 1728 and £1467 15s 6d in 1729.[28]

For all the effort put into exploiting Scotland's remaining forests, the quantities of timber extracted were generally small and the returns short-lived. In the burghs of Lowland Scotland timber from overseas continued to dominate the supply, with coastal sawmills long established at Burntisland,[29] Alloa,[30] Leith[31] and Airth,[32] the last two mills being wind-powered. With the Union of 1707, the huge timber resources of the New World had also become accessible to Scottish merchants, and the establishment of a sawmill at Glasgow in the 1720s was probably aimed at exploiting this new source.[33] During the century after 1730, however, the landscape of Lowland Scotland was to change in a way which stimulated Scottish timber production, while those few woods left in the Highlands remained adequate for the needs of those who continued to exploit them.

NOTES

1. Lythe, S. G. E., *The Economy of Scotland in its European Setting, 1550-1625*, Edinburgh, 1960, 148.

2. Anderson, M. L., *A History of Scottish Forestry*, 2 vols, London, 1967, I, 331.

3. *Ibid.*, I, 317.

4. In listing pertinents it was customary to list any item which might possibly be present. SRO GD176/19.

5. *RSSRS* 1st Series, 279-80.

6. Anderson, *op. cit.*, I, 321.

7. *RSSRS* 2nd Series, IX, 1468 (1643).

8. Anderson, *op. cit.*, I, 359.

9. *RSSRS* 2nd Series, X, 17.

10. SRO GD44/51/742.

11. Anderson, *op. cit.*, I, 322.

12. *Records of Aboyne*, New Spalding Club, 1894, 291.

13. Wailes, R., in Singer C., Holmyard, E. J., Hall, A. R. & Willis, T. I. (eds.), *A History of Technology*, 5 vols, Oxford, 1956-59, III, 106-7.

14. SRO GD1/389/8.

15. *RSSRS* 3rd Series, IV, 421.

16. *RSSRS* 3rd Series, IV, 570-76.

17. *RSSRS* 3rd Series, VIII, 148.

18. SRO GD50/160.

19. Anderson, *op. cit.*, I, 446.

20. *RSSRS* 3rd Series, III, 448.

21. Probably at Milton Eonan (GR NN5746): Stewart, A., *A Highland Parish or the History of Fortingall*, Glasgow, 1928, 92.

22. Stewart, *op. cit.*, 92.

23. *RSSRS* 3rd Series, VII, 46-7.

24. SRO GD44/39/27.

25. SRO GD44/19/25.

26. SRO GD124/17/147; SRO GD124/17/123.

27. SRO GD124/17/123.

28. SRO GD124/17/144.

29. See Chapter 1, p.

30. Mitchell, Sir A. (ed.), *Macfarlane's Geographical Collections*, *SHS* LI (1906), LII (1907), LIII (1900), I, 308 (1722): two mills on the Brathie Burn near the coast.

31. Anderson, *op. cit.*, I, 331.

32. Mitchell, *op. cit.*, I, 327. A sawmill in the village, 'which goes by wind of a figure never before seen in Scotland'.

33. *SBRS*, 'Extracts from the Records of the Burgh of Glasgow', V (1718-38), Glasgow, 1909, 152; 256, 349.

Part Two

The Age of Water Power, 1730-1830

9

The Technology of Water Power

The early stages of the Industrial Revolution have accurately been described as the Age of Water Power,[1] for despite the application of the steam engine to rotary motion during the late 18th century, water power was already being harnessed for a wide range of industries and was the subject of further design innovations well into the 19th century. Indeed, new techniques for utilising water power brought about a minor renaissance in its use during the late 19th century. Almost all of the new manufacturing techniques which appeared between 1730 and 1830 in the textile industry, in iron-working and in a multiplicity of other trades made use of the tried and tested power of water before attempting to use steam power. The nature of these applications will be considered in the chapters which follow.

Millwrights and Engineers

During the 18th century the demands of a wide range of manufacturing industries brought the trade of millwright into its own and helped to give birth to the profession of engineer. The work of Smith at Deanston, and Kelly at New Lanark, both in connection with the cotton industry, is dealt with in Chapter 20, but the virtuosity and prowess of the Scottish millwright is best illustrated by the Meikle family who, through three generations, come close to covering the entire period.

James Meikle has already been referred to in connection with the introduction from Holland of winnowing machines and pot-barley mills.[2] Of his sons, Andrew (1719-1811) is well known for his threshing machine patent,[3] but this has tended to overshadow his other achievements and those of another member of the Meikle family, Robert. The exact relationship of Robert to Andrew and to James Meikle is not clear, although it seems likely that he was Andrew's elder brother. In 1734 he turns up in Glasgow as a 'stranger millwright', already familiar with iron-rolling and -slitting machinery, and having a knowledge of surveying and model-making.[4] After settling in Glasgow as a 'wright and engine maker',[5] he produced plans and models of a number of mills for the Duke of Argyll during the mid-1740s.[6] From about 1747 to about 1768 Robert and Andrew Meikle worked together on a number of projects, mostly in connection with the textile industry.

A long association with the Board of Trustees for Manufactures started in

1747 with visits to bleachfields in the Perth area;[7] in 1751 they were taken on as consultant millwrights to the Board and were given £20 per annum to train apprentices.[8] Together they developed improved bleaching machinery in 1754.[9] Each carried out surveys of mills for the Forfeited Estates Commission,[10] and in 1768 they took out a joint patent on corn-dressing machinery.[11] Robert is also identified with a number of engineering projects, starting in 1767 with a joint survey with Watt for the proposed Forth and Clyde Canal, using a route shorter than that proposed by Smeaton.[12] At this time he was resident at Westfield, Falkirk. Thereafter his work seems to have taken him back to the west of Scotland. His name appears in connection with 'engines' for Port Glasgow dry dock (1768), a scheme for deepening the Clyde (1778), and additions to the old Glasgow Bridge (1779). Robert Meikle died in 1780, by which time he seems to have returned to Saltoun Barley Mill.[13] Had he been born some fifty or so years later, Robert Meikle might have found fame as an engineer: his later work in particular shows a range of skills far beyond those of millwright, and it is interesting to note that in the 1768 patent Andrew is identified as 'Millwright' but Robert as 'Engineer'.[14] As it was, Robert has been almost completely forgotten, overshadowed by the later achievements of Andrew.

Although he travelled widely in Scotland and in England, Andrew Meikle, unlike Robert, was based in his native East Lothian throughout his long life. Up to about 1750 his address is given as Saltoun, from then until about 1783 as Houston Mill, East Linton, and for the rest of his life as Knowes Mill, East Linton.[15] Despite his 'great throng of business',[16] he could still find time to perform work locally, free of charge; that such generosity did not go unrecognised is evident from a minute of Haddington Town Council, dated 28th June 1763:

> The Council, in regard Andrew Meikle, milnwright at Houston Waukmiln, has upon several occasions done acts of friendship to this Burgh by his advice in repairing the Town's Milns, and that without demanding any gratuity for his trouble, recommend to the Dean of Guild and his Council to admit the said Andrew Meikle ane heritable Burgess upon the town's expense.[17]

Andrew's second patent, for spring-regulated windmill sails, was taken out in 1772, but its originality has since been contested on the basis of an earlier patent (1745) to Edmund Lee.[18] Work on the threshing machine started in 1776,[19] and in 1781 he designed a new set of mills for the Burgh of Dumfries, to replace Smeaton's mills which had lately been destroyed by fire.[20]

From about 1785 Andrew worked closely with his son George: together they designed a mill for the Burgh of Linlithgow,[21] and the threshing machine patent of 1788 was taken out in their joint names.[22] The originality of the machine was disputed at the time and widely 'pirated', although towards the end of Meikle's life a subscription was raised for him in recognition of his work.[23] From 1790 until his death in 1812 less is heard of him, though it would be wrong to assume that he drifted into senility: evidence given at a Court of

Session case in 1805 suggests that, even in his mid-eighties, he still had possession of his faculties.[24] It was George Meikle who erected the first commercial
model of the threshing machine at Kilbagie, Clackmannanshire, but he is best
remembered for his ingenious water-raising wheel at Blairdrummond, Stirlingshire (1787), the sophistication of which drew praise from various quarters,
including the designer of an alternative but less efficient wheel.[25] George died
in 1811 shortly after his father. A summary of the Meikles' work appears in
Table 1.

Table 1

A Summary of the Work of the Meikle Family

1. *James Meikle*
   - 1710: Wright in Wester Keith, East Lothian.
   - 1710: Visit to Holland.
   - 1710: Established Saltoun Barley Mill.
   - 1712: Mr. McKell and brother — work in Edinburgh & Glasgow.
   - 1715: Second visit to Holland, milling machinery.

2. *Robert Meikle* (son or nephew of James Meikle)
   - 1734: 'Stranger millwright' in Glasgow — made model of engine for slitting and chipping iron, and for rolling hoops.
   - 1741: Survey of fall to Provan Mill and other mills on Molendinar Burn.
   - 1742: Petitioned Glasgow Town Council for permission to use a wind mill as a corn mill.
   - 1744-5: Worked for Duke of Argyll, including models of slit mill, lint mill, wind mill (corn and malt), thread mill.
   - 1747: (With Andrew) visited bleachfield in Perth area.
   - 1747-9: Saltoun Bleachfield.
   - 1749: Mill machinery, Whim and Rosneath, Argyll.
   - 1749-51: Mill machinery, Carlunden, Inveraray.
   - 1751: (With Andrew) engaged as millwright to the Board of Trustees for Manufactures.
   - 1752: Granted £20 per annum for taking apprentices.
   - 1752-5: Andrew Fraser from Fordyce, Banffshire, apprenticed to Robert and Andrew.
   - 1753: Thomas Carfrae taken on as apprentice.
   - 1753: Sent washing mill model by Board of Trustees for assessment.
   - 1754: (With Andrew) (millwrights at Saltoun) mechanised feed to rubbing boards.
   - 1751-63: Worked on Lord Milton's lint and barley mills at Saltoun.
   - 1762: Proposal that he be millwright for Saltoun Bleachfield.
   - 1762: Survey of River Carron.
   - 1762-3: Report on Auchnagairn Mill for Forfeited Estates Commission.
   - 1768: (With Andrew) corn dressing patent (at Westfield, Falkirk).
   - 1768: Engines for Glasgow Dry Dock.
   - 1778: Deepening of River Clyde.
   - 1779: Additions to Old Glasgow Bridge.
   - 1780: Died (at Saltoun Barley Mill).

3. *Andrew Meikle* (son of James Meikle)

Born 5th May 1719.

1747:	(With Robert) visited bleachfields in Perth area.
1747:	(With Robert) work on Saltoun Bleachfield.
1749:	Work on Bonnington yarn mill.
c. 1750:	Survey of Tyne and Colstoun Water for Haddington Tarred Wool Company.
1750:	Visited England *per* Lord Deskford and Lord Milton (Board of Trustees for Manufactures) for Tarred Wool Company (waulk mill machinery).
1751:	Assessment of Currie's improved flax bruising and fining mill at Kevock Mill.
1751:	(With Robert) taken on as millwright to the Board of Trustees for Manufactures.
1752:	Unable to complete Garvaldfoot waulkmill because of 'throng of business'.
1752:	(With Robert) granted £20 per annum to take on apprentices.
1752:	At East Linton.
1754:	(With Robert) improvement to rubbing board feed.
1754:	Attestation of fitness — waulkmill at Kilmarnock.
1755:	Report on James Hog's flax fining mill.
1759:	Report on Bonnington Mills.
1759:	Report on mills on the Perth estate (Forfeited Estates Commission).
1762:	Inspection of blue stones at the West Mill of Haddington.
1762:	Made an honorary burgess of Haddington (millwright at Houston Waulkmill, East Linton).
1768:	(With Robert) corn dressing patent.
1773-5:	John Rennie working at Andrew's millwright's shop.
1776:	Work on Thornton Mill, East Lothian.
1776:	First threshing machine, at Knowes mill, for George Meikle.
1777-9:	John Rennie working part-time.
1778:	Threshing machine plans presented to the Board of Trustees.
1779:	John Rennie doing 'overflow' from Andrews's work.
1781:	Dumfries town mills.
1785:	(With George) burgh mills at Linlithgow.
1788:	Threshing machine patent (at Knowes Mill).
1801:	Reconstruction of East Mill, Haddington.
1802:	Threshing mill, Biel Mill.
1805:	Evidence in Court of Session case (Haddington).
1811:	Died.

4. *George Meikle* (son of Andrew Meikle)

1785:	At Knowes Mill.
1785:	(With Andrew) burgh mills at Linlithgow.
1787:	Blairdrummond water-raising wheel.
1788:	Work on threshing machine.
1789:	At Alloa.
c. 1789:	Alloa burgh mills.
1795:	Lanark burgh mill (Mousemill).
1811:	Died.

The Meikles also provide a link with the engineering profession in the person of John Rennie. Rennie was born on 7th June 1761, the son of James Rennie, farmer at Phantassie, only a stone's throw from Houston Mill. According to Boucher,[26] Rennie often played truant and visited Meikle.

At the age of twelve, having completed his local education, he spent two years working with Andrew Meikle prior to going to school at Dunbar in 1775 at his own request, to learn Latin, English and Mathematics. On a visit to Dunbar, David Loch commented on Rennie's remarkable abilities; after two years at school, Rennie returned to working with Meikle, continuing his studies in his spare time. Starting with a few jobs which Meikle had insufficient time to undertake, Rennie soon became an accomplished millwright. According to tradition, his first job in 1779 was to install a threshing machine at Knowes Mill, followed by machinery for mills at Invergowrie (Dundee) and Bonnington (Edinburgh).[27] Rennie's notebook, now in the National Library of Scotland, includes a series of experiments on a flour mill at Invergowrie (1782), the content of which shows that his skills as a millwright already had a firm scientific basis.[28]

In November 1780 Rennie had started three years of study at Edinburgh University under the eminent Professor of Natural Philosophy, John Robison, a man who also took a scientific interest in water power.[29] It was Robison who recommended Rennie to Watt as a suitable person to carry out the structural and millwrighting work on the Albion Mills, London (1784), the first of many steam-powered mills.[30] Rennie's contribution to the technology of water power will be discussed further at a later stage; a summary of his most important Scottish works appears in Table 2.

The continuing importance of water power is reflected in the work of major

Table 2

John Rennie's Principal Scottish Mill Works*

1773-5: Working at Andrew Meikle's millwright's shop.

1777-9: Working part time with Andrew Meikle.

1779:   Doing 'overflow' from Andrew Meikle's work.

1779:   Work on Knowes Mill, East Lothian.

1780:   Corn (?flour) mill machinery, Invergowrie. Repair to Bonnington Mills, Edinburgh.

1781-3: Work on Proctor's Mill, Glamis. Foundry mill for Carron Company.

1783-8: Flour mill at Leith.

1807:   New mill at Water of Leith (?Dean). Report on Glasgow Corporation mills.

1809:   Mills at Perth.

1810:   Loch Leven drainage report.

* Adapted from Boucher, C. T. G., *John Rennie 1761-1821*, Manchester, 1963, 123 *et seq.*

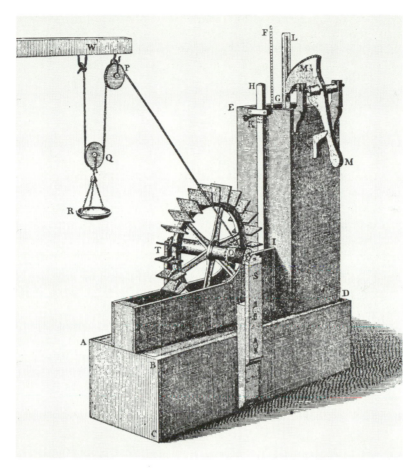

Fig 27. Smeaton's model for testing the power of undershot water wheels. *Smeaton, Reports*

engineering figures, such as Telford, Smeaton and Fairbairn;[31] of these the most important was Smeaton, whose *Experimental Enquiry Concerning the Natural Powers of Water and Wind to Turn Mills* . . . brought him the Royal Society's Gold Medal. Using ingeniously designed testing apparatus, first with paddles (undershot), then with buckets (overshot) (Figure 27), Smeaton was able to show that the best design of overshot wheel was much more efficient than the best undershot type.[32] On the basis of this he established the principle that there must be considerable losses in efficiency when a jet of water strikes the flat blade of an undershot wheel and that the work could be much better done by filling the buckets of an overshot wheel and relying on gravity rather than on impulse alone.[33] Being not only a man of science but also a practical working engineer, Smeaton was able to put his theories into practice at a number of sites. A summary of Smeaton's work in Scotland appears in Table 3.

Table 3

John Smeaton's Principal Scottish Mill Works

1769:	Dumfries Town Mills.
1769:	Luncarty Bleachfield, Perthshire.
1769:	Carron Ironworks — No. 4 blast furnace.
	No. 2 blast furnace.
	Water supply.
1770:	Carron Ironworks — Double boring mill.
1771:	Dalry Mills, Edinburgh.
1771-3:	Milton of New Tarbat, Ross-shire.
1777:	Carron Ironworks — clay mill.
1779:	Carron Ironworks — boring mill.
1779:	Leadhills mines — water engine.
1780:	Wanlockhead Mines — stamp mill, blowing wheel.

Without doubt, therefore, and notwithstanding the attention devoted to the development of the steam engine between 1730 and 1830, a great deal of attention was still being paid to technical improvements in water-driven prime movers, by a number of parties from practical millwrights to the most eminent engineers and academics of the age. The rest of the chapter will be given over to describing the nature of these improvements and the way in which they were put into practice in Scotland.

Mill Gearing

In terms of materials, the Industrial Revolution is characterised by a move from organic to inorganic materials or, more specifically, from wood to cast iron. This transition is clearly illustrated by developments in water mill machinery which underwent changes not only in materials but also, as a result, in design.

As so little has been written on the subject, it is by no means easy to tie down or ascribe to individuals developments in mill gearing between 1730 and 1830. However, broadly speaking, the wooden 'cog and rung' gearing described in Chapter 1 was still universally used in Scotland until at least the 1770s, but thereafter it gradually gave way to cast-iron shafts and gear wheels, with cycloidal teeth, in which wood was used only occasionally for alternate sets of teeth, to provide smoother, quieter running than would have been possible if iron teeth meshed with iron ones.[34] To some extent this was made possible by improvements in the techniques of metal casting and turning.

Smeaton is known to have used cast iron gears with wooden teeth in a number of mills,[35] the first of which, Brook Mill, Deptford, he designed in 1778.[36] According to Boucher, some engineers had used cast iron segments bolted onto wooden felloes, but not until 1784, with Rennie's design for the Albion Mills, London, was cast iron used throughout.[37]

According to the (Old) Statistical Account, Mr. Kelly, at New Lanark, had lately discovered a new method of erecting the great gear of large machinery in cotton mills, which would require twenty-five per cent less water, would save lives and would be applicable to all types of mill. For this he was awarded a premium by the Board of Trustees for Manufactures.[38] While the Statistical Account does not provide any further details, a brief entry in the *General View of the Agriculture of Peeblesshire* (1802) gives some indication of the rapidity with which it was disseminated. The 'improvement' is identified as being 'bevelled work', probably a reference to the transmission of power at an angle by means of cast iron gear-wheels with bevelled faces. The use of 'bevelled work' was reported to have originated less than twenty years earlier, at New Lanark, and to have been universally adopted in threshing machines and every new corn mill, that at Spittalhaugh having been the first in the county.[39] Whether or not bevelled gearing had originated at New Lanark, the example illustrates well the speed with which improvements in water mill technology could be diffused in the late 18th century.

Lastly, one further improvement in gearing should be mentioned. By taking the drive from the circumference, rather than the centre of a water wheel, it was possible to obtain much higher speeds of rotation from drive shafts and, by means of a belt-drive from the shafts, to eliminate much cumbersome and energy-draining gearing. As with other aspects of mill gearing, this innovation cannot definitely be ascribed to an individual, but Stowers[40] suggests that it was Fairbairn who first used high-speed shafts in 1818.

Water Wheels

As a material in water wheel construction, wood was far from perfect: inter-mittent contact with water caused it to rot and, the larger the wheel, the more difficult it was to find a design which was at the same time structurally sound and not excessively cumbersome. If the spokes or 'arms' were morticed into the shaft, it was considerably weakened. The use of a clasp-arm construction helped solve the problem but still failed to overcome the inherent weakness of wood as a material.[41]

In an earlier section reference was made to Smeaton's experiments on water wheel design and the conclusions which he reached. In his practical work as an engineer he was able to apply his theoretical knowledge to the full. In 1779, in his design for a furnace blowing engine at Carron Ironworks, he introduced the first cast iron water wheel shaft; in 1780 he used wrought iron for buckets.[42] By the early 19th century water wheels of all-iron construction were coming into use. Stowers has spoken of Smeaton's designs as marking the end of an era of wooden water wheel construction.[43] In reality it would be more accurate to speak of them as the beginning of the end. In the 1820s timber was still being used very widely in the construction of water wheels and other mill machinery, but in a scientific way which recognised the qualities of particular woods and made use of them in the best possible manner.[44]

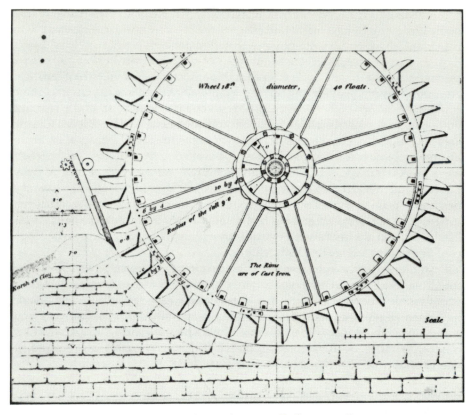

Fig 28. Smeaton's water wheel for Carron boring mill. *Smeaton, Reports*

Smeaton's theoretical findings on water wheels had a substantial influence on subsequent design practice. To make the greatest possible use of the gravitational power of water, breast-shot wheels were built with a closely fitting breast-work which prevented water from passing the wheel without contributing to its rotation. This comes out well in Smeaton's plan for a boring mill at Carron (Figure 28), but can also be seen in a great many later mills throughout Scotland. A further refinement was the depressing sluice, attributed to Rennie and first used by Smeaton at the Soho Factory in 1784.[45] The sluice, which was lowered rather than raised in the conventional manner, enabled water to be drawn off from the top of the lade or shute, thereby increasing the height and the gravitational power of water working on a breast-shot wheel.

To make the best use of the force of moving water it became customary to construct wheels with curved buckets and inlets set at an angle which minimised 'shock loss'.[46] With particularly large wheels, problems arose with air-locking as the water entered the buckets, and when tail-water was high with the bottom of the wheel running submerged.[47] This difficulty was overcome by using ventilated buckets, designed by Fairbairn and first used by him at Wilmslow, Cheshire in 1828.[48] According to Fairbairn, this measure was capable of effecting a twenty-five per cent increase in power.[49]

At least one misconception arose from Smeaton's work. In his experiments he had shown that water wheels were at their most efficient when their circumference moved at a little more than three feet per second, and it became standard practice to design wheels with a speed of about three and a half feet per second. Joseph Glynn is credited with having discovered that greater speeds could be used as the height and diameter of the wheel increased, without any appreciable loss of efficiency. Thereafter he built several iron water wheels of thirty feet or more in diameter, to revolve at six feet per second, thereby reducing the need for gearing and the load on the wheel and axle.[50] As the demands of industry led to the construction of ever-larger mills, attention turned to producing lighter, less cumbersome water wheels. In the early 1820s T. C. Hewes, a Manchester engineer, invented a 'Suspension wheel' which used circumference gearing and therefore needed only a relatively light axle. The principle used was similar to that of the bicycle wheel, relying on the tensile strength of lightweight arms, rather than the strength of heavier members under compression, to maintain stability of shape.[51] Fairbairn improved on the invention by substituting gibs and cotters for the nuts and screws which held the spokes to the centre,[52] and used suspension wheels at a number of sites, including the rightly celebrated group of four fifty-feet diameter by twelve-feet wide wheels at Catrine. Even more remarkable were the wheels proposed for Deanston cotton mill, Perthshire. A group of eight water wheels, capable of eight hundred horse power, were to be set in a building ninety feet square and surrounded by another building two hundred and sixty feet square. Only two of the wheels were erected by Messrs Fairbairn & Lillie, and a further two by the company's own engineer, William Smith. The remaining four were never built, nor was the square mill surrounding the wheelhouse.[53] Other exceptionally large wheels were built in Scotland, the very largest of which, at a cotton mill in Greenock, is descibed at great length in the *Imperial Gazetteer.*[54] Where only low falls were available, it was possible to increase power by widening the wheel. Thus at Dalmarnoch printworks, Dunbartonshire, a fall of only twenty-six inches carried a wheel sixteen and a half feet in diameter by fifteen feet broad,[55] and at Linwood cotton mill, Renfrewshire, there was an undershot wheel, fourteen feet in diameter by no less than twenty feet broad.[56]

NOTES

1. Musson, A. E. & Robinson, E., *Science & Technology in the Industrial Revolution*, Manchester, 1969, 71.

2. See Chapter 2, p.

3. See Chapter 14, p.

4. *SBRS*, 'Extracts from the Records of the Burgh of Glasgow', V (1718-38), Glasgow, 1909, 424.

5. Lindsay, I. G. & Cosh, M., *Inveraray and the Dukes of Argyll*, Edinburgh, 1973, 423, Appendix: Tradesmen.

6. *Ibid.*, 423.

7. NLS Acc.2933/350.

8. SRO NG1/1/11, 7th June 1751.

9. SRO NG1/1/12, 13th December 1754.

10. Andrew Meikle: SRO E 769/35: Report on Mill at Auchnagarden, c.1759; Robert Meikle: SRO E 769/125: Report on Mill of Auchnagairn, 1762-3.

11. See Chapter 14, p.

12. Lindsay & Cosh, *op. cit.*, 173.

13. *Ibid.*, 423.

14. *Ibid.*, 423.

15. Sources: various.

16. SRO NG1/1/12, 15.12.52.

17. I am indebted to Mr. J. N. Cartwright, Bolton, East Lothian, for drawing my attention to this information.

18. Boucher, C. T. G., *John Rennie 1761-1821. The Life and Work of a Great Engineer*, Manchester, 1963, 2, 3.

19. See Chapter 14, p.

20. See Chapter 12, p.

21. SRO GD215/1825/35 (1785).

22. *Scots Magazine* LI (1789), 211.

23. Handley, J. E., *The Agricultural Revolution in Scotland*, Glasgow, 1963, 104.

24. OSP 485:25. Haddington Burgh Council v. Haddington Tarred Wool Co.

25. See Chapter 14, p.

26. Boucher, *op. cit.*, 3.

27. *Ibid.*, 5.

28. NLS Acc 5111/25.

29. Boucher, *op. cit.*, 6; SRO NG1/1/28: £30 to Professor Robison at University of Edinburgh, for experiments on the motion and action of water. Wants to do experiments in Renfrewshire cotton mills. Thinks that he has developed a rule.

30. Boucher, *op. cit.*, 8; Musson & Robinson, *op. cit.*, 76.

31. Burne, E. L., 'On Mills. Thomas Telford, 1796', *TNS* XVII (1936-7); Wilson, P. N., 'The Water Wheels of John Smeaton', *TNS* XXX (1955-7); Smeaton, J., *Reports of the Late John Smeaton*, 3 vols., London, 1812; Fairbairn, Sir W., *Treatise on Mills and Millwork*, 2 vols., 4th Edition, London, 1878.

32. Bowman, G., 'John Smeaton — Consulting Engineer', in Semler, E. G. (ed.), *Engineering Heritage*, Vol. 2, London, 1966, 11, says that the best overshot designs were almost twice as efficient as the best undershot; Wilson, P. N., 'Water-Driven Prime Movers', in *Engineering Heritage*, Vol. 1, London, 1963, 30, gives the efficiencies of overshot and undershot wheels as 63% and 22% respectively.

33. Wilson, *op. cit.* (1963), 30.

34. The same combination of wood/iron is used to this day.

35. Wilson, *op. cit.* (1963), 30.

36. Wilson, *op. cit.* (1955-7), 33.

37. *Boucher, op. cit.*, 83.

38. *OSA* IV, 35, Lanark, Lanarkshire.

39. Findlater, C., *General View of the Agriculture of Peeblesshire*, Edinburgh, 1802, 27.

40. Stowers, A., 'Observations on the History of Water Power', *TNS* XXX (1957-9), 252.

41. Wilson, *op. cit.* (1963), 30.

42. Wilson, P. N., 'Water Power and the Industrial Revolution', *Water Power*, August, 1954, 312.

43. Stowers, A., 'Water Mills', in Singer, C., Holmyard, E. J., Hall, A. R. & Williams, T. I. (eds.), *A History of Technology*, 5 vols., Oxford, 1956-9, IV, 209.

44. See Monteath, R., *The Forester's Guide & Profitable Planter*, Edinburgh, 1824, 193-4.

45. Boucher, *op. cit.*, 79.

46. Wilson, *op. cit.* (1963), 30.

47. *Ibid.*, 30-1.

48. Stowers, *op. cit.* (1957-9), 252.

49. Wilson, *op. cit.* (1963), 31.

50. Stowers, *op. cit.* (1956-9), 205.

51. Musson & Robinson, *op. cit.*, 70.

52. Fairbairn, *op. cit.*, I, 120-1.

53. *Ibid.*, I, 128-9.

54. Wilson, J. M. (ed.), *The Imperial Gazetteer of Scotland*, 2 vols., Edinburgh, London & Dublin, N.D. (c.1875), I, 17.

55. *NSA* VIII, 224, Bonhill, Dunbartonshire.

56. *NSA* VII, 51, Houston & Killallan, Renfrewshire.

10

The Rural Corn Mill

There stand three mills on Manor Water,
A forth on Posso Cleugh,
Gin heather bells were corn and bere,
They wad hae grist eneugh.[1]

In 1730 the pattern of Scottish grain milling was still the traditional one of many small mills, each grinding oats and bere for astricted clients, in simple buildings constructed for the most part from local materials. By 1830 a far smaller number remained, and, of these, most were well-equipped mills, working for cash and utilising the products of science and industry in their design and construction. Why did such a change come about and what form did it take?

Technical Developments

Improved machinery was an important prerequisite for the more centralised manufacture of grain, and it was largely because of developments in technology that, by the end of the period, requirements could be met by a far smaller number of mills than had been necessary at the beginning; at least one contemporary writer cites it as the most important single factor in the decline of corn mill numbers.[2] Other sources point to the inefficiency of existing mills: reporting on the mill of Auchnagarden (Inverness), Andrew Meikle claimed that, given the proper machinery, it could perform the same work with half the water,[3] while a survey made in 1816 claimed that one good mill could have carried out all the work of the six 'wreched' mills in Strathfleet, Sutherland.[4]

Between 1730 and 1830 building standards showed a marked improvement. The single-storey clay, rubble or turf mill, with its roof of thatch or divots, was cramped and required frequent stoppages for rebuilding to take place. At the turf-roofed Mill of Cranston (Midlothian) the 'stooling' was very low and the pit below consequently dark and dirty. The dirt which gathered in the pit increased wear and tear on the pit wheel, and when it came to replacing a cog, access was very difficult and repairs very time-consuming. Furthermore, it was impossible to detect whether grain was spilling from the millstones down to the pit below.[5] By 1830, such mills had vanished from all but the most isolated corners of the country, and in their place had been built two- or three-storey mills, with cemented walls of rubble or ashlar, and roofs of pantile or slate. Within the mill sufficient room was available to separate the machinery onto different floors; to accomplish all the lifting which the extra height made necessary, water-powered sack hoists and grain elevators were often installed.[6] Mills equipped with two or more pairs of stones could carry out the processes of shilling and mealing on separate stones, eliminating the need for tentering between the two processes, doubling the capacity of the mill. Ample space was left for storage and, as often as not, a kiln was appended to the mill building, with direct access provided between the two. Figure 29 shows a typical 'Improved' corn mill of the early 19th century. In 1730, farms in many districts still had their own circular kilns, 'miserable hovels, covered with straw' and containing a framework of boughs (kiln-ribs) which supported a platform of heather or straw (kiln-head) upon which the grain was laid out; kilns of this type were to be found at some, but by no means all, corn mills.

In the widespread rebuilding of the 18th and early 19th centuries, kilns of this type were replaced by rectangular ones, roofed with pantile or slate. Perforated tiles took over from heather and straw in the kiln-head, and by the 1790s, in central Scotland at least, earthenware tiles had, in turn, been super-seded by perforated metal plates, or 'yetling', a speciality of Carron Company's forges.[7] According to the *General View of Forfarshire*, kiln design had become so sophisticated that, where water was available, a small bucket wheel of about four feet in diameter was, by means of a crank, made to work bellows which blew the kiln fire through iron tuyeres, in much the same way as in a blast furnace.[8]

It was in the machinery itself, however, that improvements were most marked. A scientific approach was applied to mill design: precise calculations were made as to available water-power, and gear ratios were manipulated to give high or low speeds as required. The work of John Smeaton in this field has already been discussed (Chapter 9). The materials used were those which had been found to be the most durable, and notable among them was iron. Small quantities of iron and steel had long been used for spindles, gudgeons, rinds, bands and nails,[9] but only after the pioneering work of Rennie and Smeaton was it widely used for major parts of millwork. This use of iron is well illustrated by Coll Mill (Berwickshire), which was rebuilt in 1826 to incorporate a cast iron axle seven inches square, a pit wheel of cast iron and a cast iron spur wheel with wooden cogs.[10] Iron was also coming into use for water wheels, but although its use was encouraged by early 19th century timber shortages, the latter material continued to be that more generally used until at least 1830.

Where iron was not used, it was the timber best suited to any one purpose that was used in that particular context. For the shrouding, paddles and buckets of water wheels, black or white saugh (willow) was deemed most suitable; for sluices and dams, the durability of larch under water recom-mended its use. For axletrees oak was still favoured, though this was often the first piece of wooden machinery to be replaced by iron. Sycamore, willow and

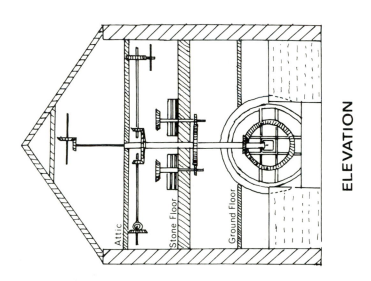

ELEVATION

Attic

Stone Floor

Ground Floor

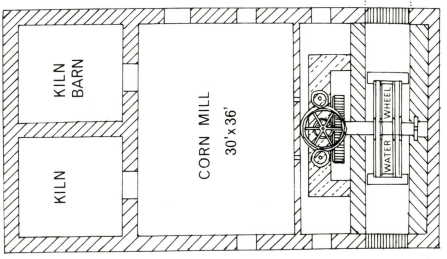

KILN
BARN

KILN

CORN MILL
30' x 36'

WATER   WHEEL

PLAN

Fig 29. Layout of a post-Improvement corn mill. *Low, 1819*

beech were all popular woods for machinery, beech being widely used to cog iron gear wheels.[11] In the early 19th century Memel pine from the Baltic came into general use.[12].

Using the most suitable and durable materials, a mill could run more efficiently, at a greater capacity, for longer periods without the necessity of a major overhaul. By drawing on skills accumulated over the previous two centuries, Scottish millwrights were able to build such mills and often added innovations of their own. In this field the work of Robert, Andrew and George Meikle was particularly notable and it was from Andrew that the engineer, John Rennie, gained his knowledge of millwrighting.

The Impact of Agricultural Improvement

Improved technology may have provided the means to reduce the number of mills, but to get closer to the cause of change one must look at the impact of developments in agricultural techniques.

The complexities of the Scottish Agricultural Revolution have been adequately dealt with elsewhere:[13] on the basis of these works it appears that the most significant changes were as follows: the drainage and enclosure of land; the creation of new steadings, roads and plantations; the amalgamation of agricultural holdings; new implements, new crop rotations and new strains of livestock. The net result of all these changes was the raising of agriculture above subsistence level and its integration into the money economy. For grain milling, the most significant changes were the new crop rotations and the draining of lochs and marshes.

Under the old system the 'infield', which was subjected to constant tillage, carried a manured crop of bere followed by two unmanured crops of oats. The 'outfield', patches of which were ploughed up from year to year, was planted with oats, and crops were taken until such time as returns ceased to justify further planting, at which juncture a fresh patch was cleared and cultivated. Although there were variations in infield rotations, such as the inclusion of beans, peas or wheat, by far the greatest acreage was occupied by oats.[14] It was this heavy dependence on oats and to a lesser extent bere, which enabled mill owners to enforce and to benefit from thirlage. As a result, corn mills came to be built wherever sufficient land was cultivated and, in some cases, even where it was insufficient. The new rotations on the other hand included such crops as turnips — which had previously been confined to the kail yard — clover and ryegrass, both previously unknown in Scotland; there was also an increase in the acreage under barley and wheat.

Early 'improved' rotations still showed an excessive dependence upon grain crops: a typical rotation at this time might be: fallow or turnips; wheat or oats; peas; barley; clover; oats or wheat. By the 1790s, however, the following were becoming more common: on rich clays fallow, wheat, beans, barley, clover, oats; on deep free loam turnips, barley, clover, oats, beans, wheat; and on light and weak soils turnips, oats or barley, clover, oats or turnips.[15] On those estates where the new rotations were introduced, the reduction in oat and bere acreages was enough to affect the viability of those mills with only small thirls, or low multure yields. At the Mill of Carsehead, Perthshire, the multures payable in 1777 amounted to only twenty-one bolls, out of which had to be paid a rent of twenty bolls.[16] According to the Old Statistical Account entry for New Monkland, Lanarkshire, poor multure yields were responsible for the decay of some of the parish's seven mills.[17] In 1754, the tacksman of Gifford Mill, East Lothian, complained that several tenants were enclosing and laying ground down to grass, thereby jeopardising his livelihood; to keep the mill working, the Barony Court had to rule that farmers were to pay the multure of ten bolls of oats and five lippies hummel corn for each ploughgate converted from grain.[18] When Robert Henry entered into a tack of the Mill of Ussie, Kincardineshire, he did so believing that the mill dues would cover the rent, but by 1821, on account of the mill's serving an area of large farms mostly under wheat, turnips and grass, mill-dues came to less than half the sum expended on rent and maintenance.[19] But for the extension of cultivation, and the higher yields made possible by new strains of oats, it is probable that many more mills would have disappeared as a result of new rotations.

Even in fertile, well-cultivated areas, the landscape of early 18th-century Scotland was pockmarked with lochs, pools and marshes. To the Improving landowner they represented a barrier to Improvement and a blight on his estate which had to be removed. The more extensive of these bodies of water had often been utilised as reservoirs for mills; in the prevailing mental climate of the Age of Improvement, the potential agricultural value of flooded land was considered much greater than any advantages which might accrue from a mill. Leslie, in his *General View of Moray and Nairn*, complains of two mills, one derelict, one little used, which prevented the Loch of Inchstellie from being drained,[20] while of Fife, Thomson reported that although one such obstruction had been removed, a further three to four hundred acres (Scots?) of good land in Kiltarlity parish was still submerged under the dams of three corn mills.[21] In the same county, four mill-dams on the Water of Motray continued to obstruct the drainage of meadow-land, despite offers of compensation to the mill owner.[22] The requirements of an overshot wheel at Luffness Mill, East Lothian long prevented the draining of a six-mile tract of high quality agricultural land alongside the Peffer Burn.[23] More often than not, lochs and ponds were finally drained, but usually to the detriment of those mills which had depended on them: in 1756, following drainage work on the Lake of Menteith, it was claimed that the Mill of Cardross, Perthshire, below it, would have insufficient water in winter to serve its thirl,[24] while the mills on the River Ore (Fife), which had previously enjoyed a steady water supply, suffered frequent stoppages after the partial drainage of Loch Ore.[25] Even more harmful was the introduction of subsoil drainage to large areas of upland, although the process had made little progress by 1830. While it is impossible to gauge how many corn mills were lost through drainage operations, the total probably stands at well over one hundred. In Aberdeenshire, the straightening of just one burn and its tributaries, and the draining of the lands beside it, led to the abandonment of no fewer than seven mills.[26]

For the Improving landowner the extension and beautification of his house and parks was as necessary a measure as enclosing fields or rebuilding steadings; indeed the proceeds from the new agriculture were often put to just such a use. One side effect of the extension of parkland was the removal of mills, and of the few which were rebuilt, all were a safe distance from the landowner's house. The Mills of Relugas, Moray, just above the junction of the Divie and the Findhorn, were removed to make way for pleasure grounds,[27] as were the Mill of Winton and the Mill of Whittingehame, both in East Lothian;[28] neither they nor the Mill of Relugas were rebuilt. A similar fate befell Kimmerghame East Mill, in Berwickshire.[29] In 1731 emparking at Taymouth Castle, Perthshire swallowed up a third of the thirl of the Mill of Taymouth;[30] some sixty years later, at the opposite end of Perthshire, two mills on a burn between Longforgan and Abernyte parishes were pulled down, once again to make way for pleasure grounds.[31]

The Decline of Thirlage

Whatever the losses sustained as a result of new agricultural practices, by far the greatest contribution to the decline of the rural corn mill came from the decay and abolition of thirlage. In Chapter 2 we saw that, while levels of production remained more or less stable, communications poor and the free market for grain small or inaccessible, thirlage did no more than ensure that the miller received enough in multures to pay his rent and the proprietor enough rent to justify maintaining the mill. Under the new agriculture, however, the suckeners' traditional resentment of thirlage was heightened by an awareness of the changed circumstances under which mills operated.

In some areas the cultivation of wastes, combined with the use of improved strains of oats, produced a situation in which multures and knaveship yielded vastly greater quantities than were, in fact, required. There were some enlightened landlords, such as Robertson of Lude, who stipulated that newly cultivated lands were to pay only one thirty-secondth in multures,[32] but on the other hand some tenants, such as those in Tulliallan parish (Fife), were obliged by clauses in their leases to grow oats rather than other unthirled crops and to pay one tenth to one eleventh in multures.[33]

The increasingly common practice of rouping mill tacks, instead of re-installing the families which had traditionally tenanted the mill itself or another in the locality, tended to push multures higher; prospective tenants of rouped mills were often led to offer sums well above their means, and more than once, when the highest bidder failed to find cautioners, mills had to be let to the second highest, or re-rouped.[34] Furthermore, those with the money to offer the highest rent were not necessarily the most skilled in milling. At the roup of the Bridge Mill of Park, Wigtownshire, in 1769, the highest bidder was a mason who 'would find it difficult to carry on to any advantage, a business to which he was not bred and of which he was entirely ignorant'. Nevertheless his high bid was accepted, with disastrous consequences for himself, the thirl and the mill owner.[35] Even if a tack did go to an experienced miller, he was often forced to exact much higher multures than were due, if only to pay his inflated rent; this was certainly the case in Halkirk parish, Caithness, where the link between augmented rents and heightened multures was clearly recognised.[36] At Milton of New Tarbat, Ross-shire the customary multure of one sixteenth malt and meal had risen by 1780 to one tenth oats and more than one ninth bere, probably for the same reason.[37] From the Old Statistical Account it is quite apparent that, by the end of the 18th century, multure rates had risen to excessively high levels (Figure 30).

For the suckeners, the tacksmen and the mill owner, the issue of multures could, and often did, 'lay the foundations for many tedious and expensive littigations (sic)',[38] especially if a dispute reached the Court of Session. In that unfortunate event a process could drag on for decades, at great cost, and without any assurance of the issue being resolved. One such process, introduced in 1780, was still going strong in 1796.[39] The rulings of Barony Courts had never been very effective in controlling abstractions and, as the Barony became less self-contained, the enhanced prestige of the tenantry was accompanied by a corresponding decline in the powers of the Barony Court. On a higher level, a dispute could be taken to a Sheriff Court, but that cost money and could result in a case being referred to the Court of Session. In at least one case involving miller and tenants, both parties withdrew and agreed to pay their own costs, rather than proceed with a potentially expensive litigation.[40] Occasionally an independent arbiter was appointed. The increased cultivation of wheat led to further disputes: bonds of thirlage tended to be full of ambiguities when it came to deciding what was, and what was not, thirled. Some millers insisted that wheat be ground at their mills, or abstracted multures paid, even if these mills did not contain the necessary machinery.[41] To sell barley for malting, or for pot-barley, farmers had to abstract it and often paid full multure for the privilege of doing so.[42]

Thirlage was also coming into disrepute among proprietors. The motivation behind Improvement was not primarily economic necessity but 'fashion, patriotism and the admiration felt by Scots of all political persuasions for a farming system that had made the English so much more affluent than themselves'.[43] Anything to do with the old system was seen as not only very passé, but positively barbaric; the 'Gothick custom' of thirlage was particularly loathsome, not only to those who owned land thirled to other landowners' mills, but to the community at large, as is manifest from the pages of the Statistical Account. Nor was thirlage simply unfashionable: it also penalised tenants for extending cultivation or for increasing productivity. Any enlightened landowner must have been fully aware of the threat which thirlage posed to the success, economic and aesthetic, of his Improvements.

On the other hand, landowners were still loth to relinquish the useful source of income obtainable from multures, or from the high rents obtainable from

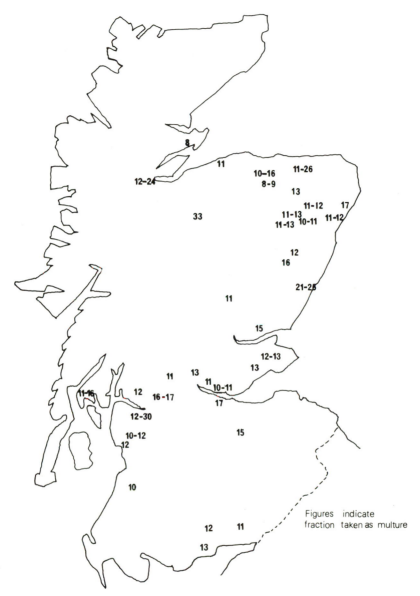

Fig 30. Multure rates, 1790s. *OSA*

mills let with them: the abolition of thirlage could lower a mill's value by twenty per cent. In 1763, faced with the potential abolition of his thirlage, the tacksman of the Mills of New Tarbat, Ross-shire asked that his rent be reduced by thirty bolls from £107 3s 4d.[44] In the event most landowners managed to find a solution which, while apparently abolishing thirlage, still left them with some of its financial benefits.

The least radical measure that a landowner could take was to lower multures from intown to outentown rates. Part of the Banff estate, Angus was thirled at intown rates to the Mill of Fyall; at the letting of the mill in 1791, however, the multures of the Mains of Banff were reduced to outsucken rates and provision was made for the rest of the thirl to be likewise converted. As compensation, the miller was to have a reduction in rent of 10s Sterling per ploughgate, or £7 10s for the whole barony;[45] by 1806, the entire thirl had been put onto outsucken rates.[46] As early as 1770, the suckeners of Innerwick and Thornton Mills were paying only outentown rates, although in this particular case it may have been traditional practice.[47] While such a measure lightened the burden of thirlage and thereby encouraged cultivation, it detracted from the value of a mill without abolishing the distasteful thirlage. A more effective step was the conversion of multures to a cash equivalent which could be paid by each of the suckeners as part of their rent. This system offered the twofold advantage of appearing to free the tenants from thirlage while ensuring that the proprietor still received the income which had formerly accrued from it. Furthermore, the fixed commutation meant that suckeners were no longer penalised for increasing their crop yields. Containing as it did something for both proprietor and suckeners, fixed commutation found support in both groups. By the 1790s it had been applied widely, notably in Aberdeenshire and the north-east. In Grange parish, Banff, very high multures of one eighth or one ninth were converted at 2s 3d in the pound rental,[48] while in Turriff parish, Aberdeenshire, a rather higher rate of 4s 6d in the pound had been fixed;[49] elsewhere in Aberdeenshire, in the parishes of Alford, Kemnay and Deer, the same system was in operation, but at unspecified rates.[50] Fixed commutations were also established in Dunning and Trinity-Gask parishes, Perthshire, and in Buchanan parish, Stirlingshire.[51]

Heritors with lands thirled to another's mill could buy their lands out of thirlage and pass on part of the expense to their tenants. In 1779 Stewart of Ascog agreed to free Lamont of Knockdow's Argyllshire lands of Towardnuiltdarich from thirlage, multures and services for £1 6s 8d Sterling per annum.[52] Those heritors bound to the Mill of Cart, Renfrewshire bought up their thirlages from the mill owner, and charged the interest to their respective tenants at 6d per acre.[53] On the Leckie estate, Gargunnock, Stirlingshire the proprietor took the mill into his own hands and, for a levy of 1s per acre, freed his tenants from thirlage.[54] Examples of this type of commutation were also to be found in Argyllshire, Ayrshire and Kirkcudbrightshire[55] (Figure 31).

A further method of ameliorating the bad effects of thirlage involved letting a mill and the rights to its multures to those thirled to it. On 30th March 1781, James Robertson of Lude made a personal appearance at his Baron Court and proposed that the Mill of Kindrochit be let to the tenants of the estate at a yearly rent of £70 5s Sterling; the tenants unanimously approved the experiment for a one-year period.[56] According to the Old Statistical Account, the heritors of Foulis Wester parish (Perthshire) had given up the high multures formerly payable at the parish's five mills and had divided the mill rents

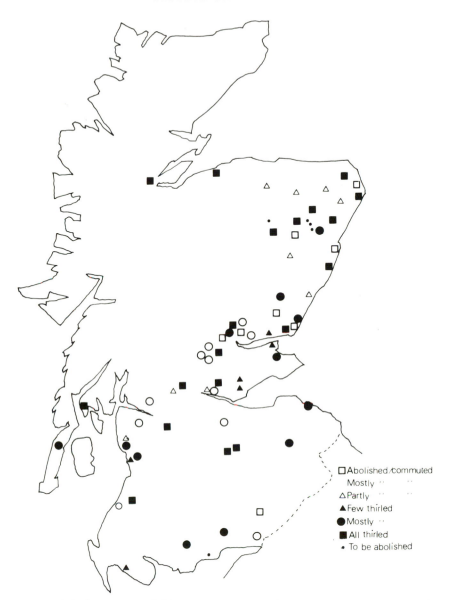

Fig 31. State of thirlage, 1790s. *OSA*

among the suckeners.[57] By the 1790s suckeners also held mills in Kirkpatrick-Fleming parish (Dumfriesshire) and Arbirlot parish (Angus).[58]

While examples of commutation, in one form or another, were to be found in most parts of Scotland, such enlightened policies were still, in the 1790s, the exception rather than the rule. Even a progressive body such as the Forfeited Estates Commission was known to refuse to free tenants from thirlage, on the flimsy pretext that since 'the mill was . . . the most convenient and adjacent the tenants could reap no advantage by being freed'.[59]

Abolition by Statute

Opposition to thirlage continued to mount; of the 848 entries in the Old Statistical Account, a great many condemned the practice, sometimes at great length, but only three condoned it. None spoke in its favour.[60]

In 1799, largely as a result of efforts by the newly formed Highland and Agricultural Society, an Act was passed which made legal provision for the abolition of thirlage.[61] The preamble which spoke of thirlage as 'checking the industry of the occupiers of the ground, and . . . occasioning troublesome and expensive litigation', suggested that suckeners be allowed to obtain a commutation for a fixed annual payment, or by buying up their thirlages outright. Under the terms of the Act, however, it was not the tenants but the owners of thirled lands, or of mills, who could apply for commutation; in the majority of cases, where the mill and the lands thirled belonged to the same proprietor, the Act offered no redress to the unfortunate suckeners.

For the proprietor who chose to take advantage of the Act, a commutation could be very expensive to obtain. In a case quoted by Handley,[62] Colonel Charles Moray, Laird of Abercairny (Perthshire), brought an action for the purchase of multures payable by some of his tenants at the Mill of Carsehead, the property of Sir Patrick Murray of Ochtertyre. Not until 1815, after the death of the original pursuer, was the case finally concluded. Almost one hundred and forty-eight acres of Moray's land was found to be thirled, from which the total annual return was estimated to be eight hundred and three bolls of grain. About a quarter was deducted for seed, and a further deduction was made for horse corn and teind, leaving thirty-eight bolls due as multures and knaveship. To this had to be added the cost of manufacture at 8d per boll and dry multure for bere; the total annual value was calculated on the average price of grain for the ten years preceding the commencement of the suit. The Lord Advocate's decision, that £1,025 2s 1d Sterling should be paid, was contested by Moray, who pointed out that the crop yields upon which the calculations were based were obtained through the use of improved methods introduced after the commencement of the suit in 1803. A sum of £860 was suggested as a fair price and the final settlement was made for the sum of £900.[63] Any landowner prepared to pay out so large a sum to free so small an area would have to be not only a very strong opponent of thirlage, but also a man of financial means.

The cumbersome working of the Act could serve only to deter potential users even further. Part of the blame lay with the 'vague and inexplicable nature of its subject',[64] and a complex legal procedure was required if a fair assessment of a thirlage's value was to be achieved. Once a petition had been brought before the Sheriff, he was to order it to be served on the other party and on the tenant of the mill in question; at the same time all other parties were to be cited, by means of an edict at the church(es) of the parish(es) in which the lands and mill were situated. If residing in Scotland, the party on whom the petition was served had to lodge answers and submit any objections to the petition, stating all claims, within forty days; those parties resident outside Scotland were allowed sixty days. Within thirty days of the expiry of this period, the Sheriff was to decide what information was relevant to the case; after a further twenty days, he was to appoint a jury for a certain day, giving them another twenty to thirty days' notice. Initially, the jury was to consist of twenty men, each either a heritor with at least £30 Sterling valued rent, or a tenant paying £30 Sterling in rent. The two parties were then to reduce the number of jurors one by one, alternately, the mill proprietor naming the first, until only nine men were left. In the absence of both parties, the Sheriff was to assume responsibility for so doing. Evidence had to be taken in writing and preserved for at least four years; once a decision was reached, it had to be entered in the Register of Sasines within sixty days.[65]

Because of its very limited terms of reference, the 1799 Act could not hope to help anyone other than those few heritors whose lands were thirled to another's mill; tenants, whose interests in land were only transient, could not raise actions to free their rented lands from thirlage. As it happened, the need for further legislation was overtaken by circumstances. On the better estates, thirlage had already been ameliorated or abolished and the Act specifically excluded situations where dry multure had already been fixed. Moreover, for all its shortcomings, the Act did help to mobilise public opinion by giving the state's backing to the already substantial anti-thirlage lobby. By 1814, Sinclair of Ulbster could state that 'few country gentlemen above the rate of a Squire Western in point of intellect, ever now think of confining their own tenants to their own mills under such preposterous bondage'.[66]

Grinding for the Open Market

As the period progressed and circumstances changed, larger, more efficient mills began to appear; once mills were freed from catering solely for the needs of astricted clients, their size and the milling capacity available in any one area could be adjusted to whatever level was required. Those grain-producing areas which had good access to ports, or to urban markets, showed a marked concentration of milling capacity: mills within ten miles of Eyemouth or Berwick exported great quantities of manufactured grain via these ports,[67] while at the opposite end of the Merse, three grain mills in Gordon parish produced ten to twelve thousand bolls of meal per annum, most of which was driven in carts up the turnpike road to Edinburgh, Dalkeith, Musselburgh and Prestonpans.[68] The meal mill at Cramond Bridge, near Edinburgh, manufactured one thousand bolls of oats per annum;[69] Clyde's Mill, near Glasgow, which was capable of grinding thirty to forty bolls per day, was almost constantly employed: in winter and spring local farmers used the mills, and in summer and autumn Glasgow grain dealers kept them occupied grinding

foreign oats, one to two thousand bolls of which were milled each year.[70] The
greater the number of large commercial mills, the less the need for the smaller,
more primitive ones. A further incentive was provided by the greatly
enhanced value which wartime shortages added to grain during the years 1793-
1803. In Midlothian, barley rose in price from 20s per boll in 1793 to 30s in
1810, while oats, from being 16s per boll in 1793, rose to 42s on one occasion
and averaged 28s for the war years.[71] As a result, it became much more
remunerative for the miller to become a manufacturer of, and dealer in, grain,
the profits accruing therefrom often being sufficient to persuade the miller to
relinquish the astriction of certain lands, particularly if that entailed
responsibilities such as transporting grain and meal. In Berwickshire, where
millers were said to despise the petty profits of thirlage, the custom was falling
into disuse by 1808,[72] and in Angus it had been totally eliminated by 1813.[73]
Inflation in rents and abnormally high profits during the wartime years led to a
spate of mill building and rebuilding which, temporarily at least, compensated
for the abolition of thirlage. Thus, in 1813, Headrick could report of Angus
mill rents that 'when leases expire, the increase [in value] is progressive'.[74]

By the early 19th century, communications in rural areas were good enough
for farmers to have a choice of mill from several within easy reach. Not
surprisingly, they chose those mills which had the most reliable water supply,
the greatest accessibility, the best machinery and the cheapest rates of
grinding. To some extent these qualities reinforced each other: a good water
supply offered a longer period during which work could be undertaken and
therefore higher profits to re-invest in machinery. Alternatively, such a mill
might cut profits to the level obtained by a mill with a poor water supply, but
in doing so, it would be able to undercut the latter on prices. If reasonably
accessible, a well-equipped mill with a good water supply and competitive
rates stood a good chance of surviving. On the other hand, a mill with an
unfavourable combination of these factors was unlikely to do so, especially
with the falling grain prices and retreating cultivation margins of the post-war
era. Proprietors who had more than one mill often allowed their smaller, less
efficient mills to decay whilst rebuilding and re-equipping the best mills on
their estates.

Besides giving the farmer a choice of mill, the abolition of thirlage also
opened up the possibility of his avoiding milling altogether. Although in many
cases thirlage had been limited to the grower's own grain needs, in many more
it applied to the whole saleable corn; without the disincentive of abstracted
multures, selling unground grain became a much more attractive proposition.
Here again improved transport facilities, in the form of turnpike roads and
canals, brought markets within easy reach of producers; the growing
importance of secondary and tertiary occupations will be considered in more
detail at a later stage. While this brought a boost to urban and port-orientated
mills, it served only to accelerate the decline of the rural mill. Just as it had
been thirlage that had made so great a number of corn mills viable, it was its
abolition that, more than anything else, led to a decline in their numbers.

Changes in Diet

Even more marked than the changes in agriculture were those taking place in industry. Aided by the Board of Trustees for Manufactures, the Scottish linen industry went from strength to strength during the 18th century, offering many opportunities for employment in its several branches. On a more general level, the push exerted by agricultural Improvement and the pull of large-scale industrial undertakings, such as the Carron Ironworks or the cotton mills of the late 18th century, led to a decrease in the numbers of those living off the land and an increase in those depending on a wage to buy their food. Existing towns, such as Glasgow and Dundee, experienced rapid growth and new communities, such as Johnstone and Stenhousemuir, appeared where there had been only open ground. The higher standard of living enjoyed by the industrial wage-earner opened up the possibility of an improved diet, one feature of which was the substitution of wheaten bread for oatcakes and barley bread; by 1830 wheaten bread had also made a lot of headway in rural areas. This change of tastes encouraged the cultivation of wheat, often at the expense of lower-priced oats, and further aggravated the already unfavourable position of the rural corn mill.

Conclusion

Between 1730 and 1830 a number of factors combined to contribute to the decline of the rural corn mill. Changes in land use, notably the diversification of crops grown, the drainage of lochans and the extension of parkland, reduced the acreage under oats or bere. Thirlage gradually fell into disuse, and in the free-market conditions which ensued, farmers were able to grind meal at the best mill available or to dispose of grain unmilled; with better com-

Table 4

Conversion of Corn Mills to Other Uses

Mill	New Use	Date
Nether Mill of Dalnotter (Dunb.)	Ironworks	1769
Fauldhouse Mill (W. Loth.)	Gunpowder Mill	1812
New Mills (Renf.)	Cotton Mill (Site)	1780
Penicuik Mill (Bank Mill)	Paper Mill	1803
Mill of Cambus (Clack.)	Distillery	1806
Mill of Brigton (Angus)	Flax-spinning Mill	1788
Mill of Struthill (Perths.)	Oil Mill	1780
Old Mill of Strichen (Ab'n)	Wool-carding Mill	c.1797
Hole Mill (Fife)	Flint Mill	pre-1833
St. Ninian's Mill* (W.Loth.)	Bark Mill	C18

*ex malt mill

munications, markets could be found further afield. Industrialisation and a move away from the land brought changes in population distribution and improved standards of living, which in turn produced a shift in diet away from meal to flour. Developments in technology not only helped make this industrialisation possible, but also enabled larger, more efficient corn mills to be built; with an increasingly wide range of other uses for water power, corn mills offering low profitability could be more usefully applied to other purposes (Table 4). Without doubt, the number of corn mills fell, although the exact number cannot be ascertained.

The last word, however, should go to David Low who, writing in 1818, recognised the decline and identified the cause:

> Common corn mills are now a less favourite and valuable possession than formerly, the number of mills with better machinery having increased in the country; and from a change in the habits of the people, a larger proportion of flour, and a smaller proportion of meal, are now being used as food. The system of forcibly upholding the rents of mills by means of thirlage begins to be generally laid aside, and with good reason, as this compelling of tenants and dependents to carry their grain to be manufactured at a certain mill, is found to be productive of many inconveniences and fruitless disputes.[75]

NOTES

1. Buchan, J. W., *A History of Peebles-shire*, 2 vols., Glasgow, 1925, I, 78.

2. *OSA* XIX, 427, Kilmany, Fife.

3. SRO E 730/35.

4. Adam, R. J. (ed.), 'Sutherland Estate Management 1802-16', *SHS* 4th Series VIII-IX (1972), I, 204.

5. SRO GD135/94.

6. See, for example, plans in Gray, A., *The Experienced Millwright*, London, 1806.

7. Sinclair, Sir J., *General Report of the Agricultural State and Political Circumstances of Scotland*, 3 vols. and Appendix, 2 vols., Edinburgh, 1814, I, 117; Headrick, J., *General View of the Agriculture of the County of Forfar*, London, 1814, 226; Robertson, J., *General View of the Agriculture of South Perthshire*, London, 1794, 51; *OSA* XI, 602, Callander, Perthshire; *OSA* XVIII, 349, Kippen, Stirlingshire.

8. Headrick, *op. cit.*, 266.

9. See, for example, SRO GD224/240, 'Account of Ironwork used for work to Rickerton Miln', November 4th, 1743.

10. SRO GD267/27/188.

11. Anderson, M. L., *A History of Scottish Forestry*, 2 vols., London, 1967, II, 145.

12. For an example of how timber was used, see SRO GD161/24, P. Fergusson to Dr. Hamilton, May 16th, 1818.

13. See, for example, Handley, J. E., *Scottish Farming in the Eighteenth Century*, London, 1953; Handley, J. E., *The Agricultural Revolution in Scotland*, Glasgow, 1963.

14. Handley, *op. cit.* (1953), 38-9.

15. Handley, *op. cit.* (1963), 122.

16. SRO GD24/1/648.

17. *OSA* VII, New Monkland, Lanarkshire.

18. SRO GD1/16/1.

19. SRO GD46/17/59.

20. Leslie, W., *General View of the Agriculture of the Counties of Moray & Nairn*, London, 1811, 35.

21. Thomson, J., *General View of the Agriculture of the County of Fife*, Edinburgh, 1800, 339.

22. *OSA* XIX, 426, Kilmany, Fife.

23. Somerville, R., *General View of the Agriculture of the County of East Lothian*, London, 1805, 302.

24. SRO GD15/832/1,4.

25. Thomson, *op. cit.*, 40.

26. Based on a comparison of General Roy's Map of Scotland (c.1747) and *OS* 1st Edition 6"/mile (1867).

27. Dick-Lauder, Sir T., *An Account of the Great Floods of August 1829 in the Province of Moray and Adjoining Districts*, Edinburgh, 1830, 91.

28. The Mill of Winton appears for the last time on William Forrest's map of East Lothian (1799). Whittingehame Mill ceased to function about the time that Whittingehame House was built and its grounds laid out, c.1827. See Shaw, J. P., 'The Making of the Landscape: the Eastern Parishes of East Lothian 1700-1971', MA Geography Dissertation, University of Edinburgh, 1971.

29. Kimmerghame East Mill appears as disused on an 1802 plan: SRO RHP197.

30. SRO GD50/16/1.

31. *OSA* IX, 138, Abernyte, Perthshire.

32. SRO GD132/3.

33. *OSA* XI, 547, Tulliallan, Fife.

34. See, for example, SRO GD10/1234: Mill of Flilarg 1790. The person involved was fined £10.

35. SRO GD72/539.

36. *OSA* XIX, 69, Halkirk, Caithness.

37. SRO GD71/216/1.

38. *OSA* V, 336, Cathcart, Renfrewshire.

39. SRO GD38/1/1194.

40. SRO GD38/1/1194.

41. *OSA* II, 125, New Abbey, Kirkcudbrightshire; *OSA* XIII, 258, Kirkpatrick-Fleming, Dumfriesshire.

42. *OSA* XIV, 260, Kilfinan, Argyll; SRO E729/8 53: Mill of Gartchonzie, Perthshire.

43. Smout, T. C., *A History of the Scottish People, 1560-1830*, London, 1969, 297.

44. SRO E787/22.

45. SRO GD83/744.

46. SRO GD83/776.

47. SRO GD6/2252.

48. *OSA* IX, 550, Grange, Banffshire.

49. *OSA* XVII, 407, Turriff, Aberdeenshire.

50. *OSA* XV, 450, Alford, Aberdeenshire; *OSA* XII, 203, Kemnay, Aberdeenshire; *OSA* XVI, 474, Deer, Aberdeenshire.

51. *OSA* XIX, 436, Dunning, Perthshire; *OSA* XVIII, 485, Trinity Gask, Perthshire; *OSA* IX, 12, Buchanan, Stirlingshire.

52. Lamont, Sir N. (ed.), 'An Inventory of Lamont Papers, 1231-1897', *SRS* LIV (1914), No. 1301.

53. *OSA* XV, 502, Kilbarchan, Renfrewshire.

54. *OSA* XVIII, 109, Garnock, Stirlingshire.

55. SRO GD170/484/2; *OSA* XII, 99, Dalry, Ayrshire; *OSA* II, 125, New Abbey, Kirkcudbrightshire.

56. SRO GD50/159.

57. *OSA* XV, 605, Foulis Wester, Perthshire.

58. *OSA* XIII, 258, Kirkpatrick-Fleming, Dumfriesshire; *OSA* III, 467, Arbirlot, Angus.

59. SRO E773/29.

60. The three exceptions to the rule being: *OSA* VII, New Monkland, Lanarkshire; *OSA* VII, 290, Mouswald, Dumfriesshire; *OSA* XIX, 427, Kilmany, Fife.

61. Act 39 Geo.III Cap.55.

62. Handley, *op. cit.* (1963), 230-1.

63. SRO GD24/1/78, /94, /667, /668.

64. *Farmers' Magazine* XVIII (1817), 319.

65. *An Act for Encouraging the Improvement of Lands Subject to the Servitude of Thirlage in that Part of Great Britian Called Scotland.* Copy in SRO GD173/21.

66. Sinclair, Sir J., *op. cit.*, Appendix II, 278.

67. Chalmers, G., *Caledonia*, 4 vols., London, 1810, II, 317.

68. *OSA* V, 75, Gordon, Berwickshire.

69. *OSA* I, 240, Dalmeny, West Lothian.

70. *OSA* V, 241, Cambusland, Lanarkshire.

71. Handley, *op. cit.* (1963), 249.

72. Kerr, R., *General View of the Agriculture of the County of Berwick*, London, 1809, 77.

73. Headrick, *op. cit.*, 266.

74. *Ibid.*, 226.

75. Low, D., *Report on Marchmont Estate.* Printed privately, 1819, 25-6 (Copy in SRO GD158/725).

11

Flour and Pot Barley Mills

The fortunes of flour and pot barley mills during the century 1730-1830 present a marked contrast to those of common corn mills. In 1730 there had been, ostensibly, only one pot barley mill in Scotland (see p.39) and no flour mills, but by 1830 machinery had been installed in corn mills, or in mills specifically for flour and pot barley, over much of Scotland.

FLOUR MILLS

Wheaten bread was by no means new to the more affluent citizens of larger burghs: it has already been noted that the Baxter Corporation of Glasgow had had a 'wheat mill' in the 17th century and that in other burghs sifting or boulting was carried out by hand.[1] Some wheat had been grown prior to 1730, notably in the better cultivated lands of eastern Scotland, but not until after that date was there an agricultural system capable of producing it on a large scale, or a market wide enough to justify so doing. What is more, it was only during the century after 1730 that mills for converting wheat into flour became by any means common.

Technology

The technology of flour mills differed from that of common corn mills in two important respects. Firstly, there was a difference in the type of millstones used: in Scottish corn mills the surface of the millstones was not cut into furrows but simply roughened to enable them to tear and bruise the grain into coarse meal. To grind flour, however, stones had to be carefully furrowed so that by the time the grain reached the hem it had been cut very fine.[2] Although no specific reference is made to such stones, they were almost certainly incorporated in flour mills from 1750 onwards and probably in a few earlier cases, such as the Baxters' wheat mill in Glasgow; because of the taste for finely ground barley or pease flour, those corn mills which possessed a second pair of stones often had them dressed in the same manner.

Whereas stones for corn mills could be obtained from one of many quarries within Scotland, those for flour mills — French burrstones, greystones and blue or Cullen stones — had to be imported from the Paris basin, the Peak District and the Rhineland respectively. During the Napoleonic Wars, when

Fig 32. The machinery of an improved flour mill. Two pairs of stones are driven from a single upright shaft via separate spindles. An extension of the shaft drives a boulting engine (K) and a sack hoist (M). *Jamieson, 1827*

Table 5

'Accompt of the Aprisment of the floure mills on Dichty Watter Belonging to the Toune of Dundee, 4 December 1780.'

The East Mill	£	s	d
Water wheel and axletrie	7	10	8
The winch, trindels, whords & rope of the butt mill	1	3	—
The inner whill, trundels, spindel and rind	2	10	—
The bridge cloves stipiels shills & plankes	3	10	—
The trouch, troues and boutt mill	4	10	—
The takel for lifting the stone		16	
The happer, crubets and lettner tries	1	—	—
The box for the whett	1	—	—
	21	19	8

The West Mill	£	s	d
The watter whill, axiltrie & iner whill	9	—	—
The trindels, spinell & rind	1	12	—
The trundels, whords, rope & winch of the bout mill	1	3	—
The tekell for lifting the stone	—	14	—
To shill plankes and lofting about the stone	1	15	
To bridge cloues & stipills	1	3	
To crubetts happer & letther tries	1	5	—
To the trouch and boutt mill	4	10	
To the box for houlding the whett	1	6	
To the troues	1	—	
	25	08	,,

Source: SRO GD205/2.

---

the price of French millstones rose to £60 a pair, local substitutes were found, such as Inverteil stones from Fife[3] and Abbey Craig stones from Stirlingshire. Like the French stones, the latter type were built up from small pieces. Over three hundred pairs were made and sold at £12-£20 per pair, but after the peace with France, imported burrstones fell to a very low price and demand for Abbey Craig stones all but disappeared.[4]

The second respect in which flour mills differed from conventional corn mills was the inclusion in the former of boulting machinery. Traditionally, flour had been sifted by hand in 'harps'. Simple, tray-like boulters were in use in Europe from the early 16th century, and more sophisticated cylindrical types had been developed before the end of the same century.[5] The cylinder, which was inclined, was lined with brush work and divided into, say, five compartments and covered with cloth or wire mesh (boulting cloth) through which flour of different grades passed separately.[6]

The boulting mill installed by 1741 at Bonnington Mills (Edinburgh) was probably of this type; the mill at Invergowrie (Perthshire) certainly had one by the 1780s.[7] Figure 32 shows the layout of a typical flour mill of the early 19th century. Developments in the Falkirk area illustrate well not only the changes in technology but also in demand; in 1730 only two hundred bolls of wheat per annum were being made into flour, and that in common corn mills with hand boulting; by the 1790s seven flour mills were grinding seven thousand bolls per annum and boulting by machine.[8] Valuations of two 18th-century flour mills are given in Table 5.

The Market for Flour

By the late 18th century, the taste for, and the ability to pay for, wheaten bread had spread into the countryside;[9] such was the demand for flour that mills were constructed in whatever localities had access to consumers, and any district which lacked them, such as Upper Clydesdale, was considered to be at a great disadvantage.[10] For the enlightened landowner the construction of a flour mill was the logical sequel to, or incentive towards, a programme of agricultural Improvement; additional income could be derived from providing the means whereby neighbouring heritors could grind their flour. In 1780 Andrew Wight reported that on General Abercromby's Glasshaugh estate, Banffshire:

> fall, lime and dung, has yielded him large crops of wheat in a country where there was none before; and in order to furnish his neighbours good flour, he has erected a windmill which, tho' expensive, was successful. But this mill not being sufficient to answer the demand for flour, he has erected another wheat mill, on the only stream of water he is in possession of. Upon the same stream he has erected a mill for pot-barley. His neighbours are much indebted to him for the conveniences of living thus afforded them at hand.[11]

In certain favoured areas, the demand for flour and other grain products turned milling into a substantial industry. During 1779 Alexander Young, who rented the Mills of Elgin for £150 Sterling per annum, ground a thousand bolls of wheat, exported one thousand four hundred bolls of barley and made great quantities of pot barley for the London market.[12] By the 1790s there were twenty flour mills on the Water of Leith;[13] on Leader Water, between Lauder and the Tweed, there were between twenty and thirty mills, some recently built to grind wheat and barley.[14] One mill near Perth ground five thousand bolls of wheat per annum, mostly for the city,[15] while by 1800 Fife's fourteen flour mills were processing some forty thousand bolls of wheat.[16] By 1813, the already substantial capacity of Forfarshire (Angus) flour mills was considered to be too small, and with demand still growing, fears were being expressed that the profits from grinding went to market-orientated mills elsewhere; more mills were planned.[17] As David Loch discovered at Melrose, the commerce generated by flour mills could bring other benefits too:

> The Duke [of Buccleuch] has erected fine . . . mills here, which enables the farmers to drive their meal and flour to the Edinburgh and Dalkeith markets, and gives the

return carts an opportunity of bringing coals, lime, timber, and all sorts of goods from the Lothians, at a moderate charge: by this means Melrose is supplied with coal and all other necessaries as cheap as if they were within four miles of the coal-pits or Port of Leith.[18]

The construction of flour mills helped the progress of the Agricultural Revolution, generated capital in rural areas and helped feed the growing concentrations of population in urban communities, both within and without Scotland. The addition of flour-milling machinery to existing corn mills almost guaranteed the survival of the latter, although in some areas pressure from the industrial users of water power brought a change in use. In rural areas at least, wheat was generally multure free, a fact which further encouraged its growth once a suitable mill was built. For the same reason, however, large quantities of wheat found their way to market unground, to be milled eventually at urban mills.

No comprehensive source is available to show the distribution of flour mills during the period, but most of those which appear on the first Ordnance Survey maps were probably in existence by 1830.

We should also take into account another element in Scottish grain milling, for besides flour mills, those for pot barley were experiencing a similar growth.

POT BARLEY MILLS

After the construction of the first pot barley mill at Saltoun (East Lothian), the process used remained a closely guarded secret and the mill enjoyed a monopoly for some forty years. According to one story, the miller at the neighbouring Mill of Keith hit upon the idea of plying a worker from the barley mill with alcohol and succeeded in extracting the necessary information.[19] Whether or not the monopoly was broken in quite this manner, the secret did eventually leak out and soon became general knowledge. Subsequently, the use of pot barley mills became widespread.

Technology

Although pot barley could be prepared by hand, with a mortar and pestle, the method was very laborious and never completely separated the husk from the kernel; a mill could produce pot barley much more quickly and effectively, with substantially less labour. The early mills consisted of two horizontal mill-stones, placed one above the other, as in an ordinary meal mill. The lower stone revolved within a circular wooden case, the circumference of which was covered with perforated sheet iron, through which dust and small 'seeds' could escape. This type of mill continued to be built until the 1770s, when a more efficient type was introduced, incorporating a vertical edge-running stone, instead of a horizontal one.[20] In either form, it could be added to any well-powered mill at no great expense. At Skaithmuir Mill, Banffshire the barley mill was to be driven off the existing pit wheel, round the edge of which was fixed a ring of cast-iron cogs. These engaged with the wooden teeth of a wood and iron spur wheel which, through a 4¼″ square iron lying shaft, drove a barley stone 3′ 10″ by 9″.[21]

Incentives to Building

From the miller's point of view, the addition of a barley mill to the machinery of a corn mill could offer an additional source of income, particularly useful in that the preparation of pot barley, unlike oatmeal, was paid for in cash not kind.[22] Furthermore, by manufacturing this commodity, the miller was compensated for any reduction in oats grown or ground and could profit from the processing of barley which might otherwise have found its way to a brewery, distillery or market, unground. In some places, barley and bere were made into pot barley as a preliminary to grinding it into flour in flour mills.[23] Obviously, a corn mill which lacked such equipment was in a relatively unfavourable position.

For the farmer and, when involved, the grain dealer, the sale of pot barley could produce a useful source of income. A greatly improved road system and a network of coastal and overseas shipping routes were used to good effect in transporting not only pot barley, but also flour and oatmeal, and, to a large extent, the markets for the three commodities coincided. Two Kincardineshire mills, using one thousand three hundred bolls per annum, sent most of their produce to the Forth ports;[24] from Currie (Edinburgh) pot barley went to Glasgow, whence some was exported to the West Indies, to be used as food for slaves.[25] A pot barley mill in Stoneykirk parish, Wigtownshire was built with a view to supplying the Liverpool market,[26] and the four hundred bolls produced annually by one Angus barley mill were shipped to London.[27] Reference has already been made to Alexander Young exporting great quantities of pot barley to the same destination from Elgin. Fife mills, which by 1800 were milling 104,000 bolls of oats, and 40,000 of wheat, also produced 25,000 cwt of pot barley per annum, from 15,000 bolls of barley.[28] Like the flour mills with which they were often built, pot barley mills helped to assure the survival of many rural corn mills, bringing money to rural areas and providing an important element in the diet of Scotland's increasingly urban population. Furthermore, for many years Scotland held a virtual monopoly of pot barley making in Britain and therefore was able to exploit markets in England, Ireland and the Colonies.

A Note on Pease Ovens

One of the more unusual purposes to which water power was put in Scottish grain milling was the pease oven, devised at some time before 1782 by John Watt or Wark at the Mill of Dripps (Renfrewshire) and applied by several other millers nearby (Figure 33). According to Semple, Wark built a 'kiln for drying peas, with an engine which goes by a water wheel, always stirring and

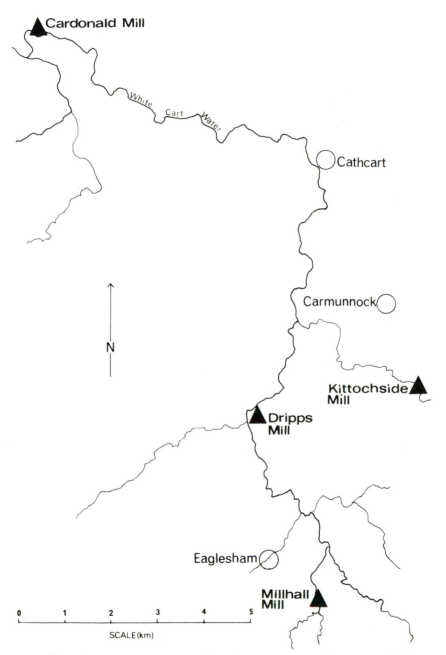

Fig 33. Mills with pease ovens, East Renfrewshire, West Lanarkshire. *Crawford, 1782.*
OSA

turning peas, and will dry about five pecks of peas in the space of one hour'.[29] As far as is known, no more is heard of pease ovens after 1795, and the invention never spread outside the immediate area.

NOTES

1. See p. 39.
2. Findlater, C., *General View of the Agriculture of Peeblesshire*, Edinburgh, 1802, 27.
3. Pococke, R., 'Tours in Scotland, 1747, 1750, 1760', *SHS* I (1887), 281.
4. *NSA* VIII, 223, Logie, Stirlingshire.
5. Clelland, J., *Annals of Glasgow*, 2 vols., Glasgow, 1816, II, 513 (footnote).
6. Singer, C., Holmyard, E. J., Hall, A. R. & Williams, T. I. (eds.), *A History of Technology*, 5 vols., Oxford, 1956-9, III, 18-19.
7. NLS Acc 5111/Box 25 No. 1.
8. *OSA* XII, 86-7, Falkirk, Stirlingshire.
9. Handley, J. E., *Scottish Farming in the Eighteenth Century*, London, 1953, 205.
10. *OSA* VIII, 120, Carluke, Lanarkshire; *OSA* XV, 18, 47, Lanark, Lanarkshire; *OSA* I, 259, Kiltearn, Ross-shire; *OSA* X, 565, Campbeltown, Argyll.
11. Wight, A., *Present State of Husbandry in Scotland*, 4 vols., Edinburgh, 1778-84, IV, 70.
12. *Ibid.*, IV, 84-5.
13. *OSA* XIX, 580, Colinton, Midlothian.
14. *OSA* I, 72, Lauder, Berwickshire.
15. *OSA* XVIII, 515, Perth, Perthshire.
16. Thomson, J., *General View of the Agriculture of Fife*, Edinburgh, 1800, 177.
17. Headrick, J., *General View of the Agriculture of the County of Forfar*, London, 1814, 266.
18. Loch, D., *A Tour through Most of the Trading Towns and Villages of Scotland*, Edinburgh, 1778, 45.
19. MacKenzie, W. C., *Andrew Fletcher of Saltoun. His Life and Times*, Edinburgh, 1935, 304.
20. Sinclair, Sir J., *General Report of the Agricultural State and Political Circumstances of Scotland*, 3 vols. and Appendix, 2 vols., Edinburgh, 1814.
21. SRO GD58/18/42.
22. In Kirkoswald parish, Ayrshire, the going rate was 1s 8d to 2s per boll: *OSA* X, 491.
23. Keith, G. S., *General View of the Agriculture of Aberdeenshire*, Aberdeen, 1811, 252.
24. *OSA* XIII, 4, Inverbervie, Kincardineshire.
25. *OSA* V, 313, Currie, Midlothian.
26. *OSA* II, 51, Stoneykirk, Wigtownshire.
27. *OSA* V, 145, Menmuir, Angus.
28. Thomson, *op. cit.*, 302.
29. Crawford, G. (revised Semple, W.), *The History of Renfrewshire*, Paisley, 1782.

12

Urban Grain Mills

During the century 1730-1830 the urban sector came to represent a much greater proportion of Scotland's population than previously: the drift from the land has already been referred to; the increase in the demands put upon urban mills was such that although most were rebuilt on a much larger scale, it was still necessary to enlist the help of the better equipped rural mills in preparing meal, flour and pot barley for the rapidly growing number of urban consumers.

Mill Rebuilding: Dumfries, Perth and Alloa

In 1730, most burgh mills were equipped to grind only meal and malt for the small thirls which they served. With the introduction of machinery to prepare flour and pot barley and the growth of large domestic markets for these commodities, burghs found it necessary to install machinery suited to such purposes, thus providing the mills with an extra source of income. As early as 1705, Dumfries burgh council engaged a Mr. Mathew Frew to build 'ane sufficient miln, capable of grinding malt, meal, flour and all other sorts of grain'. In 1707, the new mill was let, but not until 1742 was a wheat mill installed, and a proper barley mill had to wait until even later.[1] The mills were rebuilt in 1769, to a design by John Smeaton, at a cost of £633; they were accidentally burnt down in 1780, but the machinery was saved and, with a sum of £1,530 retrieved in insurance, this went a long way towards recouping the loss.[2] Within a year they had been rebuilt yet again, this time to a design by Andrew Meikle.[3] By the 1790s the mills were yielding £400 Sterling per annum in rent; in 1825, the flour, barley and meal mills were renting at £220, £60 and £171 respectively, a total of £451.[4]

The burgh mills of Perth, which incorporated separate malt, corn and flour mills, were rebuilt about 1787, and a second flour mill was added[5] (Figure 34). By the 1790s, besides grinding malt, bere, pease and oats, the mills made pot barley and ground sixty bolls of flour per day, two thirds of which was for local use. The tenants, Messrs Ramsay, Whittel and Co., rented the mills for about £800 per annum. It is interesting to note that at this period the bakers still paid multure.[6] Further building, or rebuilding, took place between 1805 and 1809 with the construction of the Lower City Mill in which oatmeal was produced.[7]

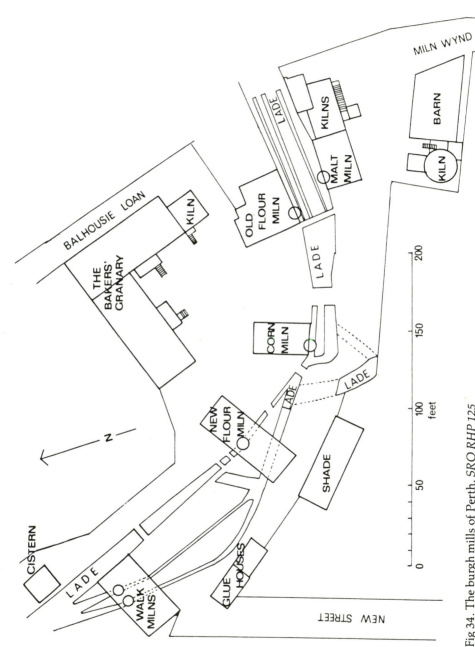

Fig 34. The burgh mills of Perth. *SRO RHP 125*

The mills of Alloa were rebuilt in 1735-6 at a cost of nearly £2,000 Scots, utilising water from Gartmore Dam;[8] in the late 18th century they were totally rebuilt in a mere twelve months to a design by George Meikle. This 'fine set of mills', 93 ft x 31 ft and 32 ft high, was equipped to grind wheat, oats, malt and pot barley, at the rate of four hundred bolls per day when necessary; two internal 19 ft diameter water-wheels drove all the machinery.[9]

Malt Milling and the Rise of Brewers

The long hard struggle to uphold thirlage over brewers had not yet come to an end by 1730. The power of a burgh to enforce thirlage over brewers depended on the number and economic strength of the brewers, the capacity of the machinery in a burgh's mills and the determination of a burgh's council or feudal superior to uphold thirlage. At Linlithgow, the brewers were still astricted in the 1790s and paid 1/16th in multures;[10] at Irvine, a converted multure of 6d per boll was paid on oats and malt alike,[11] while at Rutherglen the whole burgh was still astricted in 1793, but at a rate of only 1/40th, less than was taken at most rural mills for grinding multure free.[12] In these cases, the brewers were apparently quite prepared to pay multures. On the other hand, there were burghs where that 'rising branch of trade' was strong enough to challenge, or even ignore, thirlage. One such place was the burgh of Dalkeith. In the year 1742-3 the town's malt mill had ground 3,685 bolls yielding 119 bolls in multure; [13] apparently the brewing industry was already well established. In 1759 an Act of Parliament had been obtained for a 2d Scots duty on ale, beer and porter brewed in the town, a favourite means of raising money for public works. The brewers within the burgh were faced with the extra cost of the 2d levy and, not having the use of steel mills, which yielded twenty per cent more than conventional mills, they had to make use of the burgh's mill and pay multures there. Before very long, the imposition of the levy was having undesirable repercussions: in the period between 24th December 1760 and 24th June 1768, 14,948 bolls of malt were made in Dalkeith, but of this only 6,361½ bolls passed through the burgh's mill. The balance, some 8,586½ bolls, was abstracted, depriving the mill of £229 11s 10d in multures.[14] In March 1761 the brewers were brought before the Baron Baillie; they affirmed that they had been in the habit of grinding their malt at the mill and that some had been ground elsewhere. Having admitted to this, they were asked to pay abstracted multures but, not content with this judgment, the defenders presented a bill of advocation before the Court of Session and, in June 1762, obtained an interlocutor from Lord Auchinleck to the effect that malt made within the thirl, but sold outside it, had never been subject to thirlage. Seeking a quick settlement, the brewers, whilst still not acknowledging that they were thirled for malt, offered to grind at the burgh's mill as formerly, on condition that the Duke of Buccleuch (as pursuer and feudal superior) erected steel mills and prohibited the sale of 'foreign' ale. The Duke responded by starting a process against the retailers who had 'imported' ale, while refusing to drop that against the brewers. His next step was to turn towards the terms on which the brewers were thirled by their feu charters. However, despite the production of several such documents, and Acts of the Baron Court dated 1626, 1664, 1701 and 1705, he failed to convince the Court of Session of the existence of anything other than a thirlage of *grana crescentia*, a judgment which was upheld in interlocutors of March and July 1765. In August of that year the pursuers claimed that the tacksmen of the mills had, in the past few years, installed steel mills 'to be wrought by water' but had taken them down again as the maltsters and brewers had failed to make use of them. A further interlocutor, dated 23rd January 1766, upheld the brewers' freedom to grind their malt wherever they chose, and on 17th June 1766, in what appears to have been the last judgment in the case, only one small concession was made to the pursuers, who were asked to pay the defenders for the expense of extracting a decree.[15]

In 1752, the Burgh of Perth brought an action against Alexander Clunie and others, who had established a brewery outside the burgh and at which Clunie ground his own malt to the loss of the burgh mills. From the brewery, he imported beer into the burgh, but Perth being a royal burgh, its authorities lacked the power of a feudal superior in a burgh of barony and could, therefore, do nothing to prevent Clunie from so doing.[16] In 1824, Alloa was still attempting to maintain a thirlage of malt, although the Carsebridge and Grange breweries and one major distillery had been granted exemption.[17]

In Glasgow, the town council continued to fight their losing battle against the brewers and their steel mills. Efforts were made to improve the efficiency and reliability of the town's malt mills: in 1741, millers from the malt mill and corn mill at Townhead commissioned Robert Meikle (elder brother of Andrew) to prepare a scheme to improve the mill's water supply. The scheme was accepted and carried through by the corporation.[18] In 1744 the town had made trials of steel mills at one of its own water mills,[19] but when, in 1760, the multures of the town's four malt mills were let (at 5,600 merks), permission was granted for agreements to be made, whereby individuals could use their own steel mills.[20] In 1771 one of the mills, at Clayslap, was granted to the bakers, in perpetual feu; the demands made on the burgh's malt mills had apparently diminished sufficiently to permit such a sale. More positive evidence appeared in the next decade. On the 7th June 1780, it was noted that, although exposed to roup, the malt mills had not been set for two years past. Their unattractiveness, it was claimed, lay in the reduction in multure yields resulting from the indulgence shown in letting people in Glasgow and Gorbals use their own steel mills, instead of the city's water mills, to which they were thirled.[21] By 1795 Subdean Mill had been converted to grind cudbear[22] (see p. 349), and in 1809 Partick Mill was sold to the Slit Mill Company[23] (see p. 424), leaving only the Town Mill and Provan Mill in the hands of the corporation.

Thirlage and the Baxters

The brewers were not the only 'rising trade' to disrupt thirlage. At one time Perth had twenty-four bakers, but a 'rigid exaction of thirlage multure' drove them into the suburbs, notably to Bridgend. By the 1820s there were only six bakers left in Perth, but six in Bridgend and more than ten in other suburbs; the grist left to the burgh mills was hardly enough to pay for the counter-obligation to keep up the mills.[24] In many burghs it was the bakers, or baxters, who rented the burgh mills, for by so doing they could exempt their members from paying multures, while continuing to levy them on whoever else should make use of the mills. If the tack fell into the hands of other parties, however, the bakers would often do their utmost to avoid paying multures by grinding their wheat elsewhere.

In 1750 the Mills of Baldovan, Angus, the property of the Burgh of Dundee, were let to the incorporation of bakers for a period of eleven years at a rent of £63 per annum. In 1761, at the termination of the lease, the mills were re-let, but not to the bakers, who had subsequently expressed their disapproval by denying that the mills had a right of thirlage and by grinding their wheat elsewhere without paying abstracted multures. Only after the magistrates had brought an action before the Court of Session did the bakers grudgingly recognise the thirlage. This tack, in turn, also expired and the bakers succeeded in regaining control of the mills, on a nineteen-year tack, at £91 per annum. All their doubts as to the validity of the thirlage were suddenly dispelled and it was firmly enforced throughout the bakers' tenancy. No sooner had the tack expired, however, than the bakers were once again contesting the burgh's right of thirlage over them. Seeking to obtain confirmation of this right, the town council brought an action before the Sheriff Court; the bakers countered by asking that an action be brought on their behalf for commutation of thirlage under the recently passed Act. While the opposing parties argued the pro's and con's of their respective cases, the magistrates of Dundee raised a further case before the Burgh Court, this time against several individual bakers, for abstracted multures; the bakers' rejoinder was to raise an action of declarator and damages before the Court of Session, questioning the adequacy of the mills for grinding wheat and the capacity of the mills in meeting the needs of the thirl.

On 27th November 1801, this action and those from the Burgh and Sheriff Courts came before the Court of Session. Judgment was given on 23rd May 1804, when the Court found that the incorporation of bakers had a right to insist on purchasing their thirlage. As to the nature and extent of the thirlage, however, the Court failed to resolve any of the points at issue and, after dragging on for some time, the case was ultimately abandoned.

Meanwhile the bakers had obtained, at a greatly increased rent, another nineteen-year lease of both mills and thirlage to run from Martinmas 1804. Once again the bakers strictly enforced the thirlage, even to the extent of raising actions against those who failed to comply with it. When in 1823 the lease expired, the bakers threatened to resurrect the old court actions and press for commutation should the lease to them not be renewed. As it happened, they were out-manoeuvred by one Alexander Clark, who offered the preposterously high rent of £502 per annum, only £2 above the bakers' final bid. Clark was the owner of 'very complete and efficient' steam-powered flour mills in Dundee itself, and his motivation in taking on a lease of the then almost derelict Baldovan Mills can only be construed as a wish to see them run down further to the benefit of his own mill. While conceding that as a mere tenant he could not alter existing thirlages to Baldovan Mills, he 'considered it would be more advantageous' for astricted flour to be ground at his own mill and, in an effort to obtain the bakers' concurrence, he offered to grind their wheat at his mill for 1s 9d per boll, instead of 2s 3d levied in multure at Baldovan. Full multure would still be taken from those grinding at the latter, and those who started by grinding at one mill or the other would have to keep to that mill for the rest of the year. In effect Clark was attempting to establish a thirlage of his own at rates well above those prevailing at most free mills.[25]

Apparently he had underestimated the bakers. In the first year of the lease they abstracted between 3,000 and 5,000 bolls of wheat; in reply to processes raised by Clark, they attacked him for not keeping mill servants, locking the doors and failing to take up the burgh's offer of financial aid in rebuilding the mills. The capacity of the mills, at 14,000 bolls per annum, fell far short of the 25,000 bolls which the bakers, by their own calculations, used each year, and as long as the Mills at Baldovan were inadequate they were not obliged to grind there. On 7th February 1828, after three judgments alternately for and against the bakers had been overturned, it was finally decided that the mills were inadequate and that the multures were not, therefore, payable. The bakers also tried to gently twist the arm of their former adversary, the burgh council. In a memorial of about 1825, they pointed out that the 16,000 bolls they had to grind for the thirl's 15,000 inhabitants would yield a profit for Clark of only £281 7s once his rent had been paid. In place of multures a tax was proposed on wheat and flour entering the town, which tax the bakers would farm at £100 Sterling per annum. The town could then sell the mills, valued by the bakers at £7,000, exclusive of thirlage.

It would appear that the bakers were not far wrong in their calculations of Clark's income; at that stage the bakers were already a source of financial embarrassment to him, and by 1827 they had led him to bankruptcy. By this time the town council was anxious to dispose of so troublesome a property, but when the mills were exposed to roup, with thirlages, the bidding failed to reach the reserve price of £5,000, let alone the £7,000 at which they had been valued without thirlages by the bakers. Five months later, the bakers obtained a feu of the mills at the knockdown price of £4,000. The bakers and their astriction continued to pose problems, and Baldovan Mills were still the subject of legal proceedings in the 1860s.[26]

In Glasgow, where the bakers had their own thirlage-free mills, the relationship between bakers and burgh was, by way of contrast, exemplary. While this arrangement led to an unusually great dependence upon malt at the burgh mills, it also saved the council from the troublesome disputes which burghs such as Dundee experienced with their bakers. When in 1771 the demands on the bakers' Partick Mill became too great, no confrontation arose with the burgh; instead, the bakers purchased the town's malt and snuff mill at Clay-slap and had it fitted out as a flour mill.[27] In 1800 a combination of dry weather and ever-growing demand for flour, not only to feed the inhabitants but also to victual ships, led to a situation where there was not so much flour in the city as would feed the inhabitants for one day. Wheat had to be carted as far as Alloa for grinding.[28] Requirements had finally outgrown the productive capacity of the local water mills. In the following year, Clayslap Mill was extended and a 32hp steam engine installed for use during dry spells.[29] Water and steam power worked in a complementary not competitive way. The charge for grinding, which had been a mere 6½d in 1780, was still low in 1816 at 13½d inclusive of cartage.[30]

Glasgow's grain mills were a credit to both bakers and town. James Cleland, writing in 1816, spoke of them in the following terms:

> The Clayslap Mills, it is believed, are not inferior to any in the Empire, in point of situation, management and the internal arrangements of the machinery. The principal mill has four floors; is 207 feet long, and 41 feet wide, within the walls; it contains three water-wheels, each 17 feet diameter, and 6 feet 6 float boards; has fifteen pairs of stones, double motion, on one floor; four bolting and two sheiling machines. The mills at Partick contain four water-wheels, seven pairs of stones, two bolting and one sheiling machine so that there are seven water-wheels, twenty-two pairs of stones, six bolting and three sheiling machines, connected with the establishment. There are also four granaries; two of these are four storeys high, each 140 feet long and 35 feet wide. The kilns, and the other buildings, are proportionate to the mills. These mills are on a scale capable of grinding 3,000 bolls of wheat per week, or 156,000 per annum. In 1815, there were upward of 90,000 bolls manufactured. The granaries are calculated to contain from 30 to 35,000 bolls of grain. The millstones used in these premises are from 4 feet 8 inches to 4 feet 10 inches diameter, and 12½ inches thick. They are built on the spot, with small stones from the neighbourhood of Bordeaux, called French Burrs; they are very hard, free from sand, and are joined together with stucco cement, within an iron hoop. The grounds connected with these works extend to about fourteen acres. The value of the whole may be estimated at somewhat between 45,000 l. and 50,000 l. . . .[31]

The Glasgow bakers, free from thirlage to burgh mills, enjoyed a peaceful prosperity in marked contrast to the hundred years of conflict between their brethren at Dundee and the authorities of that town.

Competition from Steam

Reference has already been made to two steam-powered mills; only very rarely did the need for them arise. Some were built in already large com-

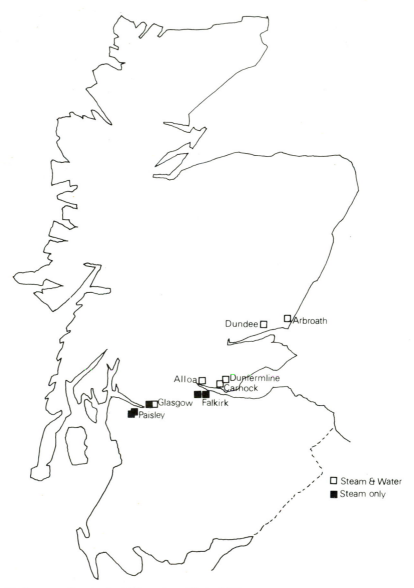

Fig 35. Steam power in Scottish grain mills to 1830

munities where rapid growth in the textile industries had boosted the population to such an extent that their needs could no longer be met by water-
powered mills alone. In other cases water power was available in only small
quantities, or at a great cost, because of competition from other users. Figure
35 shows the distribution of steam grain mills prior to 1830. Paisley, where
two steam-powered grain mills had been built by 1812,[32] was already big

enough in 1782 to support two large water-powered mill groups: Seedhill, built in 1759, incorporated two corn mills, one malt mill, two flour mills and three kilns; and Saccel Mill, around which had grown up the suburbs of Paisley, had flour, malt and barley mills.[33] Even these, however, were not sufficient to meet demand after the introduction of steam-powered cotton spinning had greatly augmented the town's population. Standing near sea level, in an area with many industrial users of water power, Paisley was not in a position to erect new water mills.

Similar circumstances operated at Dunfermline and Arbroath. The mills at Alloa and Falkirk, while not in textile-producing centres, were in areas poorly endowed with water power. Alloa's mill had to rely on an artificial water course, which first had to serve, *inter alia*, the local coal works. Even so the steam engine was installed not to replace but only to supplement water power. Falkirk's growth was closely tied to that of the iron industry, which had already occupied all the best falls in the area, leaving no alternative to using steam.

Only after the possibilities of using water power had been exhausted was the use of steam power resorted to. As later chapters will show, grain milling was not alone in this respect.

NOTES

1. McDowall, W., *History of Dumfries*, Edinburgh, 1867, 544-5.
2. *Ibid.*, 685.
3. *Ibid.*, 686; *OSA* V, 119, Dumfries, Dumfriesshire.
4. McDowall, *op. cit.*, 760-61.
5. SRO RHP125 (1787).
6. *OSA* XVIII, 515, Perth, Perthshire.
7. Butt, J., *The Industrial Archaeology of Scotland*, Newton Abbot, 1967, 42.
8. SRO GD124/17/288.
9. *OSA* VIII, 592, Alloa, Clackmannanshire.
10. *OSA* XVI, 556, Linlithgow, West Lothian.
11. *OSA* VII, 169, Irvine, Ayrshire.
12. Ure, D., *The History of Rutherglen & East Kilbride*, Glasgow, 1793, 117.
13. SRO GD224/288/1.
14. SRO GD224/375.
15. SRO GD224/375.
16. Morison, W. M., *Decisions of the Court of Session*, 36 vols., Edinburgh, 1820, III, 1986.
17. SRO GD124/17/467.
18. *SBRS*, 'Extracts from the Records of the Burgh of Glasgow', VI (1739-59), Glasgow, 1911, 92-3, 110, 140-1.
19. *Ibid.*, 174.
20. *SBRS*, 'Extracts from the Records of the Burgh of Glasgow', VII (1760-80), Glasgow, 1912, 15.
21. *Ibid.*, 599.

22. *SBRS*, 'Extracts from the Records of the Burgh of Glasgow', VIII (1781-95), Glasgow, 1913, 695.

23. *SBRS*, 'Extracts from the Records of the Burgh of Glasgow', X (1809-22), Glasgow, 1915, 15.

24. SRO GD205/2.

25. At Stockbridge Mills, Edinburgh, for example, regulars were charged only 1s 3¾d per boll, inclusive of cartage to and from the mill.

26. SRO GD205/2.

27. Cleland, J., *Annals of Glasgow*, 2 vols., Glasgow, 1816, II, 513.

28. *Ibid.*, 515.

29. *Ibid.*, 513.

30. *Ibid.*, 515.

31. *Ibid.*, 514.

32. Wilson, J., *General View of the Agriculture of the County of Renfrewshire*, Paisley, 1812, 266.

33. Crawford, G. (revised Semple, W.), *The History of Renfrewshire*, Paisley, 1782, 273, 289.

13
Brewing and Distilling

The Industrialisation of Brewing

Although for several centuries the brewing of ale had been a feature of both rural and urban life in Scotland, it was only in the 18th century that it began to take on the proportions of a factory-based industry. The individual, brewing small quantities for private use, suffered firstly from the imposition of malt taxes, then from other legislation such as the Sale of Beer Act (1795), which required the licensing of premises for the manufacture and sale of beer. Reference has already been made to the increasingly powerful place held by brewers in Scottish burghs and to the urbanisation which, by concentrating demand in the towns, favoured the development of larger units of production.

In 1765 James Rigg of the Marischal Street Brewery set up Aberdeen's first common' or 'public' brewery which, allegedly, brewed beer 'both at a cheaper rate and of a better quality' than the inhabitants of Aberdeen could brew it themselves. When the brewery was set up, almost every family in the town brewed its own ale, but within fourteen years the practice had almost disappeared, and five or six breweries had been set up on the same lines as Rigg's.[1] Nor was the process of centralisation confined to the cities: according to Singer, brewing in Dumfriesshire had fallen 'into a few hands' by 1812.[2]

Brewing, Distilling and Agricultural Improvement

As demand increased, so did agriculture's ability to supply grain; with improved techniques bere and oats were replaced by higher-yielding strains of barley which were particularly favoured on account of their finding a ready sale for pot barley making, or to brewers and distillers for malt. In Stirlingshire, for example, it was said that the many large distilleries 'are of advantage to the district, by procuring a ready sale for barley; and the culture of barley is undeniably an important article in the rotation of crops, as it is always accompanied by a rich addition of manure, and a succeeding rest under a crop of ameliorating grasses'.[3]

Many Improving landowners chose to establish towns and villages, partly with a view to resettling those displaced from the land and partly to absorb the products of the new agriculture.[4] Not surprisingly, the establishment of a brewery was a common feature of these new communities: it provided a market for locally grown barley, offered employment to some of those who had been forced off the land, and enhanced the estate's rental. Sir George Ross of Pitkerie built a brewery (which still survives) out of his own money as part of his replanning of Cromarty;[5] the brewery at Gatehouse (c.1784), while probably a private venture, had the backing of the village's founder, James Murray.[6] That most famous of Improvers, Cockburn of Ormiston, built maltings, a brewery and a distillery which, under the management of Alexander Wight, made pale malt, 'high flavoured' ale and whisky.[7] Despite the 'risk' to the morals of the cotton mill workers, a brewery was added to Catrine village about 1795.[8] Banff, Grantown and Thurso, all planned settlements, had breweries built about 1750, 1780 and in 1798 respectively.[9]

Brewing Technology

These large units of production often necessitated the introduction of power to drive machinery. The first operation, malting, required none in itself but, once malted, barley had to be ground. While brewers remained thirled, the process was carried out at whichever mill held the astriction; from the early 18th century, with the introduction of steel mills, thirlage was gradually broken and mills installed in breweries. Water power was definitely used for this purpose at Gatehouse and at Gilcomston Brewery, Aberdeenshire,[10] while at Annan (Dumfriesshire), Cambus (Clackmannanshire) and St. Vigeans (Angus) its use seems probable.[11] However, in the predominantly urban setting of breweries readily available water power was the exception rather than the rule: Gatehouse brewery could utilise the cotton mill lade, and Gilcomston stood on the site of a corn mill which had been occupied as a distillery c.1750-1770. Other breweries had to use hand-operated mills or utilise water-powered malt mills elsewhere: the brewers of Bo'ness, for example, used malt mills on the River Avon two miles away,[12] while the Crieff brewery, founded in 1791, probably used the nearby malt mill on the River Turret.[13]

In the next operation the ground malt was macerated with warm water for several hours in a mash tun. Mashing had traditionally been performed by men, with wooden instruments, but by the 1820s the process was undergoing mechanisation:

> A very strong iron screw, of the same height as the mash-tun, is fixed in the centre of this vessel, from which proceed two great arms or radii, also of iron, which [are] beset with vertical teeth, a few inches asunder, in the manner of a double comb; . . . the iron arms, which at first rest on the false bottom, are made to revolve slowly on the central screw, in consequence of which, in proportion as they revolve, they also ascend through the contents of the tun to the surface; then, inverting the circular motion, they descend again in the course of a few revolutions, to the bottom.[14]

This process may have been mechanised at the Keltybridge brewery, Fife where, in 1775, 'the work of the brewery, *and* the grinding of the malt, which is done on a steel mill', was 'all effected by a rivulet' which ran past the brewery.[15] In the absence of further evidence, it can only be assumed that other breweries mechanised the mashing process. In the larger urban breweries, mashing and the pumping of 'wort' were almost certainly being performed by steam or water power by the 1820s.

The Industrialisation of Distilling

Information on distilling is a little more readily available. Compared to brewing, whisky distilling was a relative newcomer to Lowland Scotland, originating, by different accounts, from Ireland or the Scottish Highlands. Throughout the period small-scale distilling by individuals, whether legally or illegally, continued to be practised in Scotland, particularly in the Highlands. Even in that area, however, the increase in demand for whisky in both England and Scotland was sufficient to stimulate factory production once malt taxes reached a low enough level. Similarities in the processes meant that the same mechanical techniques were applied to distilling as to brewing. Grange Distillery, Burntisland, built as a brewery in 1767, had its own water-powered threshing mill,[16] as had Kilbagie Distillery, Clackmannan.[17] Most capitalist distilleries were equipped with water-powered malt rollers, while those without adequate water supplies often used steam power for pumping liquids: James Haig and Company's distillery at Canonmills had a steam engine by 1787,[18] and Kennetpans Distillery, Clackmannan was one of Boulton & Watt's first Scottish customers.[19] Where water power was adequate, it was applied to these and other processes: the ill-fated Beauly Distillery used water power to stir the mash tuns and to pump water, wash and wort.[20] One particularly well-endowed distillery, built near Bridge of Don in 1794, had the use of a thirty-eight foot waterfall and was designed to manufacture 12,000 quarters of corn per annum.[21]

The Role of the Excise

Levels of whisky production were strongly influenced by legislative measures. The Wash Act of 1784 effectively divided Scotland into Lowland and Highland districts, which were taxed on the basis of production and capacity respectively. The commercial distilleries of Lowland Scotland had already been forced, by competition from illicit Highland stills, to seek markets outside Scotland; the Wash Act only aggravated their position. Even worse was to come. In 1786 the Wash Act was replaced by the Scottish Distillery Act, which raised the level of excise on Scottish spirits exported to England, so as to equalise the price of English and Scottish products. Prior to that time major distilleries such as Kennetpans and Kilbagie had depended entirely on the London market,[22] but with the passing of the Wash Act and then the Scottish Distillery Act, they lost their advantageous position. Further legislation, in 1788, limited the size of the still and put a premium on rapid distillation. By 1799 fast stills had come into general use in Lowland Scotland, as a result of which the basis of the duty was changed to one of 4s 10½d per gallon of spirit made for consumption at home. During the first year of the new duty (1801) a third of Scotland's eighty-seven licensed distillers gave up business, and revenue from the tax dropped from £1,620,388 to £775,750. In 1802 the duty was lowered to 3s 10½d, in response to which the number of distillers rose to eighty-eight in the following year and revenue to £2,022,409. In 1804 the excise was once again raised and the number of distillers declined once more. Because of the wartime shortages, distilling from grain was prohibited from June 1808, with serious repercussions in agriculture.[23] Spirit duty reached a peak of 9s 4½d in 1815, but fell to 6s 2d in 1817 and 2s 4¾d in 1823.

The Decline of Illicit Distilling

Those distillers who had survived the difficult war years were further encouraged by the Distillery Act of 1824, which marked the beginning of the end for the illicit distillers and the beginning of a boom in distillery building. Glenlivet Distillery, founded in 1824, was one of several built on a formerly illicit site; such was the local opposition to the suppression of illegal stills that for some time the owner carried firearms for his own protection.[24] The following year smugglers went so far as to burn down the Banks o' Dee Distillery in Aberdeenshire.[25] About sixty years later, Alfred Barnard visited some one hundred and twenty-nine distilleries in Scotland; of these, at least forty dated from the 1820s — thirteen from 1824, eight from 1825 and five from 1826.[26] The rise of legal distilleries is reflected in the increase in the gallonage on which duty was paid, from 2,225,124 gallons in 1822 to 5,981,549 gallons in 1825.[27] Not that this necessarily represented an absolute increase in total output: up to the end of the 18th century, it was claimed, duty was paid on only 1/40th of Scottish production, and not until 1821 were any concerted attempts made to stamp out illicit distillation.[28]

While it seems certain that some distilleries, such as those around Campbeltown, used steam power to crush their malt, stir their mash tuns and drive their pumps, the rural situation of the majority would suggest that water power was the general rule. This assumption is supported by the fact that so many distilleries were still using water power in the 1880s, well into the 'Age of Steam'.

By 1830 whisky distilling had come to occupy an important position in the economy of Scotland, particularly in the northern and eastern Highlands. Although the products of Scottish breweries found ready sale in London and elsewhere, the extent of these sales was hardly comparable with that of whisky. Within Scotland it had succeeded in ousting ale as the national drink. Furthermore, through malt taxes and spirit duties the government were able to benefit from the industry: before 1788, Kilbagie and Kennetpans distilleries had between them paid more excise than was raised by the land tax in Scotland, and at one time Kilbagie alone paid £500,000 Sterling in duty per annum.[29] But for the availability of water power, it is doubtful if the rural sector of the distilling industry could have been established on the scale it was. Nowhere is this more evident than on Speyside, where access to water both for making whisky and driving machinery was good, but access to coal for steam engines very poor.

NOTES

1. Clow, A. & Clow, N. L., *The Chemical Revolution*, London, 1952, 573. For a general discussion of brewing in Scotland, see Donnachie, I., *A History of the Brewing Industry in Scotland*, Edinburgh, 1979.

2. Singer, Dr. W., *General View of the Agriculture of Dumfriesshire*, Edinburgh, 1812.

3. Graham, P., *General View of the Agriculture of Stirlingshire*, Edinburgh, 1812, 349.

4. For a full account of the landowner's role in the creation of planned villages, see Smout, T. C., 'The Landowner and the Planned Village in Scotland', in Mitchison, R. & Phillipson, N. T. (eds.), *Scotland in the Age of Improvement*, Edinburgh, 1970.

5. Smout, *op. cit.*, 94.

6. Donnachie, I. L., *Industrial Archaeology of Galloway*, Newton Abbot, 1971, 55.

7. Whitehead, W. Y., *History of Ormiston*, Haddington, 1937, 41.

8. Butt, J., *Industrial Archaeology of Scotland*, Newton Abbot, 1967, 230.

9. *Ibid.*, 233 (Banff); Wight, A., *Present State of Husbandry in Scotland*, 4 vols., Edinburgh, 1778-82, IV, 385 (Grantown); Butt, *op. cit.*, 239 (Thurso).

10. SRO GD10/1266; Kennedy, W., *Annals of Aberdeen*, 2 vols., London, 1818, I, 388; SRO RHP 814.

11. *PP* 1831-2, XLII (Annan); *OSA* VIII, 592, Alloa, Clackmannanshire; *OSA* XII, 170, St. Vigeans, Angus.

12. *Caledonian Mercury*, 29th July 1775; *OSA* XVIII, 440, Boness, West Lothian.

13. *OSA* IX, 583, Crieff, Perthshire; Porteous, A., *History of Crieff*, Edinburgh, 1912, 169.

14. Accum, F., *Treatise on the Art of Brewing*, London, 1820, 47.

15. *Caledonian Mercury*, 28th August 1775.

16. SRO RHP252; Morison, W. M., *Dictionary of Decisions of the Court of Session*, 36 vols., Edinburgh, 1820, III, 1991.

17. *OSA* XIV, 626, Clackmannan, Clackmannanshire.

18. NLS Acc. 5111/27.

19. *OSA* XIV, 623, Clackmannan, Clackmannanshire.

20. SRO CS96/209, Letter Book of Beauly Distillery Company.

21. Kennedy, *op. cit.*, I, 423; *OSA* XIX, 222, Aberdeen, Aberdeenshire.

22. *OSA* XIV, 623-4, Clackmannan, Clackmannanshire.

23. Clow & Clow, *op. cit.*, 554-66.

24. Barnard, A., *The Whisky Distilleries of the United Kingdom* (1887), Newton Abbot, 1969, 219.

25. *Clow & Clow, op. cit.*, 567.

26. Barnard, *op. cit.*

27. *Ordnance Gazetteer* VI, 83.

28. Clow & Clow, *op. cit.*, 567.
29. Graham, P., *General View of the Agriculture of Kinross-shire & Clackmannan-shire*, Edinburgh, 1814, 360; *OSA* XIV, 623, Clackmannan, Clackmannanshire.

14

The Mill on the Farm

One of the principal elements in agricultural Improvement was the introduction of more efficient, less labour-intensive techniques. Improved ploughs, notably that of Small, found favour in that they could be worked by one man and two horses, instead of the team of six, eight or ten oxen or horses, and four men, required to coax along the old Scots plough.[1] The preparation of grain for milling or for animal feedstuffs was another area in which substantial labour savings could be made: both winnowing and threshing employed centuries-old techniques which were both inefficient and labour-intensive. 'The grain, as needed, was "cast in" to the barn, "thrashed" with a flail, "cleaned" with a series of riddles, and what aid a current of air passing between two doors could afford; thence it was removed to the kiln to be dried'.[2] A winnowing machine had already been introduced to Scotland;[3] between 1730 and 1830 machines, often water-powered, were developed to perform a variety of farming tasks such as turnip slicing, straw cutting, butter churning and whin crushing. However, by far the most important and most widely applied innovation was the threshing machine.

'A Capital Improvement in Husbandry'[4]

The problem of devising an effective threshing machine was one which occupied millwrights and other interested parties for much of the 18th century. The earliest machine which has been traced was that invented and patented by Michael Menzies, advocate. Menzies' machine, using the same principle as the flail, was installed to work by water power at several locations, and attracted the attention of the Society of Improvers, who sent a delegation to inspect two machines, one at Roseburn (Edinburgh) driven by a large water wheel with 'trindles' (gearing), and another at an undisclosed locality with a wheel of only three feet diameter. The mill at Roseburn succeeded in cleaning grain from straw already threshed by hand, and both mills met with the delegation's approval:

> . . . it is our humble opinion that the machine would be of great use to farmers, both in threshing the grain cleaner from the straw and in saving a great deal of labour; for one man would be sufficient to manage a machine which would do the work of six.[5]

Despite this auspicious start, it was later discovered that, to thresh the grain effectively, the flails had to work at so high a velocity that they soon broke. Before long the Menzies machine had fallen into disuse.[6] A similar machine erected by Gordon of Premnay at Licklyhead (Aberdeenshire) suffered the same fate.[7]

The next stage marks the beginning of a long line of machines which, while ultimately achieving relatively good results, was never acknowledged as perfected. In 1748 or 1758[8] Michael Stirling, farmer at Craighead, Dunblane, invented a threshing mill which utilised a scutching principle, already employed in lint mills.[9] Stirling's machine, driven by a vertical water wheel,[10] had four horizontal scutching arms and was sufficiently good for several to be set up in Scotland and England. According to the Statistical Account, the design was improved by Mr. Meikle (probably George) of Alloa who, by adding another gear-wheel, was able to put the threshing boards onto a horizontal axis and thereby permit the addition of bruising rollers.[11] In view of later developments, the intervention of Meikle is of great significance. In his General Report for Angus, Headrick describes in considerable detail a threshing mill, of a type first used near Dunblane, which had been installed at Howmuir near Forfar at a cost of £20. A Mr. Stirling is named in connection with the mill and, indeed, it resembles Stirling's original design in all but one respect: at Howmuir a horizontal water wheel was used, with blades set at an angle of 45° to meet water from a wooden flume at right angles.[12]

The *Farmers' Magazine* described, in 1807, a threshing machine costing only £10 'lately invented in Perthshire'; while closely resembling the Howmuir mill, it had the additional refinement of curved upper edges to blades which prevented water from splashing over.[13] A later edition mentions a machine invented by a Mr. Monteith at Shirrasmuir (Sheriffmuir) near Dunblane and improved by William Keir at Milnholm, Dumfriesshire. Keir's mill had cost £36 9s 1d to erect; five more had been built at a cost of £18-£37, and a sixth was under construction at Eastfield, near Bowden, Roxburghshire.[14] Despite criticisms made of them, machines using a scutching principle, apparently originating in the Dunblane area, seem to have achieved quite a wide currency. According to Sinclair, Stirling-type mills were still being used in some parts of Scotland as late as 1814, worked by water power or by oxen.[15] Perthshire in particular remained faithful to this type of machine, and when Sinclair established a fund to reward Meikle for inventing the threshing machine, the Strathearn Agricultural Society refused to subscribe, on the grounds that it was Michael Stirling, not Andrew Meikle, who had invented it.[16]

Whatever the sentiments may have been in Strathearn, it is generally Andrew Meikle who is credited with perfecting the threshing machine. 'Perfecting' is probably a more accurate term than 'inventing' for, in addition to the machines already mentioned, several others preceded that patented by Meikle in 1788 and may well have influenced it.

In 1772 or thereabouts, a Mr. Ilderton, near Alnwick, and a Mr. Smart at Wark, both in Northumberland, built machines which, instead of scutching the grain, rubbed it off. Sheaves of corn passed between an indented rotating drum, of about six feet diameter, and a number of similarly indented rollers, pressed against the drum by means of springs. The machines were far from perfect, performing very little work in a given time and bruising the grain so badly that its market value was seriously impaired.[17] A similar machine erected by Mr. Oxley at Flodden (also in Northumberland) achieved a slightly better result.[18]

While touring Northumberland, Sir Francis Kinloch of Gilmerton (East Lothian) came across the threshing machines built by Smart and Ilderton[19] and was sufficiently impressed to have models made for his own use. Back in East Lothian, Kinloch modified the design by enclosing the drum in a fluted cover and fixing four sprung pieces of fluted wood onto the circumference of the outer cylinder. In 1784 the model thus modified was sent to Andrew Meikle for tests to be carried out at Houston Mill, near East Linton.[20]

Before proceeding any further, we should go back a few years. Apparently Meikle had already been working on threshing machines and by 1778 had installed a prototype at Knowes Mill (East Lothian). At this stage he was still trying to improve on the flail principle used by Menzies: five flails, attached to a beam which was moved by a crank, threshed corn on two platforms, one on either side of the beam. In trials on 14th February 1778 the machine performed well, threshing more grain than could be done by flail; Andrew Wight, the authority on farming, was impressed by this performance, as were a number of East Lothian gentlemen who immediately brought it to the notice of the Board of Trustees for Manufactures. Some four months later, Meikle himself submitted plans of 'Machinery for threshing corn and scutching flax'.[21] A similar machine, apparently more efficient, had been developed by John Thomson at Keith Mill (East Lothian); Wight described this machine as 'simple', 'easily moved' and deserving to be made public. News of Thomson's mill had also reached the Board of Trustees, who asked that its performance be compared with that installed at Knowes Mill before Meikle was granted a premium for the latter.[22] Unfortunately, no record of their relative merits exists: Thomson seems to have returned to obscurity, while the next that is heard of Meikle is in 1784, when he received Kinloch's model for testing.

If we are to believe George Rennie, writing some twenty-seven years later, Meikle found little use for the Kinloch machine, and suffered it to remain in his shop, as a piece of 'useless lumber'.[23] When the machine was finally put to the test, it was torn to pieces in a matter of minutes; a like fate befell a full-sized machine which Sir Francis installed at Athelstaneford Mains.[24] Whatever the weaknesses of Kinloch's machine, however, it must have given Meikle food for thought, for in the following year (1785) he started work on a threshing machine based, like Kinloch's, on a revolving

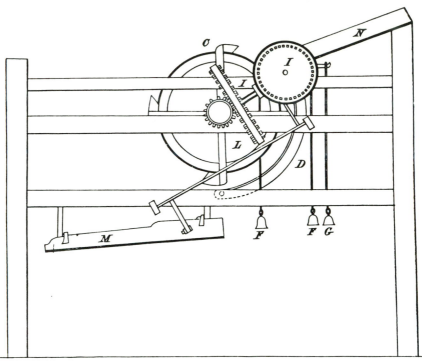

Fig 36. Patent drawing from Meikle's threshing machine. C: threshing bar. D: guard. F,G: weights to control rollers. I: gear wheels. L: threshing drum. M: dressing sieve. N: feed tray

drum, but with short scutchers, working with a close-fitting breastwork, rather than fluted surfaces.[25] In 1786 he communicated his ideas to his second son, George, millwright of Alloa who, it may be recalled, made improvements to Stirling type machines. George was much employed by James Stein of Kilbagie who, in addition to a distillery, ran an extensive farm. Unable to find enough barnmen to thresh straw for cattle litter, he engaged George to build a threshing mill. The mill which George built was identical to that devised by his father, with the exception of two fluted rollers which were added to it.[26] In agreeing to have the mill built, Stein offered to provide materials, but declined to pay for workmanship unless the mill performed satisfactorily. In the event the machine, driven by water power, 'answered so well in point of expedition and effort, that the proprietor declared he would not take a present of a common threshing by flail'.[27]

In 1787 Andrew Meikle built a second machine driven by horses at Phantassie (East Lothian), and in the following year a patent (No. 1645) was taken out[28] for a fourteen-year period (Figure 36). An advertisement was placed in the *Scots Magazine* in the following terms:

It is a species of mill, capable of being worked by two horses, or any power of wind or water equivalent to that force. The work performed is twenty-four bushels of barley or oats per hour, wheat and other grain in proportion. The corn is not only separated completely from the straw, but made ready for the market by being riddled and cleaned from chaff. No attendance is needed but for that of three men, women and boys . . . Gentlemen may either erect the machine themselves, upon a plan furnished by the Inventers; or contract with them for the whole at a fixed price.[29]

In practice, the patent proved impossible to enforce, and there were numerous infringements and further claims to have invented the machine. Additional claims were made on behalf of Oxley in Northumberland[30] and Mr. Crow of Netherbyres, Berwickshire.[31] Yet others extolled the virtues of machines based on waulkmills and oilmills.[32]

When the Meikle machine came up for consideration before the Board of Trustees, it was in competition with another, smaller machine devised by George Cotterel, ironfounder, in Leith Walk, Edinburgh.[33] Eventually, both received £20, while a third contender, John Fergusson, in Kilmadock parish, Perthshire, was given £15 for his machine. Cotterel's machine was 'soon laid aside',[34] but during the first ten years of the patent, so many threshing machines were erected that, at the end of that period attempts to enforce the patent were abandoned, as the cost would far outweigh any profits which might be made during the four remaining years.[35] Eventually, Sir John Sinclair, as president of the Board of Agriculture, established a fund and managed to raise £1,500 on Andrew Meikle's behalf.[36]

To give the Meikles their due, the use of feeding rollers and the high-speed rotation so crucial to the success of the machine were undoubtedly their own innovation. While the use of a revolving drum might have owed something to Oxley, and the use of scutchers to Stirling, it was the Meikles who successfully combined the two elements with other ingenious ideas. Above all, there is no doubt that Andrew Meikle, the foremost millwright of his century, was quite capable of inventing such a machine.

The Diffusion of the Threshing Machine

Once perfected, the threshing machine was rapidly taken up. By the late 1790s it had become well established in the Lothians, the Merse, Fife, and east-central Scotland; a few examples were beginning to appear in the Borders, Galloway, the north-east, Angus and west-central Scotland, but as yet none had reached the northern or western Highlands.[37] By 1810, they had become almost universal in the Lothians and Merse, and common in most arable parts of Dumfriesshire, eastern and north-eastern and central Scotland. In Renfrewshire and possibly elsewhere in west central Scotland, they were still fairly uncommon, and although machines had been installed on a few farms in Inverness-shire and Sutherland, none had yet reached Argyll.[38] The New Statistical Account, comprising entries written in the

1830s and early 1840s, gives a fairly detailed impression of the situation at the end of the period under consideration. Outside the northern and western Highlands and Islands, the use of threshing machines was nearing saturation point, with the exception of parts of the southern and Grampian Highlands where they were, nevertheless, not uncommon.[39]

At the same time as this spatial diffusion was taking place, a similar process was underway entailing diffusion from farms with larger arable acreages to those of smaller extent. To a considerable degree, this also involved a downward diffusion through the ranks of farming society. Thus, in East Lothian and the Merse, where large productive arable farms were the rule, the rapid adoption of the threshing mill was only to be expected. In areas of smaller farms, or less intensive arable husbandry, the first initiative generally came from heritors: the first threshing mills to be built in Caithness and Peeblesshire during the 1790s both fall into this category, the former built by Trail of Hobbister, the latter by Kerr of Kerrfield.[40] The same arrangements continued to be made for small tenants after the larger ones had installed their own machines: this was certainly true of Aberdeenshire (1811),[41] and even in East Lothian, where the threshing machine was very widely applied, the villagers of Ormiston made use of one installed at Ormiston Mill about 1823 to thresh grain from their small plots.[42] In Sutherland they were installed in extensive new steadings on the Duke of Sutherland's estates, along the narrow coastal strips; in Inverness-shire, by 1808, several heritors had built threshing mills, starting with Davidson of Cantray.[43] By the late 1830s they had reached a much smaller class of farmers: in Fordoun and Marykirk parishes (Kincardineshire) almost every farm of more than 100 acres had one,[44] in Kilmarnock parish (Ayrshire) the figure was 60 acres,[45] in Udny and Auchterless 50 acres,[46] and in Tarves, Longside and Oyne (all Aberdeenshire), 30.[47] In Boyndie parish (Banffshire) threshing machines had descended to the class of crofters,[48] and in Carstairs to pendiclers,[49] while in Ayton (Berwickshire) every farm had a threshing machine by 1834.[50]

Needless to say, by no means all these threshing machines were water-powered. The commonest were driven by two, three or four horses, but water power was found to be 'by far the cheapest and the best power to be applied to threshing mills. From the equality and gentleness of the motion, the machine will last twice as long as one drawn by horses; and as water mills generally do much more work when in motion, they do not require to be so frequently used. It is calculated that in threshing a crop of any extent, a pair of horses may be saved upon the farm, by the use of a water-mill, which cannot be calculated at less than L100 per annum'.[51] Water-powered threshing mills were commonest in those areas where topography and drainage facilitated the construction of dams and where farms had sufficiently large arable acreages to justify installation costs. Although no adequate contemporary source exists, the First Edition Ordnance Survey Maps give a fair indication of the distribution of water-powered threshing mills in 1830. As for the numbers, about 4,500 have been traced from this source, and this too can be taken as an indication of numbers in 1830. In some cases considerable efforts were made to bring water power to a steading: one mill, constructed by James Watt, millwright in Biggar, was connected by means of inclined shafts to a water wheel fifty feet below and one hundred and twenty feet distant from it. A similar example, erected at Crowhill, near Dunbar, cost some £800.[52] In the lowlands of eastern Scotland, from the Merse to Easter Ross, a few wind-powered mills were built. Despite their high cost, they were apparently 'becoming very common' in Berwickshire by 1810, while in East Lothian there were seven by the late 1830s.[53] Steam threshing mills were known as early as 1811,[54] but a combination of a shortage of skilled operators, anxieties about the use of 'fire engines' on farms, poor access to coal and high installation costs restricted them to those areas where large arable farms were unable to make effective use of water power but could readily obtain coal. In East Lothian, where they seem to have taken on most strongly, there were about eighty farms with steam threshing mills by the late 1830s.[55]

From contemporary evidence, water- and wind-powered threshing mills emerge as the cheapest forms to operate but, according to figures for Midlothian in 1811, water-powered mills at £150-£160 each were much cheaper to install than wind-powered ones at £450-£470.[56]

For those men, variously designated lotmen, barnmen and taskers,[57] who threshed by the flail, work was slow and tedious and yielded a remuneration of only 1/25th of the grain threshed, or a cash payment of 1s 3d per boll.[58] With such a gruelling occupation and with payment on a piecework basis, it is hardly surprising that the system was abused. From contemporary writings it is apparent that farmers and landowners despised and distrusted the tasker; this, with increased agricultural output and more lucrative employment opportunities elsewhere, intensified the demand for a mechanical substitute. As one might expect, the threshing mill, once perfected, spread rapidly through the Lowland districts of Scotland and was hailed as 'the most useful and profitable instrument belonging to a farm' or even as 'the greatest improvement that has been introduced . . . during the present age'.[59] The 'Code of Agriculture' lists its benefits as follows:

1. From the superiority of this mode, one-20th part more corn is gained from the same quantity of straw than by the old fashioned method.
2. The work is done more expeditiously.
3. Pilfering is avoided.
4. The grain is less subject to injury.
5. Seedcorn can be procured without difficulty from the new crops for those to be sown.
6. The market may be supplied with grain more quickly in times of scarcity.
7. The straw, softened by the mill, is more useful for feeding cattle.
8. If a stack of corn be heated, it may be threshed in a day, and the grain, if kiln dried, will be preserved and rendered fit for use.

9. The threshing mill lessens the injury from smutty grain, the balls of smut not being broken, as when beaten by the flail.
10. By the same machine, the grain may be separated from the chaff and small seeds, as well as from the straw.[60]

Although the majority of threshing mills were powered by horses, and others by wind or steam power, water power, where available, was considered to be the best option. Such was their success that by 1830 there were probably more water-powered threshing mills in Scotland than any other type of water mill, and once the initial outlay had been made, the available power could be harnessed to drive additional farm machinery.

Other Types of Farm Mill

Fanners

Fanners or winnowers were first introduced to Scotland by Andrew Meikle's father, James, in the 1700s. In its early form the machine consisted simply of a wheel, fitted with four fan blades of wood or iron, which revolved at a great speed within a drum. The strong draught thus produced issued forth from an opening in one side of the drum; when passed slowly through this draught the chaff blew to one side, while the grain fell straight down.[61] Although James Meikle was familiar with water-milling, it seems probable that this early machine was hand-driven. No more is heard of fanners until 1737, when Andrew Rodger, a farmer from the Hawick area, built a machine based on the Dutch design, and succeeded in selling fanners on both sides of the Border. By the 1790s his descendants were selling about sixty per annum, at two to three guineas each.[62]

In the meantime, fanners had come into general use in the arable districts of Scotland: machines had been installed in almost every mill, some of them possibly driven by water power. Many more fanners were to be found in farm steadings. In 1768 Andrew Meikle had taken out a patent on a machine which combined a riddle and fanners for dressing and cleaning corn,[63] and although they were not included in the prototype of Meikle's successful threshing machine, fanners, rakes and shakers were soon added; when it was advertised in 1789, the machine was said to be capable of preparing grain for market by riddling and winnowing the threshed grain, almost certainly with Meikle's own patent machine.[64]

During the next twenty-five years, fanners and riddlers came to be very common features of threshing mills, particularly where there was powerful water-powered machinery.[65] Initially winnowing still had to be completed by hand,[66] but through improvements in design and the addition of more fanners it would appear that this was no longer necessary by the early 1810s;[67] the threshing machine installed at Swellhead Farm, Maryculter (Kincardineshire) in 1836 had no less than three sets of fanners.[68] In some cases a chain and bucket system was fitted, so that grain could be returned for further winnowing.[69]

Hummelling, Bruising and Chopping

Barley proved particularly difficult to dress, in that most threshing machines failed to detach the awns (beards or spikes) from the grain, a process known as hummelling. Sometimes the chain and bucket system might be used to return the grain to the threshing machine, but in its absence barley had to be hummelled by hand. In 1810 or thereabouts a Mr. George Mitchell, millwright at Bishop Mill (Moray), designed a machine for hummelling barley, which was attached to several threshing machines including a water-powered mill at Skelbo farm, Sutherland[70] (Figure 37). According to Sir John Sinclair, those who had made use of the machine found it 'a great improvement', but to this he added a rider that 'the merit of this invention is disputed'.[71]

Sinclair's *General Report* gives details of two types of machine for bruising grain for horsefeed both of which could bruise five to six bolls of oats, wheat or barley per hour.[72] Thomson's 1778 threshing machine incorporated, *inter alia*, straw cutters, and machines of this type were in use in the 1810s, having found an application among tanners in chopping bark.[73] The water-powered threshing mill at Mount Annan (Dumfriesshire) incorporated both corn bruisers and straw cutters.[74] In Berwickshire, and probably elsewhere in the south-east, some farmers used the threshing-mill wheel to drive a pair of millstones which broke corn or beans and ground oats or barley.[75]

Whin Mills

As a widely occurring shrub, whins offered a potential fodder crop for farmers in areas of poorer quality land, although their needle-like leaves made them unpalatable. The earliest known example of a whin-crushing mill was that added to a snuff mill at Woodside, Aberdeenshire some time between 1764 and 1771.[76] Thereafter, mills on various principles were set up over an area extending from the Borders to Inverness-shire, but with a concentration in the north-east.[77] An undated document in the Gordon Castle muniments (probably late 18th century or early 19th) gives directions for preparing whins for mills:

> . . . the tender crops are cut by gardeners' scissors, hooks or short scythes, and bruised by flails, mills or engines like waulk mills or heavy stones going round on edge, as a common bark or oil mill to clear them from prickles and reduce them to a soft pulp.[78]

As with threshing mills, the majority seem to have been powered by animals.

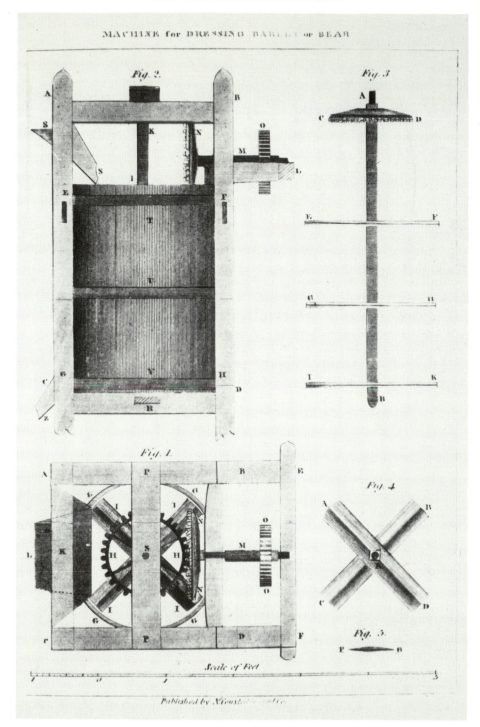

MACHINE for DRESSING BARLEY or BEAR

Fig. 2.

Fig. 3.

Fig. 1.

Fig. 4

Fig. 5.

Scale of Feet

Published by N. Constable

Butter Churns

According to Fenton, barrel and box churns were already replacing plunge churns in most Lowland counties by the 1790s.[79] The rotary motion by which they were operated was readily adaptable to water and horse power, and from the 1810s onwards there are occasional references to churn mills: Keith (1811) cites an example in Aberdeenshire, and the New Statistical Account (1837) mentions one in Ceres parish, Fife.[80] However, it was in the west, and particularly in Renfrewshire, that water power was most widely applied to churning. A 'churning mill' appears on Ainslie's map of Renfrewshire (1796),[81] and the writer of the General View for that county (1812) speaks of them as a 'most material improvement in machinery', before going on to describe their operation:

> The churn, in this case, is in the form of a hogshead, and was fixed in a horizontal position. The frame for breaking the milk is moved with a moderate velocity, on an axis passing through the centre of the churn, while the churn itself remains at rest; and to prevent the escape of the milk, apperture for admitting the axis is small and closely fitted. The whole apparatus is simple . . . the expense is small and the advantage in saving labour great.[82]

At Neilstonside Farm, a churn mill in the steading was linked to a water wheel on Levern Water by means of underground shafting, in a manner similar to the threshing mills at Biggar and Crowhill.[83] By the late 1830s demand was high enough to justify specialisation by millwrights; thus Hugh Smith at Broomlands, Paisley appears in Pigot's 1837 directory as 'manu-facturer of threshing mills and churning mills'.[84]

The Blairdrummond Wheel

Before leaving the subject of water power in agriculture, we should say something about an unusual, if not unique, application of water power which, like so many other elements in this chapter, involved the Meikle family. Blair-drummond Moss formed part of the peat-covered Forth Carselands above Stirling. In 1766, Lord Kames took on the Blairdrummond estate and by demolishing a corn mill was able to use water from its lade to carry off peats cleared from the fertile underlying Carse clays. Two methods were considered, contract labour or colonisation; the latter was settled upon, and thirteen tenants, established between 1767 and 1774, succeeded in clearing the lower part of the moss. The upper part, where peat deposits were much thicker, presented greater problems, but by digging additional channels a further twenty-nine tenants, settled between 1775 and 1782 on lots of eight acres each, were able to make further progress. When, in 1783, Mr. Drummond took over

Fig 37. Barley hummelling machine. Fig 1: plan. Fig 2: elevation. Fig 3: spindle (K in Fig 2) with arms (E,F,G,H,I,K). Fig 4: arms in plan. A footnote adds that the merit of the machine is disputed. *Sinclair, Husbandry, II. App. IV (1813)*

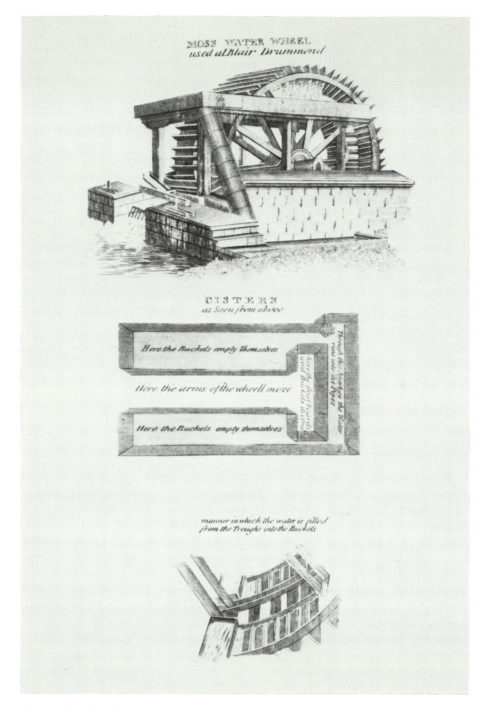

Fig 38. The Blairdrummond water raising machine. *Sinclair, General Report, App. II (1814)*

the estate, one thousand acres of the High Moss remained unclaimed, but by digging a further channel across the moss he was able to attract another fifty-five tenants to take on four hundred and forty acres of the moss between 1783 and 1785. However, to remove the remainder of the moss required considerable expense. Several engineers were employed to carry out surveys and make plans for a water supply from the nearby River Teith. A Mr. Whitworth, superintendent of the London waterworks, prepared plans of a pumping machine, but was soon upstaged by George Meikle, who presented a model of an 'exceedingly simple' machine which he and his father (Andrew Meikle) had designed. Whitworth, recognising the superiority of the machine, recommended its use in preference to his own, and in the spring of 1787 a contract was signed with George Meikle. By the end of October 1787 the wheel, with its accompanying waterworks, had been completed at a cost in excess of £1,000. Illustrated in Figure 38, it shows great ingenuity in its design. The 'driving' water was admitted laterally to a double circle of buckets on the outside of the wheel and water for draining to buckets on the inside of the wheel, lifted to the top of the wheel and dropped into a trough which fed a canal. By placing the arms of the water wheel close together between the two circles of buckets, the Meikles were able to construct a close-fitting trough which caught most of the water lifted by the buckets. According to contemporary sources, the wheel was twenty-eight feet in diameter, ten feet wide and made four revolutions per minute.[85]

The Meikles' 'Great Wheel' apparently functioned perfectly and appears with its water courses on a plan of the partially cleared moss. The last part of the moss was cleared in 1839.[86]

NOTES

1. Handley, J. E., *Scottish Farming in the Eighteenth Century*, London, 1953, 64-5, 216-7.

2. *Ibid.*, 67.

3. That of James Meikle. See p.39

4. *OSA* IV, 480, Errol, Perthshire.

5. Maxwell, R., *Select Transactions of the Honourable Society of Improvers in the Knowledge of Agriculture in Scotland*, Edinburgh, 1743, 276-7.

6. Loudon, J. C., *An Encyclopaedia of Agriculture*, London, 1825, 402.

7. *Farmers' Magazine*, III, 424-433 (1802).

8. *OSA* XX, 75 (1748); Loudon, *op. cit.*, 402 (1758).

9. See p.172.

10. *Farmers' Magazine*, XII, 74 (1811).

11. *OSA* XX, 74-5, Doune, Perthshire.

12. Headrick, J., *General View of the Agriculture of Forfarshire*, Edinburgh, 1813, 264-5.

13. *Farmers' Magazine*, VIII, 465 (1807).

14. *Ibid.*, XI, 148-53 (1809); *Ibid.*, XII, 68 (1811).

15. Sinclair, Sir J., *General Report of the Agricultural State and Political Circumstances of Scotland*, 3 vols., and Appendix, 2 vols., Edinburgh, 1814, I, 227.

16. Porteous, A., *History of Crieff*, Edinburgh, 1912, 165.

17. Loudon, *op. cit.*, 402-3.

18. Sinclair, *op. cit.*, I, 227.

19. Smart & Oxley, according to Smiles, S., *Lives of the Engineers*, 5 vols., London, 1874; Smeaton & Rennie, 205; Sinclair, *op. cit.*, I, 228.

20. *Farmers' Magazine*, XII, 485 (1813); Loudon, *op. cit.*, 403.

21. Wight, A., *Present State of Husbandry in Scotland*, 4 vols., Edinburgh, 1778-82, II, 490-92; Smiles, *op. cit.*, 205; SRO NG1/1/22, 18th February 1778, 24th June 1778.

22. Wight, *op. cit.*, II, 248; SRO NG1/1/22, 24th June 1778.

23. *Farmers' Magazine*, XII, 485 (1811).

24. Sinclair, *op. cit.*, I, 228; Loudon, *op. cit.*, 403; *Farmers' Magazine*, XII, 485 (1811).

25. *Farmers' Magazine*, XII, 488 (1811); Cartwright, J. N., 'The Meikle Threshing Mill at Beltondod', *TELA&FNS*, XI (1968), 75.

26. *Farmers' Magazine*, XII, 486 (1811); Sinclair, *op. cit.*, I, 229.

27. *Scots Magazine*, LI, 211 (1789).

28. *Farmers' Magazine*, XII, 486-8 (1811); Smiles, *op. cit.*, 206.

29. *Scots Magazine*, LI, 211 (1789).

30. Sinclair, *op. cit.*, I, 227-8.

31. Kerr, R., *General View of the Agriculture of the County of Berwick*, London, 1809, 162.

32. *OSA* V, 281; *OSA* XVI, 383, Peterculter, Aberdeenshire.

33. SRO NG1/127, 11th March 1789; 19th January, 19th March 1791.

34. *Farmers' Magazine*, XII, 487 (1811).

35. Sinclair, *op. cit.*, I, 230.

36. Handley, J. E., *The Agricultural Revolution in Scotland*, Glasgow, 1963, 104.

37. Information derived from *OSA* and pre-1800 *General Views*.

38. Information derived from post-1800 *General Views*.

39. Information derived from *NSA*.

40. *OSA* XII, Olrick, Caithness, 158; Findlater, C., *General View of the Agriculture of Peeblesshire*, Edinburgh, 1802, 25.

41. Keith, G. S., *General View of the Agriculture of Aberdeenshire*, Aberdeen, 1811, 259.

42. *NSA* II, 145, Ormiston, East Lothian.

43. Henderson, J., *General View of the Agriculture of Sutherland*, Edinburgh, 1812, 61, 134; Loch J., *An Account of Improvements on the Estates of the Marquis of Stafford*, London, 1820, Appendix 2; Robertson, J., *General View of the Agriculture of Inverness-shire*, London, 1808, 105.

44. *NSA* XI, 102-3, Fordoun, Kincardineshire; 303, Marykirk, Kincardineshire.

45. *NSA* V, 549, Kilmarnock, Ayrshire.

46. *NSA* XII, 137, Udney, Aberdeenshire; 290, Auchterless, Aberdeenshire.

47. *Ibid.*, 639, Oyne, Aberdeenshire; 672, Tarves, Aberdeenshire; 866, Longside, Aberdeenshire.

48. *NSA* XIII, 243, Boyndie, Banffshire.

49. *NSA* VI, 557, Carstairs, Lanarkshire.

50. *NSA* II, 141, Ayton, Berwickshire.

51. Sinclair, Sir J., *An Account of the Systems of Husbandry of Scotland,* 2 vols., Edinburgh, 1814, I, 86.

52. *NSA* II, 245, Innerwick, East Lothian; East Lothian County Council, *East Lothian Water Mills,* Haddington, 1970, 27; *NSA* VI, 365, Biggar, Lanarkshire.

53. Kerr, *op. cit.,* 161-2. There were four wind-powered threshing mills within three miles of Kerr's farm in Ayton parish; *NSA* II, 374, General Observations, East Lothian; *NSA* IX, 526, Ceres, Fife; Headrick, *op. cit.,* 262-3: 'A few' wind-powered threshing mills; *NSA* XII, 402, Pitsligo, Aberdeenshire; Souter, D., *General View of the Agriculture of the County of Banff,* Edinburgh, 1812, 126; *NSA* XIV, 465, Tarbert, Ross-shire.

54. Trotter, J., *General View of the Agriculture of the County of Linlithgow,* Edinburgh, 1811, 41-2.

55. Sinclair, *Systems,* I, 80-87; *NSA* II, 374, General Observations, East Lothian.

56. Sinclair, *Systems,* I, 96.

57. Fenton, A., *Scottish Country Life,* Edinburgh, 1976, 79. Trotter refers to them simply as 'flailmen': Trotter, J., *General View of the Agriculture of the County of Linlithgow,* Edinburgh, 1794, 19. An 'ode to the threshing mill', circulated when the Meikle machine first appeared, refers to them as 'supple-drivers' (*souple* — the part of the flail which strikes the unthreshed grain): *Farmers' Magazine,* XI, 59 (1810).

58. Sinclair, *Systems,* I, 90-91.

59. *Ibid.,* 95-98.

60. Loudon, *op. cit.,* 407.

61. Sinclair, *General View,* I, 230.

62. *OSA* VII, 521, Hawick, Roxburghshire.

63. Smiles, *op. cit.,* 203.

64. *Ibid.,* 206; *Scots Magazine,* LI, 211.

65. See, for example, Kerr, *op. cit.,* 164-5; Headrick, *op. cit.,* 267; Keith, *op. cit.,* 219; Singer, Dr. W., *General View of the Agriculture of the County of Dumfries,* Edinburgh, 1812, 137; Whyte, A. & Macfarlane, D., *General View of the Agriculture of the County of Dunbartonshire,* Glasgow, 1811, 75; Graham, P., *General View of the Agriculture of the County of Stirling,* Edinburgh, 1812, 114; Thomson, J., *General View of the Agriculture of the County of Fife,* Edinburgh, 1800, 131-3.

66. Kerr, *op. cit.,* 164-5.

67. Sinclair, *Systems,* I, 78.

68. *TH&AS,* XIV, 354 (1843).

69. Sinclair, *Systems,* I, 98 (footnote).

70. Henderson, *op. cit.,* 134; Sinclair, *General Report, I, 498.*

71. *Ibid.,* I, 34-5.

72. *Ibid.,* I, 247-8.

73. *Ibid.,* I, 248-9.

74. Singer, *op. cit.,* 136.

75. Kerr, *op. cit.,* 96.

76. Morgan, P., *Annals of Woodside & Newhills,* Aberdeen, 1886, 17; SRO RHP814 (1773).

77. Fenton, *op. cit.,* 141.

78. SRO GD44/45/12.

79. Fenton, *op. cit.,* 152.

80. Keith, *op. cit.,* 219; *NSA* XI, 526, Ceres, Fife.

81. GR NS522557. Latterly Netherplace Bleachworks.

82. Wilson, J., *General View of the Agriculture of the County of Renfrew*, Paisley, 1812, 89.

83. Taylor, C., *The Leven Delineated*, Glasgow, 1831, 48.

84. *Pigot & Co's National Commercial Directory of the Whole of Scotland and the Isle of Man*, London, 1837, 724.

85. *OSA* XXI, 159-168, General Appendix.

86. *Imperial Gazetteer*, I, 174. There is a model of the wheel at the National Museum of Antiquities of Scotland.

15

Lint Mills

Technology

Long before it had received the attention of the Board of Trustees for Manufactures, the preparation of flax, or lint, by hand was widely practised in
Scotland. Robertson (1808) describes the process as follows:

> After it has been duly watered and dried, the sheaves of flax are formed of the
> thickness of a man's leg and beat with mallets on a smooth stone, to separate the
> reed from the rind. Then it is separated into handfuls, such as a person can easily
> grasp; and with a wooden instrument, made into the form of a hedge-bill or large
> knife, in the right hand, and holding the lint in the left, over the end of a small
> perpendicular board set firmly in a sole, which is held down by the foot and about
> three feet high, the lint is scutched or whipped with the wooden instrument,
> turning one end of the lint after another to the stroke, and turning the inside out,
> as appears necessary until the rind has been completely separated.[1]

During the 17th century, attempts had been made to mechanise the process.
In England patents were taken out by Abraham Hill in 1664 and by Charles
Moreton and Samuel Weale in 1692.[2] In Northern Ireland a 'flax mill' is
referred to in 1717 and again in 1719.[3] The earliest reference to such a mill in
Scotland relates to one at Paisley, first let in 1726; that at Drygrange, Berwickshire seems to date from the same period.[4] However, it was only with the
establishment of the Board of Trustees in the late 1720s that satisfactory lint
mill machinery was developed.

In 1727 it was reported to the newly formed Board of Trustees that, in trials,
a flax-beating machine designed by one David Donald 'performed exceeding
well'. Donald was asked to make a full-sized version of the machine, so that
Mr. Spalden (or Spalding), lint dresser, might inspect it further.[5] The Trustees
later ordered four pairs of Donald's rollers, and by December 1729 these, fitted
to water mills, were said to 'bruise the flax exceeding well, especially at Ceres
in Fife'.[6] For the Board of Trustees, this marked the beginning of a commitment
to the development of a water-powered flax dressing industry, a commitment
which was to stand firm for a hundred years.

Besides testing Donald's rollers, the Trustees had been looking into other
ways of mechanising flax dressing. On 16th April 1728 it was agreed that
James Spalding be sent to Holland to collect models of the most efficient Dutch
dressing machines and to learn the techniques employed.[7] By July 1729 he had

completed his mission, returned to Scotland and fitted up a machine in Edinburgh. First trials in East Lothian, using horse power, had proved unsuccessful, and a further attempt at Bonnington Mills, using water power, showed little more promise. However, Spalding was of the opinion that an experienced millwright could put the machine to rights, and to this end the Trustees asked that Andrew Mitchell (?Meikle) be brought from Perth.[8] Mitchell's estimate of £48 Sterling was accepted, and by the following March the work had been completed.[9] This time the mill performed very favourably: the rollers of the machine bruised the flax at four times the speed of hand breaks or mallets and with equal effectiveness, while the scutchers (revolving blades which struck the flax) proved faster than the hand scutch, but just as effective. The mill had cost only £41 8s 2½d.[10]

The combination of rollers and scutchers proved very successful and remained the basis of Scottish flax mill design throughout their history, although minor improvements continued to be made. From the outset the Board of Trustees held an explicit faith in the superiority of water power over hand dressing despite widespread criticism.

Within a year of the mill's completion Spalding was claiming to have improved the cylinders and other parts of the machine, bringing its cost down to £13 14s and the cost of flax dressing to 18d per stone.[11] In 1735 he developed a machine incorporating three rollers instead of the customary two,[12] and in 1740 he offered to disclose a method whereby flax could be dressed at half the usual cost, but only on condition that he received a reward for work already done and a loan towards the cost of a new mill.[13] In 1747 the Trustees convened a meeting of lint raisers, dressers and manufacturers with the aim of establishing the best method of dressing flax. Rollers were, by common consent, 'the safest and most expeditious' method of breaking flax, although hopes were also held out for two imported machines. Mill scutching was approved, but only in carrying out the first three-quarters of the process; for the remainder a hand scutching method was recommended. A third process, beating or softening, was also identified; according to informed opinion, this was a vital prerequisite to heckling. Two fining mills had already been imported for this purpose, although plain, ungrooved cylinders were found to be equally suitable.[14]

With a view to testing these machines, the Trustees engaged James Currie, lint dresser at Redford Bridge, to build an experimental bruising and fining mill at Colinton. Three years later a grant of £275 Sterling had received the Royal Assent and £120 had been forwarded to Currie.[15] Nothing is heard of the relative success of the machines, and no further reference is made to fining mills until 1779, when a new machine was recommended for fine fabrics.[16] James Currie's name occurs again in 1751, this time as the contested inventor of a flax dressing machine reckoned to be 'of the utmost importance to the manufacture'. To establish the usefulness of this and a rival machine, the Trustees called in Robert and Andrew Meikle, the most prominent millwrights of the age. Andrew Meikle was asked to test Currie's machine at Kevock Mill;

no record of the result exists, although a Currie machine was installed at Newhall Mill, Penicuik in 1752.[17] Their continued interest in improving and diffusing the technology of flax dressing is evident from their decision soon after to engage the Meikles on a permanent consultative basis, on account of their ingenuity 'in inventing, as well as improving many different kinds of machinery requisite for the cheapening of labour'.[18]

As far as is known, very few illustrations exist of Scottish lint mills, but from the few written accounts it is possible to build up a picture of their exterior and interior features. Grant of Monymusk, writing in 1748, describes Hospital Mill, Fife as being 16 feet by 48 feet with a loft, a thatched roof and a 12 foot shade projecting from one side. A fall of only 3 feet 6 inches drove a wheel 17 feet by 18 inches with a 13 foot axletree.[19]

Although most lint mills were of a fairly conventional design, a mill built at Invervar, Perthshire was circular in outline, about 18 feet in diameter with an upper floor for storage. The builder, Ewan Cameron, had two lint mills at Lawers and was responsible for the construction of eighty or so mills throughout the Highlands. Cameron died in 1817 at the advanced age of 112.[20]

Grant of Monymusk's own mill, completed about 1750, had separate chambers for bruising, scutching and heckling. Bruising was carried out with three rollers and scutching with an enclosed four-bladed machine with eight apertures through which flax could be introduced.[21]

Despite the Trustees' preference for breaking by rollers, several other methods were still being used in the 1770s, the commonest being mallets or stampers, usually moved by water power but occasionally by hand; Hindford Mill, Lanarkshire used both rollers and stampers, while Cullen Mill, Banffshire, employed the Dutch Break, a method widely used on the Continent but seldom found in Scottish mills. In Grant of Monymusk's mill, as in Spalding's, the scutchers were mounted horizontally, in a manner typical of Scottish lint mills. At several mills, however, the Irish practice was adopted, with scutching arms mounted vertically on the axletree of the mill.[22] Figure 39 shows rollers and horizontal scutchers as fitted to a mill about 1810.

Many of the mills recorded in the 1772 survey performed scutching only, while, in north Perthshire, mills with rollers only were said to be of 'great use to the industrious poor'.[23] At the opposite end of the scale were mills such as that at Gorgie, near Edinburgh, which specialised in beating or softening imported Dutch flax, presumably for fine fabrics.[24]

Although the Trustees commonly blamed human failings for any shortcomings in lint mills, they still continued to improve the technology available. The 'general complaints and reflections frequently thrown upon lint mills' are dealt with later in this chapter, but they probably encouraged the Trustees to back experiments on new techniques in an attempt to 'restore the credit of these mills'.[25] When, in 1761, a new machine showed promise, the Board of Trustees readily agreed to finance the construction of an experimental mill in Fife and the installation of a second such machine at Angus Macdonald's Elie

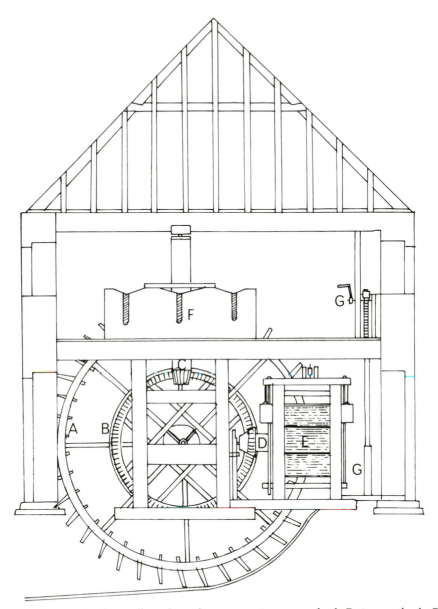

Fig 39. Layout of a lint mill, early 19th century. A: water wheel. B: inner wheel. C: upright shaft to scutchers. D: lying shaft to rollers. E: breaking rollers. F: scutching box. G: sluice control. *Gray, 1806*

lint mill for instructional purposes. Nothing is heard of this actually taking place, however; a mill of this type, fitted up at the lint mill of Drum, Banffshire, proved to be inadequate, and eventually the machine and its inventor fell into disrepute.[26]

Reference has already been made to the partial mechanisation favoured in north Perthshire (p. 173). Elsewhere, in even more marginal areas, the Board wished to encourage production and stimulate employment but, because of the small quantities of flax grown, lint mills were out of the question. The need was eventually filled by a foot-driven machine devised by the Board's principal clerk, Robert McPherson, in 1763.[27] Lord Kames, among others, held out high hopes for the new machine:

> It is zealously to be wished, and may reasonably be expected, that flax raising will be greatly promoted by this machine and will creep into every corner.[28]

Hugh Smith at Carnwath lint mill and Angus Macdonald at Elie, both experienced flax surveyors, also spoke highly of the machine and helped gain for McPherson a £100 reward.[29] However, for all its success, the foot machine was never meant to replace the lint mill, and within a few years Smith had incorporated its essential features in a water-powered version fitted up at the Board's expense on the horizontal axle of one of his existing mills.[30] Similar mills were subsequently built at Lochmaben and Cullen. A further indication of the superiority of the new design is seen in the claim that a mill on the Isle of Bute, hitherto little used, 'might be made to do double' if fitted with the new machinery.[31] On two further occasions Smith was called upon to test other new machines. In 1768 a modified version of McPherson's machine, to a design by Baillie John Reid of Tain, was installed alongside the existing McPherson-type machine. This, being the third in one building, was described as being similar to a Dutch scutcher, giving a perpendicular stroke to the flax which was held in an adjustable stock.[32] Two years later he was granted £40 for a fifth mill, with 'yetlin' rollers, to be built at Wiston, Lanarkshire.[33]

At last it seemed that the Board's faith in the lint mill was paying off. In 1773 one was reported to be scutching at a cost below half the hand rate; encouraged by this, the Board decided to seek further opinions to 'determine the propriety of encouraging or discouraging water mills'.[34] Although further improvements were made in 1773, 1778, 1782 and 1784, some mills were poorly enough designed for Smith to cite 'false principles' in design as one reason for the continuing inefficiency of lint mills.[35] Apparently most mills had been built with rollers and scutchers driven off the same axle, a practice which greatly reduced the efficiency of a mill. Having considered seeking legal powers, the Trustees finally settled for confining financial aid to those mills in which the processes were separately powered.[36]

In the lack of proper storage facilities the Trustees saw another reason for the less than perfect performance of many mills. As early as 1747 it had been observed that much more wastage occurred in damp weather than in dry, but it was not until 1761 that the Trustees began to offer financial aid for the construction of sheds, while the regular financing of sheds did not start until 1772 (Figure 40). So overwhelming was the response that by 1797 they were stipu-

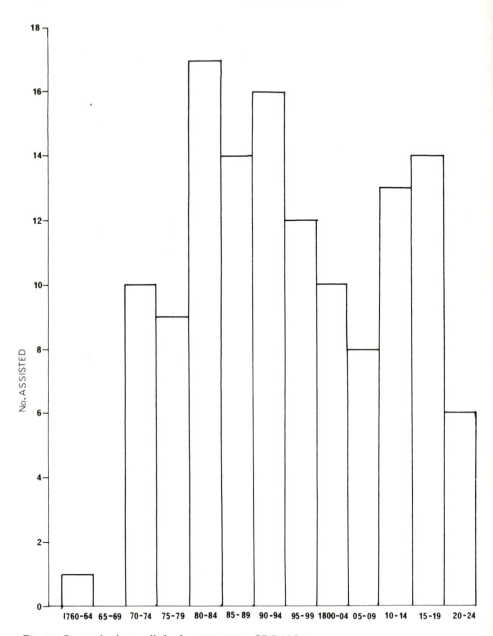

Fig 40. Grants for lint mill sheds, 1760-1824. *SRO NG1*

lating that all new mills incorporate sheds, or shades, rather than face the possibility of having to make two separate grants.[37]

   Another way of ensuring that flax to be dressed was in good condition was the provision of drying ovens, a common feature in Holland but one which was hitherto unknown in Scotland. However, when in 1785 the Trustees agreed to give Hugh Smith £12 towards an oven, they were at pains to point out that this was merely an experiment and that no money would be forth-coming for their construction elsewhere. Obviously their commitment to financing mill and shed building was as much as their budget could allow.[38]

As for the 'going graith' of the lint mill, there were no major improvements during the late 18th century. In 1790 Hugh Smith was said to be planning a lint mill on a 'new and improved plan', but at the time of his death, some four years later, the mill had not been built.[39] A supposedly novel lint mill near Panmuir, Angus, while showing some ingenuity in its design, turned out to be very similar to existing mills.[40] A hand machine for dry scutching, the invention of a Mr. Lee, was introduced to Scotland in 1815 but was dismissed by the Board of Trustees: 'Mr. Lee's machinery will be of no use in Scotland'.[41]

In later years some mills had sprung 'wipers', or blades, fitted to their scutching arms,[42] but by that time the impetus had long gone out of designing lint mills and had turned instead to larger, more complex machines in more highly capitalised branches of the textile industry.

The Workforce

While the lint mill represented an important technological breakthrough, it was of little use in itself without skilled labour to operate it correctly. To fulfil this need the Board of Trustees adopted various techniques which, broadly speaking, fell into two categories: on the one hand there were those designed to train unskilled persons and on the other those intended to diffuse and improve the skills of those already trained.

Never before in the history of Scotland had a totally new industrial process been adopted so widely and so rapidly. It was hardly surprising, therefore, that the Board's attention was focused at a very early stage on training a suit-able labour force. In 1730 Hope of Rankeillor, himself a Trustee, was promised £25 towards the cost of a mill to be built on the River Eden at Hospital Mill, Fife and to be supervised by John Ness.[43] In 1734 Jacques Housset, whom the Board brought over from Flanders, was sent to Hospital Mill to pass on his knowledge of flax raising; within a few months a programme had been instigated there, under which Housset gave training in raising and Ness in dressing flax.[44] The first person to complete the course was sent to the Glasgow Linen Society's mill at Clayslaps, Glasgow in 1735 and on to Duchal Steps, Renfrewshire the following year. By August 1737 he had moved yet again, this time to Barochin, also in Renfrewshire, leaving Duchal Steps in the care of a relative.[45]

By the end of 1736 some five or six persons, from as far north as Fochabers, had been instructed at Hospital Mill, and fourteen more were to be taken on, bringing the number up to twenty. Three more were presented in 1738, and by 1740 twenty-four raisers and dressers had been trained and sent out, though not all to established mills. While some 'raiser stations' had no mill, there were areas such as Angus where the number of mills built, with and without aid, outstripped the number of trained dressers the Board could supply, and on balance it would seem that the training scheme was not keeping pace with mill building.[46] Nevertheless, the Hospital Mill scheme illustrates the determination of the Board to create a pool of skilled labour. The scheme ran until 1753, when it was replaced by apprenticeships.[47] In 1762 John Ness, 'now reduced by old age and infirmities', asked the Board for a small pension, only to be icily rebuffed: 'the board's funds are destined for other purposes than charity'.[48]

One of the purposes for which those funds had been destined was the payment of salaries to those lint raisers and dressers whom John Ness had helped to train. Until 1737 the Board helped to finance lint mill construction; from that time onwards this practice was replaced by a £7 10s payment to each of twenty raisers. The 'raiser stations' at which they were based were to be inspected annually by James Spalding, who had been appointed 'surveyor of the raisers, dressers and hecklers of lint'.[49] In the first year only twelve appointments were made; in 1739 a further nine unpaid dressers were taken on, and in 1740 the unpaid raisers, now twelve in number, were brought onto the pay roll, bringing the number of paid raisers to twenty-four. Trained as they were, not all raisers were stationed at lint mills, and in an effort to remedy this the Board transferred the £7 10s payment from raiser to mill.[50]

The report for 1741 paints a chaotic picture of raisers without mills, mills without raisers, and raiser stations with neither raisers nor adequate mills. In that year only eighteen out of twenty-four salaries were paid and in the following year only sixteen out of twenty.[51] In 1743 it was reported that two raisers had deserted their posts and that two others had failed to raise enough flax. Three stations had to be given up because of lack of business.[52] The following year saw some improvement, with salaries paid to twenty-one of the twenty-four stations, and reports for 1745 were generally good, despite the troubled times, only one station being dropped. The following year's results were very mixed, for while one station dressed 1,000 stones of flax, and two others over 500 each, there were at least three raisers still without mills. A good year was 1747, with only four of the twenty-four stations going unpaid and only one being closed down. Six salaries were left unpaid in 1748. By this time the Board were becoming concerned about the number of mills at which raisers were needed and the number of raisers still without mills:

> those flax raisers who are not possessed of milns should be certified that they will be struck off the establishment unless they shall be provided in milns betwixt now and next Christmas, or if they cannot be provided in these at the places at which they are now stationed, that they must repair to other stations, where there are milns.[53]

For 1749 the number of stations was raised to thirty, and in the triennial plan from December that year it was proposed that their number be increased further to sixty, although in the event the salaries of the thirty were doubled instead. The Board obviously were very pleased with the progress made by their raisers:

> To these young men and to the milns lately erected is chiefly to be attributed the increase in the quantity of home grown flax.[54]

In the following four years between twenty-six and twenty-eight raisers received salaries;[55] in 1754 four stations failed to transmit certificates and a further five grew insufficient quantities of flax. The four were struck off the roll and none of the five received salaries.[56] The raiser system continued to operate in that form until 1758, by which time it was considered that flax cultivation was sufficiently well established in Perth, Forfar and Fife for salaries to be discontinued, and instead a 1s per stone premium was offered for the greatest quantities raised and dressed.[57] As from 1758 financial support for flax raisers was restricted to four mills salaried at £10 each and three at £5 each. Salaries for the four mills were discontinued in 1762 and for the remaining three in 1763.[58]

Long before the Board had given up paying lint millers or raisers, another form of sponsorship had been introduced in an effort to extend the cultivation and milling of flax. Such had been the demand for lint raisers that in December 1744 it was decided that experiments should be made with lint boors.[59] In the Low Countries, whence came the idea, lint boors bought up all the local green flax, watered and grassed it and prepared it for the spinner.[60] The duties of the Scottish lint boors were to be broadly similar, with the additional responsibility of building and operating a lint mill and storage houses. The Trustees proposed a premium of £140 per person, £100 of which was to buy up twenty acres of flax per annum for three years and £40 for building the mill. In exchange the lint boor had to undertake to 'break, bruise and swingle' at his mill all the flax brought to him, at 1s 2d Sterling per stone Amsterdam or 1s 5d per stone Tron.[61]

In setting up such an experiment the Trustees had failed to take into account several crucial differences between flax cultivation in the Low Countries and in Scotland. In the Low Countries flax cultivation was centuries old, with large acreages given over to the crop in any one locality. In Scotland, however, as Lord Kames later pointed out, the manufacture was still in its infancy, with only small and widely scattered patches under the crop.[62] It was hardly surprising, therefore, that in the first three-year period (1745-1747) the Board were unable to find anyone prepared to take on the twenty-acre undertakings expected of the first two lint boors.[63]

In the event one post was filled by two men in East Lothian and the other by three men in widely separated parts of Perthshire.[64] By 1747 interest in the idea had increased and six places were offered; of these, only five were taken up and these went to east-central Scotland where flax cultivation was already well established.[65] In the following year demand for lint boors mushroomed, but of the forty-seven applicants, only seven could be found places.[66] The cultivation of flax received stimulus enough to enable thirteen of the fifteen lint boors established by 1749 to fulfil their flax-buying obligations.[67] Early in 1750 the Board still looked favourably on the scheme:

> That the premium £140 has been of great benefite to the manufacture would appear from the great increase of the quantity of flax raised within the course of the last three years . . .[68]

On the other hand abuses of the scheme were sufficiently common for the Board to insist that lint mills be near completion and twenty acres of flax planted locally before any payment could be made; furthermore their directive to lint boors not to 'decoy or entice away' each others' servants suggests a shortage of skilled labour.[69] Before long other abuses had become apparent: in March 1750 it was claimed that lint boors were being taken advantage of by growers who charged high prices; the obligation to buy twenty acres was therefore lifted for those lint boors started that year.[70] In November, Scott of Rossie reported that lint boors were having great difficulty in keeping rates down to the prescribed 1s 2d per stone and that the twenty-acre quota was twice as high as could be managed.[71]

Seven lint boors had been taken on in 1749, a further five were taken on in 1750 but only two in 1751.[72] These were to be the last for a while. The final blow came in 1752. When Robert Balfour Ramsay of Balbirnie applied for a lint boor early that year, the Board replied that they were unable to oblige on account of

> the diminution of the funds under their management by a failure of the malt duty which they are certain of has obliged them to restrict the large premiums [lint boors] and to confine themselves to the small premium of £15 a year by way of salary to an overseer to the miln [flax raisers] — and this premium, small as it is, they can only affoord to thirty milns throughout Scotland and they are uncertain but next year the necessity of the manufacture may oblige them to withdraw it altogether.[73]

According to Durie,[74] the ill-fated lint boor experiment had cost the Trustees over £5,000.

It is not generally known that the experiment was repeated some twenty years later. In December 1771 £500 was set aside as premiums for growing flax. Despite a smaller undertaking of only five or six acres, this second attempt seems to have been even more disastrous than the first: in East Lothian the lint boors were unable to obtain the necessary accommodation, and in the Merse the lint boor had to struggle to fulfil his commitments, while the one in Midlothian neither built housing nor finished off his mill.[75] When it came to distributing the £500 set aside, only nine of the seventeen boors qualified for premiums, and the cost to the Board worked out at about 11s Sterling per stone of flax produced.[76]

We must now return to the Board's activities in training labour. In 1753 the Board's training establishment at Hospital Mill was reduced to the status of an ordinary raiser station (p. 178), and to satisfy the continuing need for skilled lint millers it was proposed that apprentices be attached to individual mills where they would be trained at the Board's expense. One of the first to receive apprentices was Angus McDonald's mill at Elie.[77] McDonald was a man held in some esteem by the Trustees, and his first apprentice, who finished in 1763, was sent to the Board's own mill on the Isle of Bute.[78] Of the four other apprentices trained at Elie one, Angus McPherson, worked in the Merse on the Board's second lint boor scheme before taking on Grangehaugh Mill, East Lothian and the post of itinerant flax-raiser.[79] While at Grangehaugh he himself trained at least six apprentices up until the 1790s, and at least one more was trained by his successor, John McPherson.[80]

Hugh Smith, another of the Trustees' close colleagues, had instructed five apprentices at Carnwath Mill by 1765 and went on to train at least three more.[81] From time to time other mills took apprentices, and the practice continued well into the early 19th century.[82] In some cases, as at Kilmartin, Argyll, the Trustees used other means to disperse lint milling skills such as paying for the transport and employment of a skilled dresser. These cases were, however, few and far between and the sponsorship was restricted to a short period.[83]

Although the Trustees continued to operate an apprenticeship scheme, the need to do so was lessened by the great mobility of lint millers who could pass on their skills at one mill before moving to another, often newly built, mill. The careers of two millers, Thomas Ness and Patrick Campbell, illustrate the point well.

Thomas Ness started his training at his father's Hospital Mill in 1741.[84] In 1750 he took a thirty-eight year tack of Lord Deskford's waulk mill at Haugh of Boyne, Banffshire. By March 1751 building work on a lint mill was almost completed and more than twenty acres of flax had been sown. Ness received £140 as a lint boor and became a raiser with salary.[85] In 1758 he was reported to have left Boyne but was apparently still there in 1762, when Lord Deskford agreed to release him to work on a three-year contract for a group of farmers who had built a lint mill at Forgue, Aberdeenshire. By 1763 he was working at Forgue and, as an itinerant flax raiser, had a salary of £10 per annum.[86] From the 1772 survey it appears that Ness had moved again, this time to a lint mill in Banffshire where he had trained the rest of the mill's workers in the art of flax dressing.[87] By 1781 he had made a further move, this time to Glenkindie, Aberdeenshire.[88]

Patrick Campbell was trained as a lint miller at the lint mill of Monzie, Perthshire, where he worked for four years (c. 1749-1753). In 1754, or thereabouts, he left to take charge of a lint mill in Angus, returning to Perthshire the following year to work at Buchanty lint mill. In 1757 he entered the service of Dr. Adam Drummond of Gardrum, at whose mill he worked until 1760. During this time he also supervised the sowing of flax seed. In 1761, with recommendations from Drummond, Campbell moved yet again, this time to Killin, where he oversaw another lint mill. After one year at this mill, he spent three years as a lint heckler before returning to lint dressing, this time at Crieff. In 1764 he was again seeking a post as the manager of a lint mill.[89]

Despite some obvious mistakes such as the lint boor scheme, the Board of Trustees achieved a fair degree of success in teaching and dispersing the skills necessary to operate the rapidly growing number of lint mills. This success was all the greater when one considers the limited assets available to them and the novelty of the technology employed, and while complaints against lint millers were common, the blame did not necessarily lie with the Board. Altogether at least fifty millers were trained at the Board's expense, an achievement which, along with a great mobility, both social and geographical, went a long way towards fulfilling the needs of the industry.

The Mills on the Ground

Numbers

The little work that has been done on Scottish lint mills has not so far established the number of mills actually built.[90] Indeed, it would be quite a daunting task to assess the number for, with the exception of early 18th-century figures and the 1772, 1782 and 1802 surveys, researchers have had no comprehensive figures to work from. Impossible as it is to identify every single lint mill ever built, it should be possible, through the voluminous minutes of the Board of Trustees[91] and other sources, such as county plans and the Old Statistical Account, to establish the minimum number of mills built by a given time, though not necessarily the number in operation. Used in conjunction with the Board's own surveys of 1772 and 1782, these figures can give some indication of 'turnover' through abandonment or change of use, while a known starting point of 1729 and the figures from the first Ordnance Survey maps (1848-1880) help to define the beginning and the end of the lint mill. Figure 41 shows the cumulative number of mills known to have been built, at five-yearly intervals from 1729 to 1829. The substantial gap between the figures for 1769 and 1774 is the result of many mills going unrecorded until the 1772 survey and, that being the case, one can safely assume that figures for the years before 1774 are higher than those plotted.

Whether or not it reflects real patterns, the growth rate is very slow for the first fifteen years, picks up between 1745 and 1754, but almost comes to a halt in the period 1755 to 1759. Growth appears to have been fairly steady between 1759 and 1769. A comparison of mills built with and without Board of Trustees funds (Figure 41) shows a broadly similar trend in both, although the latter grew faster than the former after 1759. By the time of the 1772 survey, nearly 350 lint mills had been constructed, but only 252 are recorded in the survey.[92] This deficiency can be explained in two ways. Firstly, it is possible that the survey is not as comprehensive as Hamilton and McClain have assumed.[93] In a very few cases unrecorded mills can be identified as probably working at the time of the survey: Hospital Mill was one such case.[94] Other

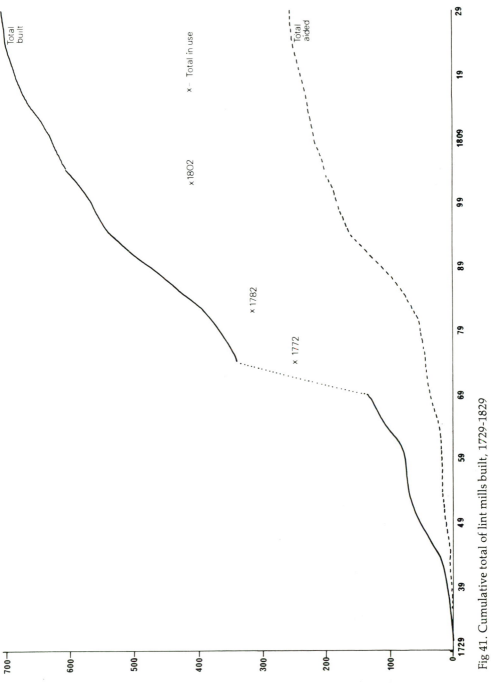

Fig 41. Cumulative total of lint mills built, 1729-1829

mills appear twice: Edinbarnet Mill, for example, was surveyed under Dunbartonshire and Lanarkshire, and (new) Mill of Gray under Angus and Perthshire.[95] It is just as likely that some mills were missed altogether. Further evidence comes from the preparation for later surveys: in 1783 the minutes state that no comprehensive survey has been carried out by that date. If that were the case, the 1772 survey represents no more than one of the reports submitted annually by riding officers. A second explanation, and one which probably accounts for a greater part of the deficit, is that many of the mills founded in the earlier part of the century had ceased to operate by 1772. These early mills in particular were often handicapped by shortages of skilled labour, technological problems and under-utilisation. Assuming therefore that the 1772 figures are approximately correct, it is clear from Figure 41 that by that time mills built without public funds far outnumbered those built with such funds.

The fifteen-year period from 1780 to 1794 witnessed a fifty per cent growth in the total number of mills, from 364 to 538. This unusually rapid growth is largely accounted for by the almost threefold increase in the number of mills built with help from the Board of Trustees (Figure 42); at the same time the ratio of aided to unaided mills changed from 1:5 to 1:2. The results of the 1782 survey show a continued deficit between mills built and mills known to be operating. The fact that the deficit has narrowed suggests that the figure for the total number of mills built has been underestimated.[96]

From 1794 to 1825 growth eases off to a level only half that experienced in the previous fifteen years, with the number of mills built with and without aid each representing about fifty per cent of the total. By the late 1820s lint mill building had almost ceased.

As demand for, and the availability of, funds for mill building decreased so, conversely, the funds for rebuilding increased. From the late 1760s onwards the Board had occasionally funded repairs to mills, though not generally to those previously helped (Figure 43). It was only after 1800, once mill building had slowed down, that the practice became common, representing a significant investent throughout the first three decades of the 19th century.

By 1830 more than seven hundred lint mills had been built in Scotland, and of these more than a third had been partially financed by the Board of Trustees. Considering that no mills had existed prior to 1729, this represented a major success for the Board's policy of encouraging mill building, even if some of these mills ran inefficiently once built. It also represented a large-scale investment in industrial plant: even assuming a very modest construction cost of £80 per mill, the total cost would amount to £56,000 excluding repairs. While part of this sum was provided by the Board of Trustees, the greater part came from private sources. The next section will attempt to identify these.

Mill Builders

From the foregoing section it is apparent that the majority of Scottish lint

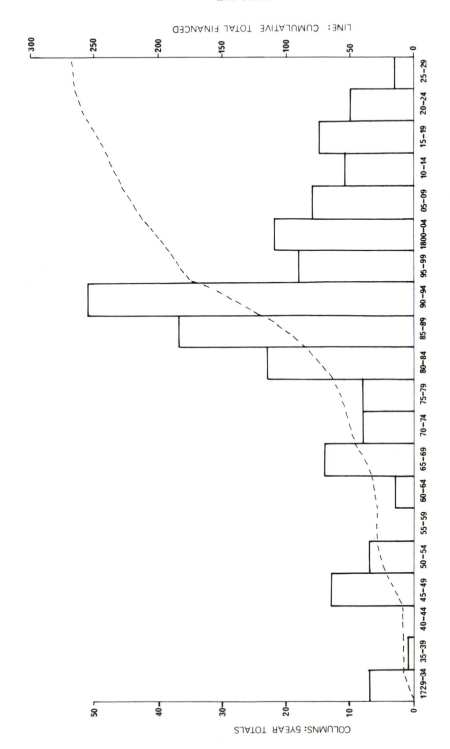

LINE: CUMULATIVE TOTAL FINANCED

COLUMNS: 5YEAR TOTALS

Fig 42. Lint mills built with Board of Trustees aid. *SRO NG1*

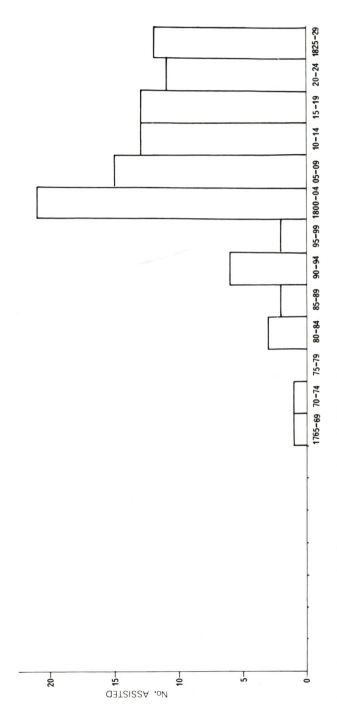

Fig 43. Lint mills repaired with Board of Trustees aid. *SRO NG1*

mills were built unaided and, although financial aid from the Board of Trustees helped in the building of a substantial minority, such assistance could only be obtained after a previous decision on the part of an individual, or group of individuals, to build. A site had to be found and progress on building had to be well advanced before any public funds were forthcoming; only a handful of mills were financed exclusively from public funds.[97]

Details of origin are available for about half of the seven hundred or so mills known to have been built. Unfortunately not all of these are precisely date-able, and in many cases one can only determine the date at which a mill is first recorded. Bearing in mind these limitations, however, it is still possible to group mills chronologically in terms of date built or date first identified and on this basis to establish the social background of those financing mill con-struction. Nor is this limitation as great as it may initially seem to be, for the 1772 survey being nearly comprehensive, all the mills first referred to in the period immediately afterwards must date from that same period.

The years between 1729 and 1745 saw, for the first time, the establishment of lint mills in Scotland. Since the technology was untried and not widely known, it is not surprising to find that almost all the mills built before 1745 were the work of landowners who were, in addition, the only group to possess, at that time, sufficient financial and natural resources to establish mills. Notable among them was Hope of Rankeillor, the well known Improver, whose Hospital Mill became the Board's training centre[98] (see pp. 177-178). In a few cases the initiative lay elsewhere: in 1735 the Linen Society of Glasgow set up a lint mill in a converted waulk mill,[99] and in Renfrewshire one early mill was financed by the magistrates of Paisley, and another by a farmer and a customs officer.[100]

Between 1725 and 1760 the social status of mill builders began to diversify. In those counties in which mills had already been established, such as Perth-shire, Renfrewshire and Midlothian, landowners were joined by tenants and workers in the textile trades such as bleachers, dyers and flax dressers. In those counties where no mills had existed before 1745 and where few were built by 1760, the pioneering work was usually left to landowners, although not always to those with the Improving status of Grant of Monymusk or Lord Belhaven, both of whom established lint mills about 1750.[101] In one or two cases workers in the textile trades built mills in these outlying areas: in Roxburghshire, for example, it was a weaver and in Banffshire a flax dresser who built the first mills in those counties.[102]

In the period 1760-1772 the pattern develops still further, with mill or farm tenants joining the ranks of mill builders in such counties as Perthshire, Angus and Lanarkshire where mills had become well-established. While this may appear to be an important development, a tenant could not usually obtain help from the Board of Trustees if an indifferent or hostile landlord failed to give his support, financial or otherwise.[103] On the other hand some landowners showed an enlightened attitude to providing credit facilities or, as at Moulin in Perthshire, entered into a cost-sharing agreement with a tenant.[104] An increasingly common practice was for the site of a proposed lint mill to be taken on feu.[105]

Areas which had been marginal prior to 1760 now showed signs of diversifying: In Aberdeenshire, for example, flax dressers often built their own mills, but in those counties which were still marginal, such as Berwickshire and Ross-shire, most of the initiative continued to come from the landowning class.

For the remainder of the 18th century, developments in established areas continued to follow the same lines as formerly. The diverse occupations which mill builders pursued began to include masons, millwrights, joiners, ministers and advocates besides the more numerous textile workers and tenants of farms and mills.[106] In these established areas landowners continued to play a role in mill building. In marginal areas it was often major landowners or other Improvers who introduced lint mills: Grant of Grant and the Duke of Gordon both built mills in Inverness-shire, as did Sinclair of Ulbster in Caithness.[107]

A certain amount of interest was also being shown by merchants and manufacturers, either individually or in partnership. The early example of the Glasgow Linen Company has already been cited; in 1756 the British Linen Company had incorporated a lint mill in their Saltoun bleachfield, and the rest of the century saw the increasing involvement of local merchants and manufacturers, particularly in the north and east.[108]

Between 1800 and 1830 the building of new mills and the cultivation of flax declined rapidly (p. 184). Merchants and manufacturers were involved in financing only one mill and landowners only a handful; for the most part construction was undertaken by farm or mill tenants in areas where flax cultivation was well established. Elsewhere, and in other social groups, interest in lint mills was waning rapidly.

Despite the occasional participation of merchants, manufacturers, local authorities and members of the legal profession, their overall significance never reached very great proportions. The vast majority of mill builders were essentially rural in background. Some owned, feued or rented land, some were involved in small-scale textile trades such as heckling, while others had experience in constructing or operating mills. In this respect Scottish lint mills were more closely allied to corn and other grain-processing mills than to the mills built to serve the other, more highly capitalised branches of the linen industry. Although the data impose some limitations, it is possible to discern a regular pattern of development, with an initial commitment by landowners and a subsequent contribution by tenants and other essentially rural groups. This progression was repeated in each area into which lint mills were introduced, up to about 1800, after which the prolonged decay of the flax-growing industry led to a gradual reduction in those areas in which new mills were built, until about 1830, by which time only a few tenants and landowners in isolated corners of central Scotland or upland Perthshire were prepared to put up money for the construction of lint mills.

Distribution

Most of our ideas about the distribution of lint mills are based on the results of the 1772 survey which, with the exception of Wares Mill, Caithness, were plotted by McClain.[109] While these distributions are probably accurate enough for the time to which they relate, they give no idea of the spatial development of the industry before or after that date. The difficulties in obtaining comprehensive figures have already been discussed. Nevertheless a fairly comprehensive list can be drawn up from manuscript sources such as the Minute Books of the Board of Trustees, the Records of the Forfeited Estates Commission and a variety of estate documents, besides published sources such as the Old Statistical Account, the New Statistical Account and county plans.

Bearing in mind their limitations, it should still be possible to obtain a clear picture of the number of lint mills built in any area by a certain time and a less clear but still useful impression of the locality of those mills actually operating.

Figure 44 shows the number of mills built or first referred to in the period 1729-1744. Most of the twenty mills built before 1745, for which locations are known, occupy a broad belt across central Scotland from Renfrewshire in the south-west to Angus in the north-east, with two eastern outliers, Aberdeenshire and Berwickshire. While there are no references to Perthshire mills, some probably did exist, but independently of the Board's activities.

The distribution of mills in Figure 45 (1745-1760) reinforces this view to some extent, with no fewer than twenty-one Perthshire mills recorded for the first time. The strongest development occurred in east-central Scotland in an area which included Midlothian in the south. Developments in west-central Scotland were less marked, but mills had begun to spread outwith the central area into south-east Scotland and from Aberdeenshire to the Moray Firth area. In Argyll the establishment of mills is surprisingly strong, owing much to the work of major landowners such as Campbell of Barcaldine.[110] Indeed the wider spread of mills generally owes much to the innovating role of enlightened landowners. As the survey of 1772 gives the first comprehensive review, the very high figures for the period 1760-1772 must reflect, to some extent, a backlog of sites from earlier periods. The pattern that emerges (Figure 46) tends to reinforce that of earlier times: a strong concentration in the central Lowlands with extensions into the straths of Perthshire and round the eastern coastal fringe. In west-central Scotland the lag in growth between 1745 and 1760 may have been more apparent than real, although the apparently strong growth in the period 1760-1772 may be partly attributable to the transfer of flax-growing premiums in 1763 from Perthshire, Fife and Forfarshire to Dunbartonshire, Lanarkshire, Stirlingshire, Renfrewshire and Ayrshire.[111] Nevertheless, it is difficult to accept that the number of mills in Dunbartonshire jumped straight from nought to eighteen in so short a time.

The diffusion outwith central Scotland continued with consolidation in Aberdeenshire and Banffshire, so that by 1772 lint mills had been built in all but five of the counties of the Scottish mainland. As for the number of mills actually working, Figure 47 shows that the counties of west-central Scotland

1729-44

Fig 44. Lint mills first recorded 1729-44

1745-59

Fig 45. Lint mills first recorded 1745-59

1760-72

Fig 46. Lint mills first recorded 1760-72

1772

Fig 47. Lint mills, 1772 survey

were on a par with those of the east by 1772, assuming, that is, that the survey is comprehensive. It is interesting to note that none of the six mills built in Argyll and only two of the ten in Midlothian are listed. Omissions apart, this suggests that most of the mills in these 'marginal' areas had been short-lived and of limited viability.

While the figures for 1773-1789 (Figure 48) may not be comprehensive, there is little chance of their including mills built before the 1772 survey. The most striking change is the widespread diffusion of mills from the central Lowlands into the Borders, Galloway and Inverness-shire. By contrast, very little building took place in the area around east Dunbartonshire which had previously experienced extensive mill construction. In Inverness-shire the Duke of Gordon and Grant of Grant were among those who built mills, but in the Borders and Galloway the initiative often lay with smaller landowners or with millers and farmers.

It would appear from Figure 49 that the area in which lint mills were still being built in the 1790s was already contracting and that the principal area had shifted on to a more polar axis, running from Buchan to north-eastern Lanark-shire. The Dumfries area and the straths of Perthshire continued to show sig-nificant new building while Kincardineshire, a county formerly with very few mills, saw extensive mill construction. It is tempting to see the sparseness of new mills in west-central Scotland as a reflection of the displacement of linen by cotton; certainly during the two decades up to 1800 the area had ex-perienced a meteoric rise in the number of water-powered cotton mills and of 'jenny' mills in Glasgow itself. What is more, the amount of linen cloth produced there was falling sharply.[112] However, much more research would be necessary to establish a direct causal relationship. Various writers have recog-nised a switch in west-central Scotland from linen to cotton, and McClain goes so far as to imply that in this area lint mills were practically extinct by the 1790s.[113]

The distribution pattern for new mills in the period 1800-1814 (Figure 50) does not really tally with such a view. By far the strongest concentration is in the poorer land of central Scotland between Edinburgh and Glasgow. Else-where too it is the more isolated mills, on poorer land, which make up the bulk of the sites: upland Perthshire, Kirkcudbrightshire and Cunninghame all figure prominently.

This 'retreat' can be ascribed to at least two forces. Firstly, the availability of good land for flax cultivation was very restricted. For some time flax had suffered the reputation of being an 'exhausting' crop which took nutrients from the soil without replacing them.[114] While this view was still being challenged in the early 19th century, it was probably the Napoleonic wars which drove flax cultivation off much of Lowland Scotland. The impact of the wars on arable cultivation is well documented[115] and can still be seen in the broad green rigs which flank the margins of present-day cultivation. And just as the need to grow food crops created a boom in grain mill construction so, conversely, it led to a slump in flax cultivation and lint mill construction. Only on the poorer

1772-89

Fig 48. Lint mills first recorded 1772-89

1790-99

Fig 49. Lint mills first recorded 1790-99

1800-14

Fig 50. Lint mills first recorded 1800-14

lands, such as those in the great empty heart of central Scotland, could flax compete. The second major factor was the mechanisation of flax-spinning which, while by no means perfected, increased the centralisation of spinning and the use of imported flax at the expense of the locally grown and spun product. Furthermore, it should be borne in mind that while the overall impression is one of decline in east-central Scotland, there is reason to believe that many existing mills, built before 1800, continued to operate at least for a decade or so after that date.

·In the post-war period (Figure 51) the further decline of flax-mill building is apparent, with an even more marked centralisation in mid-central Scotland. By 1815 Lanarkshire was the most important flax-growing county in Scotland and ranked first among those counties where new mills were being built.[116] In much of Lowland Scotland cotton had taken over the role formerly held by linen, and while the volume of the home crop fluctuated widely, the difficulties of cultivating flax can hardly have helped its position *vis a vis* cotton or imported flax. In the traditional flax-growing region of east-central Scotland mill spinning was becoming the rule, using imported flax, and often employing the sites occupied previously by lint mills.

Mid-central Scotland continued to occupy a leading role for the period that the truncated flax industry survived after 1830: of the forty or so lint mills mentioned in the New Statistical Account (c.1834-45) eleven lay in a belt between western West Lothian and north-east Lanarkshire, twelve in the Grampian area and five in south-west Scotland. By contrast only two were mentioned in Fife, five in Perthshire and one in Angus.[117] Many of these forty were little used, although one in Kirkmichael parish, Ayrshire was still dressing two hundred stones of flax per annum.[118] About an equal number of mills appear in the first Ordnance Survey maps (c.1848-1878), half of these in mid-central Scotland and a substantial part of the remainder in upland Perthshire. Over much of Scotland, however, the lint mill had long since passed into history. Figure 52 shows the distribution of all mills known to have been built in Scotland.

A Scottish Lint Mill: Grangehaugh Mill, East Lothian

No mill illustrates the points already made better than Grangehaugh Mill, East Lothian. While its situation is hardly central to the flax-growing regions of Scotland, its unusually good documentation reveals a complex history which exemplifies most of the features already referred to more generally.

Grangehaugh Mill was constructed in 1750 by Lord Belhaven, an Improving landowner and a member of the Board of Trustees for Manufactures.[119] The site chosen was on the northern side of Biel Water at the western edge of Biel estate in the parish of Stenton (Figure 53). From the remains still visible today the mill would appear to have been a two-storey, red sandstone rubble building with well-faced jambs and lintels and a breast-shot wheel of about ten feet in diameter. The ark, also in well-faced stone, fits closely around the site

1815-30

Fig 51. Lint mills first recorded 1815-30

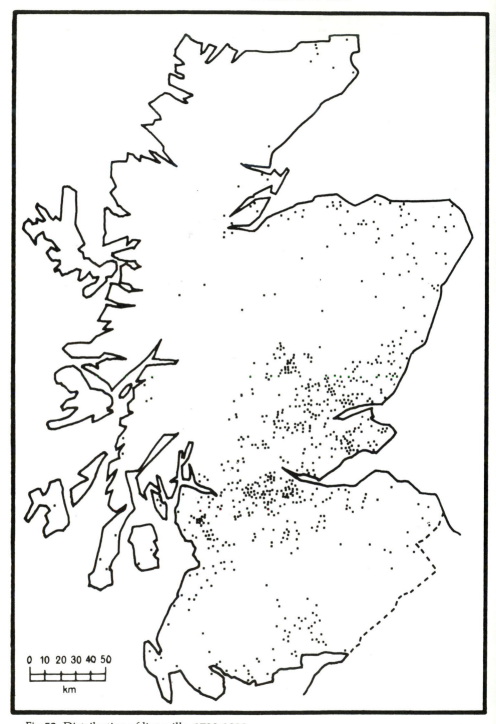

Fig 52. Distribution of lint mills, 1729-1830

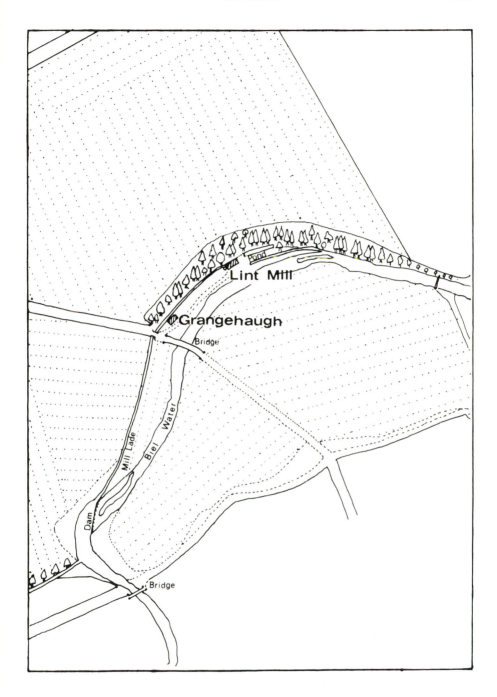

Fig 53. The environs of Grangehaugh lint mill

of the wheel, and the mill may have been the work of the Meikle brothers: by the early 1750s Andrew Meikle had taken up residence at Houston Mill, only three miles away.[120] This, with the attested expertise of the Meikles in lint mill design (p. 173), would have made him an obvious choice.

On 12th January 1750 the Board's secretary wrote to John Ness at Hospital Mill asking that one Thomas Finlayson from the parish of Stenton and shire of Haddington

> be instructed by you in all your art of breaking, bruising and swingling fflax by the miln, and in every art and mystery concerning the dressing flax by the miln and concerning the miln itself so far as you know or practise yourself; you are to pay him of wages for his work while with you at the rate of 3d each day he works; so soon he is fully instructed you are to give him a certificate under your hand testifying the same accordingly . . .[121]

Having completed his training, Finlayson entered into a twenty-one year tack of Grangehaugh Mill, to run from Whitsunday 1750.[122] On 24th July he was conditionally offered the post of raiser:

> The Trustees for the Manufactures have appointed you flax raiser at Beild with a salary of £15 by the year to take place for this current year in case you shall perform, and that any one of the flax raisers now on the establishment shall not perform the conditions required and not otherways — I therefore send you ten copies of the Trustees instructions for their stationed flax raisers and twenty copies of rules and directions for raising flax and hemp which you are to observe and distribute what copies of each you can spare to proper persons in your neighbourhood.[123]

On 22nd March arrangements were made for Finlayson to undertake the second part of his training, and the following letter was sent to John Keysar, Flanders flax raiser at Musselburgh:

> The Trustees present Thomas Finlayson from Beild in the shire of Haddington, to be instructed by you in all your art of raising flax, that is to say the preparing the ground, pulling, watering, grassing and every other part of the mystery by you known or practised. You are also to instruct him in the art of swingling by stock & hand — you are to pay him of wages for his work while with you at the rate of three pence sterling each day he works for the first month & five pence sterling each day he works for the other five months. So soon as he is fully instructed, you are to give him a certificate under your hand, testifying the same accordingly.[124]

In June 1750 the Board had considered James Brown at Beesknowe, on the Biel estate, as a possible lint boor for the following year,[125] but as tacksman of a lint mill Finlayson was a more obvious choice. Early in 1751 he was promised a post as lint boor.[126] Finlayson already had a mill, and by May of that year, having fulfilled his commitment to sow twenty acres of flax, he was given his £140.[127] On 5th March 1751 his post of raiser had been confirmed, with an obligation to raise ten acres;[128] thus, within eighteen months of starting his training, Finlayson had earned the double distinction of being both lint raiser and lint boor.

Besides dressing flax from lands rented by Finlayson (Figure 54), the mill also took in flax grown by other individuals at farms throughout the eastern half of the county. Figure 55 shows the origin of flax dressed between December 1751 and August 1752.

The wide hinterland from which flax came is probably larger than that of most flax mills and owes much to the lack of intervening opportunity and the comparatively good roads of East Lothian.[129] While the produce of the mill was small and continued to be so, it was nevertheless economically viable, making a profit of £11 0s 11¾d on crop 1751-1752, £17 14s 11d in 1753, £9 7s 4d in 1754, £28 19s 6d in 1755 and £6 12s 1d in 1756.[130] This profitability may well have stemmed from Finlayson's thoroughness, a quality which earned him a £5 premium for 'the most distinct abstract' in three successive years.[131]

An agreement dated 1754 to run during Finlayson's contract with the Board of Trustees gives some insight into the nature of the partnership between Belhaven and Finlayson. Under the terms of the agreement they were to share equally the profits on flax raised, dressed and heckled. The cost of carrying out repairs to the mill was also to be halved between them. Finlayson was not to buy any flax on his own account without letting Belhaven have a share and was to keep accounts.[132] Finlayson continued to receive a salary from the Trustees right up to 1758 when raisers ceased to be paid as such.[133] Even after this he was one of three lint millers paid at £5 per annum, a sum which he continued to receive until 1763.[134] From that time onwards, or possibly earlier, the mill was rented at £4 per annum, but after a fire in 1766 the rent was given up on condition that Finlayson repaired the damage and left the mill in good order at the expiry of his lease.[135]

In the survey of 1772 Grangehaugh Mill receives a good report. The supply of water was adequate for nine months of the year; flax was broken by rollers, while the perpendicular scutchers provided space for nine persons to work simultaneously. The loft was said to be 'prety large' and capable of holding a considerable quantity of flax, while the machinery and the 'sufficiency' of work were both considered to be good. All in all, the impression is of a large, well-run mill and, despite its small volume of business (159 stones, crop 1770), rates for scutching and heckling were kept down to 2s and 1s per stone Tron respectively.[136]

Under the lint boor scheme of 1772 both Finlayson and James Wood, a heckler from Stenton village, were accepted for posts. It soon became apparent, however, that neither would be able to find the necessary housing and accommodation;[137] in all probability Finlayson had failed to obtain a renewal of his previous twenty-one-year tack. In March 1773 the Board refused to pay them £3 per acre for the little flax they had planted,[138] and in the following July Finlayson was dropped from the scheme.[139] After this no more is heard of him.

By 1778 the mill had come into the possession of Angus McPherson. McPherson had trained at Elie under McDonald (p. 181) and had shown some success as a lint boor in the Merse, despite difficult circumstances. It is not

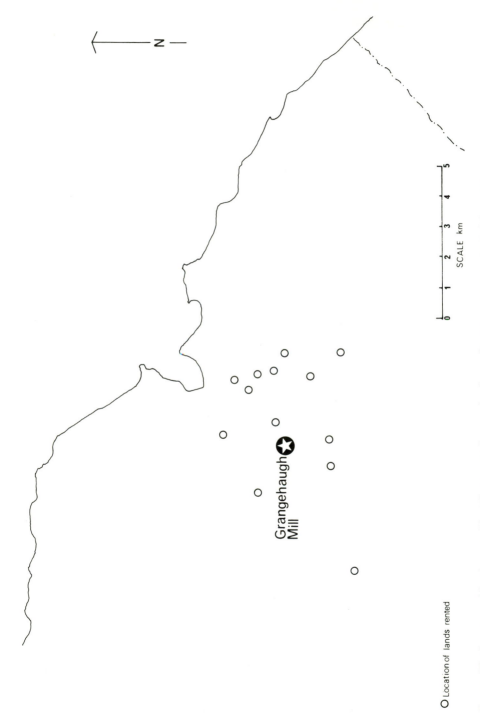

Fig 54. The location of lands rented by Thomas Finlayson for flax cultivation, 1751-2. *SRO GD6/1275*

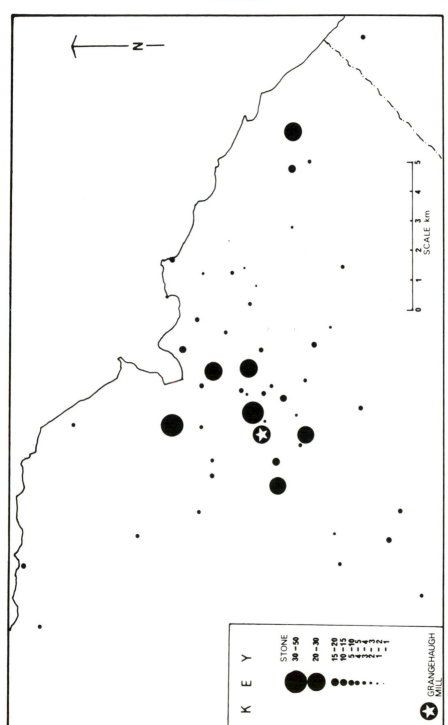

Fig 55. Origin of flax dressed at Grangehaugh lint mill, 1751-2. *SRO GD6/1275*

easy, therefore, to reconcile this with the state of affairs which existed in 1778-1779. In 1778 local farmers petitioned the Board of Trustees requesting that another lint mill be built.[140] The Board decided to make enquiries into the quantity of flax dressed at the mill, the best site for a new mill and who would build it.[141] Shortly afterwards, in a second petition, the farmers claimed that they were unable to have their 1776 crop dressed for want of a lint mill in the county.[142] The situation cannot have been rectified that year, for in January 1779 the Board received yet another complaint.[143] This lapse is not easily explained; on the basis of the low figures for 1772 it is hardly likely that demand for dressing had outstripped the capacity of the nine-port mill unless there had been a particularly severe drought. Nor does it appear to have been due to any deficiency on the part of McPherson; he had already gained a good reputation as a flax boor and a few years later, in 1782, was to be sent two apprentices, a privilege reserved for only the most favoured of lint millers. Whatever the cause, the problem seems to have resolved itself. In 1781 the old paper mill at Gifford (pp. 57-59) was converted to dress flax; this may have helped to take any pressure off Grangehaugh.[144]

By 1785 the two apprentices, taken on in 1782, had completed their training and McPherson, now the Board's itinerant flax raiser, was given two more. Subsequent evidence suggests that he continued to take on apprentices on the Board's behalf, and at its expense, until at least 1794.[145] Yet another apprentice was taken on in 1806, this time by John McPherson, probably the son of Angus.[146] The McPhersons benefited from the Board of Trustees in other respects too. In the early 1790s Angus McPherson was granted £10 to build a flax storage shed, and in 1806 another shed was built. For this latter and for renewing the mill's machinery John McPherson received £24.[147] The mill continued to operate until the second quarter of the nineteenth century, although the minutes of the Board of Trustees contain no references to the mill, or to McPherson, after 1806.[148]

Considering the mill's doubtful viability, even in the 1770s, its survival into the 1820s is very surprising. East Lothian was never a major flax-growing county, and the war years in the early 19th century must have all but driven the crop off its highly productive lands. Once the mill had closed, or possibly in its later years as a working mill, the lade was modified to supply threshing mills at Biel Grange and Beesknowe.[149] The age of flax growing was over; like so many other lint mills all over Scotland, Grangehaugh had reached the end of its useful life.

Summary

It must be acknowledged that, according to the present arrangement, the substitution of machinery in place of hand labour for preparing flax has obstructed instead of facilitating improvement in this branch of industry.[150]

In the century between 1729 and 1830 the Board of Trustees, handicapped by a small and variable budget, had mechanised flax dressing, helped finance the building of some two hundred and eighty mills and offered technical aid to others, had provided facilities and finance for the training of lint millers and had paid salaries to many of these once trained. Together with private individuals they had built over seven hundred mills using machinery previously unknown in Scotland. Why, then, is the general view, among both contemporaries and historians, one of failure?

To some extent the blame must lie with the Board of Trustees. Although they encouraged flax-growing, they could not guarantee that mills would be available to dress it or that there would be buyers to take it. The lint boor scheme, involving an investment of £140 per person over a three-year period, was at best misguided and at worst foolhardy, failing as it did to take account of Scottish conditions. However, as Naismith was later to concede, the task of co-ordinating the introduction of flax cultivation and of lint mills was an extremely difficult one.[151] Furthermore, the financing of mills was open to abuse although, to give them their due, the Trustees did try to crack down on this in later days. All things considered, however, their worst crime was to hope for too much too soon and on too small a budget.

Where, then, did the blame lie, if not with the Board of Trustees? According to Lord Kames, the root of the problem lay in 'the indolence and ignorance of the low people, and their want of honesty'.[152] Indeed, human failings accounted for many of the inadequacies found in lint mills. Lord Kames makes a criticism traditionally directed at corn millers:

> the lint miller, being under no check nor control, is tempted to defraud his customers of part of their dressed flax: and there are instances where the whole has been withheld from poor people, who it was thought would not have courage to bring a law suit.[153]

Naismith blamed the lack of skilled labour:

> The millers, keeping no more hands than what are barely necessary to expose the flax to the action of the machine, and those preparers not being deeply interested in the success of the operation, the work is often passed over in a slovenly manner, and all kinds of flax subjected promiscuously to the same treatment without any pains being taken to distinguish their different qualities.[154]

Whatever the Board's efforts in training a skilled labour force, they were, in effect, unable to overcome the problems of an essentially seasonal industry. The 1772 survey shows that at the best mills, such as Elie, labour was engaged for the whole year. In one case, at Quartalehouse, Aberdeenshire, the miller had brought an expert hand from Perthshire, and between them they had trained the rest of the labour force which had been there ever since.[155] On the other hand there were many lint millers, especially in the west of Scotland, who had to be content with hiring labour for the winter months only, and not necessarily those hired the previous year. At a Banffshire mill, referred to by McClain, the miller had managed to accommodate the problem: three of his six employees were masons who worked at their trade during the summer months and three were farmers who farmed all year round but worked at the mill in their spare time.[156] At one stage the Board sought to rectify the situation by suggesting that mills be built alongside bleachfields, the latter providing work during the summer months: this was the system adopted at Cullen, Banffshire.[157] However, the policy had to be modified after a lint mill fire at Balgersho, Perthshire, which destroyed valuable bleaching machinery in 1768.[158]

The human element in the form of either deliberate dishonesty or an un-avoidable shortage of skilled labour was only one reason for the notoriety of lint mills. Another was the physical state of the mills themselves. At an early stage lint mills gained a reputation for damaging flax; Lord Kames claimed that:

> the ordinary yield of this mill in dressed flax is so much inferior in quantity to that of stock in hand as to overbalance fully what is saved upon labour; not to mention the hurt that is done to the flax by the violent and ill-directed action of the mill.[159]

Naismith believed that the momentum of ordinary scutching mills was too great and that the horizontal action of the scutching arm was too severe.[160] He also suggested that flax dressers put too much faith in the powers of the mill: 'By relying on the execution of the mill, the attention of the man is in a great measure removed'.[161] Despite his criticisms Naismith went on to clear the basic design principle from blame:

> The application of machinery would nevertheless be of great service, under proper regulations. Notwithstanding the clamour which disappointment has raised against skutching mills, there is nothing in the construction or impetus of these engines to prevent flax being cleaned by them in the most advantageous manner, provided the previous processes have been skilfully conducted, and the flax fitted to undergo the operation.[162]

Not only the Board's experiments, but also those of Naismith himself con-firmed his view.[163]

Another shortcoming was the lack of storage facilities: 'In many places there is not sufficient house-room provided for the flax that is brought to the mill; which in a throng time is often exposed to the air for months together before the miller can reach it'.[164] Flax left out in the open often reached the mill in an unfit state, resulting in a poorly dressed product.[165] The financial aid which the Board offered for shed building (p. 175) and for experiments on drying ovens (p. 176) probably went some way towards solving this problem.

A third set of difficulties arose from the siting and situation of mills. The most serious fault in siting was a failure to have sufficient command of water. This was alleviated to some extent by the seasonal nature of the lint mill's work but, even so, many mills were seriously handicapped by dry spells, whilst low water, by slowing down the scutching arms, resulted in badly scutched flax.[166] The situation of mills was not always the most convenient for flax growers. Because of the scale and fixed capital cost (about £80-£120) of lint mills, the chances were that even in those areas where flax was widely cultivated some farmers would have to carry their flax several miles to be dressed. In more marginal areas, where a mill's hinterland was much wider (such as Grangehaugh), and communications often difficult, the effort involved must have been a strong disincentive at a time when many small farmers did not even possess a cart.[167] On the other hand there were those areas which had mills but which failed to produce a large enough crop to make them financially viable.[168] Distance from markets must have been a further disincentive, even to those farmers who had managed to get their crop to a mill. Granted, farmers in Angus, Fife or Perthshire could often sell their crop on the ground, and the flax-buying powers vested in lint boors may have temporarily alleviated the situation in a few areas, but for the most part the problem remained unresolved.[169]

A Note on Oil Mills

Although not strictly speaking a branch of the linen textile industry, oil mills logically belong with it inasmuch as their raw material was derived from flax grown for manufacture into linen. Seed, generally that unsuitable for propagation, was *rippled* or separated from the flax plant and crushed to produce an oil which found a ready market, both within and without Scotland, in the treatment of woodwork (especially furniture) in making varnish and, when mixed with ochre, in making a paint known as Spanish brown.[170]

Technology

From specifications drawn up in 1780 for an oil mill at Mill of Struthill, Perthshire, it is possible to obtain a fairly detailed picture of the mechanics of a Scottish oil mill in the 18th century. The mill was to be built in stone, fifty feet by twenty-two feet, with a slate roof. Inside, it had a ground floor and two separate lofts. From an external wheel, via an axletree, two more axletrees, one horizontal and one vertical, drove the oil press and stampers respectively. The latter were probably used to break up the seeds prior to pressing. As for the press itself, it consisted of one horizontal stone six feet in diameter by ten inches thick, upon which revolved two vertical stones, six feet in diameter by fourteen inches thick, which crushed the seed in their circular path. The whole press was enclosed in iron supplied from Carron, the same material being used for axletrees. Although this particular mill included stamps, it seems probable that some mills had only a set of vertical stones, the initial breaking being performed by hand.[171]

As far as is known, there were few major technical advances during the period when oil mills operated in Scotland. In 1766 John Craig at Linlithgow Bridge claimed to have made improvements in oil mill design and was asked by the Board of Trustees for a model and estimates for a full-sized mill.[172]

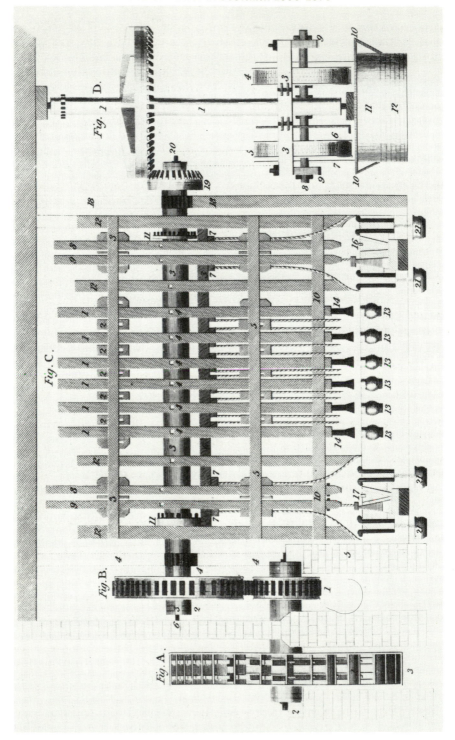

Nothing is known of the nature of these improvements or of the fate of Craig's design. In 1805 David MacVicar and George Sandeman in Perth asked the Board for encouragement to build a mill to crush lintseed oil, in return for which they offered to send a person to England to look for improvements. The Board appears to have found the application rather vague, and no more is heard of the proposed mill.[173] Figure 56 illustrates the machinery of an oil mill about 1810.

The Mills on the Ground

In the *Scots Courant* for 14th August 1719, the Duke of Atholl advertised that he had had much success in growing not only lint seed but rape seed and offered enough for one acre to anyone who would try it. As a further incentive and a means of reaping some benefit himself, he offered £20 Sterling for each boll of Scottish-grown seed sent to the 'Oyl Mill of Huntingtower' before Michaelmas 1720.[174] This is the earliest reference to a Scottish oil mill. No other sites have been positively identified prior to the 1760s, although it is probable that others had been built by then: the suggestion, in 1730, that oil-crushing machinery be modified to dress flax at Bonnington Mills indicates that the technology was already fairly well-known.[175] Craig's claim to have improved the design of oil mills adds further support to the view that other oil mills were operating in Scotland prior to 1766 (p. 209). Perhaps the most conclusive evidence is to be found in the premiums offered by the Board of Trustees in 1771 for seed producers who sent the greatest quantities of seed to the mill.

Although proposals were made in 1767 for a mill at Culcrieff, Perthshire and detailed specifications were drawn up, it would appear that it was never built.[176] However, there were at least two oil mills operating in Strathearn by 1775, one at Crieff, the other near Abernethy.[177] The next twenty years saw the construction of a dozen or so others, and while these included one at Gourock, Renfrewshire, by far the greatest number were situated in the flax-growing area of east-central Scotland and, notably, in Strathearn (Figure 57).

In contrast to their activities in connection with lint mills, the Board of Trustees had little to do with oil mills. No records exist of the aid given for mill building, although on its own estates the Forfeited Estates Commission fulfilled this role, a fact which may account for the concentration of oil mills in western Strathearn on its Perth estate. There is only one reference to the Board of Trustees offering an incentive to growers, in 1771, when premiums totalling £35 were offered to seven persons who sent the greatest quantity of flax seed of their own raising to oil mills.[178] With this one exception, the only aspect of oil milling to attract their attention was the nature of the seed used, for there was a real danger of the bad seed reserved for milling finding its way onto the

Fig 56. Machinery of an oil mill, early 19th century. A: water wheel. B: gearing. C: stampers. D: edge-runner crushing mill. *Jamieson, 1827*

Fig 57. Distribution of oil mills, 1730-1830

market as sowing seed. In 1781 a complaint was made to the Board concerning the sale of bad seed, the proprietors of Balbirnie Mill being singled out for blame.[179] By 1799, with this type of abuse in mind, the Board of Trustees had imposed a ban on the import of bad seed for milling.[180] In 1800 the legislation was modified so as to allow the importation of bad seed on condition that security was given, but this was revoked in 1804, possibly as a result of abuses.[181] Persistent complaints by oil millers failed to move the Board, although they occasionally gave tacit approval to the import of bad seed. According to the millers, most of their mills were built at a time when seed could be imported freely, and as a result of the ban they were frequently at a standstill. At a time when domestic flax cultivation was in decline the hardship must have been all the greater. The mill owners also contrasted the situation in Scotland with that in England and Ireland where there were no restrictions on the importation of crushing seed.[182] Finally, in 1810, the Board gave way and agreed to allow importation for a trial period.[183] While no details are available as to the length of the trial, in all probability the ban was dropped, for by the 1830s a mill had been built at Port Seton, East Lothian, in a situation where it would probably have used imported seed.[184]

Mill Builders

Like lint mills, oil mills were often built on the initiative of farmers and land-owners, but there was also a strong mercantile element more commonly found in the other sectors of the linen industry. This may reflect the heavier financial commitment which, in the absence of aid from the Board of Trustees, was necessary to build an oil mill. It may also be a reflection of the need for marketing facilities.

As we have seen, Scotland's first oil mill was built by the Duke of Atholl, a well-known Improving landowner. By the 1770s and 1780s, however, the initiative had passed to other groups. It was a merchant, Patrick Arnot, who built the mill at Crieff in 1774,[185] while the Mill of Struthill (1780) was a joint venture involving a farmer and a merchant (see below).[186] The rival mill, at Milnab (1780), involved three partners including James Wright, smith and farrier in Crieff.[187] The mill at Gartchonzie, near Callander, was one of two mills operated by Arthur Buchanan, a tenant farmer.[188] At the same time and in a similar manner to lint mills the interest of landowners which had been apparent in the founding of the first mills continued throughout the 18th century.[189]

Two Scottish Oil Mills: Mill of Struthill and Milnab, Perthshire

The development of the Scottish oil mill is probably best exemplified by two mills in Strathearn, the Mill of Struthill and Milnab. Both date from 1780, during the period which saw the construction of most Scottish mills, and both are well documented in the records of the Forfeited Estates Commission.

On 14th November 1780 Patrick Davidson in Drummawhance and Matthew Finlayson, merchant in Muthill, petitioned the Forfeited Estates Commission, pointing out that local flax-raising had increased greatly and that farmers were taking the trouble of saving their lint seed. The petitioners went on to propose that they be given a forty-one-year lease, timber and other aid, in return for which they would convert the Mill of Struthill to crush lint seed.[190] As the mill was one of four corn mills within a few miles of each other, the tenant was finding it hard to pay for its upkeep and was only too glad to resign his tack in their favour.[191] The Commission's factor added his approval to the venture, pointing out that in the previous year Patrick Arnot's mill at Crieff had had more seed than it could handle.[192]

The very next day the Commission was sent another petition, this time from James Wright, smith and farrier in Crieff, proposing to build an oil mill below the Nether Mill of Milnab in Crieff parish. Objections were raised on the grounds that it would flood good land, while the factor, Thomas Keir, advised against the 'encouragement' of two oil mills at the same time. In his opinion the Mill of Struthill was a more deserving project.[193] Undeterred by this rebuff, Wright wrote to the Commissioners pointing out that the Mill of Struthill was 'in a wilderness', a long way from anywhere and with only enough water to work for eight hours per day.[194]

In the meantime the promoters of Struthill Mill had drawn up detailed specifications and costings and had asked the Commission for blown or dead ash, plane, beech or oak from which to make machinery.[195] In the absence of any evidence to the contrary, it would appear that the mill received financial help from the Commission.

At Milnab, on the other hand, no financial aid was given, although the Commission supplied some timber from Drummond Park for heavy machinery.[196] It was perhaps with a view to acquiring additional capital that Wright joined with two others, John Cook and Thomas Caw; together they set about implementing an enlarged plan to include not only an oil mill but also a paper mill (cf. Chapter 22, p. 360).[197] Caw dropped out of the partnership at an early stage, but Wright and Cook succeeded in obtaining from the Commissioners a forty-one-year tack of land at Milnab, at three guineas per annum. By 1782 the mill had been completed at a cost to the partners of nearly £400.[198]

A report on the Perth Estate, compiled in 1783 by William Frend, gives some indication of the relative fortunes of the two mills. The Mill of Struthill had been sublet to one Robert Sorley at a very high rent. Like the last tenant of the corn mill, Sorley was unable to pay for the upkeep of the mill, with the inevitable result that it had 'gone to ruin entirely', putting local lintseed growers to some inconvenience. Paradoxically, Frend recommended that the mill be converted to grind meal.

In contrast, the mill at Milnab was in good order and 'likely to answer well'. The paper mill, which had not answered so well, was to be converted to a flour mill.[199] Both mills continued to operate until the 1790s, by which time Milnab was pressing three to four hundred bolls per annum, the locally grown lint seed being purchased at 18s per boll.[200] No details are available for the Mill of Struthill.[201] By 1860, when the first Ordnance Survey maps were surveyed, the Mill of Struthill had disappeared off the face of the earth, but Milnab was one of only two oil mills still operating in Scotland. Obviously Wright's faith in his site had been well-founded.

The Fate of the Oil Mills

While the period 1775-1795 appears to have been a Golden Age for Scottish oil mills, the early years of the 19th century seem to have brought an abrupt end to it. Those mills which had depended on home-grown seed must have suffered badly from the decline of domestic flax cultivation, while those using imported seed were hampered, at least temporarily, by import restrictions. Furthermore, the competition from England and Ireland, of which the petitioners had spoken in 1810, may finally have proved too much for Scottish oil millers. The mill on the Dichty near Dundee, which in the 1790s had been crushing eight hundred bolls of lint seed per annum and exporting oil to London at 1s 3d per pint, closed down shortly afterwards.[202] The oil mill at Bridge of Balgonie, Fife had gone out of production by 1830,[203] and by 1860 one mill in Auchterarder parish, Perthshire had been converted to grind farina or potato flour.[204] Many others, including Gartchonzie and the mill in Abernethy parish, had ceased to exist. As with flax scutching mills, time had run out for Scottish oil mills.

NOTES

1. Robertson, J., *General View of the Agriculture of Inverness-shire*, London, 1808, 151.

2. Singer, C., Holmyard, E. J., Hall, A. R., Williams, T. I. (eds.), *A History of Technology*, 5 vols., Oxford, 1956-9, III, 157.

3. McCutcheon, W. A., 'Water Power in the North of Ireland', in *TNS* XXXIX (1966-7), 73.

4. SRO NG1/1/2: Patterson of Drygrange asks encouragement to refit and amend a machine for flax dressing, set up by him *some years ago* on the Water of Leader. Brown, R., *The History of Paisley*, 2 vols., Paisley, 1886, I, 398; SRO NG1/1/3 20/7/1733: Petition from the town of Paisley — set up lint mill *several years ago* for 3,000 Merks. Now in disrepair. Hear that there is a better way.

5. SRO NG1/1/1 1/9/1727.

6. SRO NG1/1/2 19/9/29; SRO NG1/1/2 12/12/29.

7. SRO NG1/1/1 26/4/1728.

8. SRO NG1/1/1 18/7/29.

9. SRO NG1/1/2 28/11/1729.

10. SRO NG1/1/2 10/3/30.

11. SRO NG1/1/2 27/11/1730.

12. SRO NG1/1/4 10/1/35.

13. SRO NG1/1/6 25/4/40.

14. SRO NG1/1/8 7/11/46; 18/3/47. One of the machines mentioned at the 1747 meeting as being designed by James Hog was the subject of a report by the Meikles in 1754. The Minute books give no details. SRO NG1/1/13 4/11/55.

15. SRO NG1/1/8 12/6/47.

16. SRO NG1/1/22 13/1/79; 3/2/79.

17. SRO NG1/1/11 18/1/51; 22/2/51; 3/1/52.

18. SRO NG1/1/11 7/6/51.

19. Hamilton, H. (ed.), *Life and Labour on an Aberdeenshire Estate, 1735-1750,* Aberdeen, 1946.

20. Stewart, A., *A Highland Parish or the History of Fortingall,* Glasgow, 1928, 173.

21. Hamilton, *op. cit.,* 146-7.

22. SRO NG1/19/1: Reports Anent Lint Mills; McCutcheon, *op. cit.,* 73-5.

23. SRO NG1/1/20 24/11/73. For an estimate of the cost of such a mill, see SRO GD248/954/1.

24. SRO NG1/19/1 Edinburgh 2.

25. SRO NG1/1/16 22/1/62.

26. SRO NG1/1/16 21/1/61; 22/1/62; SRO NG1/1/19 12/3/68.

27. SRO NG1/1/17 15/8/63.

28. Home, Henry (Lord Kames), *Progress of Flax Husbandry in Scotland,* Edinburgh, 1766, 23.

29. SRO NG1/1/18 12/3/64.

30. SRO NG1/1/18 20/1/66; SRO NG1/19/1 Lanarkshire 7.

31. SRO NG1/1/18 27/11/66; 24/3/67; 4/3/68.

32. SRO NG1/19/1 Lanarkshire; SRO NG1/1/19 26/7/68; 13/8/68.

33. SRO NG1/1/19 12/2/70; 29/1/72; SRO NG1/19/1 Lanarkshire 10.

34. SRO NG1/1/20 28/7/73.

35. SRO NG1/1/20 15/12/73; SRO NG1/1/22 5/8/78; SRO NG1/1/23 31/1/82; SRO NG1/1/24 16/6/84; 30/6/84; SRO NG1/1/25 9/8/86; 29/6/85.

36. SRO NG1/1/25 28/11/85.

37. SRO NG1/1/16 21/1/61; SRO NG1/1/29 28/6/97.

38. SRO NG1/1/25 12/12/85.

39. SRO NG1/1/27 24/2/90; SRO NG1/1/28 26/11/94.

40. SRO NG1/1/33 22/1/17.

41. SRO NG1/1/33 22/11/15; 6/3/16.

42. Warden, A. J., *The Linen Trade, Ancient and Modern,* London, 1864, 30.

43. SRO NG1/1/2 17th July 1730.

44. SRO NG1/1/3 8/2/34.

45. SRO NG1/1/4 7/11/35; 29/10/36; 5/8/37.

46. SRO NG1/1/4 23/7/36; 3/12/36; 24/2/38; SRO NG1/1/5 1/2/40.

47. SRO NG1/1/12 19/1/53.

48. SRO NG1/1/17 23/7/62.

49. SRO NG1/1/4 5/8/37; 13/1/38.

50. SRO NG1/1/4 5/8/37; SRO NG1/1/5 19/1/39; 22/2/40.

51. SRO NG1/1/6 11/3/41.

52. SRO NG1/1/7 7/3/44.

53. SRO NG1/1/7 1/3/45; SRO NG1/1/8 4/7/46; 23/1/47; SRO NG1/1/9 18/1/48; 18/1/49.

54. SRO NG1/1/9 3/2/49; SRO NG1/1/10 12/1/50.

55. SRO NG1/1/10 2/2/50; SRO NG1/1/11 18/1/51; 3/1/52; SRO NG1/1/12 19/1/53.

56. SRO NG1/1/12 13/12/54.

57. SRO NG1/1/14 15/12/58.

58. SRO NG1/1/14 15/12/58; SRO NG1/1/16 22/1/62; SRO NG1/1/17 27/4/63.

59. SRO NG1/1/7 28th December 1744.

60. Home, *op. cit.*, 12.

61. SRO GD248/954/1: Description of a Lint Boor. Edinburgh 17th July 1747 12.

62. Home, *op. cit.*, 12.

63. SRO NG1/1/7 3/4/45; 5/7/45.

64. SRO NG1/1/7 12/7/45.

65. SRO NG1/1/8 12/6/47; 17/7/47.

66. SRO NG1/1/9 11/1/48.

67. SRO NG1/1/9 18/1/49.

68. SRO NG1/1/10 12/1/50.

69. SRO NG1/1/10 23/6/49.

70. SRO NG1/1/10 7/3/50.

71. SRO NG1/1/11 16/11/50.

72. SRO NG1/1/10 9/6/49.

73. SRO NG1/2/5 11/2/52.

74. Durie, A. J., The Scottish Linen Industry, 1767-1775, with particular Reference to the Early History of the British Linen Company, PhD Thesis, Edinburgh University, 1973, 103.

75. SRO NG1/1/19 4/12/71; SRO NG1/1/20 10/2/73.

76. SRO NG1/1/20 28/7/73.

77. SRO NG1/1/16 22/1/62.

78. SRO NG1/1/17 27/4/63.

79. SRO NG1/1/20 10/2/73; SRO NG1/1/25 19/12/85.

80. SRO NG1/1/25 19/12/85; SRO NG1/1/28 15/1/94; SRO NG1/1/32 9/7/06.

81. SRO NG1/1/18 18/3/65; SRO NG1/1/26 30/7/88.

82. For references to other mills taking apprentices, see: SRO NG1/1/27 30/1/91; 25/5/91; 18/8/89; SRO NG1/1/25 23/1/86; SRO NG1/1/26 5/3/88; SRO NG1/1/28 8/2/92; 13/11/93; 18/12/93; SRO NG1/1/29; 9/12/95; 20/1/96; SRO NG1/1/30 12/6/99; 25/6/09; SRO NG1/1/31 21/11/04; 27/2/05; SRO NG1/1/32 9/7/06; 2/11/10; 5/6/11; SRO NG1/1/33 29/1/12; 23/11/14; 5/3/17; SRO NG1/1/34 13/3/19.

83. SRO NG1/1/20 17/3/73.

84. SRO NG1/1/6 6/2/41.

85. SRO NG1/1/11 21/6/51.

86. NLS Acc 2933/330: Petition Alexander Morison *et al*, Forgue parish, Aberdeenshire 1762; SRO NG1/1/17 27/4/63.

87. SRO NG1/19/1.

88. SRO NG1/1/23 14/2/81.

89. SRO E 777/198/14 20/11/64.

90. For work to date on lint mill numbers, see Hamilton, H., *An Economic History of Scotland in the Eighteenth Century*, Oxford, 1963, 135; McClain, N. E., 'Scottish Lintmills, 1729-70', in *Textile History*, I, 3/12/70, 293-308; Durie, A. J. *The Scottish Linen Industry*, Edinburgh, 1978.

91. SRO NG1/1/1-36.

92. SRO NG1/1/19.

93. Hamilton, *op. cit.* (1963), 135.

94. Although not listed in the 1772 survey, Hospital Mill was known to be working in 1751 and 1774: SRO NG1/1/11 22/2/51; SRO NG1/1/21 30/11/74.

95. SRO NG1/1/19: Dunbartonshire 4 / Lanarkshire 26 / Forfarshire 22 / Perthshire 27.

96. SRO NG1/1/23 6/8/83.

97. Bonnington Mill: SRO NG1/1/2 10/3/30; Colinton Mill: SRO NG1/1/8 12/3/47; Bute Mill: SRO NG1/1/16 22/1/62.

98. SRO NG1/1/2 17/7/1730; 23/2/1731.

99. SRO NG1/1/4 21/2/35; *SBRS,* 'Extracts from the Records of the Burgh of Glasgow' V (1718-38), Glasgow, 1909, 434.

100. SRO NG1/1/3 20/7/33; 24/8/33.

101. SRO NG1/1/11 13/7/50; SRO NG1/1/10 8/6/50; Hamilton, *op. cit.* (1946).

102. SRO NG1/1/10 22/6/50; SRO NG1/1/11 21/6/51.

103. See, for example, Petition of Robert Gordon, tacksman of Cairnie Mill, Perthshire: SRO NG1/1/21 21/2/76.

104. See, for example, Quartalehouse: SRO NG1/19/1 Aberdeenshire 4; Moulin: SRO NG1/19/1 Perthshire 67.

105. See, for example, SRO NG1/19/1 Stirlingshire 12-13; Perthshire 16; Elgin 2.

106. Joiner: SRO NG1/1/27 23/6/90; Mason and Wright: SRO NG1/1/25 11/12/86; Millwright: SRO NG1/1/27 2/12/89; Minister: SRO NG1/1/27 20/1/90; Advocate: SRO NG1/1/25 19/12/85.

107. Grant of Grant: SRO NG1/1/28 8/2/92; Duke of Gordon: SRO NG1/1/26 20/2/82; Sinclair of Ulbster: SRO NG1/1/26 23/7/88.

108. British Linen Company: NLS Acc 2933/350 1/1/1749; N.E. Scotland: OSA XIII, 425, Gollactrie, Aberdeenshire; SRO NG1/1/18 19/2/68 Huntly, Aberdeenshire; SRO NG1/1/28 22/5/93 Letham, Angus; SRO NG1/19/1 Banffshire 8, Cullen; SRO NG1/1/16 22/1/62 Drum, Banffshire; SRO NG1/1/10 9/6/49 Linkwood, Moray.

109. McClain, *op. cit.,* 294.

110. SRO NG1/1/12 19/1/53.

111. SRO NG1/1/17 15/8/63.

112. SRO NG1/1/28 19/12/92. According to Alex. Munro, stampmaster in Glasgow, linen had fallen so much in favour of cotton that he could hardly pay his office rent.

113. McClain, *op. cit.,* 307-8.

114. Thomson, J., *General View of the Agriculture of the County of Fife,* Edinburgh, 1800, 206-7, 208.

115. See Handley, J. E., *The Agricultural Revolution in Scotland,* Glasgow, 1963.

116. SRO NG1/1/33 8/3/15.

117. *NSA* Aberdeenshire, 158, 305, 419, 442, 572, 982; Ayrshire 508; Banffshire 138, 164, 238, 341, 390; Dumfriesshire 184; Dunbartonshire 199; Fife 227, 385; Forfarshire 333; Kirkcudbrightshire 43, 288; Lanarkshire 401; Perthshire 293, 407, 505, 1012; Stirlingshire 118, 214,385; West Lothian 51; Wigtownshire 74.

118. *NSA* Ayrshire 508.

119. SRO NG1/1/11 13/7/50.

120. SRO NG1/2/5 22/7/52.

121. SRO NG1/2/4 12/1/50.

122. SRO NG1/1/11 22/5/51.

123. SRO NG1/2/4 24/7/50.

124. SRO NG1/2/4 22/3/51.

125. SRO NG1/2/4 22/6/50.

126. SRO NG1/1/11 18/1/51.

127. SRO NG1/1/11 22/5/51.

128. SRO NG1/2/4 5/3/51; 7/6/51.

129. East Lothian's first turnpike Act was passed in 1749.

130. SRO GD6/1275.

131. SRO NG1/1/12 19/1/53; 14/12/53; 13/12/54.

132. SRO GD6/1275: Agreement, Lord Belhaven and Thomas Finlayson, 1754.

133. SRO NG1/1/14 15/12/58.

134. SRO NG1/1/14 15/12/58; SRO NG1/1/17 27/4/63.

135. SRO NG1/19/1 Haddingtonshire 1.

136. Ibid.

137. SRO NG1/1/20 10/2/73.

138. SRO NG1/1/20 3/3/73.

139. SRO NG1/1/20 28/7/73.

140. SRO NG1/1/22 21/1/78.

141. Ibid.

142. SRO NG1/1/22 18/2/78.

143. SRO NG1/1/22 13/1/79.

144. SRO NG1/1/23 4/7/81; 1/8/81.

145. SRO NG1/1/25 19/12/85; SRO NG1/1/28 15/1/94.

146. SRO NG1/1/32 9/7/06.

147. SRO NG1/1/27 2/3/91; 9/3/91; SRO NG1/1/32 9/7/06.

148. Fowler, Greenwood & Sharp, (Map of) *Haddingtonshire*, 1825. The lint mill is shown as in use. On the first Ordnance Survey map of East Lothian (surveyed 1853), the mill is shown as disused.

149. An early 19th-century estate plan, in the possession of Mr. E. Jeffrey, Biel Grange, shows a lade running past the by then disused mill to water wheels on Biel Grange and Beesknowe farms.

150. Naismith, J., *Thoughts on the Various Objects of Industry pursued in Scotland*, Edinburgh, 1790, 219.

151. *Ibid.*, 230.

152. Home, *op. cit.*, 6.

153. *Ibid.*, 15.

154. Naismith, *op. cit.*, 220.

155. SRO NG1/19/1 Fife 9; SRO NG1/19/1 Aberdeenshire 4.

156. McClain, *op. cit.*, 301.

157. SRO NG1/1/16 22/1/62; SRO NG1/19/1 Banffshire 8.

158. SRO NG1/1/19 23/12/68.

159. Home, *op. cit.*, 15-16.

160. Naismith, *op. cit.*, 219.

161. *Ibid.*, 219.

162. *Ibid.*, 221.

163. *Ibid.*, 221.

164. Home, *op. cit.*, 16.

165. McClain, *op. cit.*, 303.

166. Naismith, *op. cit.*, 222.

167. McClain, *op. cit.*, 303-4; Home, *op. cit.*, 15.

168. McClain, *op. cit.*, 299-302.

169. *Ibid.*, 303.

170. *OSA* XXI, 53; Singer, C., Holmyard, E. J., Hall, A. R. and Williams, T. I. (eds.), *op. cit.*, III, 697.

171. SRO E 777/198/62.

172. SRO NG1/1/18 21/11/66.

173. SRO NG1/1/31 26/6/05.

174. Murray, D., *The York Buildings Company. A Chapter in Scotch History*, Glasgow, 1883, 39.

175. SRO NG1/3/2 6/2/35.

176. SRO E 777/129/4 13/7/67; SRO E 777/198/27.

177. SRO E 777/198/38; Ainslie, J., *Fife*, 1775 (Map).

178. SRO NG1/1/18 21/11/66.

179. SRO NG1/1/23 4/7/81.

180. SRO NG1/1/30 23/11/99.

181. SRO NG1/1/32 4/2/07.

182. SRO NG1/1/32 30/11/08; 8/2/09; 4/7/10.

183. SRO NG1/1/32 4/7/10.

184. *NSA* II, 298.

185. SRO E 777/198/38; *OSA* IX, 583.

186. SRO E 777/198/53 (1) 14/11/80.

187. SRO E 777/198/55; E 777/198/58.

188. SRO E 777/198/44; E 777/129/6; E 777/198/51.

189. See, for example, *OSA* IX, 94.

190. SRO E 777/198/53.

191. SRO E 777/198/53.

192. SRO E 777/198/53.

193. SRO E 777/198/55.

194. SRO E 777/129/8.

195. SRO E 777/198/53; E 777/129/7.

196. SRO E 777/198/58.

197. Ibid.

198. SRO E 777/198/62.

199. SRO E 777/252.

200. *OSA* IX, 583.

201. *OSA* VIII, 485.

202. *OSA* XIII, 493.

203. SRO R.H.P. 770.

204. O.S. 1st Edition 6″/mile, 1861, Perthshire.

16

Bleachfields

As early as the 16th century the manufacture of coarse linen cloth had become an industry of some consequence in Scotland.[1] However, so primitive were the methods employed that the Scottish product was totally unable to compete with the vastly superior linen cloth of Holland and Germany, from whom Scotland and her more prosperous neighbour, England, continued to import all but the poorest cloth. One major factor was the inferiority of Scottish bleaching: for the most part it was carried out manually by private individuals on the banks of streams or in meadows, and while a handful of bleachfields, such as that at Corstorphine, were set up before 1728, it was only after that date that attention began to be focused on the technology of bleaching as a means of improving the finished product.

Technology

The Bleaching Process: Dutch and Irish Methods

The bleaching process as practised in 18th-century Scotland consisted of boiling and soaking in alkali, wringing or mangling, then soaking in acid. This was followed by a second washing, drying and finishing either by beating or pressing.[2] Banks of boilers or 'keivs' and tubs for washing can be seen in a plan of Deskford bleachfield, c.1752 (Figure 58). While these differed only in scale from the primitive coppers used by private individuals, the other processes in bleaching saw extensive mechanisation, much of which involved the introduction of water-powered machinery.

In Scotland two distinct methods were used in bleaching: the Irish method and the Dutch method. In the light of the superior quality of Dutch bleaching, it is hardly surprising that it was this method which was adopted first. The Dutch method involved little in the way of mechanisation, as the washing process was performed by women who cleaned the cloth in large vats, no use being made of water power. Perhaps the most famous example of a 'Dutch' bleachfield was that established by two merchants, Andrew and William Gray, at Provan Mill near Glasgow. As early as 1728 cloth from the Grays' field was reported to be as white as Dutch cloth.[3] The Dutch method continued to be used for much of the 18th century and, as we shall see, large sums of money were expended in its application by the Board of Trustees.

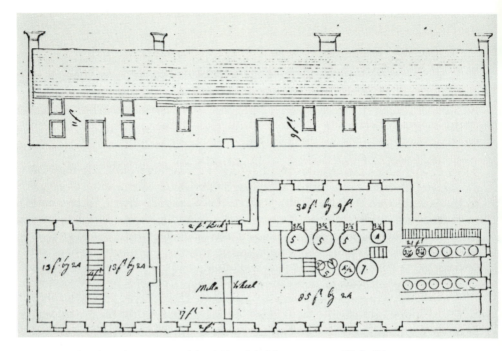

Fig 58. Bleaching house at Deskford Bleachfield, *circa* 1752. *SRO GD248/951/5*

By the early 1730s, however, another process, known as the Irish method, had appeared in Scotland. Unlike the Dutch, the Irish method utilised water power for washing, and it was from Ireland too that many of the subsequent technical advances stemmed.

Washing Mills

Mills for washing cloth were far from unknown in Scotland before 1730: in the period 1550-1730, at one time or another, there were at least three hundred waulk mills for washing or fulling cloth (see Chapter 3, p. 46), and it seems likely that Scotland was one of the sources from which fulling mills were introduced into Ireland during the 17th century.[4] It is, therefore, somewhat paradoxical to find them being re-introduced into Scotland from Ireland in the following century as 'putstock' mills or under the Irish name of 'tuke miln'.

The earliest reference to the use of the Irish method in Scotland is to a field at Ormiston, East Lothian, which one Alexander Christie was said to have founded in 1731.[5] By 1734 it was being run by John Christie and John Drummond.[6] According to the Board's committee, 'their bleaching house is large, and the coppers, keeves, pumps, tubs and tuke miln of very good workmanship'.[7] In the same year a bleachfield established by Richard Holden at Baldovie, near Dundee, had 'two mills for beating and cleansing the cloth', while in 1755 the same Alexander Christie who had founded Ormiston bleachfield had entered into an eighty-year tack from the Earl of Kinnoull for land at Tulloch, near Perth, on which he established a bleachfield with washing mills.[8]

While the comparative gentleness of the Dutch method rendered it suitable for fine cloth, the Irish method was found to be the better for bleaching the coarse cloth which represented the bulk of Scottish output. Therefore most of the larger Scottish bleachfields of the 18th century were built with washing mills, and gradually the Irish method came into general use. By the 1760s Grays' Green bleachfield, where so much private and public capital had been invested in the 1730s and 1740s, was in such a state that the bleacher had to turn down an offer of help for new capital works 'because it would cost more money — which his business will not bear, being greatly declined since the Irish method of bleaching prevailed, and he has no water for machinery in the Irish way'.[9]

Rubbing Mills

The next process to be mechanised was rubbing. The usual arrangement was to have two square boards, toothed transversely, the upper of which, moved by a crank and driven by water power, passed over the unpowered lower board in a rubbing action.[10] According to McCutcheon,[11] the process had been mechanised in Ireland by about 1740, although Gauldie gives a date some ten years earlier.[12] While the 'Irish rubbing mill', operated by two men, could do as much work in one day as could twenty women by hand, it was found to give a woolly surface to the cloth, which soon dirtied, and for that reason rubbing by hand continued to be employed for the finer fabrics.[13]

Although there are few substantiated reports of rubbing mills in Scotland before the late 1740s, it would seem that, for the coarser fabrics at least, they had become a common feature by mid-century and that the ingenuity of Scottish millwrights had been applied to making further refinements. It is not surprising to find the names of Robert and Andrew Meikle associated with these: in 1754 they claimed to have devised a means of drawing cloth through the rubbing mill by machine, an innovation which, having succeeded in its first application, had been copied elsewhere in Scotland and in Ireland.[14] In the following year they were presented with a £40 reward from the Board of Trustees.[15] It is probable that most of the subsequent rubbing mills, such as that installed at Cullen in 1762, incorporated this modification.[16] While they never became as common as the wash mill, rubbing mills continued to be installed at new and existing bleachfields throughout the 18th century and into the early 19th century: at Cullen in 1802, at Ednam, Roxburghshire in 1810, and at Coveyheugh, Berwickshire in 1813.[17] In the latter part of the period some of the larger bleachfields had two or more rubbing mills. Ness bleachfield near Inverness had two in 1791, as had Keirfield, Stirlingshire in 1827.[18]

Beetling Mills

That the finished product might have a smooth surface, it was customary to subject it to a pressing. Under the Dutch method the cloth was usually passed between rollers or calenders,[19] but at fields where the Irish method was employed the cloth, having passed over a roller, was beaten by hammers or stamps raised and lowered by cams set in a double helix on a rotating shaft (Figure 59).[20] In any one machine there could be perhaps twenty-five stamps, and bleached cloth was subjected to this treatment for at least four days.[21] Because of the great amount of effort required, beetling mills were usually water- or occasionally horse-powered.

According to McCutcheon[22] the beetling engine was introduced into Ireland in 1725, but the reference is unsubstantiated and the machine's origin obscure. Certainly the principle employed is the same as that used for some time in the paper industry and in mineral dressing (p. 54 and p. 73), and it may have been from these applications that the idea stemmed. As for the date of its introduction into Scotland, there is some confusion: Gauldie[23] claims that beetling engines were in use at Pitkerro, Angus in 1732 and at Ormiston by 1734; the report of a visit to Pitkerro in 1734 mentions two mills for 'beating and cleansing the cloth', but these were probably only washing mills.[24] At Ormiston, in 1734, there was 'a room where cloath is beetled', but there is nothing to suggest that the process was performed mechanically.[25] According to Green,[26] a Scots engineer named William Bell invented a water-driven beetling machine about 1745 and introduced it to Ireland. This corresponds with the earliest substantiated references to beetling engines in that country. In 1751 the Board of Trustees paid 40s to George Landale, millwright of Perth, for 'a model of a miln for beetling cloth after bleaching', a move which suggests that the machine was still something of a novelty.[27] Later that same year the Board decided to offer £50 for the best beetling mill fitted up in Scotland during 1752, but only 'if upon due consideration beetling cloth shall be found a proper thing to be encouraged'.[28] The Board intended to seek the opinion of manufacturers, but in the event a shortage of funds prevented the scheme from going ahead.[29]

Shortly after this, references to beetling mills begin to appear. In 1754 William Sandeman paid £102 15s 11¾d for a beetling machine at Luncarty.[30] Saltoun had a beetling machine before 1760, for in that year new equipment was installed, consisting of 'two sets of beetles and beams proportioned to move at the same time and with the same outer wheel, and these beetles made to strike perpendicular or straightways on the cloth, and not aslant as at present'.[31] Robert Meikle was sent to inspect a beetling mill at Perth, possibly that at Luncarty, and on his return he built an improved machine to his own specifications.[32] In 1761 an additional beetling mill was built at Luncarty, possibly to Meikle's design.[33]

The Board of Trustees gave financial aid for beetling engines at Denovan, Stirlingshire in 1762 and at Cullen, Strathmiglo and Saltoun Barley Mill in

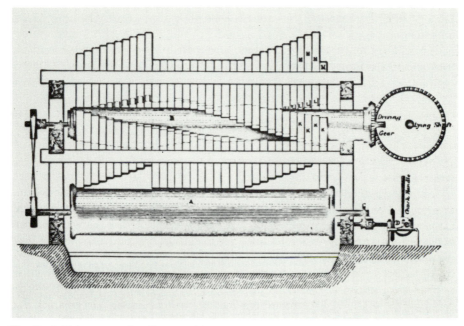

Fig 59. A 19th-century beetling machine

1763. At Saltoun bleachfield the mill had cost £86 3s 11d.[34] Beetling machines were installed at most of the major Scottish bleachfields during the remainder of the 18th century, but at some places, such as Letham, Angus, beetling was still being performed by hand in the 1790s.[35] The Board of Trustees were still providing grant aid for this purpose as late as 1823, in which year a replacement machine was installed at Dollar bleachfield.[36] As with rubbing boards and washing mills, multiple installations became common. In 1826 Keirfield, Stirlingshire had twelve sets of beetles;[37] according to Gauldie[38] there were no less than one hundred and eight sets of beetles working on the Perthshire Almond during the 19th century. The mechanisation of beetling led to a substantial reduction in the number of workers required in cloth finishing, and the increased productivity which they offered made beetling engines a worthwhile investment for the larger fields. In 1794 Joseph Read, bleacher at Linlithgow Bridge, received £10 from the Board of Trustees for designing an improved beetling mill.[39] In the following year a full-scale machine was set up with three rollers instead of the customary two and 'movements for fitting on and changing the cloth from one beam to the other'. In the opinion of the Board's inspector, the design was 'certainly new' and showed 'very considerable ingenuity'. Its greatest advantage was that it could be operated by one man instead of the three previously required, and such was the Board's approval that it offered twenty guineas to those who proposed to adopt it and a further six guineas royalty to Read for each of the first six machines installed.[40]

Read's machine was suitable only for beetling cloth and when, in 1810, coarse linens began to be bleached as yarn rather than as cloth, a modified version of the older type of beetling machine, with a fixed beam, was used.[41] A claim to further improvements was made by a Dumfriesshire man, William Steel, in 1821, but no details are available.[42]

Other Applications of Water Power

In some cases calendering was performed by water power: a calender was planned for Saltoun bleachfield in 1760, to be driven by the same water wheel as the beetles.[43] Towards the end of the 18th century large-scale mechanical calenders became widespread. The first powered calender in the Dundee area was installed at Douglasfield in 1797 by William Sandeman. This was also the first application of steam power to the process. As this source of power developed, particularly in the Dundee area, calendering premises were often set up away from bleachfields, in towns.[44]

At Ness bleachfield water power was used to drive the pumps which supplied the wash mills with water and, while there is no firm evidence, it is probable that water power was applied to the same purpose elsewhere.[45] At one new bleachfield in Renfrewshire, water power was used to grind ashes.[46]

Despite the radical changes in the chemistry of bleaching,[47] the industry's mechanical technology, once introduced, changed very little, and the heavy, cumbersome machinery which typified the bleachfield of the 18th century continued to be used into the 19th century and even the 20th.

The Workforce

As with lint mills, so also with bleachfields the Board of Trustees provided facilities for the training of a skilled workforce.

Linen bleaching was already well-established, if poorly executed, in Scotland, and in the early years of the Board's existence many of the new bleachfields were in the capable hands of the Irish bleachers such as Alexander Christie[48] or John Christie.[49] Nevertheless, most bleachers were loath to divulge their secrets and, initially at least, the Board of Trustees took a keener interest in bleaching by the Dutch method than by the Irish, for there had been no influx of Dutch bleachers comparable to that of the Irish.

Grays' Green, 1728-1748

Prior to the establishment of the Board of Trustees, a linen bleachfield had been laid out at Provan Mill, near Glasgow, by two merchants, William and Andrew Gray.[50] One of these two brothers had 'been throw the different parts of Europe where the manufacture is brought to the greatest perfection'.[51] By November 1728 linen cloth from the Grays' field was reported to be 'fully as whitned as dutch cloath'.[52]

In 1729 the Grays received a £350 premium from the Board of Trustees, and in 1738 a massive £1,000 to complete their field[53] (cf. p. 239). By that time the Board had become fully aware of the shortcomings of the first group of bleachfields to be built and financial aid had been withdrawn until such time as techniques were improved.[54] It was against such a background that the Board established its first training scheme, under the auspices of the brothers Gray, at Provan Mill.

As only the Dutch method was taught, the Grays' Green training scheme is not directly relevant to the present study. All the same, its impact was considerable and it deserves some mention, if only to put later schemes into context.

In July 1738 royal approval was given for the payment of £200 per annum as salaries to William and Andrew Gray for teaching master bleachers from other fields.[55] The conditions of the scheme were strict. Candidates normally had to be proprietors or tacksmen of bleachfields and had to make a bond for £1,000 Sterling not to divulge the information to any other person. Furthermore, they were not to employ any foreign persons at their bleachfields once the Grays' method had been adopted.[56] Despite these rigorous conditions, the prestige of Grays' Green was sufficient to draw trainees from most of the major fields then operating or proposed. This working arrangement, under which the Grays received £200 per annum, continued to operate until the late 1740s, by which time relations between the Board and the Grays had deteriorated somewhat. In 1748 Andrew Gray received two trainees, but William Gray refused to instruct either of them and wrote to the Board expressing a wish to end the arrangement.[57]

Although the training scheme had come to an end, Andrew Gray continued to work for the Board, instructing at new bleachfields and acting as a travelling inspector.[58] However, his health soon led to disagreements over remuneration: in 1749 he was said to be able to visit only those fields near Glasgow, and in the following year, having failed to make his tour of the bleachfields, Andrew Gray was taken out of the Board's employment.[59]

Other factors also came into play. As we saw, the Dutch method, while successful in bleaching fine linen, was unsuited to the cheap, coarse linen which represented the bulk of home production.[60] If the Board was to operate a training scheme of any relevance to the Scottish bleaching industry, it would have to be one which included both Dutch and Irish methods.

Saltoun Field, 1751-1765

Even before the Board had dispensed with Andrew Gray, the search for a suitable field had started. In January 1750 the Board approached William Neilson of Roslin Bleachfield, a man 'very expert in his business' and capable of bleaching to a standard 'equal to Mr. Gray'.[61] Unmoved by the £100 which the Board had offered him for passing on his skills, Neilson replied 'expressing his dissatisfaction at being put upon the same footing with the common rank of bleachers'.[62] However, a much better alternative existed, and at the same meeting at which Andrew Gray was dismissed, the Board of Trustees chose the British Linen Company's Saltoun bleachfield as the site of their next training scheme.[63]

Saltoun possessed several advantages. In February 1749 James Armstrong, then the master bleacher at Saltoun, had been given permission to inspect Andrew Gray's bleaching journal and take copies.[64] In the following month Armstrong was joined at Saltoun by one Doggan who had recently come over from Ireland, claiming to possess a new bleaching method;[65] that summer the Board had given Doggan £21 to train two apprentices.[66] Saltoun was, there-fore, one of the few fields at which both Dutch and Irish methods were practised.

In accordance with the Board's proposals apprentices were to be taken on for three years, with a maximum of four apprentices on the field at any one time. The first two years were to be given over to coarse bleaching and the third to fine; trainees were also to be taught book-keeping. Journals with day by day accounts of work undertaken were to be submitted to the Board for the second and final years of training, and each trainee had to pass the Board's own examination. Apprentices found to be duly qualified as master bleachers were to receive a certificate from the Board and a premium of £50 on setting up a field of at least two or three acres, or on being engaged as foremen at such fields. In exchange for his services the owner of Saltoun, or the instructor there, was to receive £100 per annum out of which the apprentices were to be paid 6d per day.[67]

In January 1751 the British Linen Company accepted its first two apprentices, and the salary formerly payable to Andrew Gray was transferred to it.[68] The following month a third apprentice, who was to have been trained by Andrew Gray, came to the field.[69] Later the same year the Board offered to provide help in building a house 'for the better accommodation of apprentices'.[70]

By January 1753 twelve apprentices had been taken on.[71] In June of that year the apprentices were given a 1d per day pay rise, and lapping, or folding, was added to the curriculum.[72] Instruction was given jointly by Armstrong and Doggan until 1756, when Doggan left.[73] He went on to establish Kevock Mill bleachfield, Midlothian.[74] By 1773 he was also involved with Ford bleachfield, which had been founded in 1753 by Samuel Hart, one of Saltoun's first graduates.[75] At a later date Ford was taken on by another former Saltoun apprentice, John Herdman, who had previously managed Glencorse bleach-field, some ten miles away.[76]

From 1756 until his retirement in 1765 Armstrong had sole charge of the field. For three years thereafter it was run by an Irishman, Samuel Sinclair, and on his returning to Ireland his place was taken by Archibald Horn, another ex-apprentice, who had been the manager of the bleachfield at Saltoun barley mill.[77] Long before this time, however, the Board's training scheme had come to an end: in March 1765 Armstrong was notified that as from the

Table 6

Saltoun Apprentices: Destinations

Name	Date Started	Destination
James Watson	1751	Deskford (Banff)
Samuel Hart	1751	Ford (Midlothian)
Hector Turnbull	1751	Luncarty (Perth)
John Park	1751	Arthurlie (Renfrew)
Alex Skirvine	1752	Luncarty
William Henderson	1752	Haircraigs (Renfrew)
Colin Smith	1752	Brechin
Archibald Horn	1752	Saltoun Barley Mill
Charles Baxter	1752	Melrose
Robert Nisbet	1752	Inverness
Robert Monro	1752	Culcairn (Ross)
Robert Smith	1753	Brechin
David Muir	1754	Glorat (Stirling)
William Grant	1754	Elgin
David Kennedy	1754	Irvine
William Nisbet	1756	Strichen (Aberdeen)
Robert Scott	1758	Balbirnie (Fife)
William Coldon	1759	Cullen
William Hart	1761	Ford
William Tait	1762	Inverness

following year the £50 per annum, payable for training apprentices, would be withdrawn.[78]

In all, twenty-seven apprentices had passed through Saltoun, of whom about twenty are known to have taken on bleachfields of their own, either as owners or as overseers. Table 6 shows the destinations of these twenty apprentices. It is hardly coincidental that the fields which they founded, or to which they went, represented the greater proportion of the best Scottish bleachfields of the mid- to late-18th century, and their pre-eminence must owe more than a little to the Saltoun training scheme. In a few cases former apprentices moved on after taking on the management of a bleachfield: the examples of John Herdman and Archibald Horn have already been cited. William Henderson, who took on Haircraigs bleachfield, Renfrewshire in 1754, had moved to Inverness by 1770,[79] while William Tait, who was running the same Inverness bleachfield in 1776, appears to have moved to Culcairn bleachfield, Ross-shire by 1791.[80] On the whole, however, ex-apprentices appear to have kept to their first field. Perhaps the expense of fitting up a bleachfield contributed to this stability.

While most of the Saltoun graduates met with success in their work, the most distinguished career was that of Hector Turnbull. In December 1753 Turnbull, having completed his term at Saltoun, was taken on as a partner in Luncarty bleachfield, near Perth. Such was the size of the field that the Board took the unusual course of giving him his premium of £50 despite the fact that Andrew Skirvine had already been granted the premium for that field.[81] By 1756 Turnbull had become overseer and had been asked by the Board to instruct the son of a Dundee thread manufacturer in the art of bleaching;[82] at least one other trainee was referred to Turnbull before 1773.[83] In 1777 Turnbull, still at Luncarty, was claiming to have made improvements to bleaching machinery and to have passed them on to anyone who had asked.[84]

In the same year the Board, impressed by Turnbull's performance, offered him £100 to instruct two apprentices in coarse and fine linen bleaching. Unfortunately, an agreement with the owners of the field prevented him from accepting the offer.[85]

Overall, the Saltoun apprenticeship scheme appears to have been very effective, and when it did finally come to an end it was as a result of its success rather than its failure in training skilled bleachers.

After 1765

After the termination of the arrangement with Saltoun, the Board occasionally sent apprentices to one or other of a handful of favoured bleachfields and paid for their training. The example of Luncarty bleachfield has already been cited. In 1766 James Macgregor, whose bleachfield at Milngavie employed 'the complete Irish method', was offered and accepted £50 per annum over two years to teach Irish bleaching to whoever the Board presented to him.[86] Despite their assistance in training labour, it was very rare for the Board to offer support to working bleachers of the kind they had provided for lint millers (pp. 177-180). As we shall see, bleachfields were much larger units, often backed by mercantile or manufacturing interests, and it was therefore assumed that the proprietors of bleachfields were better equipped to pay for skilled staff than were the landowners, farmers or artisans who financed lint mills. Moreover, such was the expense of site preparation and the extent and complexity of plant that most of the funds which the Board made available to bleachfields went towards those purposes, leaving very little for the establishment of a state-financed labour scheme.

The Scottish bleaching industry's skilled labour requirements were met initially by immigrant bleachers from Ireland supplemented by native Scots. In the early years, however, the quality of their work was often poor and the rates at which they operated were too high. By providing master bleachers, thoroughly trained at the best Scottish bleachfields, the Board of Trustees improved the quality of work and brought their prices down to a competitive level. In the 1740s much of the linen produced in Scotland was still being bleached elsewhere. By 1775 most of it was being bleached in Scotland, and by the 1790s some English cloth was being bleached there too.[87] Part of the credit for this turnabout must lie with the Board of Trustees and their efforts to establish a skilled workforce.

The Bleachfields

Numbers

In attempting to assess the number of water-powered bleachfields once operating, one is immediately faced with the problem of disentangling those using the Irish method from those using the Dutch. The principal source materials, notably the Minutes of the Board of Trustees, the Old Statistical Account and newspaper advertisements, cast some light on the problem, and it is fairly safe to assume that most of the larger and later bleachfields used the Irish method, unless the Dutch is specifically mentioned. Furthermore the scale of water-powered bleachfields, and their frequent recourse to advertising, lessens the chances of their going unrecorded. On the other hand there is no single source comparable to the lint mill survey of 1772. Unlike lint mills, many bleachfields continued to operate after 1830, sometimes with the addition or substitution of steam power.

Bearing all these factors in mind, it is still possible to gain some idea of the number of water-powered bleachfields operating in Scotland. In the years up to 1745 there is evidence that at least twenty-five bleachfields were established, and while some small fields, such as Carberry,[88] Midlothian, were short-lived, the vast majority survived for many years thereafter: Ormiston, Tulloch, Roslin, and Leven (Fife) all date from this period. A significant number, including Dalquhurn, Haddington, and the Grays' Green, used the Dutch method of bleaching and were not, therefore, water-powered.

Between 1745 and 1765 at least sixty-five additional fields were established, almost all of them water-powered. However, as some of the smaller bleachfields of the previous period had already gone out of use, this does not represent an absolute increase. Most significant of the bleachfields established during this period was Saltoun, whence came the bleachers who founded or operated about twenty of the other major new fields. Ironically, Saltoun itself survived for only a short period after 1765.

The period 1765 to 1790 saw the greatest number of new bleachfields, with over a hundred established between those years. Significant among them were Leven (Dunbartonshire), Huntingtower, Dollar and Inglis Green. While the trend was towards larger, more complex fields, there were some on a very small scale, such as that at Bedrule Mill, Roxburghshire.[89] According to Clow, there were about ninety bleachfields in Scotland by 1772, distributed as follows: Aberdeenshire 5; Ayr 3; Banff 5; Berwick 2; Dumbarton 3; Dumfries 3; Edinburgh 14; Elgin 1; Fife 13; Haddington 6; Inverness 1; Kincardine 1; Kinross 1; Lanark 8; Linlithgow 1; Orkney 1; Perth 6; Renfrew 3; Ross 1; Roxburgh 1; Selkirk 1; Stirling 3; Forfar 9.[90]

At least thirty more bleachfields were set up in the 1790s, including Prinlaws (1790) and Letham (Angus) (1792). By this time there was little need for additional bleachfields, and the contraction of the linen industry in some areas may have led to an overall decline.

Between 1801 and 1830 only about ten new fields were established, and

Fig 60. Distribution of water-powered bleachfields 1730-1830

these, for the most part, were in west-central and eastern Scotland. Outwith these areas the period was characterised by a marked drop in the number of fields.

Distribution

Throughout the period 1730-1830 the location of water-powered bleach-fields was closely related to the changing needs and location of the linen, and latterly also the cotton, textile industries. Over and above this, however, there was a broad pattern of diffusion and contraction. In the period up to 1745, bleachfields were most common in south-east Scotland, with minor concentrations in the Edinburgh area and the Upper Merse. Outwith the south-east there were only a very few sites in the rest of the central Lowlands and two in the Dumfries area.

However, between 1745 and 1765 bleachfields became much more widespread, and although a significant number of new fields were created in the south-east, the centre of gravity shifted to east-central Scotland. In the north-east the influence of merchants and Improving landowners is seen in the creation, for the first time, of about ten fields, while in the south-west, where only two fields were recorded before 1745, at least twelve more were created between 1745 and 1765. In the Highlands too, a handful of Improving land-owners established fields, though probably more from a 'spirit of industry' than from an actual demand for them.

Between 1765 and 1790 east-central Scotland continued to maintain the dominant position which it had established between 1745 and 1765, with at least twenty-five new fields during the period. The north-eastern area continued to increase in importance, with fifteen new fields. While fields continued to be built in all areas, there was a notable increase in the number of fields in the Highlands and Islands, particularly in Inverness-shire. With the establishment of Catfirth bleachfield in Shetland, the diffusion of Scottish bleachfields reached its zenith.

The 1790s saw a marked contraction in the building of new bleachfields. Only in east-central Scotland, where yarn bleachfields were built to serve flax spinning mills, were new fields built in any significant numbers. Elsewhere, despite the construction of a few new fields, there may have been a net reduction in the total number of fields operating. During the period 1800-1830 this was certainly the case. For the most part existing fields were able to cope with demand, and with the contraction of the linen industry many fields, particularly those in marginal areas, ceased to be financially viable. While some of the existing fields, especially those in eastern and west-central Scotland, continued to operate up to and beyond the end of the 19th century, the building and operating of bleachfields in most parts of Scotland had come to an end. Figure 60 shows the distribution of known and probable water-powered bleachfield sites between 1730 and 1830.

Finance

While the establishment of a lint mill required a certain amount of capital it was, with the aid of the Board of Trustees, within the means of a large tenant or small landowner. However, a much greater amount was needed to establish a bleachfield, especially if the field was to have water-powered machinery. True, the Board of Trustees provided some aid, often in the region of £100 or more, but this was only made available on the work being completed. Furthermore, the limitations of the Board's funds prevented them from providing anything more than a small proportion of the capital cost of larger fields, on which the total outlay could be several thousand pounds. The role of the Board was therefore only of secondary importance; first we must establish who it was that laid out the capital initially.

From approximately one hundred sites for which information is available, it would appear that they belonged to four major groups: companies and other partnerships, individual merchants and manufacturers, landowners, and persons from related textile trades.

Companies and other Partnerships

The first group comprised both true companies and less formal partnerships. Notable among early examples of the latter sub-group was the fraternal partnership of William and Andrew Gray, the two Glasgow merchants who founded Provan Mill bleachfield in 1728.[91] It was another partnership of Glasgow merchants who founded Dalquhurn bleachfield, also in 1728.[92] Family and other partnerships continued to be of some, albeit limited, significance throughout the period up to 1830, and notably between 1745 and 1790. Companies became evident in the 1740s, most significantly the British Linen Company, whose Saltoun bleachfield was founded about 1748.[93] Other early companies included Leyes, Still & Co. (Gordon's Mills, pre-1755), and Rannie, Fordyce & Co. (Deskford, 1752). For the rest of the period company-financed fields continued to represent the largest single group of new bleachfields. While it is beyond our purpose to analyse the composition of companies, the little evidence that is readily available points to a significant contribution to the formation of companies by both merchants and landowners. The partnership of Wallace, Gardine & Co. (Arbroath, 1746) consisted of three Arbroath merchants.[94] The two principal partners in Richardson & Co. (Huntingtower, 1772) were Sir John Richardson of Pitfour and Robert Smythe of Methven.[95] The firm of Sir John Mitchell & Co., founders of the ill-fated Catfirth bleachfield in Shetland, was financed by Shetland landowners,[96] and while it was 'the Linen Company at Granttown' which operated the bleachfield there, most of the initiative came from Grant of Grant himself.[97] In the case of J. King & Co. (Mid-Arthurlie) the situation was even more complex: of the two partners one, A. Brown, was a merchant and baillie in Paisley while the other, who gave his name to the company, was a bleacher but also the owner of the lands of East Carriagehall near Paisley.[98]

Individual Merchants and Manufacturers

Less common than company fields were those founded by individual merchants and manufacturers. Almost all of the fields in this category were situated in the east of Scotland and generally were smaller than company fields. The most notable exception to the rule was Luncarty, founded in 1752 by a Perth merchant, William Sandeman.[99] More typical were Arrat (A. Glegg, merchant in Montrose, 1789), Milton (G. Morrison, manufacturer in Keith, 1789), Strathendry (R. Birrel, merchant and manufacturer in Kirkcaldy) and Elgin (J. Ritchie junr, merchant in Elgin, 1785).[100] Most of the merchants and manufacturers involved were already concerned with either the marketing or production of linen and may have seen bleaching as a way of extending their interests in the industry. It is noticeable that most of the fields in this category date from the period 1765-1789, particularly the 1780s, by which time sufficient capital had been accumulated to make such an investment. After 1790, in times less certain for the linen industry and in circumstances favouring large, highly capitalised fields, individual merchants and manufacturers all but disappeared from the scene. Obviously the time when a merchant could go it alone had passed.

Landowners

The contribution of the third major group, landowners, is more difficult to assess. On the one hand, as has already been shown, landowners often formed the nuclei of companies and, on the other hand, successful merchants and manufacturers often became landowners: the example of J. King has already been cited. Besides this 'invisible' element, there is also evidence of a significant number of landowners who took the initiative to establish bleachfields on their own account. One of the earliest examples was Colonel Hamilton-Price of Raploch who, having previously set up a weaving community, founded a bleachfield at Laverockhall in 1729.[101] Although a handful of other landowners, such as Wright of Lawton, established bleachfields during the next thirty years, it was not until the 1760s that they appeared in any numbers.

In 1761 John Adam of Blairadam established a bleachfield at the new village of Maryburgh on his Fife estate;[102] Dunfermline bleachfield was founded in 1763 by the Earl of Elgin[103] and Portsoy bleachfield in 1767 by Lorimer of Portsoy.[104] After a lapse during the 1770s there was a revival of interest in the 1780s, starting with Gordon of Glendavenny's Peterhead bleachfield in 1780.[105] Among those which followed were the Laurencekirk bleachfields of Lord Gardenstone (pre-1785), Pitsligo bleachfield (1785), laid out at a cost in excess of £1,000 by Sir William Forbes of Pitsligo, Cumnock (1785), laid out by the Earl of Dumfries, Kingussie (1785), by the Duke of Gordon, Ness (1787), by Baillie of Dunain, and Thurso (1789), by Sir John Sinclair of Ulbster.[106]

After 1790 there is very little evidence of landowners laying out large sums of money on establishing bleachfields. By that time attention had turned to carding and spinning mills for wool in the Borders, the Hillfoots and north-east Scotland, for linen in east-central Scotland and for cotton over much of Scotland, but more especially in the west. Although a few landowners under-took directly to build such mills, it was more usual for them to offer sites on their estates to merchants or manufacturers. Where new bleachfields were established after 1790, it was usually on the initiative of those merchants and manufacturers as an adjunct to their spinning mills.

Textile Trade Employees

The final group, textile trade employees, came from very diverse back-grounds: threadmakers, weavers, stampmasters, a lint miller and, most commonly, bleachers. Several Irish bleachers founded their own fields in Scotland, notably in the early years of bleachfield development. The Christies (Kinchey (1734), Ormiston (1731) and Tulloch (1735)) were certainly Irish, as probably were the McWhirters (Trailflat (1776) and Dounieston (1808)).[107] One William Adair, from Lismore field, Ireland, set up at Cross-Arthurlie in 1773 after allegedly having sailed up the Clyde without seeing a single bleach-field.[108]

A few of the Saltoun apprentices went on to found their own bleachfields. One of the first, Samuel Hart, obtained a tack of land at Ford, Midlothian from Dewar of Vogrie in 1753 and built a bleachfield there.[109] Another Saltoun trainee, William Henderson, set up a bleachfield at Haircraigs, Renfrewshire in 1754 on land let to him by T. Caldwell, a Paisley merchant who had bought the estate in 1749.[110] A third apprentice, Robert Munro, seems to have been responsible for the establishment of Culcairn bleachfield, Ross-shire but in this case, as in others involving bleachers in this capacity, one suspects that more than a little help was provided by landed or mercantile interests. Most of the Saltoun apprentices took on supervisory rather than entrepreneurial roles and, while a few bleachers became partners in bleachfields, their contribution was probably skill rather than capital.

All in all there was no room in the bleaching industry for the small farmer or tradesman who became so prominent in flax milling, and for the most part it was landowners, merchants and manufacturers who established bleachfields, for it was only they who could bear the cost of setting up and running a field of any size.

The Cost of Bleachfields

The capital laid out on creating bleachfields varied enormously. A small bleachfield without machinery could cost as little as £100, whereas a fully equipped field with several acres of drying field could cost several thousands.

Fixed Capital Cost Components

Once land had been purchased, feued or let, the first task was to level the site and form irrigated greens. This alone could cost several hundred pounds: at Montrose field, where no machinery was installed, £208 had been applied to this purpose by 1754,[111] and by 1755 Samuel Hart had spent £416 on laying out the field at Ford.[112] In the case of water-powered bleachfields dams and lades also had to be constructed, although existing ones were sometimes used: Tulloch bleachfield, for example, was on the long-established Perth town lade.[113]

The site having been prepared, a number of buildings had to be constructed. A boiling house could cost £100 and a drying house anywhere between £68 (Gifford, 1754) and £500 (Saltoun, 1752).[114] In addition there had to be buildings to house machinery, keives and tubs.

Machinery could be a major item of expenditure, especially if a field was to have a full set comprising washing mill, beetles, rubbing boards and calender. Machinery and housing at Brechin bleachfield, for example, cost £238 in 1785.[115] Even after a field had been fully equipped, it was only a matter of time until a refit was necessary: repairs to machinery at Deanshaugh bleachfield, Elgin cost £147 in 1824, while £359 10s 9d was spent on renewing the machinery and drying house at Roslin in 1761, only twenty-three years after it was founded.[116]

All told, the cost of a moderate-sized field was often about £500 to £800: Douglas (1774), Deskford (1752), Glasgow (1753) and Meigle (1805) are typical examples.[117] The cost of a smaller field such as Pitsligo (1785), Strathmiglo (1756), Arthurlie (1754) or Blackland Mill (1776) was in the region of £150 to £400 while a large field could cost between £1,000 (Inglis Green, 1774), and £4,000 (Stormont, 1791).[118] The expenses involved in constructing Luncarty bleachfield (1752-1762) were as follows:

'Accompt of Money Expended upon Luncarty Bleachfield from the Beginning of the Year 1752, when it Began to be Fitted up to 4 August 1761

	£	s	d
1752 Oct — Accompt for levelling and laying out 12 acres of bleachfield and building a boiling house, with house for a water mill for washing and rubbing cloth after the Irish method	755	6	4½
1753 Laid out further before completion	470	6	0¼
A press for lapping after the Dutch method	73	3	3
1754 A house for holding a beetling machine and room for lapping cloth	175	7	7½
Beetling machine	102	15	11¼
Fencing about the waters	28	8	1
1756 Sundry new utensils, large keives etc.	26	15	8
1757 A machine for pounding ashes, with improvements on rubbing boards	47	13	8½
1758 Dwelling house	200	0	0
Sundry improvements to machines and extending bleachfield			

ground	78	13	5¼
1759 Large house for 18 tubs for 36 women to wash and rub cloth after the Dutch method, and laying out 3 acres of bleachfield	193	19	6½
1760 Large house for servants. House for rinsing and blueing cloth. 1½ acres more bleachfield	177	15	11¾
	£2,486	14	7

1761 House 36 feet by 20 feet for holding milk casks and keives for souring cloth	30	0	0
Built and finishing			
House 32 feet by 24 feet — ground floor for holding ashes etc. 2 timber floors for holding and lapping linen	150	0	0
Just starting			
House for containing new washing mill, rubbing boards and beetling mill est	120	0	0
House for bucking cloth, with boilers, keives etc.	160	0	0
Complete set — washing mill, rubbing boards and beetling machine and canal for water and miln wheel	200	0	0
Drying house, to be large	200	0	0
Dwelling house for overseer, and room for holding cloth	150	0	0
Laying out and inclosing 40 acres for dry bleaching of coarse linen	20	0	0
	£1,030	0	0'

NLS Acc. 2933/330

Such expenditure was even greater than that required for the early cotton mills, and the need for companies or other partnerships is clearly apparent. Joseph Read founded Inglis Green bleachfield in 1772 with only one other partner, and when less than five years later the latter went bankrupt the whole cost of £1,000 which had been expended on the field fell on Read.[119] When, in 1787, John Baillie of Dunain agreed to lay out a bleachfield for Donald Macintosh, he expected to spend about £200. However, by 1790 the bleachfield, though still incomplete, had cost some £900, and to repay this Macintosh was forced to pay a cripplingly high rent which soon led to his bankruptcy.[120] Fortunately the Scottish bleacher, undercapitalised as he often was, could usually obtain some help from the Board of Trustees, and it is to their contribution that we must look next.

Extent and Purpose of Aid

We have already seen the extent to which the Board of Trustees provided aid towards the construction of lint mills. The capital required in establishing a bleachfield was much more and, as might be expected, the contribution of the Board was correspondingly greater.

Initially, from 1727, this aid took the form of a £50 per acre grant. This very high level of assistance meant that in the case of the one field, Dalquhurn, the proprietors received no less than £600, while another field, Cameron, received £450. In all, only seven bleachfields benefited from the scheme before the £2,000 allocated to it ran out:

Gorgie	6 acres	£300
Grays' Green	7 acres	£350
Cupar	4.5 acres	£225
Dalquhurn	12 acres	£600
Cameron	9 acres	£450
Aberdeen	1 acre	£50
Tipperlin	?	£25
		£2,000 [121]

Besides the benefit to only a few fields, and that to an excessive extent, there was no assurance that the fields, once established, would operate effectively or that they would continue in business for any length of time.

By the late 1730s the policy of the Board of Trustees had changed to ensure a more equitable distribution of funds. Even so, only a few fields benefited — four between 1735 and 1739, two between 1740 and 1744, and six between 1745 and 1749. In the late 1730s some very large grants were still being awarded, notably to Grays' Green, which was given £1,000 in 1738 towards construction and improvements.[122] Ormiston received a further £200, Roslin £150 and Tulloch £300;[123] altogether these four received more aid than did some thirty-four separate fields in the period 1780-1789.

The early 1750s saw a fourfold increase in aid through which thirty-one fields were granted sums varying from £20 to £200. Much of this went to investment in drying houses towards which, for example, Saltoun field received £200 and Ayton £100.[124] The scale of aid to any one field was still falling in the late 1750s, during which a little over half the sum made available in the previous five years went to twenty-three fields. Here again, drying houses accounted for a substantial proportion of the aid.

Up to about 1760, aid had been directed, for the most part, towards earthworks and buildings. Thereafter, however, funds were made available for the increasingly complex machinery which bleachers were having to install. In 1762 Deskford bleachfield received £50 towards rubbing boards and other improvements, while another £60 went towards the cost of a set of beetles at Saltoun Barley Mill bleachfield.[125] In 1768 Ormiston received £50 towards a washing mill and a lignum vitae cylinder.[126] Between 1760 and 1769 twenty-nine fields shared a total of £1,840. During the early 1770s the aid to fields, buildings and machinery rose to £1,245 shared among twenty bleachfields. In the late 1770s the value of aid fell back sharply but recovered slightly between 1780 and 1794. A fairly large proportion of the aid granted during this period went towards the extension and renewal of buildings and machinery, although some new fields were still being created.

After 1794 aid fell to a very low level and remained there. On the one hand the financial impetus had passed to various kinds of spinning mill while, on the other hand, the funds at the Board's disposal were being increasingly directed towards the revitalised woollen industry. In the thirty-five-year period 1795-1830 less was paid out in grants to bleachfields than in the five-year period 1750-1754.

Policy

Three main points of policy emerge from the minutes of the Board of Trustees.

Firstly, as with lint mills, aid towards bleachfields was granted only after most of the work had been completed. While this virtually eliminated the misuse of funds, it meant that the work had to be financed either by credit or that, if capital was available, there was no need for the aid in the first place.

A second point of policy was to restrict the number and total value of grants to any one field, so that deserving projects were often turned down solely on the grounds that money had already been given towards other works at the field in question. There were, of course, exceptions, particularly in the case of highly successful fields. Thus Luncarty received £375 in four instalments between 1752 and 1764, Deskford £400 in seven instalments from 1753 to 1821, and Ormiston £800 in six instalments from 1734 to 1768.[127] Grays' Green, which received no less than £1,350, has already been mentioned, but the most remarkable breach of policy was at Roslin bleachfield near Edinburgh. Roslin bleachfield was founded in 1738 by William Neilson. That year he received £150 towards setting up the field;[128] in 1747 the Board granted him a further £100, this time for repairs and improvements.[129] By 1750 he had gained an excellent reputation as a bleacher and was approached, unsuccessfully, by the Board as a possible successor to the Grays[130] (p. 227). In 1752 he was given an additional £100 and in 1759 £200, the latter amount being for a drying house and repairs.[131] In 1761 he received a further £100 towards the same the total sum expended by him being £359 10s 9d.[132] In 1771, when David Ross, a new bleacher there, applied for aid, he was turned down on the grounds that £750 had already been granted to the field, but the following year his request for aid towards the cost of a washing mill, rubbing boards and other bleaching machinery was accepted and £100 given towards the £314 13s 10d which had been laid out to that end by 1773.[133] By the late 1770s ownership of the field had changed once again. In 1779 the new occupants, John and Walter Biggar, were given £50.[134] Finally, in 1808, £60 was granted to Samuel and Charles Read, tacksmen of Roslin bleachfield, for work on machinery there.[135] In all Roslin had been given financial assistance on no fewer than nine occasions, amounting to £900.

The third policy concerned the distribution of bleachfields. On the whole the Board were reluctant to support fields in areas such as Renfrewshire where bleaching was already well established, and on several occasions aid was withheld on these grounds (for example N. Arthurlie, Paisley and Irvine).[136]

However, here again there were exceptions: the Board's attitude towards Stormontfield, founded by two Perth merchants in 1789, was initially one of indifference, and when it was approached for aid, it was withheld on the grounds that there were already sufficient fields in the area. Nevertheless, a testimonial by Lady Henderland and a favourable report by the Board's own surveyor were sufficient to persuade it to give the field £300 over three years.[137]

Overall, the financial contribution of the Board of Trustees must have been of significant proportions, coming at a time when many Scottish bleachers were seriously under-capitalised. However, it cannot really be considered crucial, as most fields had laid out money before the Board provided any return, and at least the larger, better capitalised fields could have survived without it. All the same, the Scottish bleaching industry would have been noticeably the poorer without the £16,243 which the Board provided between 1728 and 1830.

A Scottish Bleachfield: Saltoun, East Lothian

As the most important and one of the best documented fields in Scotland, Saltoun is an obvious choice to examine in detail. Since other aspects of the field have already been considered, we shall concentrate on the establishment and construction of the field. The British Linen Company, for whom the field was built, had been founded in March 1745 by Lord Milton and two merchants, William Tod and Ebenezer McCulloch. On 5th July 1746 it was given a Royal Charter.[138] As the best Scottish bleachfields such as Grays' Green and Roslin were already constantly employed, the company was forced, initially, to send its cloth to other Scottish fields or even to London.[139] Before long, however, the problems of doing so had become evident and the company had to seek an alternative. In the words of the company's minutes:

> The managers represented that the price commonly paid the bleachers in this country for whitening of linen was so great a charge on the manufacturers that without a saving in that article, they could bring no quantities to the London market, at a price equal to the foreign; that the only method which had occurred to the directors and managers was for the company to take a field for bleaching coarse linens, and to employ some skilled bleacher to manage the same at a certain salary or proportional part of savings that might arise to the company, betwixt the price that bleaching might cost and the price now paid to the bleachers in the country; that they represented that the Lord Justice Clerk had agreed to erect a bleachfield for this purpose, and enter into tack with the company, at the rate of twenty shillings sterling yearly, for each acre of ground that might be employed in the field, and of seven pounds ten shillings per cent per annum, for the money laid out by his lordship in erecting the same.[140]

The choice of Lord Milton's estate was an obvious one. Firstly, besides being a founder member of the British Linen Company, he served on the Board of

Trustees for Manufactures and could be relied upon to obtain financial aid from it. Secondly, his estate in East Lothian was only fifteen miles from Edinburgh, still, at that time, the centre of the linen industry and of the company's activities. Thirdly, he had access to the resources required: good haugh land beside Saltoun Water, water-powered potential on the same stream and, in Robert Meikle, then resident at Saltoun, a first-rate millwright. Last but not least, he had capital. In the event Lord Milton lent the money for the field's construction interest-free and allowed the company to use the field rent-free until such time as it became profitable.

Although the company had had to wait until September 1747 for a quorum, the decision had already been taken and construction work started in 1746.[141] Before the end of that year progress had been made on preparing earthworks and water works, while George Merylees had done some smith work. During 1747 construction work was in full swing. By June of that year Robert Meikle, aided by a workforce which included his brother Andrew, had completed the brass, iron and woodwork of the upper mill, the first two at a cost of £12 1s 4½d and the last, including axletree, stock and two wheels, at £18 11s. Besides the washing mill, the upper mill also housed rubbing boards, probably to the Meikles' own improved design (see p. 223).

Between August and September 1747 one hundred and twenty-three cartloads of timber were brought from Prestonpans; in that same year sixty-nine bars of iron were purchased from Messrs. Fall, merchants in Dunbar, and twelve from Mr Caddel, merchant in Cockenzie. In all £653 0s 8d was laid out on the field during 1747.

Work continued into 1748, and Robert Meikle's attention now turned to the Lower Mill. By October he had completed the iron and brass work and had blocked out the woodwork. Before the end of 1748 he had added a lint mill to the machinery. By May of that year a great number of cartloads of iron, deals, rough timber and other materials had been brought to the field including eight loads of brick from Lord Milton's Brunstane Estate, just east of Edinburgh. During July and August fifty-five cartloads of deals and logs came from Port Seton, and one cart carried a plane tree from Brunstane.

Slating work on the mills and dwelling house was carried out by a Dalkeith slater, Thomas Burns, using slate from Auchinleck. Estimates at the time put the number of slates required at 28,000; a cart could carry two hundred and fifty. Tiles, probably imported via Port Seton, were used in roofing shades. Lime for plastering the roofs and for cementing stonework probably came from Herdmanston limeworks near Haddington. In all, £793 16s 5d was expended on the field during 1748.

Although the field began to operate in that year, construction work continued until 1750. The establishment of the field had involved the carriage of tiles, bricks and trees from Brunstane, timber from Leith and Prestonpans, timber and iron from Port Seton, timber, scaffolding and iron from Fisherrow, slates from Auchinleck, stone from Tranent and elsewhere, iron from Dunbar, trees from Saltoun Parks, lime from Herdmanston and sand from locally dug pits. There is evidence of at least four hundred cartloads of materials going to the field; the total is probably a lot higher. In all, by the end of 1750, Lord Milton had laid out £2,123 13s 6d.[142] The completed field, with later additions, appears in Figure 61.

Work on establishing the field finished in 1750. After that date repairs and additions continued to be made; those to the bleaching and drying greens are detailed in Figure 61. In 1752 the Board of Trustees gave £200 towards a drying house costing £509 11s 3d.[143] Some eight years later, following a visit of inspection to a beetling mill at Perth, Robert Meikle prepared one to his own design and installed it at Saltoun.[144] Between 1750 and 1762 Lord Milton spent £536 10s 6d on repairs and additions to the field.[145] Innovations were also made in the chemistry of bleaching, and during 1752 experiments were made in the use of oil of vitriol (H_2SO_4) from John Roebuck's Prestonpans works.[146]

The field finally closed down in 1772. By that time the machinery comprised three water wheels, three washing stocks, two sets of rubbing boards, three beetling engines and two lignum vitae rollers.[147] Although Lord Milton tried to sell the field, it would appear that no buyer could be found, for by 1777, when Mostyn Armstrong's map of the Lothians was produced, there was no longer a bleachfield at Saltoun.[148]

Despite its short life the impact of Saltoun continued to be felt in the work of skilled ex-trainees at bleachfields all over Scotland. For that reason alone it must be considered the most important single field in the history of Scottish bleaching.

In summarising the development of water-powered bleachfields in Scotland between 1730 and 1830, three questions have to be answered: firstly, how did the industry develop; secondly, what was its impact on the economy as a whole and thirdly, to what extent was this impact a product of the application of water power?

The development of the bleaching industry in Scotland between 1730 and 1830 was of considerable proportions. Indeed, for the first time, something developed which truly could be called an industry and which could be identified in many of its features as the precursor of factory production. The technology used turned a simple, small-scale activity, carried out by hand, into a sophisticated craft in which the application of mechanical power created a capital-intensive industry in which the process could be carried out cheaply and on a large scale at any one site. The application of chemical science also revolutionised the process by removing its dependence upon plant and animal materials and by permitting bleaching to be carried out rapidly indoors, instead of outdoors over several months at the mercy of the weather.

The workforce showed an unprecedented degree of specialisation, and at the larger fields they were employed in considerable numbers. Both features were typical of factory production and, as one might expect, bleachfields produced some of the earliest examples of purpose-built industrial housing.

Because of the need to carry out field levelling, canal digging, building and

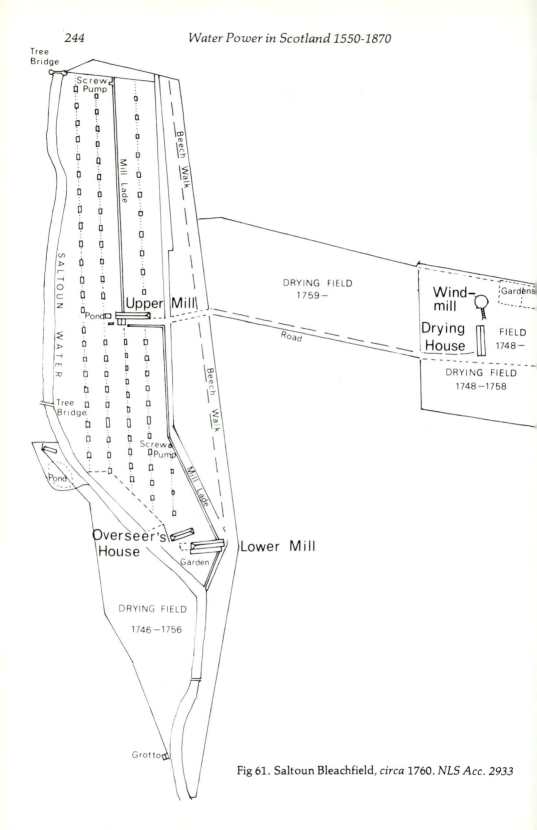

Fig 61. Saltoun Bleachfield, *circa* 1760. *NLS Acc. 2933*

the installation of expensive machinery, the capital required to establish any but the smallest bleachfields was usually beyond the means of the ordinary landowner, farmer or artisan. The only industries which had required such investment before then were the mining and smelting of lead and silver and the mining of coal. In the former case finance had come from the Crown and in the latter from landowners made wealthy by export sales of coal. In the case of the bleachfields the money tended to come from individual merchants and land-owners or from co-partneries comprising either or both groups. While these were by no means the first examples of such companies,[149] it was only with the financing of bleachfields that they became common in Scotland. In the light of later developments, namely cotton and linen spinning, this familiarity with joint-stock organisation and the capital accumulated by them, becomes of even greater significance. Devine[150] has recognised in the textile finishing industries a link between the capital accumulated in colonial trade and the capital later laid out in the cotton industry. Taking a conservative estimate of £500 as the average unit cost, something in the region of £100,000 must have been laid out on bleachfields in Scotland between 1730 and 1830.

To turn to the second question, what was the impact of the bleaching industry on the Scottish economy between 1730 and 1830? Undoubtedly it was of major importance. In 1730, while the linen industry was already of signifi-cant proportions, all processes were still carried out by hand, in small-scale units. Although the quality of work was poor at all stages of production, it was in bleaching that the greatest improvement was needed, since only by sending cloth abroad could it be finished to a quality and at a price that made it competitive. However, through the work of the Board of Trustees and that of individual millwrights, bleachers and scientists, a bleaching industry was established which in terms of rates and quality of work could equal that of Holland or anywhere else. As the bleaching process could now be carried out within Scotland and cloth could be bleached more cheaply, the capital accruing from bleaching remained in the country, often to be re-invested, and the manufacturer could be more certain of getting his web back again in a shorter period. Because of its labour requirements the linen bleaching industry was able to go some little way towards absorbing surplus workers at a time when radical changes in agriculture were throwing great numbers off the land. The significance of the bleaching industry in the accumulation of capital has already been discussed.

Finally, to what extent was the impact of the bleaching industry due to the application of water power? In terms of scale of operation and quality of finish the use of water-powered machinery was of major importance, though not the only factor. Although the initial capital outlay might be great, machinery could soon pay for itself, either through savings on wage labour or by achieving economies of scale. In one example, cited by Durie,[151] the beetling engine installed at Saltoun in 1760 double beetled 288,458 yards of cloth and

486 table cloths between March 1761 and March 1762. The cost of doing this by hand at the Edinburgh lapping house would have been £329; deducting £91 per annum for running costs, the beetling engine made £238 per annum extra and in three seasons would have paid for itself.

While some bleachfields followed the Dutch method of bleaching and did not therefore require water power, their competitiveness was based on the high quality of their work and of the cloth which they bleached. It was, however, the coarse linen industry which made the greatest contribution to the Scottish economy, and a crucial stage in its manufacture was a bleaching process which utilised mechanical power. In a few cases horses provided it, and in the 19th century the steam engine came into use. For the most part, however, water provided the power and continued to do so, in some cases, until the middle of the 20th century.[152]

One should not over-emphasise the significance of water power in the development of the bleaching industry as a whole. One might equally cite the availability of suitable sites with clear water near centres of population, the availability of capital to establish fields, the active co-operation of the Board of Trustees, the application of chemical science or the existence of markets for finished cloth in England, Scotland and the colonies. On the other hand the contribution made by water power should be recognised as being greater than is generally acknowledged. Indeed, without it the bleaching industry might never have assumed the proportions it did, nor might it ever have contributed so much to the economic development of Scotland between 1730 and 1830.

A Note on Plash Mills

During the early 19th century bleachfields for linen yarn began to replace traditional cloth bleachfields. Stimulated by the vastly augmented output made possible by the mechanisation of spinning many large yarn bleachfields were set up in east-central Scotland, but the process was also carried out at small-scale yarn washing or plash mills. Whilst these came to be associated with spinning mills, their origin goes back to an earlier period, and the earliest recorded plash mill was not situated in the heartland of flax mill-spinning but further south in Edinburgh.

In 1748 the Board of Trustees were presented with two similar requests for financial aid in connection with machinery to clean yarn by water power. According to the first, Messrs. Cheap & Neilson, manufacturers in the Canongate, claimed that they could clean yarn for Osnaburghs in half the usual time, while the second petition from Messrs. Bell & Murray, manufacturers, made much of the cheapness, relative to manual methods, with which yarn could be cleaned using water power.[153] Only a week later a third petition was submitted by John Forester & Co., Stirling, but in the Board's Minute Books this is overshadowed by a detailed account of Messrs. Cheap & Neilson's methods.

According to their estimates, public boilers could clean coarse linen yarn at

3½d per pound, but their mill could clean an equal quantity for ¾d in a far shorter time. The Board were sufficiently impressed to put forward £50 towards the cost of an experimental mill, the total cost of which was to be £112 7s; little did they realise that the eventual cost was to be more than twice this sum.[154]

The site chosen was at Bonnington Mills, Edinburgh, where less than twenty years earlier James Spalding had built his experimental lint mill. By July 1748 work was under way, and Messrs. Cheap & Neilson were claiming the balance of the £50 offered to them.[155] However, the choice of site was not a wise one: according to a report prepared by Hope of Rankeillor, the position of the mill, the projected fall and height of the trows were such that it seemed unlikely the mill would ever work. As the yarn mill had been built on the tail lade of an existing corn mill, it could only operate when the corn mill was at work;[156] by August 1748 the projected cost of the mill had reached £300, forcing the Board to take it over on their own account and complete it at public expense.[157]

Following the submission of Hope's report, two millwrights Landale and Muckle (Meikle) were called in. Meikle started by making a model of the mill; by July 1749 hopes were being expressed that the yarn might soon be completed and, in anticipation of this, rates for yarn washing were drawn up.[158] Notwithstanding this apparent optimism, the Board were still conferring with both Andrew and Robert Meikle later that month, having instructed them to work only on those parts of the mill which could be moved elsewhere. A further indication that all was not well came from the Board's moves to find an alternative site at Canonmills, but by the time negotiations were concluded in January 1750, the mill at Bonnington had been completed at a cost of £251 10s 3d.[159]

No more is heard of the mill, other than that it was still functioning in 1758.[160] By that time the plash mill had become well established elsewhere, in east-central Scotland. According to Hay's *History of Arbroath*, Nether Mill, near Arbroath, was converted to wash yarn about 1740, a function which it continued to perform until 1863.[161] Whilst it seems improbable that such a mill existed at so early a date, a report dated 1760 confirms that several plash mills had been built by that year:

> Milns are used in Angus for cleaning coarse yarns and therefore the cleaning in general is proposed at first rather than confining them to ashes.[162]

The writer went on to suggest that the linen industry might benefit from the wider adoption of this technique and proposed that, for a trial period no coarse yarn should be sold unwashed in Fife, Angus and Perthshire. Although the scarcity of mills at that time would have made the experiment impracticable, additional mills were built from time to time, though only rarely with the assistance of the Board of Trustees. By 1790 there were probably thirty or so plash mills at work in Scotland, by far the largest concentration of which was on the Dighty Water, near Dundee where, from there having been only a single mill in 1760, numbers had risen to seventeen by 1790.[163]

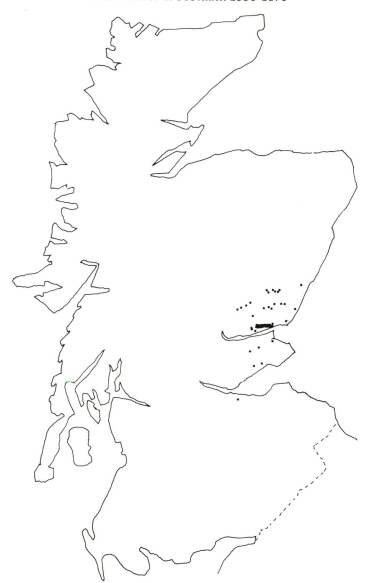

Fig 62. Distribution of plash mills, 1730-1830

With the mechanisation of flax spinning and the construction of spinning mills, coarse yarn production soared and the need for plash mills increased correspondingly. As most of these spinning mills were situated within the existing coarse linen region, the overall distribution of plash mills was little changed and continued unchanged throughout the remaining life of the Scottish linen industry (Figure 62). In all, about fifty plash mills were built in Scotland during the period 1730-1830.

NOTES

1. Durie, A. J., The Scottish Linen Industry, 1707-1755, with Particular reference to the Early History of the British Linen Company, Edinburgh University PhD, 1973, 10.

2. Gauldie, E., 'Mechanical Aids to Linen Bleaching in Scotland', *Textile History*, I, 130 (No. 2, Dec. 1969).

3. SRO NG1/1/1 8/11/1728.

4. McCutcheon, W. A., 'Water Power in the North of Ireland', *TNS* XXXIX, 80 (1966-7).

5. SRO NG1/1/2 7/5/1731.

6. SRO NG1/1/3 19/7/1734.

7. Ibid.

8. SRO NG1/1/3 18/1/1734; SRO NG1/1/4 18/7/1735.

9. SRO NG1/1/18 18/3/1765.

10. McCutcheon, *op. cit.*, 79.

11. *Ibid.*, 79.

12. Gauldie, *op. cit.*, 133.

13. NLS Acc. 2933 Box 329 f.1.

14. SRO NG1/1/12 13/12/1754.

15. SRO NG1/1/12 17/1/1755.

16. SRO NG1/1/16 22/1/1762.

17. SRO NG1/1/31 15/12/1802; SRO NG1/1/32 4/7/1810; SRO NG1/1/33 3/7/1813.

18. SRO GD128/3/1; SRO CS96/2072.

19. Gauldie, *op. cit.*, 140.

20. McCutcheon, *op. cit.*, 78.

21. *Ibid.*, 78.

22. *Ibid.*, 78.

23. Gauldie, E., 'Water-Powered Beetling Machines', *TNS* XXX, 125 (1966-7).

24. SRO NG1/1/3 18/1/1734.

25. SRO NG1/1/3 19/7/1734.

26. Green, E. R. R., *The Industrial Archaeology of County Down*, Belfast, 1963. Cited by Gauldie, *op. cit.* (1969), 139.

27. SRO NG1/1/11 12/7/1751.

28. SRO NG1/1/11 15/11/1751.

29. SRO NG1/1/11 24/1/1752.

30. NLS Acc. 2933/330.

31. Durie, A. J., *op. cit.*, 365-6.

32. *Ibid.*, 366.

33. NLS Acc. 2933/330.

34. SRO NG1/1/16 22/1/62. Later withdrawn. See SRO NG1/1/18 27/3/1764; SRO NG1/1/17 4/2/1763; SRO NG1/1/17 5/8/1763; SRO NG1/1/17 16/7/1763.

35. SRO NG1/1/28 13/6/1792.

36. SRO NG1/1/34 8/7/1823.

37. SRO CS96/2072.

38. Gauldie, *op. cit.* (1969), 139.

39. SRO NG1/1/28 17/12/1794.

40. SRO NG1/1/29 20/5/1795; 17/6/1795; 20/1/1796.

41. Gauldie, *op. cit.* (1966-7), 126.

42. SRO NG1/1/34 19/6/1821.

43. Durie, A. J., *op. cit.*, 366.

44. Gauldie, *op. cit.* (1969), 140-1.

45. SRO GD128/3/1.

46. Crawford, G. (revised Semple, W.), *The History of Renfrewshire*, Paisley, 1782.

47. For a full account of the role of chemistry in bleaching, see Clow, A. & Clow, N. L., *The Chemical Revolution*, London, 1952.

48. Ormiston, 1731; Tulloch, 1735.

49. Kinchey, 1734.

50. *SBRS*, 'Extracts from the Records of the Burgh of Glasgow', V (1718-38), Glasgow, 1909, 290.

51. *Ibid.*, 290.

52. SRO NG1/1/1 8/11/1728.

53. SRO NG1/1/1 10/1/1729; SRO NG1/1/4 23/6/1738.

54. Perth, Irvine, Ednam, all SRO NG1/1/4 13/1/1738.

55. SRO NG1/1/4 23/6/1738.

56. SRO NG1/1/4 26/1/1739.

57. SRO NG1/1/9 10/6/1748.

58. SRO NG1/1/9 17/6/1748; SRO NG1/1/9 6/1/1749.

59. SRO NG1/1/9 27/1/1749; SRO NG1/1/11 23/11/1750.

60. SRO NG1/1/11 23/11/1750.

61. SRO NG1/1/10 12/1/1750.

62. SRO NG1/1/10 20/7/1750.

63. SRO NG1/1/11 23/11/1750.

64. SRO NG1/1/9 24/2/1749.

65. SRO NG1/1/9 24/2/1749.

66. SRO NG1/1/10 9/6/1749.

67. SRO NG1/1/11 23/11/1750.

68. SRO NG1/1/11 18/1/1751.

69. SRO NG1/1/11 8/2/51.

70. SRO NG1/1/11 15/11/51; SRO NG1/1/11 24/1/1752.

71. SRO NG1/1/12 19/1/1753.

72. SRO NG1/1/12 15/6/1753.

73. Durie, *op. cit.*, 357.

74. SRO NG1/1/13 23/12/1756.

75. SRO NG1/1/12 16/11/1753; SRO NG1/1/20 20/1/1773.

76. SRO NG1/1/29 20/5/1795; SRO NG1/1/23 26/6/1782.

77. Durie, *op. cit.*, 356-7; SRO NG1/1/16 22/1/1762.

78. SRO NG1/1/18 18/3/1765.

79. SRO NG1/1/12 13/12/1754; SRO NG1/1/19 17/1/1770.

80. SRO NG1/1/21 7/2/1776; SRO NG1/1/27 2/3/1791.

81. SRO NG1/1/12 26/12/1753.

82. SRO NG1/1/13 5/3/1756.

83. SRO NG1/1/20 17/2/73.

84. SRO NG1/1/21 2/7/77; SRO NG1/1/22 3/12/1777.

85. SRO NG1/1/22 3/12/77; SRO NG1/22 11/3/1778.

86. SRO NG1/1/18 14/3/1766; SRO NG1/1/18 24/3/1767.

87. *OSA* XVII, 638.

88. SRO NG1/1/5 18/1/1740.

89. SRO NG1/1/20 15/12/1773; SRO NG1/1/22 27/1/1779; SRO NG1/1/26 8/8/1787; SRO NG1/1/21 30/11/74; SRO NG1/1/18 14/3/1766.

90. Clow & Clow, *op. cit.*, 180.

91. *SBRS*, Glasgow V, 290.

92. SRO NG1/1/1 9/8/1728.

93. Durie, *op. cit.*, 351.

94. SRO NG1/1/12 17/1/1755; SRO NG1/1/12 1/12/1752; SRO NG1/1/8 19/12/1746.

95. *NSA* X, 1034.

96. SRO NG1/1/19 22/1/1772.

97. SRO NG1/1/20 26/1/1774.

98. Crawford, G., *op. cit.*, 171, 267.

99. SRO NG1/1/11 3/1/1752.

100. SRO NG1/1/27 29/7/1789; SRO NG1/1/27 2/12/1789; SRO NG1/1/26 10/12/1788; SRO NG1/1/25 14/11/1785.

101. SRO NG1/1/1 24/1/1729.

102. SRO NG1/1/16 21/1/1761.

103. SRO NG1/1/17 5/8/1763.

104. SRO NG1/1/18 24/3/1767.

105. SRO NG1/1/22 8/3/1780.

106. SRO NG1/1/25 22/6/1785; SRO NG1/1/25 29/6/1785; SRO NG1/1/24 21/2/1785; SRO NG1/1/27 17/6/1789; SRO GD128/3/1.

107. SRO NG1/1/3 19/7/1734; SRO NG1/1/2 7/5/1731; SRO NG1/1/4 18/7/1735; SRO NG1/1/21 7/2/76; SRO NG1/1/32 6/7/1708.

108. *NSA* VII, 335.

109. SRO NG1/1/12 16/11/53.

110. SRO NG1/1/12 13/12/1754; Crawford, *op. cit.*, 265.

111. SRO NG1/1/12 15/11/1754.

112. SRO NG1/1/12 17/1/1755.

113. SRO NG1/1/4 18/7/1735.

114. SRO NG1/1/12 2/8/1754; SRO NG1/1/11 3/1/1752.

115. SRO NG1/1/24 21/2/1785.

116. SRO NG1/1/35 29/6/1824; SRO NG1/1/16 31/7/1761.

117. SRO NG1/1/21 7/12/74; SRO NG1/1/12 1/12/1752; SRO NG1/1/12 13/7/1753; SRO NG1/1/31 11/12/1805.

118. SRO NG1/1/25 29/6/1785; SRO NG1/1/13 27/8/1756; SRO NG1/1/12 19/7/1754; SRO NG1/1/22 28/1/1778; SRO NG1/1/21 26/2/1777; SRO NG1/1/27 2/3/1791.

119. SRO NG1/1/21 26/2/1777.

120. SRO GD128/3/1.

121. SRO NG1/1/1 10/1/29.

122. SRO NG1/1/4 26/1/1739.

123. SRO NG1/1/4 28/6/1738; SRO NG1/1/4 23/6/1738; SRO NG1/1/4 12/12/1735.

124. SRO NG1/1/11 3/1/1752; SRO NG1/1/19 22/11/1769.

125. SRO NG1/1/16 22/1/1762; SRO NG1/1/16 22/1/1762.

126. SRO NG1/1/18 26/7/1768.

127. Luncarty: SRO NG1/1/11 24/1/1752; SRO NG1/1/13 14/11/1755; SRO NG1/1/14 24/1/1749; SRO NG1/1/18 27/3/1764; Deskford: SRO NG1/1/12

1/12/1752; SRO NG1/1/12 19/1/1753; SRO NG1/1/12 17/1/1755; SRO NG1/1/17 4/2/1763; SRO NG1/1/17 27/4/1763; SRO NG1/1/31 15/12/1802; SRO NG1/1/34 10/7/1821; Ormiston: SRO NG1/1/3 19/7/1734; SRO NG1/1/4 28/6/1738; SRO NG1/1/8 12/6/1747; SRO NG1/1/10 9/6/1749; SRO NG1/1/12 26/3/1753; SRO NG1/1/19 28/7/1768.

128. SRO NG1/1/4 23/6/1738.

129. SRO NG1/1/8 12/6/1747.

130. SRO NG1/1/10 12/1/1750; SRO NG1/1/10 20/7/1750.

131. SRO NG1/1/12 24/11/1752; SRO NG1/1/14 24/1/1759.

132. SRO NG1/1/16 23/1/1761.

133. SRO NG1/1/19 12/3/1771; SRO NG1/1/20 1/12/1773.

134. SRO NG1/1/22 17/2/1779.

135. SRO NG1/1/32 6/7/08.

136. SRO NG1/1/23 26/2/1783; SRO NG1/1/24 16/6/1784; SRO NG1/1/24 23/6/1784.

137. SRO NG1/1/27 1/7/1789; SRO NG1/1/27 8/7/1789; SRO NG1/1/27 9/12/1789.

138. Durie, *op. cit.*, 204.

139. *Ibid.*, 349.

140. NLS Acc. 2933/350: Minute of the Court of Proprietors of the British Linen Company, 7th September 1747.

141. Durie, *op. cit.*, 351.

142. NLS Acc. 2933/350.

143. SRO NG1/1/11 3/1/1752.

144. Durie, *op. cit.*, 366.

145. NLS Acc. 1933/350.

146. SRO NG1/1/12 19/1/1753. See also Clow & Clow, *op. cit.*

147. Durie, *op. cit.*, 367.

148. Mostyn Armstrong, (Map of) The Lothians, 1777.

149. See Scott, W. R., *Joint Stock Companies to 1700*, 3 vols., Cambridge, 1910-12.

150. Devine, T. M., Glasgow Merchants in Colonial Trade, 1770-1815, Strathclyde University PhD thesis, 1972.

151. Durie, *op. cit.*, 366.

152. Gauldie, *op. cit.*

153. SRO NG1/1/9 11/1/48.

154. SRO NG1/1/9 18/1/48.

155. SRO NG1/1/9 15/7/48.

156. SRO NG1/1/9 22/7/48.

157. SRO NG1/1/9 4/8/48.

158. SRO NG1/1/10 23/6/49; 21/7/49.

159. SRO NG1/1/10 12/11/50; 23/11/50.

160. SRO NG1/1/14 14/7/58.

161. Hay, G., *History of Arbroath*, Arbroath, 1876, 406.

162. NLS Acc. 2933/330.

163. *OSA* V, 218, Mains of Fintry, Angus.

17

Flax Spinning Mills

Technology

Much attention has been given by historians to three inventions which revolutionised the cotton spinning industry in the late 18th century: Hargreaves' spinning jenny and Arkwright's water frame of 1769, and Crompton's mule of 1779.[1] While the cotton industry was of undoubted importance in Scotland, as in England, only limited emphasis has been placed on the invention which led to the mechanisation of spinning in Scotland's other major textile industry, linen.

Substantial quantities of flax were already being spun by hand in Scotland when, in 1787, two Darlington men, Kendrew, an optician, and Porthouse, a clockmaker, invented and patented a machine to spin flax.[2] In the same year Messrs. Walters, Sim & Thom, threadmakers, obtained a licence and machinery from Kendrew and Porthouse which they used to establish an eight-frame, three-storey spinning mill on the Haugh of Bervie, Kincardineshire, with a view to producing yarn for thread.[3]

During late 1787 and 1788 experiments with the machine were carried out in a former corn mill at Brigton, Angus, to ascertain its usefulness in producing yarn for Osnaburgs, the coarse staple cloth of eastern Scotland. The experiments proved successful, and in 1789 work started on a new four- or possibly five-storey mill nearby.[4] In November 1790 the proprietors attempted to recoup some of their costs by petitioning the Board of Trustees, but despite a favourable report, the £300 which the Board had promised had to be forfeited on the grounds that the machinery was patented.[5]

A few of the later mill-spinners attempted to circumvent this denial of funds by constructing, or claiming to have constructed, machinery of their own design. Neilson, Greenhill & Co. of Kirkland Mill, Fife made such a claim in 1791, but were denied aid for refusing to make their invention available to the public.[6] A similar claim was made in 1794 by Alexander Aberdeen & Co., owners of a mill at Letham, near Arbroath. Although they promised to allow public access, no reply is recorded to the Board's query as to just how free access was to be.[7] Either or both machines may simply have been modifications of Arkwright's machinery, or may even have infringed the Kendrew and Porthouse patent.

As the latter machine was of simple design, it could be readily constructed or modified by millwrights. At Brechin, for example, Thomas Jamison, 'a clever workman, but an unsteady man', built the machinery for a four-frame mill in 1796.[8] However, despite the enthusiasm shown in the 1790s, the Kendrew and Porthouse spinning frame had a major defect. According to Gauldie, 'hand spinners of flax had been accustomed to moisten their flax as they worked, to keep it flexible'.[9] Since the Kendrew and Porthouse machine spun flax dry, the yarn which it produced was brittle and subject to frequent snapping. The fault was diagnosed at an early stage,[10] and although a form of wet spinning was developed in France about 1800, it was not until 1825 that James Kay of Preston, Lancashire patented a wet spinning process.[11]

Flax heckling, a process similar to carding in wool or cotton manufacture, separated the 'line', or long fibres, from the 'tow', or short fibres. The latter, once separated, could be carded and spun like cotton, and at least one tow carding mill was built, on the River Carron in Dumfriesshire.[12] In some cases individual mills specialised in tow spinning, some moving to tow after the difficulties of spinning 'line' became apparent. Heckling had been mechanised by the 1820s, but for the most part it was still performed by hand in 1830, skilled hecklers having an exalted status similar to that once enjoyed by weavers.

Competition from Steam

Many of the early flax spinning mills had been badly sited, necessitating the later addition of auxiliary steam engines to supplement water wheels during dry spells. At Kinghorn, Fife, three flax and cotton spinning mills had been erected on the outflow from a small loch. Within a year or so it was realised that not only had the fall been underestimated but also that the loch would soon be drained. At one of the mills a colliery engine was installed, presumably to pump back water, but it proved so troublesome that it had to be abandoned. Boulton and Watt engines were later added to the other mills, with greater success.[13] At Glamis, Angus, auxiliary steam power was installed in 1820,[14] and by 1834 twelve of the thirty-six mills surveyed by the Factory Commission were using auxiliary steam engines, while at many of the remaining mills owners complained of seasonal variations in water supply.[15] It should be borne in mind, however, that the survey was being carried out with a view to introducing a shorter working day, so the claims may not have been entirely genuine. Some of the same mills which ostensibly suffered from water shortages in the 1830s continued to increase their exploitation of water power until the 1860s, without any resort to steam (Chapter 29, p. 521).

At Dundee, Arbroath and Kirkcaldy, towns with very little exploitable water power, mills powered entirely by steam were built. During the 1790s three or four such mills were built in Dundee but with limited success and, although others were tried in the 1800s and 1810s, it was not until the 1820s that steam became a serious competitor to water power.[16] Steam power was about to be introduced in Fife about 1800,[17] but it was apparently not until 1807 that the

Table 7

Water and Steam Power in Scottish Flax Spinning Mills, 1838

	No. Mills	No. Engines	H.P.	No. Wheels	H.P.	Engines & Wheels	H.P.
AYRSHIRE							
Kilbirnie	1	1	20	—	—	1	20
Beith	2	2	26	—	—	2	26
ABERDEENSHIRE							
Aberdeen	4	10	428	3	200	13	628
MIDLOTHIAN							
Malleny	2	1	30	2	30	3	60
Musselburgh	2	2	61	—	—	2	61
Leith	1	1	30	—	—	1	30
Prestonholm	1	2	55	1	30	3	85
FIFE							
Dunfermline	4	3	56	1	12	4	68
Kinghorn	3	5	103	3	13	8	116
Kirkcaldy	10	11	139	—	—	11	139
Dysart	1	—	—	1	20	1	20
Leslie	5	1	14	6	122	7	136
Edenbank	1	1	8	1	12	2	20
Kettle	1	—	—	1	6	1	6
Markinch	3	—	—	5	107	5	107
Leven	6	3	44	5	110	8	154
Largo	1	1	14	1	15	2	29
Cupar	5	3	44	4	58	7	102
Dairsie	2	—	—	2	26	2	26
Pitscottie	1	1	8	2	26	3	34
Blebo	1	1	8	1	14	2	22
LANARKSHIRE							
Glasgow	2	2	40	—	—	2	40
RENFREWSHIRE							
Greenock	2	—	—	2	100	2	100
Port Glasgow	1	2	92	—	—	2	92
WEST LOTHIAN							
Blackburn	1	1	16	1	16	2	32
PERTHSHIRE							
Perth	1	1	15	—	—	1	15
Woodend	1	—	—	1	25	1	25
Blairgowrie	7	—	—	7	109	7	109
Rattray	4	—	—	4	89	4	89

Table 7 (continued)

	No. Mills	No. Engines	H.P.	No. Wheels	H.P.	Engines & Wheels	H.P.
ANGUS							
Dundee	46	58	1333	—	—	58	1333
Lochee	4	5	64	3	18	8	82
Arbroath	18	25	341	—	—	25	341
Tarry	2	1	6	2	6	3	12
Colliston	2	—	—	2	6	2	6
Friockheim	1	1	7	1	10	2	17
Hatton	2	2	12	2	13	4	25
Inverkeillor	3	2	18	3	28	5	46
Montrose	6	7	267	—	—	7	267
Brechin	4	—	—	4	76	4	76
Kinnaber	1	—	—	1	8	1	8
Tannadice	2	—	—	4	42	4	42
Glamis	1	1	10	1	18	2	28
Ruthven	2	—	—	2	35	2	35
Logie	2	1	14	2	44	3	58
KINCARDINESHIRE							
Bervie	5	—	—	5	23.5	5	23.5
Stonehaven	1	—	—	1	8	1	8
Auchinblae	1	1	7	1	13	2	20
Laurencekirk	1	—	—	1	9	1	9

first steam-powered mill was built, at Kirkcaldy. The first steam-powered mill at Arbroath was established about 1806.[18]

During the 1820s no fewer than twenty-six steam mills were built in Dundee, and the first comprehensive figures, those for 1838, show Dundee in a commanding position, with Kirkcaldy and Arbroath taking second and third places. Nevertheless, water power still accounted for more than thirty per cent of the power used in Scottish flax spinning mills.[19] The results of the 1838 survey are shown in Table 7.

Distribution and Chronology

As has already been noted, the first Scottish flax spinning mill was built near Inverbervie, Kincardineshire in 1787 and the second at Brigton, Angus in 1788. From this time onwards almost every mill of this type was to be built in east-central Scotland (Figure 63). There were several reasons for this. The east of Scotland was already well established as the locus of coarse linen manufacture; the dry process spinning of the Kendrew and Porthouse machine was better suited to these products than to the finer textiles of the west. Even before the mechanisation of spinning, home-grown flax had failed to meet demand and additional supplies had had to be imported from the Baltic and elsewhere; the

Fig 63. Distribution of water-powered flax-spinning mills to 1830

east of Scotland was well placed in relation to these sources. Added to this, there were already merchants dealing in flax and manufacturers giving out work to spinners and weavers. Their capital, access to raw materials and control of the existing labour force put them in a good position to utilise the new flax spinning machinery. All in all, the east of Scotland was the obvious area for the development of mechanised flax spinning.

One negative aspect also contributed to the concentration of flax spinning mills in east-central Scotland: in the west, linen production was already in decline and a new staple, cotton, had absorbed labour, capital and the best water-power sites.

Such was the consistency with which the industry remained centred on one area that there is little to say of changes in distribution within the period 1787-1830. The first spate of mills, about thirty or so, built before 1800, were widely scattered, with little noticeable concentration. Some, such as Kirkland and Kinghorn in Fife, and West Barns in East Lothian, combined flax with cotton spinning.[20] Some were unwisely sited in relation to raw materials or, as has already been noted, to water power. Until 1800 the influence of steam-powered mills on the survival of water-powered ones was negligible. By 1800 much of the euphoria of the previous decade had evaporated, and between that date and 1820 fewer mills were established than during the previous thirteen years. Among the newer mills there was a tendency to utilise rivers offering adequate water power within reasonable reach of ports and therefore raw materials, notably the Ericht in Perthshire, the Esk, Lunan and Dighty in Angus, and the Leven and Eden in Fife. Although there was a move towards larger mills, this was not a universal trend: Lornty Mill, Blairgowrie, built in 1814, had only four spinning frames.[21] As yet, steam power still offered little opposition.

The 1820s brought a revival in building, with as many mills built during that decade as in the previous two. By this time concentration was becoming apparent, and competition from steam was beginning to be felt. Once the use of steam power and flax-spinning machinery had been mastered, port-based mills at Dundee, Arbroath, Montrose or Kirkcaldy were much better placed than water-powered mills inland and, while the cost of coal had to be borne by steam-powered mills, they at least were untroubled by fluctuations in water supply. Some country mills were forced to close while others, although installing auxiliary steam power, were still handicapped by the additional cost of carrying coal overland. For well sited mills, however, the relative cheapness of water power was enough to guarantee their survival, as well as the construction of new mills after 1830.[22] Even in 1838 water power was still competing successfully with steam (Table 14).

In all, about ninety water-powered flax spinning mills had been built in Scotland by 1830. An additional twenty or so mills, mostly built in the 1830s, will be considered in Section Three.

Sources of Finance

The Landowner

For Scottish landowners the prospect of establishing a flax spinning mill offered few attractions. The textile mills which they had been building since 1730 were generally on a small scale, both physically and in terms of capital investment; they utilised local raw materials, complemented rather than competed with agriculture, and were of little or no detriment, aesthetically or economically, to the estate. Flax spinning mills failed to satisfy any of these criteria: they were large, required substantial capital investment, competed with agriculture for labour and, at a time when landowners were already becoming disenchanted with industrialisation, might well have seemed detrimental aesthetically in terms of the building itself and the influx of workers, or economically in terms of the work taken away from hand-spinning and the inflationary effect on farm and estate workers' wages.

Besides all these drawbacks, the landowner could never hope to match the business acumen, existing contacts and access to capital enjoyed by merchants and manufacturers. On the other hand the landowner, by joining a partnership or allowing others to build mills on his land, could find some benefits. Although the high wages offered by spinning mills drew industrial labour away from the land, the presence of a large industrial workforce ensured a ready market for agricultural produce. While spinning mills took work from spinners, they gave it back to weavers. By augmenting the estate's rental, the establishment of a spinning mill might well be to its benefit, economically or even aesthetically, provided that overall control of development rested with the landowner, who could make it the nucleus of an existing or projected planned village.

The earliest case of involvement by a landowner is also the most interesting. The Brigton Mill of 1789, although financed and run by Dundee interests headed by the mathematician James Ivory, also involved the landowner William Douglas. Besides making a corn mill available for experiments, Douglas built the village of Douglastown to house spinning-mill workers.[23] When, in 1803, the company was disbanded, he paid off its debts and in the following year bought the mill at a public sale. He continued to run the mill until 1808 when he took in partners at £800 each. Some seven years later poor trade and bad debts forced the mill to close once more; Douglas again paid off its debts and ran the mill himself until 1817, when he finally withdrew. The mill and the village were advertised for sale, initially at an upset price of £3,000, subsequently at £2,000. The mill was eventually bought and continued to operate until the mid-1830s, when it finally closed down.[24] Douglas was much more typical of the 18th than the 19th-century landowner in his dedication — probably misguided — to a favourite project.

The only other landowner who is known to have been actively involved in flax mill spinning was George Dempster of Dunnichen. While Dempster was better known for his exploits in the cotton industry (p. 321), he was a member of the partnership which built a flax mill alongside the cotton mill at Stanley, Perthshire.[25] He may also have been involved in either or both of the spinning mills operating at his village of Letham in 1813.[26]

Merchants and Manufacturers

In contrast to the passive role of the landowners, that of the merchants and manufacturers was central to the development of flax spinning mills. Some reference has already been made to the advantages enjoyed by merchants and manufacturers when it came to establishing such mills (p. 257). In addition, it should be said that spinning was a major cost component in the manufacture of flax, offering an incentive to mechanise the process and thereby increase profits or undercut competitors. Although large sums might be required to establish a flax spinning mill, initial losses could be offset by profits from other processes in textile manufacture.

Of those merchants and manufacturers involved in mill building, the majority already had close links with the textile industry. Mark Stark, who founded Brucefield Mill, Dunfermline and Prestonholm Mill, Midlothian, both in 1793, had previously run a bleachfield at the former site.[27] The Baxters at Dundee and Alexander Aberdeen & Co. at Arbroath were already linen manufacturers when they built their spinning mills, while two of the partners in Grandholm Mill, Aberdeenshire had backgrounds in the bleaching and woollen industries (p. 263).

While most merchants and manufacturers were based at coastal towns, the need for water power led them to build mills miles inland. Thus a Montrose company built their mill four miles inland at Logie;[28] Baxters and Neilsons, both from Dundee, built mills at Glamis and Kirkland respectively.[29] Kirkcaldy merchants and manufacturers, such as John Fergus, built their mills to the north, on the River Leven.[30] One important inland centre, Forfar, was also very deficient in water power; James Laird & Co., manufacturers there, built a mill five miles away on the Esk at Murthill.[31]

Despite the creation of rural spinning mills, the yarn produced there still went back to the manufacturers' town bases, and particularly to Dundee. In many cases it was a struggle to find even enough local labour for the spinning mill itself, so there was little prospect of weaving taking place there too. Furthermore, the organisation of the industry was still centred on the towns and ports as the move back to them showed once steam power became practicable. Even Blairgowrie, a growing community with an established weaving population, sent yarn to Dundee.[32]

Tenants and Artisans

Bearing in mind the need for capital, knowledge of the trade, and control over other stages in manufacture, it is hardly surprising that very few tenants or artisans were able to build flax spinning mills. The two rare examples that follow show the contrasting fortunes of a weaver and a millwright.

James Smith, the eldest son of a millwright, trained and worked as a weaver before giving it up at the age of seventeen to work in his mother's meal shop. Four years later he decided to build a flax spinning mill at Strathmartine, Angus, on land tenanted by his uncle. Tradesmen's bills for the construction of the mill came to £407, but for the most part no written contracts were entered into. The mason, who was due £67, received only £40, the remainder of his account being paid as sixteen bolls of meal, a quantity of sugar and some cheese. The millwright also received part of his payment in kind. Other tradesmen received part of the money due to them, but Smith was unable to pay their accounts in full, and only thirteen months after construction had started his assets were sequestrated.[33]

In contrast David Grimond enjoyed considerable success. The Grimond family had occupied a lint mill on Lornty Burn, north of Blairgowrie: Charles Grimond was granted £15 in 1803 to repair the lint mill of Lornty and build a shed.[34] This mill was almost certainly the one in which David Grimond, a millwright by trade, installed four spinning frames in 1814, although McDonald claims that the mill was built from scratch.[35] The profits from the mill, about £5-£6 per week, may have been re-invested in a second mill, Brooklinn, which David Grimond built on the tail lade of Lornty Mill, probably in 1820.[36] At one time or another the Grimond family controlled four of the twelve mills in the Blairgowrie area.[37] As with William Douglas among landowners, David Grimond was very much the exception to the rule among tenants and artisans. With very few exceptions Scottish flax spinning mills were the work of merchants and manufacturers.

The Board of Trustees

Before leaving the subject of mill financing, something should be said about the role of the Board of Trustees, if only to illustrate the way in which developments had overtaken it.

Reference has already been made to the Board's reluctance to provide financial backing for flax spinning mills, on the grounds that the machinery was patented (p. 253). There were other grounds on which the Board refused help. It had seldom given backing to large-scale projects, the raw material was imported, and the mechanisation of the process deprived hand-spinners of their livelihood. By the mid-1790s merchants and manufacturers had accepted that the Board was not going to provide help; in any case, it is doubtful whether they either wanted or needed the small amount of aid which the Board could have given, had it wished to.

The mid-1790s also saw the emergence of a long-standing point of contention between the mill-spinners and the Board of Trustees. In July 1795 eight mill-spinners, including Robert Fall & Co., merchant owners of West Barns Mill, petitioned the Board for the abolition of the Act under which reels of yarn were confiscated for containing too little.[38] The regulation, which had originally been introduced to prevent fraud, was easy to comply with when small quantities were being spun by hand, but almost impossible under millspinning. However, the Board was adamant: 'this application cannot upon any account be listened to'.[39] In 1800, after a second petition, this time from millspinners in Fife, a committee of enquiry was appointed, which eventually found in their favour.[40] Despite the ruling, the Act continued to be enforced. During 1806 the Board's inspector was refused access to at least one mill, and by 1808 a group of mill-spinners were preparing to lobby Parliament for the Act's abolition.[41] The battle dragged on until finally, in 1823, the Board's powers of inspection, including that of linen yarn, were abolished.[42]

As far as flax spinning was concerned, the Board had outlived its usefulness. The protection, guidance and support which it offered were of great value to the small-scale manufacturer of the 18th century, but in an age of large-scale capitalist mill-spinners such activities, by a group largely made up of land-owners and members of the legal profession, were seen as restrictive and obsolete.

Had the Board been more flexible in its approach, it could have found a useful role in controlling working conditions. Indeed, part of the reluctance among mill-spinners to allow inspection might have been due to the abysmal conditions under which their employees worked. As it was, the Factory Commission and the Royal Commission on the Labour of Children in Factories assumed this role from the 1830s onwards, and it is only through their work that we know just how bad these conditions could be.

The Workforce

The mechanisation of flax spinning brought about important changes in the distribution, quantity and quality of work. Prior to mechanisation, spinning had been performed by individuals at home, or occasionally in small workshops. Although manufacturers already had some control of those employed, workers — generally female — were free to work their own hours and lived in communities scattered over a wide area. The effect of mechanisation was to concentrate spinning in a relatively few localities, denying work to those in many other localities where spinning had formerly been performed. From Meigle parish, Perthshire it was reported in the New Statistical Account that machinery had put an end to hand-spinning and that old women in particular had been reduced to poverty for want of work.[43]

On the other hand the increase in output engendered by mechanisation created more demand for weavers, and in several instances weaving re-absorbed some of the labour deprived of spinning work. In Collace parish, Perthshire, according to the New Statistical Account, the spinning wheel had been entirely superseded and spinsters had taken up the loom, using yarn which agents brought by cart from Dundee.[44] The same changeover had occurred in the Forfar area by 1812.[45]

While the mechanised spinning industry was less labour-intensive, there were still problems in recruiting workers. An average mill might need about forty or fifty workers, and larger ones a hundred or more. The dependence upon water power meant that mills were often built in areas with only a scattered rural population, much of it already employed in agriculture or weaving. There are also reasons for believing that there was a reluctance to work in such unpleasant, strictly regulated conditions. The evidence given to the Royal Commission on the Labour of Children in Factories not only casts some light on these conditions, but also shows the way in which a labour force was found. In some cases children as young as five years of age were hired for a few months or several years. Orphans from charitable institutions in Edinburgh and Perth were sent to work in mills, sharing bothies with adolescent female employees. To fulfil a certain work quota, a working day, nominally thirteen or fourteen hours, might be extended up to twenty-one hours during low water. Clocks were removed from within the mill and workers were locked in.[46] Generally speaking, workers in country mills suffered longer hours and poorer living conditions than those in towns. Because of the isolation of many mills it was difficult to find alternative employment.

With the exception of children the majority of mill employees were young women, the same women who might otherwise have worked at hand-spinning. The writer of the Old Statistical Account for Dron parish, Perthshire complained of the shortage of female servants brought about by the increase in linen manufacture and the recent introduction of spinning.[47] There is also some slight evidence of people displaced from the land finding employment in spinning mills.

Through time conditions in spinning mills improved. At Trottick Mill, Angus, for example, the mill owner ran a school which child employees could attend during working hours.[48] The practice of accommodating workers in bothies began to give way to building houses as the scale of mills increased. Besides the example at Douglastown (p. 259), villages grew up at Haugh Mill, Fife and at Craigo and Logie, Angus.[49] At Prinlaws, Fife a village created to house bleachfield and spinning mill workers contained seven hundred and sixty inhabitants by the mid-1840s. The houses, each with its own garden, were 'neatly built, and ornamented with shrubs and evergreens'.[50] At Blair-gowrie some mill workers lived beside the mills and others at the existing communities of Blairgowrie and Rattray.[51]

A Scottish Flax Spinning Mill: Grandholm Mill, Aberdeen

On 20th February 1792 the firm of Leys & Co. entered into an agreement with John Paton of Grandholm, under which the company cut a lade over a mile in length to carry water from the River Don to a projected bleachworks and flax spinning mill.[52] The three partners, Thomas Leys, Alexander Brebner and James Hadden, had previous contacts with the textile industry. Leys was a member of the family which, in 1749, had established a bleachfield at Gordon's Mills under the firm of Leys Still & Co., later Leys, Masson & Co.[53] Alexander Brebner was his brother-in-law, and James Hadden was the son of Alexander Hadden, a hosiery merchant in Aberdeen and a woollen manufacturer at Gordon's Mills and Garlogie.[54]

The original flax spinning mill stood seven storeys high and contained three hundred and eighty-six windows;[55] two water wheels developed eighty horse power.[56] To facilitate access, the company built bridges on the River Don and the Aberdeenshire canal.[57] In 1805 the water supply was augmented by the construction of a dam across the Don, at the intake to the lade; thereafter additional wheels were installed to give a further forty-three horse power.[58] A fireproof wing was added to the mill in 1812,[59] and in all nearly £30,000 was spent on modifications to the mill between 1805 and 1820.[60]

According to Kennedy, writing in 1818, the mill contained two hundred and forty spinning frames, producing 10,000 spindles of yarn per week. Part of the machinery was used to twist yarn for coloured thread. The heavy yarns were sent south for weaving, mostly to Fife and Angus, while the rest of the yarn was woven by the company.[61] An additional fireproof building, for heckling by power, was built in 1822-3; a third building, for weaving and tow carding, was constructed in 1826 and extended in 1830.[62] All this additional machinery put a strain on the available water power, for although the company had one hundred and fifty horse power at its disposal, it had become involved in expensive litigation over water rights, which started in 1816 and dragged on for many years thereafter, eventually to be settled by compromise.[63] With these problems to consider, plus the variable flow of the River Don, the company, like several others, installed auxiliary steam engines of fifty and sixty horse power, one of which ran in tandem with one of the water wheels during low water.[64] The mill continued to operate long after 1830, eventually being used as a woollen mill.[65]

With the mechanisation of spinning, the Scottish linen industry made a further move from being primarily a domestic industry dispersed over a large area to a factory industry concentrated in relatively few localities. The move towards a more capital-intensive industry, which had started with mechanised flax scutching and which had developed further with the mechanisation of bleaching, took a major step forward. In those areas where mills were built, new villages were created and others expanded to house both mill-workers and the additional workforce required in weaving and bleaching. The need for commercial skills and the large amount of capital required to establish and run a spinning mill precluded involvement by the tenants and artisans who had contributed to the industry at earlier stages; landowners, lacking capital, expertise or, for that matter, interest, were also excluded. In almost every case the initiative to build flax spinning mills came from merchants and manufacturers, working individually or collectively, and such was their power and influence that they could ignore or even overrule the Board of Trustees, the body which had supported and guided the industry during its earlier days.

The adoption of fixed quotas of production, in a highly competitive market, was in conflict with the variable capabilities of water power and led initially to the imposition of excessively long hours and eventually to the introduction of steam power either as a supplement or as an alternative. While the better-sited water-powered mills continued to function up to and beyond 1830, the industry had already become primarily urban by that date, which led to a further concentration of population and a decline in rural industry. The Age of Water Power was coming to an end. The Age of Steam had already begun.

NOTES

1. See Chapter 20, pp. 317-8.

2. Mann, J. de L., in Singer, C., Holmyard, E. J., Hall, A. R. & Williams, T. I. (eds.), *A History of Technology*, 5 vols., Oxford, 1956-9, IV, 291-2.

3. Warden, A. J., *The Linen Industry Ancient & Modern*, London, 1864, 489-90; *OSA* XIII, 4.

4. Warden, *op. cit.*, 511; *NSA* XI, 218.

5. SRO NG1/1/27 17/11/90; 19/1/91; 26/1/91.

6. SRO NG1/1/27 2/2/91.

7. SRO NG1/1/28 11/6/94.

8. Black, D. D., *The History of Brechin to 1864*, 2nd Edition, Edinburgh, 1867, 272.

9. Gauldie, E. (ed.), 'The Dundee Textile Industry 1790-1885', *SHS* 4th Series, VI (1969), xx.

10. See, for example, *OSA* V, 218 on Trottick Mill, Angus.

11. Mann, *op. cit.*, 292-3.

12. SRO NG1/1/35 29/6/24.

13. Warden, *op. cit.*, 510.

14. *NSA* XI, 348.

15. *PP* 1834 XIX 80180, Replies by Manufacturers to Queries.

16. Warden, *op. cit.*, 588-9, 592.

17. Thomson, J., *General View of the Agriculture of the County of Fife*, Edinburgh, 1800, 307.

18. Warden, *op. cit.*, 565.

19. *PP* 1834 XIX, 82-3.

20. Butt, J., 'Valuation of Scottish Cotton Mills by Sun Fire Insurance Office c. 1795', *EcHR* 2nd Series, XXIII (1970), 262-3.

21. MacDonald, J. A. R., *A History of Blairgowrie*, Blairgowrie, 1899, 168.

22. See Chapter 29.

23. Although Warden attributes the village to James Ivory & Co., an earlier source, the New Statistical Account, names Douglas himself as its founder: *NSA* XI, 225.

24. Warden, *op. cit.*, 511-3.

25. *OSA* XVIII, 515.

26. Headrick, J., *General View of the Agriculture of Forfarshire*, Edinburgh, 1813, 210-1.

27. *OSA* XIII, 433; SRO GD45/16/450; SRO NG1/1/18 8/12/67.

28. *NSA* XI, 267.

29. Gauldie, *op. cit.*, xx-xxi.

30. SRO NG1/1/19; *PP* 1834 XIX, 66-7. John Fergus & Son, manufacturers in Kirkcaldy, established a bleachfield at Tyrie in 1772 and a flax spinning mill at Leslie before 1834. John Fergus & Sons also had a cotton mill at Kinghorn in 1796: Butt, *op. cit.*, 263.

31. SRO CS96/767.

32. *NSA* X, 921.

33. SRO CS96/419.

34. SRO NG1/1/31 6/7/1803.

35. MacDonald, *op. cit.*, 168. A lintel bears the date 1755, possibly that of the original lint mill.

36. *PP* 1834 XIX, 164. 1820 is the second of two dates given by Grimond. The first, 1815, ties in with the commencement of spinning at Lornty.

37. *Ibid.*, 165, Oakbank Mill; MacDonald, *op. cit.*, 169, Ashbank Mill.

38. SRO NG1/1/29 8/9/95; Act 13th Geo 1st Cap. 26.

39. *Ibid.*

40. SRO NG1/1/30 28/5/1800; 4/2/1801; SRO NG1/1/32 9/7/1806.

41. SRO NG1/1/32 9/7/1806; 24/2/1808.

42. Warden, *op. cit.*, 472.

43. *NSA* X, 236.

44. *Ibid.*, 215-6.

45. Headrick, *op. cit.*, 189.

46. *PP* 1832 XV, 338-92, Royal Commission on the Labour of Children in Factories.

47. *OSA* IX, 466.

48. *PP* 1832 XV, 364.

49. Logie, Craigo: Butt, J., *The Industrial Archaeology of Scotland*, Newton Abbot, 1967, 62; Haugh Mill: Lewis, S., *Topographical Dictionary of Scotland*, 2 vols., London, 1846, I, 536.

50. Lewis, *op. cit.*, II, 170.

51. Wilson, J. M. (ed.), *The Imperial Gazetteer of Scotland*, 2 vols., Edinburgh, London & Dublin, N.D. (c.1865), I, 174-5, II, 645.

52. Morgan, P., *Annals of Woodside and Newhills*, Aberdeen, 1886, 58.

53. *Ibid.*, 58.

54. *Ibid.*, 65, 67.

55. *Ibid.*, 59.

56. *Ibid.*, 63.

57. *Ibid.*, 59.

58. *Ibid.*, 63.

59. *PP* 1834 XIX, 10.

60. Morgan, *op. cit.*, 64.

61. Kennedy, W., *Annals of Aberdeen*, 2 vols., London, 1818, II, 199-200.

62. *PP* 1834 XIX, 10.

63. Morgan, *op. cit.*, 59-63.

64. *PP* 1834 XIX, 10-12.

65. Butt, *op. cit.* (1967), 200.

18

Woollen Mills, 1730-1785

Introduction

The century between 1730 and 1830 saw the transformation of the Scottish woollen industry from one in which most of the processes in manufacture were performed by hand to one in which almost all were performed by machine. Within the period, however, it was not until 1785 that most of this mechanisation took place, and while the industry prior to this date shows indications of the way in which it was to develop thereafter, it was in many other respects little different from that of the late 17th century. For this reason and because of the sheer scale of the industry between 1730 and 1830, it is convenient to consider the periods before and after 1785 in two separate chapters.

Technology

Unlike any other type of 18th-century textile mill, the waulk mill and its technology were by no means new to Scotland (see Chapter 3). It is therefore doubtful whether any technical advances were made in the years immediately after 1730. By mid-century, however, there is some indication of attempts to improve waulk mills by utilising English designs.

A company of Glasgow merchants, with a manufactory at Camlachie, petitioned the Board of Trustees in 1745 for help in building an English-style waulk mill, claiming that a 'perfect fulling mill' was 'a thing utterly unknown in this country'.[1] Eventually, in 1754, a mill was built at a cost of £380,[2] but in the meantime a second mill, at Haddington, had been constructed by Andrew Meikle, using information gathered on a tour of England financed by the Board of Trustees.[3] From the little technical information available from the time, it would seem that one of the major advantages of English waulk mills was the use of multiple fulling stocks: the mill at Haddington had two and the Camlachie company, in its petition, mentions the use of several in any one mill. By inference the Scottish mills of the time had only one fulling stock. It is also tempting to see the introduction of English designs as a change from more primitive falling-stocks with the feet or hammers dropping vertically and hanging-stocks with the feet pivoted at their ends (Figure 64), but there is no concrete evidence to confirm this theory.[4] Whatever was the case various im-

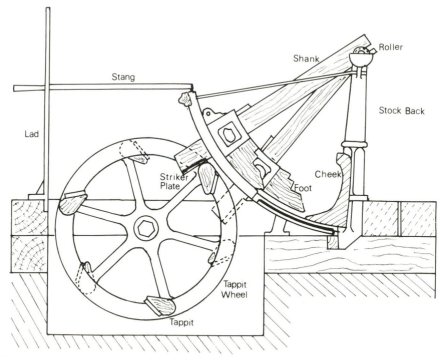

Fig 64. 19th-century fulling mill machinery

provements were incorporated into the Camlachie and Haddington mills, and possibly into another waulk mill which Andrew Meikle built for the ill-fated Garvaldfoot manufactory, Peeblesshire in 1752-3.[5]

No further refinements seem to have taken place by 1783 when George Mercer, a small-scale manufacturer at Wilderhaugh, Galashiels, claimed to be building a waulk mill on 'a new and improved plan'.[6]

In addition to these minor modifications to fulling mills, the period 1730-1785 saw the introduction, or rather the re-introduction, of other finishing machinery. In Chapter 3 reference was made to a gig mill and a frizzing mill, installed at New Mills and Restalrig respectively (p. 51). It was also suggested that these machines may have gone out of use after the early 1700s; whether or not this was the case, a gig mill was certainly in use at Haddington during the 1750s, and a frizzing mill had been installed by the 1770s. The Haddington mill also incorporated what was probably Scotland's first water-powered 'teazer', a machine which removed foreign bodies from the wool and opened out the fibres.[7]

While these additional applications had been found for water power, it is doubtful whether any but the most extensive woollen manufactories such as those at Kilmarnock, Camlachie or Haddington were able to put them into use. In the vast majority of Scottish waulk mills, the fulling stock itself remained the only water-powered machine until after 1785.

Mill Builders

Landowners

With the exception of guild mills in burghs, almost all the waulk mills built in Scotland prior to 1730 had been the work of landowners. In the depressed circumstances in which the woollen industry found itself after the Union and with enough existing mills to handle the coarse cloth still produced, it is unlikely that many waulk mills were built by landowners before mid-century. From about 1750, however, a new wave of mill-building started, in which landowners played a significant part.

While most of the earlier rural mills had been intended to serve the needs of individuals or custom weavers, the new waulk mills were often conceived as part of a larger venture, foreshadowing the development of integrated woollen mills after 1785 and reflecting a more general 'Improving' movement among landowners.

The Haddington Tarred Wool Company of 1750 included several landowners such as Lord Milton and Lord Deskford; a second company, occupying the same site, was dominated by landowning interests. The history of the Tarred Wool Company is considered at length later in this chapter. In this case the involvement of landowners was indirect: the mill was capitalised collectively by landowners and other parties.

None of them provided the site, nor could any of them expect to derive particular benefits for his estate through its presence. In short, it was more a business enterprise than a personal project.

A similar type of manufactory was established at Hawick about mid-century by three landowners, who took into partnership a Dunfermline weaver.[8] Although the original product was to be carpets, by the 1780s the finest wool was being set aside for making blankets, which found a ready market, and inkle-work had been started. Wight, visiting Hawick in 1782, found the partners starting work on 'a fulling mill upon a most complete plan, adjacent to a fall of water'.[9]

Besides these 'business enterprises', other manufactories of a similar type were developed as individual projects. James Dickson, the owner of Ednam estate, Roxburghshire, envisaged a canal from Berwick to Ednam and his estate as a great centre of industry. To that end, in 1765 he established a woollen cloth manufactory, fitted with the best machinery and manned by skilled workers from Yorkshire. The principal products were English blankets. Besides the manufactory he built ' a neat village' of brick houses with pantile or slate roofs. Only £200 was subscribed towards the Berwick canal, but the manufactory enjoyed a modicum of success, though hardly on the scale originally envisaged.[10]

The 5th Duke of Argyll, who started a woollen manufactory near Inveraray in 1774, was very similar to Dickson in his motivation, but worked in a much less favourable environment. Auspicious beginnings persuaded other Argyll landowners to subscribe and, by 1775, £700 had been raised. In November of that year attempts were made to find a manager; William Inglis, a manufacturer from Lanark, took the post on a nine-year contract with a salary of £100 per annum. From a minimum supply of four hundred stones of wool Inglis had to produce carpets, coarse cloth, Kendal 'cottons' and stockings. Over £500 was laid out in 1777 and 1778 on building a factory house and several other buildings, including a waulk mill. Although Inglis proved to be a poor manager, the manufactory struggled on, largely through the efforts of the Duke of Argyll. The local population increased, and a school was built for workers' children, but in 1785 Inglis failed and handed over the factory and machinery, now in a very run-down state, to two Glasgow manufacturers. The woollen manufactory stumbled on through a succession of crises and managers until the early 1800s when, despite the repeated intervention of the Duke, it finally closed down.[11]

A smaller, less ambitious project, the building of a waulk mill, was undertaken by a few other Highland landowners: Grant of Grant at Craggan, Inverness-shire in 1750,[12] Campbell of Barcaldine at Lismore, Argyll in 1759,[13] and the Forfeited Estates Commission at the Kirktoun of Strowan, Perthshire, in 1765.[14]

Merchants and Manufacturers

Two groups of merchants and manufacturers, definable but not always distinct, were involved in the development of wool textile mills during the period 1730-1785. On the one hand there were a number of fairly substantial merchants who became members of partnerships involved in wool manufacture, although this was not their prime area of interest. On the other hand there were small-scale waulker manufacturers who combined the operation of a waulk mill with other stages in wool manufacture, wool trading or even farming.

Members of the first group were active in the central Lowlands, notably in the west. In 1746 six or eight of the 'most opulent and respectable merchants and inhabitants' of Kilmarnock established a woollen manufactory in the town to make carpets.[15] By 1754 a waulk mill had been added, at a cost of £100.[16] At Camlachie, near Glasgow, a group of Glasgow merchants established a woollen manufactory in, or shortly after, 1745. Finding that the woollen industry was 'quite unknown in all its steps' in the Glasgow area, they petitioned the Board of Trustees for assistance in acquiring machinery and skilled workmen from England.[17] By 1754 they had built a waulk mill at a cost of £380.[18] In the east of Scotland William Caddell, a Cockenzie-based merchant, became one of the shareholders in the second Haddington Tarred Wool Company.[19]

The second group, while numerically greater than the first, were usually of far lesser stature financially. Indeed, they owe their status as merchants or manufacturers largely to the loose connotation of the terms in a Scottish context; anywhere else they might not have qualified for the title. Some of them combined this work with other activities. In the light of subsequent developments it is significant that most of them were to be found in the Borders; most of the evidence comes from Loch's *Tour*. At Yetholm, Roxburghshire, Andrew Kerr, a tenant farmer, was also described as 'manufacturer and clothier'. According to Loch, he 'does a great deal of business in the dressing and dying way, as well on his own account as for all the country around; he is capital in all branches of his business; he has good education, and endowed with a more than ordinary share of knowledge and good sense. He has a waulk mill and houses of his own property sufficient to carry on his work to a large extent'.[20]

At Melrose, John Lyell, 'merchant, manufacturer and clothier', manufactured cloth with wool purchased from the Duke of Buccleuch's tenants, and had 'a good waulk mill' of his own construction.[21] Alexander Hopkirk, 'a noted clothier', had a waulk mill at Dryburgh, Berwickshire;[22] William Darling at Cumledge Easter Waulkmill was described as 'dyer and woollen manufacturer', and George Mercer of Wilderhaugh, Roxburghshire as 'clothier and dyer' in 1783.[23] Elsewhere in the Borders, at Galashiels, where there had been three waulk mills since the 16th century, and at Peebles small 'waulker-manufacturers' collectively rented waulk mills or held them in feu.[24]

Tenants and Artisans

Between 1730 and 1785 there are very few cases of tenants or artisans building waulk mills. In 1739 the tenant of North Berwick mills had a waulk mill built at a cost of £47 19s 7d, using capital advanced by and repayable to his landowner.[25] The only other example which has been found was at St. Andrews, where Robert Russell, feuar of Seamills and sub-tacksman of the town's flour mills, successfully petitioned the council to allow him to build a waulk mill and washing mill immediately below the flour mill.[26]

In addition to these two, the small waulker-manufacturers of the Border counties, who were certainly active during the third quarter of the 18th century, might be included as much in this category as in the previous one, but they were differentiated from the run-of-the-mill waulker by their broader involvement in woollen manufacture and by the subsequent developments which stemmed from their early initiatives.

Already, by 1730, there was an adequate stock of waulk mills in Scotland; immediately thereafter the woollen industry survived, but hardly flourished, and in the twenty years up to 1750 only one waulk mill is known to have been built. When, after 1750, building finally recommenced, most mills were associated with ventures larger than artisans were able to finance. Admittedly, a Dunfermline weaver was a member of the partnership which established the carpet manufactory at Hawick, but his contribution was more probably one of skills than of capital. Only after 1785 did tenants and artisans begin to play an active role.

The Board of Trustees

From its instigation in 1727, the Board of Trustees had a mandate to support the development of three sectors of the Scottish economy, namely fisheries, the linen industry and the woollen industry. The budget allocated to the woollen industry was from the first a small one, and at least until 1785 it very much came second to linen in the aid afforded to it by the Board.

At an early stage the Board of Trustees introduced a scheme under which persons could contract to sort and manufacture a certain quantity of wool.[27] However, with inferior livestock and poor marketing there was little prospect of the Board's reviving the industry.[28]

As for a commitment to mill-building, this did not come until about 1750, and then possibly through devious means. In 1750 the Haddington Tarred Wool Company persuaded the Board to finance a visit to England by Andrew Meikle, who had already undertaken work for it in connection with the linen industry.[29] Meikle was to inspect the best English waulk mills and bring back models. In the event, the Board not only paid for the visit and the models, but also gave the company a contribution towards the cost of constructing its mill, to an extent equivalent in value to an unfulfilled quota of woollen cloth previously contracted for by the company.[30] It may have been more than co-incidence that this, the first waulk mill to receive financial aid from the Board, included among its shareholders two of the Board's foremost members, Lord Milton and Lord Deskford.[31]

The case of the Tarred Wool Company seemed to set a precedent for the Board's providing financial and technical aid. In 1753 they granted £100 towards the £254 laid out on a mill by Andrew Brown for William Douglas & Co., at Garvaldfoot, Peeblesshire. Two years later, however, the company was struck off the Board's list for failing to provide any of the woollen cloth contracted for.[32] In 1754 a grant of £40 was given towards a £100 mill at Kilmarnock, and in 1755 a like sum was provided towards a £380 mill at Camlachie, Glasgow, but only on condition that it dressed coarse tarred wool at reasonable rates.[33] Andrew Meikle, who had undertaken research and construction work for the Haddington company, attested to the completion of the Kilmarnock mill and appears to have acted in an advisory capacity at Garvaldfoot, even though his 'throng of business' delayed the mill's completion.[34]

From the 1750s no further assistance was given to waulk mill-building until the 1780s, and then only grudgingly.[35] During the intervening twenty years the Board's attention and finances had been fixed on the linen industry. However, one cannot place all the blame for lack of interest on the Board, for its attitude was merely a reflection of that of Scotland as a whole. Without improvements in livestock husbandry and technology, and with few mills being built anyway, there was little justification or scope for it to provide aid. The emphasis placed on linen was probably well-founded, for while pamphleteers occasionally bemoaned the lost status of the woollen industry, the potential markets, the scope for improvements in production and the overall public interest were probably greater in linen than in wool at that time.

Distribution and Chronology

An attempt to assess the distribution and chronology of waulk mills between 1730 and 1785 is fraught with difficulties, most of which stem from an 'information vacuum' between the early and late 18th century.

In Chapter 3 we saw that, at one time or another between 1550 and 1730, something like three hundred waulk mills operated in Scotland. Just how many of these were still active in 1730? We do not know; major sources such as the Register of the Great Seal and Poll Tax Returns stop short of 1730, while others such as the Old and New Statistical Accounts come too late. Of the few strictly contemporary sources, General Roy's map is accessible only as a poor redrafting which shows no more than forty sites, while the Scottish Record Office's GD series of estate papers mentions only fifty or so, including several identified by Roy. Some of these may have been mere place names, perpetuating the memory of mills already defunct. Just to complicate matters further, many of the mills mentioned by these and other sources were not necessarily built after 1730: they may well have been established much earlier, but were simply not previously recorded.

Without a lot of additional research it is not possible to build up a reasonably comprehensive distribution map. Instead it will have to suffice to show those mills already recorded before 1730 and still operating, those first identified between 1730 and 1785 and those definitely established within that period (Figure 65). This information will, in turn, be added to the distribution map for the much better documented period from 1785 to 1830. However incomplete information might be, some understanding of developments between 1730 and 1785 is needed to set the scene for the major developments which were to take place after 1785.

This is best done by considering the contemporary evidence for activity of a more general nature in the Scottish woollen industry; as the process of fulling was already mechanised in all areas except the remoter parts of the Highlands and Islands, this should give a fair reflection of the distribution of working waulk mills.

While the protestations of merchants and manufacturers about the adverse effects of the Union might have led one to believe that the Scottish woollen industry died in 1707, there is little evidence to support this. As we saw in Chapter 3, the manufacture of fine woollen cloth was ailing long before 1707, and was extinct by 1730. The coarse woollen industry, on the other hand, involved a low-price, low-quality commodity which was not entirely directed towards the open market and was therefore practically immune to the English competition which had helped to wreck the fine cloth industry. Furthermore, the opening up of English colonial markets more than compensated for the loss of European outlets.

Fig 65. Distribution of waulk mills, 1730-1785

Gulvin, in *The Tweedmakers*, gives the following information on the industry's distribution:

> In 1733 Patrick Lindsey admitted that Kilmarnock, Stirling, Aberdeen and Edinburgh were not unimportant centres of woollen manufacture and that Musselburgh and Galashiels were also manufacturing for the open market. By the 1760s Postlethwayt found 'many hundreds' of looms at work in the Stirling area and a number around Alloa. By then woollens were also expanding at Edinburgh and in the Lothians. At Aberdeen woollens were declining relative to linens, but the old cloths were still made 'to a great amount' and the stocking trade was thriving.[36]

In addition to the coarse traditional cloth, the manufacture of light worsted fabrics was appearing among urban clothiers, partly in response to the needs of colonial markets.[37]

In which areas, then, did the manufacture of woollen cloth decline and in which did it expand? In the Borders the pattern seems to have been one of redistribution. Pococke, travelling through Jedburgh in 1760, found that the town's former woollen manufacture had 'quite decayed',[38] but at Hawick a carpet manufactory had been established about mid-century[39] and it had also taken to making blankets by the early 1780s.[40] At Selkirk, a woollen manufactory which later became the site of a major spinning mill was established in 1767.[41] Loch's *Tour* of the late 1770s depicts a thriving woollen industry in several of the Border towns and villages, notably at Galashiels where 2,200 stones of wool per annum were being used to make blankets and Galashiels greys.[42] In 1780 Lord Gardenstone 'found in this village a number of very industrious people'.[43]

In the west of Scotland, notably in Ayrshire, the woollen industry continued to operate, and in Kilmarnock and Maybole manufactories were established.[44]

In the Lothians wool lost a little ground to linen, and even the manufacture of broadcloth and blankets at Haddington experienced mixed fortunes (pp. 276-8).

In Fife and Angus one would have expected the linen industry to affect the fortunes of the woollen industry to a greater extent; in both counties there had been large numbers of waulk mills prior to 1730, and some may have been converted to dress flax or to serve other purposes. On the other hand Dalkeith and Haddington were still sending wool north to Fife in the late 1770s, and a broadcloth manufactory, proposed for Dundee in the 1770s, offers further evidence that the woollen industry was more resilient than might have been supposed.[45]

In the north-east, where competition from linen was less marked, wool was still being imported from southern Scotland in the 1770s.[46] In the Highlands there is evidence of the extension of the woollen industry, with the establishment of the Inveraray manufactory and the building of waulk mills at Lismore in Argyll, Craggan in Inverness-shire, Strowan in Perthshire and Ullapool in Ross-shire.[47]

Broadly speaking, the distribution of woollen manufacture in Scotland was, with the exception of developments in the Highlands, little different from that of the 17th century, even though the products were more diverse; most of the changes in distribution were to take place in the years between 1785 and 1830, although the vitality of waulker-manufacturers in the Borders was already apparent, as were the beginnings of regional specialisation, such as the Ayrshire carpet manufacture. All in all, the woollen industry — and by implication waulk mills — if not flourishing to the same extent as linen, was still functioning in most areas during the period 1730-1785, a fact which goes some way towards explaining its forceful revival in the period 1785-1830.

A Scottish Woollen Mill: the Tarred Wool Company's Mill, Haddington

Before concluding this chapter it is worth examining in more detail one of the mills which, in many ways, characterised developments in the use of water power in the woollen industry between 1730 and 1785. The most interesting, and certainly the best documented, is the Tarred Wool Company's mill at Haddington.

The closure in 1713 of the New Mills manufactory near Haddington may have brought an end to the Scottish fine woollen industry, but not to the woollen industry as a whole in the Haddington area. The town continued to function as a market for coarse wool, produced in the uplands to the south, and the manufacture of coarse cloth still took place in the town. In the 1730s part of this manufacture was located in the Nungate, a suburb of Haddington, and the town's waulk mill, which predated New Mills, continued to operate.[48]

In 1750 a new venture was started in the town. Unlike New Mills it produced coarse cloth and, on account of the then current practice of tarring wool to protect sheep from infection, it went under the title of the Tarred Wool Company.

Prior to its establishment, three Haddington clothiers, Alexander Maxwell, Henry Hepburn and William Lawson, had contracted with the Board of Trustees to produce two thousand stones of woollen cloth at 1s per stone.[49] In 1750 they were joined by other parties, notably Lord Milton and Lord Deskford, and a company was formed to last for two nineteen-year periods with a stock of £6,000 divided into one hundred and twenty shares. The first advance of capital was to one-fifth.[50]

Although the company was successfully established, it found itself 'at a great loss for want of a waulk mill'.[51] In June 1750 Alexander Maxwell, one of the founder members, petitioned the Board of Trustees, 'proposing to send Andrew or Robert Meikles to England to procure models of the best waulk-mills used there for enabling them to erect a proper one, if the Board would defray the expense of the journey and of the model'.[52]

To this the Board agreed. Having visited England and returned with models of the best waulk mills there,[53] Andrew Meikle was employed to survey the

River Tyne and Colstoun Water and report on a suitable site. In Meikle's opinion the best location was on the Tyne, a little to the west of Haddington's east mill; the mill 'would be sufficient and constantly a going mill with that fall, except in the event of an extraordinary drought, and a high speat in the water'.[54] The Tarred Wool Company petitioned the Burgh Council, asking for a feu of a site of eighty square feet and for financial aid, 'as the burgh must reap great benefit and advantage by the said manufactory being carried on within this town'. Although the site had already been promised to James Spalding for a lint mill, Lord Milton was able to use his influence as a member of the Board of Trustees, and in the event the Council unanimously agreed to accommodate 'so beneficial a trade as the manufactory of tarred wool', offering the Company a feu at £2 Scots per annum, provided that safeguards were laid down for the town's malt mill and waulk mill. On this basis the Tarred Wool Company built a two-stock mill, a freese mill and a teazer, all driven by water power.[55] The total cost of Meikle's visit to England, the construction of models and of the waulk mill came to £390 18s 3d. According to the testimonies of three clothiers, the mill 'answered extremely well'. The Board made £100 available from its model fund.[56]

While little information is available on the Company's fortunes, it does not seem to have prospered. In 1754 the two thousand eight hundred stones which the Company had contracted for had to be reduced to two thousand four hundred,[57] and by 1758 the first company had collapsed and given way to a new one.[58] The new partnership comprised landowners such as Lord Milton and Lord Colstoun, a merchant, William Cadell and a local minister. Management was in the hands of George Sawyers and Henry Hepburn, clothiers in Haddington.[59] By August 1759 all the shareholders' capital had been called in, including over £500 needed to buy the waulk mill and other effects from the old company.[60]

At one stage a water-powered 'willow' was installed, to prepare wool for carding, but this was later removed and the process performed by hand. The friese mill was extensively used, not only by the Company itself, but also by other manufacturers from as far away as Dunglass, sixteen miles to the east.[61] The power to drive these machines was made available by the removal of the second stock shortly after 1750. During droughts the town's malt mill ran by day and the waulk mill by night.[62]

The new company lasted longer than its predecessor, making broadcloths and blankets. A sample of its cloth, a heavy, well-felted brown material, is contained in the Saltoun Papers at the National Library of Scotland.[63] According to various sources,[64] the Tarred Wool Company continued to produce woollen cloth until 1775 or 1789. The earlier date seems the more likely, for in that year the manufactory building was advertised for sale or let. The description contained in the advertisement gives a detailed picture of the equipment at the mill:

> in the first floor, a dye house with three large boilers, dyestuff-cellar, and drying stove, a fulling mill with two fulling stocks, press shop with two presses, a shear

shop containing two pairs of shear-boards, &c. In the second floor, a weaving shop, burling shop, reeling and warping room, freizing mill, scribling room with a good ware room and lodging room for the manager. In the upper floor, a drying house forty feet by twenty feet, and wool lofts eighty feet by twenty feet.[65]

The confusion over the date of the Company's disbandment may stem from the fact that one of its members, George Sawyers, took over its running in 1775 and continued to make high-quality blankets until 1789.[66]

When Loch visited the town in the late 1770s he found the woollen industry in a healthy condition. Of the six thousand stones of wool brought into Haddington during 1776, five thousand stones were manufactured locally, the remainder going to Fife. The principal products of the town were broadcloths, sold at 4s to 10s 6d a yard, narrow cloths at 1s 6d to 6s, and English-style blankets at 4s to 18s each. The goods manufactured there, mostly for the Edinburgh and Glasgow markets, were valued at £5,000 Sterling per annum, compared with £2,800 for the raw wool, including that exported to Fife. The town also had a flourishing dyestuffs industry, notably in woad, four tons of which were produced per annum.[67]

After Sawyers' departure the mill was sold to William Wilkie, who brought skilled workers from Yorkshire and attempted unsuccessfully to continue the woollen manufacture.[68] In 1795 he leased the premises to Hay Smith for a thirty-eight year period; Smith installed additional machinery to grind mustard and dystuffs, including indigo.[69] In 1803 he became bankrupt and the mill was leased to James Dawson, who used it as a woollen manufactory with two fulling stocks and carding, raising and scribbling machines.[70] The manufactory seems to have closed down for good in 1814, following a legal case over water rights. The town's own waulk mill continued to operate until mid-century when, for want of business, it too closed down.[71]

In following the history of the Tarred Wool Company's mill we have moved well beyond the period 1730-1785, to which we return in the next chapter.

NOTES

1. NLS Acc. 2933/328/ f.1.
2. SRO NG1/1/12 13/12/54.
3. SRO NG1/1/11 7/7/51.
4. For other examples of vertical stamps, see chapters on paper, bleachfields, lead mining and minor users of water power.
5. SRO NG1/1/12 15/12/52; 16/11/53.
6. SRO NG1/1/23 22/1/83; 2/7/83.
7. OSP 485:25 Haddington Town Council v. Haddington Tarred Wool Company.
8. Wilson, R., *A Sketch of the History of Hawick*, Hawick, 1825, 252.
9. Wight, A., *The Present State of Husbandry in Scotland*, 4 vols., Edinburgh, 1778-84, IV, 606.

10. *OSA* XI, 303, Ednam, Roxburghshire; Burleigh, J., *Ednam and its Indwellers*, Glasgow & Dalbeattie, 1912, 198.

11. Lindsay, I. G., & Cosh, M., *Inveraray and the Dukes of Argyll*, Edinburgh, 1973, 273-5.

12. SRO GD248/125/47.

13. SRO GD170/416 (1759).

14. Miller, A. H. (ed.), 'A Selection of Scottish Forfeited Estates Papers, 1715; 1745', *SHS* LVII (1909), 209.

15. Aiton, W., *General View of the Agriculture of the County of Ayr*, Glasgow, 1811, 59.

16. SRO NG1/1/12 13/12/54.

17. NLS Acc. 2933/328.

18. SRO NG1/1/12 13/12/54; SRO NG1/1/13 19/12/55.

19. Loch, D., *A Tour through Most of the Trading Towns and Villages of Scotland*, Edinburgh, 1778, 48.

20. *Ibid.*, 47

21. *Ibid.*, 45.

22. *Ibid.*, 46.

23. SRO NG1/1/23 22/1/83; SRO NG1/1/24 10/12/83.

24. Loch, *op. cit.*, 44-5, 51.

25. SRO GD110/764.

26. Kettelbey, C. D. M., *Tullis Russell, 1809-1959*, Markinch, 1967, 12.

27. SRO NG1/1/1 8/12/1727.

28. Gulvin, C., *The Tweedmakers*, Newton Abbot, 1973, 31.

29. SRO NG1/1/10 8/6/50.

30. SRO NG1/1/11 7/6/51.

31. NLS Acc. 2933/354 6/4/1758.

32. SRO NG1/1/12 16/11/53; SRO NG1/1/13 19/12/55.

33. SRO NG1/1/12 13/12/54; SRO NG1/1/13 19/12/55.

34. SRO NG1/1/12 15/12/52.

35. SRO NG1/1/23 22/1, 2/7, 6/8/83.

36. Gulvin, *op. cit.*, 32.

37. *Ibid.*, 32.

38. Pococke, R., 'Tours in Scotland, 1747, 1750, 1760', *SHS* I (1887), 344.

39. Wilson, *op. cit.*, 252.

40. Wight, *op. cit.*, IV, 606-7.

41. Craig-Brown, T., *The History of Selkirkshire*, 2 vols., Edinburgh, 1886, II, 176.

42. Loch, *op. cit.*, 44-51.

43. SRO NG1/1/22 9/8/80.

44. SRO NG1/1/12 13/12/54.

45. Loch, *op. cit.*, 5, 9; SRO NG1/1/21 5/3, 30/7/77.

46. Loch, *op. cit.*, 5, 9.

47. Inveraray: Lindsay & Cosh, *op. cit.*, 274 (1777-8); Lismore: SRO GD170/416 (1759); Craggan: SRO GD248/125/47 (1750); Strowan: Miller, *op. cit.*, 209 (c.1765); Ullapool: *Ibid.*, 97 (c.1760).

48. Gray, W. F. & Jamieson, J. H., *A Short History of Haddington*, Edinburgh, 1944, 114.

49. SRO NG1/1/10 20/12/49.

50. NLS Acc 2933/354: Contract of Co-partnery, 1750.

51. SRO NG1/1/10 8/6/50.
52. *Ibid*.
53. SRO NG1/1/11 22/5/51.
54. OSP 485:25.
55. *Ibid*.
56. SRO NG1/1/11 3/1/52.
57. SRO NG1/1/12 13/12/54.
58. NLS Acc 2933/354: General Meeting of the Proprietors of the New Company for Tarred Wool at Haddington 6 April 1758.
59. *Ibid*.
60. NLS Acc 2933/354: George Sawers to Lord Milton, 20 July 1759.
61. OSP 485:25.
62. *Ibid*.
63. NLS Acc 2933/354.
64. Gray & Jamieson, *op. cit.*, 166; OSP 485:25.
65. *Caledonian Mercury*, April 19th 1775.
66. Gray & Jamieson, *op. cit.*, 116.
67. Loch, *op. cit.*, 9.
68. Martin, T. C., 'Old Haddington', *TELA&FNS* XII (1970), 57-8.
69. OSP 485:25.
70. *Ibid*.
71. Martin, *op. cit.*, 58.

19

Woollen Mills, 1785-1830

Technology

With the exception of fulling and the few innovations which had been introduced to a handful of mills during the previous hundred years, the Scottish
woollen industry of 1785 was still unmechanised. By 1830, however, so many
new inventions had been applied that every one of the numerous manufacturing processes could be performed by water-powered machinery. In
describing this process of innovation, it is impossible to follow a logical
chronological sequence without losing track of the sequence of operations by
which wool was manufactured. For this reason, it is better to consider each
process in order of manufacture.

Teazing

Wool, having been sorted and washed, had to be disentangled before
slubbing and carding. This process, known as teazing, was one of the first to
be mechanised after 1785, using a machine known as a teazer or willy. One
was installed at the Tarred Wool Company's Haddington mill at an unknown
date,[1] possibly before 1785, and a hand-driven 'willow' was subsequently purchased by Galashiels manufacturers.[2] The first water-powered teazer to which
a date can be assigned was one proposed by George Mercer at Wilderhaugh
Burn Mill, Galashiels: in 1787 he offered to pass on information concerning a
water-powered teazing machine of his own design, in exchange for help from
the Board of Trustees in constructing it. Although the Board asked Mercer for
an estimate, they later decided that the machine was unsuited to the purpose
and presumably gave no help towards its development.[3] In 1790 Andrew
Pringle, millwright at Brunstane Mill, Midlothian, claimed to have perfected a
water-powered teazer. The machine was referred to Galashiels manufacturers
and their favourable response persuaded the Board of Trustees to award him
£30.[4] At about the same time Alexander Brodie, a native of Peeblesshire who
had made his fortune in London, incorporated teazing machinery in a mill at
Innerleithen.[5]

In 1791 there was a second petition from Mercer, in which he too claimed to
have perfected a water-powered teazing machine; on this occasion a grant was
provided towards this and other water-powered machinery.[6] Whether the

successful design was the work of Pringle, Mercer, a combination of both or simply a plagiarism from elsewhere, by 1800 teazing machines had been installed elsewhere in Galashiels, in Berwickshire, Kirkcudbrightshire, the Hillfoots and as far north as Ross-shire.[7] It may also have been applied in an early woollen mill at Duntocher, Dunbartonshire.[8] By 1810 it had been brought into use in most of the Scottish counties and continued to spread thereafter, as mills were established or refitted.

Scribbling and Carding

Having been teazed and oiled, the wool underwent two carding processes, scribbling and carding proper. Traditionally carding had been a slow and laborious manual process using wooden cards with metal teeth. Cylindrical cards, turned by a crank, were introduced to England in 1748, and in 1775 Sir Richard Arkwright patented a carding machine for cotton.[9] The first wool carding machines were set up in Yorkshire in the early 1770s, using machinery patented by Bourn,[10] and by the late 1780s Arkwright machinery was available, the patent having been overturned.[11]

In 1784 George Mercer had visited the North of England, and in the following year he succeeded in obtaining a £30 Board of Trustees grant towards a dyehouse, a large woad vat, and scribbling machines similar to those which he had seen at Kendal and Leeds.[12] In the same year three other Galashiels manufacturers, who had probably seen Mercer's scribbler, successfully petitioned the Board for aid towards installing such machines.[13]

Although there was a further application from Galashiels in 1788,[14] it would appear that these early scribblers were driven by hand, for in 1791 George Mercer again petitioned the Board, this time for aid to bring a water-powered scribbler from England, to assemble it and to provide someone to train his son and himself in its operation. All this would suggest that a water-powered version of the machine was hitherto unknown in Scotland.[15]

At about the same time, scribblers were independently introduced elsewhere in Scotland. In 1791 John Archibald and another manufacturer in Tullibody asked for assistance in procuring scribbling and carding machines, but the money offered was not taken up until the late 1790s, when members of the Archibald family established a mill at Menstrie, Stirlingshire.[16] During the 1790s scribbling machinery was installed at mills in Selkirkshire, Roxburghshire, Berwickshire, Ayrshire, Stirlingshire, Nairn and Ross-shire.[17] During the early 19th century it came into general use in Scotland.

Carding machines, which performed the second carding process, followed close on the introduction of scribbling machines. Charles Baird, one of the partners in Stoneywood Mill, Aberdeenshire, brought two carding machines from Rochdale in 1790, and these were assembled by a Mr. Matthew Young. Soon afterwards the same Matthew Young fitted up machinery for Messrs. Kilgour at Kinmundy, Aberdeenshire, and in 1797 he and Robert Ogston established a woollen mill at Strichen.[18] Brodie's mill at Innerleithen also incorporated water-powered carding machinery.[19] George Mercer soon added a carding machine to his mill, and in 1792 William Thomson, 'engineer and mill-wright', having recently returned from Yorkshire and Lancashire, informed the Board that he could make and install a full set of carding and spinning machinery for wool at £170-180.[20] Carding machinery was introduced to several counties during the 1790s and became general between 1800 and 1830.

Double carding engines are first mentioned at Dalmellington, Ayrshire, in 1796,[21] and another such machine, apparently introduced from Lancashire, was being used at Jedburgh in 1807.[22] Many others were installed during the early 19th century, but the significance of 'double' is not clear.[23] In 1813 James Darling at Cumledge, Berwickshire claimed to have substituted a roller, covered with filleting cards, for the crank used formerly for taking wool off the last roller (doffer) of the machine. Three machines incorporating these improvements were successfully applied at Jedburgh, but it is difficult to ascertain the authenticity of Darling's claims.[24]

The doffer of the carding machine had spaces in the card clothing which covered its surface, in which the wool accumulated in webs about four inches wide. A final cylinder, with fluted surface, gathered these webs into ropes of about half an inch in diameter.[25] Until the 1830s these were joined together or 'pieced' by hand before being spun.[26] Combing, a process in worsted manu-facture equivalent to flax heckling, was mechanised by 1822 at Crookholm, Kilmarnock.[27]

Slubbing and Spinning

Just as the carding process was divided into two parts, so also was spinning. The first stage, slubbing, gave the untwisted 'ropes' from the carding machine a loose twist, using a machine known variously as a slubber, roving machine or billy. The billy, adapted from the cotton industry, was initially driven by hand, but water-powered machines had appeared in Scotland by the late 1790s.[28] Slubbing billies came into general use in the early 19th century, but it seems unlikely that they were ever fully adapted to water power.

The second part of the spinning process, the spinning itself, also used a machine borrowed from the cotton industry. The machine in question, the jenny, had been patented by James Hargreaves in 1770,[29] and had been applied to the Edinburgh woollen industry by the late 1770s.[30] The jenny was a hand-powered machine and remained so throughout the period, although a claim to have devised a water-powered jenny was made in 1816.[31] The water frame, by means of which water power was applied to the cotton industry, was unsuited to the short fibres used by most of the Scottish woollen industry,[32] but the spinning mule was successfully applied by W. & D. Thomson at Rosebank Mill, Galashiels in 1814.[33] In 1816, at about the same time as it was being applied at Leeds, William and Simon Bathgate, millwrights in Galashiels, claimed to have devised a water-powered machine which could spin at half the cost of the jenny.[34] The mule was only slowly introduced, and was still comparatively rare in 1830. Machines for twining and reeling yarn were installed at various mills during the early 19th century, but do not appear to have been water-powered.[35]

Weaving

Little need be said about weaving in the present context, for the power loom did not appear in the woollen industry until the mid-19th century. In 1830 wool was still being dyed after weaving rather than earlier in its manufacture, as came to be the case more recently. Picking machines, to remove foreign bodies from woven cloth, were in use by the mid-1820s, but were probably not water-powered.

Fulling

Little change seems to have taken place in the long-established technology of cloth fulling or waulking. A fulling mill 'on a new construction', the invention of George Pringle, millwright in Earlston, was erected at Dryburgh by the Earl of Buchan about 1789,[36] but although many new mills were constructed thereafter, no further improvements seem to have taken place.

Raising

After fulling, the surface of the cloth was raised by means of teazels, used individually or mounted collectively on frames. Raising or gig mills had appeared in Scotland in the 1690s and were in use at the Haddington Tarred Wool Company's mill some time after 1750.[37] Thereafter, they are not mentioned again until 1790, when one was proposed at Jedburgh.[38] From Galashiels there were applications for aid towards raising machines in 1792 and 1794,[39] but in a petition dated 1807 Richard Lees claimed to have just introduced it to the town.[40] Gig mills or raising machines are referred to in several subsequent petitions from Galashiels, where there seems to have been little if any of the resistance encountered in England.[41] Although they may have been introduced to other areas outside the Borders, there is nothing in the Minutes of the Board of Trustees to confirm this.

Shearing

Once the surface of the cloth had been raised, excessively long fibres were cropped or sheared. Traditionally, large hand shearers were used, but a shearing machine on which several pairs of shears were driven by water power was patented in France in 1784 and in England, by J. Harmer of Sheffield, in 1787. Opposition by workers prevented its widespread use in England until after 1815.[42]

The first machine to be brought to Scotland was installed at Galashiels in

1811 by Richard Lees, using a new and powerful water wheel.[43] According to Lees, a man or a boy could operate four to six pairs of shears at once, and machines of this type were introduced to Peebles in 1812, Selkirk in 1813 and Jedburgh in 1816.[44] Lees later brought from England a 'perpetual backer' which was to be used with a cropping machine.[45]

A more sophisticated machine, the principle of which was later applied to the lawnmower, stemmed from a design patented by an American, Samuel Dorr, in 1794. Later versions of this were patented by two Englishmen, Lewis and Collier, in 1815 and 1818 respectively.[46] In 1820 James Patterson brought what he described as an American Cropper to Galashiels, describing it as cheaper and more efficient than the earlier type.[47] Lewis-type cropping machines were also being used in the town by the late 1820s.[48]

Beyond the Borders, cropping machines of one type or another are known to have been introduced to Banffshire and Dumfriesshire before 1830 and were probably in use elsewhere.[49]

From the preceding account of the mechanisation of the woollen industry, the dominant role of Galashiels manufacturers is clearly evident. While this may be partly due to better documentation through their frequent recourse to the Board of Trustees, it is also true to say that they set the pace for mechanical innovation in the Scottish woollen industry throughout the period. As will become apparent in subsequent sections, this was not the only respect in which Galashiels, or more broadly speaking, the Borders, led the industry.

Competition from Steam

More than any other sector of the textile industry, wool manufacture maintained its dependence on water power well into the 19th century. As many of the sites which it occupies were in close proximity to uplands with good water catchment qualities, water power was readily available in adequate quantities. Furthermore, these areas offered little competition from other users, so that as the number of mills and the range of water-powered processes increased, the industry was able to take up almost all the water power available in its area. Some districts, notably the Borders, were far removed from coal supplies, at least until the coming of the railways. The earliest steam-powered mills were built in the Stirling-Hillfoots area. Stirling itself had a long-established woollen industry but very poor water resources in its immediate vicinity; the town's first steam-powered mill was founded about 1811.[50] In the Hillfoots towns and in Alloa, a water-powered industry was created on very limited supplies, and before 1830 the expansion of the industry necessitated the application of steam power.

A similar set of circumstances applied in other major urban centres such as Kilmarnock, Ayr, Glasgow and Aberdeen, but in the Borders steam power was very late in arriving: the first steam mill in Galashiels was not started until after 1830, by which time all the available water power in the town had been taken up.[51] Of ten mills in the Hawick area in the late 1830s, only one was powered by steam.[52] Outside the main manufacturing districts the more isolated mills continued to use water power alone long after 1830.

The 1839 Factory Returns show that in the mills surveyed there were one hundred and sixteen water wheels against only thirty-seven steam engines, the former producing 1198 horse power out of a total of 1822 horse power.[53]

Mill Builders

Landowners

By the 1780s the contribution which landowners could make towards the development of the textile industries was relatively small. The process of mechanisation already outlined, with corresponding increases in the scale of individual units, meant that an integrated woollen mill required not only substantial capital but also a great deal of technical and commercial expertise. Merchant and waulker manufacturers were much better equipped for this, while in the case of smaller, more specialised mills, such as those engaged in waulking or carding, textile trade artisans, and particularly waulkers or dyers, were becoming sufficiently well-established to undertake mill-building on their own account. At the same time, the landowner still had a role to play in deciding whether a mill should or should not be built, and as title-holder to land, his reluctance or willingness to grant tacks or feus could decide the fate of a proposed mill. For a small landowner, the additional income and other benefits which favoured the estate development might lead him to look favourably on mill development, but the larger, more prosperous landowner could afford to be more discriminating and might consider the aesthetic loss to be greater than any potential economic benefit. Wilson, writing in the mid-1820s, contrasts the attitudes of landowners at Hawick and Galashiels: for some years, falls of water in the Hawick area could not be made use of 'owing to a whim of the late Duke of Buccleuch'. 'His Grace seems to have forgotten that the manufacturers and their workers were the principal consumers of the produce of his land.' At Galashiels, however, where ninety-nine year leases were readily available, 'Mr. Scott of Gala, and his father, whose views seem to have been equally sound and liberal, have raised a town which is likely to become the Leeds of Scotland'.[54] Without detracting from their achievement, it should be added that the Scotts of Gala were able to bring this about without themselves laying out any capital.

Financial and other incentives from landowners were sometimes a pre-condition for aid from the Board of Trustees;[55] by providing this, a landowner could promote the development of the woollen industry on his estate without any direct involvement. At Kingussie, on Speyside, a small woollen company was founded in 1805 and received a £100 grant from the Board of Trustees on condition that it obtained 'encouragement' from the Duke of Gordon prior to making further claims.[56] A second petition in 1807 was turned down, but by

1808 the Duke of Gordon was affording the company 'various conveniences', and in 1810 it was successfully petitioning the Board for a further £100.[57]

Above and beyond this general role, there were cases in which the landowner played a more active part in the establishment of woollen mills. Broadly speaking, these cases involved either localities in which the mechanised industry had not yet been established, or they were connected with the development of planned villages. Almost all took place in the 1790s or early 1800s.

The earliest example of an integrated mill built by a landowner was Caerlee Mill, Innerleithen (c.1790), one of the first mechanised mills in Scotland. Its founder, Alexander Brodie, was hardly typical of Scottish landowners: he had started his working life as a blacksmith in Traquair parish, Peeblesshire and made his fortune as an ironmaster in Shropshire, before returning as landowner to his native county. The mill was built on four storeys, with water-powered carding and roving machinery on the lower floors, jennies on the top floor and a separate waulk mill. The decision to build was based more on philanthropy than on sound economic judgement, and its eventual success, under a Galashiels manufacturer, was achieved only after a number of tenants had failed to run it profitably.[58]

On the Black Isle, David Urquhart of Braelangwell built a woollen mill in 1796, at a cost of £1,000, with a view to introducing industry to Cromartyshire and thereby staving off emigration. Machinery to teaze, scribble, card and spin wool started operating in January 1797, and a manager was brought from the south. Nothing is heard of the mill after 1799, but it still stands today.[59]

In Galloway landowners played an active role in organising companies to operate woollen mills during the late 18th century.[60] One such co-partnership, a leading member of which was Lord Daer, had a mill at Old Kirkchrist which had once been a distillery and which was to have been a cotton mill before a downturn in trade persuaded the proprietors to install machinery for teazing, scribbling and carding wool instead.[61]

This first category of landowner, concerned with introducing the mechanised industry to new areas, overlaps with a second group which was engaged in establishing villages. At Grantown-on-Spey, Grant of Grant established a woollen manufactory with eight looms and a carding machine,[62] whilst in Caithness Sir John Sinclair persuaded Alexander Walker, an Aberdeen manufacturer, to settle at Halkirk and carry on the manufacture of wool, on condition that Sir John provided £250 towards machinery.[63] At the opposite end of the country, in Dumfriesshire, General Dirom of Mount Annan built a large woollen mill on a good fall of water adjacent to his new village of Brydekirk.[64] James Little, who took on the mill, promised in 1800 to pursue the woollen manufacture 'on a scale much greater than has yet been attempted', but in making so brash a claim lost the opportunity to obtain help from the Board of Trustees.[65] Nevertheless, the mill enjoyed greater success than most of those established by landowners.

Initiatives of the type outlined above represented only a small proportion of the woollen mills built during the period 1785-1830. In choosing to build them, landowners seem to have been motivated by the potential economic and social benefits of having woollen mills on their own estates under their own control. In this respect, in their dedication to a particular project, and in their blindness to economic realities, they represented the remnants of the 18th-century Improving movement, a movement out of touch with the harshly competitive economic climate of the early 19th century. Managers with a knowledge of the trade came and went, but it was not until control passed to experienced manufacturers that the surviving mills became competitive. Many estates, particularly those where improved breeds of sheep had been introduced, could and did support small carding mills, but as will become apparent later, the initiative to create these came from mill tenants and textile trade workers rather than from a dying race of Improving landowners.

Merchants and Manufacturers

As with linen, so also with wool, merchants and manufacturers made up the bulk of mill builders between 1785 and 1830. The twofold division used in the previous chapter also holds good for this period, although many of those who started out as small-scale clothiers or waulker-manufacturers had achieved the status of merchants or manufacturers by the 1830s.

There was a very fine dividing line between the waulkers and dyers, who might be categorised as tenants or artisans, and the small waulker-manufacturers of the late 18th century. Several of those who described themselves as manufacturers were probably men of very limited financial means who saw the development of carding and other manufacturing processes as a means of diversifying their interests. Unfortunately it is not possible to gauge the level of control which they already had over manufacturing; in some cases it must have involved little more than buying cloth from weavers, fulling it and putting it through the first stage of marketing.

John McKay, who in 1789 described himself as 'woollen cloth manufacturer' in Cluny parish, Aberdeenshire, did not even have a waulk mill and had to look to the Board of Trustees for help in building one.[66] In 1794 John Young, 'woollen manufacturer' at Cortachy, Angus, also had to enlist the help of the Board, this time in purchasing a scribbler costing no more than £40. Even with this help it appears that he had given up 'manufacturing' by 1797.[67]

Not all of the small manufacturers were quite so impecunious and some, from modest beginnings, managed to develop into large-scale manufacturers. Besides the waulker-manufacturers of Galashiels, one of the best examples is that of the Darling family at Cumledge, Berwickshire. William Darling was a dyer and woollen manufacturer at Cumledge Easter Waulkmill when he decided to 'extend the woollen manufacture' with the help of his sons. In 1797 he applied for a grant towards water-powered scribbling, carding and slubbing machinery at an estimated cost of £127.[68] A fifty per cent grant was provided, and although Darling seems to have underestimated the cost, his son James installed further machinery, successfully ran the woollen mill and made improvements in carding mill design. The mill continued to operate until the 1960s.[69] It is at Galashiels, however, that the transition from waulker-manufacturer to capitalist-manufacturer is clearest. By 1790 there were already five waulk mills in Galashiels: Upper, Mid and Nether Waulkmills, which had been in existence since at least the 1580s, Wilderhaugh, built in 1783 by George Mercer, 'clothier and dyer', and Buckholmside, built by Pringle of Torwoodlee in 1788[70] (Figure 66). The waulkers who tenanted these mills, individually or collectively, had already attained the status of manufacturer by taking in, fulling and marketing woven cloth. For various reasons they were able to assume a wider control over the industry in the late 18th and early 19th centuries. As we have seen, they had a keen awareness of technical advances; since the machinery was relatively inexpensive, and since they already controlled water-powered sites, it was only a small step to install the new water-powered machinery, particularly where it was financed jointly. As much of the machinery was for yarn preparation, the employment of hand- then jenny-spinners was a natural step to take, and by supplying this yarn to weavers they could complete the cycle of control over the industry.

By 1805 all five waulk mills had been adapted or rebuilt to house preparing, carding and finishing machinery. At Wilderhaugh and Buckholmside mills water-powered preparing and carding machinery was installed by the waulker-manufacturers who already tenanted them, in 1791 and 1793 respectively.[71] Mid Mill was rebuilt to a height of sixteen feet in 1793, Waulkmillhead (Upper Mill) to twenty feet in 1802 and Nether Mill to twenty-two feet in 1805; all three, as rebuilt, were about forty-two feet in length by about twenty-eight feet in breadth. These three mills and a fourth, Weirhaugh, established in 1797, were each held jointly by four waulker- or dyer-manufacturers. The mill sites were held on ninety-nine year tacks from Scott of Gala.[72]

From 1805 there are signs of certain of these small manufacturers reinforcing their positions by founding new mills. Of these only one, Huddersfield (1818) was jointly financed; the four partners included George Patterson, co-founder of Waulkmillhead, and Robert Walker, founder of Ladhope Mill. Another partner, John Gledhill from Huddersfield, was the only English manufacturer to invest in the Galashiels industry during the period. David and William, sons of William Thomson (co-founder of Weirhaugh Mill), established Linburn Mill in 1805; Richard Lees (co-founder of Mid Mill), established his own mill, Galabank, in 1818 and Robert Sanderson, presumably a relative of Hugh Sanderson (co-founder of Weirhaugh Mill) built Galabank Mill, a three-storey, sixty-five feet by twenty-eight feet structure, in 1826.[73]

Through deaths, bankruptcies and other events those mills established jointly before 1805 gradually passed to individual owners. Mid Mill was under the sole control of the Cochranes by 1831, but in most cases the consolidation of ownership was not completed until the 1840s, 50s or 60s.[74] However, the small waulkers and manufacturers of the late 18th century had already become

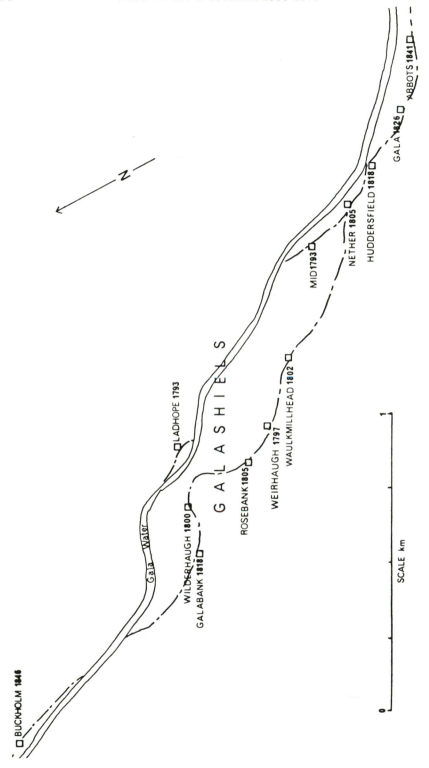

Fig 66. Galashiels woollen mills. *Hall (1898)*

capitalist manufacturers by the 1830s, and while, at some centres, woollen mills were still taking on custom work, those at Galashiels were producing solely for the open market.

Although the majority of woollen mills were built by small-scale waulker-manufacturers, merchants and manufacturers of more substantial means were involved in a number of projects, most of them large in scale. In some cases woollen manufacturers had already accumulated sufficient funds to make substantial investments at an early stage. David Irving, manufacturer at White-shiels, near Langholm, had laid out more than £2,000 on establishing a woollen mill there by 1799, in which year he took in a partner from Kendal and started the firm of Irvine & Co. to manufacture druggets or coatings.[75] In most cases, however, woollen manufacturers were too poorly financed to make such a heavy investment, and where larger mills were built in the years immediately before and after 1800, their backers usually had other sources of mercantile or manufacturing income. Daniel Clark, merchant in Campbeltown, built a woollen mill at Auchalick, Argyll, 'on a pretty large scale',[76] while at Duntocher, Dunbartonshire, the Duntocher Wool Company, a basically mercantile group, established a large woollen mill about 1787. The Dalnottar Iron Company, from whom the land was sublet, had a controlling interest in the woollen company and in a second company, established in 1788 on a capital of £8,000.[77] In the 1790s the company was employing over three hundred workers and was capable of producing one hundred thousand yards of cloth per annum.[78]

Another early mill, Stoneywood, involved a variety of interests. The two major partners, Charles Baird and Alexander Smith, were respectively a silk buyer and a paper manufacturer; among the other partners were Thomas and Robert Kilgour, manufacturers in Kinmundy, and Thomas Black, druggist in Aberdeen.[79]

Lastly, at least two other large woollen mills in the north-east had mercantile origins. James Knowles was a member of a long-established Aberdeen merchant family trading in wool, corn and hosiery. In 1805, while in Rotterdam, he leased Cothal Mills, near Aberdeen, and took one Crombie, a local weaver, into partnership to manufacture high-quality woollen cloth for sale through his Dutch contacts. At a later stage the partnership was augmented by Alexander Rhind, an Aberdeen merchant with real estate and shipping interests.[80] An Elgin merchant, Alexander Johnstone, established a woollen mill at Newmill in the late 1790s. According to Gulvin, he 'dealt in oatmeal, fish, whisky, snuff, tobacco and beer as well as English cloths, and sold flannels on commission for a Rochdale firm, hats for a Manchester business, cloth for Prest's of Leeds, crockery and, for a while, insurance'.[81] Although the mill was initially intended to card wool for local needs, manufacturing for the market soon came to predominate. By 1807 he had installed four carding engines, a slubbing billy, four spinning jennies, six broad-looms and a fulling mill, to which he proposed to add a slubbing billy, two spinning jennies, four broad-looms and a second fulling mill.[82] By 1811 Messrs Johnstone & Sim, as the company had come to be known, were manufacturing two thousand stones of wool per annum into narrow cloth. All processes, from carding to pressing, were carried out at the same works, while four additional carding mills, owned by the company, prepared wool for private individuals in the Moray area.[83]

These examples, which represent the majority of the large early woollen mills, show the importance of mercantile and manufacturing capital at that time and in that type of mill. However, the impact of these mills was small when compared with those built or occupied by smaller manufacturers or waulkers. Although they were large in terms of physical scale, their contribution to total output was relatively small, and numerically they were relatively few. Cothal and Newmills became important, long-lasting establishments but Auchalick soon died out, Duntocher was converted to spin cotton, and even Langholm, where Whiteshiels mill was situated, went over temporarily to cotton manufacturing.[84] Their most important role was one of innovation. Cothal Mills and Newmills introduced fine cloth manufacture to their respective areas, whilst Duntocher produced worsted. Whiteshiels brought to Scotland a type of cloth previously only manufactured in the Kendal area of Westmorland; Stoneywood brought the carding machine to the north-east, and Auchalick brought machinery to the west Highlands.

By 1815 many of the manufacturers who had started on very limited means had accumulated sufficient capital or credit to build large mills of their own: in the Hillfoots it was the Archibalds, Patons and Drysdales, at Bannockburn the Wilsons, at Hawick the Nixons, Wilsons, Scotts and Pringles, and at Galashiels the various manufacturing families already referred to. For the merchant manufacturer there were new areas to exploit, but the more successful of the small manufacturers stayed with the woollen industry, eventually taking on the status of large-scale manufacturers.

Tenants and Artisans

In 1790 John Naismith suggested that:

> some good fulling mills, occupied by tenants properly accomplished for the business, would lend greatly to the advancement of the woollen manufactory. Those tenants would not only be capable of giving a good finishing to the cloth, upon which others employed them, but they would be naturally disposed to apply any stock they might be able to command, either in employing people to manufacture woollen cloth, or in purchasing from the little manufacturers in the neighbourhood such raw undressed cloth as might be offered for sale, in order to give employment to their mills.[85]

To some extent the results which Naismith wished to see were already coming about with the rise of the waulker-manufacturer; before the end of the period his ideas were also to see fruition in a much wider context, with the involvement of lesser waulkers and dyers not only in establishing woollen manufactories but also in building waulk mills.

Waulk mills were built by dyers at Berryscar (Dumfriesshire) in 1799, Fort William (Inverness-shire) in 1808 and Stanleybank (Ayrshire) in 1819.[86] Fullers and dyers installed carding machinery, or even a full set of preparing and spinning machinery, at Kirkconnel (Dumfriesshire) and at Killearn (Stirlingshire).[87] Killearn was still held by the same family some forty years later, by which time four hundred hundredweight of wool per annum was undergoing all processes including weaving.[88] Members of the same trade were responsible for at least five carding mills in Perthshire, of which one, established at Blackford in 1802, was enlarged in 1825 and, under the same family, was manufacturing wool into blankets at the time of the 1834 Factory Commission.[89] There were doubtless many other instances, especially in areas marginal to large-scale woollen manufacture, but petitions to the Board of Trustees, the most important source of information on such matters, seldom gave details of applicants' backgrounds.

Two other examples from the textile trades show something of the variety of backgrounds from which mill builders might be drawn. James Kirk had been a foreman with the Edinburgh woollen manufacturers Jackson & Co. before taking a tack of the waulk mill at Gifford. In 1798 he applied for aid to set up a wool manufacture there or, more specifically, for a carding machine at an estimated cost of £50.[90] It seems unlikely that his plans ever reached fruition, for only seven years later there was a second petition, from another person, for a full set of machinery on the same site.[91]

About 1800 a West Linton weaver, Alexander Alexander, built a carding mill at Carlops, Peeblesshire, to manufacture coarse Tweeddale wool into felts for Midlothian papermills. According to Findlater, he proposed to diversify production into serges and other coarse woollen goods as capital, credit and markets grew.[92]

In a few cases persons described as millers or millwrights established woollen mills. John Miller, tenant of Newmill of Arnbeg, Argyll, added carding machinery to his meal mill about 1811,[93] whilst at Dunphail Mills, Nairn, William Sutherland, the miller, obtained a grant towards a carding mill in June 1828, only to have it razed to the ground in the floods of the following autumn.[94]

In Edinburgh an enterprising millwright, Alexander Hamilton, built machinery at St. Leonards Hill to grind printers' ink and to card wool for hat manufacturers, at a total cost of only £157. The mill's water supply was derived from surface water off the streets of Edinburgh and from springs in the Meadows area.[95]

A variety of circumstances favoured the development of small-scale woollen mills by tenants and artisans. Textile employees already had some knowledge of the trade, millwrights had the requisite skills to construct machinery, and millers had leases on buildings and water power which could be applied to driving fulling, preparing or carding machinery. Waulkers were particularly well placed. On the whole the areas in which tenants and artisans built mills had not yet been monopolised by large-scale manufacturers; the spread of sheep farming, using improved breeds, provided a readily available raw material. Many of their mills involved only a partial mechanisation of wool manufacturing, enabling them to draw upon existing spinning and weaving skills while using their own modest assets to install preparing and carding machinery. However, success stories such as those at Killearn and Blackford were exceptional, and despite the survival of many of these mills through most of the 19th century, there were new applications for aid after 1810, suggesting that in wool, as in linen, the early years of the 19th century belonged not to the artisans, mill tenants or other small men but to larger, better financed manufacturers.

The Board of Trustees

The demand for and the supply of Board of Trustee funds for the woollen industry contrasts strongly with the situation in the linen industry. In the latter, only very limited funds were made available for mill-spinning, and these during the earliest years of its development. Finance for the woollen industry, however, grew from very small proportions to oust bleachfields and lint mills as the largest sector of the Board's expenditure.

Initially the Board was reluctant to provide help: in 1783 it turned down George Mercer's first petition for aid towards a waulk mill and only accepted a second one on the strength of recommendations from Scott of Gala and Pringle of Torwoodlee.[96] A similar application from Robert Walker in 1788 was turned down, despite recommendations, on the grounds that the Board was 'not in the practice of assisting in the erection of waulk mills'.[97] However, within a few years the Board had begun to look more favourably on the reviving woollen industry, and continued to make a contribution to financing buildings and machinery until the 1830s.

The decision to back the woollen industry rather than linen owed something to the Board's attitudes towards imported raw materials, scale of unit and spatial distribution. Until the early 1800s the woollen industry used a raw material largely produced in Scotland. In both the southern Uplands and the Highlands improved breeds of sheep, notably the Cheviot and the Blackface, enhanced the quality and increased the quantity of wool available. In the Highlands the replacement by sheep of cattle and people alike had commenced on a few estates during the late 18th century and accelerated in the early 19th. This also encouraged, if it did not guarantee, the involvement of Scotland's landowners, a group favoured by the Board of Trustees and one whose active co-operation had been sought over a prolonged period. Their backing for a project could persuade the Board to loosen its purse-strings, and where a landowner's co-operation was not already forthcoming the Board could stipulate it as a precondition of financial aid.

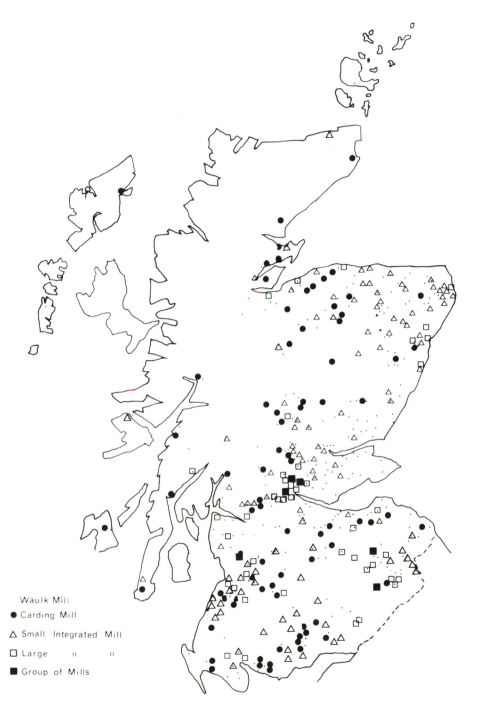

Waulk Mill
● Carding Mill
△ Small Integrated Mill
□ Large   "   "
■ Group of Mills

Fig 67. Distribution of water-powered woollen mills, 1730-1830

As to scale of unit, the woollen industry in its early stages of mechanisation usually entailed small units which were inexpensive to establish and which could be set up and run by people of limited means. Consequently, the limited funds at the Board's disposal could be used to the benefit of a large number of sites over a wide area. There was also the possibility of partial mechanisation; the Board can hardly have failed to notice the decline in hand spinning brought about by the mechanisation of cotton and flax spinning, and while a handful of mills were built to card locally grown tow, the potential for wool carding mills was much greater. This attribute of the woollen industry was particularly significant for the Highlands, where the Board had previously shown reluctance to introduce processes which might reduce rather than increase employment.

Initially the Board favoured small units, even to the extent of declining to help more expensive projects, but gradually the scale of finance increased as individual units became larger and more expensive, until by the 1820s it was regularly paying out sums of £100 or £200 to projects costing £1,000 to £3,000.

Closely related to the question of scale was the dispersion of the industry. Since widely available raw materials could be partially or totally manufactured by relatively inexpensive machinery in small mills, there was a steady process of diffusion which was still going on in 1830. By that time woollen mills of one kind or another had become well established in and adjacent to most upland areas as far north as Lewis and Caithness (Figure 67). This fitted in well with the Board's long-standing preference for dispersion rather than concentration. Unfortunately, in pursuing its policy the Board tended initially to back projects of doubtful viability in outlying areas rather than supporting other, more economically sound ventures in established manufacturing centres. Before long, however, this policy, like that on scale of unit, had been dropped in recognition of the need to subsidise repeated heavy investment in individual mills. Assistance was given not only to several mills in any one area but also to the same mills on more than one occasion.

Initially flax spinning, with its imported raw materials, its heavy capital investment, its large units of production and tightly defined distribution presented quite a different set of characteristics. However, the features which favoured wool rather than linen in the eyes of the Board of Trustees were already losing significance in the 1820s as the more highly developed sectors of the woollen industry took on the same attributes as had prevented the Board from financing flax spinning. Whether or not the Board was aware of this, it continued to provide grants which by 1830 totalled over £18,000, a not insignificant contribution to the industry's resurgence.

Distribution and Chronology

In the previous chapter something was said of the difficulties involved in assessing the number of waulk mills operating during the period 1730-1785. Although this particular problem applies to a lesser degree for the period 1785-1830, the broadening of the range of water-powered processes poses several new ones.

The first problem concerns sources. Most of the mechanisation took place in the period 1800-1830, but in the areas most affected, notably the south-west and the Moray-Aberdeen region, cartographic sources are generally too early, too late or insufficiently detailed to show all sites: the best surveys of Kirkcudbrightshire and Wigtownshire were made before 1800, whilst the first-edition Ordnance Survey maps (c.1850-1880) exclude some short-lived mills but include others, established after 1830. Published sources offer more help: the Statistical Account picks up the majority of waulk mills still operating in the 1790s as well as most of the early integrated mills; the General Views of Agriculture give some information on the early 1800s but with few exceptions fail to identify sites individually. The New Statistical Account gives a good breakdown of sites to parish level but again often fails to give their status and exact location. The best source by far is the Minute Books of the Board of Trustees, but even here there are pitfalls. While they give details of the machinery proposed and the grants offered to a great many mills, they fail to indicate whether the machinery was ever installed or whether the grant was taken up. In some cases confirmation comes from other sources, but in several instances there is equally strong evidence that some projects were never realised.

The second problem concerns the status of mills. Between a small country waulk mill and a large, fully mechanised spinning mill there was a wide range of mills for scribbling, carding, jenny spinning, mule spinning and combinations of these. Furthermore the scale of carding and spinning mills could vary enormously from a single-storey mill with one carding engine to a three- or four-storey mill with several carding engines and spinning mules.

To make the most of the sources available, waulk mills, being the longest established, will be looked at first, followed by carding mills, then spinning mills.

Waulk Mills

From cross-referencing between maps of the 16th to 19th centuries it would appear that many earlier waulk mills were still in use during the period 1785-1830. At the same time it is also apparent that a number of mills were lost completely during the low ebb in the woollen industry in the first three quarters of the 18th century, or were converted to other purposes such as flax scutching.

In the 1780s and 1790s a few new mills were set up: Cluny (1789) in Aberdeenshire, Tillicoultry (1790) and Alloa (1794) in the Hillfoots, Wilderhaugh (1783), Buckholmside (1788), Dryburgh (1789) and Innerleithen (1790) in the Borders and Moffat (1796), Kirkinner (1797), Langholm (1799) and Berryscar (1799) in the south-west all belong to this group.[98] As waulk mills and the woollen industry in general were already well established in these areas, this implies that the industry was growing or that the use of fulling in cloth manufacture was on the increase. The real situation probably involved both elements. In all the areas concerned wool from improved breeds of sheep was either grown or manufactured. There is good reason to believe that the influence of waulker-manufacturers was on the increase and that several of the waulk mills which they established during the 1780s and 1790s were, or were to become, part of integrated mills where carding and latterly spinning were also performed by water power. At one major centre of innovation, Galashiels, four out of the five waulk mills had already been incorporated into integrated mills by 1800.[99] In all of these areas, but particularly in Aberdeen-shire, the survival of earlier waulk mills is apparent.

The Statistical Account contains several references to existing waulk mills in Fife, Angus and Perthshire but little evidence of new ones. Many of the established mills had probably been adapted for washing linen yarn (i.e. plash mills): at least one new waulk mill, at St. Andrews, was intended primarily for this purpose.[100]

In Ayrshire and the west of Scotland there is little sign of activity during the 1780s and 90s. In Ayrshire there were probably sufficient mills already, and an early specialisation in carpet manufacture might go some way towards explaining the lack of new mills. Over the whole area cotton had become the major textile industry, while in the more isolated areas flax was still of some importance.

The Lothians were still an important wool-manufacturing area, with a substantial number of existing waulk mills. Nevertheless, the lack of new developments suggests a relative decline in the area's status. In the Highlands there was not as yet any sign of the waulk mill extending its range into areas of manual waulking.

By the early years of the 19th century the only waulk mills still being built in the Borders and the Hillfoots were those which formed part of integrated mills. With the move towards production for market, the industry tended to concentrate in those areas with mechanised carding and spinning facilities; at the same time it seems likely that there was a corresponding decline in custom work and the waulk mills which catered solely for it.

In the north-east, Galloway, Stirlingshire and west Perthshire there was a slight increase in the number of waulk mills, and while some were integrated with carding mills, these were not generally so large-scale or so market-orientated as the integrated mills of the Borders and Hillfoots. Alongside a revival in the woollen industry there was a decline in the linen industry in these areas; the reduction in home cultivation of flax, the extension of sheep farming and the mechanisation of wool carding all contributed to a transfer of weaving skills from linen to wool and a corresponding increase in the demand for the services of waulk mills. In Galloway the cotton industry which had shown signs of developing in the late 18th century was also in decline.

In Fife, Angus and east Perthshire flax still dominated textile manufacture, whilst in west-central Scotland a similar situation pertained with regard to cotton. In both areas there was very little new waulk mill-building except on upland margins, and there was probably a net decline in numbers in operation. The Lothians too saw a decline in numbers, but a few new mills were being built in parts of the Highlands where formerly there had been none.

Between 1815 and 1830 the trend towards centralisation in the Borders and Hillfoots continued. In the north-east a few new mills were built and carding machinery added to, or substituted for, existing fulling machines. Developments in Galloway followed similar lines, although here there may have been a small net decline. The relative importance of east-central and west-central Scotland continued to fall, with a consequent reduction in the total number of mills, but in Ayrshire a few new ones were built as individual units for small manufacturers in the south or as components of integrated mills in the north. In both districts of Ayrshire the flax industry underwent further decay, while in the north of the county the influence of cotton was also waning.

In west Perthshire and Stirlingshire the revival which had begun between 1800 and 1815 continued to gain strength; in the more isolated areas waulk mills were built as individual units or with carding machinery, but in more accessible areas, such as Bannockburn, they formed part of integrated mills. In the Highlands the waulk mill continued to break new ground, and by 1830 it had spread as far as the Outer Hebrides.

Changes in the distribution and numbers of waulk mills between 1785 and 1830 may be summarised as follows. In the Borders, Ayrshire and the Hillfoots there was a net increase in numbers, but within each area fulling tended to concentrate in those centres where carding and spinning also took place. The Highlands saw a small net increase involving a widening distribution of individual waulk mills; west Perthshire and Stirlingshire experienced a similar increase, except that here it involved small manufactories. In Galloway and the north-east there was a rough stability in numbers, with some re-siting and the development of small integrated units around waulk mills. In the Lothians there was a net decline, despite the failure of linen and cotton industries to take root, but in east-central and west-central Scotland the success of linen and cotton respectively may have contributed to a decline in waulk mill numbers in all but upland areas.

In all there were probably about three hundred waulk mills operating in Scotland between 1785 and 1830, including those in integrated mills (Figure 63).

Carding Mills

From its introduction in 1790, the carding mill soon spread across the established wool manufacturing districts of Scotland. Carding machinery appears to have arrived almost simultaneously at four separate localities, Innerleithen,

Duntocher, Galashiels and Stoneywood,[101] but only in the case of Stoneywood is it possible to identify a subsequent process of diffusion.[102]

By whatever means, carding machines had spread to a few dispersed sites by 1800, mostly in the Galloway-south Ayrshire area and the Borders, but also in the Hillfoots, the north-east, along the Moray Firth to the Black Isle, and the more accessible parts of Highland Perthshire. In the central Lowlands linen and cotton still held sway but the latter, which had been established in Galloway, was already on the decline there, as demonstrated by the decision to install machinery for wool rather than cotton at Old Kirkchrist, Kirkcudbrightshire.[103] By 1800 there were already carding mills in each of the areas which were subsequently to dominate the Scottish industry, and some sites, notably in the Borders, were to become integrated mills. Even so, there were probably no more than twenty-five machines in the whole country at that time.

Between 1800 and 1815 at least three tendencies can be detected in the distribution of carding mills. In those areas such as the Borders where they had gained a strong footing by 1800, there was a move towards the accretion of other manufacturing processes to the existing carding mills and the creation of new integrated mills. Spinning, which had been performed at a number of carding mills by means of hand-driven jennies, was firstly adapted to water power at Galashiels in 1814.

In areas such as Highland Perthshire and the Moray Firth Lowlands, where perhaps one or two mills had been established before 1800, there was a process of consolidation, with more carding mills being built. The third tendency was the colonisation of, on the one hand, areas such as Stirlingshire and north Ayrshire where linen or cotton had formerly been the predominant textile industry and, on the other hand, areas which had formerly had little organised industry, such as the northern central Highlands. Growth in the former area was much more marked than in the latter.

In reality developments were by no means as distinct as the preceding account suggests, for in any one region at least two of these processes might be at work. Thus, in the Borders colonisation was taking place in the upper reaches of Tweeddale at the same time as accretion in manufacturing villages such as Galashiels, whilst in the Moray Firth area Elgin had fully integrated Newmills at the same time as colonisation was taking place in upland areas.[104] Between 1800 and 1815 carding machinery was installed in at least one hundred and twenty mills in Scotland.

Between 1815 and 1830 the regions where integrated mills were already established gained in strength and, generally speaking, carding machinery was installed only as a component of integrated mills. The process of accretion had, therefore, come to a temporary end, although new integrated mills were still being built and the process was to start afresh after 1830 with the mechanisation of weaving.

Elsewhere there was little evidence of consolidation, but further colonisation was quite apparent. In the west the cotton industry was becoming increasingly centralised as the centripetal force of Glasgow grew; this is reflected in the establishment of woollen mills in north Ayrshire, most of them integrated and at least one, at Dalry, housed in a former cotton mill.[105] In the east a similar process of substitution was taking place in areas marginal to the linen industry which, like cotton, was becoming increasingly centralised, in this case on Dundee. New mills were established in Kincardineshire, the Lothians and even west Fife.[106]

Colonisation in the Highlands gained a greater momentum than it had achieved before 1815, with particularly marked development in the eastern and northern Grampians, with one site as far west as Stornoway.[107] Generally speaking, these Highland mills contained only carding machinery, although several had hand jennies and a few had waulk mills.

Between 1815 and 1830 carding machinery was installed in at least one hundred mills, and during the entire period 1785-1830 there were no fewer than three hundred mills with carding machinery, including those already established as waulk mills and those containing spinning machinery. Throughout the period hardly any carding mills were established in the Glasgow area or in Fife and Angus, the respective centres of the cotton and linen industries.

Spinning Mills

The distribution of water-powered wool spinning mills is particularly difficult to define. As we saw, a number of carding mills had hand-powered machines for spinning or even for weaving, while a few, from an early stage, performed all operations in the manufacture of woollen cloth without using water power for any process except preparing and fulling. Furthermore, since water-powered wool spinning was not perfected until 1814, only those areas in which wool manufacture was well established had adopted the new method by 1830.

The most helpful approach is to work backwards from a period when distributions and numbers are well known. The 1838 Factory Returns[108] list a total of one hundred and twelve woollen mills, of which about a hundred were partially or totally water-powered. Discounting those mills built after 1830, including those in northern Scotland, such as Holm Mill, Inverness, and Newmills, Elgin, which were not enumerated, and taking into account any mills which might have gone out of production between 1814 and 1830, one arrives back at a total of about one hundred for the period up to 1830.

In contrast to the wide distribution achieved by waulk mills and carding mills, that of spinning mills was strongly concentrated in the principal centres of the industry — the Borders, Ayrshire, Galloway, the Hillfoots/Stirling/west Perthshire area and eastern Aberdeenshire (Figure 63). Within these areas concentration was most apparent in the Borders — Galashiels and Hawick had ten mills each — and the Hillfoots. At the other extreme, few communities in south Ayrshire had more than one mill. As one might expect, these areas coincide with those in which the Board of Trustees was making the heaviest investment between 1814 and 1830. During the period 1785-1830 at least five hundred water-powered woollen mills of one type or another were operating in Scotland (Figure 63).

A Case Study: the Hillfoots Woollen Mills

Introduction

The choice of a site for more detailed consideration is not an easy one to make. The concentration of mills in certain favoured districts suggests that an examination of a small area would be more revealing than one concerned with an individual site; of the potential areas of study, Galashiels provides the best instances of innovation and had the most mills, but the consideration already given to it in this chapter and by other writers, such as Hall,[109] would make a second account repetitive. Hawick, the other major woollen centre in the Borders, has been written about to a lesser extent, but still lies within an area which is comparatively well documented. In contrast, relatively little is known of the Hillfoots district which, with twenty mills within a five-mile radius, was second only to the Borders as a wool-manufacturing centre. In view of this poor state of documentation for such an important area, the Hillfoots district is an obvious choice for a case study of Scottish woollen mills between 1785 and 1830.

Historical Background

By the late 18th century Clackmannanshire or, more precisely, the Hillfoots district (Figure 68) already had a small woollen industry based on serges, and although Stirling had traditionally been the local centre for woollen manufacture, Alloa had its own waulk mill by 1785 and Dollar parish had two by the 1790s.[110] As yet the villages of Menstrie, Alva and Tillicoultry had no such mills, but the 1790s brought developments which were to turn the Hillfoots into a major manufacturing district.

In 1791 two local 'manufacturers', John Archibald at Tullibody and John Wilson at Alloa, successfully petitioned the Board of Trustees for a grant towards the purchase of scribbling and carding machinery.[111] Although the offer was not taken up immediately, the same funds were offered again in 1794 to John Wilson for a waulk mill and preparing machinery, possibly on the site of the existing Alloa waulk mill.[112] As will emerge later, Archibald had not given up woollen manufacture but was developing interests elsewhere. At Tillicoultry the first carding machine was hand-driven and a later one horse-driven.[113] In the mid-1790s Thomas Harrower built an open-air fulling machine, powered by Tillicoultry Burn,[114] and at about the same time three brothers, John, Duncan and William Christie, built the first integrated mill in

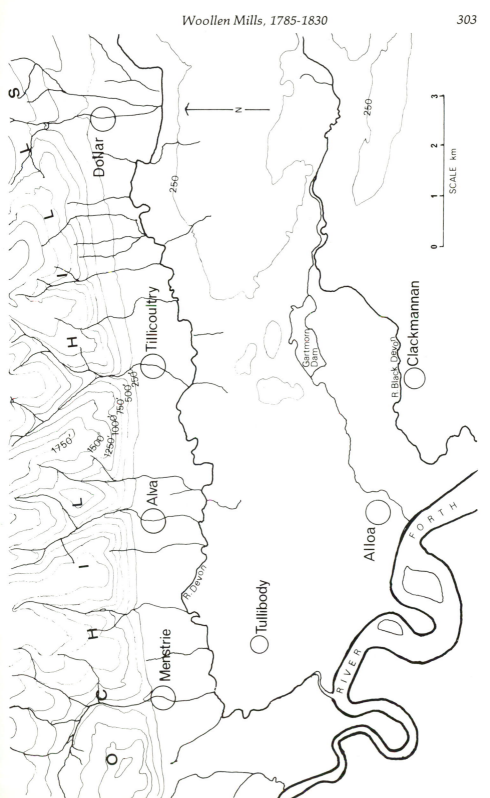

Fig 68. The Hillfoots district, Clackmannanshire

Tillicoultry at the (Old) Mill of Castle Mills. In 1801 they obtained a £50 grant towards carding and spinning machinery, a waulk mill, press and dyeing vats.[115] At Alva in 1798 Robert and James Matthew installed teasing and carding machinery in a mill leased from Johnstone of Alva. A petition for machinery, supposedly new and costing £335, was submitted to the Board of Trustees in 1804.[116] Further west again at Menstrie, John Archibald who, with John Wilson, had petitioned the Board in 1791, established a woollen mill in partnership with his two brothers, William and Robert.[117]

By 1800, therefore, water power had been applied to woollen manufacture in all the places which were subsequently to achieve such importance. The application of machinery so soon after its introduction to Scotland shows an initiative on the part of small manufacturers similar to that found in the Borders, but although good falls were available, the volume of water was small, a factor which was to be of significance in the industry's later development.

1800-1830

Minor Centres: Menstrie

Although no further water-powered mills were established at Menstrie, the Archibalds' mill continued to grow. William left in 1806 to establish his own mill at Tillicoultry, and Robert took on an existing mill in 1817, leaving John and two of his sons, Peter and Andrew, to run the mill at Menstrie (Table 8).[118] Two other sons, John and William, ran other woollen mills in the Hillfoots area. The Menstrie mill was extended to the east in 1810, and in 1813 John Archibald obtained a grant for machinery from the Board of Trustees.[119] A second application, for a further £150, was submitted by Andrew Archibald in 1816, but by 1810 he had emigrated, leaving the mill in his father's hands once more.[120]

The grants had apparently been put to good use; when the mill was visited in 1819, it housed three teasing machines, three scribbling machines, three carding engines, six slubbing billies, two jennies, three reeling and twining machines, ten looms, two waulk mills and twelve pairs of shears.[121] However, the meagre water resources available to the mill could not drive this and additional machinery; by 1834 steam power had been installed, and the irregular supply of water provided no more than half of the required ten horse power.[122]

Over the years the mill's products changed, for although it was already making blankets and plaidings in 1819, the serges and coarse cloth, traditional products of the district which the mill still made then, had given way to shawls by 1834.[123] By 1841 the mill was employing fifty workers.[124]

Table 8

The Archibald Family

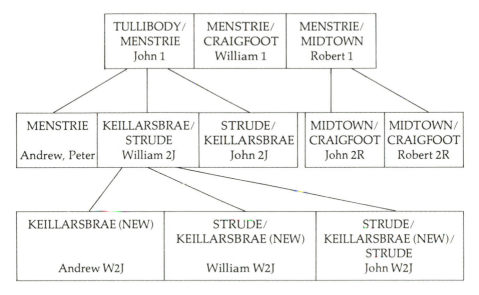

TULLIBODY/ MENSTRIE John 1	MENSTRIE/ CRAIGFOOT William 1	MENSTRIE/ MIDTOWN Robert 1	

MENSTRIE Andrew, Peter	KEILLARSBRAE/ STRUDE William 2J	STRUDE/ KEILLARSBRAE John 2J	MIDTOWN/ CRAIGFOOT John 2R	MIDTOWN/ CRAIGFOOT Robert 2R

KEILLARSBRAE (NEW) Andrew W2J	STRUDE/ KEILLARSBRAE (NEW) William W2J	STRUDE/ KEILLARSBRAE (NEW)/ STRUDE John W2J

Minor Centres: Alloa

According to Gibson, Keilarsbrae (Old) Mill, Alloa had been founded, predictably, by a Mr. Keilar; whether or not this was the case, it was occupied in 1815 by James Wilson, possibly a relative of John Wilson (see p. 302).[125] Although Wilson obtained a grant of £150 in that year, he went bankrupt soon afterwards and the machinery was sold off.[126] By 1819 William Archibald, one of John Archibald's sons, had taken on the mill which, notwithstanding its 'indifferent looking' appearance, housed an excellent set of machinery, covering all processes from teasing to fulling.[127] Of the total cost, £105 had been covered by a Board of Trustees grant.[128] During his occupancy, William added two storeys to the existing single-storey mill.[129]

While William had been at Keilarsbrae Mill, two of his sons, John and William, had been at their uncle John's mill at Alva (Table 15). At some stage John senior and William senior changed places, and subsequently William senior built a second mill at Keilarsbrae, referred to as Keilarsbrae New Mill, for John and William junior and a third son, Andrew. When this failed, one of the sons, John, rejoined his father at Alva.[130]

From this account it should already be evident that the activities of the Archibald family were extremely complex. According to the 1834 Factory Commission Report, Keillarsbrae Mill, occupied by William Archibald, had been built in 1821 and enlarged in 1824 and 1831. As John senior's mill at Alva was not built until 1825, this probably refers to the earlier of the two mills at Keillarsbrae, in which case 1821 would be the date at which the additional two storeys were built. If one were to assume this, Keillarsbrae New Mill was not founded until after 1834, and was probably steam-powered.[131] The Keillarsbrae Mill referred to by the Factory Commission derived a steady six horse power from water power, with a reservoir to regulate the flow during dry spells. No steam power was required.[132] In 1819 the mill had specialised in carpet and stocking yarns, but by 1834 it had moved over to blankets and worsteds.[133]

Besides the Keillarsbrae mills, Alloa had only one other water-powered woollen mill, Kincraig, established in 1812, first used for woollen manufacture in 1814 and enlarged in 1819.[134] John Paton, the mill's founder, was a member of what was later to become an important wool manufacturing family; in 1816 he obtained a £150 grant[135] which seems to have been well employed, for the 1819 report comments on the 'excellent machinery' which performed all processes from teasing to fulling. At this stage the mill was doing a thriving trade in yarn for carpet weavers and coarse country cloths,[136] but here again there was a move towards more market-orientated production, and by 1834 it was specialising in stocking yarns. As elsewhere in the Hillfoots, difficulties had arisen over water supplies, for although the mill had ten horse power for most of the year, only half as much was available during dry summers, while in prolonged droughts the stream had been known to dry up completely for two or three weeks at a time.[137] It should be borne in mind, however, that in submitting evidence to the Factory Commission, manufacturers wished to emphasise the need for long working hours; had the position at Kincraig been really serious, a steam engine would have been installed long before 1834.[138]

Minor Centres: Dollar

Despite their long association with the woollen industry, the textile manufactures of Dollar were dominated in the early 19th century by the extensive bleachfields which specialised in bleaching table linen for Dunfermline manufacturers.[139] The first woollen mill was built about 1805 by Messrs. Gibson, Pitcairn and Burns, under the management of William Wilson.[140] In 1806 Robert Pitcairn & Co. were offered £65 towards existing carding and spinning machinery and for a double carding engine, a billy and two jennies yet to be installed.[141] This first mill was demolished about 1818 to make way for a second one.[142]

Dollar's second woollen mill reflected the general move from custom work to manufacturing for the market: the first mill had carded and spun country wool[143] but its successor, built by William Drysdale, the son of an Alva woollen manufacturer, performed all processes from carding through spinning and weaving to fulling. By 1821 over £400 had been invested in machinery, £55 of which had come from the Board of Trustees.[144] Water provided six horse power but was described in 1834 as irregular. By the early 1840s the mill had become a subsidiary of an Alva mill and was concentrating on carding and spinning.[145]

While Menstrie, Alloa and Dollar could be described as wool manufacturing communities, it was at Tillicoultry and Alva that the industry took on most successfully.

Major Centres: Tillicoultry

Despite Tillicoultry's long-standing associations with woollen cloth manufacture, the industry had reached a low ebb by the 1790s. At that time there were only twenty-one weavers in the parish and, according to the stampmaster, only seven thousand yards of serge and an equal quantity of plaiding passed through his hands each year.[146] The first signs of revival came in 1798 when John Christie, 'an ingenious and energetic native of the village', with two of his brothers, Duncan and William, built a woollen manufactory at Old Mills of Castle Mills.[147] In 1801 they obtained £50 from the Board of Trustees towards a waulk mill, press, dyeing vats and carding and spinning machinery.[148] Initial successes prompted the Christies to build a second mill, Midtown, about 1805, towards the machinery of which £67 was granted in 1807;[149] but the success was short-lived. In 1815 William Christie, who appears to have taken overall control of the mills, obtained a grant of £150. In all probability the money was needed to pay off debts on capital investment or to finance an over-ambitious project; whatever the case, William Christie went bankrupt shortly afterwards and emigrated to America.[150] Thereafter the mills lay empty for a year or two.[151]

In the meantime, since the founding of Midtown Mill, other mills had been built in the village. William Archibald left Menstrie Mill in 1806 to start his own mill at Tillicoultry (p. 304). The mill in question was Craigfoot, on the very edge of the Ochils at the upper end of the village. To secure an adequate water supply, he had to build a new dam high up in the glen with a very long lade, part of which ran twenty feet below ground level.[152] According to Gibson, women in the village, objecting to pollution from Craigfoot's waulk mill, twice demolished the dam under cover of darkness before arrangements were finally made to carry off the polluted water in a sewer.[153] William Archibald died in 1826, but the mill was carried on for a further thirteen years by his widow. In 1838 it was replaced by a new mill with a thirty-five foot diameter water wheel.[154]

Tillicoultry's fourth mill, referred to by Gibson as the 'horse mill' or 'company mill', was established above Castle Mills in the early 1810s by a group of Alva-based manufacturers trading under the name of James Balfour & Co.[155] On this site the company built a waulk mill and probably other water-powered machinery. Although little is known of the mill's early history, the company, still intact despite changes in membership, obtained grants in 1822 and 1829 totalling £131 towards carding, spinning, weaving and fulling machinery costing £727.[156] As it stood in 1833, the mill was of three storeys, seventy-five feet by thirty-four feet, with a tiled roof.[157]

The next mill was founded by James Dawson, a local woollen manufacturer,

Table 9

Board of Trustees. 1819 Woollen Mill Survey. Hillfoots

	1	2	3	4	5	6	7	8	9	10
Year aided	1813	1816	*	1814	*	1815	1818	1816	1815	1819
Sum	£90	£150	£50	£65	£80	£150	£75	£150	£150	£105
Teas. mach's.	3		1	1	1	1	1	1	—	1
Scrib.　,,	3		2	2	1	3	1	1	—	1
Card.　,,	3		2	2	2	2	1	2	—	1
Slub.　,,	6		3	3	1	4	2	1	—	1
Sp. Jennies	2		—	—	4	—	1	4	—	4
Reel. & Twin. ,,	3		1	2	1	1	1	2	—	1
Looms	10		6	8	6	8	6	3	—	3
Waulk mills	2		1	—	1	2	1	1	—	1
Dye-houses	1		—	—	—	—	—	—	—	—

1. John Archibald, Menstrie
&
2. Andrew Archibald, Menstrie. All belongs to John Archibald
3. W. & R. Harrower, Alva. Formerly J. Harrower & Sons
4. R. Drysdale & Son, Alva
5. Wm. & David Drysdale, Alva
6. Wm. Christie, Tillicoultry. Bankrupt. Gone to America
7. Robert Archibald, Tillicoultry
8. John Paton, Alloa
9. J. Wilson, Keillarsbrae. Bankrupt. Machinery sold
10. William Archibald, Keillarsbrae

on a site adjacent to Craigfoot Mill. Gibson dates it to 1811 or 1812, but evidence from the Factory Commission and the minutes of the Board of Trustees suggests that it was not built until 1821.[158] Dawson installed a full set of preparing, spinning, weaving and fulling machinery at a cost of £554, £85 of which was borne by the Board of Trustees.[159] In 1827 additional machinery costing £400 and two new water wheels were about to be added.[160] By Hill-foots standards Dawson's mill, with seven or eight horse power, was moderately well endowed with water power;[161] it was still in the family in 1834, producing blankets, plaidings and tartan shawls.[162]

Before proceeding any further, we should return to Tillicoultry's first two mills after the bankruptcy of William Christie in 1815. In 1817 the Christies' Midtown Mill was purchased by Robert Archibald, co-founder of Menstrie Mill.[163] Here Archibald installed a new set of machinery (Table 9), for which a grant of £75 was awarded,[164] and although the mill-house was described as 'poor' in 1819, some improvements were made in 1821 and 1826;[165] Robert Archibald continued to operate the mill with his two sons, Robert and John. In

1839 they were among the first woollen manufacturers to make use of William Smith's self-acting mule, and in the same year John and Robert took over Craigfoot Mill, which had been run by their uncle William's widow.[166] The new company, J. & R. Archibald, continued for several years; John Archibald died in 1848, and in 1851 the mill finally passed out of the family.[167]

In 1819 Midtown Mill was producing coarse cloth for local use,[168] but it seems probable that some change in products and markets had taken place by the 1830s. Although there were the usual problems with water supply, no steam engine had been installed by 1834 to supplement the four to seven horse power available from the burn.[169]

The earlier of the Christies' two works, the Old Mill of Castle Mills, also found a new occupant in 1817. Robert Walker had founded a mill in Galashiels but had been forced to sell to creditors in 1811. Some six years later he re-appeared at Tillicoultry, and installed a full set of machinery at Old Mill of Castle Mills at an estimated cost of £386, £80 of which was provided by the Board of Trustees.[170] In 1820 or, more probably, 1824 his eldest sons, James and George, founded a new mill, with machinery costing £682; additional machinery, costing £583, was installed about 1830.[171] The dimensions of the mill were given in 1833 as seventy feet by thirty-two feet by thirty-eight feet high, but despite its size the mill had only an irregular eight horse power at its disposal.[172] In 1834 it was producing blankets, plaidings and tartan shawls, the last of which had been introduced to Tillicoultry some ten years earlier.[173] Andrew Walker, younger brother of George and James, established another mill, the New Mill of Castle Mills, in the late 1820s and laid out £170 on its machinery.[174]

In 1825 James and David Paton, members of the important wool-manufacturing family, had built a mill at Tillicoultry to produce soft tartan shawls, blankets and twilled flannels.[175]

Thus, between 1795 and 1830, Tillicoultry had been transformed from a small village in which a little cloth was produced by hand to a thriving manufacturing town, with eight large woollen mills producing a range of products which included fashionable shawls and tartans of high quality. At the time of the New Statistical Account the woollen industry in Tillicoultry consumed 30,000 stones of wool per annum and employed three hundred men, one hundred and twenty women and one hundred and forty children.[176]

Major Centres: Alva

In the late 18th century, when the manufacture of serges at Tillicoultry was at a low ebb, the same product was being successfully produced at Alva, despite initial customer resistance. Indeed, production at Alva was confined to serges and blankets until the introduction of shawl manufacture in 1829.[177] Unfortunately the industry at Alva is not so well documented as at Tillicoultry.

Little is known of the origins of Alva's first mill, but it is known to have been acquired later by the Drysdale family who had founded the village's second mill in 1802. By 1814 machinery grants had been awarded to two branches of the family, Robert Drysdale and Son and William and David Drysdale. According to the 1819 report, both mills made blankets and coarse cloth for country use, and both had a full set of preparing, spinning and weaving machinery, but only William & David Drysdale's mill had fulling machinery;[178] of an additional £418 laid out on this mill during the early 1820s, £65 was met by the Board of Trustees.[179] William Drysdale junior, who may have belonged to either branch of the family, received £155 in two machinery grants during the 1820s, and was running two mills in Alva by 1834, one being the town's first mill, the other a mill built by him about 1827. Both mills had an irregular ten horse power water supply but no steam power.[180] William Drysdale junior had also established the second mill in Dollar about 1818.

By 1834 the Drysdales' first mill, built in 1802 and added to in 1820, was under the firm of William Drysdale and Sons, but here too it is not clear how this William Drysdale was related to the rest of the family. Yet another member of the family, Thomas Drysdale, spent £421 on machinery at Alva in 1829 and obtained a grant of £84 from the Board of Trustees; this machinery might have been installed at a new or existing mill. David Drysdale had been one of the partners in the Company Mill, Tillicoultry.[181] There is evidence, therefore, of the Drysdales building two or possibly three mills at Alva, and occupying another, already built. Much more research would be required before the family's business interests could be disentangled.

In comparison with the Drysdales' activities, the rest of the Alva woollen industry is relatively straightforward. In 1807 James Harrower & Sons established a mill at Alva, a grant of £50 being made towards the machinery; a further £90 was given to their successors, William and Robert Harrower, in 1817.[182] According to the 1819 report, buildings and machinery were both excellent.[183] At the Harrowers' mill, as at others in Alva, the products at that time consisted of blankets, plaidings, serges and coarse cloth, but by 1833 worsted shawls were being produced as well.[184] Another mill in Alva was occupied in 1821 by James Ritchie, William Rennie and James Balfour, three of the principal partners in the Company Mill, Tillicoultry.[185] A seventh mill, Strude, was established in 1825 by yet another member of the Archibald family, and started production on 12th April 1826.[186] Initially, it was occupied by John Archibald, son of the Menstrie Mill co-founder of the same name.[187] For a while his two nephews, William and John, were also at Strude, but their father, William, who had been at Keillarsbrae Old Mill, changed places with his brother John at Strude and founded Keillarsbrae New Mill for his two aforementioned sons and a third son, Andrew. When this proved unsuccessful, one of the three brothers, John, returned to Strude Mill, now occupied by his father.[188] In 1834 Strude Mill was producing yarn for shawls.

These, then, are the seven mills known to have existed in 1838. By the time the New Statistical Account was written, an eighth mill had been built; at that time the mills consumed 480,000 lbs. of wool per annum and gave employment to five hundred and sixty-five people.[189]

In the Hillfoots as in the Borders, the backbone of the woollen industry was made up of initially small-scale manufacturers. While they were not as quick as the Borders in adopting new machinery, they did manage to build up a substantial coarse cloth manufacture and had sufficient business acumen by the late 1820s to transfer into more profitable lines such as shawls and tartans, just as manufacturers in the Borders had moved into tweeds.

But there was at least one major difference between the two areas: whilst the Borders possessed abundant water power, that available to the Hillfoots was very limited. On the other hand the latter area was situated adjacent to coalfields and could therefore use auxiliary steam power more cheaply than could the Borders. At Alva a dam was constructed to store water, but despite this measure the average fall there produced only six horse power in 1838; the average for Tillicoultry, at 7.7, was little better.[190] These figures compare poorly with averages of 8.4 at Galashiels, 15.5 at Hawick and 17.3 at Selkirk.[191] It is therefore hardly surprising that steam power was applied much earlier and more generally in the Hillfoots than in the Borders, although the evidence given to the Factory Commissioners suggests that those mills which installed steam engines did so only during the phase of rapid expansion after 1830. Prior to that the Hillfoots woollen industry, like that of Scotland as a whole, was very largely water-powered.

NOTES

1. OSP 485:25: Haddington Town Council v. Haddington Tarred Wool Company.

2. Martindale, J. G., 'The Rise and Growth of the Tweed Industry in Scotland', in Jenkins, J. G. (ed.), *The Wool Textile Industry in Great Britain*, London, 1972, 273.

3. SRO NG1/1/26 27/6/87, 27/6/87.

4. SRO NG1/1/27 10/2/90: 8/12/90.

5. Findlater, C., *General View of the Agriculture of Peeblesshire*, Edinburgh, 1802, 218; *OSA* XIX, 598, Innerleithen, Peeblesshire; Buchan, J. W., *A History of Peeblesshire*, 3 vols., Glasgow, 1925, II, 217.

6. SRO NG1/1/27 2/2/91.

7. Galashiels: SRO NG1/1/28 29/2/92, 15/1/94; Tullibody: SRO NG1/1/28 10/12/94; Braelangwell, Ross-shire: SRO NG1/1/29 8/2/97; Greenlaw, Berwickshire: SRO NG1/1/29 26/6/99; *OSA* VI, 34, Newhills, Aberdeenshire; *OSA* XV, 287, Longside, Aberdeenshire; *OSA* XV, 80, Twynholm & Kirkchrist, Kirkcudbrightshire.

8. Duntocher, established in 1785, was reputedly one of the first mechanised woollen mills in Scotland: Devine, T. M., 'Glasgow Merchants and Colonial Trade, 1770-1815', Strathclyde University PhD, 1972, II, 378; *OSA* V, 229, Old Kilpatrick, Dunbartonshire.

9. Richards, R. T. D., 'The Development of the Modern Woollen Carding Machine', in Jenkins, *op. cit.*, 73-4.

10. Mann, J. de L., in Singer, C., Holmyard, E. J., Hall, A. R. & Williams, T. I. (eds.), *A History of Technology*, 5 vols., Oxford, 1956-9, IV, 298.

11. Richards, *op. cit.*, 74.

12. Hall, R., *The History of Galashiels*, Galashiels, 1898, 422; SRO NG1/1/25 23/1/86: three scribbling machines erected by Mercer.

13. Hall, *op. cit.*, 422-3.

14. *Ibid.*, 424.

15. SRO NG1/1/27 2/2/91.

16. SRO NG1/1/28 10/12/91, 28/5/94; SRO NG1/1/30 11/12/99.

17. SRO NG1/1/28 15/1/94; SRO NG1/1/29 23/5/98; SRO NG1/1/29 26/6/99, 13/2/99, 8/6/96, 8/2/97; SRO NG1/1/30 20/11/99.

18. Morgan, P., *Annals of Woodside & Newhills*, Aberdeen, 1886, 191.

19. Findlater, *op. cit.*, 218.

20. Hall, *op. cit.*, 301; SRO NG1/1/28 25/1/92.

21. SRO NG1/1/29 29/6/96.

22. SRO NG1/1/32 8/7/07.

23. For further information on carding machinery, see Richards, R. T. D., *op. cit.*, 71-84.

24. Richards, *op. cit.*, 79.

25. McKechnie, K., *A Border Woollen Town in the Industrial Revolution*, London, 1974, 53.

26. Gulvin, C., *The Tweedmakers*, Newton Abbot, 1973, 101.

27. SRO NG1/1/34 10/7/22.

28. SRO NG1/1/30 27/11/99; SRO NG1/1/29 29/11/97.

29. See Chapter 20.

30. Loch, D., *A Tour through most of the Trading Towns and Villages of Scotland*, Edinburgh, 1778, 1.

31. SRO NG1/1/33 21/2/16.

32. Mann, *op. cit.*, 299.

33. Hall, *op. cit.*, 394.

34. *Ibid.*, 429.

35. SRO NG1/60/54/1.

36. *Scots Magazine* LI (1789), 618.

37. See Chapter 3, p. 51; Chapter 18, p. 277.

38. SRO NG1/1/27 23/6/90.

39. SRO NG1/1/28 29/2/92; Hall, *op. cit.*, 426.

40. SRO NG1/1/32 16/12/07.

41. Mann, *op. cit.*, 304.

42. *Ibid.*, 304.

43. SRO NG1/1/32 26/6/11.

44. SRO NG1/1/33 29/1/12; 13/1/13; 7/2/16.

45. SRO NG1/1/33 19/6/16.

46. Mann, *op. cit.*, 305.

47. SRO NG1/1/34 23/5/20.

48. SRO NG1/1/35 7/7/1829.

49. SRO NG1/1/34 10/7/22; SRO NG1/1/35 29/6/24.

50. SRO NG1/a/32 10/7/11.

51. See Chapter 29, p. 517.

52. *NSA* III, 405, Hawick, Roxburghshire.

53. *PP* 1843, LVI, 359.

54. Wilson, R., *A Sketch of the History of Hawick*, Hawick, 1825, 287-8.

55. SRO NG1/1/32 6/7/08.

56. SRO NG1/1/31 11/12/05.

57. SRO NG1/1/32 8/7/07; Robertson, J., *General View of the Agriculture of Inverness-shire*, London, 1808, 314; SRO NG1/1/32 4/7/10.

58. *OSA* XIX, 598, Innerleithen, Peeblesshire; Findlater, *op. cit.*, 218.

59. SRO NG1/1/29 8/6/96; 8/2/97; 14/2/98; SRO NG1/1/30 13/2/99; Hume, J. R., *The Industrial Archaeology of Scotland*, 2 vols., London, 1976-7, II.

60. Donnachie, I., *Industrial Archaeology of Galloway*, Newton Abbot, 1971, 68, 75-7.

61. *Ibid.*, 68; *OSA* XV, 80, Twynholm & Kirkchrist, Kirkcudbrightshire.

62. Robertson, *op. cit.*, 314.

63. SRO NG1/1/31 26/1/03; *Farmers' Magazine* V, 8 (1804).

64. Donnachie, *op. cit.*, 74; Singer, W., *General View of the Agriculture of the County of Dumfries*, Edinburgh, 1812, 62-3.

65. SRO NG1/1/30 9/5/1800.

66. SRO NG1/1/26 11/2/89.

67. SRO NG1/1/28 28/594; SRO NG1/1/29 25/1/97.

68. SRO NG1/1/29 25/1/97.

69. SRO NG1/1/29 7/2/98; SRO NG1/1/31 19/12/04; SRO NG1/1/33 30/6/13; 24/11/13; Hume, J. R., in *Scottish Society for Industrial Archaeology Newsletter*, No. 4, Pt. 1, May 1972; Hume, J. R., *op. cit.* (1976-7), I, 75.

70. SRO NG1/1/23 2/7/83; Hall, *op. cit.*, 395.

71. *Ibid.*, 391, 395.

72. *Ibid.*, 399-402.

73. *Ibid.*, 387, 394, 404, 405.

74. *Ibid.*, 382-407.

75. SRO NG1/1/30 3/7/99; *OSA* XXI, 245-6, Langholm, Dumfriesshire (Addenda).

76. SRO NG1/1/32 21/12/08.

77. Thomson, G., 'The Dalnottar Iron Company', *SHR* XXXV (1956), 19-20; Devine, *op. cit.*, II, 378.

78. *OSA* V, 229, Old Kilpatrick, Dunbartonshire.

79. Morgan, *op. cit.*, 190-1.

80. Gulvin, *op. cit.*, 58.

81. *OSA* X, 635, Spynie, Moray; Gulvin, *op. cit.*, 58.

82. SRO NG1/1/30 17/12/1800; SRO NG1/1/32 8/7/07.

83. Leslie, W., *General View of the Agriculture of the Counties of Moray & Nairn*, London, 1811, 400-1.

84. *NSA* VIII, 25-6, Old Kilpatrick, Dunbartonshire; Donnachie, *op. cit.*, 95-6.

85. Naismith, J., *Thoughts on the Various Objects of Industry pursued in Scotland*, Edinburgh, 1790, 479.

86. SRO NG1/1/30 5/6/99; SRO NG1/1/32 3/2/08; SRO NG1/1/34 15/6/19.

87. SRO NG1/1/29 13/2/99.

88. *NSA* VIII, 70, Killearn, Stirlingshire.

89. SRO NG1/1/31 6/7/03; *PP* 1834, XIX, Factory Commission, 163-4.

90. SRO NG1/1/29 7/3/98.

91. SRO NG1/1/31 11/12/05.

92. SRO NG1/1/31 30/6/02; Findlater, *op. cit.*, 218.

93. SRO NG1/1/32 10/7/11.

94. SRO NG1/1/35 17/6/1828; Dick-Lauder, Sir T., *An Account of the Great Floods of August 1829, in the Province of Moray and Adjoining Districts*, Edinburgh, 1830, 73.

95. SRO NG1/1/33 5/7/15.

96. SRO NG1/1/23 2/7/83.

97. SRO NG1/1/26 23/7/88; 6/8/88.

98. Wilderhaugh: SRO NG1/1/23 22/1/83; Buckholmside: SRO NG1/1/26 23/7/88; Dryburgh: *Scots Magazine* LI (1789), 618; Innerleithen: *OSA* XIX, 598; Cluny (Perthshire): SRO NG1/1/29 29/6/96; Tillicoultry: Gibson, W., *Reminiscences of Dollar, Tillicoultry and other Districts adjoining the Ochils*, Edinburgh, 1883, 171; Alloa: SRO NG1/1/28 10/12/94; Moffat: SRO NG1/1/29 2/3/96; Langholm: SRO NG1/1/30 3/7/99; Berryscar: SRO NG1/1/30 5/6/99; Kirkinner: SRO NG1/1/29 28/6/97.

99. Hall, *op. cit.*, 382-407.

100. SRO NG1/1/29 14/6/97; 28/6/97.

101. Innerleithen: Findlater, *op. cit.*, 218; Galashiels: SRO NG1/1/28 15/1/94; Duntocher: Devine, *op. cit.*, 378; Stoneywood: Morgan, *op. cit.*, 190.

102. Morgan, *op. cit.*, 191. A carding mill, built at Old Mill of Strichen, c.1797, was founded by Matthew Young, who had been brought to Stoneywood to install machinery.

103. Donnachie, *op. cit.*, 68; *OSA* XV, 80, Twynholm & Kirkchrist, Kirkcudbright-shire.

104. Newmill: SRO NG1/1/30 17/12/1800; Tammore, Banffshire: SRO NG1/1/31 6/7/03; Peebles: SRO NG1/1/31 3/2/1802; Romanno Bridge: SRO NG1/1/32 5/7/09.

105. *NSA* V, 233, Dalry, Ayrshire.

106. Edenbank: SRO NG1/1/34 4/7/20.

107. SRO NG1/1/34 10/7/21.

108. *PP* 1839, XLII, Factory Returns.

109. Hall, *op. cit.*

110. Bremner, D., *The Industries of Scotland* (1869), Newton Abbot, 1969, 208; *OSA* XV, 164, Dollar, Clackmannanshire.

111. SRO NG1/1/28 30/11/91.

112. SRO NG1/1/28 10/12/94.

113. Gibson, *op. cit.*, 13.

114. *Ibid.*, 171.

115. SRO NG1/1/31 8/7/01.

116. SRO NG1/1/31 13/6/04.

117. Gibson, *op. cit.*, 177.

118. *Ibid.*, 177-8.

119. *PP* 1834, XIX, Factory Commission, 30.

120. SRO NG1/1/33 3/7/16; SRO NG1/60/54/1: Survey of Woollen Machinery and Mills.

121. SRO NG1/60/54/1.

122. *PP* 1834, XIX, 30-31.

123. SRO NG1/60/54/1; *PP* 1834, XIX, 30-31.

124. *NSA* VIII, 230, Logie, Stirlingshire.

125. SRO NG1/1/33 5/7/15.

126. SRO NG1/60/54/1.

127. Ibid.

128. SRO NG1/1/34 29/6/19.

129. Gibson, *op. cit.*, 193.

130. *Ibid.*, 193.

131. In 1834 Alloa had six woollen mills, four of which were steam-powered: *NSA* VIII, 48, Alloa, Clackmannanshire. Both Old and New Mills were still functioning in the 1860s: Bremner, *op. cit.*, 207-8.

132. *PP* 1834, XIX, 28-9.

133. *Ibid;* SRO NG1/60/54/1.

134. *PP* 1834, XIX, 29-30.

135. SRO NG1/1/33 3/7/16.

136. SRO NG1/60/54/1.

137. *PP* 1834, XIX, 30.

138. Similar hard luck stories came from manufacturers on the Ericht in Perthshire and the Don in Aberdeenshire.

139. *OSA* II, 164, Dollar, Clackmannanshire.

140. Gibson, *op. cit.*, 13.

141. SRO NG1/1/32 9/7/06.

142. *PP* 1834, XIX, 218-9.

143. Gibson, *op. cit.*, 13.

144. SRO NG1/1/34 10/7/21.

145. *NSA* VIII, 110, Dollar, Clackmannanshire.

146. Bremner, *op. cit.*, 208.

147. *Ibid.*, 208; Gibson, *op. cit.*, 171.

148. SRO NG1/1/31 8/7/1801.

149. Gibson, *op. cit.*, 171-2; SRO NG1/1/32 8/7/07.

150. SRO NG1/1/33 5/7/15.

151. Gibson, *op. cit.*, 178.

152. *Ibid.*, 179.

153. *Ibid.*, 179-80.

154. *Ibid.*, 181.

155. *Ibid.*, 172, 181. The term 'Horse Mill' referred to an earlier horse-driven carding mill.

156. SRO NG1/1/34 10/7/72; SRO NG1/1/35 7/7/29.

157. SRO NG1/60/52/16.

158. Gibson, *op. cit.*, 181; *PP* 1834, XIX, 33-4; SRO NG1/1/34 10/7/22.

159. SRO NG1/1/34 10/7/22.

160. SRO NG1/1/35 10/7/1827.

161. *PP* 1834, XIX, 33-4.

162. *Ibid.*, 33-4.

163. *Ibid.*, 33; Gibson, *op. cit.*, 175.

164. SRO NG1/1/34 30/6/18.

165. SRO NG1/60/54/1; *PP* 1834, XIX, 31-3.

166. Bremner, *op. cit.*, 209; Gibson, *op. cit.*, 181.

167. Gibson, *op. cit.*, 181.

168. SRO NG1/60/54/1.

169. *PP* 1834, XIX, 31-3.

170. SRO NG1/1/34 4/7/1829.

171. Gibson, *op. cit.*, 180; SRO NG1/1/35 28/6/1825; SRO NG1/60/52/14.

172. SRO NG1/60/52/14.
173. *PP* 1834, XIX, 35-6.
174. Gibson, *op. cit.*, 181; SRO NG1/1/36 5/7/31.
175. *PP* 1834, XIX, 34-5; SRO NG1/1/36 5/7/31.
176. *NSA* VIII, 73, Tillicoultry, Clackmannanshire.
177. Bremner, *op. cit.*, 210.
178. SRO NG1/60/54/1.
179. SRO NG1/1/34 10/7/22.
180. *PP* 1834, XIX, 218-9.
181. SRO NG1/60/52/16.
182. SRO NG1/1/32 6/7/08; SRO NG1/1/33 1/1/17; *PP* 1834, XIX, 221.
183. SRO NG1/60/54/1.
184. *PP* 1834, XIX, 221.
185. SRO NG1/1/34 10/7/21.
186. *PP* 1834, XIX, 222.
187. Gibson, *op. cit.*, 193.
188. *Ibid.*, 193.
189. *NSA* VIII, 188, Alva, Stirlingshire (Clackmannanshire).
190. *PP* 1839, XLII, 315.
191. *Ibid.*, 315.

20

Cotton Mills

Compared with the long-established linen and woollen industries, cotton was a relative latecomer to Scotland. By 1730 a little cotton was being used both by itself and with linen yarn; the first cotton printfield was established in Glasgow in 1738.[1] By mid-century cotton manufacture had taken root in west-central Scotland, utilising the skills developed in the production of fine linen.

In the second half of the 18th century its growth gathered further momentum: cotton wool imports rose from 105,831 lbs in 1755 to 466,589 lbs in 1770. By the end of the 1770s carding and spinning machinery, the first of its kind in Scotland, had been introduced,[2] giving cotton an advantage over linen and wool which helped enable it to take over from linen in west-central Scotland and threaten it elsewhere.

Technology

During the late 18th century three important innovations revolutionised cotton spinning. In 1764 James Hargreaves, a weaver at Stanhill, near Blackburn, Lancashire, invented the spinning jenny, a machine which, driven by a hand crank, reproduced the actions of a manual spinner to produce several spindles of yarn simultaneously. Initially it was used for both warp and weft, but latterly was found to be better suited to the latter. A patent was taken out in 1769, but as Hargreaves had already sold a few machines, it was found to be invalid.[3]

A few weeks prior to Hargreaves' application for a patent, another cotton spinning machine had been patented by Richard Arkwright. Whilst Hargreaves' machine had been original in its design, Arkwright's appears to have been only the culmination of work by a number of parties. In its operation it required more power than did the jenny, but produced a strong yarn suitable for warp, thereby complementing it. In his patent specification Arkwright had envisaged that the machine would be powered by horses, but its more general use of water power soon earned it the name of water-frame.[4] In 1775 Arkwright took out a patent on a carding machine, developed from designs by Bourn and by Paul; this also showed machinery for drawing and roving.[5]

A third machine, designed by Samuel Crompton but never patented, combined features of both the jenny and the water-frame. The 'mule', as it was called, could produce yarn for both warp and weft but was initially only hand-driven.[6]

The first cotton mill in Scotland was at Penicuik, Midlothian. In 1774 one Peter Brotherstone wrote to the Board of Trustees regarding a carding machine which he claimed to have lately invented.[7] Whatever the authenticity of Brotherstone's invention, he was amply rewarded for it and was offered incentives to prepare models of cotton-spinning machinery.[8] On 21st June 1777 he obtained a sub-tack of land immediately below the waulk mill of Penicuik[9] and by July 1778 had set up a mill with water-powered carding, roving and spinning machinery.[10] This time there was no doubt as to the source of the machines' design, for Arkwright was threatening to close down the mill for having infringed his patent.[11] In the Lord Advocate's view the patent did not extend to Scotland;[12] the mill continued to function unmolested, and a second was added, although this had been converted to paper-making by 1805, in which year the 'little mill' underwent a like change.[13]

Elsewhere in Scotland others were attempting to breach the Arkwright patents. In the late 1770s a group of Sheffield men, headed by James Kenyon, succeeded in buying off some of Arkwright's workers, who understood the construction and operation of Arkwright's machines, with a view to establishing a mill on the Marquis of Annandale's Scottish estate. Although Kenyon failed to find a suitable site there, he obtained a ninety-nine year lease of ground at Rothesay, on the Earl of Bute's estate, and having initially carried out trials on water frames in Rothesay lint mill, built a cotton mill there about 1778.[14] By 1779 he too was threatened by Arkwright, but had the backing of the Lord Advocate's earlier ruling and the additional incentive of a twenty-guinea premium from the Board of Trustees.[15] According to Sinclair,[16] the experimental work at the lint mill predated the Penicuik mill, but the first purpose-built mill at Rothesay was almost certainly of a later date. The lint mill was latterly converted for housing, but what is assumed to have been the cotton mill still stands.[17]

During the early 1780s several other 'pirate' ventures were attempted. In 1784 the Arkwright patent expired and in 1785 his patents on preparing machinery were set aside.[18] In England too there had been blatant infringements of the patent, and from 1785 Arkwright became active in the Scottish industry, which he saw as a potential rival to his English competitors.[19]

Even the earliest Scottish cotton mills were able to make use of improved versions of Arkwright's machines, and once they had become well established, they were further modified and added to. Willowing or scribbling machines were adapted from those already used in the woollen industry, whilst for the next process in manufacture, that of batting, a power-driven scutcher was developed in Scotland by Neil Snodgrass in 1797.[20] Various improvements were made to carding in England, and in Scotland by James Smith, manager of Deanston Mill, Perthshire.[21] Roving, too, underwent several improvements, culminating in the development of the bobbin and fly frame by Henry Houldsworth of Glasgow in 1825.[22] In 1790, William Kelly, manager of New Lanark

Mills, succeeded in applying water power to some of the operations of the mule, but a self-acting mule, patented in 1792, was soon given up as too cumbersome;[23] not until about 1830 was an effective design developed.[24] James Smith was one of those who had made modifications to the spinning mule.[25] An improved version of the throstle was developed after the Napoleonic Wars, and by 1830 this, in turn, had undergone further modifications.[26]

In England, a power loom was developed by Cartwright in 1786, improvements to which were patented in 1787 and 1792.[27] Besides numerous English design changes, there were at least three Scottish attempts to develop an effective power loom. Alexander Robb, Minister of Tongland, Kirkcudbrightshire, constructed a model which prompted the Board of Trustees to offer him encouragement to build a full-sized version in Edinburgh, but although he received twenty-five guineas plus costs, it was conceded that there were still problems to be surmounted.[28] John Austin, in Glasgow, claimed to have invented a water-powered loom in 1804,[29] but in the long term the most important Scottish work was that of Robert Miller, who developed a machine in Glasgow in 1796, and contributed to the first successful application of the power loom in 1798.[30] The first power looms in Scotland were installed at Milton Printfield, Dunbartonshire; by 1814 there were two hundred and thirty-four at Catrine, five hundred being installed in Lanarkshire and a total of one thousand five hundred already installed in Scottish mills, most of them in west-central Scotland.[31] A major breakthrough came in the 1820s, during which decade the number in operation rose from two to ten thousand.[32]

From the very start, Scottish cotton mills were substantial buildings, but an even greater scale of building soon became normal. Dovecothall Mill, built about 1780, was 'three stories high, having twenty-three windows in front and twenty-four on the back side, viz. three rows, with eight windows in each row. The outer great wheel is sixteen feet in diameter, and three feet thick . . . The mill within has two rows of frames, with twenty-eight in a row, each frame having twenty-four spindles . . . on the one side and twenty on the other total 2,464.'[33] A larger mill, 112 feet by 31 feet by five storeys, with 136 windows, was built at Johnstone about 1782, the machinery of which was powered by a water wheel six feet broad and eighteen feet in diameter[34] (Figure 69). At Greenock, the wheel which drove the machinery of a cotton mill was at one time the largest in the world: seventy feet two inches in diameter, one hundred and seventeen tons in weight and capable of two hundred horse power.[35]

Although most of the early cotton mills were water-powered, several used hand-operated jennies. Manufactories of this kind existed at Spinningdale in Sutherland and at East Kilbride in Lanarkshire.[36] Elsewhere, certain mills used water power for carding, and sometimes roving, only, much as in the same manner as early woollen mills. In the 1790s there were carding and roving mills at Kilwinning (Ayrshire), Flemmington (Lanarkshire) and Luncarty (Perthshire), all of them associated with jenny spinning. At Catrine, where water-powered spinning had started in about 1787, a jenny factory was added

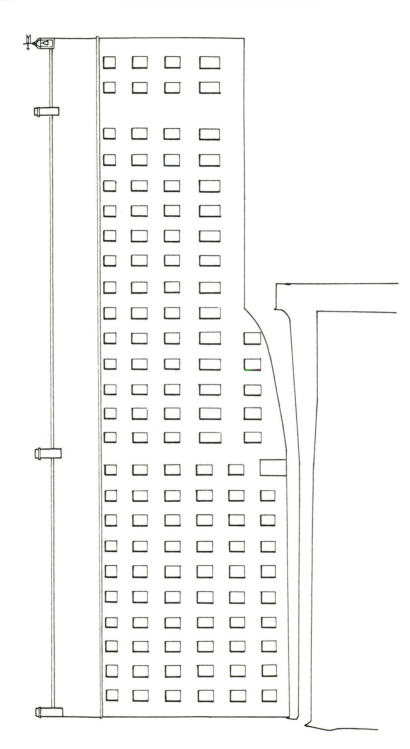

Fig 69. Old Mill, Johnstone, *circa 1790. SRO RHP 276/2*

in 1790, the cotton for which was carded and roved by a mill on the spinning mill tail race.[37]

The application of steam power to the cotton industry was of insignificant proportions until 1800. According to Hills, Boulton and Watt sold only one textile mill engine in Scotland in 1798, three in 1799 and five in 1800. Even taking into consideration the incomplete nature of Hills' figures, some of these engines were for use in flax mills, so that a total of about ten steam engines in the cotton industry would be quite feasible. By 1800 there were already some sixty or so water-powered cotton mills in Scotland. During the 1800s and 1810s steam gained ground, mostly in the Paisley-Glasgow area, but as far north as Aberdeen, where the first cotton mill engine was installed about 1803.[38] During the 1820s a spate of mill-building in the Paisley-Glasgow area took steam power into the lead, but water-powered mills were still being built in favoured areas. The first comprehensive figures for 1835 show that water power was still producing 2,480 of the 5,680 horse power available to Scottish cotton mills, compared with a 6,094 horse power contribution to the 32,607 horse power used in Northern England.[39]

Sources of Finance

The Landowner

Although the same considerations applied to cotton mills as to flax-spinning mills, some late 18th-century landowners were sufficiently well disposed towards cotton mills to consider developing them on their land.

In Galloway, a cotton mill was built at Newton Stewart by a company, the principal partners in which were David Dale, the Glasgow manufacturer, and Sir William Douglas, owner of the estate. The business was carried on for several years but, proving unprofitable, was sold to another company at half the original cost.[40] David Dale also shared a partnership in Catrine cotton mill with the landowner, Claud Alexander of Ballochmyle. In 1801 it was taken over by James Finlay & Co.[41]

The nearest that a landowner came to taking on the role of entrepreneur was at Stanley, Perthshire, where George Dempster of Dunnichen, founder of Letham village, established a mill with Perth merchants, on land feued from the Duke of Atholl.[42] Dempster, who was also a partner in the ill-fated Spinningdale venture, was by no means typical of Scottish landowners, coming as he did from a merchant family.[43]

Merchant Landowners

In the context of the cotton industry there are a significant number of mills which were established by partnerships in which at least one leading partner appears to have been a landowner. Whilst the examples already cited show that this was sometimes quite genuinely the case, the majority, on closer inspection, turn out to be merchants, or members of merchant families who, having accumulated capital in the textile, tobacco or other trades, invested it in land and subsequently took to manufacturing on their newly acquired estates.

Patrick Barron, a partner in the firm of Gordon, Barron & Co. which was founded in 1785 to spin cotton by Arkwright machinery, owned the lands of Woodside, Aberdeenshire, on which the company's mill was built, but was also a merchant in Aberdeen.[44] Peter Speirs, who co-founded Culcreuch cotton mill, Stirlingshire with a group of Glasgow merchants, was the son of Alexander Speirs, a major figure in Glasgow's colonial trade.[45] However, in seeking to establish the mill, he was certainly acting in his capacity as landowner. Prior to this, he had already carried out improvements on the estate, laying out plantations and making enclosures. Partly as a result, the population of Fintry parish in which the estate lay had fallen from 891 in 1775 to 348 in 1791. A new village was founded near the mill, and by 1811 the population of the parish had recovered to 1,003.[46] Robert Dunmore was the owner of Ballindalloch estate, also in Stirlingshire. He ran an important textile printing business in Glasgow, and in 1780 was a partner in a printfield at Pollokshaws, in cotton mills at Spinningdale and Duntocher, and at another printfield beside the River Endrick, the last mentioned being on his own estate. In 1790 he entered into a partnership with James and Archibald Buchanan, to build a cotton mill on his estate, and subsequently built the village of Balfron to house mill workers and weavers.[47] The benefits to the landowner of having large spinning mills on his estate are well brought out by the writer of the *General View* of Stirling-shire:

> It cannot be questioned that these establishments are of advantage to the agricultural interests of the district in which they are set down. They afford a convenient asylum and the means of subsistence to the small occupants who have been ejected from their farms, to make way for tenants of proper skill and capital, who are now so generally introduced. They increase the consumption of the produce of the ground, and furnish a ready market for every article that is produced on the farm.[48]

On the other hand the tenant farmer, engaged in a still only partly mechanised agriculture, found himself competing for the services of farm workers with spinning mills which could offer higher wages.

In the 1780s and 1790s many landowners would have liked to see cotton mills on their estates, and even offered financial incentives to would-be mill builders.[49] The same attitude is echoed by the parish ministers who contributed to the (Old) Statistical Account, or at least those who had not yet witnessed the less savoury aspects of cotton mills. However, setbacks to trade, the increasing concentration of the industry in west-central Scotland, and a declining interest among landowners in matters economic left the further development of cotton mills in the hands of merchants and manufacturers.[50]

Merchants and Manufacturers

The contribution of merchants and manufacturers to mill developments was nowhere more marked than in the cotton industry. Mercantile interests already controlled the import of raw cotton and the export of finished goods. Several of their number had already begun to invest back into manufacturing operations, notably in calico printing, and to move from simply importing raw cotton to importing and spinning yarn was an equally obvious step, once the technology for mass production became available. In a slightly different capacity, John and Archibald Buchanan had been engaged in importing yarn from England for spinning in Scotland before establishing the Adelphi cotton works at Deanston, Perthshire; Archibald Buchanan had the additional benefit of having been apprenticed to Sir Richard Arkwright at Cromford.[51]

Besides a mercantile involvement which developed via printing, there is at least one instance of cotton mills being established as a direct outgrowth of printing as a principal activity. William McAlpine, a calico printer from Glasgow, moved to the Perth area in the late 18th century and founded printfields at Cromwellpark and Stormontfield to both of which were later added cotton mills.[52] Other merchants, not necessarily involved in importing cotton or exporting yarn, also took an interest in the millspinning of cotton. Robert Fall, who established a cotton mill at West Barns, near Dunbar, was a general merchant with several interests, including the West Barns grain mills, leased from the Burgh of Dunbar.[53] The Birtwhistle family, which had two cotton mills at Gatehouse of Fleet, had been Yorkshire cattle dealers, buying livestock in Galloway. They bought an estate near Kirkcudbright, with the intention of establishing a cotton mill there, but eventually settled for sites at Gatehouse.[54] For manufacturers it was an even more obvious step to take. Those who became involved in millbuilding usually had existing interests in the manual spinning and weaving of fine linen. As many in west-central Scotland had already moved over to cotton, a transfer into mill-spinning enabled them to tighten control and increase production of yarn, while utilising and extending their established weaving workforce to work the yarn into cloth.

In some instances merchant and manufacturer were the selfsame person; even when this was not the case, the complementary interests of merchant and manufacturer, the one importing, finishing and marketing, the other spinning and weaving, often led to partnerships in which both elements were present. For both groups, the profit to be made from mill-spinning was highly attractive: raw cotton, at 5s per pound, sold at £9 18s 6d when ready for weaving.[55] The high fixed-capital cost and long-term credit requirements at high risk discouraged other parties but were available to merchants and manufacturers from their own assets or at low interest rates through banks. In addition to the skilled workforce which they already controlled, manufacturers were able to draw mill labour from the population which Improved agriculture was driving off the land.

The most successful and the best known of the manufacturers turned mill-spinners was David Dale, whose activities deserve consideration at length. Dale started his working life as herd boy at Stewarton, Ayrshire before training as a weaver. His work as a weaver took him to Paisley, Hamilton and Cambuslang; as an extension to this he became a small-scale linen dealer, buying up locally produced home-spun yarn.[56] Through time this assumed a much grander scale, with Dale importing linen yarn from France and Flanders to be woven by cambric weavers in his own employ.[57] In 1783, Arkwright, whose water frame was still supposedly under patent, came to Scotland and met Dale who by this time had mercantile, manufacturing and banking interests. The two became partners in what was probably the first Scottish mill to legally use the Arkwright machinery, on one of the prime water-power sites in Scotland at New Lanark.[58] Construction work on the first mill started in April 1785, and spinning commenced in March 1786.[59]

Arkwright provided training facilities for skilled workers, but dropped out of the partnership soon after his patent was overturned. A second mill was built in the summer of 1788 and was nearing completion when, on 9th October 1788, it was burnt down; the mill was rebuilt during 1789, and two more were added during the 1790s.[60]

Although Dale is best known for having established New Lanark works, he helped to set up several other mills over a wide area. The first, at Blantyre, was co-founded with James Monteith in 1785;[61] the second, at Catrine, was a joint enterprise with the landowner Claude Alexander of Ballochmyle, started in 1787,[62] and Newton Stewart, in collaboration with another landowner, Sir William Douglas, started in 1793.[63] This last mill was said to have cost £20,000 but failed to achieve the success enjoyed by New Lanark, Catrine and Blantyre. After several years of production it was sold to another company for about half the original cost;[64] they, in turn, were forced to give up, and after it had lain empty for some years it was sold at one twentieth of the original cost to Lord Garlies, who used it as a source of stone for building cottages and farmhouses.[65]

Newton Stewart was not the only imprudent venture entered into by Dale: a jenny factory at Spinningdale, Sutherland, co-founded with George Dempster of Dunnichen and other landowners, had a short and troubled life before it was burnt out and abandoned in 1809.[66] A small 'branch of the cotton manufacture', introduced to the parish of Kilmore and Kilbride, Argyll, suffered from a dearth of fuel and was probably soon given up.[67] Despite these setbacks, Dale's more successful ventures were enough to save him from bankruptcy, a fate suffered by not a few early cotton mill owners.[68]

Other Parties

The contribution made to cotton mill development by tenants and artisans was negligible. In Rerick parish, Kirkcudbrightshire, a company of farmers led by a 'patriotic gentleman' subscribed £1,200 towards a cotton mill at Heston Bay, but this was an isolated instance.[69] Mechanised carding and spinning were entirely new to Scotland when cotton mills first appeared, and for some time thereafter the technical knowledge and skills required were beyond those of the rural millwright or carpenter. The new material, being of foreign growth, could not be grown by Scottish farmers and was unlikely, for that reason, to interest them in mill development. The scale which individual units of production assumed, from an early juncture, put the capital requirements beyond the means of most tenants and artisans, even if they were to work collectively. These limitations, in conjunction with the favourable position of merchants and manufacturers, help to explain why so few tenants and artisans managed to establish themselves as cotton manufacturers.

In the late 18th century, the enthusiasm for cotton mills was such that it attracted investment from sources outwith the industry. The examples of the Birtwhistles, who were cattle dealers, and Fall, who was a general merchant, have already been cited. In one other case a surgeon in Gatehouse of Fleet, John Paple, took up cotton spinning with his brother-in-law, John Smith, in 1791. After difficulties in finding securities, a mill was built at Gatehouse on a one hundred and fifty feet by one hundred feet feu, at a cost of £1,102. Papple soon found himself in financial difficulties, and by 1795 he was faced with sequestration.[70]

Although the earliest cotton mills, built in violation of Arkwright's patents, obtained moral, if not financial, support from the Board of Trustees, the Board's attitude soon became one of opposition, and by 1784 it was expressing the opinion that

> it is not advisable to go largely into the encouragement of the cotton manufacture, because as the raw material is not the produce of this country, it cannot become so beneficial as the linen and woollen branches.[71]

This policy, which was also to be applied to flax-spinning mills, may also have owed something to the fact that cotton mills were usually controlled by merchants and manufacturers and not by the more landward groups with which the Board tended to identify.

Distribution and Chronology

Despite difficulties in distinguishing between water-powered and hand-powered cotton mills, the location and dates of most Scottish cotton mills are relatively well documented, allowing a fairly accurate picture of distribution and chronology to be built up.

As we saw, the first cotton mill to be built in Scotland was on an inland site,

Fig 70. Distribution of water-powered cotton mills founded 1778-89

in south-east Scotland at Penicuik. However, the siting of the next few mills —
Rothesay (1778), Dovecothall (1780), Busby (1781), Old Mill, Johnstone
(1782) and Woodside, Glasgow (1784) — shows that the centripetal force
exerted by Glasgow as a trading and manufacturing centre was already
making itself felt. Whilst the earliest mills had been quite modest in scale, an
increase in size was already apparent, and during the mid-1780s several very
large mills were built, though not in the immediate vicinity of Glasgow:

Woodside (Aberdeenshire), Catrine (Ayrshire), Annan (Dumfriesshire), Gatehouse I (Kirkcudbrightshire), Blantyre and New Lanark (Lanarkshire) and Deanston and Stanley (Perthshire) all dated from about 1785 (Figure 70). This widespread dispersal, against the trend towards nucleation in the Glasgow area, reflects the need for water power; most of these mills, and especially Stanley and New Lanark, occupied prime sites on substantial rivers. Glasgow merchants and manufacturers had a part in several of these mills, and most had the backing of Sir William Arkwright, who was seeking to use Scottish mills against his English competitors. The judicious siting of these mills, on good improvable falls of water, compensated for their distances from Glasgow and helped them to compete successfully until well after 1830. While this outward movement was taking place, the position of Renfrewshire as the leading cotton-spinning district of Scotland was reinforced by the erection of additional mills — Laigh Mill, Johnstone (1785), Gateside (1786), Old and New Mills, Lochwinnoch (1788 & 1789). According to the *Scots Magazine* of April 1788, Scotland had nineteen of the one hundred and forty-three water-powered cotton mills in Britain, distributed as follows: Lanarkshire 4; Renfrewshire 4; Perthshire 3; Midlothian 2; Ayrshire, Galloway, Annandale, Bute, Aberdeenshire and Fife, one each.[72] The total of four sites for Renfrewshire is inaccurate, in that at least five mills were already in operation there by 1788.

During the 1790s the two contrasting trends of dispersal to outlying districts and nucleation in the Glasgow area developed further. In the east of Scotland one mill at Kirkland (Fife), one at West Barns (East Lothian) and no fewer than four at Kinghorn (Fife) were built to manufacture both cotton and linen yarn, using Arkwright and Kendrew & Porthouse machinery.[73] In the area between Glasgow and Perth, where there had formerly been only one mill, at Deanston, two mills were built in Perth itself, three were built near Perth by a Glasgow calico printer, two between Perth and Crieff by Crieff manufacturers and three at Condorrat, Culcreuch and Ballindalloch in south-west Stirlingshire. In Dumfries and Galloway, a region well situated for importing cotton, mills were established at Gatehouse of Fleet, Newton Stewart, Creetown, Twynholm, Castle Douglas, Wigtown, Rerick and as far inland as Langholm. In Renfrewshire at least fourteen new mills were founded, bringing the county total to twenty-one, by far the largest number of mills in any one county and certainly the greatest concentration (Figure 71).

From the mid-1790s the dispersal of cotton mills which had taken place in the previous ten years came to a halt, and very few new ones were started beyond a twenty-mile radius of Glasgow. In the east, the mechanisation of flax spinning gave linen a new impetus; a mill at Brechin, built to spin cotton, was converted to flax, a flax-spinning mill was added to the existing cotton mill at Stanley, and Fife mills at Kirkland and Kinghorn gave up cotton spinning to concentrate on flax. In the south-west, cotton still held sway, and at least one new mill was built, at Langholm. However, another proposed mill, at Twynholm, was dropped in favour of a woollen mill. From this time onwards

Fig 71. Distribution of water-powered cotton mills founded 1790-99

cotton declined in importance, and in the south-west wool came to be increasingly important. The large Arkwright mills of the mid-1780s continued to operate, and in some cases additional mills were built on established sites.

The application of steam power, though initially on only a very small scale, eventually confirmed Glasgow's place as the principal seat of cotton manufacture in Scotland. During the first thirty years of the 19th century very few new water-powered mills were built in Scotland, even in the Glasgow area

Fig 72. Distribution of water-powered cotton mills founded 1800-1830

(Figure 72), but in Glasgow itself, and in the Paisley area, there were no fewer than one hundred and sixteen cotton mills, all but four of which were steam-powered.[74] Although several mills which had formerly used Arkwright machinery were refitted with spinning mules, the growth of the cotton industry after 1800 came almost entirely from the application of steam power.

Developments in the distribution of Scottish water-powered cotton mills present a rapid series of events: an initial preference for west-central Scotland

Fig 73. Distribution of water-powered cotton mills, 1778-1830

before the mid-1780s; a small number of large, widely dispersed but well sited Arkwright mills in the mid-1780s, with more mills in the Glasgow area; an explosion of sites consolidating and extending the range of the Arkwright mills from the mid-1790s and a rapid contraction in the range of new growth, this being largely confined to the Glasgow area from the late 1790s. In all, there were slightly more than one hundred water-powered cotton mills in Scotland (Figure 73).

Water power in the Scottish Cotton Industry: The Cart Basin, Renfrewshire

In considering the role of water power in the Scottish industry, one tends to think of the large rural mills, such as New Lanark, Catrine and Deanston, which were built during the mid-1780s. Whilst these were of major importance, they are already fairly well documented and are not altogether typical of the industry in Scotland. Surprisingly little, however, has been written in secondary works about the Renfrewshire cotton mills, despite some excellent source materials and an abundance of mills — about one quarter of the Scottish total — within this one small county. Renfrewshire, or more precisely, the district drained by the Cart River system, is of further interest in that its proximity to Glasgow helped the water-powered industry to establish itself, survive and grow from 1780 to 1830 and beyond. Most of the examples used in earlier sections were quite deliberately drawn from other districts. By looking at the Cart Basin in depth, it should be possible to gain further insight into the general points already made and into the specific characteristics of the industry in the area, thereby redressing the balance within the chapter and within the literature of the Scottish cotton industry.

In 1780 the Cart Basin was already well placed to receive the new cotton mills. It had well-established textile interests in the form of bleaching and printing, besides a substantial population of weavers, already accustomed to working on the fine fabrics. Its proximity to Glasgow made contact with the means of import and export, as well as with manufacturing and commercial interests, relatively easy, whilst water power was readily available from streams rising in the Renfrewshire Hills and flowing to the flat lowlands beside the River Clyde.

The area's landowners were also well-disposed towards industrial growth, and during the second half of the 18th century several new villages had been created: in 1769 the Earl of Eglinton had the old village of Eaglesham demolished and rebuilt on 999-year feus. By 1782 Eaglesham had sixty-eight houses and fifty looms.[75] Gavin Ralston of that ilk, who obtained the lands of Arthurlie by marriage, feued off the village of Newton Ralston on the road from Ayrshire to Glasgow.[76] In 1781 Sir John Houston of that ilk started feuing off land for a new village above the existing village of Houston, and by July 1782 all thirty-eight feus had been taken up.[77] Under the most ambitious scheme, initiated in 1781 or 1782, George Houston of Johnstone feued off land for a new town with a main east-west street over seven hundred and fifty feet in length, north-south streets over one thousand five hundred feet in length and street widths of forty feet.[78] By 21st October 1782 nine houses had been completed, two more were under construction and a further forty-two sites had been feued off.[79] The new town of Johnstone had the further good fortune to have been the site chosen for what must have then been the largest cotton mill in Scotland. William Semple, writing of the town in 1782, did not fail to recognise the potential symbiotic relationship between town and mill and between landowner and manufacturer:

. . . it may well be considered that this town will be of very great service to the workmen at the cotton mill, especially in lodgings, vegetables, etc; on the other hand, the mill will be of great service to the said town, by employing a number of their boys and girls who must otherwise be idle for some time.[80]

In addition to these planned settlements, several estates had been bought up by merchants and manufacturers, as will emerge later.

Thus, in its formative years, the Scottish cotton industry found in the Cart Basin an area very receptive to new industry. The first of several cotton mills was built on Levern Water, at Dovecothall, in 1780. The mill, a three-storey, eight-bay structure housing 2,464 spindles, was jointly financed by Samuel Ramsay, John Leviston and John Love, merchants in Glasgow, John Clurdsley, merchant in Preston, Lancashire, and Jonathan and William Haugh, described as manufacturers at Dovecothall.[81] According to tradition, it was Jonathan Haugh who obtained the necessary technical knowledge by spying on an English water-frame mill.[82] A second mill, the fourth in Scotland, was set up on the White Cart Water by William Ferguson, merchant in Glasgow, who had purchased the lands of Newmills in 1780 and who used the site of corn and lint mills for a three-storey works housing one thousand two hundred spindles.[83] The site of this mill, and a later one, built about 1790, was later known as Busby. A third and much larger mill, on the Black Cart Water, was built at Johnstone in 1782 by Messrs. Corse, Burns & Co., and a large extension was added in 1787[84] (Figure 74). George Houston, founder of the town of Johnstone, built Laigh Mill below Old Mill in 1784 and, by constructing a dam immediately below the Bridge of Johnstone, managed to jeopardise his neighbour's water supply, thereby precipitating the first of several disputes over water regulation.[85] By the early 1790s the two mills at Johnstone housed 11,672 spindles, with space for a further 11,000.[86] These mills, with an additional mill on the Levern at Gateside (1786),[87] gave Renfrewshire a head start in cotton spinning at a time when the large rural mills, set up with Arkwright's backing, were just beginning to appear. Some indication has already been given of the complex interaction of merchant, manufacturer and landowner; the first mill at Lochwinnoch brings it out particularly well. In March 1788 William McDowall (a West Indies merchant) signed a contract of co-partnery with George Houston (a Renfrewshire land-owner, connected with Johnstone and Laigh Mill) and George Burns (a merchant manufacturer in the linen trade). McDowall also owned the lands of Lochwinnoch, and could expect to benefit through the augmentation of his estate's rental and by the increased demand for its produce. Houston, related to McDowall by marriage, had a useful partner in the latter. As owner of the Loch of Lochwinnoch, the waters of which fed the cotton mills on Black Cart Water, McDowall was later to build a dam across the mouth of the loch and refuse to allow an adequate flow of water into the river until firms agreed to pay a higher rent for its use; McDowall's mercantile connections could ensure a secure supply of raw cotton for the company's mills. Burns, with access to

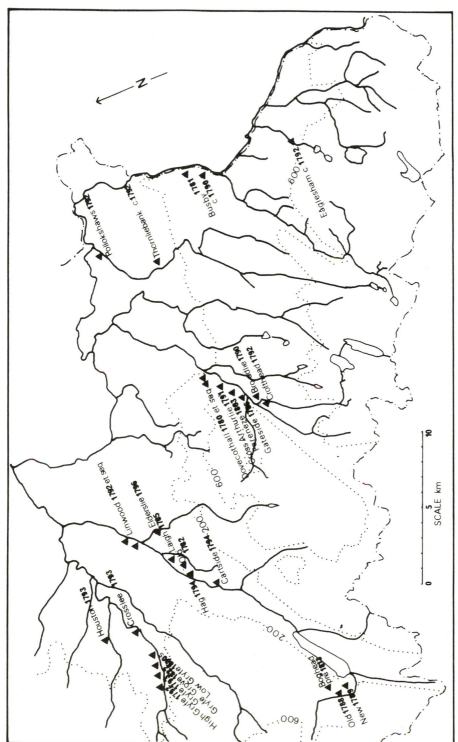

Fig 74. Water-powered cotton mills in the Cart Basin, Renfrewshire

weavers and markets for cloth, had a good knowledge of the trade and was a useful addition to the partnership.

In at least one case a landowner with mercantile connections was able to benefit from the cotton boom without joining a partnership. In the summer of 1792 Archibald Speirs, the son of a merchant, Alexander Speirs, was offering 'several respectable stances for cotton mills' in Neilston parish. Water was to be provided free of charge, and feus would be granted on the most reasonable terms. Similar terms were offered on the Water of Old Patrick, near Elderslie, and in 1796 Speirs is found to be granting the use of the cotton mill of Elderslie to Corses, Buchanan, Findlater & Co; the implications are that he had built the mill at his own expense and was now leasing it out.[88]

During the boom years of the early 1790s, the Cart Basin cotton industry went through a period of rapid growth. A second mill was built at Lochwinnoch in 1789 or 1790, and on the White Cart and its tributaries new mills were established at Busby (c. 1790), and at Pollockshaws, Thornliebank and Eaglesham (all c.1792). On the Levern, Broadlie and Cross-Arthurlie mills were started in 1790, and Crofthead failed to materialise only because landowner and the would-be builders failed to reach agreement.[89] On the Black Cart construction started on a mill at Linwood in 1792, and a village of the same name was founded adjacent to it. 1794 saw the building of Hag and Cartside Mills, both near Johnstone. As most of the best sites on the Levern, Black Cart and White Cart were already occupied by cotton mills, bleachfields and printfields, attention turned westwards to the Gryfe Water and its tributaries. The first mill on the Gryfe was built in 1792, and a second mill, adjacent to it, followed in 1793. Beside the mills the village of Bridge of Weir, founded in 1792, grew up.[90] Lower down the river a third mill, Crosslee, was built in 1793 and a village of the same name was established beside it. In the same year a cotton mill was set up on a tributary of the Gryfe, near to the planned village of Houston.

In contrast to the flurry of activity in the early 1790s, the second half of the decade saw only two new mills, Elderslie, which was built and let out by Archibald Speirs, and Levern (1798) beside the old Dovecothall mill. Fereneze, the last water-powered cotton mill for some time, was rebuilt on the site of a burnt-out flax mill about 1803. By this time the application of steam power was making it possible for mills to be built in Glasgow itself, rather than on water-powered sites outwith the city. With most of the best water-powered sites already occupied, further development seemed unlikely. Although the 1820s saw vigorous mill growth within the Cart Basin at Johnstone and Paisley, all the mills were steam-powered. However, this is not to imply that water power was abandoned in favour of steam. Existing mills continued to use water power, and many were extended: Thornliebank was added to in 1806 and again in 1809;[91] a new mill was built at Gateside to hold 10,560 mule spindles, 1,344 water-twist spindles and ninety-five carding engines;[92] Crofthouse Mill was extended in 1818;[93] Gryfe Grove Mill was established in

1822,[94] Busby was extended in 1823[95] and Crosslee in 1824.[96] In 1825 Cartside Mill was almost doubled in size and the water frames were replaced by mules.[97] Eaglesham Mill was extended in 1826,[98] Broadley in 1827.[99] A small mill on the Gryfe, near Bridge of Weir, was founded during the 1830s.[100] Between 1812 and 1831 the number of spindles in the six Levern mills increased from 57,000 to 78,280.[101]

Only in a few cases did expansion involve the addition of steam power. At Houston Mill, a thirty-three per cent expansion required the installation of a small engine for dry spells but, as the proprietor conceded, it would have been unnecessary had he been prepared to buy land further up the burn where reservoirs could have been constructed.[102] Expansion at New Mill, Lochwinnoch necessitated the addition of a steam engine for dry spells, and at Linwood a twenty horse power engine was installed to supplement the forty-eight horse power available from water power.[103] As late as 1838, well into the 'Age of Steam', twenty-eight water wheels were still producing seven hundred and ninety-seven horse power, 41.5% of Renfrewshire's total. Fifty steam engines produced 1,124 horse power, of which 333 horse power was concentrated in the town of Paisley.[104] Figure 74 shows the distribution and date of foundation of water-powered cotton mills in the Cart Basin.

Water-powered mills had helped to establish or augment settlements from Bridge of Weir in the north-west of the county to Eaglesham in the south-east (Figure 75). Barrhead, in 1827, illustrates this well:

> Barrhead, you must understand, has undergone a considerable metamorphosis with these thirty years back, when it was in its infancy; for 30 or 40 years and perhaps 30 families were not in it all, now there is a street half a mile in length, built on each side, with a secession chapel which was founded perhaps 30 or 40 years ago . . . Fifty years ago and there was perhaps but one small cotton factory on the Levern, and now there are 6 large ones within 2½ miles of each other, besides 3 or 4 printfields, 2 weaving factories, and bleachfields numerous and extensive. Thirty years ago and perhaps there was only one public . . . house in this village . . . and now there are certainly 30, there being, it is estimated, one for every 25 or 30 families. Thirty years ago and there was but one school in it, and there are in the village and neighbourhood 6 or 7.[105]

By the 1830s Neilston parish's six mills were employing 1,381[106] people, while over the Cart Basin as a whole, water-powered cotton mills probably provided jobs for at least 4,500 people.

Clearly, therefore, water power continued to play a very important role in the Renfrewshire cotton spinning industry well into the 19th century. Although much larger water-powered mills were working in 1838, those of Renfrewshire were the most numerous, and more significant in illustrating the relative attractiveness of steam and water power. In the light of the continuing role of water power, it is, perhaps, not altogether surprising to find that by 1850 Renfrewshire cotton mills, including the predominantly steam-powered weaving mills, derived one thousand and thirty-nine horse power from water power, but only nine hundred and three horse power from steam.[107]

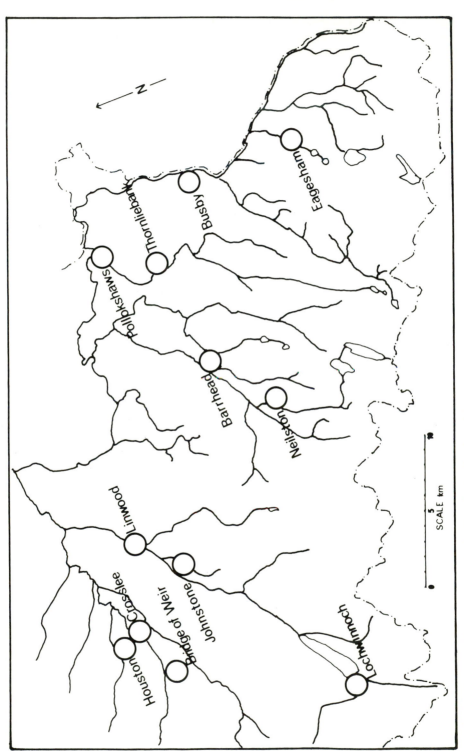

Fig 75. Cotton mill communities in the Cart Basin, Renfrewshire

For a brief period during the late 18th century, the water-powered cotton-spinning industry was at the forefront of Scottish industrial development; in west-central Scotland it continued to function alongside a rapidly growing steam-powered industry until well after 1830. Despite its short life, it left behind some of the most substantial remains of any water-powered industry in Scotland: whole towns and villages from Woodside in Aberdeenshire to Gatehouse in Kirkcudbrightshire owe their origin or success to water-powered cotton spinning, whilst in several localities the mills themselves survive to this day. At New Lanark, the mill village *par excellence*, one can still see the mills themselves, workers' housing, a school and all the other institutions which played a part in the lives of the mill workers. In addition to mills and mill villages, the houses of weavers who once wove yarn from the mills are scattered over much of central and south-western Scotland.

Factory production, already implicit in the bleachfields of the 18th century, finally came to fruition in the cotton mills of the 1780s and 1790s, to which bleaching, printing and power-loom weaving were eventually appended. The scale of most units was enormous, probably bigger than in any previous industry, with the exception of the larger mining and metallurgical enterprises. Cotton mills were exceptionally large in several respects: physically, in terms of the capital invested, the employment generated, and the scale on which water power was utilised.

The response to cotton mills was mixed. Some, such as Taylor, saw nothing but good in them, and pointed to the work which they created for the young and for those displaced from the land, the contribution which they made to Scotland's wealth, the market which they offered for the produce of Improved agriculture, and the establishment of new dependent settlements. For them the development of mechanical technology and the increasing scale of production were a source of wonder. At the other extreme there were those, such as Naismith, who saw nothing but harm in the mechanisation of cotton spinning. They pointed to the bad, cramped working conditions and the long hours which the mill employees, especially children, had to endure; far from enriching Scotland, they saw cotton as impoverishing her by depriving home-based spinners, hecklers and carders of work and replacing Scottish-grown flax and wool with imported cotton. In agriculture they saw inflated wage rates brought about by unfair competition from spinning mills, and in factory production they saw a dangerous risk being taken in concentrating so much capital in so few sites. Between these two extremes lay a range of opinion, each individual stance depending on whether the person concerned was a mill owner, factory worker, landowner, minister, wool merchant or whatever else. The truth of the matter, if one can speak of such, included something of both extremes, although for those with the benefit of hindsight, Naismith's view has been the more attractive. Whatever the opinions of the time, cotton mills were a physical reality and one which had repercussions on the textile industry as a whole. They led to the creation of several new printfields and stimulated the mechanisation of flax and wool spinning. The establishment of a water-powered spinning industry in the late 18th century paved the way for an even bigger one, based on steam power, in the early 19th, with its attendant problems of health, sanitation, civil disorder and rapid urban growth, far beyond those engendered by the water-powered cotton-spinning industry in Scotland.

NOTES

1. Clow, A. & Clow, N. L., *The Chemical Revolution*, London, 1952, 224.

2. At Penicuik, Midlothian: SRO NG1/1/22 8th July 1778.

3. Mann, J. de L., in Singer, C., Holmyard, E. J., Hall, A. R. & Williams, T. I. (eds.), *A History of Technology*, 5 vols., Oxford, 1956-9, IV, 278-9.

4. *Ibid.*, 277-8.

5. *Ibid.*, 280-1.

6. *Ibid.*, 279-80.

7. SRO NG1/1/21 30 November 1774.

8. SRO NG1/1/21 25 January 1775.

9. SRO GD1/575/1.

10. SRO NG1/1/22 8 July 1778.

11. Ibid.

12. SRO NG1/1/22 7 July 1779.

13. SRO GD1/575/1.

14. Reid, J. E., *History of the County of Bute*, Glasgow, 1864, 103; *Scots Magazine* LXXVI (1814), 904; *PP* 1834 XIX 26 Factory Commission; SRO NG1/1/22 15 December 1779.

15. SRO NG1/1/22 7 July 1779, 15 December 1779.

16. *Scots Magazine* LXXVI, 904.

17. *PP* 1834 XIX, 26-7; Butt, J., Donnachie, I. L., Hume, J. R., *Industrial History in Pictures, Scotland*, Newton Abbot, 1968, 37.

18. Bremner, D., *The Industries of Scotland* (1869), Newton Abbot, 1969, 275-6.

19. *Ibid.*, 275-6.

20. Mann, *op. cit.*, 283.

21. *Ibid.*, 284.

22. *Ibid.*, 285.

23. *Ibid.*, 287-8.

24. *Ibid.*, 288.

25. *NSA* X, 1237, Doune, Perthshire.

26. Mann, *op. cit.*, 291.

27. *Ibid.*, 300.

28. SRO NG1/1/26 23 January 1788, 11 February 1789.

29. SRO NG1/1/31 29 February 1804.

30. Mann, *op. cit.*, 300; Smout, T. C., *A History of the Scottish People, 1560-1830*, London, 1969, 405.

31. *Scots Magazine* LXXVI, 905-6.

32. Smout, *op. cit.*, 405.

33. Crawford, G. (revised Semple, W.), *The History of Renfrewshire*, Paisley, 1882, 172.

34. *Ibid.*, 257.

35. Wilson, J. M., (ed.), *The Imperial Gazetteer of Scotland*, 2 vols., Edinburgh, London & Dublin, n.d. (c.1875), II, 17.

36. *OSA* VIII, 362, Creich, Sutherland; *OSA* II, 421, East Kilbride, Lanarkshire.

37. *OSA* XI, 142, Kilwinning, Ayrshire; *OSA* V, 241, Cambuslang, Lanarkshire; *OSA* XV, 531, Redgorton, Perthshire; *OSA* XX, 176, Sorn, Ayrshire.

38. *PP* 1834, XIX, Factory Commission.

39. Chapman, S. D., *The Cotton Industry in the Industrial Revolution*, London, 1972, 19.

40. Smith, S., *General View of the Agriculture of Galloway*, London, 1813, 329.

41. *NSA* V, 140, Sorn, Ayrshire.

42. *OSA* XVII, 556, Auchtergaven, Perthshire.

43. Smout, *op. cit.*, 408.

44. Morgan, P. *Annals of Woodside & Newhills*, Aberdeen, 1886, 20-21.

45. Devine, T. M., Glasgow Merchants and Colonial Trade, Strathclyde University PhD., 1974, II, 382-3.

46. Ibid., II, 383.

47. Ibid., II, 368-378.

48. Graham, P., *General View of the Agriculture of Stirlingshire*, Edinburgh, 1812, 349.

49. See, for example, *Caledonian Mercury*, 28 February 1793: 'Situation for a Cotton Mill or Any Work requiring a Command of Water'.

50. For a further development of the pro's and con's of textile mills from the land-owner's point of view see Shaw, J. P., 'Rural Industry: Water Power and Textiles', in Parry, M. & Slater, T. (eds.), *The Making of the Scottish Countryside*, London, 1980.

51. Devine, *op. cit.*, II, 376-7; Smout *op. cit.*, II, 385.

52. Turner W. H. K., 'The Textile Industry of Perth and District', *TIBG* XXIII (1957), 125.

53. Butt, J., 'Valuation of Scottish Cotton Mills by Sun Fire Office', *EcHR* 2nd Series, XXII (1970); OSP 290:19 Brown v. Johnston.

54. Butt, *op. cit.*, (1970).

55. Bremner, *op. cit.*, 279.

56. Smout, *op. cit.*, 385.

57. Hamilton, H., *An Economic History of Scotland in the Eighteenth Century*, Oxford, 1963.

58. Butt, J., *Industrial Archaeology of Scotland*, Newton Abbot, 1967, 69-70.

59. *OSA* IV, 34, Lanark, Lanarkshire.

60. *Ibid.*, 34.

61. Wilson, *op. cit.*, I, 176.

62. *OSA* XX, 176, Sorn, Ayrshire.

63. *Caledonian Mercury*, January 31st 1793.

64. Wilson, *op. cit.*, II, 510; Smith, *op. cit.*, 329.

65. Wilson, *op. cit.*, II, 510.

66. *NSA* XV, 20, Creich, Sutherland.

67. *OSA* XI, 121, Kilmore & Kilbride, Argyll.

68. *OSA* XV, 530, Redgorton, Perthshire; Devine, *op. cit.*, II, 370.

69. *OSA* XI, 45, Rerick, Kirkcudbrightshire.

70. CS 96/813.

71. SRO NG1/1/24 21 July 1784.

72. *Scots Magazine* L (1788), 159.
73. Butt, *op. cit.* (1970).
74. *PP* XLII Factory Returns.
75. Crawford, *op. cit.*, 219.
76. *Ibid.*, 170.
77. *Ibid.*, 106.
78. *Ibid.*, 258.
79. *Ibid.*, 257.
80. *Ibid.*, 257.
81. *Ibid.*, 172.
82. Taylor, C., *The Levern Delineated*, Glasgow, 1831, 56.
83. Crawford, *op. cit.*, 207.
84. *Ibid.*, 257; *PP* 1834 XIX Factory Commission.
85. SRO RHP 276/3 (1788); SRO RHP 658/1 (1790).
86. *OSA* XII, 74, Paisley Abbey, Renfrewshire.
87. *OSA* II, 141, Neilston, Renfrewshire.
88. Devine, *op. cit.*, II, 380-2.
89. Taylor, *op. cit.*, 56.
90. *NSA* VII, 51, Houston & Killallan, Refrewshire.
91. *PP* 1834 XIX 215-6.
92. Taylor, *op. cit.*, 58.
93. *PP* 1834 XIX 194-5.
94. *NSA* VII, 51, Houston & Killallan, Renfrewshire.
95. *PP* 1834 XIX 187-8.
96. *Ibid.*, 181-2.
97. *Ibid.*, 202-3.
98. *Ibid.*, 177-9.
99. *Ibid.*, 190-1.
100. *NSA* VII, 51, Houston & Killallan, Renfrewshire.
101. Taylor, *op. cit.*, 60.
102. *NSA* VII, 52, Houston & Killallan, Renfrewshire.
103. *NSA* VII, 103, Lochwinnoch, Renfrewshire; *NSA* VII, 337, Neilston, Renfrew-shire.
104. *PP* 1839 XLII 306-7.
105. *Glasgow Free Press*, 8 September 1827, quoted by Taylor, *op. cit.*, 72.
106. *PP* 1839 XLII 306-7.
107. *PP* 1850 XLII Factory Returns.

21

The Textile Industry:
Minor Users of Water Power

Besides being used extensively by several sectors of the textile industry, water power was also applied in a small way to a number of other branches, each involving no more than forty sites. As none of these justifies a chapter on its own account, they are to be dealt with collectively in this, the last of the chapters on the textile industry.

Printfields

Technology

Whilst printfields were of more than minor importance to the textile industry, those using water power were relatively few. In the most primitive form of textile printing, patterns were pencilled onto the cloth and painted by hand. This method was still being used in Paris in the mid-18th century. Block printing, with wooden blocks, probably started in mediaeval times and may predate the printing of books. Although attempts were made to mechanise block printing, they were not attended with success.[1] Brass and copper faces were later added to prolong the life of blocks, and by 1769 engraved copper plates were being used at Pollokshaws and by 1771 at Carmyle[2] (both near Glasgow). In 1782 Fereneze, a large printfield on the Levern Water (Renfrewshire), had a mill for polishing copper plates,[3] but the application of water power to the printing process had to wait for the cylinder printing process, patented in 1783 and 1784 by Thomas Bell, a Scot, resident at Walton-in-Dale, near Preston, Lancashire. Earlier patents, by Keen & Platt in 1743 and by Aitken in 1772, had apparently not been put to effective use. Bell should be seen as perfecting, rather than originating, the cylinder machine, much as Meikle perfected the threshing machine or Arkwright the carding machine. Further patents, incorporating additional improvements, were taken out by Slater in 1784 and by Paul in 1796.[4]

Scottish printers were quick to take up the new invention, and by the early 1790s cylinders were being used at fields on the Dunbartonshire Leven, the Endrick, the Glazert and probably elsewhere.[5] Water power was soon applied to driving these cylinders, clearing the way for a vastly increased output of printed cloth, just at the time when the mechanisation of cotton spinning was beginning to put pressure on the slow and hitherto unmechanised printing process. According to the (Old) Statistical Account for Bonhill, Dunbartonshire, printers there had

> . . . constructed some presses to be driven by water, one of which, driven [i.e. operated] by two men, can print twenty to thirty dozen handkerchiefs in an hour. These presses at first, were almost wholy employed in printing handkerchiefs; but of late they have improved them, so as to print two or more colours upon the finest linens and muslins, leaving sprigs of flowers to be put on afterwards by the block printers. At the printfields upon the Leven they have contrived, of late to do a great deal of work by machinery driven by water, which formerly was done by hand, and at great expense.[6]

Despite the savings in time and labour which the use of cylinders made possible, they did not entirely displace block printing. As the quotation shows, it was being used for finer work in the 1790s, and as late as the 1830s Ruthvenfield, Perthshire still printed about 1,300,000 yards of cloth — about two thirds of its output — by block each year, whilst Denovan, Stirlingshire used blocks almost to the exclusion of cylinders.[7]

Although most printfields had good falls of water at their disposal, the very large throughput of the Leven fields, and at least one of those on the Glazert, none of which had much of a fall at their disposal, led to the addition of auxiliary steam power.[8] In the 1830s, Ferryfield printfield, Dunbartonshire had a wheel twenty feet in diameter and seven feet in breadth, but a fall of no more than twenty inches, supplemented by two steam engines of ten and fourteen horse power. At Dillichip, a water wheel fifteen feet six by eleven feet three had a fall of only twelve to fourteen inches, although in this case the extreme breadth of wheel provided enough water power without a steam engine.[9]

Sources of Finance

As with the associated process of bleaching, the establishment and running of a printfield required large amounts of capital. For the field itself, a large extent of the land was required, with a supply of clear water, initially for bleaching and watering only but latterly to drive machinery as well. Capital had to be available to tide the printfield owner over until such a time as work on the cloth was paid for; much of the work of a printfield was highly skilled, with printers earning 17s to 21s per week by the 1790s,[10] and with a total workforce of perhaps two to three hundred a large wage bill had to be paid out. In these circumstances the Scottish textile printing industry was dominated from the very start by mercantile and manufacturing partnerships, with ample capital and established interests in textile manufacturing, bleaching and/or marketing. Conversely, manufacturers who had taken up printing in its pre-mechanisation days might extend their activities into cotton spinning once that became a factory-based industry. Messrs. Crum were textile manufacturers before taking on Thornliebank printfield (c. 1779) and a cotton mill on the same site (c. 1792).[11] The short-lived Endrick printfield had a particularly complex parentage. Robert Dunmore, the West Indies merchant and Stirlingshire landowner, has already been mentioned in connection with cotton mills (Chapter 20, p. 322). His father, Thomas Dunmore, had been a partner in Pollokshaws printfield during the 1770s, and in 1780 Robert took over his late father's place in the partnership. In 1791 he and John Monteith, a linen merchant and manufacturer, took control of the field.[12] Dunmore already had 'an agency for manufacturing calicoes' on his estate, and in 1790 he had taken a 999-year lease of the lands of Duniechip, beside Endrick Water, Stirlingshire, from Charles Park of Parkhill. Two years later the lease was converted to a feu, in Dunmore's name, at £14 8s 9d, and in the same year he in turn feued the lands at £61 3s 6d per annum to a partnership of eight Glasgow merchants which included Monteith (his partner at Pollokshaws) and Dunmore himself, under the firm of John Monteith & Co.[13] According to the (Old) Statistical Account, every part of the field's machinery was 'new and approved', including sixteen water-powered printing machines and seventy-two block-printing machines. The management of the field was in the hands of a Swiss, M. J. F. Moriar.[14] After about ten years Dunmore was forced into bankruptcy and his estate was sequestered. However, the field continued to operate until about 1812, when the partnership was dissolved. Robert Dalglish, the brother of one of the partners, purchased the machinery and transferred it to Lennoxmill printfield, then lying vacant, where he began a printing business with his younger brother, Alexander, and a third party, Patrick Falconer.[15] Robert Dalglish, born in 1770, had trained in the textile trade at the warehouse of Andrew Stevenson, a Glasgow muslin manufacturer. The running of the printfield was left to Alexander Dalglish, while Robert pursued an administrative career which eventually elevated him to Lord Provost of Glasgow.[16]

Distribution and Chronology

As with so many other branches of the textile industry, the earliest recorded Scottish printfields were in the Edinburgh area: Gorgie and Bonnington, both on the Water of Leith, were in operation by the late 1720s, probably with English printers.[17] However, the City of Glasgow's protest against a government ban on the wearing of printed or stained cloth, in 1719, suggests that the industry was already established there by that date.[18] In the years up to the invention of water-powered textile printing (c. 1795), the development of a substantial fine linen and muslin industry in the west of Scotland helped determine the distribution of a developing printing industry which was almost exclusively confined to the Glasgow area, a distribution which was reinforced by the predominance of the Clyde as a route for the import of raw cotton and export of finished goods. In the east, a few printfields such as Cupar, Balgersho and Tullich dealt with fine linen goods.[19]

Fig 76. Distribution of water-powered printfields, 1730-1830

The distribution of printfields during the water-powered stage reflects a number of influences, notably the distribution of other, related, textile manufacturing processes: cotton spinning was superimposed on the fine linen industry of west-central Scotland, but with the mechanisation of spinning after 1778 the distribution was extended southwards into Galloway and north-eastwards as far as Aberdeen. The distribution of cotton weaving spread in a similar manner, particularly to the Perth area which already had an established fine linen industry. As bleaching was one of the processes performed by printfields, mechanised printing was often taken up on sites already employed in fine linen bleaching, as at Dalquhurn (Dunbartonshire), Crofthead (Renfrewshire) and Ruthvenfield (Perthshire), or at established printfields such as Fereneze (Renfrewshire). The distribution of printfields was further influenced by the availability of clear water for bleaching and dyeing purposes in sufficient quantity to drive bleaching and printing machinery. The pattern which emerges is shown in Figure 76.

In the Glasgow area the Leven already had bleachfields and a printfield (Cordale) prior to the introduction of mechanised printing. It had clear water from Loch Lomond and from tributary burns, though the falls available were of no great height. It was conveniently placed for Glasgow and the Clyde. Levenbank printfield was established in 1784 by Messrs. Watson & Arthur;[20] another field, probably Levenfield, followed shortly thereafter. In 1791 Messrs. Stirling, proprietors of Cordale printfield, purchased the bleachfield at Dalquhurn and fitted it up for printing.[21] By 1811 there were five printing companies on the Leven, occupying at least six fields.[22] The biggest fields, Cordale and Dalquhurn, did half of the work carried out in Dunbartonshire. A map dated 1824 shows eight mills on the Leven, of which six were printfields, the other two being bleachfields.[23] By the late 1830s all eight sites were engaged in printing,[24] as was a ninth, on a tributary burn (Figure 77).

Further east, Old Kilpatrick parish had two printfields, Milton and Cochno, by the early 1790s, and by 1835 printing had spread into the adjacent parish of New Kilpatrick, where there were three printfields.[25] Around the southern and eastern margins of the Campsie Fells the same favourable circumstances were to be found as in the Vale of Leven, but with good falls compensating for the small volume available. Printfields were established on the Endrick at Endrick-bank (1792), and on the Blane at Blanefield. On the Glazert an important group of printfields was created in Campsie parish at Kincaid (1785), Lennox-mill (1786) and Lillyburn (1831), besides two smaller fields, Alloch and Haugh-head. According to the (Old) Statistical Account, there was sufficient water to drive printfield machinery at all seasons; Kincaid had a fall of twenty-two feet.[26] Further downstream another printfield was established at Bellfield in Kirkintilloch parish.[27] On the Carron, which rose in the eastern end of the Campsies, there were fields at Herbertshire (1783) and Denovan (1800) although only the former used water power.[28] To the south of Glasgow, particularly in Renfrewshire, several new fields were founded, though not all of them were water-powered. Further north, a group of printfields developed on the Tay, the Almond and the 'Town Lade' to the north-west of Perth. William McAlpine, a calico printer from the Glasgow area, founded a printfield at Cromwellpark (1785) and a second field at Stormont shortly afterwards.[29] Others followed (Figure 78). By 1785 Perth had already established itself as the centre of an important bleaching district, and the inclusion of Perth in the area influenced by the Glasgow-based cotton industry helped foster the development of printfields.

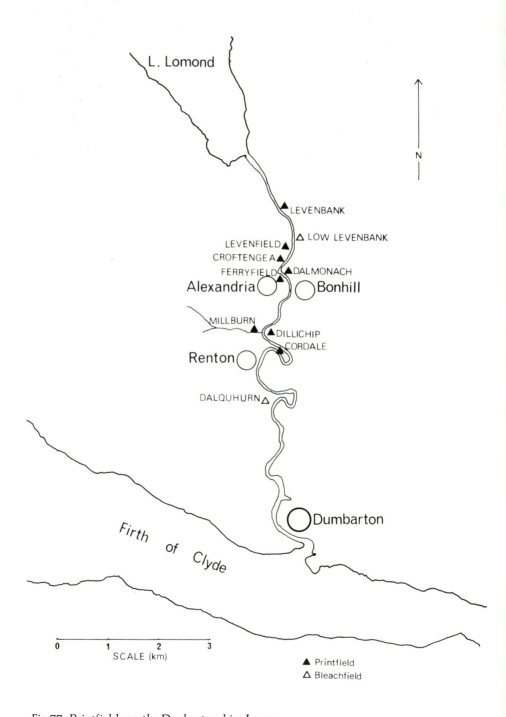

Fig 77. Printfields on the Dunbartonshire Leven

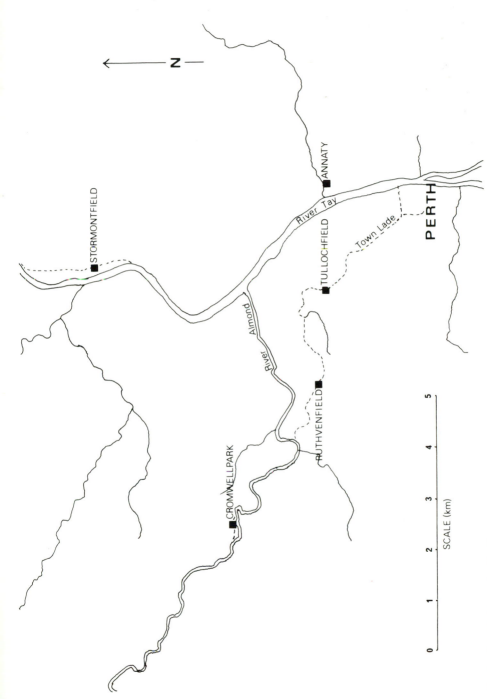

Fig 78. Printfields in the Perth area

Within each of these areas the role played by Glasgow-based capital was crucial; outside, in areas not thus favoured, and lacking an established cotton industry, with poor access to Glasgow and without clear water in sufficient volume, very little development took place. Altogether there were probably about thirty water-powered printfields in Scotland.

Impact

The mechanisation of calico printing helped to break a bottleneck in the manufacture of printed cottons which had been aggravated by the vastly increased output of yarn made possible by the introduction of mechanical cotton spinning. Although not so labour intensive as manual printing, each field created about two hundred jobs for men, women and children, which helped to absorb those displaced from other sectors of the economy, notably agriculture. In Old Kilpatrick, for example, two hundred and eighty of the five hundred and ninety-five employed in printfields in the early 1790s came from outside the parish.[30]

The need to house such large numbers of workers led to the creation or enlargement of hamlets and villages in the printing districts: in the Vale of Leven, Renton, founded in 1782 by Mrs. Smollet of Bonhill, owed much of its success to the presence of printfields.[31] Lennoxtown, alias Newton of Campsie, owed its existence to the printfields established in its neighbourhood from 1785 onwards:

> Lindsay, Smith & Co. (founders of Lennoxmill printfield) had the terrace of Whitefield erected. Demand was soon followed by supply, and the Newton of Campsie, as distinguished from the Clachan, or old town, rapidly sprang up and developed into a thriving village, as the new houses were occupied as soon as they were finished. Shops followed, to supply the necessaries of life . . . A spirit of activity and progress became general and characterised the people of the district in all their dealings.[32]

Despite the relatively small number of sites involved, the scale of operations at each site gave some importance to printfields, not only within the development of water power in Scotland but also in the landscape as a whole.

Mordants and Dyestuffs

As mordants and dyestuffs were essential elements in the work of print-fields, it seems reasonable to include the former within this chapter and to follow one with the other, even though the range of dyestuffs produced related to a far wider spectrum of textiles than those passing through printfields.

Woad, used to produce a blue colour in woollen cloth, was grown and prepared in Scotland. The leaves were dried, ground, rolled into bales, dried and ground again and finally fermented.[33] On his visit to Haddington in 1778, Loch found that William Ramsay and Robert Davie grew and prepared about four tons of woad per annum, but no reference was made to a mill.[34] Another plant leaf, indigo, was imported from the West Indies and yielded a blue dye which, according to its price, was used with or as well as woad. Hay Smith, who took a tack of the Tarred Wool Company's Haddington mill in 1795, installed additional machinery for grinding indigo and other dyestuffs.[35] Another blue dye, Prussian blue, was manufactured in Portobello from 1785 by a Newcastle company and was introduced to Campsie alum works by Charles Macintosh, but there is no certainty that water power was ever used in its preparation.[36]

Generally wool dyeing was carried out on a domestic basis, or integrated with waulk mills, but in some cases, as at Morangie (Ross-shire) and Douglas (Lanarkshire), there were separate mills for this purpose.[37] For dyeing yellow, various substances, including weld, fustic and bark were employed, but no reference has been found to the use of water power in this context.[38] For reds, cochineal, derived from a South American insect, was used.[39] A lichen dye, crottal, had been long used in the Highlands, and in 1758 the brothers Cuthbert and George Gordon and Messrs. William Alexander & Co. in Edinburgh entered into partnership to manufacture the dye commercially under the name of Cudbear, at Leith. The Leith works closed down in the late 1770s and the business transferred to Glasgow, where a works had been established in 1771 by John Glassford, James Gordon, John Robertson *et al*, under the management of George Mackintosh. The process of manufacture is outlined by Clow.[40]

George Mackintosh, the son of a Ross-shire tenant farmer, started work as a junior clerk in the Glasgow Tan Work Company. Realising the profitability of boot and shoe making, he set up his own business and by 1773 had five hundred employees. His other interests included glassmaking and the East Indies trade, but these he abandoned to take up cudbear manufacture, the start of a long association between the Mackintosh family and the mordant and dyestuff industries.

In October 1777, George Mackintosh, on behalf of the Cudbear Company, notified Glasgow Burgh Council that he had been offered the tack of Subdean Mill, one of the town's malt mills, by the then tenant, Duncan Stewart.[41] The purpose to which Mackintosh wished to put the mill was probably pounding the lichen with ammonia.[42] On November 11th, 1777 the Council agreed to a tack, at £7 per annum for the remaining four years of Stewart's lease and at £18 for the next fifteen years. As a condition of the lease, Mackintosh was to put up a partition between cudbear and malt machinery, besides promising to provide good service and carriage for those using the malt mill.[43] Cudbear could produce a variety of colours from bright pinks and reds through purples to bright blues in silk and wool but not cotton. It could also improve the yellowish reds derived from madder. The trade was eventually killed off by the popularity of greys and blacks in the 1840s, and the works finally closed down in 1852.[44]

Mackintosh crops up again in 1785, this time as co-founder of Scotland's first Turkey red dyeworks. The dye, derived from madder, produced a bright red colour, but the manner of its preparation had eluded Scottish dyers until a Frenchman, Pierre Jacques Papillon, who had once been a dyer in Turkey, came to Glasgow in search of financial backing.[45] The backing came from a number of parties, including George Mackintosh and David Dale. Papillon was to work at the newly founded Dalmarnock works, but by 1787 he had parted company with Mackintosh and had set up business at Rutherglen Bridge.[46] Papillon was obviously upset by a Government premium of £2,500 which in 1786 had gone to another Frenchman, M. Borelle, who had set up in business with his brother in Manchester.[47] As Papillon saw it, the premium was to have been shared with Borelle, but the latter had taken it all and absconded with it.[48] Despite this setback, Papillon stayed in Scotland, and by 1789, having sunk his entire capital in enlarging his dyeworks and building a new mill, he petitioned the Board of Trustees for some reimbursement and for funds to bring his wife and family over from France.[49] The Board offered him £200 over three years, on condition that the process was revealed to a competent judge (Dr. Black), approved by him and kept from the public during Papillon's lifetime, or at least while he remained in business. Dr. Black's approval came in May 1790, and the money was handed over.[50]

Mackintosh's Dalmarnock Works continued to prosper,[51] and by 1830 Turkey red was being produced at a number of localities in the Glasgow area.[52] Charles Mackintosh, son of George, was a co-founder of a works producing the mordant alum at Hurlet (1797) and Campsie (1808), both of which seem to have used water power at one time.[53] A mill on the River Kelvin ground potash, one of the substances used in alum manufacture.[54]

One of the most widely used sources of colouring was logwood or dyewood, derived from American timber and first used in England in the 16th century.[55] In 1720 two wrights, William Balloch and James Tripney, sought permission to use the Drygate Burn in Glasgow to drive a wood-rasping mill for the preparation of logwood dyes,[56] but according to the (Old) Statistical Account the earliest chipping and rasping mills were those built on the Kelvin by John Duncan in 1760.[57] Subsequently, dyewood grinding machinery was installed at Chapel bleachfield (Renfrewshire), Arthurston Mill and Little Dunfin (Dunbartonshire), Alloa (Clackmannanshire) and Denny (Stirlingshire).[58] Very little is known of these mills. According to the New Statistical Account, the last-mentioned mill belonged to John Gray & Son, and was engaged in chipping, rasping and grinding dyestuffs, besides providing liquor for colours to manufacturers of fancy woollen, cotton and linsey-woolsey articles. The mill, and a branch factory in Castle Rankine Glen, provided work for twenty-one people. The distribution of dyestuff mills was closely related to that of their customers. In all, there were probably no more than twenty-five or so such mills in Scotland between 1730 and 1830 (Figure 79).

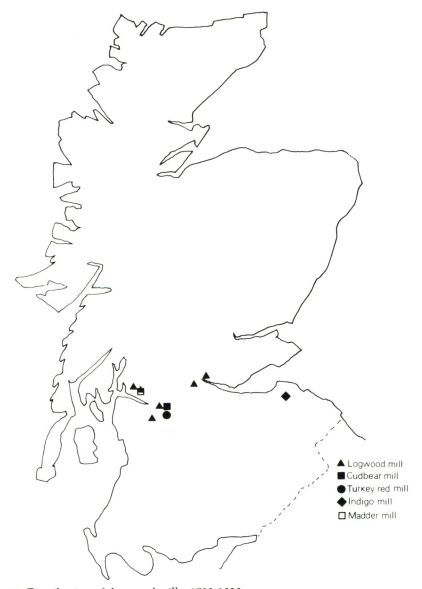

Fig 79. Distribution of dyewood mills, 1730-1830

Thread Mills

Thread twisting by machine was first introduced to the Paisley area in the 1720s, but despite its success it remained exclusively hand-driven for some time. The first suggestion that water power might have been used comes in 1755 when James Alexander, a wright in Kilbarchan (Renfrewshire), produced 'a machine to go by water' which, it was claimed, could twist thread better,

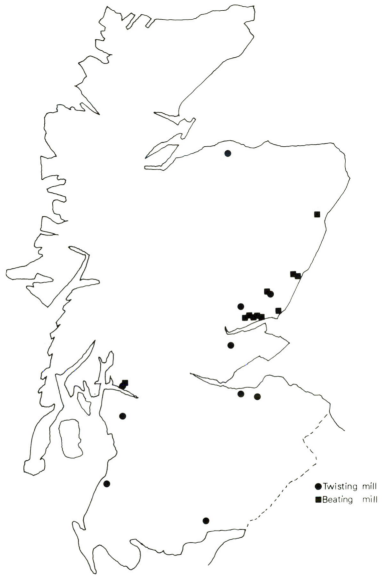

Fig 80. Distribution of water-powered thread twisting and beating mills, 1730-1830

quicker and cheaper than could existing methods. In the years which followed
the Board of Trustees awarded £20 to him in recognition of his work.[59] By the
early 1760s two types of machine had been brought into use. One, possibly
derived from Alexander's design, twisted the thread while another, based on
the already common stamping mill, softened and glossed the dry thread. Two
well documented mills on opposite sides of Scotland are known to have been
in operation. At Strathmiglo (Fife) William Carrick, a west of Scotland man,

had a small cloth bleachfield and 'a water mill for twisting thread';[60] at Dalquhurnfield (Dunbartonshire) the bleacher, Charles Scott, concerned at the decline of Dutch bleaching (i.e. without machinery), decided to introduce the manufacture of thread. He had a lade dug from the Leven, seven hundred and fifty yards long, ten feet wide and seven feet deep, and on a fall of only three feet he built a large mill which housed seven thread twisting mills, each of forty-eight spindles, and ten mauls for beating the thread. Something like £500 was laid out on this ambitious venture, and by 1763 thread making was employing forty men and women.[61]

At about the same time James Spalding, still at Bonnington Mills, proposed that thread-twisting machinery be installed in an existing plash mill there. According to Spalding, thread makers were generally small-scale producers, with dispersed premises and limited capital. In addition to their basic equipment, they each had to pay high wages to workers who performed the laborious work of turning the mill. In Spalding's opinion, one water-powered machine at Bonnington could perform the work for all the thread makers in Midlothian or, indeed, Scotland.[62] Although Spalding's plan may never have been taken up, there was certainly a thread-twisting mill at Dumfries by the late 1760s[63] and a beating mill, which had cost nearly £100, at Greenburn, near Aberdeen, by 1774.[64]

By 1800 there were water-powered thread mills at Kirkoswald (Ayrshire), Pencaitland (East Lothian), Elgin (Moray) and Pettyvaich (Banffshire),[65] but the most marked development was in the coarse linen area of Angus. Between 1760 and 1790 five thread-beating mills were built on the Dighty;[66] Mill of Craigo and Mill of Logie, both in Logie Pert parish, had thread-beating machinery, as had a mill in St. Vigeans parish.[67] Elsewhere in the county there were thread mills in the parishes of Monifieth and Lundie and at the village of Letham.[68]

With the mechanisation of spinning, thread making was absorbed into spinning mills, and the few thread mills which had been built (Figure 80) soon fell out of use.

Hemp Mills

Hemp, a coarse imported fibre, which was used in sail and rope manufacture, came into use in Scotland before 1730. During one stage in its processing it was beaten, in the same way as flax, and water power was sometimes applied to this process.

In 1711 the proprietors of a sail cloth manufactory, which had been established at Leith in 1708, applied to Edinburgh Burgh Council for permission to use Bonnington Mills for beating mills, workshops and bleachfields. The partners obtained a thirty-eight year tack of the mills, with power to build a hemp mill, but there is no certainty that their plans were carried out.[69] On the west coast, at Greenock, a ropework and sail cloth factory, with its own hemp mill, was founded in 1725-6, and another mill was built at a ropework in Port

Glasgow some time after 1740.[70] There were hemp manufactories at Inverness from 1766[71] and there were certainly rope and sail works around the coasts of Scotland, but there is little to suggest that they had hemp mills. In all, there were probably no more than ten such mills in the whole of Scotland, most of them on the east coast or the Firth of Clyde.

NOTES

1. Vincent, C. W. (ed.), *Chemistry as Applied to the Arts and Manufactures*, 8 vols., London, n.d. (c. 1875-80), III, 673-4.

2. Clow, A. & Clow, N. L., *The Chemical Revolution*, London, 1952, 195, 226.

3. Crawford, G. (revised Semple, W.), *The History of Renfrewshire*, Paisley, 1782.

4. Vincent, *op. cit.*, III, 674.

5. *OSA* XI, 319, Campsie, Stirlingshire; *OSA* XVI, 117, Kilearn, Stirlingshire; *OSA* III, 442, Bonhill, Dunbartonshire.

6. *OSA* III, 442, Bonhill, Dunbartonshire.

7. *NSA* X, 1035, Tibbermore, Perthshire; *NSA* VIII, 384, Dunnipace, Stirlingshire.

8. *NSA* VIII, 224-5, Bonhill, Dunbartonshire.

9. *Ibid.*, 224-5.

10. *OSA* XV, 356, Campsie, Stirlingshire.

11. Clow & Clow, *op. cit.*, 225.

12. Devine, T. M., Glasgow Merchants and Colonial Trade 1770-1815, Strathclyde University PhD., 1972.

13. Cameron, J., *Parish of Campsie*, Kirkintilloch, 1892, 14.

14. *OSA* XVI, 117, Kilearn, Stirlingshire.

15. Cameron, *op. cit.*, 14.

16. *Ibid.*, 15.

17. Clow & Clow, *op. cit.*, 224.

18. *SBRS*, 'Extracts from the Records of the Burgh of Glasgow', V (1718-38), Glasgow, 1909, 74-5.

19. Cupar: SRO NG1/1/21 7/12/74; Balgersho: *Caledonian Mercury*, 25th March 1775; Tulloch (Perth): *Caledonian Mercury*, 27th February 1775.

20. Irving, J., *History of Dunbartonshire*, 3 vols., Dumbarton, 1919-24, III, 424.

21. Clow & Clow, *op. cit.*, 225; Irving, *op. cit.*, III, 423.

22. Whyte, A. & McFarlane, D., *General View of the Agriculture of Dunbartonshire*, Glasgow, 1811, 273.

23. SRO RHP 967/4.

24. *NSA* VIII, 224, Bonhill, Dunbartonshire.

25. *NSA* VIII, 58, New Kilpatrick, Dunbartonshire.

26. Cameron, *op. cit.*, 8-48; *NSA* VIII, 254-5, Campsie, Stirlingshire; *OSA* XV, 319, Campsie, Stirlingshire.

27. *NSA* VIII, 200, Kirkintilloch, Dunbartonshire.

28. *NSA* VIII, 384, Dunipace, Stirlingshire.

29. Turner, W. H. K., 'The Textile Industry of Perth and District', *TIBG* XXIII (1957), 125.

30. *OSA* V, 234, Old Kilpatrick, Dunbartonshire.

31. Wilson, J. M. (ed.), *The Imperial Gazetteer of Scotland*, 2 vols., n.d. (c.1875), II, 653.

32. Cameron, *op. cit.*, 12.

33. Jamieson, A., *A Dictionary of Mechanical Science*, 2 vols., London, 1827, I, 248.

34. Loch, D., *A Tour through Most of the Trading Towns and Villages of Scotland*, Edinburgh, 1778, 9.

35. OSP 485:25: Haddington Burgh Council v. Haddington Tarred Wool Co.

36. Clow & Clow, *op. cit.*, 209.

37. *NSA* XIV, 295, Tain, Ross-shire; Forrest, W., (Map of) Lanarkshire, 1813.

38. Jamieson, *op. cit.*, 248.

39. Clow & Clow, *op. cit.*, 119.

40. *Ibid.*, 210-1.

41. *SBRS*, 'Extracts from the Records of the Burgh of Glasgow', VII (1760-80), Glasgow, 1912, 509-10.

42. Clow & Clow, *op. cit.*, 211.

43. *SBRS*, Glasgow VII, 511, 544.

44. Clow & Clow, *op. cit.*, 213-4.

45. *Ibid.*, 214-5.

46. *Ibid.*, 217; SRO NG1/1/26 6th February 1788.

47. Clow & Clow, *op. cit.*, 217.

48. SRO NG1/1/26 6th February 1788.

49. SRO NG1/1/27 4th March 1789.

50. SRO NG1/1/27 16/12/89, 20/1/90, 19/5/90.

51. Clow & Clow, *op. cit.*, 218.

52. *OSA* III, 442, Bonhill, Dunbartonshire.

53. Clow & Clow, *op. cit.*, 239-40.

54. *OSA* XIV, 283, Govan, Lanarkshire.

55. Clow & Clow, *op. cit.*, 199.

56. *SBRS*, Glasgow V, 92.

57. *OSA* XIV, 283, Govan, Lanarkshire.

58. Taylor, C., *The Levern Delineated*, Glasgow, 1831, 7; *OSA* III, 442, Bonhill, Dunbartonshire; *OS* 1st Edition 6"/mile Dunbartonshire 1860; *NSA* VIII, 161, Luss, Dunbartonshire; *OSA* VIII, 592, Alloa, Clackmannanshire; *NSA* VIII, 118, 129, Denny, Stirlingshire.

59. SRO NG1/1/13 25/7/55, 23/1/56.

60. NLS Acc.2933/330/f.2 (1762).

61. Ibid. (June 1763).

62. Ibid., f.3 (March 1763).

63. SRO NG1/1/19 9/12/68.

64. SRO NG1/1/21 7/12/74.

65. *OSA* X, 492, Kirkoswald, Ayrshire; *OSA* XVII, 40, Pencaitland, East Lothian; SRO NG1/1/29 22/11/1797, 21/11/1798.

66. *OSA* V, 218, Mains of Fintry, Angus.

67. *OSA* IX, 33, Logie Pert, Angus; *OSA* XII, 170, St. Vigeans, Angus.

68. *OSA* XIII, 494, Monifieth, Angus; *OSA* VII, 281, Lundie, Angus; SRO NG1/1/28 13/6/92.

69. *SBRS*, 'Extracts from the Records of the Burgh of Edinburgh', XIII (1701-18), Edinburgh, 1967, 219.

70. Crawford, *op. cit.*, 78, 86.

71. SRO E.769/87/2; *NSA* XIV, 22, Inverness & Bona, Inverness-shire.

22

Paper Mills

In Alistair Thomson's Edinburgh PhD, 'The Paper Industry in Scotland, 1700-1861', paper mills have been covered already in greater depth than is possible here. Some overlap in sources is inevitable, but any information which has come directly from Thomson's work is acknowledged as such, and note is taken of any further evidence which extends or which contradicts his findings.

Technology

The water-powered stamping machinery which Scottish paper mills were using in 1730 was much the same as that used during the previous century. However, by 1830 the industry had been revolutionised by the introduction of two new types of machinery. The first of these, the Hollander, had been developed in the Netherlands during the 17th century and consisted of a drum, fitted with iron knives or teeth, which revolved on a close-fitting metal or stone bed-plate[1] (Figure 81). By mechanising rag pulping it reduced the time and labour needed to produce paper. The Hollander must have been a well kept secret: according to Thomson, it is not known to have been introduced to Scotland until 1789.[2]

While the Hollander doubtless increased the output of cut rags, the traditional vat, in which paper was still made by hand, sheet by sheet, continued to hold up production. In some mills the problem was overcome by installing more vats,[3] but only with the introduction of the paper machine was the bottleneck removed. The machine was patented in France by Nicholas Luis Robert in 1799, and in England by John Gamble, brother-in-law of Leger-Didot who had promised to buy, but had not paid for, the French patent. In London, Gamble showed the still imperfect machine to the Fourdrinier brothers who, with Brian Donkin, started to improve on it. By 1806 it was ready to go onto the market but in 1810 the Fourdriniers went bankrupt, having sunk over £60,000 on the machine's development. The unfortunate Fourdriniers failed to reap any benefit on account of the complexities surrounding the patent.[4]

The first Scottish mill to install a machine was that of Lewis Smith, at Peterculter, Aberdeen, where there was one in use by 1811.[5] At the same mill a second machine was added some ten years later,[6] and during the 1820s machines were installed in a number of other mills.[7] A list of all the paper mills

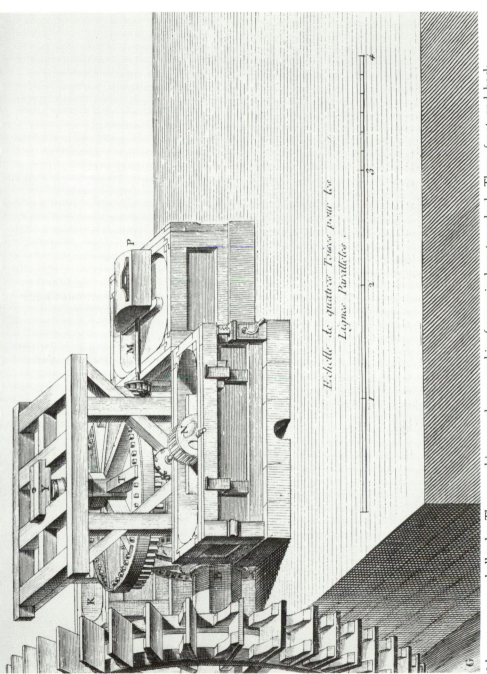

Echelle de quatre Toises par les
Lignes Parallelles.

Fig 81. 18th-century paper hollander. Three machines are shown working from a single water wheel. Those front and back (N, K) have been opened up to expose the mechanism. *Diderot, L'Encyclopédie*

Fig 82. Vats and paper machines in water-powered paper mills, 1832. *Paper Mills in Scotland, 1832*

in Scotland, published in 1832, gives details of the number of machines and vats in each (Figure 82). Of fifty-two working mills, twenty-three had paper machines; of these, eighteen had no vats and five had both machines and vats. Only seven mills had two machines. At the opposite end of the spectrum were no fewer than fourteen one-vat mills.[8]

The introduction of the paper machine helped bring about several important changes in the industry. Firstly, it helped to eliminate the smaller country mills where production levels did not justify, or capital run to, installing a machine; the preceding figures show that by no means all of these mills had been eliminated by 1832. Secondly, it reduced the amount of labour required to produce a given quantity of paper. The New Statistical Account makes several references to this: in New Kilpatrick parish (Dunbartonshire) a mill which had formerly employed twenty-two men and several women in making twenty reams per day was able to produce three times the quantity with a reduction of seven in the number of male employees.[9] The third change, the converse of the second, was a greater demand for mechanical power, precipitating the introduction of steam power. Already, in 1803, an engine was in use at Lasswade,[10] and in that year a wholly steam-powered mill was built at Aberdeen.[11] For the most part, however, and particularly in those mills away from coalfields, water power continued to be applied.[12] As with bleaching, the need for clean process water militated against the urbanisation of the industry. As late as 1843 the ratio of steam to water power was only 1:1.4.[13]

Sources of Finance

In 1730 there was only a very small paper industry in Scotland, so that little capital or business expertise was available for its further development. While the various branches of the textile industry could draw upon the accumulated assets of established manufacturers, the paper industry owed its existence largely to those who marketed or consumed paper — printers, booksellers and stationers. The rise of printing in Scotland was reflected in the establishment of a plethora of newspapers: the *Edinburgh Gazette* in 1699, the *Edinburgh Courant* in 1718, the *Glasgow Journal* in 1729, the *Scots Magazine* in 1739, the *Aberdeen Journal* in 1748, and a great many others thereafter.[14] Faced with the necessity of importing paper from England, several marketers or users of paper set up their own mills. On the Midlothian Esk an Edinburgh stationer, Richard Nimmo, established a paper mill at Low Mill, Penicuik, formerly a waulk mill.[15] John Boyle, a bookseller and printer, set up Stoneywood Mill, Aberdeen in partnership with Richard Hyde, a dyer, in 1770.[16] In the Perth area the introduction of paper making was almost entirely the work of Messrs. Morrison & Lindsay. James Morrison, a Perth printer who also carried out work for the University of Edinburgh, went into partnership with his brother-in-law, Henry Lindsay. In 1792 they obtained a fifty-eight year lease on the paper mill of Ruthven, and by the mid-1790s they also had two paper mills in Methven parish.[17] Whilst the Ruthven mill specialised in coarse paper, the two Methven mills also made writing and printing papers of which some of the best went to London.[18] One of Morrison's pupils, Robert Tullis, became a stationer, bookseller and printer at Cupar before setting up his own paper mill at Auchmuty, on the Fife Leven, in 1810.[19]

Whether imaginary or real, the profits to be had from paper making attracted interest from a wide variety of sources. An English paper maker, Bartholomew Smith, took over a former waulk mill at Culter, Aberdeenshire in 1750, just two years after the establishment of Aberdeen's first newspaper.[20] In Strathearn, the Forfeited Estates Commission encouraged several parties to set up mills: a young Crieff merchant, Patrick Arnot, built a paper mill for coarse paper about 1763, only the third such mill north of the Forth. By 1765 he had laid out £200 Sterling on the project and had plans for a second one nearby.[21] A paper mill at Waulkmill, Auchterarder, costing £400 Sterling, was built about 1775 by James Barnet in Castle Mains and John Ferguson at Shinafoot — probably a farmer and millwright/waulker partnership.[22] Members of two Scottish finance houses were persuaded by the manager of a small, established mill to set up an extensive five-vat mill at Polton, Midlothian, but after a large sum had been laid out and one, then another English paper maker had been hired (both died), the mill was given up in 1772, following the bankruptcy of one of the two firms.[23]

During the course of the 18th and early 19th centuries the development of the industry gave rise to firms whose prime concern was papermaking and who had sufficient capital and accumulated knowledge to establish or take over other mills. Two examples will suffice.

James Craig began papermaking at Balerno about 1812 with his son-in-law, a Mr. Hill, as partner.[24] In 1820 he took over a paper mill at Newbattle, Midlothian, and during the late 1820s or early 1830s his brother John took on Moffat Mill, near Airdrie.[25] Of James's four sons, Thomas and George took up papermaking at Portobello, while Robert stayed on at Newbattle. David, the youngest, took over Portobello in 1849-50.[26] In 1846 the three brothers obtained land and water rights for a mill at Caldercruix, Airdrie, which was in production by 1848, powered by two large water wheels.[27]

The Cowan family entered the papermaking business in 1779 when Charles Cowan, merchant in Leith, bought the long-established Penicuik (later Valley-field) paper mill. About 1804 the firm bought Penicuik corn mill and converted it into a paper mill (Bank Mill). Valleyfield was sold to the Government in 1811 to house French prisoners of war, but was repurchased in 1818; a third paper mill, Low Mill, Penicuik,[28] and a fourth, Melville Mill, Lasswade,[29] had been taken on in the interim. By 1832 the family had interests in Kate's Mill, Colinton and were still operating their three Penicuik mills.[30] According to Thomson, the Cowans also had a mill at Bullionfield, Dundee, founded in 1850.[31] A similar development took place with regard to the skilled workers who actually made the paper. The services of a good paper maker were highly valued, and in an age of social mobility he could rise to being a partner and eventually owning his own mill. At Robert Tullis's Auchmuty Mill, Fife, one of the ten shares was allocated to Alexander Grieve, formerly at Balerno paper mill. Grieve became manager at Auchmuty when production started in 1810, and six years later he built his own small mill at Balbirnie, which was still in the family in 1862.[32] .

Lastly, something should be said of the landowner's role. Very rarely were landowners so foolhardy as to venture into papermaking on their own account: Alexander Copland was apparently doing so in the 1790s on his Dalbeattie, Kirkcudbrightshire estate,[33] but for most landowners a textile mill was a much safer option when it came to finding an application for unharnessed water power. Despite this reluctance to participate directly, there is ample evidence of a favourable disposition towards the industry in the form of the long leases on mill sites, at low rents, which several paper makers are known to have enjoyed. At Culter, Patrick Duff of Premnay gave Bartholomew Smith a six by nineteen year 'improving lease' of a waulk mill with its outbuildings and a fall of water for £60 Scots per annum,[34] whilst at Crieff Patrick Arnot obtained a three by nineteen year lease on an eleven-foot fall from James Porteous, minister at Monzievaird, for £2 Sterling per annum.[35]

In at least one case, the favourable disposition extended to paper makers on other estates. In 1767 Sir John Clerk of Penicuik entered into a contract with William Annandale, proprietor of Auchendinny paper mill, under which the former undertook not to remove or seek compensation for the latter's mill dam, one end of which impinged on Clerk's estate,

> in order to encourage him the better to carry on that branch of manufactory of paper-making which is so usefull and beneficiall to the country.[36]

Considering that Clerk already had two paper mills on his own estate, and at a time when water rights were all too often the subject of prolonged legal battles, this seems to have been a particularly magnaminous gesture.

Distribution and Chronology

Before considering the geographical distribution of the paper industry in Scotland, and the way in which that pattern developed between 1730 and 1830, something should be said of the factors which lay behind it.

The first requirement was water power, initially to drive stampers, latterly to drive Hollanders and eventually paper machines too. As water power was available in sufficient volume in most parts of Scotland, this was not, in itself, much of a constraint on the spread of the industry. Although clean water was needed for papermaking, this could be drawn from springs, rather than from the river which provided the driving power. Thus several mills, each with their attendant pollution, could use falls on the same watercourse in areas favoured by other circumstances.

One of the most important of these other circumstances was proximity to raw materials. During the period under consideration these raw materials were rags, almost all of them linen, and whilst the manufacture and use of linen cloth in Scotland favoured the development of a paper industry, the volume of rags needed was enormous: in the 1790s Crieff paper mill consumed over two hundred hundredweight of rags per annum, and by the late 1830s Herbertshire Mill, Stirlingshire was using twenty-six hundredweight per day.[37] So enormous were the requirements of the industry that most of the larger mills were closely tied to major urban centres, the more isolated mills having to scavenge over a large area. One Berwickshire mill had agencies in Berwick (itself a major source of rags), Wooler, Alnwick, Jedburgh, Kelso and Duns.[38] Even mills near to cities had to advertise:

> Bartholemew Smith, paper-maker from England, who has now rented and set agoing on the Burn of Culter a papermill, where he can serve the country in paper, fine and coarse, brown paper, pasteboard, pressing cards for dysters &c., gives notice that he buys rags of all kinds of flax and hemp by the stoneweight, and designs for that end to come to Aberdeen every Friday. Mr Smith expects that, as his undertaking is so beneficial to the country, every person will be careful to save their materials for his work, which formerly were thrown away as useless.[39]

Some ingenious papermakers found substitutes. Robert Walker, at Balernobank, Midlothian, was using leather refuse in 1812; in the late 1830s Carrongrove Mill, Stirlingshire was using old ropes.[40] It was, however, only after 1850 that realistic substitutes were found for rags.[41]

In that it used rags drawn from urban areas, any paper mill situated close to its raw materials was also close to its markets. Printing was growing rapidly in importance, and various grades of paper were being applied to a wide range of purposes: 'calender paper' for pressing cloth, cartridge paper for hosiery manufacturers, coarse paper for sheathing ships, millboard, brown and blue paper, writing paper, tissue paper — all were made in Scotland and found ready markets.[42] As most mills were near towns and most towns near navigable water, paper could easily be exported to London, a market which became increasingly important as the output of the Scottish industry increased. As early as 1765, even an inland mill such as that at Crieff found its product readily marketable in Glasgow and London, despite the extra cost of overland transport.[43]

Lastly, a paper mill had to have access to labour. The amount required varied with the size of the mill: during the 1790s a small one-vat mill at Saltoun (East Lothian) employed only eight workers, whilst a seven-vat mill at Ayton employed ten times that number.[44] Four mills in Lasswade parish provided work for two hundred and sixty people and four in Colinton for ninety-two people.[45] In 1809 four Berwickshire mills employed two hundred.[46] Generally speaking, a highly mobile population, the unskilled nature of much of the work (children as young as eight were employed)[47] and the proximity of most mills to existing centres of population prevented the need for labour from assuming any great importance in determining the distribution of paper mills.

Of the eighteen or so mills founded between 1550 and 1730, it is doubtful whether more than seven were still in production at the end of that period (Figure 83). Of these seven —Cathcart, Cathcart (Millholm),[48] Penicuik,[49] Yester,[50] Jinkabout,[51] Bogsmill[52] and Redhall[53] — all but two were in the Edinburgh area, perpetuating the city's dominant role first established in the 1590s. In the twenty years to 1750 little happened to change this: paper

Fig 83. Distribution of paper mills, 1730-1749

production languished,[54] no new mills were established in the 1730s, and of the eight founded during the 1740s, four were in the Edinburgh area (Figure 83). Within that area, however, a shift of emphasis was apparent. On the Water of Leith, where most of the earlier mills had been built, there was fierce competition for millsteads among a great many potential users, and a move to the North Esk, starting with Penicuik mill in 1709, and Auchendinny by 1745, was not unexpected.[55] For reasons unknown, the section of the Water of

Leith above Colinton, where falls were more readily available, was not exploited until much later. Outside the Edinburgh area, the growing status of Glasgow as a business and commercial centre was reflected in the establishment of three mills in addition to those already operating at Cathcart.[56] Away from these two centres only one mill, and that of doubtful provenance, was built, at Larbert near Falkirk.[57] Between 1750 and 1780 there were important changes in the range of Scottish paper mills, although the Edinburgh area maintained its dominance (Figure 84). Two additional mills were started on the North Esk — Polton (1750),[58] and Melville (1763) — and there were further developments to the west at Midcalder (1761),[59] to the north-east at Portobello (1775),[60] and to the east at Saltoun (1773), the last being a former lint mill only a few miles from the Scots White Paper Company's Yester Mill, which was itself soon to be converted into a lint mill.[61] To some extent developments outside the Edinburgh area reflected a reoccupation of rag-catchment areas first exploited in the late 17th century: Culter Mill (1750) and Stoneywood (1770) drew from and sold to Aberdeen, as had Gordon's Mills, while Broomhouse (c.1760) bore a similar relationship to an area centred on Berwick, as had the grey-paper mill at Ayton.[62] In addition to these, however, there is evidence of paper mills breaking new ground, drawing on raw materials from less densely populated but hitherto unexploited districts: Crieff (1763, 1780),[63] Tongland (Kirkcudbrightshire c.1766),[64] Galston (Ayrshire pre-1770),[65] Waulkmill, Auchterarder (1775)[66] and a mill on the River Avon in Stirlingshire[67] all come into this category. The 1750s and 1760s saw a rapid increase in the output of paper, but after 1770, when only three small mills came into production and at least one went out of use, output dropped back slightly.[68] The last two decades of the 18th century saw further increases in the number of Scottish paper mills but few changes in distribution (Figure 85). In the Edinburgh area there was renewed interest in the Water of Leith, and of four new mills established on it, three were above Colinton, on a stretch of water hitherto little used by the paper industry;[69] on the Esk, three mills were added.[70] In the other established papermaking districts, further developments took place: in the Glasgow area a second mill was built at Balgray;[71] near Aberdeen, two more mills were built at Stoneywood (1786, 1796);[72] whilst in Berwickshire a paper mill at Millbank, Ayton, has started by 1785.[73] The Perth-Strathearn area, where papermaking had only started in the 1760s, assumed greater importance, with two mills in Methven parish and one at Ruthven by the mid-1790s.[74] Another formerly under-exploited area, that around Falkirk and Stirling, achieved much greater status with new mills at Sauchie (1787), Herbertshire (1789), Falkirk (pre-1799) and three mills in Lecropt parish, Perthshire.[75] A second mill was built in Galloway, this time at Dalbeattie (1780),[76] but the only area where new ground was broken was in the central Borders, where a mill was founded at Langholm some time before 1799.[77]

The pattern of development between 1780 and 1800 was largely a continuation of that started in the previous thirty years. This failure to break

Fig 84. Distribution of paper mills founded 1750-1779

new ground may have been partly due to the lack of further urban centres from which raw materials could be drawn. One might have expected further developments in Ayrshire, where there was only one mill, or in Moray, Fife and Angus, where there were none, but presumably these areas could be provided for by mills around Glasgow, Aberdeen and Perth. In all, about twenty new paper mills were founded between 1780 and 1800.

Fig 85. Distribution of paper mills founded 1780-1799

While the last two decades of the 18th century had been important ones for the Scottish paper industry, the first three of the 19th, measured in terms of new mills, were much more so. Of the forty or so mills first recorded between 1800 and 1830 (Figure 86), the majority were in well-established papermaking districts, but although Edinburgh and, to a lesser extent, Aberdeen continued to dominate the industry, the central region between Edinburgh and Glasgow increased its relative importance, and Linlithgow, for the first time, became a

Fig 86. Distribution of water-powered paper mills founded 1800-1830

papermaking centre.[78] Berwickshire, and to some extent Galloway, on the other hand, failed to keep pace with the growth of the industry. The most noticeable departure from the existing pattern was in Fife, where three mills — Rothes (1806), Auchmuty (1810) and Balbirnie (1816) — were established on the River Leven.[79] Elsewhere, new mills were set up at Crook of Devon (Kinross-shire)[80] and Overton, on the Shaws Water Aqueduct, Greenock.[81] A list of Scottish paper mills, published in 1832, gives some idea of the distri-

Fig 87. Distribution of water-powered paper mills, 1730-1830

bution of working mills at the time (Figure 82). In all, there were probably about one hundred paper mills at work in Scotland between 1730 and 1830 (Figure 87). Whilst the paper industry was closely tied to centres of population, it remained conservative in its distribution, showing only a slight shift towards west-central Scotland in response to changing population distributions. However, the Edinburgh area offered other advantages: the capital city continued to be a major publishing and administrative centre, and it was well placed for importing raw materials from Europe and exporting paper to London. Competition for falls may also have been less in the east than in the west, and this consideration, along with access to English markets, may have had a bearing on the development of the Berwickshire and Aberdeen districts.

Papermaking on the Midlothian Esk

In choosing an area to illustrate in more detail the development of the Scottish paper industry between 1730 and 1830, the obvious choice must be that area centred on the Rivers North and South Esk in Midlothian. From a single mill in 1730, papermaking grew until paper mills had become the greatest single user of the rivers' water power, and the industry established there held a dominant position which was never subsequently challenged by any other area. The proximity of Edinburgh was crucial to the success of papermaking on the Esk. It already had its own paper industry, utilising the Water of Leith, and provided at the same time a source of rags, a market for paper and access to an even larger market in London. Edinburgh also provided a mixed bag of entrepreneurial skills which by one means or another found their way into the paper industry.

While the Water of Leith ran closer to Edinburgh, it already supported a multitude of users at the beginning of the period and no less than seventy-one mills by the 1790s.[82] Although additional mills were established on the upper reaches of the river, it seems likely that the high cost of falls and the already polluted water made the Esk a more attractive location. With the exception of grain mills and a few waulk, lint and bleaching mills, the Esk had few industrial users to compete with paper.

Since the paper industry before 1830 depended on a ready supply of rags for its raw material, it was advisable to locate mills close to urban centres, thereby minimising transport costs. By Scottish standards Edinburgh was a very large centre of population, with a steady turnover of clothing suitable for papermaking and, through its port of Leith, access to rags drawn from a much wider area. Penicuik (Valleyfield), Springfield, Lasswade and Melville mills all had rag stores in the city itself, whilst Polton and Auchendinny had stores in Leith.[83]

This close association with Edinburgh extended beyond raw materials and markets to include the sources of finance for running mills. Edinburgh and Leith merchants played a significant part in establishing and running paper mills. John Hutton, merchant in Edinburgh, founded Melville Mill some time before 1763,[84] and from 1756 had a share in Springfield Mill.[85] In 1793, following his bankruptcy, Melville Mill and its contents were put up for sale, and by 1805 the mill was in the hands of another Edinburgh merchant, John Pitcairn of Pitcairn, later to become the first chairman of the directors of the Commercial Bank of Scotland (1810), and Chairman of the Edinburgh Chamber of Commerce (1820).[86] The connection between Eskside paper mills and banking is one which will be taken up again later. In 1814 the mill was

taken on by D. & A. Cowan, owners of paper mills in Penicuik.[87] Their pre-
decessor, Charles Cowan, had been a merchant in Leith before taking on
Valleyfield Mill (Penicuik) in 1779.[88] Another Leith merchant family, the
Cadells, controlled Auchendinny Mill from 1782.[89] One of the Cowans' mills,
Bank Mill, was said to have taken its name from its having made paper for
Scottish banknotes,[90] and at least one other mill, Polton, made them for the
British Linen Bank about 1768.[91] Polton had been founded by a Mr. Hunter
and a Mr. Guthrie, members of the Edinburgh finance houses, Forbes, Hunter
& Co. and Arbuthnot & Guthrie. The mill was run jointly by two companies
until 1772, when the latter house went bankrupt and the former sold the mill
off.[92]

The connection between the Esk paper industry and Edinburgh printers,
publishers and stationers was much more marked. The earliest mill on the
river (Valleyfield, 1709) was linked with a succession of printers to the crown.
Its founder, Andrew Anderson, was the first such and his widow, who
succeeded him, held the same office.[93] At a later stage, the mill was held by
Richard Watkins, printer to the king and one-time occupant of Yester Mill; he,
in turn, was followed by another king's printer, his nephew, Adrian
Watkins.[94] Walter Ruddiman of the *Caledonian Mercury* and Robert Fleming
of the *Edinburgh Courant* co-founded Springfield Mill with an Edinburgh
bookseller, John Aitken, in 1742.[95] Ruddiman's brother held the post of printer
to the University.[96]

Besides these examples of investment by those who consumed paper, there is
also evidence of expansion from within the industry. The development of the
Cowan empire has already been referred to. From within the industry's
workforce we find Archibald Keith, a mould maker, buying up machinery in
1795 from John Hutton's Melville Mill, to set up his own small mill on the
South Esk near Newbattle.[97] Perhaps the most unlikely link involved two
distillers, John Haig and his brother-in-law John Philp, owners of two cotton
mills at Esk Mills, one of which was converted to papermaking about 1805 by
the occupant of the mills, John White, who was also another of Haig's
brothers-in-law.[98]

Chronology

The first paper mill on the Esk was founded in 1709, but it was not until the
1740s that any further mills appeared (Figure 88). During the 1710s a few more
mills had been built on the Water of Leith, but graphs prepared by Thomson[99]
show a very depressed industry suffering badly from English competition, and
only after 1745 did output begin to rise steadily. Between 1740 and 1750 five
mills were built on the Esk, at Springfield, Lasswade, Auchendinny, Low Mill
and Polton,[100] but not until 1763 was the next mill, Melville, built.[101] During
the period 1740-70 about half of the new paper mills established in Scotland
were on the Esk,[102] an indication of the area's importance within the industry,
and yet another example of Scottish industrial growth starting in the

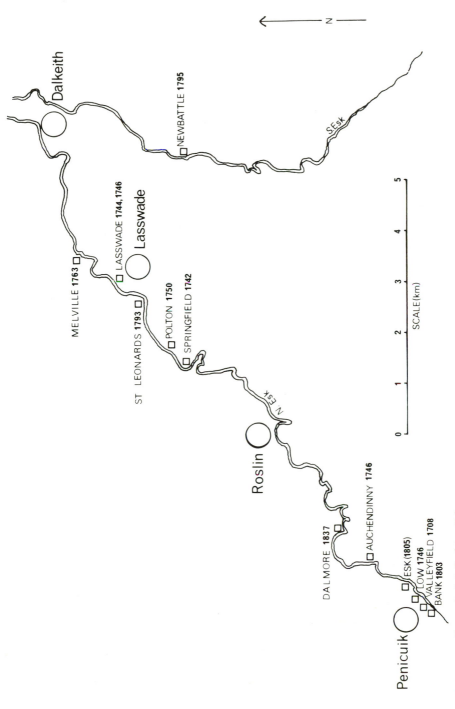

Fig 88. Paper mills on the Midlothian Esk

Edinburgh area. Thomson's graphs show total paper production and that of white paper, an Esk Valley speciality, falling back during the 1770s, in line with the generally depressed state of the economy.[103] The immense increase in output during the 1780s involved no new mills on the Esk, possibly because existing ones had been working below capacity, although in the 1790s two more mills, St. Leonard's and Newbattle, came into production,[104] and by 1805 a further two, Bank Mill and Esk Mill, had been added.[105] The first half of the 19th century was marked by consistent growth in Scottish paper output,[106] but not until the 1830s were the next mills established at Dalmore and Kevock.[107]

The vitality of the Esk Valley paper industry is reflected in the increasing scale of production and the adoption, in the early 19th century, of paper machines. According to the (Old) Statistical Account, output from paper mills in the Edinburgh area, including several on the Water of Leith, had risen from 6,400 reams in 1763 to 100,000 reams in 1791.[108] As early as 1767 the mill at Polton had five vats,[109] suggesting a very large capacity, whilst Melville Mill, with four vats in 1793,[110] and six by 1814,[111] must have been one of the largest such undertakings in Scotland.[112] A rather unusual papermaking machine developed in Scotland was installed at Springfield Mill in 1816, at a time when only one Fourdrinier machine was in use in the country.[113] Of the next seven Fourdrinier machines installed between 1820 and 1825, four were in Eskside paper mills;[114] by 1832 the nine mills then in production on the river had ten machines, one third of the Scottish total, but only four of the now almost obsolete vats, out of a national total of sixty-eight.[115]

The rise of the paper industry brought with it increased populations. In Lasswade parish employment in the paper industry rose from thirty or forty in the early 1740s to two hundred and sixty (at four mills) in the early 1790s and 'several hundreds' (at three mills) by 1843.[116] The population of Penicuik parish rose from 890 in 1755 to 1,132 in 1772 and 1,721 in 1793. While part of the increase between the last two dates was attributable to the Esk Mills cotton mills (employing about five hundred workers), further growth during the early 19th century was largely due to the paper industry which, despite the substitution of the paper machine for the more labour-intensive vats, had about four hundred employees by 1839.[117]

Conclusion

Between 1730 and 1830 perhaps only just over one hundred sites were involved in paper making in Scotland, but its development provides a useful barometer of the development of the Scottish economy during that period. Thomson[118] has shown how the output of paper related to fluctuations in the economy, and Smout[119] has referred to it as a 'buoyant little industry, casting a vivid shaft of light on . . . cultural and economic change'.[120] Besides reflecting the development of the economy in general, the paper industry also typified the industries of the period in its extensive use of water power, a source of power which was widely applied well into the 19th century, even in those areas such as Fife and Midlothian where coal was readily available.

Despite a considerable widening in the industry's distribution between 1730 and 1830, its dependence upon raw materials drawn from, and manufactured products destined for, towns, prevented it from reaching deeply rural districts. Throughout the period the area around Edinburgh continued to dominate the industry, even after a shift of population towards the west might have been expected to bring a corresponding change in its own distribution. At the same time, paper mills seldom employed enough workers within a small enough area to bring about the establishment of mill villages, except in Midlothian, where Balerno or Penicuik (originally an estate village) might be cited as examples.

NOTES

1. Coleman, D. C., *The British Paper Industry, 1495-1860: A Study of Industrial Growth*, Oxford, 1958, 63.

2. Thomson, A. G., *The Paper Industry in Scotland*, Edinburgh, 1974, 42.

3. *Caledonian Mercury*, 4th May 1793.

4. Coleman, *op. cit.*, 180-7.

5. Keith, G. S., *General View of the Agriculture of Aberdeenshire*, Aberdeen, 1811, 586.

6. Cormack, A. A., *Our Ancient and Honourable Craft*, Aberdeen, 1933, 30.

7. Shorter, A. H., *Paper Making in the British Isles*, Newton Abbot, 1971, 201.

8. Anon., *Paper Mills in Scotland*, Edinburgh & Glasgow, 1832.

9. *NSA* VIII, 58, New Kilpatrick, Dunbartonshire.

10. Svedenstierna, E. T. (translated Dellow, E. L.), *Svedenstierna's Tour of Great Britain 1802-3*, Newton Abbot, 1973, 133.

11. Morgan, P., *Annals of Woodside & Newhills*, Aberdeen, 1886, 204.

12. See, for example, the water wheel from Culter Paper Mill at the Royal Scottish Museum, Edinburgh.

13. Thomson, *op. cit.*, 159.

14. Clow, A. & Clow, N. L., *The Chemical Revolution*, London, 1952, 259-60.

15. Wilson, J. J. *The Annals of Penicuik*, Edinburgh, 1891, 123.

16. Morgan, *op. cit.*, 176-7.

17. Bell, S. S., *Dictionary of the Decisions of the Court of Session from November 1808 to November 1833*, 2 vols., Edinburgh, 1842, II, 1134; *OSA* X, 617, Methven, Perthshire.

18. *OSA* XVIII, 515, Perth, Perthshire; *OSA* XVII, 637, Tibbermuir, Perthshire; *OSA* X, 617, Methven, Perthshire.

19. Kettleby, C. D. M., *Tullis Russel, 1809-1959*, Markinch, 1967, 4, 7.

20. Morgan, *op. cit.*, 203.

21. SRO E 777/201/4.

22. SRO E 777/201/5.

23. Waterston, R., 'Further Notes on Paper Making Near Edinburgh', *BOEC* XXVII (1949), 56-7; Thomson, *op. cit.*, 99.

24. Craig, R. & Sons, *A Century of Paper Making, 1820-1920*, Edinburgh, 1920, 7.

25. *Ibid.*, 7, 25.

26. Baird, W., *Annals of Duddingston & Portobello*, Edinburgh, 1898, 451.

27. Craig, *op. cit.*, 47-8.

28. Wilson, *op. cit.*, 120-123.

29. SRO GD51/11/22/3, /5.

30. Anon., *Paper Mills in Scotland*.

31. Thomson, *op. cit.*, 200, note 123.

32. Kettleby, *op. cit.*, 33-4.

33. *OSA* XI, 61, Urr, Kirkcudbrightshire; Thomson, *op. cit.*, 94.

34. Cormack, *op. cit.*, 15.

35. SRO E 777/201/4/(2).

36. SRO GD18/1328.

37. *OSA* IX, 583, Crieff, Perthshire; *NSA* VIII, 128, Denny, Stirlingshire.

38. Thomson, *op. cit.*, plate 14.

39. *Aberdeen Journal*, 8th January 1751. Quoted by Morgan, *op. cit.*, 203.

40. SRO NG1/1/33 16th December 1812; *NSA* VIII, 127, Denny, Stirlingshire.

41. See Chapter 29, p.513.

42. *OSA* XVII, 55, Lecropt, Perthshire; *NSA* I, 600, Crammond, Midlothian; *NSA* VIII, 127, Denny, Stirlingshire; *NSA* XII, 111, Peterculter, Aberdeenshire; *OSA* XVII, 637, Tibbermuir, Perthshire; *OSA*, XVI, 373, Peterculter, Aberdeenshire.

43. SRO E 777/201/4(2).

44. *OSA* X, 257, Saltoun, East Lothian; *OSA* I, 79, Ayton, Berwickshire.

45. *OSA* X, 279, Lasswade, Midlothian; *OSA* XIX, 580, Colinton, Midlothian.

46. Kerr, R., *General View of the Agriculture of the County of Berwick*, London, 1809, 455.

47. *OSA* I, 79, Ayton, Berwickshire.

48. *OSA* V, 336, Cathcart, Renfrewshire.

49. Waterston, *op. cit.*, 48.

50. NLS Acc 4862/151/f.l.

51. According to Waterston (*op. cit.*, 49), it was founded in 1714. Probably still working in 1730.

52. Waterston, *op. cit.*, 50.

53. *Ibid.*, 53. Founded 1718. Probably still working 1730.

54. Thomson, *op. cit.*, 74.

55. Waterston, *op. cit.*, 54.

56. Thomson, *op. cit.*, 116, Table 8: Dalmuir 1747; Balgray 1746. The third mill, Dawsholm, though not mentioned by Thomson, was certainly in existence by 1747: NLS Acc. 2933/328.

57. General Roy, Map of Scotland.

58. Thomson, *op. cit.*, Table 8.

59. SRO GD51/11/122/(24) (Melville); Thomson, *op. cit.*, Table 8 (Mid Calder).

60. Hume, D., *Decisions of the Court of Session, 1781-1822*, Edinburgh & London, 1839, No. 389.

61. Thomson, *op. cit.*, 116; NLS Acc 2933/224; SRO NG 1/1/22 22/7/78; SRO GD1/16/1.

62. Cormack, *op. cit.*, 15; Morgan, *op. cit.*, 176; Thomson, *op. cit.*, Table 8.

63. *OSA* IX, 583, Crieff, Perthshire.

64. Thomson, *op. cit.*, 52.

65. *Ibid.*, 123.

66. SRO E 777/201/5.

67. Hume, *op. cit.*, 504.

68. Thomson, *op. cit.*, 74.

69. *Ibid.*, Table 8.

70. *Ibid.*, 120. Esk Mill was not converted to paper making until 1805. Chapter 20, p. 463.

71. Thomson, *op. cit.*, 121. The mill in New Kilpatrick parish was probably that at Dawsholm, founded c.1747 (see note 56).

72. Thomson, *op. cit.*, 149, note 40.

73. *Ibid.*, 123.

74. *OSA* X, 617, Methven, Perthshire; Bell, *op. cit.*, II, 1134.

75. Thomson, *op. cit.*, Table 8; *OSA* XVII, 55, Lecropt, Perthshire.

76. Thomson, *op. cit.*, 122.

77. *OSA* XXI, 245, Langholm, Dumfriesshire (Addenda).

78. Trotter, J., *General View of the Agriculture of Linlithgowshire*, Edinburgh, 1811, 200. Loch Mill established by this date.

79. *NSA* IX, 673, Markinch, Fife.

80. Thomson, *op. cit.*, 131.

81. Anon., *Paper Mills in Scotland*, No. 73.

82. *OSA* XIX, 580, Colinton, Midlothian.

83. Shorter, *op. cit.*, 195.

84. SRO GD51/11/122/(24), (5).

85. Waterston, *op. cit.*, 55.

86. *Caledonian Mercury*, 25th March 1793; Waterston, *op. cit.*, 58; SRO GD51/11/122/(5).

87. Waterston, *op. cit.*, 58.

88. Wilson, *op. cit.*, 120-1.

89. Waterston, *op. cit.*, 54.

90. Wilson, *op. cit.*, 121.

91. Thomson, *op. cit.*, 101.

92. Waterston, *op. cit.*, 56-7; Thomson, *op. cit.*, 99.

93. Wilson, *op. cit.*, 120-1. See Chapter 4, page 77.

94. Waterston, *op. cit.*, 48.

95. *Ibid.*, 55.

96. *Ibid.*, 55.

97. Thomson, *op. cit.*, 120.

98. SRO CS96/803.

99. Thomson, *op. cit.*, Figure 8, Figure 9.

100. *Ibid.*, 120, 211-2; Wilson, *op. cit.*, 123; Waterston, *op. cit.*, 54.

101. SRO GD51/11/122/(24).

102. Thomson, *op. cit.*, 75-6.

103. Hamilton, H., *An Economic History of Scotland in the Eighteenth Century*, Oxford, 1963, 314-323.

104. Thomson, *op. cit.*, 120.

105. Wilson, *op. cit.*, 121; SRO GD1/575/1.

106. Thomson, *op. cit.*, Figure 8.

107. *Ibid.*, 210-1.

108. *OSA* VI, 551, Edinburgh, Midlothian.

109. Waterston, *op. cit.*, 56.
110. *Caledonian Mercury*, 25th March 1793.
111. Waterston, *op. cit.*, 58.
112. See Thomson, *op. cit.*, Figures 2, 3 for plans of both mills in 1795.
113. *Ibid.*, 162, 177.
114. *Ibid.*, 177.
115. Anon., *Paper Mills in Scotland*.
116. *OSA* X 279, Lasswade, Midlothian; *NSA* I, 334, Lasswade, Midlothian.
117. *OSA* X, 422, Penicuik, Midlothian; *NSA* I, 44, Penicuik, Midlothian.
118. Thomson, *op. cit.*, Chapter 3.
119. Smout, T. C., *A History of the Scottish People, 1560-1830*, London, 1969, 251.
120. *Ibid*.

23

Coal Mining

Coal mining between 1730 and 1830 is probably the industry in which one might least expect to find water power being used: it was to the drainage of coal mines that steam power was first applied, and Newcomen-type engines had already reached Scotland by 1730.[1] During the remainder of the 18th century further developments, notably those by Watt, produced an engine capable of rotary motion and therefore of raising coal.[2]

However, on closer examination it appears that water power continued to find an application in the Scottish coal industry up to and beyond 1830, not only on small, isolated coalfields such as Brora (Sutherland) and Canonbie (Dumfriesshire), but also on the major coalfields of Fife, the Lothians and west-central Scotland.

Technology

The technology of mine drainage by water power was already well-established by 1730: simple 'rag and chain' and 'bucket and chain' systems were widely used during the 17th century, particularly on the Fife coalfield, whilst more sophisticated barrel pumps, of a type used with steam engines, were to be found on a few water-powered sites during the early 18th century.[3] This latter type, the so-called 'bob engine' or 'water engine', was the machine most commonly used between 1730 and 1830, but other ingenious types were also devised: that at Byreburn, near Canonbie,[4] bore a resemblance to the water-bucket pumps used at Leadhills, described more fully in Chapter 24.

An illustration dated 1738 shows a water engine in Strathore, Fife, consisting of a water wheel connected to two pumps by means of cranks and beams (Figure 89). The design has obvious affinities to that of steam-powered beam engines, but it has not been established which of the two came first.[5] The capacity of pump varied with the power available and the volume of water to be cleared, but generally a cylinder of between nine and fifteen inches in diameter was used. The importance attached to water power in its application to coal mining is reflected in the involvement of Smeaton, Rennie and Meikle.[6]

During the course of the 18th century, water power found new applications in coal mining:

> In Scotland, particularly at the Alloa colliery, a machine was introduced about the year 1740 for drawing coals, upon a simple and very ingenious construction. It

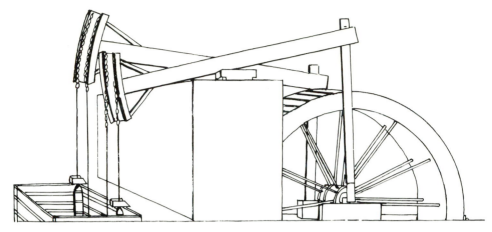

Fig 89. Colliery water engine at Strathore, Fife, *circa* 1736

consisted of a water-wheel of about eighteen feet diameter, and three feet broad, divided vertically, so as to have two sets of buckets; the one set placed reverse to the other, so that when water was set upon one side of the wheel it turned forwards; then the water was stopped upon this side, a valve allowed the water to flow upon the other division of the wheel, which made the wheel move backwards; this produced an alternate motion of the ropes in the pit; and with a strong lever the machine was quite under command. This is still the cheapest and best machine for coal drawing, where a plentiful supply of water can be got.[7]

It should be remembered that at this time the steam engine was still only capable of producing a reciprocating action,[8] and where rotation was necessary, resort had to be made to water, wind and animal power. In the north-east of England this often led to the cumbersome arrangement, still common in the 1800s, of using a steam engine to raise water to feed a water wheel which in turn worked coal-haulage gear.[9] No example of this unlikely combination has been found in the Scottish coal industry, though such a system was used in other contexts, notably at Carron Ironworks.[10]

From Clerk of Penicuik's 'Dissertation' it would appear that water power might also find an application in mine ventilation, but there is little reason to believe that it was ever thus used in Scotland.[11]

In coal mining, more than in almost any other industry, means other than water power could be, and were, used. In the case of drainage, a level, permitting water to drain off naturally, was always preferred where topography allowed, but as shallower seams were worked out and deeper ones exploited, this often became impracticable, and other techniques had to be resorted to. On the Marquis of Abercorn's Duddingston estate (Midlothian), one of the lessees of the coals, John Biggar of Woolmet, replaced an existing bucket and chain system with a level, three miles long, which emerged at sea level. By 1776 a water engine had been introduced to allow the Great and Starhead seams to be worked twenty fathoms below the level, and continued to operate until at least 1791. Steam, or 'fire', engines were also being used during the late 18th century.[12]

Where topography did not favour the use of levels, a 'horse gin' might be introduced, but as this depended on a bucket and chain system, only a small volume of water could be cleared, and this to a limited depth.[13] Horse gins were also expensive to run.[14] Windmills were occasionally applied to mine drainage: at Cranston, Midlothian, about 1782, Sir John Dalrymple installed not only a water engine to drain his coals but also a windmill which worked pumps, ground wheat and prepared pot barley.[15] Sir John Clerk commended windmills as cheaper than steam engines and just as effective, but later commentators stressed their susceptibility to the vagaries of the weather and the necessity of having elevated sites.[16]

As we saw, the steam engine had already appeared in Scotland by 1730 and took on an ever more dominant role as the 18th century progressed. Clerk hailed it as 'one of the noblest inventions of this or the last age',[17] but this sense of wonder at its mechanical ingenuity was tempered by a concern over the expense incurred in installing and running it. In 1770 Alexander Thomson, overseer of the Alloa coalworks, claimed that a 'fire engine' to drain newly discovered coals at Coallyland would cost £3,000-4,000, compared to a mere £400 for a level:

A fire engine is attended with great expense yearly besides the extraordinary expense of making and repairing new boylars, beams, pumps etc.[18]

For anyone running a small colliery there was the additional drawback that a 'fire engine' consumed large quantities of the very substance which its use made accessible. As late as 1812 water wheels were still being recommended for small mines in preference to 'expensive' steam engines.[19] Alexander Thomson was not alone in casting doubts on the usefulness of steam engines; water, where available, was the preferred source of power during the early part of the period,[20] and according to Duckham's admittedly conservative estimates, there were only fourteen or fifteen steam engines at Scottish collieries by 1769 and only eighty or so by 1800, not all of these latter necessarily still in use at that date.[21]

A similar range of alternative sources of power was available for raising coals. On the Midlothian coalfield, and doubtless elsewhere, coals were still being carried to the surface manually in 1830.[22] Horse gins were widely used during the early part of the period, but with the same drawbacks as those used in drainage. At Bo'ness, in 1740, a two-horse gin, 'of the best Newcastle sort', was recommended as a second choice to a water gin, and there is no doubt that water power would have been cheaper: according to calculations made in 1735, a water gin at Alloa could save £2,416 16s Scots per annum in labour, and could raise an extra £1,944 worth of coal.[23] In 1776 it was estimated that even a steam engine/water wheel combination could be operated at little more than three-fifths of the cost of a horse gin.[24]

No example has been found of wind power being employed in this context;

Sir John Clerk thought that it might be a good, though possibly dangerous, means of raising coals.[25] Steam power was a relative latecomer to winding. Duckham suggests that Scotland's first steam winding engine was erected at some time between 1777 and 1790; only a few more are recorded during the 1790s. Thereafter numbers are difficult to assess, but they continued to grow, mostly at the expense of horse gins.[26] As for water power, it was still recognised as a viable alternative in the early 19th century, but the Age of Steam had truly arrived, and even Robert Bald, having spoken highly of the water gins, had to concede that 'no more will be erected, excepting in situations where there is a good natural fall of water'.[27]

Sources of Finance

As with other sectors of the Scottish economy, control of the Scottish coal industry underwent a period of transition between 1730 and 1830. However, the nature of mineral rights meant that overall control continued to lie with the landowner, even though the individual tacksman or company might make all the necessary capital investment. In the case of collieries using water power, it was almost invariably the landowner who provided the capital needed to set up the machinery. This is much as one might expect; even where the coals were held in tack, mining remained an adjunct of the estate, to the extent that a landowner might provide expensive equipment such as drainage and haulage machinery in much the same way as he might supply the 'large graith' for tenanted corn mills. Most of the water engines and water gins were in the east of Scotland, where landowners tended to keep a close hold on coalmines, and in any case the lessee of a mine would have to make arrangements with the owner to obtain a supply of water before even contemplating the use of water power. Most of the few instances where the expense was borne by a tenant were in the west of Scotland: it was a Mr. Barker, lessee of minerals from the Duke of Buccleuch, who sank a pit shaft and built a water engine at Knockenjig near Kirkconnel, Dumfriesshire,[28] and the proprietors of a bleach-works at Arthurlie, Renfrewshire who apparently ran the small water-powered colliery on the Levern near Crofthead as a means of keeping their works in coals.[29]

Distribution and Chronology

Without doubt, some of the water engines and water gins established before 1730 were still in active use at that date. The Prestons of Valleyfield were still pursuing their Court of Session case in 1740, suggesting that their water engine was still being employed.[30] The (Old) Statistical Account refers to at least two more possible sites: at Clackmannan, a water engine driven by a lade from the Black Devon may be the one shown on a map dated 1713 (Figure 17), or at least a direct successor to it, whilst on the Durie estate in Fife, another engine, admittedly defunct by the 1790s, may have been of 17th-century origin.[31]

Evidence from other sources suggests the continued use of water engines at Kirkland, Fife, Tulliallan, Fife and Alloa, Clackmannanshire.[32] It need hardly be stated that all these survivals lay on the Fife-Clackmannanshire coalfield, where the use of water power in the coal industry had shown the strongest development during the period up to 1730.

Between 1730 and 1760 at least five additional water engines were erected. The first, at Balgonie, on the Fife Leven, was built about 1730-31;[33] at Alloa an earlier water engine, threatened with flooding from old workings, was supplemented by a machine with eight-inch diameter pumps and an eighteen-foot diameter wheel on an old pit shaft called Dickie's Sink.[34] About 1740, another eighteen-foot diameter wheel, fitted with reversible buckets, was installed for raising coals.[35] The workings on which these two engines were placed were apparently exhausted by 1764, but other engines were to follow.

At Cluny Bridge, Fife, a water engine was erected in 1738 or 1739 by one Stephen Row for the 10th Earl of Rothes.[36] This may well be the engine which appeared on Ainslie's 1775 map of Fife, and that mentioned by Thomson (1800)[37] as being on the River Ore. Duckham believes that Row was an Englishman and cites the Cluny Bridge engine as an example of English influence on the Scottish coal industry.[38] While this may have been true in this particular case, there was no shortage of Scottish initiative: at a later date John Rennie took an interest in the subject, and Andrew Meikle was consulted in connection with a water engine for the Leslie and Dadham coals.[39] In 1739, William Adam, the architect, built a coalworks at Pinkie, with a horse gin to provide drainage. This proving inadequate, he devised a scheme to utilise the waters of the River Esk to provide the motive power. A lade about a mile long was dug from the river to the southern edge of the hill on which Inveresk village stood. Encountering a bed of sand at this point, he sank a fifty-foot shaft to the bedrock and cut a channel four feet wide by six feet high, from the bottom of the shaft for a distance of eight hundred feet before returning the lade to surface level by means of a second shaft.[40] Apparently coal owners were still prepared to go to considerable expense to bring water power to collieries, much as they were prior to the invention of the steam engine. In William Adam there was at least one Scot with the technical expertise to bring it about.

Lastly, there is an unconfirmed reference in Payne's *Studies in Scottish Business History* to an engine built at Brora about 1748.[41] On the basis of the distribution of water engines before 1730 (Figure 18), it is not surprising to find that four of the six known additions between 1730 and 1760 were on the Fife-Clackmannanshire coalfield. The builder of the Pinkie water engine had close associations with the district, and the inspiration for the Brora engine may also have come from the same area.

The concentration of new engines on the Fife-Clackmannanshire coalfield is somewhat less marked between 1760 and 1800, but still apparent. Of the fourteen or so sites first identified during this period, no fewer than six lay within this area: a second engine was installed at Balgonie, in 1785,[42] and no fewer than three were erected at Balbirnie,[43] whilst at Backbank, north of Alloa, one was built at some time prior to 1799.[44] The sixth, the fall for which was taken over by Kirkland cotton and flax works, is first referred to in the late 1780s but may date back to the 17th century.[45] While this last mentioned had already ceased to function by 1790, and that at Backburn was no longer in use in 1820, two of the three Balbirnie engines and the one at Balgonie were still in use in 1830.[46]

Outside the Fife-Clackmannanshire area, there were two additional sites in Midlothian at Duddingston (pre-1776) and Cranston (1782);[47] At Craigheads, in Kilbarchan parish (Renfrewshire), the water-powered mine had already ceased to operate by 1782, whilst two near Lochwinnoch, in the same county, first appear on Ainslie's 1796 map.[48] At least two water engines were being used in the vicinity of Muirkirk ironworks during the late 18th century.[49] A report on the West Lothian coalfield, compiled in 1845, speaks of a water-wheel pump north of Oatridge in Ecclesmachan parish as having functioned 'at a very early period':[50] although no date is given, the fact that it was still remembered in 1845 suggests that it was still working no earlier than the second half of the 18th century. Lastly, something should be said of the unusual water engine at Byreburn, in Canonbie parish (Dumfriesshire). The engine, invented by a Mr. Keir, first appears in the (Old) Statistical Account, at which time it was said to have been newly constructed.[51]

With the exception of the two Midlothian sites, it was only in Fife and Clackmannanshire that water power was being used in large collieries. Of the Midlothian engines, Duddingston was assisted by a steam engine and Cranston by a windmill; elsewhere water power was only used at a handful of small-scale mines.

During the first three decades of the 19th century, only four new water engines are known to have been constructed: New Sauchie (Clackmannanshire), Douglas Water (Lanarkshire), Smithyhaugh (West Lothian) and Brora (Sutherland).[52] Of these, only Smithyhaugh, which dated from about 1825, is known to have originated within the period. The engine at Brora is particularly interesting in that it used water power for both pumping and winding:

> A powerful water-wheel keeps the mine dry and a small water-wheel with reverse buckets draws the coal to the bank. The pumps are in two lifts with $9\frac{1}{2}$ inch barrels, and the engine manages the whole growth in three hours out of the twenty-four.[53]

By the 19th century, water power was no match for steam in the Scottish coal industry, and it is significant that, with the exception of New Sauchie, where a well-established infrastructure already existed, the few sites established between 1800 and 1830 were at small-scale collieries or on small, isolated coalfields. Nevertheless, some existing sites, notably on the Fife Leven and in the Alloa area, continued to use water power until at least mid-century, and three sites in these areas are first recorded only in the New Statistical Account.[54]

Taking the period 1730-1830 as a whole, the distribution of water engines

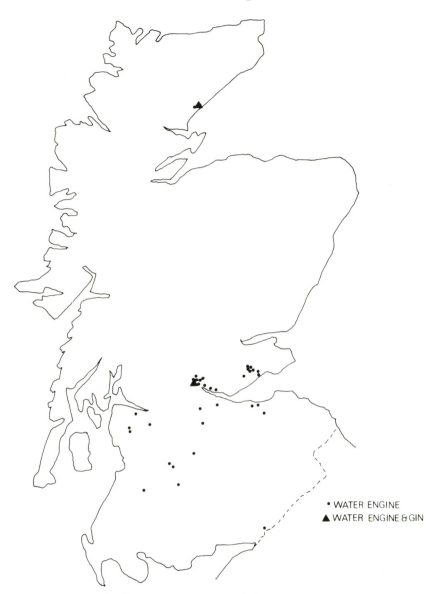

Fig 90. Distribution of colliery water engines and gins

falls into four major areas (Figure 90). Firstly, the Fife-Clackmannanshire coal-field, where the use of water power was already a prominent feature of the industry prior to 1730: here water power continued to offer a viable alterna-tive to steam power, utilising quite powerful falls on the Leven, Ore and Devon or existing artificial reservoirs such as Garmorn Dam (Alloa) and Peppermill Dam (Kincardine). More water engines were used in this area than in all the rest of Scotland, and although this might be interpreted as conservatism, the way in which the technology of pumping and winding by water power was developed in the area argues against such a view. The second area, the Lothians, comprises a group of three water engines to the east of Edinburgh and three to the west.[55] Here there was no tradition of water-powered mine drainage, although one of the area's greatest authorities on mining, Sir John Clerk, looked favourably upon it. The smaller mines continued to depend on levels or horse gins, while larger, deeper workings took readily to using steam power. In the third area, Renfrewshire, where coal mining developed relatively late in comparison with the east, steam power would have been the norm, although topography and drainage characteristics favoured the use of water power in some small-scale workings. The small, isolated collieries in the Southern Uplands, which make up the fourth group, were similarly disposed towards the use of water power, even though it seems to have arrived at a late stage. The limited production from these collieries must also have militated against the use of steam power on the grounds of cost and coal consumption. The same considerations applied to the outlying coalfield at Brora.

The coal industry was the first in Scotland to make use of steam power which was available as an increasingly effective alternative to water power throughout the period. In the face of this competition, the continuing interest shown in the development of water-engine design and the construction of some thirty or so engines between 1730 and 1830 suggests that, in Scotland at least, the advent of the steam engine did not bring an immediate end to the age of water power.

Case Study: Balgonie and Balbirnie

It has just been suggested that water power could still find a place in Scottish coal mining well after the advent of steam power. Nowhere is this more evident than at Balbirnie and Balgonie.

In 1731 Andrew Marshall, wright to Erskine of Carnock, installed a water engine on the 5th Earl of Leven's Balgonie colliery.[56] This was by no means the first water engine in the area: the Register of the Privy Seal contains passing reference to engines on the Wemyss and Durie estates, and during the 1710s David Landale of Burns built one, fitted with pumps, in Markinch parish.[57] The choice of Andrew Marshall as wright is an interesting one; Erskine of Carnock was one of the parties to a protracted Court of Session case over water supplies to collieries in west Fife (Chapter 5, p. 69) and, as his wright, Marshall could be expected to have a considerable body of relevant knowledge. The total cost of the engine, which apparently had pumps driven by beams and cranks, was £3,995 16s 6d Scots; according to the (Old) Statistical Account, it had nine-inch working barrels which drained the coal to a depth of thirty fathoms.[58]

In 1732 the coal, with its engine, was leased to John and Alexander Landale, almost certainly relatives of the David Landale who had been involved in the earlier water-engine.[59] In practice, the Balgonie engine was not powerful enough and was overcome by excessive water in the workings.[60] The Landales replaced it with a windmill fitted with eight-inch diameter pumps which dried the coal to a depth of sixteen fathoms,[61] but in 1740 George Balfour had had a level dug to drain his nearby Balbirnie coal, thereby enabling him to undersell coal from Balgonie. The local market was unable to support both collieries, and with transport costs too high to justify exporting, Balgonie was forced to close down in 1743.[62]

Another thirty years were to pass before water power was again used at either Balgonie or Balbirnie. The Balfours continued to use their coal level, but by the late 1770s it would appear that something else was needed, for in 1775, and again in 1778, plans were drawn up for a water engine.[63] An engine with two fourteen-inch barrels was installed about 1780; by 1794 another two had been brought into use with eleven- and fifteen-inch barrels.[64]

In the meantime, the abandoned Balgonie workings had re-opened and, possibly in response to the Balfours' initiative, the Earl of Leven had engaged a Leeds engineer, John Green, to look into ways of clearing the workings of water.[65] In November 1784 he advised that they 'should prosecute the Landales' plan' and erect a water engine to the north-east of the windmill. According to Green, the coal could be worked to a depth of forty or fifty fathoms with a water wheel of thirty feet or more in diameter driven by the River Leven; to suggestions that a steam engine should be used instead he replied that 'supposing myself a tack(s)man for 20 years [I] would not be debar'd the water of Leven for five thousand pound'.[66] In 1785 the water engine was constructed with a twenty-six foot diameter wheel and two pumps of twelve and a quarter inch barrel which, it was hoped, would drain the coal to a depth of thirty fathoms.[67] In practice these hopes were not immediately fulfilled. As there was already a level to a depth of five fathoms, the water engine had only to raise the water by twenty-five fathoms; this, it was envisaged, would be achieved by using two separate lifts of twelve and a half fathoms, the first feeding into a cistern from which the second drew water. However, by April 1787 the engine pit had only been sunk to twenty-two fathoms, six fathoms above the 'pavement' of the coal. Such had been the volume of water encountered that an extra set of seven-inch pumps had been installed at the lower level, and this proving inadequate, two sets of twelve-inch pumps had been applied, but all to no avail. At that time it was feared that the engine 'must soon go to ruin', and it was recommended that a level be dug to the foot of the engine pit.[68] By whatever means, the problem was eventually overcome, for the engine is mentioned in the (Old) Statistical Account (1794) and was almost certainly one of the three water engines on the Leven referred to by Thomson (1800), the two others being at Balbirnie.[69] During the early 19th century, water power continued to be used at both collieries. Balgonie in particular found a new *raison d'être* as a supplier of coal to the ill-fated Balgonie (or Leven) ironworks, the partners in which took it in tack in 1802.[70] In 1803 the ironworks company suffered its first bankruptcy,[71] having laid out £1,000 on improving the colliery, and in 1805, when the iron-works and colliery were re-let, the partners were given the right to put a new water engine on the same stretch of the River Leven as the existing one, and a second one to drain to a greater depth.[72]

For all its good intentions, the ironworks company allowed the water engine to fall into decay, and by 1808, when the company suffered another sequestra-tion, the wheel of the engine was reported to be 'an entire wreck'. As a tem-porary measure to help clear the water hampering work at the colliery, it was suggested that the buckets be patched with Scots fir until a new wheel could be prepared at an estimated cost of £180.[73] The engine was patched up, and the company resurfaced for a second time, but by 1813 it was evident from a report by James Scott that the superficial repairs of a few years earlier had been totally inadequate:

> The axle-tree and arms . . . are totally decayed, and the rings and buckets which have within these few years been attached to these rotten supports, are ready every moment to tumble to pieces by their own weight, so that a sufficient power of water cannot be applied without risking the destruction of the whole.
>
> The stonework which supports the water wheel, and which has likewise within these few years undergone a superficial repair, has been so imperfectly executed that the water, insinuating itself betwixt the old and new work, has thrust out the former, so as to rub upon the water wheel, and it is impossible to warrant her going on for twenty four hours.
>
> The beams are evidently rotting in many places, and altho a coating of paint prevents an examination of every part, the presumption is strong that they are totally insufficient. In short, a radical repair is absolutely necessary, if it is intended to save the coalliery; and this repair will embrace every part of the present machinery, the pumps excepted.

The cost of repairs was put at £450 plus £200 worth of mason work.[74] As a last desperate measure Thomas Lewis, the lessee, was offered exemption from rent on the ironworks for the year 1813-14, on condition that he spent £2,000 on repairs to the colliery over a three-year period. However, by this time the iron-works was once more in trouble: in January 1814 Lewis proposed to abandon it; the colliery, already troubled by embezzlement and labour shortages, suffered a roof fall in the 'seven-foot' coal, and this too had to be given up.[75] This time the ironworks company failed to re-emerge.

It would seem that the colliery, its fortunes no longer tied to those of the ironworks company, was put in order: from 1817 the coal was worked by the Tyne Ironworks, and in 1823 it was sold to Balfour of Balbirnie.[76] That the water engine was rebuilt is evident from a plan of the River Leven dated 1830, which also showed two water engines on the Balbirnie coal.[77]

It would appear that at least one of the Balbirnie engines was rebuilt shortly after 1830: a plan by D. Fernie, Cupar, dated 1831, shows a high breast-shot wheel over thirty feet in diameter by five feet eight inches wide, of a light-weight construction, which incorporated curved buckets and cross-over bracing bars.[78] In view of the long period over which water power had been used, and the advanced design of the wheel, this was almost certainly a replacement for a redundant water engine. At the time of the New Statistical Account the Balgonie coal was being drained by two water engines, one of twenty-five fathoms draught, two fathoms below the coal, the other draining twenty acres of a lower seam;[79] as late as the 1850s the two Balbirnie engines were still in use but the Balgonie engine, though still visible, had ceased to function.[80]

In the Balgonie-Balbirnie area the use of water power in the coal industry had started before 1730 and continued for some time after 1830 well into the age of steam. While the water engine at Balgonie had suffered from its associations with the iron company, this in no way invalidated water power as a competitor to steam power, as experiences at the more successful Balbirnie pit show.[81] But coal was not the only extractive industry to use water power: in the next chapter we consider lead mining which, unlike coal mining, did not have immediate access to coal for steam engines.

NOTES

1. See Chapter 5, page 71.
2. See Dickinson, H. W., *A Short History of the Steam Engine*, Cambridge, 1938.
3. See Chapter 5, page 70.
4. *OSA* XIII, 608, Langholm, Dumfriesshire; *NSA* IV, 486, Canonbie, Dumfriesshire.
5. Duckham, B. F., *A History of the Scottish Coal Industry*, Vol. 1 (1700-1815), Newton Abbot, 1970, 68.
6. Smeaton: Ashton, T. S. C. & Sykes, J., *The Coal Industry of the Eighteenth Century*, Manchester, 1929, 58; Rennie: NLS Acc.5111/25/1: Water Engines at Balbirnie c.1784; Meikle: SRO GD288/315, /317.
7. Bald, R., *A General View of the Coal Trade in Scotland*, Edinburgh, 1808, 88-9.
8. See Dickinson, *op. cit.*
9. Bald, *op. cit.*, 89.
10. See Chapter 25, page 433.
11. SRO GD18/1069: Sir John Clerk, 'A Dissertation on Coal and Coal Mining', 1740.
12. SRO RHP600 (1776); Hume, D., *Decisions of the Court of Session, 1781-1822*, Edinburgh & London, 1839, 510-1; Duckham, *op. cit.*, 75-6.
13. See, for example, SRO GD237/71/1: Memorandum of Sheriffhall Coals, January 1760; Bald, *op. cit.*, 6.
14. SRO GD18/1069: Clerk, 'Dissertation'.
15. Wight, A., *Present State of Husbandry in Scotland*, 4 vols., Edinburgh, 1778-84, IV, 634. For other examples of wind pumps, see Chapter 27 (lime works) and Chapter 29 (slate quarries).
16. SRO GD18/1069: Clerk, 'Dissertation'; Bald, *op. cit.*, 8.
17. SRO GD18/1069: Clerk, 'Dissertation'.

18. SRO GD124/17/559: Memorandum, Alexander Thomson, overseer of the Coalworks of Alloa and Coallyland to the Trustees of the Mar Estate.

19. Singer, W., *General View of the Agriculture of Dumfriesshire*, Edinburgh, 1812, 36-7.

20. See, for example, SRO GD237/71/1: Memorandum of Sheriffhall Coals, January 1750.

21. Duckham, *op. cit.*, 83; Duckham, B. F., 'English Influences in the Scottish Coal Industry, 1700-1815', in Butt, J. & Ward, J. T. (eds.), *Scottish Themes. Essays in Honour of Professor S. G. E. Lythe*, Edinburgh, 1976, 33.

22. Duckham, *op. cit.* (1970), 94.

23. SRO GD75/530: Proposals for additions and alterations in working the Duke of Hamilton's main coal at Bo'ness, 14th February 1740.

24. Smeaton, J., *Reports of the Late John Smeaton*, 3 vols., London, 1812, II, 375.

25. SRO GD18/1069: Clerk, 'Dissertation'.

26. Duckham, *op. cit.* (1970).

27. Bald, *op. cit.*, 90.

28. Brown, J., *The History of Sanquhar*, Dumfries, 1891, 341-2. This took place after 1830 and is therefore not strictly speaking within the scope of this chapter. However, as water power was of such minor significance in the coal industry after 1830, it has been included.

29. Taylor, C., *The Levern Delineated*, Glasgow, 1831, 66.

30. OSP 4:87, 80:7.

31. Chapter 5, Figure 18; *OSA* XIV, 615, Clackmannan, Clackmannanshire.

32. Chapter 5, Figure 18; Kincardine: *OSA* XI, 553, Tulliallan, Fife; Kirkland: SRO RHP615 (c.1790); Alloa: SRO GD124/17/559 (c.1730).

33. SRO GD26/5/334.

34. SRO GD124/17/559. Although a water engine could not be built to Sorocold's design, it is evident that a more primitive type of machine was constructed, using water from Gartmorn Dam: *NSA* VIII, 27, Alloa, Clackmannanshire.

35. Developments at Alloa are particularly complicated. SRO GD124/17/559 refers to an existing machine and gives detailed costings for a new one which had already been built (Dickie's Sink). Bald (*op. cit.*, 88-9) implies that the Alloa winding engine was built c.1740. By 1764 these workings had been exhausted and Coallyland Pit opened, to be drained by a Newcomen Engine (*NSA* VIII, 27), but in the meantime (c.1760), it appears that another colliery, at Carsebridge, had been set up. This certainly had a water engine in the 1830s (*NSA* VIII, 28), but it has not been ascertained how far back this goes. Duckham quotes *OSA* VIII, 592 and Bald, 89, to the effect that in 1774 a single wheel was both draining the mines and winding the coals, although *OSA* VIII, 592 specifically states that, by the 1790s at least, two separate wheels were employed. In either case, the pre-1764 workings (on which the 1740 winding engine had been sited) had not been re-opened. This later example must have been elsewhere, possibly at Carsebridge.

36. Duckham, *op. cit.* (1970), 80.

37. Thomson, J., *General View of the Agriculture of Fife*, Edinburgh, 1800, 21.

38. Duckham, *op. cit.* (1976), 32.

39. Meikle: SRO GD288/315, /317; Rennie: NLS Acc.5111/25/1.

40. *NSA* I, 250, Inveresk, Midlothian; Pococke, R., 'Tours in Scotland, 1747, 1750, 1760', *SHS* I (1887), 311.

41. Payne, P. L. (ed.), *Studies in Scottish Business History*, Edinburgh, 1967.

42. *OSA* XII, 539-40, Markinch, Fife.

43. *Ibid.*, 543. These may include the engine(s) on the Cadham/Leslie coal, projected in the 1770s and built by the late 1780s: SRO GD288/299, /300, /301, /315, /317; SRO RHP23784, 23740-1, 23697, 23704.

44. SRO RHP221 (1799), 'Back Bank Engine Pit', with tail lade to R. Devon (NS906961); SRO RHP291 (1820), 'Old Mill Pit'.

45. SRO RHP615, n.d. (c.1790).

46. SRO RHP770 (1830).

47. Duddingston: Hume, *op. cit.*, 510-1; SRO RHP600 (1776); Cranston: Wight, *op. cit.*, IV, 634.

48. Crawford, G. (revised Semple, W.), *The History of Renfrewshire*, Paisley, 1782, 133; Ainslie, J., (Map of) Renfrewshire, 1796.

49. Hume, J. R., 'Water Mills of the River Ayr', *AAC* 2nd series, VIII (1967-9), 44.

50. Forsyth, C., 'On the Mines, Minerals & Geology of West Lothian', *TH&AS* 3rd Series, II (1845-7), 257.

51. *OSA* XII, 608, Langholm, Dumfriesshire; *NSA* IV, 486, Canonbie, Dumfriesshire.

52. New Sauchie: SRO GD124/17/587: Report on the books of Alloa Colliery Nov. 1828-9; Douglas Water: Forrest, W., (Map of) Lanarkshire, 1813; Smithyhaugh: Forsyth, *op. cit.*, 233; Brora: Adam, R. J., 'Sutherland Estate Management, 1802-16', *SHS* 4th Series, VIII, IX (1972-3), VIII, 147.

53. Adam, *op. cit.*, 147.

54. Dollar: *NSA* VIII, 85, Dollar, Clackmannanshire; Carsebridge: *NSA* VIII, 28, Alloa, Clackmannanshire; Camlarg: *NSA* V, 312, Dalmellington, Ayrshire.

55. For the sake of convenience, a water engine at Slamannan, Stirlingshire, which first appears on the first Ordnance Survey maps, is included in this group.

56. SRO GD26/5/334, /329.

57. SRO GD26/5/323, /324.

58. Ibid. *OSA* XII, 539-40, Markinch, Fife.

59. *OSA* XII, 539-40, Markinch, Fife; Duckham, *op. cit.* (1970), 77.

60. *OSA* XII, 539-40, Markinch, Fife.

61. *Ibid*; SRO GD26/5/363. *OSA* gives the depth as 14 fathoms, but the 16 fathoms mentioned in a report of 1787 is probably the more accurate.

62. *OSA* XII, 539-40, Markinch, Fife.

63. SRO RHP23697, 23704.

64. *OSA* XII, 543, Markinch, Fife. At least one of these may have been built at Cadham Colliery, where the Balfours are known to have installed a water engine in the 1780s: SRO GD288/299.

65. SRO GD26/5/352; Duckham, *op. cit.* (1976), 32.

66. SRO GD26/5/352.

67. *OSA* XII, 539-40, Markinch, Fife.

68. SRO GD26/5/363: The Report of the Balgonie Coal, April 1787.

69. Thomson, *op. cit.*, 21; *OSA* XI, 539-40, Markinch, Fife.

70. SRO GD26/5/371/1. The ironworks are dealt with in more detail in Chapter 25.

71. Duckham, *op. cit.* (1970), 146.

72. SRO GD26/5/371/1.

73. SRO GD26/5/371/2 (Nov. 12th 1808).

74. Ibid. (May 19th 1813).

75. Ibid. (1813-14).

76. Duckham, *op. cit.* (1970), 146.

77. SRO RHP770.
78. SRO RHP23781.
79. *NSA* IX, 659, Markinch, Fife.
80. *OS* 1st Edition 6″/mile Sheet 24 (1856).
81. SRO GD26/5/368/7.

24

Mining and Metallurgy: Non-Ferrous Metals

Whilst the mining of non-ferrous metals shared with coal mining a need for drainage, and to some extent haulage facilities, additional processes, notably crushing, washing and smelting, had to be carried out before a finished product was arrived at. As we saw earlier, water-power had been applied to the industry prior to 1730, but only at the two adjacent centres of Leadhills and Wanlockhead had lead mines been exploited to any extent. The years after the Union of 1707 had seen a revival in prospecting, with great, if often misplaced, expectations of riches, further prompted by the spectacular success of the Alva silver mines.[1] Although these hopes were, in many cases, ill-founded, several productive veins were discovered and exploited, a process which was to continue until well after 1830. In those cases where reasonably productive workings remained active for a number of years, water power was usually employed in one capacity or another.

Technology

Drainage

Throughout the period 1730-1830 lead mining operations were persistently hampered by flooded workings. As with coal mining, a number of techniques could be called upon to remedy the situation, but considerations of geology, topography and situation relative to fuel supplies made some options relatively more attractive, others less so, than in the coal industry.

Day levels were extensively used in the Leadhills-Wanlockhead district and to a smaller extent elsewhere; however, the hard upland rocks in which lead ore occurred made excavation a much more difficult task than in the softer lowland rocks of the coalfields. At Wanlockhead the Friendly Mining Society tried for some time to cut a new level, but by 1736, having proceeded in the wrong direction for forty fathoms, they had been forced to start again, at a cost of £11-12 per fathom.[2] A level to the Scots Mining Company's Susanna vein at Leadhills took no less than twenty-three years (1772-1795) to excavate, even though the distance covered was less than a mile.[3] To make matters worse, veins of lead ore were much more elusive than the extensive, often gently sloping seams in which coal occurred: a vein might cross a mine working vertically,[4] branch off in different directions or disappear entirely, only to reappear at several fathoms' distance. Thus the necessity to work below level came about more immediately and more generally than in coal mining, and if workings were not to be abandoned, some means had to be found of raising water to the level.

Hand pumps might be used as a short-term expedient where volumes of water were small, but their limited capability and their intensive use of labour usually led to the introduction of a more powerful agency. Water engines, already developed for use in the coal industry, were an obvious choice: the Wanlockhead mines had one by 1730[5] and no fewer than five by 1743.[6] In 1763 preparations were being made to place one on the Miln Vein at Leadhills,[7] and on a tour of inspection in 1779 John Smeaton found one on the Susanna Vein, below Poutshiel level:

> This engine has a twenty-four feet water-wheel overshot, and draws a column at two lifts of thirty-one fathoms, the bores of the pumps being 7½ inches working barrels; it makes a five feet stroke, and when I saw it, made 5½ strokes in each barrel per minute.

A second wheel, thirty feet in diameter, was being constructed above the first, with a view to 'drying' a further thirty fathoms below the existing engine sump. Both engines were situated underground.[8] In his report on the flooded Islay mines in 1770 Alexander Shirreff, manager of the Leadhills mines, recommended the use of 'properly placed' water engines in conjunction with a system of levels.[9]

Water-powered drainage was not, however, without its problems. The Leadhills-Wanlockhead mining district, situated as it was at the headwaters of the Clyde and the Nith, had no command of large streams but managed to compensate for this, to some extent, by the establishment of an elaborate system of watercourses which fed not only water engines but also dressing and smelting installations.[10] Even so, the available water sometimes failed to meet requirements or dried up completely. It was in these circumstances and despite the cost of bringing fuel to the mines that steam engines were installed at both Leadhills and Wanlockhead in the late 18th and 19th centuries. At Wanlockhead a steam engine, apparently only the second Watt machine in Scotland, was placed on Margaret's Vein in 1778;[11] an additional engine was put to work on the same vein in 1787.[12] Between 1800 and 1827 no fewer than five steam engines were established on Beltongrain and Cove Veins, with an aggregate of 268 horse power.[13] Nevertheless steam did not quite displace water power, for in 1822 a water wheel was still in use on Old Glencrieve Vein.[14] The Susanna Vein at Leadhills carried at least one steam engine from 1792, but here too water power continued to find a place: on the Gripps level, for example, there were two water wheels in use in 1791.[15]

The extensive use of steam power had only been made possible by the high prices which lead was fetching. The boom started about 1790, and by 1809 prices had reached £32 per ton. After the Peace of 1815 they fell back to £16 per ton and recovered to £24-25 until 1821, when they settled down to £18-19 until 1827. With the removal of tariffs, cheap Spanish lead from the Sierra Morena brought prices down to a mere £11 per ton.[16] By 1824 the lessees of Wanlockhead were proposing to form a new company with more capital to help overcome drainage difficulties. At the time it was admitted that they could not afford 'the enormous expense' of running two large steam engines on Beltongrain Vein, and that they were only being kept going as an incentive to the new company.[17] In the event, the falling price of lead precipitated the abandonment of steam power and the reinstatement of water power in the form of water pressure engines.

The water pressure engine or 'Hungarian Machine' enjoyed widespread use in Germany during the early 18th century, and in 1765 William Westgarth installed the first machine in Britain at the Coal Cleugh lead mines in Northumberland.[18] Subsequently it was improved by Smeaton and Trevithick: as early as 1779 Smeaton was advocating its use at Leadhills, but it was apparently not applied in Scotland until the price slump of the 1820s and early 1830s forced companies to abandon steam power.[19] The first Scottish water engine, by Deans of Bolton, was installed at Wanlockhead about 1833. The National Library of Scotland's copy of Smeaton's *Reports* contains a pencilled account of the engine, initialled L.D.B.J. and dated December 1834. According to the writer, the engine was 'undoubtedly most perfect and powerful in all respects beyond belief. The fall of water is 28 fathoms and the diameter of the cylinder is 13¾ inches, the length of stroke 18 feet and the number of strokes varies from 3.6 to 4.2 in a minute. The engine is at present raising about 12,000 lb of water and machinery and works with great ease and regularity. The expense was about £600 Sterling — the repairs in two years amounted to a mere trifle and the only attendant required is a boy to supply grease occasionally . . .'[20] By the 1850s a second engine had been brought into use, but on the Old Glencrief Vein a conventional water wheel pump was still being used in the 1860s.

Leadhills was slower to install water pressure engines, largely on account of a protracted legal dispute over water rights between the Leadhills Company and the Scots Mining Company. This dragged on from 1828 to 1861 and was eventually resolved by the Scots Mining Company's resigning its lease to the Leadhills Company.[21] By 1864 the latter had installed water-powered machinery totalling 550 horse power and including four water pressure engines.[22] A much simpler device, the water bucket pump, was brought into use at Wanlockhead during the mid-19th century; its remains can still be seen today.[23]

Haulage

In lead mining the use of water power in haulage was even less common than in the coal industry. Horizontal or sloping adits were widely used in addition to vertical shafts, and with water at such a premium in the two major mining centres, the opportunity to use it in this capacity seldom arose. The only examples to be identified date from a later period: Leadhills, in 1864, had four water wheels for drawing ore to the surface and one water engine, possibly by the Newcastle engineer W. G. Armstrong, who is known to have applied it to rotary motion elsewhere.[24] Steam-powered winding gear is known to have been used at Wanlockhead in the 1830s.[25]

Mine Ventilation

It may be recalled from the previous chapter that Clerk of Penicuik recommended the use of water power in ventilating coal mines. The Penicuik muniments contain an unusual sketch of a combined water wheel and trompe, the latter being applied not only to the hearth of a smelter but also to providing a supply of clean air to a mine[26] (Figure 91). John Rennie's notebook has an interesting reference to a ventilating machine for lead mines devised, and possibly installed, by Mr. Stirling (the Scots Mining Company's manager); in Rennie's view it was basically a Catalan forge or trompe.[27] It is tempting to link this with the drawing.

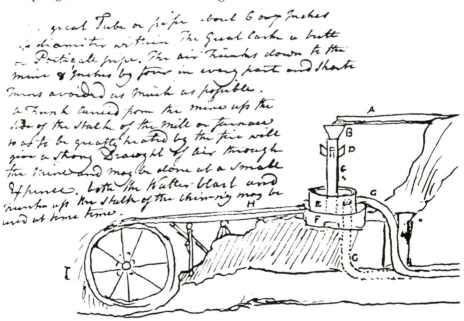

Fig 91. Water wheel and trompe. The intention was that the passage of water down the cylinder (C) would draw in air through the inlets (D) and thereby ventilate the mine. There is no certainty that the device would have worked. *SRO GD18/5955*

Ore Crushing and Dressing

Not all of the material brought to the surface contained lead, and before it could be smelted, all extraneous matter had to be removed. This was achieved by breaking down the material into small particles and washing the crushed product in such a way as to separate off the galena. A stamp mill had already been used by Sir Bevis Bulmer in the late 16th century (p.77). This, the simplest form of crushing machinery, utilised the same cam and pestle principle as was used in paper making, bleaching and a variety of other industrial processes. Alexander Telfer, who with his brother William had taken over the Friendly Mining Society's share of the Wanlockhead mines in 1734, was by 1743 using 'a machine that goes with a large wheel for beating and stamping of such coarse ore and spar as could not be done to advantage another way'.[28] In 1780 John Smeaton drew up plans for another stamping mill at Wanlockhead, but from contemporary sources it would seem that at Lead-hills, and doubtless elsewhere, at least part of the crushing was still being undertaken manually.[29]

During the early 19th century, more powerful machines, not unlike outsized malt rollers, came into fairly common use,[30] and it was doubtless a crushing mill of this type that was constructed by 'experienced German miners' at Tyndrum about 1840.[31] At Carsphairn a thirty-foot diameter water wheel was used to drive crushing machinery about 1845.[32] According to Phillips & Darlington, edgerunners and horizontal millstones were sometimes used to pulverise the ore into a fine powder, but this was more generally true of silver and gold ores than of those of lead;[33] no examples have been uncovered in Scotland. Once crushed, the metal-bearing particles were separated out in water by means of sieves, cisterns and buddles, all of which relied on the relatively greater density of these particles. It is difficult to ascertain when water power was first applied to this purpose in Scotland; a 'wash mill' at Leadhills appears on Forrest's 1813 map of Lanarkshire and on later plans,[34] but no other authenticated examples have been found for the period up to 1830.

Smelting

During the 18th and early 19th centuries the two principal means of smelting lead were the smelting hearth and the reverberatory furnace; of these, only the former used water power. According to Smout,[35] the reverberatory furnace used eight times as much coal as the smelting hearth and utilised no peat. This added fifty per cent to the cost of smelting and made air furnaces very unpopular unless there was a chronic shortage of water to drive the bellows of a blast furnace. Notwithstanding this deterrent, comparative trials were held from time to time. In 1735 experiments at Leadhills, involving 'mills' belonging to the Earl of Hopetoun and a Mr. Lowthian, and a 'furnace' belonging to the Scots Mining Company, showed that while the furnace produced slightly more lead (64 cwt as against 61 and 62 cwt), the cost at £3 18s 5d, was almost three times as high as the £1 6s 11½d expended at the Earl's mill and the time taken ninety-four hours as against only sixty at the mills.[36] Again, in 1792, the Lead-hills Company had recently taken to using a reverberatory furnace which,

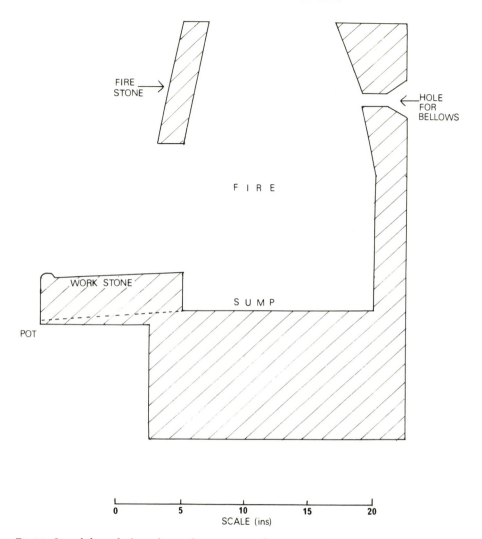

FIRE
STONE →

HOLE
FOR
BELLOWS

F I R E

WORK STONE

SUMP

POT

0   5   10   15   20

SCALE (ins)

Fig 92. Scotch hearth, based on a description in the Hopetoun leadmining papers

while avoiding the problems experienced by the Scots Mining Company's smelter, had difficulties of its own.[37]

It should be stressed that these were isolated occurrences; the general practice, from Strontian in the north to Blackcraig in the South, was to use the open or 'Scotch' hearth (Figure 92). Pococke, on one of his tours of Scotland (1747-1760), came across them in Leadhills:

> They do not smelt with a furnace but in smelt mills on common hearths blown with bellows. They smelt it with coal, turf and lime — a horse load of coal, twelve stone, two loads of turf, and one load of lime of eight bushels. They used the coal of Douglas eight miles off.[38]

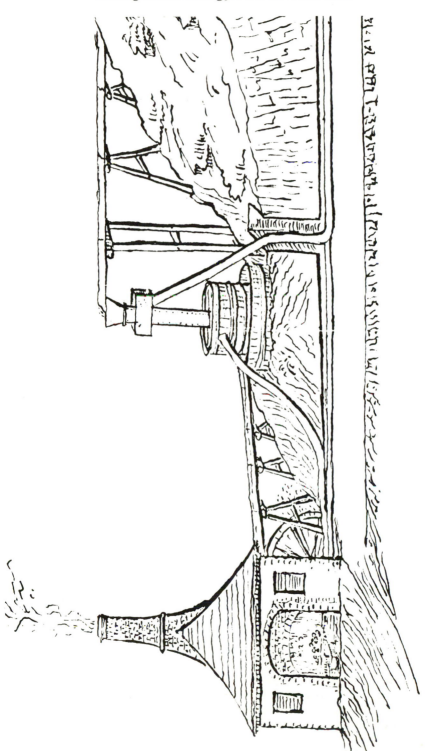

Fig 93. Trompe and smelter, a variation on Fig 91

PLAN   ELEVATION

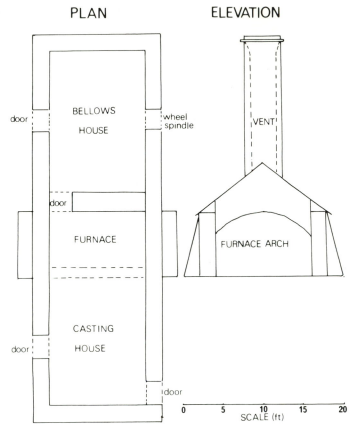

Fig 94. Plan and elevation of a lead smelter at Blackcraig, Kirkcudbrightshire

Some indication of the appearance and layout of 18th-century smelters can be gained from two contemporary plans (Figures 93 and 94). At a later period smelters became more complex: by the 1860s Leadhills had two roasting furnaces, one reverberatory furnace, four ore hearths and one slag hearth, the blast to the hearths being provided by a water wheel working two air cylinders.[39]

Whilst smelting on site reduced the volume of material to be transported by two thirds, and doubled its value per ton,[40] a dependence on water power exposed smelting to the same problems encountered in draining by that means. In 1741 Alexander Telfer was complaining that, as a result of another company's decision to replace a surface gin with an underground level, his smelting mills would lose their water supply and would be 'laid quite idle except in the time of great rains; or unless they were thrown down and new ones built lower down the water, which . . . could not be done under £1,500 Stg'.[41] During the year 1783-4 the Tyndrum smelter was out of action for a total of eighteen weeks on account of frosts and repairs following spells of bad weather.[42]

In view of the albeit temporary vogue for steam power in draining and haulage, it is perhaps surprising that no instance has been found of its use in smelting. Perhaps the ability to stockpile ore made a smelter shutdown a less serious event than the accumulation of water in workings, which could close otherwise productive workings for several years.

Shot Mills

Shot mills are known to have existed at Creetown from about 1780 and at Leadhills from 1834.[43] Regrettably, no technical details have survived in relation to either mill.

In all, and notwithstanding its temporary subservience to steam power, water power was of crucial importance to a number of processes in the mining and manufacture of lead, an importance which was maintained for a considerable period after 1830.

Sources of Finance.

During the late 16th and early 17th centuries the 'El Dorado' myth had been a powerful force in motivating prospecting in Scotland. After the Union of 1707 and the Rebellion of 1715, Scotland's more stable political climate and her closer association with England brought about a renewed interest, further prompted by Sir John Erskine of Alva's silver finds.[44] Undeterred by a high failure rate, successive would-be miners continued to show an unfounded optimism throughout the period.

The Landowner

Whilst few Scottish landowners had the requisite capital to work directly lead mines on their own lands, this was no deterrent to prospecting, for in the event of ores turning up, an individual or company could generally be found to take on their exploitation, still leaving the landowner with one sixth of any lead produced.[45] In the 1790s the Earl of Stair was actively prospecting in the New Luce area of Wigtownshire, while at the opposite corner of the Scottish mainland Sir John Sinclair of Ulbster, having already found what he believed to be a promising vein, had taken matters one step further by referring the matter to a London-based company, with detailed proposals for a lease.[46] All too often, however, supposedly promising finds turned out to be too small or too inaccessible to exploit, and even when mines were established, these were not infrequently given up after only a few years.[47]

Where ores showed more potential for sustained exploitation, landowners might occasionally work them directly through a manager: for several years the Earl of Hopetoun worked an area at Leadhills east of Glengonnar Burn, before leasing it to the Leadhills Mining Company in 1772.[48] However, the family's accumulated wealth and lead-mining experience must have set it apart from the majority of Scottish landowners. Sir Alexander Murray of Stanhope, having acquired the Ardnamurchan peninsula, invested some of his own capital in developing the Strontian lead mines before transferring them to a company in 1724.[49] Murray also took a tack of mines on Campbell of Shawfield's Islay estate, about 1730, although the manner in which he worked them showed a singular lack of concern for their prosperity:

> . . . Stanhope Murray took a lease from Shawfield, and promis'd to keep a certain number of myners constantly at work and cary on the work in a regular mineral order; but he never came himself, but trusted the work to an Ilay gentleman, who had no manner of skill of the matter. All he did was . . . to let bargains to a few of the country people, who had litle skill and litle good encouragement. But they promis'd to deliver ore at the Former price, and continued for 2 or 3 years poutering up and down the country, until Shawfield saw his country abused to little purpose. He got quit of them, and carried on the work in his own name by his factor there.[50]

Although some landowners did try to go it alone, it was a more customary practice, and certainly a safer one, to set up a company and take shares in it. As this aspect belongs more properly to the next section, no more will be said on the matter in the present context. Suffice to say that lead mining, with its heavy investment in capital and skills and its extremely high financial risks, was not an area into which the majority of Scottish landowners could afford to venture alone.

Companies

By 1730 the company, working on an *ad hoc* basis or with wider commitments, was already the customary unit of organisation in the Scottish lead-mining industry, which had become one of the first sectors of the Scottish economy to attract English capital. At that time the Wanlockhead mines were being worked by two firms, the Friendly Mining Society and the Company for Smelting Down Lead with Coal. The former was said to be made up of a number of gentlemen of London, Newcastle and Edinburgh, but the latter had its origins in the North-East of England.[51] The Scots Mining Company was, initially, Scottish in name only, for although Sir John Erskine of Alva held the original lease, and promoted the company, the majority of its shareholders were London merchants; indeed, on at least one occasion it was referred to as the London Company.[52]

Undoubtedly these companies held excellent credentials and sufficient expertise to carry out their work in 'a regular mineral order'. At Strontian, however, mining during the 1730s was dominated by 'mine adventurers' of more dubious skill and integrity. The company headed by the Duke of Norfolk, to whom Sir Alexander Murray leased the mines in 1724, had some semblance of respectability with General Wade, two Glasgow merchants and Sir Alexander himself numbered among the dozen or so partners.[53] Another partner, however, Sir Archibald Grant of Monymusk, had misappropriated funds from his own 'Charitable Corporation for the Relief of the Industrious Poor', and only his return to Scotland and subsequent contribution to agricultural Improvement redeemed his name in history.[54] Notwithstanding this 'flaw', the company seems to have shown serious intent for, if we are to believe Murray himself,

> they . . . erected several necessary buildings at Strontian, such as a smelting miln with four common hearths, a bridge on oaken piles [a]cross [th]e river, a handsome house for their manager, clerks and office, besides others with their workmen, stores etc. . . .[55]

Although the company made a loss, and smelted only 244 tons of lead over four years, it was saved by the arrival of the hapless York Buildings Company.

Originally founded as the Company of Undertakers for Re-using the Thames Water in York Buildings, the company later turned its attentions to Scotland which, in the years after the 1715 Rebellion, appeared to be a land of readily exploitable natural resources. Besides the Strontian lead mines, it took on the Earl of Winton's forfeited estate in East Lothian (including coal and salt works), built saw mills and iron mills in Strathspey, and took a lease of the Tartreven (Hilderston) lead and silver mines in West Lothian.[56] Invariably its ventures ended in disaster, although it proved remarkably persistent: not until 1829, after a lifetime of more than one hundred and fifty years, was the company dissolved by Act of Parliament. True to form, the company's activities at Strontian demonstrated the usual knack for loss-making. To start with, the previous lessees had obviously seen them coming and gave them a sub-tack at £3,600 per annum in cash, over and above the customary one sixth of all lead raised; the Duke of Norfolk's Company also received a sum of £6,000, said to have been spent on the works to date.[57] In the first two to three years £40,000 was invested, and by 1733 Murray of Stanhope felt able to give the following enthusiastic account of the company's impact on the area:

> The York Buildings Company have . . . enlarged the whole work by augmenting the number of their clerks, overseers, smelters, artificers, miners and labourers: and their several buildings proportionally, namely for air furnaces, an Almand furnace, and an essay furnace: a smelting miln with two common hearths, a slag hearth, a spacious storehouse, key and cooperidge: a furnish'd house for their Gov(erno)r or any of the court of assistants, another for their manager, a well furnish'd dispensary, several lodging houses for workmen in Strontian, besides another sett of buildings for them at New York, which lyes more contiguous to the grooves; a brewhouse, malt barn and kiln, stables, workhouses, peat-barns, and timber and coal yards; & several biggings upon the grooves for smiths, carpenters &c., from whence they have made the roads for leading the ore to the smelting milns & furnaces at a great labour & expence; besides levell'd & paved or laid with gravel, all the passages & streets in Strontian, whereby it is become wholesome and pleasant.[58]

Fig 95. Strontian, Argyll. A major lead-mining centre, though many of the features shown here did not exist. *Murray (1740)*

Murray reinforces his glowing description with an illustration of Strontian showing the company's good works (Figure 95).

While much of what Murray had to say was probably true, it did not take long for things to turn sour. In a petition dated 29th July 1734, Charles Murray asked the Court of Session to allow him to take over the mines while the now bankrupt company underwent sequestration. By this time any effort on the part of the company had been given up, for in the words of the petitioner it had 'totally neglected the whole works and workmen, in so much as the number of their workmen are vastly reduced, and many of them have been miserably starv'd, even to death, by want and neglect'. At one time six hundred men had been employed; by 1734 'even the two hundred poor workmen, who are now only left of a vastly greater number so starv'd or forced from the works, are likewise in imminent hazard to starve, and to perish for want of provisions, and payment of their just debts, which they have gained with the sweat of their brows in the service of the publick'. In the absence of repairs to roofing timbers, the workings were in danger of falling in; dwellings, which alone had cost £10,000 Sterling, were going to ruin, as were the smelting houses and mills. Highland workers, faced with starvation, were in a bad enough position, but the possible fate of the English smiths, carpenters and masons was thought to be even worse.[59]

In 1737 Francis Grant, brother of Sir Archibald, was put in charge of the mines with an undertaking to furnish the company with lead at £8-£8 5s per ton, or more than £3,000, but despite this apparent change of fortunes the mines were abandoned and the workmen dismissed at Christmas 1740. Grant's ton, or more than £3,000 but despite this apparent change of fortunes the mines were abandoned and the workmen dismissed at Christmas 1740. Grant's claim was settled at £3,070, paid in bonds which to all intents and purposes were worthless.[60]

It is perhaps worth noting that in addition to the Strontian and Islay mines, Sir Alexander Murray set up the Morvern Leadmining Company to exploit the Lurga mines on the Duke of Argyll's estate, while Archibald Grant, in partnership with a Colonel William Burroughs, also sank large sums in the Morvern lead mines, before giving up in 1737.[61]

All too often workings at the smaller fields involved brief periods of activity by short-lived companies but, in marked contrast, the two largest and most consistently productive areas were each dominated for much of the period by a single company: the Scots Mining Company at Leadhills and Messrs. Ronald Crawford, Meason & Company at Wanlockhead. The origins of the Scots Mining Company have already been referred to. Shortly after 1715 they took on the north-western sector of Leadhills and continued to work it until 1861. The lease of the south-western sector was acquired in 1772 from a Mr. Marchbank & Company who had worked it since 1747. The area to the east of Glengonnar Burn, comprising the south-eastern and north-eastern sectors, had been worked directly by the Earl of Hopetoun, but was let in 1772 to a company headed by a Mr. Popham from Darlington. In 1805 the company lost control of these sectors, and the north-eastern sector was taken on by the Scots Mining Company which now controlled three-quarters of the Leadhills field. After the Leadhills Mining Company takeover of the south-eastern sector in 1828, a long legal wrangle developed over water rights, a battle which the Leadhills Company finally won, with the backing of the Earl of Hopetoun; in 1861 the Scots Mining Company resigned its lease, and the entire field passed into the hands of the Leadhills Company.[62] Between 1768 and 1793 the Scots Mining Company had also leased the Tyndrum mines in succession to a number of other companies.[63]

Messrs. Ronald Crawford, Meason & Company obtained a lease of the entire Wanlockhead field in 1755, initially for a period of nineteen years. This was subsequently extended by Act of Parliament to 1812, and a further thirty years was obtained thereafter. The original partnership consisted of Ronald

Crawford (an Edinburgh lawyer), his brother John (a lead merchant in Rotterdam) and Gilbert Meason, whose family had long associations with the management of the mines. During the company's protracted working life, overall control changed hands: as late as 1830, by which time the firm was being referred to as the Wanlockhead Company, a Mr. Meason was still acting as agent, but by 1835 three of the four shares in the company were held by the Marquess of Bute, the fourth belonging to a Mr. McLeod. At the end of the Company's lease, in 1842, the Marquess held all four.[64]

Without doubt the interest shown by the English provided much needed funds and technical skills for developing fields, although it would appear that Scottish involvement grew as the period progressed. Notwithstanding the frequency with which companies were formed and disbanded, the relative security and financial strength offered by company status was of crucial significance to the development of Scottish lead mining. If company mining was a risky business, attempts at mining by individuals were even more fraught with danger, and could be ruinous to those concerned.

Individuals

Despite the risk of sinking a fortune in speculative mining, without finding any mineral deposits to defray costs, there was no shortage of individuals prepared to try their hand at it. In a few cases their searches paid off: in 1741 Sir Robert Clifton of Clifton, a Nottinghamshire baronet, discovered lead at Tyndrum on the Breadalbane estate after searching for ten years.[65] At Wanlockhead, Mr. Wightman, an ex-member of the Smelting Company, worked part of their field from 1734 until 1747, while the area which had been let to the Friendly Mining Society was mined by Alexander and William Telfer during the same period.[66] This last-mentioned example shows that individual lessees were not necessarily under-capitalised, for in 1743 Alexander Telfer was employing two hundred and forty men and running three water engines.[67] More typical, however, were the mines in Lochaber and on Islay, where prospecting and working were carried out in a much more haphazard way.

James Griffiths from Swansea first heard of good appearances of copper in Lochaber from a former Strontian miner he had met in Ireland. While the miner refused to divulge the exact location without accompanying Griffiths to the spot, the latter was assured that it lay on the Duke of Gordon's estate and so accordingly negotiated a lease to run for fifteen years, a considerable achievement for a man who was already sixty-five years of age. The lease was signed in mid-November 1756; Griffiths lost no time in recruiting workers and bringing them to the site. On 5 December 1756 the miner arrived, only to inform him that the deposits lay on the other side of the burn — on the Forfeited Estates Commission's Lochiel estate. The following day Griffiths penned a hasty note to William Frasier W.S. asking him to 'soften up' the Commissioners, especially Provost Drummond of Edinburgh; this was followed in February 1757 by a formal request for a lease, explaining that he had found lead or copper in Lochaber which *might* extend into the Lochiel estate. The lease was granted, but despite the powers which were granted to erect smelting mills and water engines, no more is heard of Griffiths or the mines, and it can only be assumed that his efforts were to no avail.[68]

The Islay mines had already been worked by several parties, including the proprietor Campbell of Shawfield, prior to Squire Haily taking a tack about 1738. Like his predecessors, Haily made the mistake of entrusting the workings to a local man, Archibald Maclean, who knew little of mining, and his tenancy came to an ignoble end with the smelt mill being stopped and the tools laid up in the granary at Glasco Beag.[69] The next tenant, Captain William Thyne, had the backing of a company, but returned to England and gave up his Scottish interests with the onset of the '45, only months after taking them on. That neither managed to make any impact is evident from a report of about 1760 which concludes with the words '. . . that no sufficient tryall has been made, nor no regular work carried on . . . is very clear and obvious to any man of skill that see[s] it'.[70]

A later tenant, Charles Freebairn, put more energy (and capital) into working his tack, but by 1770 it had become apparent that the capital was not his own to spend:

> Since Mr. Freebairn undertook the working and carrying out of the foresaid mines, he had occasion to borrow considerable sums for the support of the work from Mr. William Hogg, banker in Edinburgh, and Mr. Hogg of late having stopped payment, his creditors are now pushing Mr. Freebairn for payment of that debt, which brings Mr. Freebairn under the necessity somehow to dispose of the tack of that valuable subject in order to operate his relief with those of Mr. Hogg's creditors to whom he stands engaged, and to whom he has granted security upon his tack to the extent of the value of one fourth of said tack.[71]

Not altogether surprisingly, Freebairn proposed that the tack be sold off in shares. Lead mining was far too risky a venture for an undercapitalised individual to engage in.

Distribution and Chronology

The use of water power is so much tied up with the industry as a whole that consideration has to be given to the overall distribution and chronology of lead mining in Scotland between 1730 and 1830. For the sake of convenience the period is divided into three stages, 1730-1760, 1760-1800 and 1800-1830.

In the years up to 1760 the Highlands saw intermittent activity in Morvern, Lorne and Lochaber, with some long-term exploitation on Islay and at Strontian and Tyndrum (Figure 96); of these last three, Islay and Strontian had been worked prior to 1730, but mining at Tyndrum did not start until 1741. Smelters were used at all three although lead was also at times exported unrefined.[72] No instance has been found of water power being used in mine

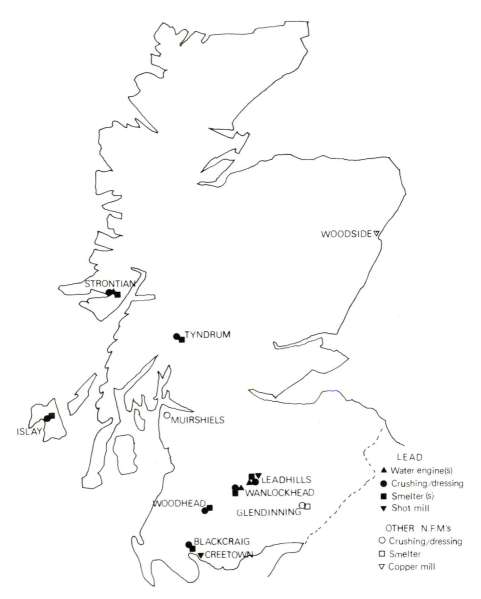

Fig 96. Distribution of water power in non-ferrous mining and metallurgy

drainage. In the Grampians lead ore was worked in a small way at Glenesk, though only at the very start of the period.[73] In the Central Lowlands an attempt was made to work mines at Kemback, Fife from 1748, but with little success; the ore was sent unrefined to Holland.[74]

Needless to say, the two Southern Upland centres, Leadhills and Wanlockhead, continued to be extensively exploited, with water power finding a use in mine drainage, smelting and, in the case of Wanlockhead, ore crushing.[75] As yet the Galloway ores remained enexploited.

Between 1760 and 1800 interest in the Highlands waned, although the Tyndrum mines continued to work steadily and those at Strontian and on Islay intermittently. The Islay smelter had been closed down before 1760, and it is by no means certain that it ever re-opened.[76] Exploration in Caithness brought to light potentially workable ores on Sir John Sinclair of Ulbster's estate,[77] but in the absence of evidence to the contrary it must be assumed that they were never exploited to any extent. From 1771 an attempt was made to work a lead mine near the east end of the village of Glamis, Angus, but, although some lead was extracted, the cost of working it became so high that it was eventually abandoned.[78]

In the Southern Uplands Leadhills and Wanlockhead continued to dominate Scottish lead mining. Water power was used in the same capacity as before, but towards the end of the century high prices for lead made the application of steam power to drainage feasible. In Galloway a soldier working on the Military Road to Portpatrick is said to have discovered the Blackcraig (Kirkcudbrightshire) mines in 1763.[79] A company for exploiting lead mines in Galloway had already been set up in 1758; in 1764 a lease was taken from Patrick Heron of Heron, and an augmented company known as the Craigtown Mining Company was formed, Heron being one of the partners. In the same year a rival firm, the Blackcraig Mining Company, obtained a lease from Heron's neighbour, Patrick Dunbar. The Craigtown Company prospered and by 1780 had built itself a smelt mill nearby and a lead shot mill at Creetown. The Blackcraig Company was less successful initially, but persisted; plans were drawn up for a smelter in 1792 (Figure 94), but it seems unlikely that it was ever built.[80] By the 1790s production at the two mines was on the decline: according to Wilson, production averaged four hundred tons per annum for a long time, but by 1793 it had fallen to thirty tons.[81] Several other trials elsewhere in Galloway failed to develop into long-term production.

The 19th century started with record prices for lead, but the peace of 1815 and later the removal of tariffs brought a slump in prices from which there was only a slow recovery from the mid-1830s onwards.[82] The Islay mines had been abandoned by 1819, not to re-open until the 1860s.[83] In 1806 the Strontian mines were still being worked in a businesslike manner, with a smelter and several sinkings, some apparently carrying water-powered drainage equipment.[84] The mines were shut down in 1815 but re-opened on a small scale two years later, under the auspices of the estate's proprietor. In 1836 the mines were re-let, but soon closed.[85] The Tyndrum mines worked intermittently during the early 19th century; by 1840 they were in the hands of 'experienced German miners' who had built a large crushing mill and an inclined railway to bring ore from the mines.[86] In Strathglass, Inverness-shire, mines were wrought on a small scale in the early 19th century but the remains of an engine house and sluices which Wilson found in 1920 probably date from a later period.[87]

The Wanlockhead and Leadhills mines continued to be worked, although the slump in prices and, at Leadhills, a protracted dispute over water rights affected their viability.

Prior to the slump, steam power had been widely used in drainage, but by the 1830s a move back to water power was apparent, in the form of water pressure engines. Smelting, crushing and dressing operations used water power, and in the 1830s a shot mill was erected at Leadhills. In Galloway the Blackcraig mines were worked intermittently but ceased to function in 1839 when the dressing and smelting plant was dismantled. The Creetown shot mill also closed down and was converted to make potato starch.[88]

Some note should also be taken of two other Galloway mines, first worked in the 1830s and 1840s. The Woodhead mines were discovered in 1838, and by 1844 a village had been established with school and library. Crushing, dressing and smelting plant were installed, the crusher being driven by a thirty-foot diameter water wheel; there were hopes that it might become a second Leadhills.[89] The Cairnsmore mines had been worked to a small extent prior to 1845, but only then, with their being leased to a company, did large-scale workings commence. Smelting was carried out elsewhere.[90]

In comparison with some other sectors of the economy, notably textiles and grain-based industries, the lead industry's use of water power was confined to a small number of localities and involved relatively few installations. Nevertheless, this does not diminish its importance to the industry. In drainage it allowed workings to continue below day levels, removing volumes of water which would have been beyond the capacity of hand-operated pumps or horse gins; steam engines, while perhaps more powerful, were a luxury which could only be afforded if production remained consistently high, if price levels held up and if coal was reasonably accessible. At Wanlockhead the introduction of powerful water pressure engines in the 1830s revived the use of water power. Again, in crushing and dressing, it was the relative strength of water power compared to animal and human power which recommended its use; furthermore, as dressing required 'process water' in any case, water brought to a site could be used to perform both functions.

Smelting by water power was already well established by 1730; it enabled mining companies to produce a commodity more valuable than unsmelted ore and one which, by the consequent reduction in bulk, could be more readily transported. Although an alternative existed in the form of the reverberatory furnace, its heavy fuel consumption militated against its use in an industry which was often sited at some distance from suitable fuel supplies. The establishment of shot mills, again water-powered, represented a further extension of the activities of mining companies into the production of a commodity manufactured from smelted lead.

Without any question, lead mining involved a very high financial risk even when, as was generally the case, the risk was shared among a number of partners. Chance finds might indicate ores which could be profitably worked on a large scale over many years, or very limited quantities, the extraction of which could sink a company deep into debt in a few years. In the majority of cases production never achieved a scale or consistency which could justify the installation of water-powered machinery, but at the few sites where reserves did prove to be adequate, the use of water power in a variety of capacities did much to ensure the industry's survival.

A Note on Other Non-ferrous Metals

Although lead was successfully worked at a number of localities, the extraction and smelting of other non-ferrous ores never developed to any extent. The Hilderston silver mines were leased by the York Buildings Company, along with mineral rights to other Hopetoun lands in the Bathgate Hills. Joshua Place, who was put in charge of operations, so impressed the Company's Governor that he was allowed to take out a further twenty-one year lease from 1749.[91] Various minerals were worked in the south-west corner of the Ochils: on the Airthrey estate fifty barrels of silver ore were extracted between 1761 and 1764, but the mine was abandoned as unprofitable. At about the same time a company formed by Charles Erskine made a mine with a day level in an attempt to find silver in the once productive glen above Alva; as a result of their efforts they found not silver but cobalt, and while this found a use in blue glazing at the Prestonpans potteries, the workings were soon exhausted. For a short period in the first half of the 18th century an English company worked a copper mine in the Mill Glen of Tillicoultry, whilst in the hills above Dollar mines once yielded both copper and lead.[92] In none of these cases, however, was activity sufficiently sustained or large-scale to justify the use of water-powered drainage or smelting equipment. Under their tack of the the Currie (Midlothian) copper mines, Richardson Terrand and Micah Shields were empowered to erect smelt mills and make dams and sluices for the working of the mines, but at its expiry in 1758 they had exhausted their funds without even leaving enough to restore the ground where they had worked.[93]

Several other instances of small-scale copper and silver mines could be cited,[94] but with only occasional vague references to water power. Wilson speaks of a smelting works at Alloa, erected by the Caledonian Mining Company at some date after 1805, to smelt copper from the Airthrey Hill mine,[95] whilst Morgan's *Annals of Woodside & Newhills* contains an intriguing passing reference to a 'copper mill' at Woodside, Aberdeenshire, converted from a waulk mill prior to 1744 by the tenant, Alexander Smith.[96]

Paradoxically, it is the less common minerals which provide the most positive evidence of the use of water power. Barytes was mined in Perthshire, Arran, Kirkcudbrightshire and near the Ayrshire-Renfrewshire border.[97] In the last mentioned area Muirshields Mill, above Lochwinnoch, was being used to crush barytes in 1857 and may have been so used earlier in the century.[98] Britain's only antimony mine, in Glendinning, Dumfriesshire, was discovered in 1760, but was not regularly worked until 1793 when the landowner (Sir

James Johnstone of Westerhall) and two other partners formed the Westerhall Mining Company. Between 1793 and 1798 the mine yielded a hundred tons of ore worth £8,400. A water-powered smelter was built on site and a village (Jamestown) was founded, with a granary, a school and the customary library. By 1800 activity had ceased, and not until 1888 were the mines reopened.[99]

NOTES

1. Smout, T. C., 'Lead Mining in Scotland 1650-1850', in Payne, P. L. (ed.), *Studies in Scottish Business History*, Edinburgh, 1967, 105. The mine is reputed to have made £4,000 per week for a period of thirteen to fourteen weeks: Forsyth, R., *The Beauties of Scotland*, 5 vols., Edinburgh, 1806, IV, 10.

2. SRO GD18/2656: Report on Wanlockhead Mines by Robert Scot, overseer of coal mines at Loanhead, 1736.

3. Harvey, W. S., 'Lead Mining in 1768: Old Records of a Scottish Mining Company', *IA* VII (1970), 317.

4. The Susanna vein 'goes down near vertical': Pococke, R., 'Tours in Scotland, 1747, 1750, 1760', *SHS* I (1887), 41.

5. Smout, *op. cit.*, 106.

6. SRO GD18/2679: Answers to Memorandum in Relation to the Lead Mines at Wanlockhead, 3rd April 1743.

7. Hopetoun Lead Mining Papers, IV 87/1: State of the Scotch Mine Company's Works at Leadhills, 1st November 1763.

8. Smeaton, J., *Reports of the Late John Smeaton*, 3 vols., London, 1812, II, 403-4. The existing engine was probably that for which preparations were being made in 1770: Hopetoun Lead Mining Papers IV 87/2: State of the Scotch Mine Company's Works at Leadhills, March 1770.

9. Smith, G. G., *The Book of Islay*, Edinburgh, 1895, 459-461.

10. See, for example, SRO RHP1336/1 (1838).

11. Brown J., *The History of Sanquhar*, Dumfries, 1891, 428-9.

12. *Ibid.*, 428-9. It was probably this engine which John Rennie saw in 1791: NLS Acc. 5111/25/7.

13. Brown, *op. cit.*, 430-6; *NSA* IV, 301-2, Sanquhar, Dumfriesshire.

14. Hopetoun Lead Mining Papers, IV/56: Robert Martin to Alexander Williamson.

15. NLS Acc. 5111/25/7.

16. Smout, *op. cit.*, 106.

17. SRO GD224/649/1: Meason to McLaren, 9th & 19th August 1824.

18. Jamieson, A., *A Dictionary of Mechanical Science*, 2 vols., London, 1827, I, 486-8; Phillips, J. A. & Darlington, J., *Records of Mining & Metallurgy*, London, 1857, 46; Smeaton, *op. cit.*, II, 409.

19. Phillips & Darlington, *op. cit.*, 46; Smeaton, *op. cit.*, II, 409-10.

20. Smeaton, *op. cit.*, II, 411.

21. Wilson, G. V., *Special Report on the Mineral Resources of Great Britain*, XVII, *Lead, Zinc, Copper and Nickel Ores of Scotland*, Edinburgh, 1921, 11.

22. Murray, A., *The Upper Ward of Lanarkshire*, 3 vols., Glasgow, 1864, III, 48.

23. Downs-Rose, G. & Harvey, W. S. , 'Water Bucket Pumps and the Wanlockhead Engine', *IA* X (1973), 129-147.

24. Murray, *op. cit.*, III, 48; Phillips & Darlington, *op. cit.*, 49.

25. Smeaton, *op. cit.*, II, 411.

26. SRO GD18/5955/ A-B.

27. NLS Acc. 5111/25/7.

28. Brown, *op. cit.*, 425; SRO GD18/2679: Answers to Memorandum . . ., 30th April 1743.

29. Smeaton Plans, No. 111: Stamp Mill for lead mines. Plan and elevation 1:24 (1760); Smout, T. C., *A History of the Scottish People*, London, 1969, opp. p.384.

30. Phillips & Darlington, *op. cit.*, 118-121.

31. *NSA* X, 1081, Killin, Perthshire.

32. *NSA* IV, 280-1, Carsphairn, Kirkcudbrightshire.

33. Phillips & Darlington, *op. cit.*, 121-2.

34. SRO RHP 360/3 1851: Washing mill, SRO RHP1336/1 1838 Washing station.

35. Smout, *op. cit.* (1967), 109.

36. Hopetoun Lead Mining Papers, Class III 50/4.

37. Ibid., Class IV 56.

38. Pococke, *op. cit.*, 41.

39. Murray, *op. cit.*, III, 48.

40. Smout, *op. cit.* (1967), 107.

41. SRO GD18/2657: Alex Telfer to Sir John Clerk, 16 Feb. 1741.

42. Smout, *op. cit.* (1967), 108.

43. Donnachie, I. L., *The Industrial Archaeology of Galloway*, Newton Abbot, 1971, 122; *NSA* VI, 336, Crawford, Lanarkshire.

44. Forsyth, *op. cit.*, IV, 10; Smout, *op. cit.* (1967), 105.

45. Although one sixth was the customary rate, new workings with unproven capabilities might be set at a lower rate. See, for example, SRO GD44/39/29: Lease for 15 years, paying 1/10th of lead or copper extracted during the first 7 years.

46. *OSA* XIII, 584, New Luce, Wigtownshire; *OSA* XX, 537, Thurso, Caithness.

47. For some Galloway examples, see Cunninghame, J. H., 'Geonostical Description of the Stewartry of Kirkcudbrightshire', *TH&AS* New Series VIII (1843), 731.

48. Clow, A. & Clow, N. L., *The Chemical Revolution*, London, 1952, 365.

49. Murray, D., *The York Buildings Company. A Chapter in Scotch History*, Glasgow, 1883, 68.

50. Smith, *op. cit.*, 457.

51. Brown, *op. cit.*, 424-5.

52. Hopetoun Lead Mining Papers, IV 87/1.

53. Murray, D., *op. cit.*, 68-9.

54. *Ibid.*, 77.

55. Murray, A., *The True Interest of Great Britain, Ireland and Our Plantations*, London, 1740. Notes accompanying plan of Loch Sunart.

56. Murray, D., *op. cit.*, 69.

57. *Ibid.*, 70.

58. Murray, A., *op. cit.* (1740), Notes accompanying plan of Loch Sunart.

59. NLS 29/1/1 vii.

60. Murray, D., *op. cit.*, 76.

61. Wilson, *op. cit.*, 83; Murray, D., *op. cit.*, 77. Burroughs had been Grant's accomplice in the Charitable Corporation affair.

62. Wilson, *op. cit.*, 11; Clow & Clow, *op. cit.*, 366.

63. Wilson, *op. cit.*, 93.

64. Brown, *op. cit.*, 430; Wilson, *op. cit.*, 11; Donnachie, *op. cit.*, 117; Clow & Clow, *op. cit.*, 368-9.

65. Wilson, *op. cit.*, 93. The lease of the Breadalbane minerals was taken out in 1730.

66. Wilson, *op. cit.*, 428-9.

67. SRO GD18/2679. By 1743 William Telfer had died, leaving only Alexander to run the mines.

68. SRO GD44/39/29.

69. I.e. 'Little Glasgow' — presumably so named by the Glasgow company which had once worked the mines.

70. Smith, *op. cit.*, 457-8.

71. *Ibid.*, 466.

72. References have already been given for the Strontian and Islay smelters. That at Tyndrum is first mentioned in 1744, when Sir Robert Clifton bought £300 worth of timber for his smelting mill: SRO GD112/9/45: Charge of Breadalbane, Crop 1743 and Money Rent Mart. 1744. Following the closure of the Islay smelter, lead was sometimes exported unrefined; when Pennant visited Islay in 1769, an air furnace was being used: Wilson, *op. cit.*, 67.

73. Headrick, J., *General View of the Agriculture of Forfarshire*, Edinburgh, 1813, 14; *OSA* V, 367, Lochee, Angus.

74. *OSA* XIV, 305, Kemback, Fife.

75. SRO GD18/2679.

76. Smith, *op. cit.*, 458.

77. *OSA* XX, 537, Thurso, Caithness.

78. Headrick, *op. cit.*, 14.

79. Wilson, *op. cit.*, 48.

80. Donnachie, *op. cit.*, 119-22. Donnachie gives details of the Craigtown Company's employees in 1780, including seven smelters. The smelting mill appears on John Ainslie's map of Wigtownshire, 1782 (NX435646).

81. Wilson, *op. cit.*, 49.

82. Smout, *op. cit.* (1967), 105-6.

83. Wilson, *op. cit.*, 67.

84. SRO RHP72.

85. Wilson, *op. cit.*, 83.

86. *Ibid.*, 95; *NSA* X, 1081, Killin, Perthshire.

87. Wilson, *op. cit.*, 108.

88. *Ibid.*, 49; *NSA* IV, 341, Kirkmabreck, Kirkcudbrightshire.

89. *NSA* IV, 280-1, Carsphairn, Kirkcudbrightshire; Cunninghame, *op. cit.*, 730.

90. Wilson, *op. cit.*, 52.

91. Murray, D., *op. cit.*, 67.

92. Forsyth, *op. cit.*, IV, 10-11.

93. SRO GD41/440.

94. See Butt, J., *Industrial Archaeology of Scotland*, Newton Abbot, 1967, 94.

95. Wilson, *op. cit.*, 141.

96. Morgan, P., *Annals of Woodside & Newhills*, Aberdeen, 1886, 17.

97. Butt, *op. cit.*, 94.

98. *OS* 1st Edition 6"/mile (NS309634).

99. Singer, W., *General View of the Agriculture of Dumfriesshire*, Dumfries, 1812, 23-4; Donnachie, *op. cit.*, 131-2.

25

The Iron Industry

The iron industry occupies a crucial position within the Industrial Revolution: the successful substitution of coke for charcoal in iron smelting provided one of the preconditions, while one of the characteristics of the Revolution itself was the replacement of wood by iron as the single most important material. In the words of Mantoux:

> The history of iron and steel is not that of a single industry, but can, from a certain point of view, be identified with that of 'Great Industry' itself.[1]

In the Scottish iron industry the period 1730-1830 was one of transition. Small beginnings had already been made in the smelting and working of iron; from the late 1720s charcoal smelting developed on an unprecedented scale, and from the 1760s, with the establishment of Carron Works, coke smelting was introduced. During the late 18th and early 19th centuries coke smelting spread to other localities, but the second major advance, Neilson's hot blast, while originating in Scotland, came too late to have any appreciable impact before 1830.[2]

With the possible exception of coalmining, steam power tends to be more closely identified with iron than with any other industry. However, in a Scottish context the correlation does not altogether hold true for, prior to 1830 at least, water power also made a significant contribution to the industry's development.

Technology

Smelting : Charcoal and Coke

In the absence of any evidence to the contrary, it would seem that the first blast furnaces to be introduced into Scotland were those built by George Hay in Wester Ross during the early 17th century (Chapter 6). Apart from possible changes in scale and efficiency, there is no reason to believe that the charcoal furnaces of 1730 were materially different to those of Hay's time. Alternating layers of charcoal, ore and limestone were melted down in the furnace and drawn off at the bottom, the heat being intensified by a draught or blast provided by bellows activated by a water wheel through cranks or cams.

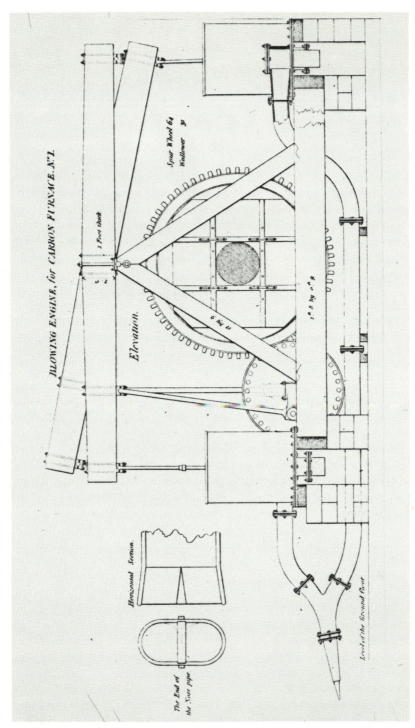

Fig 97. Smeaton's cylinder blowing engine for Carron No.1 Furnace. Smeaton, Reports (1812)

The introduction of coke smelting is already thoroughly documented,[3] and there is no point in considering the matter in any depth in the present context. Suffice to say that it was perfected by Abraham Darby at Coalbrookdale Works, Salop, in 1709. From Coalbrookdale, knowledge of the process spread only slowly, not reaching the Black Country until the 1750s. Through the agency of two West Midland industrialists, using English skilled labour and ideas drawn from Coalbrookdale itself, coke smelting was introduced directly into Scotland with the establishment in 1759 of Carron Ironworks, Stirling-shire.

Apart from differences in scale,[4] Carron's first blast furnaces were not unlike those of contemporary charcoal furnaces. The first advance in the technology, as opposed to the chemistry, of iron smelting came in 1766 when a third and fourth blast furnace were designed to be blown by cylinders (already used in England) instead of the customary bellows[5] (Figure 97). As Carron Works is to be dealt with at length in a later section, no more need be said for now, save that, with modifications, cylinders were used during the remainder of the period on all Scottish blast furnaces.[6]

In 1776 the second steam engine to be built by Messrs. Boulton and Watt was installed at John Wilkinson's New Willey Ironworks, Salop, the first time that steam power had been applied to blowing a furnace.[7] In Scotland water power did not cease to be a viable alternative, according to a letter dated 1784:

> the machinery moved by it goes more steadily, is not so liable to accidental stop-pages, has less tear and wear, and is more under the command of the founder, which enables him to adapt the blast to suit the quality of the metal he is smelting.[8]

Whatever the advantages of water power may have been, Scotland's second coke smelting iron works (Wilsontown, 1779) used steam power, as did the third (Clyde, 1786).[9] At Muirkirk (1787) the use of water power was contemplated, but whilst it was later applied to other purposes at the works, it was once more steam power which provided the blast.[10] In fact, out of the ten iron smelting works built between 1779 and 1830, only Balgonie (1801) used water power, and this for a single blast furnace.[11]

It is not too difficult to see why steam power was so readily adopted. According to Farey's calculations, the four blowing engines at Carron Works required a steady seventy horse power.[12] This in itself was beyond the capabilities of most rivers in areas accessible to coal, iron ore and limestone, but when it is considered that such a force had to be sustained for days, if not months, on end, then the requirement became almost impossible to fulfil, as Carron Company itself found to its cost.

Cast Iron Processes

Iron straight from the furnace was unsuited for most purposes, all the more so in the case of coke-smelted iron on account of the high level of impurities. However, a re-smelting furnace known as a cupola had come into use in

Fig 98. Distribution of blacking mills, 1730-1830

England about 1702, and as this involved no direct contact between fuel and iron, it was well adapted to improving the quality of coke-smelted iron to the standard required for casting.[13] Water power provided the blast for a number of re-smelting furnaces, although where air furnaces were applied to this purpose, no power was required.[14] As re-smelting furnaces were less demanding in their use of power than were blast furnaces, a wider range of sites could be utilised and notwithstanding other locational factors, the need to

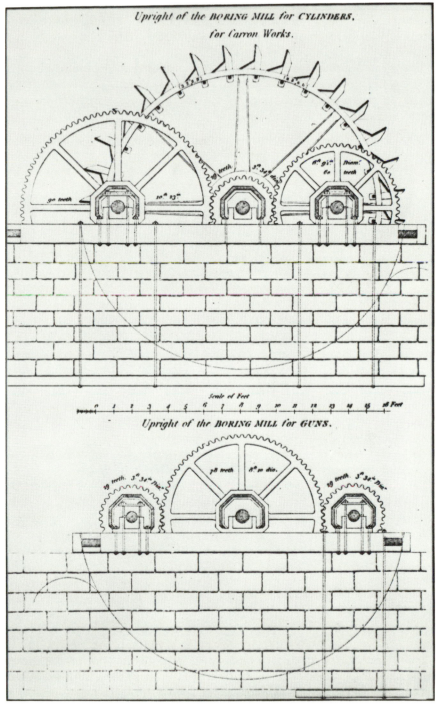

Fig 99. Smeaton's cylinder and gun boring mills for Carron Ironworks. *Smeaton, Reports (1812)*

substitute steam power could be obviated. A foundry attached to the cotton works at Catrine, Ayrshire was able to use a fifteen horse power water wheel to not only blow the cupola but also to drive machine tools.[15]

The preparation of ground charcoal for sprinkling over moulds also made use of water power. Several charcoal or 'blacking' mills are known to have existed in the Carron area (Figure 98); the ingenious construction of one particular mill caught the attention of M. Faujas de St. Fond in 1784:

> . . . it consists of a kind of mortar of cast iron, several feet in diameter, closely shut with a wooden cover, perforated in the middle to admit the passage of a vertical cylinder, which forms the principal mechanic power of the machine, being turned round on its own axis by a wheel, which is moved by water. Two iron bars pass horizontally through the bottom of the vertical axis, in the manner of a cross, and they may be raised or lowered at pleasure, by means of several holes, at different distances, in the axis. This cross divides the area or capacity of the mortar into four portions, two of which are occupied by two iron balls, nearly as large as ordinary bombs, but entirely solid, and of a polished surface. The moment the axis is put in motion, the balls begin to roll round after each other, and thus speedily bruise the charcoal . . . The two other spokes are furnished with teeth in the manner of a rake, which stir up the charcoal from the bottom of the mortar and turn it on every side.[16]

At Durie, Fife, a more conventional edge-runner was used.[17] One of the earliest machine tools to be devised for working cast iron was the boring mill. Traditionally it has been used to bore guns and cannon, but the higher standard of work required to bore steam engine cylinders drew attention to the imperfections of existing techniques. John Smeaton designed a boring mill to replace an existing one at Carron about 1769 (Figure 99); this, and a subsequent modification, are dealt with in a later section.

Although a few rural foundries used water power, the majority of those in towns and cities used steam power, if any power was required.

Before moving on to the subject of malleable iron, a brief note should be made of yet another aspect of iron manufacture to use water power. Smeaton's *Reports* contain directions and observations dated 1777 regarding a fireclay mill to be built on the tail lead of Carron Works; the machinery proposed included rollers, to turn at 50 r.p.m. and either stampers or edge-runners to prepare the clay.[18]

Malleable Iron Processes

Re-smelting could produce an iron suited to casting, but for any article which had to be reshaped during its manufacture, a less brittle type of iron was required. As these articles represented the majority of iron objects used in 18th-century Scotland, the production of a type of iron which could be hammered into the shape required was an important part of the industry as a whole.

The method used in Scotland for much of the period was as follows: iron from the blast furnace was heated and stirred, while a blast of air, usually provided by water power, was directed onto it. Carbon impurities in the iron combined with the oxygen in the air blast, leaving a purer form of iron. The building in which this took place was referred to as the forge and the melting hearth as the finery.[19] From the finery, the wrought iron 'bloom' was hammered into a block shape under a tilt hammer (generally water-powered), and then reheated, without blast, on a charcoal hearth known as a chaffery. Once reheated, the bloom was once more put under the tilt hammer and re-shaped into a marketable form.[20]

In 1734 the York Buildings Company's Coulnakyle works had two hammer wheels and two fineries, with wheels and a chaffery.[21] In Ayrshire another forge, dating from the 1730s, had two wheels, one of which drove the bellows, the other the tilt hammer.[22] Both examples were, however, atypical of normal 18th-century practice in that most of the requirements of the Scottish malleable iron industry were met by imported wrought iron, which required only a second reheating, without blast. Nor was the trip hammer widely applied before the last quarter of the 18th century, for in most cases the scale of production and the size of the articles produced did not warrant its use.

The introduction of coke smelting put pressure on the production of malleable iron in much the same way as did the mechanisation of spinning on weaving. In 1762 John Roebuck of Carron Company obtained a patent (No. 780) for making wrought iron with coke,[23] but results were disappointing. Another patent (No. 1351) was granted to an Englishman, Henry Cort, in 1783; Carron Company was approached by Cort in 1784 and again in 1786, but no agreement was reached on either occasion and a great opportunity was passed over.[24] Cort's process, known as puddling, was of course successful. According to Clow and Clow, it was not introduced to Scotland until the 1830s, but other sources reveal it was being used at Muirkirk by 1809.[25]

Although the trip hammer could produce certain items, such as spades and shovels, it was ill-adapted to making strips and sheets of metal. In England a slitting mill had been patented by Bevis Bulmer (of leadmining fame), but in Scotland such mills are not heard of until 1734, when the City of Glasgow granted Robert McKell (Meikle?), 'stranger milln wright', £3 Sterling for making and perfecting a model of a machine for slitting and chipping iron, and rolling iron hoops.[26] Several private individuals contributed a like sum, and it was observed that the model would be of value should the town ever set up such a machine 'at large'. An iron working company had already been set up in Glasgow (1732), and in 1738 the company established a slitting mill, the first in Scotland, below the Mill of Partick on the River Kelvin.[27]

The basic constituents of a slitting mill were two fluted rollers which could be adjusted to cut the iron into strips of the required width. The rolling mill, with plain rollers, produced a sheet of iron more easily than could a trip hammer, but although it is known to have come into use in Scotland during the 18th century, no date has been established for the first mill of this type.

The period 1730-1830 also brought improvements in steelmaking with the development of the crucible process by Benjamin Huntsman.[28] A process at Carron, which Grahame describes as the conversion of pig iron into wrought iron, sounds not unlike the crucible process: iron, which had been beaten into plates one inch thick, was broken into pieces two inches square which were scoured in an iron cylinder driven by a water wheel. When finished, they were put into fireclay pots and brought to a welding heat. In this state they were brought under the hammer and wrought into blooms.[29]

One of the applications of crucible steel was the manufacture of edge tools. In 1778 Loch found one such manufactory at Rutherglen:

> A great deal is done here in iron work of all kinds. They have a grinding mill for their edge tools, which goes with water, after the Sheffield manner, and is the only one in Scotland.[30]

Robert Bryce, the owner of the works, gained a high reputation for his products in the west of Scotland.[31]

The various applications of water power in the iron industry are summarised in Figure 96.

Sources of Finance

With so wide a range of units, from small country spade mills to huge integrated works, it might be expected that a similarly wide range of social groups would be involved. However, in most cases the source of finance reflects the capital-intensive nature of the industry and the high level of technical and entrepreneurial knowledge required.

The Landowner

Examples of landowners contributing to the financing of iron works are decidedly uncommon. In small, rural mills where some involvement might have been expected, instances are few enough: Lord Cathcart is reputed to have established a forge on the River Ayr about 1732,[32] and the inclusion of the Dalkeith 'iron mill' on the estate's rent roll suggests that it had been founded by the Dukes of Buccleuch.[33] Other than these, no cases have been found. Foundry work seems to have held no attraction whatsoever, and although a handful of landowners entered into smelting company partnerships, this was at a relatively late stage in the respective companies' histories: in the late 1720s or early 1730s Sir Duncan Campbell of Lochnell appears to have joined an Irish company which had established an iron works in Glen Kinglass on his estate,[34] and in 1804 the Earl of Leven and Melville helped to resurrect the ill-fated Leven ironworks on his Balgonie estate.[35] Butt cites a few other examples but rightly concludes that 'landowners generally adopted a passive role once industrial developments had been launched, unless they were compelled to intervene to safeguard their income from mineral royalties or their amenity'.[36]

One other instance of landowner initiative is worth recording, if only because it never came to fruition. In 1759, Lord Errol as lessee of the York Buildings Company's Callendar estate (Stirlingshire), had granted a feu charter of the two Lower Mills of Larbert to Carron Company, which had subsequently abandoned the mills and included their fall in a new cut to their works. At a late date further reservoirs and lades were dug, some affecting the Callendar estate. In 1781 Lord Errol's lease had expired, and shortly thereafter Sir William Forbes purchased the estate, with land along the southern side of the River Carron. If Forbes is to be believed:

> the inducement which . . . [he] had in making the purchase was the quantity of coal which the lands contained and the falles of water which rendered the situation very eligible for erecting works for the purpose of smelting and milling metals.

However, Carron Company's use of the river denied him access to water power and led to the matter being raised in the Court of Session. While it is difficult to establish just how genuine Forbes was in his intentions, and how far he would have been able to carry them out, correspondence during the early months of 1784 gives some credence to his claims. Whatever his true motives, the works was not built and Carron Company to continued to use the river as before.[37]

Altogether the level of skill required was too high, the financial commitment and risk too great and the benefits to an estate too dubious for the majority of landowners to take more than a passing interest in the iron industry.

Companies and Partnerships

Between 1730 and 1830 the Scottish iron industry was so overwhelmingly dominated by companies and partnerships that it is necessary to break this category down into smaller groups. The subdivision which most readily suggests itself is one between investment in iron smelting on the one hand and forges and foundries on the other.

The renewed wave of English interest in the natural resources of Scotland following the Union and the 1715 Rebellion was just as evident in the iron industry as in lead mining. However, the two industries differed in that it was fuel rather than ore which initially attracted English ironmasters to Scotland. Naturally the York Buildings Company managed to get in on the act, with the usual disastrous consequences. In 1728 they had purchased 60,000 fir trees in Strathspey, valued at £7,000,[38] from Grant of Grant and as a sideline set up a blast furnace and forge at Coulnakyle, using ore from the Lecht mines, fourteen miles away. The company showed its characteristic flair for loss-making, and by Christmas 1732 the iron works had an accumulated debt of £6,935 6s 11½d (Scots?); Grant's factor, John Grant of Burnside, obtained judgements against the company in 1734-5, and by 1739 the works had ceased to exist.[39] Fell has claimed that the York Buildings Company also possessed the

Glen Kinglass iron works between 1727 and 1731,[40] but evidence from else-where suggests that throughout its short history (1725-c.1735) the iron works belonged to an Irish company. Here too it was timber which first attracted the company: the original partners, Roger Murphy, tanner in Enniskillen and Dublin, and Captain Arthur Galbraith, from Dublin, obtained timber rights in 1721-1723, started the iron works at a later date and were eventually joined by other Irish and Scottish co-partners.[41]

The York Buildings Company was not the only English firm to burn its fingers at the beginning of the period. Just as lead mining attracted attention from the North Pennines, so iron smelting created interest from Furness. A long association with Scotland started in 1727 when a partnership headed by Thomas Rawlinson of Whittington entered into an agreement with John Macdonnell of Invergarry to carry on the 'trade, mistery and business of making pigg iron and other iron'. With the exception of one Scot (Charles Ormiston from Kelso), all nine partners either were members of the Rawlinson family or came from the Furness-Whitehaven area. Although Thomas Rawlinson does not appear to have had any experience in iron making, the management of the Invergarry works was entrusted to him. Before long the company found that any advantage accruing from the proximity of fuel supplies was more than offset by problems of attracting skilled labour, distances from ore supplies — despite strenuous efforts to find ore locally, most continued to come by ship, boat and waggon from Cumbria — and difficulties in finding a market for the works' poor-quality pig iron. The blast furnace closed down on 9th February 1736 and by Autumn 1736 the works had been totally abandoned.[42]

From this very shaky start, the Furness area's involvement in Scotland was eventually put onto a firmer footing. In 1752, a partnership consisting of Richard Ford, his son William, Michael Knott and James Backhouse obtained a lease of woods and lands from Sir Duncan Campbell of Lochnell with a view to starting an iron furnace and forges at Bonawe. Unlike the partners in the Invergarry works, the firm already had ample experience in the industry, with works at Newlands, in Furness, where a dearth of charcoal had put a stop to any further expansion.

The Bonawe furnace was established in 1753 and under a firm known initially as Richard Ford & Company, or the Newlands Company, but latterly as the Lorne Furnace Company, continued to operate until 1874.[43] For all its longevity the works never extended beyond the production of pig iron, with the one exception of shot-casting.[44] According to McAdam, the works had been founded in 1730 by an Irish company, using fuel from the Glen Kinglass woods, but this is almost certainly a case of mistaken identity, the company and the works having been at Glen Kinglass itself.[45]

Another Furness iron company, known as the Duddon Company or Jonathan Kendall & Company, established a furnace and forge at Inverleckan (later Furnace) on the Duke of Argyll's estate. The date of its foundation is uncertain: there is some reason to believe that there was already an iron works here in the 1750s but evidence from some sources points to 1775 as the correct date. By the 1790s the works had passed into the hands of the Latham family, also from Furness, and closed down in 1813.[46]

The introduction of coke smelting to Scotland brought English influences from other quarters, but the persistence of the North-West of England as a source of capital is reflected in the establishment in 1795 of a coke smelting works at Glenbuck (Ayrshire) by a Workington firm, under John Rumney, which was succeeded in 1805 by another company from the Cumbrian coast coalfield, headed by Patrick and Peter Hodgson of Whitehaven.[47]

Scotland's two major water-powered iron works, at Carron and Balgonie, were dominated by English capital. Carron, which will be discussed at greater length in a later section, was founded by two Englishmen, Samuel Garbett and John Roebuck, and a Scot, William Cadell. Garbett and Roebuck had already been in partnership in Birmingham as consultant chemists and in refining gold and silver. Together they set up sulphuric acid works in Birmingham (1746) and Prestonpans (1749), and it was at Prestonpans that they met with William Cadell, merchant in Cockenzie. The iron works was founded in 1759; thereafter the three original partners were joined by four others, relatives of Cadell and Roebuck. Charles Gascoine, Garbett's son-in-law, first gained a foothold in the company with a one twenty-sixth share in 1764, and by 1776 had succeeded in ousting all three founding partners.[48]

Carron was unusual among Scottish iron works in that it was a totally integrated unit, taking responsibility for mining its raw materials, smelting them, turning out cast and wrought iron artifacts and even marketing them. The Leven iron works, at Balgonie, Fife was not only more typical, but also involved a combination of existing smelting and manufacturing interests.

By a series of agreements between April 1801 and May 1803, Lord Balgonie (later the Earl of Leven) let the coal and ironstone of Balgonie to a partnership comprising George Losh, William Losh and John Robinson, of the Team Iron Works, Gateshead, Joseph Wilson and Henry Martin of the London banking house of Hatton & Martin, and Alexander Barker, Joseph Cooper, his son Samuel P. Cooper and John Anderson, all of the Leith Walk Iron Foundry. Anderson and the Coopers soon left the partnership, but the remainder formed a company to mine and smelt iron, under the title of the Leven Iron Company; to this end they took a thirty-eight year lease, including one of the corn and lint mills of Balgonie, bringing the total rent payable to £1,300 per annum. A blast furnace, powered by the River Leven, was built, but by Martinmas 1803 the company owed more than £2,750 in rent. Later the same year the company's assets were sequestered. In November 1804 the Commissioners of Creditors of Leven Iron Company agreed to accept an offer from John Losh of Woodside, Carlisle to pay off his brother's remaining debts (£1,320) and in 1805 George Losh obtained a new lease, to run for sixty years, with John Losh and James Losh, barrister in Newcastle, acting as cautioners. George ran the company until 1808, but by this time its affairs were in such a state that despite contributions from James and John, £1,428 8s 6d was still due in rent. George Losh was declared bankrupt. The works was exposed for sale on 7 September 1808, at an upset price of £5,000. No offers were forthcoming, but George Losh offered that sum on condition that all moveables, excluded from the sale price, were included. The creditors agreed unanimously to accept. What they did not realise at the time was that Losh did not have £5,000 to spare. He was rescued yet again by his family, John and William Losh, and by Thomas Thomson of Markinch, who appears to have owned the works until 1810. In July of that year it was purchased by John Surtees and Thomas Lewis of London for £7,350. George Losh continued as manager and, with money put up by his brother James, contributed to the financing of the new company. The iron works' unhappy history dragged on until 1814 when Thomas Lewis, as head of the partnership, was forced to abandon it.[49] Other instances of English influence can be found among steam-powered smelting works, although the Scottish contribution was greater than evidence solely from water-powered works would suggest.[50]

A mercantile presence can be found in three major malleable iron works: Smithfield, Dalnotter and Cramond. The earliest of the three, Smithfield, had been founded about 1732, with workshops for nailmaking and smith work at Broomielaw Croft. In 1738 the company acquired land in Kelvinhaugh as the site for an iron-slitting mill, and although a goldsmith and two wrights are mentioned in connection with the purchase,[51] it is clear from other sources that the partnership was dominated by Glasgow merchants: in 1763 the partners were named as John Murdoch, James Denniston, Allan Dreghorn and Thomas Dunlop, all merchants in Glasgow; Allan Dreghorn was one of the 'Wrights' named in 1738.[52] The works produced nails, adzes, axes, hoes, spades, shovels, chisels, hammers, bellows and anvils, all of which were in demand among Glasgow's colonial trading partners.[53] After the outbreak of the American War of Independence the works changed hands twice, and during the 1780s the mill appears to have been converted to process grain.[54]

The other west-coast works, Dalnotter, was founded in 1769 by three Glasgow merchants — George Murdoch, Peter Murdoch and William King — together with two Newcastle men, George Hudson and James King, both of whom already had experience of steelmaking. Between 1769 and 1774 both Englishmen and one Scot, George Murdoch, left the company but four additional partners were taken in. The products manufactured and the markets supplied were broadly similar to those of the Smithfield Company. The works started in the Nether (corn) Mill of Dalnotter, but two more mills were acquired in 1773, one of which, a corn mill, became a forge; the other, a waulk mill, became a slitting mill. In 1813 the works was sold to William Dunn, who eventually used the site for cotton manufacture (see p. 430); a small iron works under James Marr continued to use some of the higher falls in making spades and shovels.[55]

The Cramond iron works, on the opposite side of Scotland, also had close links with local merchants. The Smith and Wright Work Company of Leith had been founded in 1747 by William Moyes, wright in Leith, but had passed into the hands of a larger partnership by 1749. Some time before 1752 the company took a lease of Cockle Mill, a corn mill on the River Almond which they converted to roll and slit iron, and a second mill, Fairafar. Two of the partners, namely James Macdowall (textile manufacturer) and David Strachan (merchant in Leith), already had territorial interests in the Cramond area; no fewer than seven of the remaining partners were described as merchants in Edinburgh, one as a sea captain, another as an excise officer and one, the last to be admitted, as a farmer's son.[56] In 1759 the two mills were sold to Dr. John Roebuck, who was soon to co-found Carron Works, and Cramond continued under Carron control until 1770, when it was sold to one of its partners, William Cadell junior.[57] Under the Cadells, Fairafar Mill was finally converted for use in iron manufacture; two other mills, Peggy's and Dowie's, were also brought into use.[58] A new company was formed in 1847 and yet another about 1862. The iron works finally closed down about 1870.[59]

Before moving on, it is worth noting that members of the Smithfield, Dalnotter and Cramond companies co-operated in setting up a major iron smelting and bar iron works at Muirkirk, Ayrshire in 1787 at a time when the imported bar iron on which they had formerly depended was rising in price.[60] Besides his involvement in Cramond and Muirkirk, Thomas Edington was also instrumental in setting up Clyde Ironworks, near Glasgow, in 1786.[61]

Information on the ownership of foundries is less easily come by, though in those cases where water power was used there appear to be links with textile manufacture, still Scotland's most important industry during the early 19th century, and a major user of cast iron in the years following mechanisation. In some cases association is obvious: cotton mills at Catrine, New Lanark and Deanston all had requirements sufficient to justify their own water-powered foundries.[62] At Woodside Printfield, Aberdeenshire, the use of a foundry established in 1826 was also extended to members of the public:

> Gordon Barron & Co., having found it necessary to establish a foundry for the convenience of their works at Woodside, and having completed the same on an extensive scale, beg to inform the public that they are now ready to furnish every sort of cast-iron work and machinery on the shortest notice and most reasonable terms. As their new machinery requires such nicety and exactness, they have engaged an experienced founder from one of the first foundries in England, and from specimens already seen they can confidently assert that the work executed at their foundry will be found inferior to none in the country.[63]

Durie Foundry, on the Fife Leven, was established in 1809 by John Baird, a leading partner in the Shotts iron (smelting) works, David Russell, factor on the Durie estate, and three local textile manufacturers —David Alison and Robert McDowall, both at Millfield, and Robert Biset at Prinlaws. By the end of 1812 David Russell had become the sole partner; following his bankruptcy in 1817, the foundry was purchased by the Dundee merchant Henry Balfour.[64]

Elsewhere the association of foundries with the textile industry is more one of location than control, although a closer examination may reveal a broader relationship. It should be emphasised, however, that the link between iron foundry and textile mill ownership applies only to those few instances where water power was used; in all probability it would not hold good if extended to foundries in general. Lastly, small rural spade and sickle mills are occasionally found to have been run by companies, as at Robert Grindlay & Company's Upper Banton sickle works near Kilsyth, Stirlingshire,[65] but as such instances are relatively uncommon and as information is scarce, nothing further will be said of them in the present context.

Individuals

If companies were only rarely to be found running small rural spade and sickle works, then this was the one sector of the iron industry to which individual tradesmen, such as smiths or wrights, could contribute. Unfortunately the scarcity of information already mentioned extends to these small works as a whole, but the few cases where details are available cast some light on the subject. The iron works at Dalkeith occupied a mill owned by the Duke of Buccleuch, but during its long existence the business appears to have been in the hands of tenants. First recorded in 1720, the mill was run for many years by James Gray before passing to his nephew, David Hutchison. He in turn was succeeded by his son, but with a decline in trade the mill was converted to grain milling. The products of the mill consisted of sheet iron and all kinds of heavy smith work, including furnace doors and frames which were supplied to Saltoun Bleachfield.[66]

The mill at Crawick Bridge, Dumfriesshire is particularly well documented. In 1774 John Rigg, from Dalston in Cumbria, was induced to set up a shovel mill by a Mr. Barker, the then lessee of coal pits in the Sanquhar area.[67] On his tour of Scotland Loch noted that:

> a tilt mill is erected here for making spades and all such implements for country use in the iron way, equal to any in Britain.[68]

The mill was still in the Rigg family in the 1830s, making solid steel spades and shovels on two water-powered tilt hammers.[69] The requirements of the mining industry might also have encouraged James Anderson, a blacksmith, to build an iron-beating mill at the foot of Heugh Mills, Dunfermline, some time before 1769.[70]

In terms of capital investment the contribution of individual artisans was infinitesimally small beside that of companies backed by mercantile or manufacturing interests. Nevertheless, they did provide for the specialised needs of particular areas, notably in the production of spades, shovels and sickles.

Distribution and Chronology

Considerable difficulties arise in trying to assess the distribution of water power in an industry involving a fairly small number of sites with an enormous range in scale and type of production, all within the wider context of an industry which also used steam power to a great extent. Too fine a breakdown would lose sight of any pattern, and the only solution must be to follow the twofold division between smelting and other processes already used in the previous section.

Smelting

Within the iron smelting sector a clear-cut distinction can be made between the distribution and chronology of the earlier charcoal furnaces and the later coke ones. Of the charcoal iron works (Figure 100), the first three, at Glen Kinglass, Coulnakyle and Invergarry, were all established towards the end of the 1720s. All three were poorly sited in relation to iron ore: only Coulnakyle used Scottish ores, and even these had to be brought fourteen miles overland to be smelted. Both Glen Kinglass and Invergarry had to rely on ore imported with great difficulty from Cumbria; in two cases transport difficulties were aggravated by the choice of inland sites. The attraction of their sites lay rather in the availability of timber for charcoal production and other purposes, and had it not been for this, it is highly unlikely that such inaccessible sites would have been chosen. All three had gone out of production by the end of the 1730s.

Following the demise of the first group of Highland iron works, a further decade elapsed before any more were founded. Including as they did the '45 Rebellion, the 1740s were hardly conducive to English investment in the Highlands, nor was the fate of the earlier works much of an incentive to other iron masters. When it did arrive, the second generation of charcoal iron works shared with the first an attraction towards Highland forests as a potential source of fuel, but seems to have learned from the failure of its predecessors by choosing more accessible sites: Bonawe (1753) and Inverleckan (c. 1750/1775) were both situated further south on coastal sites. Inverleckan closed down in 1813, during a trade depression, but Bonawe continued to operate until 1874, some one hundred and twenty-five years after the introduction of coke smelting to Scotland. Speaking of the charcoal iron works as a whole, the dearth of timber in Lowland Scotland and the relative abundance in the Highlands made the latter area an obvious choice for siting charcoal iron works. A preference for the west reflects the need to have access to imported ores. As for the widely held belief that these works were responsible for destroying Highland forests, recent research by Lindsay[71] points to the contrary yet more plausible conclusion that they followed a sensible policy of careful woodland management.

The two water-powered coke-fired ironworks, Carron (1759) and Balgonie (1802), represent the two extremes of a much wider range of works, the majority of which were steam-powered. Carron had two, then four, blast furnaces, the product of which was manufactured into wrought and cast iron

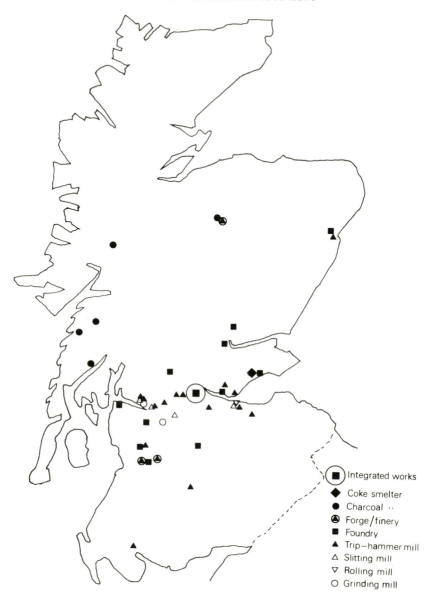

Fig 100. Distribution of water power in the iron industry, 1730-1830

goods on site, before being transported and marketed by the company itself. Balgonie, in contrast, closed down in 1814, after a short and difficult existence, and never consisted of more than a single blast furnace. The site of Carron Works was carefully chosen to optimise access to fuel, limestone, iron ore and water power, all of which were available locally, and markets which were readily accessible by sea. The steam-powered smelting works which followed Carron from 1779 onwards tended to be situated further south and west, generally close to their raw materials, yet freed from the restrictions on location imposed by water power. Balgonie, the most north-easterly of the Scottish coke-fired iron works, was no worse than its competitors with regard to raw materials and, lying within a few miles of the sea, had easier access to markets than most. Its earlier closure owed much to the persistent financial difficulties of its owners.

Foundries and Forges

As only a few foundries used water power, their distribution cannot be taken to be representative of foundries as a whole, nor is it always possible to determine whether or not a foundry did, in fact, use water power.[72] Were the locations of all pre-1830 foundries known, it would at least be possible to fit known users of water power into a wider pattern, and perhaps form some conclusions on that basis, but in the absence of such knowledge attention must be confined to the characteristics of confirmed water-powered sites. The origins of iron founding go back well before 1730, and in the early 17th century George Hay was said to be casting cannon in Wester Ross (see p. 88). During the period under consideration the production of ordnance continued to be a major application of cast iron, and from its foundation in 1759 Carron Works made it one of its specialities. However, it was the use of cast iron in millwork, in agricultural and textile machinery and, paradoxically, in the manufacture of steam engines which provided work for the majority of water-powered iron foundries, most of which date from the early 19th century.

It has already been suggested that there was a noticeable correlation between the distribution of the water-powered textile industry and that of water-powered foundries (p. 425). In addition to those examples already cited, several other foundries can be used to illustrate the point. One at Perth, established in 1802 and rebuilt about 1820,[73] lay in an area noted for its bleach-fields; Blairgowrie, with its dozen or so flax spinning mills, also had an 'iron turning' mill,[74] whilst at Barrhead in the heart of the Renfrewshire cotton manufacturing district, Clark & McAllister, 'Engineers and Millwrights', operated a water-powered foundry.[75] In some cases the connection with steam engines is stated explicitly: Henry Balfour at Durie Foundry and A. & W. Johnston, whose foundry occupied part of fall no. 4 on the Shaws Water Aqueduct, Greenock, are both listed in Pigot's 1837 directory as 'Engine and Machine Makers'.[76] It should be remembered, of course, that the converse was also true: Glasgow's steam-powered St. Rollox foundry, for example, produced *inter alia* waterwheels and mill gearing.[77]

By no means all water-powered foundries owed their existence to the market for textile machinery and steam engines. At Carmichael Mill (Lanarkshire) James Paterson, the miller, set up a small foundry to manufacture parts for threshing machines,[78] and at Clockmill, Berwickshire, James Ferguson's foundry turned out agricultural machinery.[79] Whilst Carmichael Mill probably served a fairly small area, products from Clockmill have turned up as far north as Perthshire.[80] Unfortunately it has not been possible to confirm that either foundry used water power, though in both cases this is a strong possibility.

Malleable Iron Works

In defining the distribution of water-powered malleable iron works, it is useful to distinguish between those where bar iron was produced and those where it was manufactured into artifacts.

At least six sites fall into the first category. In the 1730s Coulnakyle was producing bar iron from its own pig iron, as was Inverleckan in the second half of the 18th century; at Terreoch (Ayrshire) a forge was set up in 1732, using iron which may have been smelted in the Highlands.[81] Predictably, bar iron production came within Carron Company's all-embracing scope, and at Muirkirk where the blast was to have been provided by water power, but where steam was used instead, a canal had been cut and a reservoir built on the River Ayr to help transport raw materials to the works; this was in turn applied to driving a bar iron forge and rolling mill within the works.[82] Cartographic evidence suggests that water power might also have been used in a forge at Wilstontown (Lanarkshire, 1779).[83] Of these, only Terreoch did not use iron smelted on site. For much of the period 1730-1830 manufacturers of wrought iron goods made use of bar iron imported from Sweden, Russia and England. Coulnakyle and Terreoch had a very short existence, Carron used up its own output, and not until the 1780s did the rising price of imported bar iron prompt a group of users to combine in setting up Muirkirk iron works, and even this did not obviate the need for imports.[84] Although the manufacture of bar iron was confined to a few sites, most of them also engaged in smelting, the utilisation of bar iron took place at more numerous, more widely scattered locations. A further subdivision, between major and minor users, aids clarity.

The four major malleable iron users cover a long period: Smithfield (c. 1738-c.1780), Dalnotter (1769-1815 *et seq*), Cramond (c.1750 *et seq*) and Carron (1759 *et seq*) almost span the entire century 1730-1830. Leaving aside Carron, the location of the other three reflects the need to have access by sea for imported bar iron and exported goods. The importance of mercantile capital in their formation also influenced their location: Cramond and Smithfield grew out of smaller works in Leith and Glasgow respectively, and it was principally the need to use water power which drew them away from their original sites. Carron, of course, shared their accessibility to shipping but was able to furnish its own raw materials.

The minor users of bar iron were altogether more restricted in the scale and range of their production and in the areas which they served. Taken as a group, they occupy an exceptionally long period: at least two 'Iron Mills', at Dalkeith and near Charlestown (Fife), date from before 1730, whilst others, such as Barbules (Lanarkshire), were not established until after 1830. In the intervening century there were no additions until the late 1760s, when a spade and shovel mill was set up at Dunfermline: a second one was established at Crawick Bridge (Dumfriesshire) in 1773 and a third at Aberdour (Fife) by the 1790s.[85] In 1792 the Board of Trustees granted £10 towards the cost of a proposed sickle mill at Newton Stewart, but there is no certainty that it was ever built.[86]

The early 19th century brought an acceleration in the establishment of both types of mill, over an area extending from Aberdeen to Galloway. The location of sickle mills seems to have owed as much to the initiative of individuals as to any other factor: certainly within lowland districts geographical variations in the intensity of grain cultivation were not sufficiently great to justify the construction of a mill in one area rather than another. The distribution of spade and shovel mills corresponds to some extent with mining areas, though some of the spades must have found their way into agricultural or at least horticultural use. Concentrations of spade and shovel mills, if any there were, developed in the Falkland-Monklands area, where mining activity and a developing iron industry might go some way towards explaining their presence, and to a lesser extent in north-west Dumfriesshire, an area with less easily defined attractions. At least two small mills manufactured edge tools: one at Rutherglen was already in existence by the late 1770s but the other, at Drumglass, Kirkintilloch, may only date from the 1830s.[87]

Taken as a whole, there were probably about eighty water mills applied to various aspects of the iron industry between 1730 and 1830. All of those identified are plotted in Figure 96.

Case Study: Carron Iron Works

Time and time again Carron Company has cropped up in this chapter, and many of its characteristics recommend it for more detailed examination. Carron was the first coke smelting iron works in Scotland, the largest producer before 1830, the only totally integrated works, the greatest user of water power within the industry, and one of the greatest within the Scottish economy as a whole.

Carron Works was founded by two Englishmen — Samuel Garbett and John Roebuck — and a Scot, William Cadell. Roebuck the scientist, Garbett the entrepreneur and Cadell the merchant joined with four others, including Cadell's son William, in a partnership to form an iron works which was to use Darby's coke smelting process, and in the winter of 1758-9 trials were carried out on various Scottish ores. Those from Bo'ness were found to be the best, and a search then began for a site near Bo'ness with good access to coal, charcoal, water power and markets.[88] A site at Carron was chosen where they could:

> . . . have the entire command above [and] below the works of a fall of water equal in quantity to what would most probably be wanted for two furnaces [and] superior in power, or height, of its fall and its proximity to sea carriage, to any other . . .[89]

To ensure a high standard of workmanship, building labour and materials were brought from England. The bellows, the water wheel, shaft, hearthstone and iron plates all came from Birmingham. Bricks were transported from Stourbridge, Worcestershire.

As a supplement to the works and as a source of income while the works was under construction, Roebuck bought the iron slitting mill at Cramond for £1,010. Roebuck also planned the new works, to consist of four blast furnaces, four air furnaces, one boring mill, one double forge, one forge for drawing salt pans, one forge for drawing out metal scraps from Holland and one slit rolling mill.[90] All except the air furnaces were to be powered by the waters of the River Carron.

A huge lade was cut from the river, requiring the construction of two hundred and fifty yards of banking, and on Boxing Day 1760, after problems engendered by bad labour, inefficient communications, subsidence and bad weather, the first furnace was put on blast; the second furnace started on 4th September 1761, and in the same month a boring mill, for guns and cylinders, was completed. A forge, with three fineries and two hammers, was constructed by Sheffield workers after the completion of the first furnace. Fineries and hammers were completed by November 1762, and thenceforth they were allocated specific tasks, such as making brewers' squares for the London market, broad iron for rolling into salt pan and boiler plates, and mould boards for ploughs.[91] In 1766 a decision was taken to build two more blast furnaces. Furnaces one and two had used traditional wood and leather bellows but Garbett, impressed by the use in England of cylinders instead of bellows, sent workmen to Rotherham and consulted John Smeaton.[92] Smeaton, one of the greatest engineers of the 18th century, had put the use of water power onto a scientific footing with the publication in 1759 of his *Experimental Enquiry into the Natural Powers of Wind and Water to turn Mills*. This was only the beginning of a long association with Carron Company which was to last for twenty years. It was decided to use the Rotherham method, with three cylinders, the pistons of which were connected to a crank fixed in the centre of the water wheel axle. Initial success prompted the company to start work on the casting of cylinders to blow number four furnace in the same way, but after the crank of number four had broken at least twice in 1767, Smeaton was called in once more.[93]

Since the works had first begun, inadequate water supplies had been a problem at Carron. Originally the blast furnaces and the boring mill had been built on Stenhouse Mill lade, but the supply of water, adequate for a corn mill, was much less than that needed by a large iron works. To improve the supply and fall, the company dug a lade from Larbert and built reservoirs which fed the water wheels of the iron works. As the works expanded, however, it became apparent that this too would provide only part of the works' total needs, and so bad was the situation in the dry summer of 1765 that part of the works had to be closed down for want of water. After considering several solutions, the company finally decided in favour of a steam engine, which was installed in August 1767. Like many before it, this steam engine was employed to pump water, in this case back into the reservoirs, so that it could be used to power the wheels a second time. As an additional measure, the banks of the existing Carron pool were raised. The engine, which pumped back four hundred and forty cubic feet of water per minute, helped a little, but even with another reservoir above Larbert which could hold six days' supply, there was just not enough water to keep the works running.[94] By January 1769, as the writer of the following report makes clear, the situation was desperate:

> . . . the quantity and application of that quantity of water, . . . I reckon a subject of the utmost importance to, tho' a subject little understood by, Carron Company. Daily experience proves the sources of the Carron greatly inferior to the call of the furnaces, and the expectation of a supply by rains and a wet summer season will fall greatly short of the hopes of most of the Gentlemen since, from my own observations, I can produce conviction of the floods in Carron running off so quickly in that season that, in four or five days, there shall remain no marks of the smallest increase of the summers source and run of the river.
>
> The assistance of the reservior at Larbert has fallen much short of the calculations made upon it, and the dependence on the fire engine has hitherto been very precarious.
>
> It is generally allowed that the sources of Carron are barely sufficient for the supply of water for the two furnaces during summer — and that the other parts of the works must be supplied with forced water — the expense of which to keep insured the quantity wanted, must be so great that it may be doubted whether any of the company's works on the present head of water, besides the blast furnaces, are able by their produce to repay the expense.[95]

Again the company sought Smeaton's advice, this time to find ways of saving water. First he introduced a new four-cylinder blowing engine at number one furnace. For the first time iron, instead of wood, was used for the water wheel's axle, marking the beginning of a long transition in water mill machinery from wood to iron. At the same time, number one blowing engine incorporated several traditional features: the cranks to the cylinders were driven from the water wheel by a wallower and spur wheel with wooden cog and rung gearing, while the spur wheel itself was of a heavy, wooden 'clasp arm' construction. The addition of a fourth cylinder brought number four up to the capacity of number one.[96]

The blowing engine for number two furnace, designed later that year, shows several improvements on number one. By using an overshot wheel, in his judgement the most efficient type, Smeaton was able to reduce the wheel to a size which would revolve sufficiently fast to eliminate the need for gearing. Secondly, in place of the two beams working cylinders at either end, number two had four beams and the cylinders all placed at the opposite end of the crank.[97]

Through these and other alterations, Smeaton hoped to make number two twenty-five to thirty-three per cent more efficient than before and twenty per cent more efficient than his earlier number one blowing engine. The water wheel of number two appears to have incorporated some metal parts but there is no confirmation that this was the case. To prevent water from falling out of the buckets too early and thereby reducing the wheel's power, a close-fitting wall or breast was to be built around the lower quadrant of the wheel, while the wheel was widened as far as the breadth of the lade would allow.[98] This last feature anticipated the textile wheels of the 19th century which, by maximising breadth, could generate the greatest possible power from any one fall.

Smeaton's attention was then turned towards the boring mill which, in times of low water, was using two thirds of the river's flow. Smeaton suggested the use of a six-foot fall instead of the existing twenty-foot. With this reduction the existing wheel would have required 1697 cubic feet of water per minute. Smeaton promised to design a wheel so efficient that it would require only 660 cubic feet on a seven-foot fall. Except for an only partially successful device to support the cutting head, the gun- and cylinder-boring mills themselves incorporated little in the way of new technology. The wheels and gearing, however, were superbly thought out and incorporated many novel features which were to be of great value in the years to follow. Two eighteen-foot diameter wheels worked with a seven-foot fall; the rims and axles were to be of cast iron. Here too a close-fitting wall or breast was built around the lower upstream quarter of each wheel. The gearing, unlike that of number one blowing engine, was of iron, and instead of the conventional cog and rung gearing, interlocking iron cogs were used.[99] In the same year Smeaton also helped in the design of a blacking mill for charcoal, and[100] in 1777 he gave directions for the construction of a clay mill[101] and a blowing machine for a fifth furnace.

Charles Gascoine, who had married Garbett's daughter, eventually became manager at Carron, and it was during his time there that most of these changes were undertaken. The provision of satisfactory boring mills was particularly important, since without them the company would have been unable to break into the very lucrative ordnance market, a market which was to guarantee the survival of Carron works through the late 18th and early 19th centuries. Despite Smeaton's improvements, the River Carron still failed to supply the quantity of water needed, and in the 1770s the lade was repaired and the furnace pools expanded. The existing steam engine was repaired and a new one installed in 1780. For the rest of the century, the water power remained sufficient.[102]

Shortly after the completion of the new boring mills, they were modified to bore guns solid, instead of hollow.[103] By altering the mills in this way (and incidentally infringing Wilkinson's patent of 1774), Carron was able to make a product which found a ready market in Spain and among private merchants. In 1778, after thorough testing, the first of the famous Carrons, which became known as Carronades, were produced.[104]

Saint-Fond's description of the works, written in 1784, gives a detailed picture of production at Carron and deserves to be quoted at length:

Above one hundred acres of land have been converted into reservoirs and pools, for water directed from the river, by magnificent dams built about two miles above the works, which after turning eighteen large wheels for the several purposes of the manufacture, fall into a tidal navigation that conveys their castings to the sea. These works are the greatest of their kind in Europe and were established in 1760. At present the buildings are of vast extent: and the machinery, constructed by Mr. Smeaton, is the first in Britain, both in elegance and correctness; there are sixteen hundred men employed, to whom is paid weekly above 650L sterling; which has greatly enriched the adjoining country: 6500 tons of iron are smelted annually from the mineral with pit-coal and cast into cannon, cylinders, etc.

In the founding of cannon the works have lately arrived at such perfection that they make above five thousand pieces a year, many of which are exported to foreign states; and their guns of new construction are the lightest and neatest now in use, not excepting brass guns. The present proprietors are a chartered company, with a capital of 150,000L sterling, a common seal etc. but their stock is confined to a very few individuals. A man attended us at the gate, who said that he was ordered to conduct us everywhere, with the exception of the place where the cannons were bored, which no stranger was permitted to see.

He conducted us first into an immense court, surrounded with high walls and vast sheds. This place was covered with cannons, mortars, bombs, balls and those large pieces which bear the name Carronades. Amid these machines of war, these terrible instruments of death, gigantic cranes, capstans of every kind, levers and assemblies of pullies, serving to move so many articles of enormous weight, are erected in situations convenient for that purpose. The various movements, the shrill creaking of pullies, the continuous noise of hammers, the activity of those arms which gave impulsion to so many machines; everything here presents a spectacle as new and interesting.

The large buildings where the cannons are bored are not at a great distance from the first yard. We passed close by them, but were politely told, that particular processes and machines unknown to every other establishment of the kind, rendered it necessary to keep that place concealed from strangers. We thought this was very reasonable and followed our conductor to another quarter.

He conducted us to the works for smelting the ore; where four furnaces, of forty-five feet in height, devoured both night and day enormous masses of coals and metal. One may from this judge the quantity of air necessary to feed these burning gulphs, which disgorged, every six hours, whole floods of liquid iron. Each furnace is supplied by four air pumps, of a great width, where the air, compressed into iron cylinders, uniting into one tunnel, and directed towards the flame, produces a sharp rustling noise, and so violent a tremor, that one not previously informed of it would find it difficult to avoid a sensation of terror. These wind machines, this species of gigantic bellows, are put in motion by the action of water. Such a torrent of air is indispensably necessary to support, in the highest state of ignition, a column of coal and ore forty-five feet high; and it is so rapid and active, that it projects a vivid and brisk flame more than ten feet above the top of the furnace.

An open area, of very great extent, built in the form of a terrace, and on a level with the upper apperture of the fire places, is appropriated to the reception of the supplies of ore and coals; and on this platform are also spacious areas, where the coal is prepared for use.

There is such a numerous series of these places for making coke, to supply so vast a consumption, that the air is heated to a considerable extent, and during the night the sky is entirely illuminated with the flames. The supplies of ore are on the same terrace with the coals. A canal, dug at a great expense, and which communicates with the sea, serves to carry all the materials used here, and to transport its manufactured productions.

We visited the place where the crude iron is refined in reverberatory furnaces, to be afterwards cast into mortars, cannons, howitzers, bombs, balls etc. We saw also, that where the moulds are prepared, and another place where they are dried. We were also conducted into a vast fabric which suggested the most pleasant of ideas, for its productions consisted of the various implements of agriculture, the arts and domestic use, . . . the greater part of these productions are sold at so moderate a rate that a man of very slender fortune may here procure many articles of necessity, and even of ornament, which cannot be obtained elsewhere at three times their price. But labour and workmanship are, in this place, assisted by so many machines and ingenious processes, that its commodities are executed, both in a shorter time, and with greater perfection, than in other establishments of the same kind.[105]

Water power continued to be used for the blast furnaces until the 1830s, when a ninety horse power steam engine was installed to provide the blast.[106] In the 1850s water power was still being used to grind fire clay, bore cylinders, and grind and polish cast metal,[107] while as late as 1868 a water turbine provided power for the engineering workshop.[108]

Carron Company represents more than just another water-powered factory. It was the first major iron works in Lowland Scotland, and the first in the whole of Scotland to use coke smelting. For over twenty-five years it was the only one. Production and marketing, from the mining of coal, ore and limestone, to the distribution of Carron products in Carron-owned ships, came to be concentrated in one industrial unit, a feat exceptional for anywhere in Britain at that time.

The need to house its employees (1,200 by 1769,[109] 1,600 by 1784[110]) led to the creation of irregularly laid out villages at Larbert, Stenhousemuir, West Carron, Carronshore (once the port of Carron) and Cuttyfield, where previously there had been a 'meer moor', with 'not a single house' upon it.[111]

Above all, the products of Carron, particularly metal parts for mill-work, helped, in no small way, to bring about the transformation from wooden to iron machinery, so characteristic of the Industrial Revolution: all this with water power, with steam playing only a small subservient role.

NOTES

1. Quoted by Clow, A. & Clow, N. L., *The Chemical Revolution*, London, 1952, 327.

2. Corrins, R. D., 'The Great Hot-Blast Affair', *IA* VII (1970), 233-263.

3. See especially Raistrick, A., *A Dynasty of Ironfounders*, London, 1953; Gale, W. K. V., *The British Iron & Steel Industry*, Newton Abbot, 1967, 29-34.

4. *Scots Magazine* LXI 372 (1799): one furnace at Carron was forty-five feet high; *RCAHMS*, Argyll Vol 2, *Lorn*, Edinburgh, 1975, 284.

5. Campbell, R. H., *Carron Company*, Edinburgh, 1961; Schubert, H. R., in Singer, C., Holmyard, E. J., Hall, A. R. & Williams, T. I. (eds.), *A History of Technology*, 5 vols., Oxford, 1956-9, VI, 103, dates the invention to 1762.

6. See, for example, blast furnaces for the Clyde Ironworks, 1788, in Clow & Clow, *op. cit.*, opposite page 363.

7. Dickinson, H. W., *A Short History of the Steam Engine*, Cambridge, 1938, 73-4.

8. SRO GD171/110: John Mackenzie to William Forbes, Edinburgh, 3rd February 1784.

9. Butt, J., *Industrial Archaeology of Scotland*, Newton Abbot, 1967, 110.

10. Hume, J. R., 'Water Mills of the River Ayr', *AAC* 2nd Series VIII (1967-9), 44.

11. Butt, *op. cit.*, 110. See page 423 *et seq.*

12. Farey, J., *A Treatise on the Steam Engine*, London, 1827, 276.

13. Schubert, *op. cit.*, 101-2.

14. *Ibid.*, 102.

15. Hume, *op. cit.*, 48.

16. *Scots Magazine* LXI (1799), 375. A similar principle was used in grinding flint: see Chapter 27, page   .

17. SRO CS96/817, p.96.

18. Smeaton, J., *Reports of the Late John Smeaton*, 3 vols., London, 1812, I, 382-3.

19. Gale, *op. cit.*, 21-2.

20. *Ibid.*, 24-5.

21. SRO GD248/135/1.

22. Hume, *op. cit.*, 45.

23. No. 780: Woodcroft, B., *Alphabetical Index of Patentees of Inventions* (facsimile edition), London,, 1969.

24. Campbell, *op. cit.*, 59.

25. Clow & Clow, *op. cit.*, 350; Hume, *op. cit.*, 44.

26. *SBRS*, 'Extracts from the Records of the Burgh of Glasgow', V (1718-38), Glasgow, 1909, 424.

27. *Ibid.*, 495.

28. Gale, *op. cit.*, 35-6.

29. Graham, P., *General View of the Agriculture of Stirlingshire*, Edinburgh, 1812, 348.

30. Loch, D., *A Tour through Most of the Trading Towns and Villages of Scotland*, Edinburgh, 1778, 33-4.

31. Ure, D., *The History of Rutherglen & East Kilbride*, Glasgow, 1793, 119.

32. Hume, *op. cit.*, 45.

33. SRO GD224/282/1 (1720).

34. *RCAHMS*, Lorn, 280.

35. Butt, J., 'Capital and Enterprise in the Scottish Iron Industry, 1780-1840', in Butt, J. & Ward, J. T. (eds.), *Scottish Themes — Essays in Honour of Professor S. G. E. Lythe*, Edinburgh, 1976, 69.

36. *Ibid.*, 74.

37. SRO GD171/110.

38. See Chapter 26, page 444.

39. Murray, D., *The York Buildings Company. A Chapter of Scotch History*, Glasgow, 1883, 64; Fell, A., *The Early Iron Industry of Furness & District*, Ulverston, 1908, 379; Butt, *op. cit.* (1967), 105.

40. Fell, *op. cit.*, 379-80.

41. *RCAHMS*, Lorn, 280.

42. Fell, *op. cit.*, 343-387.

43. *Ibid.*, 390-1; *RCAHMS*, Lorn, 283.

44. Fell, *op. cit.*, 413.

45. MacAdam, W. I., 'Notes on the Ancient Iron Industry of Scotland', *PSAS* XXI (1886-7), 124.

46. Fell, *op. cit.*, 411-2; *OSA* V, 287, Inveraray, Argyll.

47. Butt, J., 'Glenbuck Ironworks', *AAC* 2nd Series, VIII (1967-9), 68-75.

48. Campbell, *op. cit.*, 7-14.

49. SRO GD26/5/371/1: Ironworks 1803-5; SRO GD26/5/371/2: Ironworks 1804-14; SRO CS96/203: Sederunt Book, Creditors of Balgonie Iron Co.

50. Butt, *op. cit.* (1976), 76.

51. *SBRS*, Glasgow V, 495.

52. *SBRS*, 'Extracts from the Records of the Burgh of Glasgow', VII (1760-80), Glasgow, 1912, 139.

53. Devine, T. M., Glasgow Merchants and Colonial Trade 1770-1815, Strathclyde University PhD., 1972, II, 339.

54. Thomson, G., 'The Dalnotter Iron Company', *SHS* XXXV (1956), 11.

55. *Ibid.*, SRO RHP187 (N.D.) identifies the Nether Mill of Dalnotter as a grinding mill; *Pigot & Co's National Commercial Directory of the Whole of Scotland and the Isle of Man*, London, 1837, 339; OS 1st Edition 6″/mile.

56. Cadell, P., *The Iron Mills at Cramond*, Edinburgh, 1973, 29-36.

57. *Ibid.*, 4-6.

58. *Ibid.*, 11; Peggy's Mill became a paper mill in 1815.

59. Cadell, *op. cit.*, 29-36.

60. *Ibid.*, 18-19.

61. Thomson, *op cit.*, 19.

62. Hume, *op. cit.*, 48; Butt, *op. cit.* (1967), 67.

63. Morgan, P., *Annals of Woodside & Newhills*, Aberdeen, 1886, 260.

64. SRO CS96/817.

65. SRO NG1/1/34 20/5/23.

66. SRO GD224/282/1; *NSA* I, 503, Dalkeith, Midlothian; NLS Acc. 2933/320.

67. Brown, J., *The History of Sanquhar*, Dumfries, 1891, 368.

68. Loch, *op. cit.*, 40.

69. Brown, *op. cit.*, 368-9.

70. Henderson, E., *The Annals of Dunfermline*, Glasgow, 1879, 505, gives the date as 1777, but the mill is mentioned by Pennant, T., *A Tour in Scotland, 1769*, 2nd Edition, London, 1772, 213. According to Henderson, 'a good trade in this kind was carried on for some years'.

71. Lindsay, J. M., 'The Commercial Use of Highland Woodland 1750-1870: a Reconsideration', *SGM* XCII (1976).

72. Possible sites: Clockmill, Duns; Newmill, Elgin; Millbank, Thurso.

73. Butt, *op. cit.* (1967), 114.

74. *OS* 1st Edition 6″/mile.

75. Pigot, *op. cit.*, 712; *OS* 1st Edition 6″/mile; *NSA* VII, 317, Neilston, Renfrew-

shire.

76. Pigot, *op. cit.*, 406, 701; *NSA* VII, 437, Greenock, Renfrewshire.

77. See, for example, SRO GD267/17/7.

78. *NSA* VI, 531, Carmichael, Lanarkshire.

79. Pigot, *op. cit.*, 305.

80. Fieldwork: Cambusmichael (St. Martin's parish, Perthshire), May 1978.

81. Hume, *op. cit.*, 45.

82. *Ibid.*, 44.

83. SRO RHP498 (1856).

84. Hume, *op. cit.*, 44.

85. Dalkeith: SRO GD224/282/1 (1720); Dunfermline (Iron Mill): see Chapter 7, page 89; Barblues: Butt, *op. cit.* (1967), 144; Dunfermline (Heugh Mills): Pennant, *op. cit.*, 213; Crawick Bridge: Brown, *op. cit.*, 368-9; Aberdour: *OSA* IV, 327, Aberdour, Fife.

86. SRO NG1/1/27 17/11/90; SRO NG1/1/28 8/2/92.

87. Rutherglen: Loch, *op. cit.*, 33-4; Ure, *op. cit.*, 119; Kirkintilloch: Pigot, *op. cit.*, 341.

88. Campbell, *op. cit.*, 7-9, 28.

89. SRO GD58/16/19, p. 44.

90. Campbell, *op. cit.*, 30-33.

91. *Ibid.*, 35-6.

92. *Ibid.*, 36-7.

93. *Ibid.*, 37.

94. *Ibid.*, 42-4.

95. SRO GD58/16/19, pp. 49-50.

96. Smeaton, J., *op. cit.*, I, 359, 364.

97. *Ibid.*, 364-6.

98. *Ibid.*, 364-6.

99. *Ibid.*, 376-9.

100. *Ibid.*, 382-3.

101. *Ibid.*, 412.

102. Campbell, *op. cit.*, 44-5.

103. *Ibid.*, 88.

104. *Ibid.*, 90.

105. *Scots Magazine* LXI (1799), 371-5.

106. Bremner, D., *The Industries of Scotland* (1869), Newton Abbot, 1969, 43.

107. Wilson, J. M. (ed.), *The Imperial Gazetteer of Scotland*, 2 vols., Edinburgh, London & Dublin, N. D. (c.1875), I, 253.

108. Bremner, *op. cit.*, 43.

109. Pennant, *op. cit.*, 244.

110. *Scots Magazine* LXI (1799), 371.

111. Pennant, *op. cit.*, 224; Wilson, *op. cit.*, I, 253.

26

Saw Mills

By 1730 sawmills had already become a feature of Highland and Lowland Scotland, those in the former utilising the remnants of natural woodland, those in the latter, where few good stands of timber remained, working with imported timber on coastal sites (Chapter 8). During the hundred years from 1730 to 1830 both sources continued to be exploited but a third, the product of estate Improvement, became available on a small scale in the late 18th century and was still increasing in relative importance in the 1830s. To some degree it was the application of existing and improved water-powered machinery which allowed the level of exploitation to be sustained and increased.

Technology

Frame Saws

The basic machinery of the frame saw mill was of a simple form, consisting of one or more saw blades, mounted vertically within a frame which moved up and down between guiding slots. This reciprocating motion was achieved by means of a rod and crank mechanism linked to the axle of a water wheel; although gearing might be used, sufficient speed could be obtained by the use of an unusually small water wheel, perhaps only four or five feet in diameter and occasionally only three feet.[1] The piece of wood to be cut was placed on a long low bench fitted with rollers and by means of a ratchet mechanism was made to pass through the frame. Figure 25 shows the machinery and structural timbers of a two-frame saw mill, possibly that built at Fochabers (Moray) about 1754. Plans of a more advanced type of frame saw mill appear in Gray's *Experienced Millwright*.[2]

Within this basic homogeneity of design there were considerable variations in sophistication: in 1757 the saw mills at Carrie (Perthshire) were described as

> perhaps the most Gothick thing of their kind in the world. The saws are one fourth of an inch thick, and at the most moderate computation destroy at least one fifth part of all the timber manufactured that way.[3]

By 1824 it was possible for a saw miller at Conan (Ross) to order frame saws four feet three inches long and only about one tenth of an inch thick.[4] Doubtless this refinement owed something to improvements in metallurgy. As early as 1734 there were already mills with more than one frame: the York Buildings Company's Old Mill at Abernethy, Inverness-shire had two frames and their New Mill three.[5] Usually separate frames would be reserved for each of the two principal sawing processes — removing backs (i.e. squaring off), a process known as slubbing, and the finer work of deal cutting. The saw mills of Tynessie (Inverness-shire), founded in 1765, had no fewer than seven frames by the 1790s, moved by four water wheels,[6] whilst the wind and water mills at Garmouth had thirty-six to forty and thirty to thirty-six respectively by the same date.[7] A number of blades might be mounted on any one frame. By the early 19th century one saw mill at Monymusk, Aberdeenshire had four frames with forty-two saws,[8] and at Rothiemurchus, Inverness-shire there were several packs of saws which could cut a squared log into deals in a single operation.[9]

The buildings themselves also became more sophisticated. For much of the 18th century wooden buildings, often of a temporary nature, seem to have been common,[10] although a certain amount of stonework would have been used to carry the axletree. Stone-built mills certainly existed and were considered to be superior. One such, Grant of Grant's mill at Muchrach (Inverness-shire), was described in 1769 as

> a good one of the kind. She is mason work up to the beams, of which she is much the better, as timber between wind and water spoils very soon.[11]

During the 19th century stone-built mills came to be more common, but were still by no means universal.

Circular Saws

The early 19th century brought the introduction of saw mill machinery of a different kind, with one or more disc-shaped saw(s), often belt-driven and normally with gearing. The saw bench continued to be used, but the use of gearing and the less cumbersome cutting mechanism meant that circular saws could utilise less powerful falls, or could even be appended to existing mills of other types.

Circular saws had been long used in Holland to cut wood for veneering, prior to their introduction to England, probably in the 1790s, by Walter Taylor.[12] Between 1805 and 1813 Marc Isambard Brunel took out a series of patents including one, dated 1808, for circular saws,[13] and from what little evidence is available they seem to have reached Scotland shortly thereafter. The earliest reference traced relates to one at Garmouth (Moray) in 1815, and by the early 1820s they were being used at a number of localities including Closeburn (Dumfriesshire), Jerviswood (Lanarkshire) and at Blairdrummond and Invermay (Perthshire).[14]

As with frame saw mills, multiple blades were employed at some sites: by 1829 the mill at Pitcroy, Moray had a saw bench 11′6″ by 4′6″ which carried two circular saws; Inver saw mill, Perthshire, had three and the Rothiemurchus mill ten.[15] Because of their limited size, circular saws were readily adopted as a means of exploiting thinnings and as yet immature plantations for estate purposes, or in the production of barrel staves. For coarser work frame saws were still preferred, and in some instances (as at Rothiemurchus) both types were used.

Although water power was the type of motive power most frequently used, it came nowhere near to holding a monopoly. Throughout the period hand-sawing over saw pits continued to play a part, but its inferior performance in terms of cost[16] and speed[17] ensured that it was confined to those areas where the volume of work was too small to justify the use of a saw mill. Several appear on mid-19th century Ordnance Survey maps. Wind-powered saw mills, probably of Dutch origin, were already in use in Scotland by the 1630s[18] and were still considered to be a viable alternative to water power over two hundred years later: the Garmouth Mill has already been referred to, and at the time of the New Statistical Account there were wind-powered saw mills at Ceres (Fife) and at Peterhead.[19] A woodturning wind mill at Crieff was only demolished about 1854.[20]

The first reference to steam power in saw-milling comes in a notice published in the *Edinburgh Advertiser* of 31st December 1803:

> The builders in and around Edinburgh, finding it necessary to erect steam engine mills for sawing timber, engineers willing to contract therefore will please give in estimates and proposals . . . to John Weir, Writer in Edinburgh.[21]

Whether or not this particular mill was built, steam saw mills had been established at Fisherrow (Midlothian) and Beansford (Stirlingshire) by 1807,[22] at Aberdeen by 1818[23] and a few other coastal and urban localities by 1830. In inland rural areas and wherever else adequate falls of water were available, water power continued to be used. The advent of steam railways and portable steam mills eventually encouraged the spread of steam power, but the dispersed nature of the industry helped ensure that water power was still being used for some new mills in the second half of the 19th century.

Wood Turning and Boring

Besides being used in sawing timber, water power also found a number of other applications in connection with woodland products. These can be divided into two major categories, those which were closely related to industries not based on woodworking and those which, by further processing timber, enhanced its value. Applications in the first category are dealt with elsewhere: logwood mills, using imported timber, in Chapter 21, charcoal mills for ironfounding in Chapter 25 and both bark mills for tanneries and charcoal mills for gunpowder works in Chapter 27. Principal among the applications in the second category were mills for turning and boring wood.

Wood-boring mills had been used on the Continent for a long time, employing techniques similar to, if less sophisticated than, those in iron-boring

Fig 101. Horizontal boring mill. Here it is being used to bore cannons, but the same technique would have been applied to wooden pipes. *Biringuccio (1540)*

(Figure 101). Boring mills were being used in both Abernethy and Rothiemurchus forests about 1770 in making wooden water pipes for London.[24] Wood-turning by water power seems to have been a later development. Doubtless pole- and treddle-lathes were being used throughout the period, but the earliest references to the use of water power only date from the early 1840s. At Camserney, Perthshire, a wheelwright had a mill for making spokes and bobbins, while at Dowally, in the same county, one James Fraser, 'ingenious mechanic and wheelwright', had contrived a mill in which a saw mill, threshing mill, turning lathes, a grindstone and the blast for a smithy hearth were all driven by a single water wheel.[25]

Organisation

As the three types of saw mill, using natural woodland, imported timber and plantations exhibit such different characteristics in terms of origins and organisation, they are dealt with separately in this and the next section, in an order which corresponds roughly to their chronological sequence.

Mills for Natural Woodland

During the period under consideration, the owner of any type of woodland, be it natural or planted, faced a choice between exploiting directly, on his own behalf, or letting out the woods to contractors, usually on a fixed quota and term. The utilisation of natural Highland woodland furnishes examples of both options.

In January 1728 the York Buildings Company bought 60,000 fir trees from the Abernethy forest on the Grant estate in Speyside for £7,000, the wood to be cut over a period of fifteen years and the money to be paid in instalments up to 1734. The company, having obtained a premium to provide main masts and other timber, commenced operations and sent specimens to London for assessment. Although a good report was sent back, the timber was considered to be unsuitable for main masts, but as an agreement had already been entered into, the company had to make the best of its predicament.[26] Operations started with one hundred and twenty working horses, waggons and 'elegant' temporary wooden houses. In addition to an existing saw mill at Coulnakyle, the company built a more powerful one of its own, besides small mills in the woods themselves. Roads were constructed to carry timber to the mills.[27]

Having invested heavily in the woods, the company soon discovered that the value of the woods came nowhere near to the price paid; inevitably it soon found itself in considerable difficulties. According to Anderson:

> . . . the company suffered heavy losses — £27,914 in four years. Up to 1731 Sir John Grant had been paid in four instalments and a fifth was due in 1732, when the governor of the company, Colonel Horsey, visited Strathspey where he was promptly arrested and had to pay or go to jail. The money was paid and the balance reduced to £2,000. The company introduced a method of payment by promissory notes. These were left unpaid and bought up to the amount of £400, on the basis of which an action was raised in 1734-5 and twenty sawmills and other equipment poinded. By 1737 the company had gone.[28]

The company's plans for buying up woodland were not confined to Strathspey: a plan by Joseph Avery, surveyed between 1725 and 1730, shows woods bought by them in connection with their iron manufacture, including woods to the west of Inverness on the Chisholm and Lovat estates.[29]

Later in the 18th century woods on Speyside were let to a variety of contractors. Between either 1745 or 1755 and 1765 John Gordon of Cluny and Alexander Shand were exploiting the forest of Glenmore, apparently on behalf of the Duke of Gordon. Timber from the forest was floated down the Rivers Luinach and Spey to Fochabers, where a saw mill had been built.[30] In 1771 two Englishmen purchased part of the forest of Abernethy from Grant of Grant, on a nineteen-year term, 12,600 trees to be cut per annum at an annual rent of £1,000.[31]

Probably the most ambitious scheme since the days of the York Buildings Company started in 1784, under the title of the Glenmore Company. The principal partners, Mr. Osbourne and Mr. Dodsworth, timber merchants in Hull, purchased the forest of Glenmore from the Duke of Gordon on a twenty-six-year term for a sum quoted variously as £10,000 and £20,000.[32] Timber from the forest was floated down the Spey to Garmouth, in the form of planks, deals and masts. By 1788 the company had two saw mills at Garmouth, one wind-powered, the other water-powered, besides labourers' houses and a dockyard. From Garmouth wood was transported, in ships built at the dock, to Hull, to the Royal Naval Yards at Deptford and Woolwich, and to Scottish markets extending from Aberdeen to the Isle of Skye.[33] Osbourne and Dodsworth fared much better than the York Buildings Company: according to Elizabeth Grant of Rothiemurchus, 'they made at least double off it'.[34]

On the Robertson of Strowan estate in Perthshire, the Forfeited Estates Commission let out the woods of Rannoch on three-year terms and on the basis of fixed tonnages, but kept overall control of its saw mills. These will be dealt with in more detail in a later section.

Although saw mills were commonly provided by woodland owners them-selves, the remaining areas of natural forest in the Highlands were normally let out to contractors, where this proved feasible. However, neither practice was invariably followed: the second saw mills at Coulnakyle and Garmouth were both company-built, and instances of direct woodland exploitation by land-owners are no less readily found. On Deeside, where there were already several saw mills by 1730, the Earl of Fife and Duff of Culter reached an agreement about 1746 whereby timber floated from the former's forests was sawn at a mill on the latter's estate.[35] At a later juncture, in 1769, Farquharson of Invercauld was both cutting and marketing his own timber. In Pennant's words:

> the value of these trees is considerable; Mr. Farquharson informed me that by sawing and retailing them he has got for eight hundred trees five and twenty shillings each: they are sawed at an adjacent saw mill into plank ten feet long, eleven inches broad and three thick, and sold for two shillings apiece.[36]

Early 19th-century evidence indicates that the Grants of Rothiemurchus controlled forestry work on their estate: William Grant organised felling on a methodical basis and, in place of the small saw mills scattered throughout the woods, built a large saw mill on the River Druie near its confluence with the Spey, where all the sawing was carried out. One man had charge of the mill, another of the woods.[37] During the 1780s, if not earlier, Grant of Grant was receiving £400 per annum from his own factor, Mr. Macgregor, for the liberty of cutting two thousand trees for deals and two thousand for other purposes. A saw mill had been erected, and both sawn and unsawn timber was floated down the Spey to the sea.[38]

Provided that he had a saw mill with the requisite labour supply and reason-ably accessible markets, there was no reason why the owner of natural wood-land should not fell, saw and even market its timber himself. On the other hand, by selling off blocks of standing trees for set terms, he could be assured of an income from it without having to involve himself directly.

Mills for Imported Timber

Cleared of the best of its natural woodland, and with as yet poor communications with the Highlands, central and southern Scotland had taken to importing timber from Scandinavia and the Baltic well before 1730, and

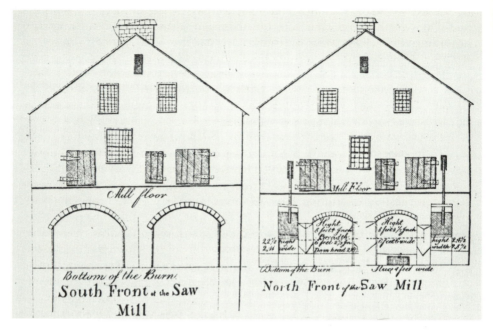

Fig 102. Saw mill on Molendinar Burn, Glasgow, *circa* 1760. *SBRS, Glasgow VII*

while much of this was sawn prior to leaving its country of origin, a few mills had been built on coastal sites in Scotland by that date. Additional supplies, notably timber from the New World and some carried by sea from the Highlands, provided further work for coastal mills. As timber had to be brought to these mills by sea, it was to be expected that operations would be handled by merchants rather than by landowners, but available evidence suggests that their control over the trade did not necessarily extend to saw-milling, and that a far wider range of interests might be involved.

On the Molendinar Burn, in Glasgow, a mill had already been built before 1730 by a member of the Hammermen, William Telfort, probably with a view to using imported timber from the Americas.[39] The mill was still in existence in 1731, but no more is heard of it thereafter. In 1749 proposals were put forward for a wind-powered mill,[40] and in the following year two wrights, William Fleming and William Murdoch, petitioned the burgh authorities, asking that they be allowed a piece of ground sixty feet by thirty-six for a mill on the Molendinar Burn, opposite the Skinners' green (Figure 102). In 1756, the mill having been completed, extra ground was made available between the mill and the Clyde for storing unsawn timber.[41] Before long, however, the burgh had reason to doubt the wisdom of allowing the mill to be built there: in November 1761, following complaints from the inhabitants of Bridgegate, an attempt was made to ease Fleming, now the sole proprietor, out of the mill, apparently without success. A second complaint regarding the 'intolerable stench' occasioned by the mill dam's holding back 'the whole filth and nastiness' carried down by the burn, resolved the council to remove the dam and force Fleming to 'flit'; in 1769 it was agreed that the mill, now apparently the burgh's property, should be put up to roup, but not until 1771 was an occupant found, one Thomas Burton, skinner.[42] The reaction of the inhabitants of Bridgegate has not been recorded for posterity, but they can hardly have been pleased at the mill's falling to a use notorious for creating 'filth and nastiness' of its own.

A more direct and less unhappy association with a burgh council is to be found at St. Andrews, where the 'common mills' advertised to let in 1793 included a saw mill.[43] At Eyemouth a saw mill was established by Thomas Hill, cooper in Berwick, about 1820, almost certainly as a source of barrel staves, although the inclusion of threshing and bark-grinding machinery shows an enterprising diversification of interests.[44] A tidal saw mill at Burntisland, which appears on a map dated 1843, was apparently of 17th century origin and was the property of the Wemyss estate.[45] Notwithstanding the existence of water-, wind- and steam-powered mills on a number of coastal sites, there are very few authenticated instances of such mills belonging to timber merchants. William Robertson's mill at Leven, Fife, reputed to be the best in Scotland in 1769, appears on Ainslie's 1775 map of Fife and was almost certainly the mill which was 'opened' in May 1807 by a Mr. Balfour who already had a mill at Kirkcaldy.[46] The founder of Jerviswood sawmill, Lanark started another mill, at Kincardine, Fife in 1825 as an extension to his timber business.[47]

Mills for Estate Plantations

Ornamental plantations around country houses had already been created before 1730, but only during the ensuing century did more extensive, commercial plantations become a feature of the Scottish landscape at large. The multiplicity of planters has already been thoroughly catalogued by Anderson, and it would be pointless to go over the same ground again. Instead, attention will be focused on the relatively few estates on which plantations had been laid out early enough and on a sufficiently large scale to justify the establishment of sawmills by 1830.

It should come as no surprise to find that two notable Improvers, Grant of Grant and the Earl of Haddington, were associated with the earliest saw mills in this category. Grant had inherited the Monymusk estate in 1713 and started planting in 1717. By 1754 he had an estimated two million well advanced trees besides many young ones, and in 1768 he established a saw mill for cutting the largest trees into planks.[48] By 1790 regular consignments were being sent to John Christie and to Robert Innes, merchant in Aberdeen, as well as to much of south and west Aberdeenshire.[49] Detailed figures for the year June 1792 to June 1793 show that in spite of a rather unreliable water supply and a lot of time consumed in sharpening saws, the mill managed to cut several thousand feet of timber over the twelve-month period.[50]

Up to this time the mill had been run by the estate itself, but a series of advertisements during the early 19th century indicates a change of approach. The first, in April 1806, makes no reference to a saw mill, but suggests that timber might be floated on the River Don to the head of the Aberdeenshire Canal; a second, in April 1808, mentions a saw mill site on the River Don with an established lade, and others, from November 1808 to April 1814, refer to a four-frame mill of forty-two saws.[51] Salesmanship apart, it is unlikely that so powerful a mill could have worked off the troublesome water supply used in the 1790s or that such difficulties would have arisen had the earlier mill been on the River Don. The omission of any reference to a mill in the 1806 advertisement and the mill's apparently incomplete condition in April 1808 suggest that a new, more powerful mill had been built as an incentive to prospective lessees; the site chosen was probably that of a former corn mill, Ord Mill, where a saw mill was damaged during the floods of 1828.[52]

In having such extensive mature plantations at their disposal, and in being under the economic necessity of exploiting them, the Grants of Monymusk were not typical of 18th and early 19th-century landowners. By way of contrast, the Earls of Haddington, while not unaware of the economic potential of their plantations, were in a more comfortable position financially and could therefore afford to exploit their plantations in a more leisurely fashion. In 1707 planting had begun on the famous Binning Wood, and at a later date a smaller plantation was made on a poor, sandy area known as the Warren, both on the Tyninghame, East Lothian estate.[53] Apparently there was sufficient mature timber for the estate to have its own saw mill by 1775,[54] but thereafter its fate is difficult to follow: Forrest's 1799 map of East Lothian shows something which may represent a second mill beside Knowes (corn) mill, but between then and the mid-19th century, when a saw mill was built adjacent to Tyninghame village, information is completely lacking. Whilst Tyninghame plantations were nowhere near so extensive as those at Monymusk, they were sufficiently large and mature to support a saw mill.[55] Obviously some exploitation was going on in the mid-1770s but probably at a fairly slow pace. Certainly the Earls of Haddington would not have felt constrained to let their plantations out to contractors or to provide a sawmill for their convenience.

Generally speaking, it was not until the early 19th century that estate saw mills began to appear in any quantity and then, for the most part, at the landowner's own initiative. Monteath (1824) cites two interesting examples: at Closeburn, Dumfriesshire planting had begun in 1774, and by 1792 there were three hundred acres under woodland; by 1824 circular saws were being used to cut large and small timber for all purposes.[56] On the Blairdrummond estate planting had begun in 1715 under Drummond of Blair and had continued under Lord Kames after 1767;[57] according to Monteath, Home Drummond of Blairdrummond, M.P., had very recently built a saw mill which he found to be of great usefulness.[58] As yet most of the timber being cut from plantations was destined for estate purposes, but even leaving aside the more extensive mature plantations such as those at Monymusk, interest was already being shown by others, foreshadowing a much more widespread trend after 1830: by 1811 plantations around Loch na Bo, Moray, dating from 1773, were sufficiently mature to have brought an offer to build a saw mill nearby,[59] whilst in Clydesdale there were plantations enough for a timber merchant to set up his own mill (Jerviswood Mill) in 1824.[60]

On the Seaforth estates in the Beauly area attempts were made to set up a partnership involving both landowner and timber merchants. In 1813 representations were made to Wilkinson & Thornby, timber merchants in Hull, regarding the setting up of a partnership and saw mill to exploit the plantations two and a half miles from the sea at Dingwall. A stream of water running through the plantations was well adapted to driving a saw mill, and Lord Seaforth was prepared to build one and to join in any partnership which might be set up.[61] Whether or not this particular project came to anything, saw mills had certainly been set up by 1824 and markets had begun to develop: in January of that year John Jardine, who had charge of the mills, could claim that 'our mills are constantly growing and doing well, but not equal to the demand'. During the first three months of 1824 the mills sent squared timber and pit props to Sunderland, barrel staves to Banff and elsewhere and deals, lath and roofing timber to Stornoway.[62] Anderson[63] gives an interesting example of just how much an enterprising landowner might do in the absence of commercial interest:

> In March 1809, Sir James Naismith of Posso (Dawyck) in Peeblesshire offered for sale a fir wood of one hundred acres, twenty-five miles from Edinburgh together with a sawmill which he had recently erected. The timber was of a large size fit for shipbuilding. The offer was repeated in December 1809. Four years later in July 1813, the New Posso Fir Wood of one hundred acres was still on offer, but meantime the owner had opened the New Posso Timber yard in Leith Walk, where sales of timber of all sizes, equal to any Norway timber, were under the charge of Mr. Haviland. It is thus clear that Sir James had been constrained to run his own estate mill.

Distribution and Chronology

Mills for Natural Woodland

By 1730 sawmills had already been established among the more accessible Highland remnants of natural woodland in Upper Deeside, on Speyside, near Loch Rannoch and on rivers debouching on the Inverness-Beauly coast: the Ness (including Loch Ness), the Beauly and its tributaries. Indeed, for much of the period to 1830, and within the obvious constraints of the distribution of woodland itself, large-scale exploitation was only carried out in those areas having ready accessibility to markets which, in an age of inadequate land transport, involved movement by sea. Certainly a market could be found locally, but not usually on a scale large enough to justify the construction of saw mills. Where only local demand had to be met, a sawpit could be used, as was the case throughout the period in a number of localities.

The fact that it was to the east rather than to the west coast that timber went can be ascribed to several factors. Firstly, all the major Highland river systems run towards the east coast, enabling a more extensive area to be tapped on that side of the country. Secondly, and for reasons not unrelated to the first factor, the east had already been subject to southern influences to a greater degree than had the west, all the more so as the 18th century progressed. In cultural rather than geological terms the Highland Line is sometimes drawn so as to exclude the Moray Firth Lowlands. This, in turn, relates to the distribution of markets: London, the destination for a not inconsiderable proportion of the timber sawn, was easily reached via the east coast, and whilst Scotland's population took on a more westerly distribution during the period, most of the major centres of population — Edinburgh, Perth, Aberdeen — were on the east coast. Lastly, and perhaps only tentatively, it might be suggested that the primarily eastern distribution of saw mills owed something to the use to which woodland was put: we saw in the previous chapter that most of the charcoal-smelting ironworks were situated in the Western Highlands, and while their use of timber would not preclude the establishment of saw mills, it could conceivably have predisposed landowners to look to smelting, or possibly tanning, rather than to sawmilling as an outlet for their woodland products.

Of course there are exceptions to every rule, and a few West Highland saw mills have been found. That in Glen Barisdale,[64] a small remote valley in Inverness-shire, is the most difficult to account for, although its apparently early 19th-century origin puts it in a period when the north-western Highlands were relatively accessible. The garrison at Fort William, an indisputably Lowland presence, had a saw mill on the River Arkaig, and although it had been abandoned by the 1790s on account of its distance from Fort William, another mill had been set up on Loch Arkaig by 1808.[65] At Inveraray, an unusual instance of a landowner-planned west Highland town, the Duke of Argyll commissioned Robert Meikle to design a set of mills incorporating, *inter alia*, two frame saws, but there is no certainty that these were ever built.[66] Doubtless there were other saw mills in the West Highlands, and the apparent imbalance between east and west may stem partly from differences in the quality of documentation.

Returning to the east, there are interesting variations in distribution which, to some extent, follow a chronological sequence. The earliest recorded mills were well up-valley, close to the woods themselves: by the late 1720s there were saw mills on Upper Deeside in Glenlui, at Prony and at Invercauld; on Speyside above and below Loch Morlich and at Coulnakyle; on Loch Ness at Alltsigh, at Cannich in Strathglass, and near Amat in Strath Cuileannach.[67] At about the middle of the 18th century there was a move towards building saw mills near to tidal water, to which timber could be floated down. The Culter mill, which took logs from the Earl of Mar's forests in Braemar, was fairly short-lived (c. 1745-55),[68] but the Fochabers and Garmouth mills (c.1756, pre-1779) at the mouth of the Spey continued to saw logs from the Duke of Gordon's forests and elsewhere on Speyside until well into the 19th century.[69] On the Beauly an extensive saw mill was built in 1765, about seven miles from the sea and near to the site of an earlier mill. According to the (Old) Statistical Account, the mill consisted of three buildings with a total length of one hundred and twenty-six feet, within which seven saws were driven by four wheels. Timber was floated down the Rivers Glass, Cannich and Beauly over a range of thirty to forty miles; planks from the mill were carried overland for three miles to avoid a waterfall, then floated a further four miles on rafts to a woodyard at Lovat, where vessels of fifty to ninety tons burthen could load. By 1819 the mill, which had sawn timber to the value of £200,000, had closed down.[70] All this down-river activity did not bring an end to saw-milling at or near to the woods themselves, although the late 18th and early 19th centuries did see a greater concentration of saw-milling at estate level, as the example of Rothiemurchus, already cited, shows. During the early 19th century the position is complicated by early Highland plantations coming to maturity, and several of the many saw mills mentioned by Dick-Lauder in 1829 may fall into this category.[71]

While there are difficulties in estimating the number of saw mills at work on natural forest timber during the period 1730-1830, a conservative estimate would put the total at about sixty.

Mills for Imported Timber

The distribution of mills for imported timber, the smallest category of saw mills, is closely and predictably related to coastal sites and, hardly less predictably, to centres of population. Edinburgh had at least seven saw mills on the Water of Leith, and Glasgow and Leven (Fife) had at least one each.[72] The number of saw mills handling both foreign and Scottish seaborne timber was proportionally far smaller than the share of the market taken by imported timber might suggest. In all probability only a small amount of such timber ever passed through Scottish water-powered sawmills; much of it was sawn in its country or district of origin. Of the remainder, some would be sawn over pits. During the early 19th century accessibility to the sea and to urban markets, which had fostered the establishment of saw mills in the first place, made seaborne coal equally accessible and led to the introduction of steam-powered saw mills, a move which was precipitated by the enormous demands of another coastal industry, fish packaging — by the early 1820s over five million barrel staves were being used annually, only a small proportion of which came from timber grown and sawn in Scotland.[73]

Altogether, and including one or two sites such as Perth (pre-1792)[74] and Eyemouth (c.1820),[75] where some more locally grown timber may have been used, there were probably no more than twenty mills of this type at work between 1730 and 1830.

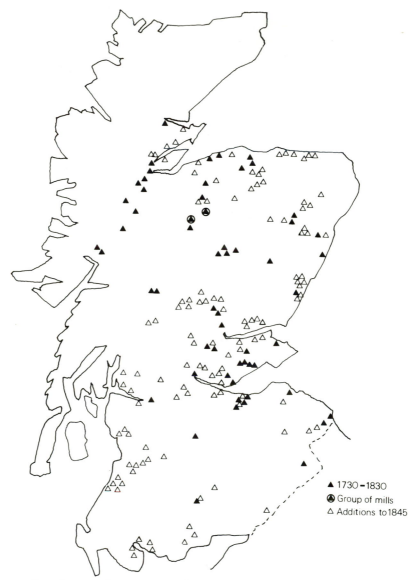

Fig 103. Distribution of water-powered saw mills, 1730-1845. Several of the mills first recorded 1830-1845 almost certainly predated 1830

Mills for Estate Plantations

The last of the three types of mill to appear was that concerned with the exploitation of plantations. The earliest mills to have been identified were those at Monymusk (1768)[76] and Tyninghame (pre-1775);[77] a third at Ayton (pre-1771)[78] may also have been an estate mill. By the 1790s perhaps an additional five or six mills had come into use, with a possible dozen or so more by 1830, giving an admittedly conservative total of about twenty mills. Estate saw mills were unusual among users of water power in that their development did not reach its height until the 1830s and '40s: the New Statistical Account refers to eighty or so saw mills, of which at least seventy fall into the category of estate mills, and whilst some may have been founded before 1830, recurring references to the recent origin of so many mills give the impression that these earlier examples constituted only a small minority. The further development of saw mills, up to 1870, is dealt with in Chapter 30.

With regard to the distribution of estate sawmills before 1830, the most important, and perhaps obvious, factor must have been the location of estates belonging to landowners who, during the 18th century, were active arbori-culturalists. To some extent the choice of forestry as an alternative to agriculture reflects the presence of poorer quality land: thus the Adams of Blairadam planted on the eastern flank of the Cleish Hills, the Grants of Monymusk on the slopes of Cairn William, and the Dukes of Atholl on the steep valley sides of Strathtay. However, it would be misleading to attach too much significance to this factor; forestry was as much a matter of fashion for the 18th-century landowner as were all the other aspects of Improvement, even though it might also be a genuine object of scientific and economic interest. The land chosen for planting by the Drummonds and Homes of Blair-drummond or by the Earl of Haddington for the Binning Wood at Tyning-hame, was hardly marginal agriculturally. In fact the high value of certain uplands as sheepwalks, notably in the Borders, could be a deterrent to planting. Further research into this subject is required.

The distribution of all types of saw mill, including those first recorded in the New Statistical Account, appears in Figure 103.

Type Sites: Loch Rannoch and Blairadam

Introduction

Two contrasting sites have been chosen for more detailed consideration. The first, Loch Rannoch, involves two mills, exploiting, and perhaps over-exploiting, the remnants of natural woodland in Highland Perthshire. The mills and the woods were let out by the Forfeited Estates Commission, which held the Robertson of Strowan estate during this period. The second site, Blairadam, had a mill built to utilise plantations on a Lowland estate under the direction of the landowner himself, right at the very end of our period. The contrast between the two also extends to the nature of the information.

For Loch Rannoch, much of the material relates to the working of the mills themselves, and to the circumstances in which they were let, while the material on Blairadam gives a rare insight into a landowner's reasons for building a saw mill on an estate containing extensive mature plantations, at a time of depressed timber prices. The latter account is taken from a description of the estate, printed privately in 1834. As only one source is used, and in order not to lose any of the original meaning, the extract is quoted verbatim, with the exception of a few minor abridgements and changes in punctuation.

Loch Rannoch

According to Anderson,[79] saw mills were established at Carrie beside Loch Rannoch about 1741, but not until 1749 does any information on their operation come to light. On returning from Holland to find Carrie saw mill without a tenant, Captain Robertson proposed and obtained a three-year tack of both woods and saw mill, dated 19th December 1749. Under the terms of the lease he was entitled to cut 1,798 logs — it was reckoned that three logs could be cut from one tree — for deals and 898 for boards, to be dressed at the mills, besides fifty loads of boards to be dressed with the axe. To feed and run the mill, Robertson provided ten men and six horses, but hardly had his term begun when the Forfeited Estates Commission intervened in an attempt to remove him. A deadline was set at Whitsunday 1750, but he was still in occupation at August 1750; on the 22nd of that month the Sheriff of Perth pronounced an interdict against him, prohibiting him from cutting any more wood. While not disputing his removal on principle, Robertson insisted on either compensation for the four hundred logs which had yet to be cut, or a delay in his removal to Whitsunday 1751.[80] In the event, the Commission relented, extended the term and offered compensation for the house and boats which Robertson had built.

Three-year tacks seem to have been the norm: in April 1751 a tack of two thousand trees, with the use of the saw mills, was granted to John Robertson of Tulliebelton (merchant and Provost of Perth) and Alexander Campbell of Coricharmaig for £350.[81] At Whitsuntide 1754 the mills were again let, this time to one Alexander Cameron. During his three-year tack Cameron was entitled to cut 1,200 logs for deals, 600 for boards, and 200 from lying timber. Tenants in Camaghouran and Carrie were exempted from rent on condition that they cut and carried logs and boards.[82]

By the end of Cameron's term, difficulties were emerging. For some time the best trees (about six hundred to each lease) had been picked out, leaving only inferior ones, six hundred of which would not make up the two hundred tons on which the rent was calculated. Furthermore, in May 1757 a report by James Small, factor on the Struan estate, and George Sandeman, joiner in Perth, showed in just how bad a state the sawmills were:

> The two sawmills at present are in very bad order, each having only one frame and one saw, each saw being so thick as to make the saw draught half an inch thick, which consumes a good deal of the best of the wood and the saws being too quickly fed, the deals are very roughly sawn, and by the insufficiency of the moving frames, are very inequal cut in thickness, some deals two inches thick at one end and bare inch at the other which not only wastes a good deal of timber, but proves hard labour and a great drawback in working of it.

Small and Sandeman recommended that one of the mills be given up and the other rebuilt to a higher standard:

> The same strength of water that drives the thick saw at present will drive two if not three saws, of the common thickness used in Holland, Leith etc. and when the water is plentiful, both the frames and all the saws could go. This will be less expensive to government as it is only keeping up one miln instead of two, and less expense to the tacksman, as it is keeping only two millers, instead of four, and less trouble in attending and looking after one mill than two.[83]

Their recommendation was acted upon; work started on a new mill, and until such a time as it was completed the price of timber, on which the rent (for two hundred tons) was based, was lowered to 12s sterling per ton. By Sandeman's original estimate the new mill was to have cost about £195, but by February 1759 the mill, now nearing completion, had cost approximately £350.[84] The other mill was dismantled or left to rot.

By July 1759 another tack had been granted, this time to Alexander McDougall, but there was still the problem of the poor quality of the remaining timber. Under the tack, the Commissioners had offered an £8 Sterling subsidy towards the sawmiller's wage, and the tonnage had been reduced to one hundred and fifty, but when the tack came up for renewal in 1762, McDougall asked that it be reduced further to one hundred tons.[85] The new mill suffered from winter freezing and summer drought; in 1764 the tenant asked for help in building a reservoir to alleviate the latter problem. There were also difficulties in marketing. A report dated 1766-7 states that a recently constructed road from Braemar to Blair Atholl had provided access to Perthshire for the better quality Deeside timber, thereby entirely destroying the market for the Rannoch product. According to the report, the tacksman of the sawmill had so much timber on hand that he had given up his tack, and the Commissioners were hard pressed to find a new tenant at the old rent.[86] It was suggested that a road from Rannoch to Crieff might help alleviate the problem, but when Pennant visited the mill in 1769, deals were only finding a local market, to which they were carried on horseback.[87] In any case trees were now becoming too scarce to admit of exportation further afield. Between 1769 and 1772 the mill itself was a cause for concern: first the wheels broke, then the flooring, joists and roof collapsed simultaneously.[88] Although the tonnage had apparently been raised from the one hundred proposed by McDougall, by 1773 the then tacksman, Alexander Cumming, was making a loss and asked that the tonnage be once more reduced to one hundred tons at 18s. Whether or not Cumming had his way, he was still tenant of the saw mill in 1778, but a further depletion of standing timber seems to have led to severe restrictions on quotas, with a consequent loss of markets, for in that year Cumming asked that he be allowed *at least* fifteen tons of wood, as without this his last customer, the Earl of Breadalbane, would purchase imported timber at Perth instead.[89] In 1784, at the end of the Commissioners' period of control, the mill still stood. The exploitation of the Rannoch woods was perhaps not so exploitative as it might have seemed. According to Lindsay, the Commissioners did attempt — though with mixed success — to control the types of tree cut by their tenants; the restrictions on quotas he sees as a conservation measure rather than one of necessity, and the decline of the woods he ascribes not only to selective felling but also to environmental factors and grazing patterns.[90]

Blairadam

'If wood had continued at nearly the price which it bore during the war, I doubt whether it would have been advisable to have erected a sawing mill; but it had diminished in value to less than half and reasonable apprehensions were held of its falling still lower. This would have a serious effect on an Estate, where so large a portion of it had been devoted to the growth of timber; so that some expedient became necessary to secure against the consequences resulting from the gradual diminution of the value of timber, not only as a matter of present profit, but as tending to embarrass or even defeat the means of keeping the woods in order. What naturally occurred for the purpose of adverting these mischiefs was the erection of a sawing-mill, a measure which received great encouragement from there being a means of placing it in a spot where the water which served the beetling-mill of the bleachfield, could be applied to work the sawing-mill. If the water thus obtained had been sufficient at all times for the purposes of working the sawing-mill we should have been relieved from the consideration of an important part of this subject . . .

'After three years experience of the working of the mill (notwithstanding there has been during that time much improvement in the machinery), the different matters for consideration are, 1st Still farther improvement in the machinery. 2nd A more effectual and constant supply of water. 3rd The best course by which to convey the wood to the mill. 4th The best mode of regulating the labour in working the mill. The three first heads raise the question of how far it is advisable to add to the expense which has already been bestowed upon the mill. It seems to be quite clear, if there can be a constant supply of timber from the woods, and a constant sale for it at the mill when worked up, at sufficient prices, then an effort at some expense is advisable to secure the unremitting working of the mill in order that making good the orders by hand-sawing may be put an end to. But if it does not appear that there can be a constant supply to the mill from the woods, or a constant demand for the article by the country, then I think it would not be advisable to incurr much additional expense, but to regulate the acceptance of orders by the power to execute them by means of the mill only.

'. . . I think it would appear that, by judicious and cautious management, the supply from the woods may be made sufficient for a good many years to come, to keep the mill in full working, at the same time improving the staple and condition of the woods. How far the country will meet the supply which may thus be produced, with adequate prices, I have no means of judging. At the same time, I am not aware of any reason for doubting that the demand will be sufficient to satisfy the proceeding with such further expansion as may be required: first for improving the machinery, secondly for increasing the quantity of water, thirdly for making a proper approach to the mill from the great body and bulk of the wood from whence the supply is to come. As to the fourth point of consideration, it requires no particular observation here.

'The wood rental, or the annual produce of the wood cut on the Blair-Adam Estate, has come to be an object of considerable importance. According to the returns of the last three years, the exact average, annually, is £900 and for every purpose of reasoning on this subject, it may be taken as that sum.

'If the production of this rental had been left to the system of sale in the rough, by roups, and to individual purchasers, it is almost certain, (with the falling prices), that the rental could not have been procured. At any rate it is quite clear that it could only have been procured by a great additional exhaustion of the staple commodity with all the consequences; such as too great rapidity of thinning, irregularity of thinning . . . additional expense of clearing out after cutting, and the keeping of the woods, the passages through them and all the appendages in order.

'Under such circumstances it became advisable to find a steady, permanent customer, not liable unnecessarily to exhaust the capital or staple, and perhaps of a description to produce as much rental for less waste of commodity. It is in this character, of a steady customer, that the sawing-mill is to be considered, and the expense incurred by the erection of the sawing-mill . . . should . . . be reckoned as money sunk to obtain a good fixed customer. . . . the net expenditure upon it to this time has been £693 . . . Deducting . . . £88 of interest, the sum paid to obtain the custom of the mill . . . is £605. My conjecture is . . . that the whole expenditure, even including the operation of clearing the dam of mud, would be covered by . . . £800 or £850. The question for consideration then is whether it is advisable at this expense, to secure this means of supporting the present wood rental.

'It is to be observed that in order to enable the sawing-mill to serve the country, by executing orders according to agreement, it is necessary to complete those orders, when there is a deficiency of water, by hand-sawing. This absorbs the profit of the mill, and I am clearly of the opinion that that mode of executing the orders must be given up, and orders only taken which can be executed by means of the mill. The immediate effect of this is the reduction of the rental. But there is another observation to be made, important to the consideration of this point, that the sum sunk to obtain the customer does not procure one to take the amount of the whole wood rental (£900). Of that sum part is taken at roups for the rough material, and from private purchasers.

'On looking at the returns of the last three years, I think the fair proportion is to ascribe £600 to the sawing-mill and £300 to the other customers, so that taking the worst view, £600 a year will be got by the advance of the further sum necessary to complete the mill. If this rental should be made permanent by the working of the saw-mill alone, without the aid of hand-sawing, it is certainly in every respect an advisable arrangement.

'. . . Besides other circumstances, in addition to the leading one of having procured a customer, there is an important circumstance to be adverted to, namely that if it continues to effect the purpose of consuming a certain fixed quantity of the staple commodity annually, it secures the means of conducting the regular cutting of the wood, and consequently all that relates to keeping the woods in order, on a regular footing . . .

'. . . According to the sawing-mill account of 1830, the profit was £113. Against the mill was charged the interest of money laid out and . . . certain other expenditures in the course of that year, which, according to the view taken here of its being a free mill, or a purchased customer, should not be set against it. All these items might bring the gain of, or the saving of staple by the sawing-mill up to £200. Taking it thus, the sawing-mill furnishes £600 of the rental . . . by the expenditure of £400 worth only, of the staple or raw material. The attempt should be made to get the sawing mill to supply the whole of the wood rental . . . Thus, on £900 of rental there would be a saving . . . of one third of raw material, that is £600 of raw material would bring the rental of £900.

'The two following years, 1832 and 1833, the profit was reduced to nothing when interest of money and expenditure on improvements were set against the profits of the mill. This defect, I have no doubt, will be redeemed by the application of sound discretion to the manner of conducting the work of the mill in future. There are reasons assigned for this variance in profit in the last two years. They are stated to be expenditure on improvements on the machinery and stoppage of water by the building of the sluice, the drought of the season is another. This last is a risk not to be averted, and should not be reckoned upon — the two others cannot recur; but there is a fourth . . . , namely that in the two last years the wood principally worked upon at the mill were large measurable trees. It is stated that in the preceding year, when there was a profit, smaller woods were worked up . . . There is a reasonable expectation of a sufficiency of wood to keep the mill at work at the greatest profit; the Blair-Adam woods having a large proportion of trees of that size coming forward. . . . Fir trees, about fifty years of age or, in other words, large measurable trees, are getting to be rare upon the estate.

'It is of great importance to secure purchasers, and to supply them with what they require . . . but this should . . . be regulated by sound discretion, and it is better to let purchasers know that they cannot have an article than to make an exertion to provide them with it, when the effect is exhausting the commodity and defeating the profitable use of the mill. Deliberate consideration and pre-concerted arrangements, therefore, should be made for supplying the sawing-mill in future, both as to the character of the wood in size and species and quality, and the due proportions being settled as far as possible by anticipating the places of the woods from which they are to be taken throughout the season, . . . and no deviation permitted without deliberate consultation and direction.

'. . . The deficiency of water should be remedied, if it can be done at reasonable expense. The failure of this power does much mischief and particularly if large measurable wood is to be principally worked up at the mill, because the want of power stops the mill, and makes it necessary to have recourse to sawing by hand. . . . There is no means of increasing the quantity of water which flows into the dam. The first suggested means for economising the water is by making a compensation dam or pond near the mill, either by widening the mill-lead to a certain extent, west from the beetling house, or by digging a reservoir out of the solid ground, immediately to the north of the mill lead and west of the beetling house. It is expected, by such an operation, that the water which comes through the lead and which must be turned aside and lost, when the mill is stopped for any occasion of putting the saws to rights, putting on the logs or the like, that the water collected in the reservoir, would keep the mill going until there was time to go to the dam to open the sluice. But if the reservoir is made sufficient in capacity to hold all the water which will flow through the mill lead for the longest period of suspension of work by the mill, then in that case the necessity of workmen going to the dam to open and shut the sluice will be entirely superseded.

'. . . I therefore propose to submit it specifically to the consideration of an engineer, how far it is advisable to incur the expense of making the compensation pond so large as to hold water sufficient to allow the sluice at the dam to be kept open for the longest period of the work at the mill being suspended.

'The other means of obtaining an addition of water by collection is by raising the spill water at the dam, so as to give an additional surface of water of eighteen inches deep. . . . This too should be made the subject of a report by an engineer, but the attention of the engineer should be particularly called to the means and at what expense, the accumulation of mud could be taken out of the dam, and how it could be kept under in future.

'Improvement of the machinery is likewise a fit subject for consideration by an engineer; and whether the construction or enlargement of the present wheel (now that the claims on the water by the bleachfield are at an end), or whether an overshot wheel of large diameter, doing the work with much less water, might be adopted with advantage and effect, and at what sum? Another means to render the sawing mill more effectual to its purpose is the easy transportation of the rough material to the mill.'[91]

NOTES

1. See, for example, *OSA* XIII, 522, Kiltarlity, Inverness-shire.
2. Gray, A., *The Experienced Millwright*, London, 1806.
3. SRO E 783/58/6 (1).
4. SRO GD46/17/65.

5. SRO GD248/135/1.

6. *OSA* XIII, 522-3, Kiltarlity, Inverness-shire.

7. *OSA* XIV, 394-5, Speymouth, Moray.

8. Anderson, M. L., *A History of Scottish Forestry*, 2 vols., London, 1967, II, 112.

9. Grant E. (Lady Strachey), *Reminiscences of a Highland Lady*, Revised Edition, London, 1960.

10. *Ibid*.

11. SRO GD44/29/8.

12. Jamieson, A., *A Dictionary of Mechanical Science*, 2 vols., London, 1827, II, 913; Gilbert, K. R., *The Portsmouth Block-Making Machinery*, London, 1965, 2.

13. No. 2844 7/5/1805; No. 2968 23/9/1806; No. 3116 14/3/1808; No. 3529 28/1/1812; No. 3643 26/1/1813; see Woodcroft, B., *Alphabetical Index of Patentees of Inventions* (Facsimile Edition), London, 1969.

14. SRO CS96/141; Monteath, R., *The Forester's Guide & Profitable Planter*, Edinburgh, 1824, 200; Anderson, *op. cit*., II, 108.

15. Dick-Lauder, Sir T., *An Account of the Great Floods of August 1829, in the Province of Moray and Adjoining Districts*, Edinburgh, 1830, 251; SRO GD237/130/4; Grant, *op. cit*., 254-5; *NSA* XIII, 139, Rothiemurchus, Inverness-shire.

16. See *NSA* X, 713, Dull, Perthshire.

17. See *OSA* VIII, 407, Kilmallie, Inverness-shire.

18. Huntly, Charles, Marquis of (ed.), 'Records of Aboyne', *New Spalding Club* (1894), 291.

19. *NSA* IX, 526, Peterhead, Aberdeenshire; *NSA* XII, 357, Ceres, Fife.

20. Porteous, A., *History of Crieff*, Edinburgh, 1912, 189.

21. Anderson, *op. cit*., II, 110.

22. NLS Acc. 5111/18/f.4.

23. Kennedy, W., *Annals of Aberdeen*, 2 vols., London, 1818, II, 505.

24. Anderson, *op. cit*., I, 510-1.

25. *NSA* X, 997, Dunkeld & Dowally, Perthshire; *NSA* X, 774-5, Dull, Perthshire.

26. Murray, D., *The York Buildings Company, A Chapter in Scotch History*, Glasgow, 1883, 57-9; Anderson, *op. cit*., I, 441.

27. *OSA* XIII, 133, Abernethy & Kincardine, Inverness-shire; SRO GD248/135.

28. Anderson, *op. cit*., I, 441.

29. Plan at Inverness Museum.

30. SRO GD44/29/8.

31. Anderson, *op. cit*., I, 442.

32. *Ibid*., I, 442; *OSA* XII, 135, Abernethy & Kincardine, Inverness-shire; Grant, *op. cit*., 147.

33. SRO RHP669; *OSA* XIV, 394, Speymouth, Moray.

34. Grant, *op. cit*., 147.

35. *OSA* XVI, 375, Peterculter, Aberdeenshire.

36. Pennant, T., *A Tour in Scotland, 1769*, 2nd Edition, London, 1772, 113.

37. Grant, *op. cit*.

38. Wight, A., *Present State of Husbandry in Scotland*, 4 vols., Edinburgh, 1778-82, IV, 389-90.

39. *SBRS*, 'Extracts from the Records of the Burgh of Glasgow', V (1718-38), Glasgow, 1909, 152, 256, 349.

40. *SBRS*, 'Extracts from the Records of the Burgh of Glasgow', VI (1739-59), Glasgow, 1911, 306.

41. *Ibid.*, 320, 444, 478-9.

42. *SBRS*, 'Extracts from the Records of the Burgh of Glasgow', VII (1760-80), Glasgow, 1912, 74-5, 188, 287, 347.

43. *Caledonian Mercury*, 14th January 1793.

44. SRO GD267/27/3786/2; *NSA* II, 331, Eyemouth, Berwickshire.

45. Young, A., *History of Burntisland*, Kirkcaldy, 1913, 32, 37.

46. SRO GD44/29/8; Anderson, *op. cit.*, II, 118.

47. Anderson, *op. cit.*, II, 108; *Pigot & Co's National Commercial Directory of the Whole of Scotland and the Isle of Man*, London, 1837, 632.

48. Anderson, *op. cit.*, I, 554; *OSA* III, 66, Monymusk, Aberdeenshire.

49. SRO GD1/32/24.

50. SRO GD1/32/23.

51. Anderson, *op. cit.*, II, 111-2.

52. Dick-Lauder, *op. cit.*, 340.

53. Anderson, *op. cit.*, I, 526.

54. *Caledonian Mercury*, 9th October 1775.

55. Anderson, *op. cit.*, I, 523.

56. Monteath, *op. cit.*, 200.

57. Anderson, *op. cit.*, I, 546-7.

58. Monteath, *op. cit.*, 200.

59. Leslie, W., *General View of the Agriculture of the Counties of Moray & Nairn*, London, 1811, 34.

60. Anderson, *op. cit.*, II, 108; Pigot, *op. cit.*, 632.

61. SRO GD46/17/41.

62. SRO GD46/17/65.

63. Anderson, *op. cit.*, II, 111.

64. *Ibid.*, II, 107.

65. *OSA* VIII, 407, Kilmalie, Inverness-shire.

66. Lindsay, I. G. & Cosh, M., *Inveraray & the Dukes of Argyll*, Edinburgh, 1973, 173.

67. Glenlui: SRO GD124/17/144 (1728); Prony: SRO GD124/17/123/2 (1725); Invercauld: SRO GD124/17/123/2 (1725); Loch Morlich: SRO GD44/29/8 (pre-1715); Coulnakyle: SRO GD248/135/1 (1727); Alltsight, Cannich, Amat: Joseph Avery, (Map of) Woods Purchased for the York Buildings Company's Iron Manufactory (Inverness Museum).

68. *OSA* XVI, 375, Peterculter, Aberdeenshire.

69. SRO CS96/141.

70. Southey, R., *Journal of a Tour of Scotland, 1819* (Facsimile Edition), Edinburgh, 1972, 113; *OSA* XIII, 522-3, Kiltarlity, Inverness-shire.

71. Dick-Lauder, *op. cit.*

72. Edinburgh: *OSA* XIX, Colinton, Midlothian; Glasgow: *SBRS*, Glasgow, V, 152, 256, 349; *SBRS*, Glasgow, VI, 306, 320, 444, 478-9; *SBRS*, Glasgow, VII, 74-75, 188, 287, 347; Leven: SRO NG1/1/18 8/12/67; SRO RHP770 (1830).

73. Monteath, *op. cit.*, 201.

74. Anderson, *op. cit.*, II, 109.

75. SRO GD267/27/3786/2.

76. *OSA* III, 66, Monymusk, Aberdeenshirj.

77. *Caledonian Mercury*, 9th October 1775.

78. Armstrong, Captain, (Map of) Berwickshire, 1771.

79. Anderson, *op. cit.*, I, 446.

80. SRO E 783/26/1-2.

81. Anderson, *op. cit.*, I, 446.

82. SRO E 783/41.

83. SRO E 783/76/2.

84. SRO E 783/50/2; SRO E 721/4 207-8.

85. Millar, A. H. (ed.), 'A Selection of Scottish Forfeited Estates Papers 1715; 1745', *SHS* (1909), 234.

86. SRO E 729/8.

87. Pennant, *op. cit.*, 92.

88. SRO E 783/60/196-7.

89. Millar, *op. cit.*, 246.

90. Lindsay, J. M., 'The Commercial Use of Highland Woodland, 1750-1870: a Reconsideration', *SGM*, XCII (1976).

91. Youngson, A. W., *Remarks on Blairadam Estate*, 6 vols. (printed privately), 1834, II, 67-80.

27

Minor Users of Water Power

In following a thematic approach to the utilisation of water power, it is inevitable that a few minor uses, which do not fit comfortably into any category, will be left over. For the most part these involve either industries which are too small and too poorly documented to merit a chapter on their own account, or industries which only occasionally used water power. The purpose of this chapter is to tidy up these loose ends; to give some sense of order, they are grouped into users of organic and inorganic raw materials.

Users of Organic Raw Materials

Snuff Mills

Scotland's tobacco trade has been well researched, and documented in some detail by a number of writers: its growth during the first three quarters of the 18th century and the disruption arising from the American War of Independence are written up in every economic history of Scotland. Although the bulk of tobacco imported into Scotland was re-exported,[1] a snuff-milling industry grew up at a number of localities; unfortunately, in contrast to the tobacco trade itself, very little has been written on the subject. For the most part, snuff mills seem to have been small units, though the quality of the premises used might vary considerably: a mill in Peterculter parish, Aberdeenshire was described as a small, low, square thatched building,[2] whereas an apparently more substantial mill at Woodside, Aberdeenshire had two storeys.[3] In making an offer to take on a derelict Glasgow mill for snuff-milling, Ninian Bryce was very specific about the accommodation required: an additional floor above the existing ground floor, to house grinding and drying rooms, the grinding room to have four windows and a partition, broken by a door giving access to the drying room, which in turn was to have a large 'brace piece' and vent, two windows, places for receiving tobacco, a staircase and a door. Both rooms were to be well 'boxed' and lined with timber and plastering; an additional room, with a fireplace and two windows, was to be made available for Bryce himself.[4]

Of snuff mill machinery prior to 1830, little is known. A reference to 'pots'[5] suggests that stampers were used, but the fact that the grinding room of Ninian

Bryce's mill was to be on the first floor points to the use of horizontal or even edge-running stones.[6] The number of 'pots' or 'mills' varied from site to site. The mill at Dawsholm, Dunbartonshire[7] had three mills in 1748,[8] and that at Woodside had seven at one time.[9] Evidently this machinery required little force to move it: the Culter mill was driven by an eight horse power water wheel, whilst Millhole Mill, Dumfries, once an 'easy going and swift going' malt mill which had been rendered 'miserably useless' by the draining of its dam, was still powerful enough to drive snuff-milling machinery.[10] In only one instance, at Cupar in the 1830s, was auxiliary steam power used.[11] A further indication of the limited scale of snuff mills can be drawn from the number of workers employed — often three, two or even one[12] — and from the additional uses to which snuff mill premises might be put: barley milling and papermaking at Dawsholm,[13] papermaking at Cathcart,[14] barley and wheat milling at Dalry,[15] and fulling, whin breaking and meal and barley milling at Woodside.[16]

Diverse parties might be involved in establishing snuff mills. A mercantile connection is, predictably, noticeable: Ninian Bryce, who had previously run a snuff mill on the Kelvin, identified himself as 'merchant' when applying to lease Todd's Mill,[17] the mill at Logie, Angus was held by a merchant in Montrose,[18] and Spylaw Mill, Edinburgh was reputed to have been built by a tobacco and snuff merchant, James Gillespie.[19] Two mills at Leslie and at Cupar, Fife belonged to the owners of nearby flax-spinning mills,[20] and at Stoneywood, Aberdeenshire a snuff mill was purchased by Charles Smith, papermaker, in 1810.[21] Mills in the Linlithgow area and on the Dighty Water, Angus were estate-owned about 1750,[22] whilst at Muggiemoss, Aberdeenshire a snuff mill was established by Charles Davidson, millwright, as an adjunct to his fulling and flax-beating mills.[23] For all the advantages possessed by merchants, the outlay required to set up a snuff mill was small enough to be within the means of a wide range of other persons.

The longevity and widespread distribution of snuff mills comes as something of a surprise. With the exception of one probably earlier but undated mill to the west of Edinburgh,[24] the earliest references to snuff mills date from the 1740s. By about 1750 there were mills in Dumfries and in the vicinity of Edinburgh, Glasgow, Dundee, Aberdeen and Linlithgow.[25] By 1775, mills had begun to congregate around Edinburgh and, to a lesser extent, Glasgow, but two new mills, at Logie (Angus)[26] and Alloa,[27] lay at a considerable distance from either. Tobacco imports between 1752 and 1775, whilst almost entirely directed towards the Clyde, also found their way in small quantities to a number of other ports, from Aberdeen to Dumfries, suggesting that snuff mills in these localities obtained at least part of their requirements from directly imported tobacco.[28] From the number of mills which come to light in the (Old) Statistical Account and other late 18th-century sources, it is evident that the disruption caused by the American War of Independence had not brought an end to snuff-milling in Scotland. Nine mills are mentioned for the first time, though these may date from before 1775. In all, there were at least twenty-five

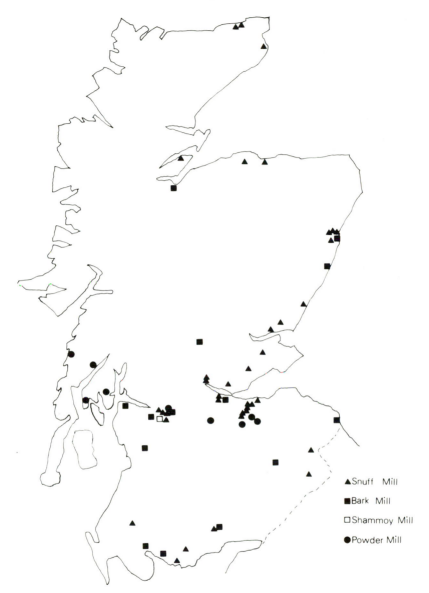

Fig 104. Minor organic users of water power, 1730-1830

mills working in Scotland, five of them on a ten-mile stretch of the Water of Leith.[29] In the Upper Merse, tobacco had established itself as a field crop, part of which was processed at snuff mills near Jedburgh and Stitchill (Roxburgh-shire).[30] The mill at Logie, which had formerly obtained its tobacco through the port of Montrose, was now, on account of restrictions, obliged to bring tobacco from Glasgow via the Forth and Clyde Canal.[31]

Even in the early 19th century snuff-milling persisted, with new mills at

Boag's Mill (Edinburgh, 1816) and Mugiemoss (Aberdeen, 1817).[32] Most of the more isolated mills had passed out of use by 1830 but in more populous districts, notably around Aberdeen, Edinburgh and Glasgow, several continued to function. In Colinton parish, to the south-west of Edinburgh, a new snuff mill was under construction as late as 1839.[33]

Taken as a whole, the distribution of snuff mills (Figure 104) reflects both the sources from which their raw material was derived and the markets for which their products were destined. As might be expected of an industry dependent on a largely imported raw material, mills tended to be sited close to ports, the remainder, relying on the home-grown crop, being close to growing areas. Coincidentally, most of the major centres of population were also port towns. In this respect Edinburgh, Glasgow and Aberdeen stand out, but it was on the Water of Leith that snuff-milling made the greatest impact: in the 1850s there were still five snuff mills around Colinton, and as late as 1890, of only three snuff mills still active, two were on the Water of Leith.[34]

Leather-Working

In view of the importance to Scotland of livestock raising and marketing, particularly in cattle and sheep, the utilisation of hides in leather manufacture was a predictable line of development. The entire manufacturing process is too long and complex to describe here in full,[35] and attention will be confined to those stages which used mechanical power. In this respect the two principal areas of concern are scouring and the preparation of bark for use in tan pits.[36] As scouring generally took place in fulling mills, it is very difficult to establish when water power was first used for this purpose. While this use of fulling mills may conceivably have dated back to the introduction to Scotland of the waulk mill itself, the earliest authenticated case to come to light was as late as 1769, when John Sawers gave a nineteen-and-a-half-year tack of a 'skinner work' and a waulk mill at Bell's Mills, Edinburgh to John Cox, skinner in Linlithgow, for £37 Sterling.[37] The 1773-4 *Edinburgh Directory* lists not only Cox but also James Forrester, leather dresser at Silver Mills; he too was using a waulk mill. In 1791, John Lindsay, skinner in Edinburgh, built a beating mill at Coltbridge Mill and subsequently obtained £20 towards costs from the Board of Trustees for Manufactures.[38]

Brunstane Mill, Edinburgh illustrates the links between fulling and skinnery work particularly well: in 1781 or thereabouts it was taken on as a woollen cloth manufactory; from about 1794 until 1802 it was run as a skinnery by Peter Wilson, and from 1802 to 1810 the mill was used for both purposes.[39]

By 1805 the Cox family had purchased Gorgie Mill. In the following year Robert Cox, son of John Cox, took on the waulk mill of Musselburgh for a three-year term, but under strict conditions laid down by the magistrates of the town. Besides ensuring that a waulker lived permanently at the mill, and that any damage to cloth was made good, he was to see that:

all persons resorting to or employing the said mill shall be served there honestly and readily according to and in the priority of time they shall bring their clothes, skins, leather or other goods to be manufactured, cleaned or scoured there.

Furthermore, he was

expressly restricted from dying any kind of goods in the said waulkmill and from drying, beating, washing manufacturing or waulking any hemp or linen yarn what-ever, whereby the woollen cloth manufactures within the town and territories of Musselburgh can or may sustain damage.

Another clause prohibited him from altering or adding to the machinery of the mill without the consent of the magistrates and council.[40] Shortly thereafter, Robert Cox took a sub-tack of a fall on the Water of Leith at Balerno, and built a mill 'for the waulking of leather'; by 1815 the family business, still based at Gorgie Mill, had grown into a company.[41]

Although the preponderance of evidence comes from the Edinburgh area, it should not be assumed that only here did skinners make use of, or build, waulk mills. The cleaning and scouring of skins and leather seems to have been much more closely linked to the woollen industry, which used the same water-powered machinery, than to other branches of leather-working, such as tanning, premises for which were often at some distance from exploitable falls of water. Before moving on to bark-milling, it is worth noting that Semple, in his 1782 revision of Crawford's *History of Renfrewshire*, mentions a 'shamoy mill for shamoying leather' at Pollokshaws, the first of its kind in Scotland.[42]

Bark, particularly that of the oak tree, had long been used by Scottish tanners as a source of tannin, often to the detriment of woodland resources. In 1665 the Council Register of the Burgh of Aberdeen refers to a bark mill,[43] and in 1720 James Paull, tanner, leased land at the foot of Old Vennel, Glasgow as the site for a bark mill, the town's first.[44] The Aberdeen mill may have been the same water-powered mill which appeared on a map of 1773, but from the description given of the land intended for the Glasgow mill — a plot twenty-one feet in diameter — there can be little doubt that it was horse-powered. As only a small amount of power was required to drive a bark mill (the 'miserably useless' Millhole Mill, Dumfries was converted to bark-milling in 1778),[45] the use of horse mills remained a feature of Scottish tanneries until the introduction of steam power. Where water mills were used, they were often situated at some distance from the tanneries themselves, the latter's need for a good draught to dry hides not always being compatible with the site characteristics of good falls, even if such characteristics ensured a steady supply of process water. Nevertheless bark mills were more closely linked with tanneries than were leather-working mills, and some tanneries, such as those at Inverness and Gatehouse-of-Fleet, had water power on the premises.[46]

As for the type of machinery used, it is possible that either horizontal or edge-running stones were employed; in 1805 the Board of Trustees for Manufactures were asked to contribute towards the cost of a steel mill for bruising (rather than grinding) oak bark, and the use of a former malt mill (St. Ninian's Mill, Linlithgow) suggests that such machinery may have been used at a preliminary stage.[47] To ensure that the bark was well 'ragged',[48] it had to be well dried, for which purpose a kiln was often used. 'Improved' mills, resembling those used in coffee grinding, came into use only in the third quarter of the 19th century.[49]

As might be expected, bark mills were often established by persons already connected with leather-working. Thus, it was the partners of the Glasgow Tannery who built the town's first water-powered bark mill about 1740,[50] and the former Deacon of the Glovers and Skinners who converted Millhole Mill, Dumfries to bark-grinding in 1778.[51] However, there were as always exceptions to the rule: the Eyemouth bark mill was established about 1820 by a Berwick cooper as part of a saw mill:[52] Ninian's Mill, used as a bark mill from 1773, was one of the Common Mills of Linlithgow and was therefore the burgh's property,[53] whereas both the tannery and bark mill at New Galloway were advertised in 1780 as part of the Robertson of Ardoch estate, the rent payable being £2 10s Sterling per annum.[54]

Table 10

Summary of Scottish Bark Mills

Site	First Recorded	A	B	C	Notes
Glasgow	1740			x	Also had major overseas markets. ? Only tannery in Glasgow, 1740.
Aberdeen	1773	x		x	Possibly the mill mentioned in 1665.
Linlithgow	1773		x		Converted to flint-grinding, 1789.
Inverness	1774	x	x		Tannery also on site.
Paisley	1782	x			Three tanneries in Paisley by 1782.
Dumfries	1778	x	x		At confluence of three routes from N., W., and Ireland.
Gatehouse	1785	x	x		Tannery also on site.
Kilmarnock	1785	x			
Muiravonside	1792		x		Near Linlithgow.
Eyemouth	1820				Probably related to marketing centre at Berwick.
Crieff	1837	x	x		Probably much earlier. One time major Tryst. 1st tannery c.1765. Three by late 1830s.
New Galloway*	1780	x	x		
Abbeyhill*	1775			x	
Selkirk*	1837	x			
Stonehaven*	1823				

A: cattle-rearing district. B: on drove road. C: major urban centre.
*possibly water-powered.

Any attempt to ascertain the distribution and chronology of water-powered bark mills has to contend with the problem of separating out the all too common horse mills. In practice this proves to be almost impossible without confirmation from cartographic or other similarly explicit sources. Even plans should be treated with caution in that the provision of a water supply may only have been in connection with process water.

Leaving aside considerations of drainage and topography, the factors affecting the distribution of both types of bark mill, and by inference tanneries themselves, are basically the same, and whilst tanneries were to be found in almost every market town, at least three additional locational factors can be identified as possibly having encouraged development, namely the presence of urban centres in cattle-rearing areas or on major drove roads, and those which, by their very size, had sufficiently large populations to provide a market for leather but also, as a by-product of meat consumption, a supply of hides. The results of applying these three considerations to the distribution of known and probable sites are shown in Table 10, which also summarises their chronology. Distributions are shown in Figure 100.

Gunpowder Mills

As consumers of charcoal, gunpowder mills have been included in this section, even though their use of sulphur and saltpetre might equally qualify them as users of inorganic raw materials.

Water power was used at several stages in gunpowder manufacture. The first involved the preparation of the three ingredients. Charcoal, after having been carefully cleaned and checked for impurities, was ground in the manner already described (Chapter 25, p. 418); sulphur was ground under edge-runners, and saltpetre was used in the form in which it came from the refinery. Once prepared, the ingredients were generally given an initial mixing prior to the more crucial business of incorporating, in which the ingredients were thoroughly mixed together to a regular consistency, either in stamping mills or, latterly, edge-runners revolving in a bowl-shaped trough. Small quantities of water were used to bind the grains together.[55]

In the larger gunpowder works, several separate mills might be used, each well removed from the next to minimise the damage from explosions. At Stobs Mills, Midlothian they were sited between natural projections or artificial mounds, planted with trees. Water power from four damheads drove ten water wheels, one of which was twenty feet in diameter.[56] At the smaller works such a spacing out of mills was out of the question: one works at Fauldhouse, West Lothian was housed in a converted corn mill.[57]

Disregarding an intriguing yet brief reference to a 'powder mill' on the Water of Leith in 1701,[58] we may say that it was not until 1794 that the first gunpowder mill was built in Scotland, at Stobs Mill, Midlothian. Its founders, an English company headed by Messrs. Hitchiner and Hunter, took a lease of ground near Gorebridge belonging to Dundas of Arniston and Dewar of Vogrie. By the late 1830s the works had grown to occupy a three-quarter mile stretch of the North Esk, and a village with seventy inhabitants had been built to house some of the company's fifty to sixty employees.[59] A second works, at Roslin, Midlothian, had come into production by 1805,[60] and by the 1840s, under Messrs. Hay & Merricks, had become the largest such works in Scotland, employing sixty workers, half of whom worked in the company's cooperage in the next mill up the valley.[61] Both Stobs Mills and Roslin survived well beyond the end of the 19th century.

During the early years of the century a large military and civil market for gunpowder encouraged the establishment of further works: Marfield Mill, Midlothian and Fauldhouse Mill, West Lothian both appear as gunpowder mills on Knox's 1812 map.[62] Fauldhouse, a corn mill, had been taken over and converted by O'Neil & Co. in 1812, and from Martinmas 1814 it was held on a forty-seven year tack by William Christie.[63] There was still a gunpowder mill here in 1817, but no reference is made to it in Pigot's 1837 *Directory*, and by 1855 it was once more a corn mill.[64] Marfield mill blew up in 1830, killing several workers, and no more is heard of it thereafter.[65]

The second generation Scottish gunpowder mills were all situated in Argyll, and all were established about 1840. Clachaig (Dunoon) Works was founded by Robert Sheriff,[66] Loch Fyne (Furnace) Works by Sheriff and his son, also Robert,[67] Kames Works by a Glasgow company,[68] and Melfort by Harrison, Ainslie & Co., proprietors of the Bonawe Ironworks.[69] The location of these works shows a marked change from market to raw material orientation, though at least one of them had a contract for imported Norwegian charcoal.[70] Each of the four works had several water-powered grinding and incorporating mills. The distribution of all eight works appears in Figure 100.

Miscellanea

A number of very minor users of water power, with perhaps only one or two mills of each type in the whole of Scotland, can be mentioned only very briefly.

In 1829 Tasker, Young and Co. established the first of at least four sugar works in Greenock to use water power, on the lowest fall of the eastern branch of the Shaws Water Aqueduct.[71] A rice mill later occupied another fall;[72] the New Statistical Account mentions an 'excellent' rice mill at Ormiston in Eckford parish, Roxburghshire, which had been built some years before but which was not yet in active use.[73] At least two mills were employed in grinding ink powder: one, on the west bank of the Kelvin, also ground potash,[74] whilst the other, at St. Leonard's Hill, Edinburgh, also teazed and carded wool for hat manufacturers.[75]

The former Tarred Wool Company's Haddington mill was used at one time in the early 19th century as a mustard works.[76]

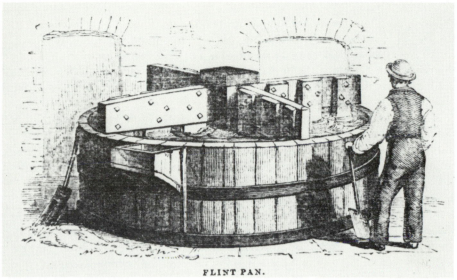

FLINT PAN.

Fig 105. Flint mill machinery, 19th century. *The Useful Arts and Manufactures of Great Britain, SPCK, London, n.d.*

Users of Inorganic Raw Materials

Flint Mills

During the period 1730-1830 an important glass and pottery industry developed in Scotland, centred on Glasgow and the Firth of Forth.[77] Although water power may have been used latterly in preparing clay and colours, and in driving other machinery, its major contribution to the industry was in grinding flint. In glassmaking, flint (silicon dioxide) was used with lead to produce a clear, lustrous 'flint glass' which was sixty per cent lead silicate. In pottery-making lead silicate (using flint) was employed as a glaze, and flint was also used as a body in the manufacture of stoneware.[78]

The earliest type of flint mill had stampers, but from the 1720s and '30s a safer, more complex method was available, in which calcined flint was ground under water in vats, the grinding action being achieved by means of stirrers which pushed runner stones of chert or quartzite over the flint undergoing grinding[79] (Figure 105). Most, if not all, of the Scottish mills were probably of this latter type. The machinery could also be applied to grinding china clay.

In terms of both distribution and organisation, flint mills were closely linked to the potteries which they served. On the southern shore of the Firth of Forth a major group of potteries grew up in the Prestonpans-Portobello area. At Prestonpans a pottery had been founded in 1751 by William Cadell and Samuel Garbett, both latterly of Carron Works.[80] Other potteries followed. According to the (Old) Statistical Account, the parish had two flint mills which, in the absence of adequate streams, used a tide mill at Morrison's Haven and a colliery level at Cuttle to drive their machinery.[81] At a later date, Hamilton

Watson, earthenware manufacturer in Prestonpans, used a mill belonging to the Earl of Wemyss, two miles to the east of Prestonpans.[82] An undated early 19th-century estate plan shows a flint mill at Sea Mill, below Seton House, and this is almost certainly the mill used by Hamilton Watson. A plan in the Hopetoun Muniments, dated 1831, shows a flint mill at Ormiston, about five miles inland from Prestonpans.[83]

In 1771 William Jamieson obtained a feu from Baron Mure of lands beside the Figgate Burn at what was later to become Portobello. Here he built a pottery and, in 1775, a flint mill.[84] As at Prestonpans, other potteries followed.[85] Jamieson's pottery, like those of the Cadells, produced white stoneware,[86] hence, presumably, the flint mill. By 1799 Portobello had grown from almost nothing to a community of three hundred inhabitants, most of whom were employed in works producing bricks, jars, tiles, brown pottery and white stoneware.[87] To help his trade, Jamieson had built a harbour at the mouth of the Figgate Burn about 1788.[88] According to Baird, the burn drove several water wheels for pottery and for a flax (?scutching) mill which was converted to making white lead about 1800.[89] Between Prestonpans and Portobello there were other potteries and at least two other flint mills, one, above Brunstane Mill (working 1812)[90] and the other adjacent to the waulk mill at Musselburgh. This latter seems to have been a speculative venture on the part of the Burgh Council. The idea was certainly under consideration by 1806; by the early 1830s the mill, let in two parts, was bringing in £70 per annum and was still being used for the same purpose in the 1850s.[91]

Another group of potteries and flint mills developed further up the Forth at Bo'ness. According to Salmon, a pottery had been founded in Bo'ness by William Cadell in 1766.[92] In 1784 John Roebuck purchased it and, in place of the coarse pottery then being produced, took to importing better clay and flint for the production of white and cream stoneware. In 1789 Ninian's Mill, Linlithgow was leased by the burgh to Roebuck for use in grinding flint. The mill was later the subject of a legal dispute which was eventually settled in 1794, the year of Roebuck's death.[93] Subsequently the pottery passed through several hands, but flint continued to be ground in the district. According to the (Old) Statistical Account, a Mr. Reid, owner of Linlithgow Bleachfield, had a flint mill nearby to which raw materials were imported from Gravesend from which flint went to Glasgow, Ireland and his own pottery at West Pans, East Lothian.[94] Strange as it may seem, the ground flint was not apparently used locally. A flint mill on the River Avon, referred to in the (Old) Statistical Account for Muiravonside, Stirlingshire, may be the same mill.[95] In Bo'ness and Carriden parish a mill had been built on the Avon to grind malt for the town's breweries, but was being used to grind flint for local potteries instead.[96]

On the north side of the Firth of Forth, in Abbotshall parish, one mill (probably Hole Mill) had been converted to serve the Kirkcaldy potteries by 1833,[97] and a second, Balwearie Mill, was converted from corn-milling some time after 1855.[98] Further to the north-east, a mill near Leven was grinding flint about 1830.[99]

Fig 106. Distribution of water-powered flint mills, 1730-1830

A plan dated 1773 suggests that water power may have been used at a pottery at Clayhills, Aberdeen, but no confirmation of this can be found in other sources.[100]

Considering the number of potteries in the Glasgow area, it is surprising to find no reference to flint mills prior to 1840, when North Woodside Mill was converted from grain-milling.[101] In the early 1830s Verreville Pottery was importing some of its ground flint from Ouseburn (Newcastle), a practice which it may have shared with other Glasgow potteries. The works also had on its premises steam-powered grinding machinery.[102] By 1865 Garrioch Mills, just upstream from North Woodside, were also grinding flint.[103] A flint-glass works and the Clyde Pottery were both founded in Greenock about 1816,[104] and a second pottery followed in 1820.[105] A map in the Boundary Reports (Scotland) (1831-2)[106] shows a flint mill on the Cartsburn, and the same mill appears on the first Ordnance Survey maps (1864): information from other sources shows that it was linked with Clyde Pottery,[107] and it may have originated some ten to fifteen years earlier. Figure 106 shows the distribution of flint mills.

Limeworks

The widespread use of lime as a means of neutralising acid soils led to the construction of kilns wherever fuel and limestone could be had at close range.[108] Only rarely was water power used, and even then usually only as a means of draining quarries. However, the earliest recorded use of water power in the lime industry relates to a very unusual, possibly unique,[109] means of preparing limestone, in a district where suitable fuel was not readily available. The first indication that such a mill was being contemplated comes in a letter of about 1763, in which George Clark, one of the Commissioners for the Forfeited Estates, reported that he had found a millwright who could build a limestone-stamping mill on the Perth estate.[110] The man in question was almost certainly Charles Leandles, who was employed in the mid-1760s by the Commission to find a suitable site and to make estimates. Although Leandles did much travelling, another millwright had been taken on by 1767, and it was probably he who built the mill,[111] not on the Perth estate but near Kinloch Rannoch on the Robertson of Strowan estate.

The mill, which seems to date from 1766 or 1767, consisted of three iron-shod stampers which delivered eighty-four blows per minute. Small pieces of limestone were fed into a sloping trough of water which carried them down, under the stampers and onwards to a receptacle from which large fragments were excluded by means of a grate. Pennant visited the mill on 2nd August 1769, but was not impressed:

> Saw a stamping mill, calculated to reduce limestone to a fine powder, in order to save the expense of burning, for manure . . . I did not find that this project answered, but was told that the benefit the land was to receive from it would not appear till the third year.[112]

Apparently the Commissioners' expectations were eventually fulfilled,[113] but there was still room for improvement in the design of the mill. In March 1770 Lord Kames suggested that a premium be awarded for the best improved design for the mill; already, in January 1769, one John Gwyn had submitted proposals for an improved mill, to cost £100, incorporating a fly wheel and capable of delivering two hundred and sixteen blows per minute.[114] No evidence has been found as to whether Gwyn's, or anyone else's, plans were carried out or, for that matter, how long the mill continued to function. If Forsyth[115] is to be believed, the mill came to a sad end, 'unfortunately carried away by the burn which had worked it'.[116]

The 1782 edition of Crawford's *History of Renfrewshire* refers to a lime-works on the Crossford estate, Lochwinnoch, which the proprietor, William Dowall, was running in conjunction with George Houston of Johnstone:

> The water is taken out with a large engine, being very curiously supplied with water conveyed a great way in wooden roans thereto, and falling perpendicularly upon the upper side of the great wheel.[117]

A paper on the use of power in limestone quarries (c.1834) identifies three other works at which water power was used. At the Cumbernauld lime-works, where seventy men were employed and eighty thousand bolls of lime produced per annum, a combined mine and quarry was drained by a water wheel which, by means of shafts working on inclined planes, raised water upwards of fifty feet in three lifts.[118] A smaller works at Kilnhead, near Annan, was drained by a water-powered chain pump with a steam engine kept in reserve for dry spells.[119] By far the most interesting of the three, however, was the Closeburn works, Dumfriesshire. By 1834 the twenty-one foot deep limestone beds at Closeburn had ceased to be worked as a quarry, and a mine had been dug with a main passage five hundred yards long and numerous branches. The first two hundred yards had rails on which waggons containing a ton of limestone were pushed to the minehead, where they were attached to a chain, connected to a ten horse power water wheel, and hauled in teams up an inclined plane to the kiln head. The same wheel was also used to drain the mine. The kilns, six in all, had several novel features including a blast-pipe to hasten combustion, the air for which was blown by the water wheel. According to the New Statistical Account (1834), water was brought six miles to the works; one wheel worked the railway and the other drained the mine, blew the kilns and drove a sawmill.[120] In the same parish an Old Red Sand-stone quarry was also drained by water power.[121]

Ochre Mills

Ochre, a blood-red coloured iron ore, was used in its natural form for drawing and under the name of 'reddle' for sheep marking. Mixed with oil, it was widely used in outdoor paintwork.[122] In Scotland, ochre was worked at Lamancha (Peeblesshire) and at Durie (Fife); both sites had grinding mills. The Lamancha mill was erected by Captain Cochrane on his Peeblesshire estate as part of a works where ochre was calcined, ground and levigated by titration with water. Ground ochre or 'Spanish Brown' was sold in batches of not less than quarter hundredweights, either in powder form or mixed with linseed oil. The mill was certainly in operation during the 1790s, but according to the *General View* of Peeblesshire (1802), no paint had been manufactured for some years.[123] On the Durie estate in Fife, a four-foot bed of ochre was worked for many years, much of the material ground at the mill being exported.[124] In the late 1830s the mill had three employees.[125]

Monymusk Lapidary Mill

Grant of Monymusk has already been referred to in connection with lint mills, saw mills and lead mining.[126] His other projects included an ironworks at Monymusk, which never came to fruition, and a stone-polishing mill there, which was built, but which had only a very short and troubled existence.

On 12th November 1765 a contract was signed between Archibald Grant and one Henry Eilbeck, jeweller and lapidary at Whitehaven, Cumberland, under which Eilbeck was to settle with his family at the Kirktown of Monymusk and pursue the trade of polishing and cutting stones for twenty-one years, giving instruction to at least six apprentices. In return, Grant undertook to build him a house and mill, to advance money for machinery and to raise a subscription on his behalf among the gentry of Scotland. Grant's intention seems to have been to make use of locally occurring gemstones and to provide employment for children living at the Kirktown.

From the start, however, the enterprise was doomed to failure. By July 1766 the house and mill were still not complete and Eilbeck had not been allowed to supervise the building work as promised. A saw mill had been built adjacent to the lapidary mill, and sharing its water, so that only in times of flood could both function properly. By late 1767 Eilbeck had finally moved to Monymusk, but was evidently dissatisfied with the state of affairs. The promised subscription had not been forthcoming, the machinery of the mill was still incomplete, his first apprentice he describes as 'very indifferent', and he had been subjected to the 'insults and abuse' of Grant's servants. Eventually, in February 1768, the agreement was abandoned, there being no certainty as to whether the mill was ever completed.[127]

Miscellanea

As with the mills in the first section of this chapter, there are a few in the second which were so uncommon as to justify no more than a passing reference.

In Stair parish, Ayrshire, the New Statistical Account refers to a mill used for two unusual purposes. Near a stone quarry William Herron, proprietor of the Dalmore estate, had discovered a deposit of graphite, and having been advised to build a mill to pulverise it, did so but, in the words of the Account, this 'did not proceed'. This probably took place in 1821, the date shown on the mill. Between 1822 and 1826 it was converted to teaze, card and spin wool, but this too was given up on the death of the proprietor and all the machinery removed, save that which had been installed for stripping and polishing Water of Ayr stone (whetstone). At the time of the New Statistical Account only one man was employed at the mill.[128] The New Statistical Account also mentions two unusual applications of water power in Midlothian: in Colinton parish a snuff mill also contained machinery for grinding magnesia, and at Dalkeith a water wheel on the River Esk was used to pump up water for the town's use.[129] Legal and cartographic evidence suggests that water power may have been used to pump sea water into salt pans at Joppa (Edinburgh): in 1791 the Marquis of Abercorn was said to have 'made additions to the machinery of his salt pans, and applied the water to the service . . . of these'. A late 18th-century plan shows a lade running from near Duddingston House (home of Lord Abercorn) to the saltworks.[130] One of the falls of the Shaws Water Aqueduct was applied to a chemical works, but the exact purposes to which the water power was put are not known.[131]

NOTES

1. *SRO* GD51/354/2: 1766: 32,400 hogsheads of tobacco imported

   31,626   ,,   ,,   ,,   exported
   1771: 50,224   ,,   ,,   ,,   imported
   48,749   ,,   ,,   ,,   exported.

2. *NSA* XII, 110-1, Peterculter, Aberdeenshire.

3. Morgan, P., *Annals of Woodside & Newhills*, Aberdeen, 1886, 17.

4. *SBRS*, 'Extracts from the Records of the Burgh of Glasgow', VII (1760-80), Glasgow, 1912, 108-9.

5. Morgan, *op. cit.*, 17.

6. *SBRS*, Glasgow, VII, 108.

7. Now part of Glasgow.

8. NLS Acc.2933/328/f.3: Memorial, James Graham of Dawsholm.

9. Morgan, *op. cit.*, 17.

10. Quoted by Shirley, G. W., *The Growth of a Scottish Burgh*, Dumfries, 1915.

11. *NSA* IX, 11, Cupar, Fife.

12. One employee: *OSA* IX, 33, Logie Pert, Angus (Mill of Logie). Two employees: *NSA* VIII, 58, New Kilpatrick, Dunbartonshire (Dawsholm).

13. NLS Acc.2933/328/f.3: January 1748.

14. *Pigot & Co's National Commercial Directory of the Whole of Scotland and the Isle of Man*, London, 1837, 697.

15. Smeaton, J., *Reports of the Late John Smeaton*, 3 vols., London, 1812, I, 423.

16. Morgan, *op. cit.*, 17.

17. *SBRS*, Glasgow, VII, 108.

18. *OSA* IX, 33, Logie Pert, Angus.

19. Geddie, J., *The Water of Leith from Source to Sea*, Edinburgh, 1896, 76.

20. SRO RHP770; SRO RHP247/1.

21. Morgan, *op. cit.*, 180.

22. Linlithgow: SRO E 707/2: Rental, c.1747-8; Dighty: SRO E 707/2: Rental, 1751.

23. Morgan, *op. cit.*, 187.

24. Mitchell, Sir A. (ed.), 'Macfarlane's Geographical Collections', *SHS* LI (1906), LII (1907), LIII (1908), III, 631.

25. Sources: various.

26. *OSA* IX, 33, Logie Pert, Angus.

27. *OSA* VIII, 592, Alloa, Clackmannanshire.

28. SRO GD51/354/1.

29. *OSA* XIX, 580, Colinton, Midlothian.

30. Jedburgh: Map at Queen Mary's House Museum, Jedburgh; Stitchill: Gunn, C. B. (ed.), 'Records of the Baron Court of Stitchill, 1655-1807', *SHS* L (1905), 210.

31. *OSA* IX, 33, Logie Pert, Angus.

32. Boag's: Geddie, *op. cit.*, 115; Mugiemoss: Morgan, *op. cit.*, 187.

33. *NSA* I, 125, Colinton, Midlothian.

34. Geddie, *op. cit.*, 68.

35. See Vincent, C. W. (ed.), *Chemistry as Applied to the Arts & Manufactures*, 8 vols., London, n.d. (c.1875-80), VI, 310-46.

36. Mechanical knives for scraping hides were invented in the 1820s: Jamieson, A., *A Dictionary of Mechanical Science*, 2 vols., London, 1827. Beating and rolling machines for finishing hides appeared in the early 1840s: Dussauce, H., *A New & Complete Treatise on the Arts of Tanning, Currying & Leather-Dressing*, London & Philadelphia, 1865, 259.

37. SRO GD1/189/17.

38. SRO NG1/1/27 1/6/91; 26/6/91.

39. OSP 512:1.

40. SRO GD1/189/26.

41. SRO GD1/189/27; SRO GD1/189/30.

42. Crawford, G. (revised Semple, W.), *The History of Renfrewshire*, Paisley, 1782, 185.

43. *SBRS*, 'Extracts from the Records of the Burgh of Aberdeen', III (1643-1747), Edinburgh, 1872, 222.

44. *SBRS*, 'Extracts from the Records of the Burgh of Glasgow', V (1718-38), Glasgow, 1909, 80-1, 85.

45. Shirley, *op. cit.*

46. Gatehouse: SRO GD10/126 (1785); Inverness: SRO RHP672 (1774); SRO RHP530 (1855).

47. SRO GD215/1825 (Ninian's Mill); SRO NG1/1/31 27/11/05.

48. I.e. reduced to a condition resembling tobacco — a mass of fibres, but with little dust.

49. Vincent, *op. cit.*, VI, 326.

50. *SBRS*, 'Extracts from the Records of the Burgh of Glasgow', VI (1739-59), Glasgow, 1911, 46.

51. Edgar, R., 'An Introduction to the History of Dumfries', in Reid, R. C. (ed.), *The Records of the Western Marches*, I, Dumfries, 1915, 111.

52. SRO GD267/27/3786/2 (1819); *NSA* II, Eyemouth, Berwickshire.

53. SRO GD215/1825.

54. *Edinburgh Advertiser*, 11th July 1780.

55. Vincent, *op. cit.*, V, 145-50.

56. *NSA* I, 53, Temple, Midlothian.

57. SRO GD266/72.

58. *SBRS*, 'Extracts from the Records of the Burgh of Edinburgh', XII (1689-1701), Edinburgh, 1962, 282.

59. *NSA* I, 53, Temple, Midlothian; *NSA* I, 183, Borthwick, Midlothian.

60. *Scots Magazine*, LXVII (1805), 965.

61. *NSA* I, 353, Roslin, Midlothian; *OS* 1st Edition 6″/mile.

62. Knox, J., (Map of) Midlothian, 1812.

63. SRO GD266/72.

64. Forrest, W., (Map of) West Lothian, 1818; *OS* 1st Edition 6″/mile.

65. Wilson, J. J., *Annals of Penicuik*, Edinburgh, 1891, 118.

66. *NSA* VII, 612, Dunoon & Kilmun, Argyll.

67. Fraser, A., *Lochfyneside*, Edinburgh, 1971, 34.

68. *NSA* VII, 366, Kilfinan, Argyll.

69. *RCAHMS*, Argyll, vol. 2, *Lorn*, Edinburgh, 1975, 292.

70. *NSA* VII, 612, Dunoon & Kilmun, Argyll.

71. Smith, R. M., *History of Greenock*, Greenock, 1921; Weir, D., *History of the Town of Greenock*, Greenock, 1829, 92; *PP* 1872, XXXIV, River Pollution Commission (Scotland), 169-71.

72. Fall 6: *Hutcheson's Greenock Register, Directory & General Advertiser for 1845-6*, Greenock, 1845, 75.

73. *NSA* III, 230, Eckford, Roxburghshire.

74. *OSA* XIV, 253, Govan, Lanarkshire.

75. SRO NG1/1/33 5/7/1815.

76. Martine, T. C., 'Old Haddington', *TELA&FNS* XII (1970), 58.

77. See Clow, A. & Clow, N. L., *The Chemical Revolution*, London, 1952, 269-326; Fleming, J. A., *Scottish Pottery*, Glasgow, 1923; McVeigh, Patrick, *Scottish East Coast Potteries, 1750-1840*, Edinburgh, 1979.

78. Clow & Clow, *op. cit.*, 273, 290-1, 318-9.

79. See Wailes, R., 'Water Driven Mills for Grinding Stone', *TNS* XXX (1966-7), 95-119; Stephen, W. M., 'Two Flint Mills near Kirkcaldy, Fife', *IA* II (1966).

80. *OSP* F31:30.

81. *OSA* XVII, 74, Prestonpans, East Lothian.

82. SRO CS96/807 (1838); SRO RHP3387.

83. SRO CS96/807.

84. Hume, D., *Decisions of the Court of Session, 1781-1822*, Edinburgh & London, 1839, 510.

85. See Baird, W., *Annals of Duddingston & Portobello*, Edinburgh, 1898.

86. *Ibid.*, 438-9.

87. *Ibid.*, 309.

88. *Ibid.*, 304.

89. *Ibid.*, 305.

90. Knox, J., (Map of) Midlothian, 1812.

91. SRO GD1/189/26 (1806); *PP* 1835, V, Municipal Corporations (Scotland); *OS* 1st Edition, 6″/mile.

92. Salmon, T. J., *Bo'ness and District, c.1550-1850*, Edinburgh, 1913, 153.

93. SRO GD215/1825.

94. *OSA* XIV, 556, Linlithgow, West Lothian.

95. *OSA* I, 200, Muiravonside, Stirlingshire.

96. *OSA* XVIII, 440, Bo'ness, West Lothian.

97. *NSA* IX, 157, Abbotshall, Fife.

98. *OS* 1st Edition 6″/mile; Stephen, *op. cit.*, 172.

99. SRO RHP770.

100. SRO RHP814.

101. Hume, J. R., *The Industrial Archaeology of Glasgow*, Glasgow & London, 1974, 54-5.

102. SRO CS96/393 153.

103. *OS* 1st Edition 6″/mile.

104. Smith, *op. cit.*, 229.

105. Clow & Clow, *op. cit.*, 323.

106. *PP* 1831/2 XLII, Boundary Reports (Scotland).

107. Weir, *op. cit.*, 94.

108. See Butt, J., *Industrial Archaeology of Scotland*, Newton Abbot, 1967; Hume, J. R., *The Industrial Archaeology of Scotland*, 2 vols., London, 1976-7.

109. A second mill was proposed at Pitlochry but was apparently not built.

110. SRO E777/139/2.

111. SRO E 728/48/(1).

112. Pennant, T., *A Tour in Scotland, 1769*, 2nd Edition, London, 1772, 100-1.

113. SRO GD18/5934.

114. SRO GD18/5933.

115. Forsyth, R., *The Beauties of Scotland*, 5 vols., Edinburgh, 1806, IV, 265.

116. *Ibid.*, IV, 265.

117. Crawford, *op. cit.*, 160.

118. Carmichael, J., 'An Account of the Principal Limestone Quarries of Scotland', *TH&AS*, New Series XI (1838), 71.

119. *Ibid.*, 416.

120. *Ibid.*, 76-8; *NSA* IV, 87, Closeburn, Dumfriesshire.

121. *NSA* IV, 87, Closeburn, Dumfriesshire.

122. Jamieson, *op. cit.*, II, 734.

123. *OSA* XXI, 53, Newlands, Peeblesshire; Findlater, C., *General View of the Agriculture of Peeblesshire*, Edinburgh, 1802, 22.

124. Lewis, S., *Topographical Dictionary of Scotland*, 2 vols., London, 1846, II, 458.

125. *NSA* IX, 272, Scoonie, Fife.

126. See Chapters 15, 24, 26.

127. SRO GD345/1027.

128. *NSA* V, 638, Stair, Ayrshire; SRO NG1/1/35 4/7/1826; Hume, J. R., 'Mills of the River Ayr', *AAC* (1969), 50.

129. *NSA* I, 125, Colinton, Midlothian; *NSA* I, 459, Dalkeith, Midlothian. Water power from the River Esk (Angus/Kincardineshire) was being used in 1868 to pump water for the burgh of Montrose: Act 31 & 32 Victoria Cap. 123 XII.

130. Hume, D., *op. cit.*, 510; SRO RHP582.

131. *OS* 1st Edition 6″/mile (1864).

28

Water Management Schemes

Although it could be argued that any dam built to store water for a mill involved a measure of water management, it was not until the late 18th and early 19th centuries that serious attempts were made to regulate water flow on whole rivers and on behalf of the owners of mills along their banks. The powers of a proprietor controlling the headwaters of a river had already been used, and not always to the advantage of mills downstream, to control the availability of water, but the water management schemes to be considered here were carried out by the mill owners and tenants themselves.

Rivers and streams had always been subject to seasonal and shorter-term fluctuations in volume. Where the only users of water power were small corn and textile mills, working for a local, often tied market, as was generally the case for much of the 18th century, a mill stoppage was a source of inconvenience but nothing more serious; there were always other tasks to be carried out, few people were employed by any one mill, and most mills had adequate surplus capacity to enable them to complete their quota of work once water levels returned to normal. Not so, however, for the large industrial mills of the late 18th and 19th centuries, which might each employ several hundred workers and which were geared to maximising output. For them, slow running or stoppage meant loss of profitability, a loss which was sometimes compensated for only by the pernicious system of working 'mill hours', that is to say, extending working hours so as to maintain the production level which would have been achieved with full water. By the second quarter of the 19th century several additional factors had further enhanced the desirability of water management schemes. Although steam power had offered an alternative means of achieving rotary motion since the 1780s, it was only in the 1820s that it began to be extensively used in Scotland; the new steam-powered factories could choose sites well placed for labour, raw materials and markets; they could be built on a scale large enough to house substantial numbers of machines, including those recently introduced, with potential for expansion in the event of further mechanisation. Not for them the stoppages occasioned by low water. Overall, and notwithstanding the additional cost of fuel, they stood a far greater chance of running profitably than their water-powered counterparts which were tied to riparian sites, often encumbered with outmoded machinery, and unable to install extra capacity without introducing auxiliary steam power, the fuel for which was probably more expensive than that supplied to the better situated steam mills.

Government attempts to regulate working hours in the textile industries were to the detriment of mill owners and were vehemently opposed by them. Latterly, the drainage of uplands which had formerly regulated day-to-day stream flow led to much quicker run-off and periods of intense activity interspersed with idle spells.

The vast majority of mills, right down to the level of corn mill, now had to work within a market economy and against ever stronger competition from steam power. In these circumstances, the only solution, short of giving up or converting to steam power, was to formulate schemes to regulate stream flow.

The Work of Robert Thom

In a Scottish context, work on such schemes was dominated by one man, Robert Thom. Thom was born at Tarbolton, Ayrshire in 1775 and studied at the Andersonian Institution in Glasgow.[1] He became manager of and partner in Blackburn cotton mill, West Lothian,[2] and in 1813 had purchased Rothesay cotton mills with William Kelly, manager of New Lanark Mills. In 1826, on Kelly's death, he became sole partner. As early as 1800 the mills had two steam engines of ten and twenty horse power, but in his plans for expanding the works Thom relied exclusively on making more effective use of the available water power. In 1821 he devised an elaborate system of aqueducts leading into Loch Fad (the mills' 'reservoir'), the storage capacity of which was doubled. The flow of water was regulated by automatic sluices of his own design, and by these means he was able to increase the available water power to a regular seventy horse power.[3] An account of the water works has been written by John Ferrier, and this should be referred to for further details.

Word of Thom's achievements soon spread to other quarters. In March 1824 he submitted a plan for 'improving the waterfalls on the line of the River Almond'. Although he was now resident in Rothesay, he still had an interest in the Blackburn cotton mill, on the Almond. Thom's plan indicated that he had already considered building a reservoir prior to moving to Rothesay, and had found several suitable sites above Blackburn. According to his calculations, a reservoir could yield 600,000 cubic feet of water per day, for eight weeks during the greatest droughts. Such a volume of water could provide a steady twenty horse power from a twenty-foot wheel for twelve hours per day. On Wednesday, 2nd June 1824, a meeting of interested parties was held in the Royal Exchange Coffee House, Edinburgh. A letter from Thom was read to the meeting and a number of resolutions were passed. The gist of these resolutions, eight in all, was that each individual should bear a proportion of the cost, as determined by two independent arbiters, and subject to unanimous support being obtained for the plan. Parties to the agreement were not to be bound for more than the £3,000 cost and £100 per annum land rent estimated by Thom; tenants were to pay their contribution to the proprietors of their

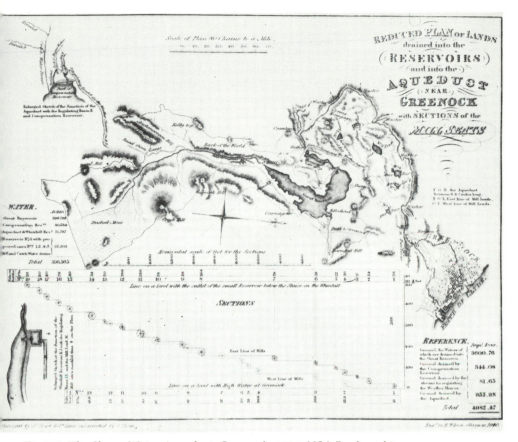

Fig 107. The Shaws Water Aqueduct, Greenock, 1827. *NSA Renfrewshire*

mills. However, for all the initial enthusiasm, nothing seems to have come of the scheme.[4]

In August 1827 Thom was asked by the City of Glasgow to find how best to improve the reservoirs and water courses of the Molendinar Burn, so as to increase the available water power as far as possible. His report, submitted in 1830, indicated that the greatest problem would be in reaching agreement with the proprietor of the head lochs with regard to their expansion, but that otherwise there would be no other insuperable problems. For his services Thom received £52 16s 6d.[5]

By far the most ambitious of Thom's schemes, and his greatest achievement, was the Shaws Water Works at Greenock. Unlike any other major scheme, it involved the creation of an entirely new water course where none had existed before. Before its establishment there were no water mills in the town of Greenock itself, yet Thom confidently asserted that, by implementing his plan, Greenock could derive as much power from water as did Glasgow from steam.

Not only did Greenock not have any water power: even water for domestic and processing purposes was in short supply. James Watt, having surveyed the area, had concluded that only small reservoirs could be constructed, as did John Rennie at a later date. In 1821 Thom was asked to inspect the area with a view to procuring a supply of water but, being occupied with work at Rothesay, he was unable to oblige. Following a second approach, in 1824, he carried out a survey and submitted a report. Thom had been commissioned only to provide a means of supplying water for domestic and processing uses, but in addition to this he showed how water could be laid on to thirty-one millsteads on two artificial water courses with a total fall of over five hundred feet.[6]

To implement the scheme, a joint-stock company was set up with a capital of £31,000 and incorporated by Act of Parliament on June 10th 1825,[7] under the title of the 'Shaws Water Company', the name being that of the principal feeder stream. At the crux of Thom's plan was the Great Reservoir (later renamed Loch Thom), an artificial lake of two hundred and ninety-six and three-quarter acres, high above Greenock on the upper reaches of the Shaws Water. The Great Reservoir was closed off by a sixty-foot-high dam and, with a compensation reservoir and six auxiliary reservoirs, held 337,000,000 cubic feet of water (Figure 107). From the compensation reservoir an aqueduct skirted Dunrod and Shaws Hills, care having been taken to minimise the height lost — over its five-and-a-half-mile-course it fell by only twenty-six feet — ending in the Long Dam, five hundred and twelve feet above sea level and at the head of the falls. In all, the works had cost £90,000. Initially two separate lines of falls were planned, but the more westerly one was never built. A branch of the eastern lead was eventually added.[8]

On 16th April, 1827, amidst great ceremony, water started to flow from the Great Reservoir to the eastern line of falls. The *Greenock Advertiser* recorded the event with justifiable pride:

> The 16th of April, will long remain a memorable day in the annals of Greenock. Rapid as was its advance from the obscurity of a fishing village to the consideration which belongs to the first sea port in Scotland, we trust it is destined from this day to exhibit a still more rapid progress as a manufacturing town, for which it has acquired facilities it did not before possess — and, we may add, which no place in the United Kingdom now possesses in the same eminent degree.
>
> To form an immense artificial lake, in the bosom of the neighbouring alpine regions, and lead its liquid treasure along the mountain summits, at an elevation of more than five hundred feet above the level of the sea, till, in the immediate vicinity of the town, it should be made to pour down a resistless torrent, in successive falls, for the impelling of machinery to a vast extent — this, in a few words, was the magnificent conception of Mr. Thom; and never, probably, did the first trial of so novel and extensive an undertaking demonstrate its capability and entire adaptation to its purpose or excite such unalloyed and universal gratification.
>
> In conclusion, we cannot help remarking, as a most singular circumstance, that the birth-place of Watt should have become the theatre for exhibiting the earliest practical demonstrations, on an extensive scale, of a great mechanical power,

rivalling the utility of his own; and been the means of adding another name to the bright record of ingenious men who have proved at once the benefactors of their country and of mankind.[9]

Such euphoria was, perhaps, a little premature. Certainly the Works represented a great technical feat, but at the time of opening there were only four mills on the nineteen falls of the eastern line: the paper mill of James Walkinshaw, the sugar refinery of Tasker, Young & Co., the Associated Bakers' grain mill, and the power loom manufactory of McNab & Co.[10] Additions were made, and by 1845 eleven falls were occupied by a wide variety of industries, some new to the district (Table 11), but the higher falls, numbers thirteen to seventeen, proved difficult to let, and it was not until 1881 that they were brought into use to drive a turbine in a woollen mill on fall twelve.[11] In 1852, during a prolonged drought, the mills were stopped for six weeks, Loch Thom was run dry, and two thousand persons were made idle. Some indication of the investment made in mills and water works can be gathered from the fact that £350,000 worth of capital was said to have lain idle during the closure.[12]

The water company had never made much of its obligation to supply water for domestic and industrial purposes, and only in 1865, when the town itself bought out the shareholders for twice the face value of their share capital, was

Table 11

Shaws Water Aqueduct. Occupants of Falls, 1845

Fall No.	Height	H.P.	Type of Mill	Occupant
1	26'	46	Saw mill	Jas. McLean & Co.
2	26'	46	Barley, Corn, Flour	Not Known
3	17'	30	Flour mill	Bakers' Mill Co.
4	26'	6	Paint mill	J. Fyfe
		12	Logwood mill	Robert Reyburn
		18	Foundry	Adam & Wm. Johnstone
5	NO INFORMATION			
6	19'	34	Rice mill	Thos. Dodson
7	28'	50	Sailcloth mill	Gourock Ropework Co.
8-9	63'	160	Cotton spinning mill	Shaws Water Cotton Spinning Co.
10	NO INFORMATION			
11	33'	42	Dyewood mill	Henry & John Reid
		18	Dye, Carding & Milling	Robert Houston
12	29'	53	Worsted manufacture	Neill, Fleming & Reid
13-17	VACANT			
18	30'	54	Paper mill	Walkinshaw & Co.

Source: *Hutcheson's Greenock Register, Directory & General Advertiser for 1845-6*, Greenock, 1845

the problem resolved.[13] Under its control, the embankment on Loch Thom was raised, at a cost of £47,000, and two new reservoirs, completed in 1872, were built on the headwaters of Gryfe Water, one to provide compensation water for mill owners, the other for domestic use, the cost of the two reservoirs amounting to £160,000.[14]

The use of turbines in the late 19th century brought a new lease of life to the mills and their eventual decline owed much more to demands for domestic and process water than to the abandonment of water power. The practical difficulties encountered by the water company should not be allowed to detract from Thom's brilliance in planning and executing a scheme of such size and ingenuity. In the absence of locally available coal for steam engines, his work gave indigenous industries such as sugar-refining, grain-milling and rope-making a chance to expand, besides attracting others such as worsted manufacture and papermaking. As one of the last great proponents of water power, Robert Thom helped to ensure its continued viability well into the Steam Age.

Water Management in East Renfrewshire

The cotton industry of the Cart Basin, Renfrewshire has already been dealt with in some detail, and an attempt made to show how water power continued to play a significant part during the first half of the 19th century. However, little was said of the importance of water management schemes in sustaining the viability of water power in the Cart system and elsewhere in east Renfrewshire.

Levern Water, a stream not large enough to merit the name 'river', had begun to attract cotton mills in the early 1780s, and by the end of the 18th century it supported a thriving textile industry based on cotton mills, bleachfields and printfields.[15] Needless to say, water storage facilities were soon required. According to the (Old) Statistical Account, a consortium of cotton mill, printfield and bleachfield owners along the Levern had taken a lease within the preceding few years of land at the headwaters of the stream, with liberty to build a dam about sixteen feet high. The land above the dam, being level and having numerous springs, was flooded to the extent of one mile by half a mile (Figure 108). During the greatest droughts this body of water, known as the Long Loch, was said to be capable of driving all the machinery in the works erected and still erecting, with only a three-inch raising of the sluice.[16] In 1804 the proprietors of mills on the Levern took a fifteen-year lease of Commore Dam, downstream from the Long Loch, renewable for a further term at Whitsunday 1823: one of the mill proprietors, a Mr. Graham, produced a holograph memorandum of agreement among the members of the association. In 1821 it was decided to renew the lease on the Long Loch and to seek a lease of Hairlaw Bog to make a reservoir; this was obtained in January 1822.[17] According to Taylor (1831), the Long Loch could provide sixteen weeks' water to the mills on the Levern, Hairlaw Dam another eight to nine

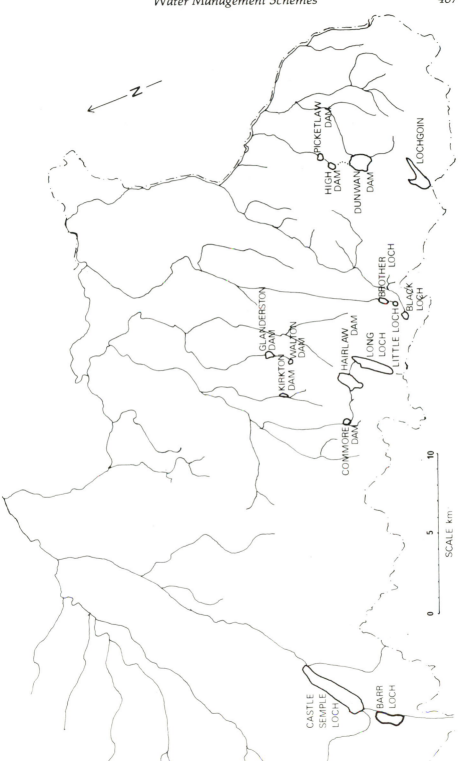

Fig 108. Water regulating reservoirs in east Renfrewshire

weeks and Commore Dam a further three.[18] Water was let to mill proprietors in shares of £20 per annum, the number of shares depending on the scale of each works: a cotton mill, for example, might pay for five shares. The total yield, about £800 per annum, went to the proprietors of land under reservoirs. The sluice at Commore Dam, which was used to regulate flow, was operated by Thomas Gemmel, farmer at Commore, who received £12 per annum for his troubles.[19]

Mearns Moor, to the east of the Levern, had been divided in 1799, with the exception of Black Loch and Brother Loch extending to eighty-six acres, which in 1812 were rented by mill owners on Capelrig Burn and White Cart Water at £62 per annum.[20] By the late 1830s Eaglesham parish, to the east of Mearns, had no less than two hundred and thirty-seven acres of hill land under reservoirs which regulated the flow to mills at Eaglesham village and Busby in Renfrewshire, and at Fenwick in Ayrshire.[21] At the time of the New Statistical Account, Renfrewshire had more than nine hundred acres of storage reservoirs.[22]

Leven—Dighty—Carron

The River Leven (Fife) carried a prodigious number of mills (Figure 109), mostly connected with flax-spinning and linen-bleaching, and in Loch Leven possessed one of the finest potential natural reservoirs in Scotland. An initial meeting of mill proprietors, in October 1824, had resolved to install sluices on the outlet from the Loch so as to regulate flow, and by 1827 an Act of Parliament had been obtained[23] 'for recovering, draining and preserving certain lands . . . in Kinross and Fife; and for better supplying with water the mills, manufactories, bleachfields and other works situated on or near the River of Leven'. A new cut was made from the Loch to the river, with sluices, spill-waters, embankments, ways and bridges; the surface level of the Loch was lowered by four and a half feet. The work was finally completed in June 1833 and the total cost, some £60,000, was met from perpetual dues based on an assessment of the enhanced value of each fall.[24]

In 1836 a Bill was drawn up for a water management scheme on Dighty Water, Angus, a stream noted for its linen bleachfields. For the purposes of the Bill, proprietors and tenants of falls were declared to be a body corporate, with one vote allocated to the mill tenant and one to the mill proprietor for each foot of fall. Once the cost of improvements became known, a committee would allocate proportions on the basis of water power installed and water volume used.[25]

Carron Ironworks, the best-known user of water power on the River Carron, had its own reservoirs from the start (Chapter 25, p. 432) but in its upper reaches the river was also applied to a number of other mills, notably for paper and woollen manufacture. By the early 1830s agricultural improvements on the Campsie Fells had begun to jeopardise the once steady flow of water, and proprietors of mills formed a society which, by subscription, raised

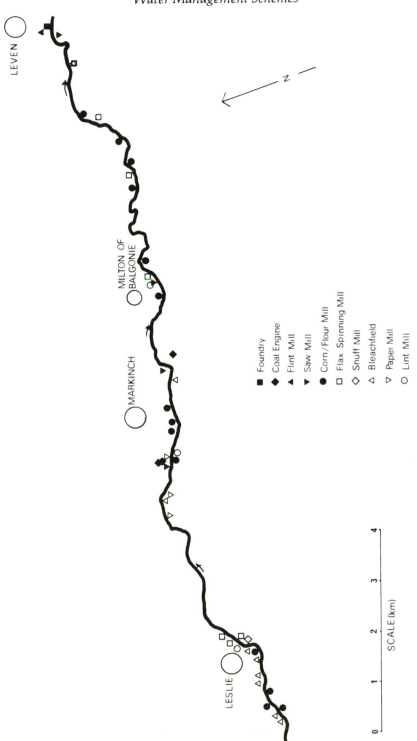

Fig 109. Water mills on the Fife Leven, 1830. *SRO RHP770*

£2,000 to build a twenty-two-foot-high embankment on a tributary stream, Earl's Burn, behind which a sixty-acre reservoir would be formed.[26] Compared to the sums laid out on the Leven and Shaws Water schemes, the £2,000 for the River Carron seems remarkably small, and the dam's construction, 'moss upon moss' with stone on the upper side, was a cheap yet far from satisfactory means of holding back so large a volume of water. On 24th October 1839, after a period of heavy rain, the dam gave way, partly under its own weight and partly under that of impounded water, causing much damage.[27] Not until 1847 was a report on a new dam submitted to the mill proprietors and occupants; this offered a number of more realistic options, with costs ranging up to £30,000.[28]

Conclusion

One could go on indefinitely giving examples of water management schemes,[29] but the few, more spectacular examples already cited should be sufficient to make a number of points regarding the state of water power in the first half of the 19th century.

Perhaps the most remarkable feature is the fact that mill owners and tenants were prepared to co-operate in this way. The records of the Court of Session are peppered with cases of disputes among mill proprietors, occupants and landowners. As congestion increased on the most favoured streams, disputes became all the more common and competition fiercer, yet in the 1820s and '30s those parties with interests in mills did a complete about-face, working together, often going to the trouble of obtaining an Act of Parliament, and investing perhaps several thousand pounds in promoting a source of power already written off in some quarters. The influences discussed at the beginning of this chapter go some way to explaining this radical change in attitude. Besides these incentives, the new steam-powered factories could be seen as a common adversary and the furtherance of water power as a common goal, all the more so if the mills in question were unable to benefit from cheap, locally available coal. This last consideration also applied to Greenock, where no mills or natural water courses had existed, but where the rise of Glasgow's steam-powered industry was viewed with some disquiet. It should be remembered too that water power was cheap, all the more so in relative terms, if considerable sums of money had already been sunk in developing industry on exploitable water courses. Furthermore, the drainage and topography of Scotland was (and is) such that fairly extensive upland reservoirs could be established on the headwaters of most of the heavily utilised rivers, either by acquiring land which was cheap and little used, or by modifying existing lochs.

However, seen within the broader context of Scottish industrial development and notwithstanding the effort put into, and in some cases the success achieved by, such schemes, they were going against the tide of history. Water power, having experienced such remarkable growth over the preceding century, and having laid the foundations of a well-developed industrial economy in Scotland, was about to enter a prolonged period of decline. The Age of Steam Power had arrived.

NOTES

1. Ferrier, J., 'The Water Cuts of Robert Thom', *TGAS* New Series, XV (1966), 130.

2. SRO GD247/46/68.

3. Ferrier, *op. cit.*, 130-2.

4. SRO GD247/46/68.

5. *SBRS*, 'Extracts from the Records of the Burgh of Glasgow', XI (1823-33), Glasgow, 1916, 267, 393, 407.

6. Weir, D., *History of the Town of Greenock*, Greenock, 1829, 98-100.

7. *Ibid.*, 100; Smith, R. M., *History of Greenock*, Greenock, 1921, 41.

8. Weir, *op. cit.*, 100-1; Clark, S., 'The Shaws Water Falls in Greenock', in *SSIA Newsletter*, VII Pt 3/VIII Pt 1 (Spring 1976), 13.

9. Weir, *op. cit.*, 104-5.

10. Smith, *op. cit.*, 42.

11. Clark, *op. cit.*, 9.

12. Smith, *op. cit.*, 43.

13. Clark, *op. cit.*, 10.

14. Smith, *op. cit.*, 44.

15. See Chapter 20, p. 332 *et seq.*

16. *OSA* II, 141, Neilston, Renfrewshire.

17. Bell, S. S., *Dictionary of Decisions of the Court of Session from November 1808 to November 1833*, 2 vols., Edinburgh, 1842, II, 1056.

18. Taylor, C., *The Levern Delineated*, Glasgow, 1831, 46.

19. *Ibid.*, 67.

20. Wilson, J., *General View of the Agriculture of Renfrewshire*, Paisley, 1812, 124.

21. *NSA* VII, 385, Eaglesham, Renfrewshire.

22. *NSA* VII, 539, General Remarks, Renfrewshire.

23. Beath, D., *Reminiscences of Leslie & Neighbourhood*, Kirkcaldy, 1912, 14; 7th & 8th Geo. IV Cap. 105.

24. Kettleby, C. D. M., *Tullis Russel 1809-1959*, Markinch, 1967, 41.

25. SRO GD16/27/364.

26. *NSA* VIII, 130, Denny, Stirlingshire.

27. *Ibid.*, 130; SRO GD58/18/64.

28. SRO GD58/18/64.

29. Further research, beyond the scope of the present enquiry, would be useful, if only to determine how many of these schemes were implemented and the extent to which they enabled mill owners and tenants to postpone or avoid the need to use steam power.

Part Three

Water Power in the Age of Steam, 1830-1870

29

Water Power in the Age of Steam

It cannot be denied that in relative, if not in absolute terms, water power in Scotland was in decline during the mid-19th century. Further improvements and diversification in the design of steam engines made them all the more competitive; the use of steam power in railways revolutionised the movement of goods, including coal, the price of which fell sharply in each locality through which a railway passed.[1] By 1870 a close network of railways linked not only the principal towns and cities of Scotland but also many minor communities. 1830 marks a major watershed in Scottish industrial history with the introduction of Neilson's hot blast which helped to bring about the meteoric rise of the Scottish pig-iron industry,[2] to the extent of its replacing textiles as the most important sector of the economy. Textiles, in contrast, had a not so easy time; cotton in particular declined in importance. This huge shift in emphasis had major implications for the use of water power, for whilst the textile industry made widespread use of it, the iron and engineering industries had already gone over almost entirely to steam by 1830. Furthermore, the huge amounts of power which could be produced by steam engines made it possible for industrial units to grow far beyond a size sustainable by water power, in localities accessible to markets and, through the medium of railways and steam navigation, raw materials. In such circumstances the use of water power might be expected to have wasted away, as some writers have implied. However, in spite of its decline relative to steam power, it would be wrong to write it off completely. So much momentum had been built up over the previous hundred years and so much capital had been invested in water power that many existing mills continued to operate and some new ones were built. What is more, the sharpened competitive edge created by the success of steam led to the development of new, more efficient means of utilising water power, which brought greater viability to mills dependent on it and otherwise unable to compete with their steam-powered counterparts.

Technology

Although the attention of most parties had turned to the improvement of steam power by 1830, there was still room for work on water power. William Fairbairn's *Mills and Millwork*, while not exclusively devoted to water power, had gone into four editions by 1878 and Joseph Glynn's *Power of Water* into five by 1875.[3] Nor was this interest of an entirely academic nature: both Fairbairn and Glynn were working engineers who continued to build water wheels and other water-powered machines during this period. In Scotland, the improvements made in water wheel design prior to 1830 were incorporated into a number of mills built or renovated thereafter. The largest water wheel ever erected in Scotland, some seventy feet in diameter, was installed in a mill at Greenock about 1839.[4] At Blairgowrie, Perthshire, two 19th-century flax-spinning mills (Keithbank and Westfield) still have their water wheels, one fourteen feet wide and eighteen feet in diameter, by Carmichael & Co. of Dundee, the other, thirteen feet wide and twenty feet in diameter, by Thomson Bros. of Dundee: at Erichtside Works, Blairgowrie, a nineteen foot by twenty-four foot diameter breast-shot wheel, also by Thomson Bros., was installed in 1871.[5]

In addition to the water wheel, new ways were developed of using water. Allen[6] identifies three types of water-powered prime movers:

1. Water wheels.
2. Water turbines.
3. Water pressure engines.

Reference has already been made to the success of water pressure engines in lead mining during the mid-19th century (Chapter 4, page 393). Elsewhere they found applications in driving hoists, capstans, winches and other small machinery requiring comparatively little power.[7] Joseph Bramah's hydraulic press, developed in the early 19th century, was used in a number of industries. At Granton (Edinburgh) the world's first railway vehicle ferry used the water pressure of the city's domestic water mains to lift carriages on and off the ferry-boat.[8] According to Allen, 'the applications of hydraulic power in the 19th century seem to have been almost limitless'.[9] However, by far the most significant innovation, from the point of view of industrial users of water power, was the water turbine. As the development of the water turbine is of only marginal relevance to the present work, the subject can be dealt with only briefly.[10] During the mid-19th century three types of turbine, outward-flow, inward-flow and axial flow, came into use. Turbines were also designed with mixed flow. A second classification can be based on a distinction between reaction and impulse turbines, the former, generally, being fully immersed, worked by the flow of water, the latter only partially immersed, being moved by its impact.

The first real move towards a turbine came in 1824 with Ponselet's use of curved veins on undershot water wheels, an innovation which achieved much higher efficiencies than were possible with conventional designs and which was, in effect, an unenclosed impulse turbine. In 1827 Fourneyfon developed an outward-flow turbine which, when full, ran as a reaction turbine and, when not, as an impulse type. Both inventions were made in France, but in the 1830s another line of development started in Scotland. 'Barker's Mill', the principle of which is still used in lawn sprinklers, had been known of for some time but only as an object of curiosity. The reaction principle on which it operated was used by James Whitelaw, a Glasgow engineer, in his 'Scotch Turbine', details of which were first published in 1833.[11] In 1839 a patent was taken out and the firm of Messrs Whitelaw & Stirrat started to manufacture them. 'Scotch turbines' were installed at a number of localities in Great Britain. Early Scottish examples included one used to power a threshing mill near Glasgow (c.1839), a cotton-spinning mill near Paisley (c.1840), two woollen mills on the Shaws Water Aqueduct (c.1840, 1841), a bleachfield near Paisley (c.1840) and Culcreuch cotton mill, Stirlingshire (1841). Experiments by eminent engineers indicated an efficiency of between 74 and 74$\frac{1}{4}$ per cent.

In 1843 Whitelaw included a number of testimonials in a sales booklet. A typical example, from J. & W. Fulton, Glenfield, near Paisley, read as follows:

> Gentlemen: We have worked your patent water-mill for upwards of two years, and it is whirling away the same as it did the first hour it was started; indeed we can see no reason why it should not continue to do so without repair for 50 years to come; and although we threw off or put on a machine of two or three horses' power, which we often have occasion to do, the regulators act so nicely that it scarcely alters its speed.
>
> It is admired for its smallness and simplicity by every one who sees it, and we are often amused with the remarks of strangers. When they see the machinery going they look for a water-wheel or steam-engine, but can see neither the one nor the other, and cannot understand where the power comes from, as the water-mill is placed underground in a covered pit, 10 feet square by 5 feet deep, and the building at the sides of the pit is all that is required.
>
> We cannot speak from experience, whether a water-wheel on the old principle or one of yours, works best, as the trouble and expense of building an arc and erecting an overshot-wheel always prevented us from getting the use of our water-fall, which is 44 feet in height; we cannot, however, conceive how a water-wheel could be made to do its work better than the machine we have got.[12]

Despite the success of Whitelaw's turbines in the 1840s and early 1850s, the ready availability of coal, and therefore steam power, concentrated attention in Britain on developing steam engines rather than water turbines. However, in New England, in France and elsewhere in Europe, further innovations were made. As early as 1826 Poncelet had proposed an inward-flow reaction turbine; in 1838 Hood had built one of several in New York State and had taken out a patent under which Francis devised a more sophisticated version. In 1843 Jonvial produced an axial-flow turbine.[13] If Britain as a whole was now looking to steam power, there were still districts, such as Cumbria and parts of Scotland, where water power could still be more viable. The same applied to Ireland, and it was perhaps no coincidence that the next major development in the British Isles originated there. James Thomson of Annaghmore, later Professor of Engineering at Queen's College, Belfast, having carried out experiments on turbines in the late 1840s, took out a patent on the 'Vortex', an inward-flow reaction turbine, the name of which came from its adjustable

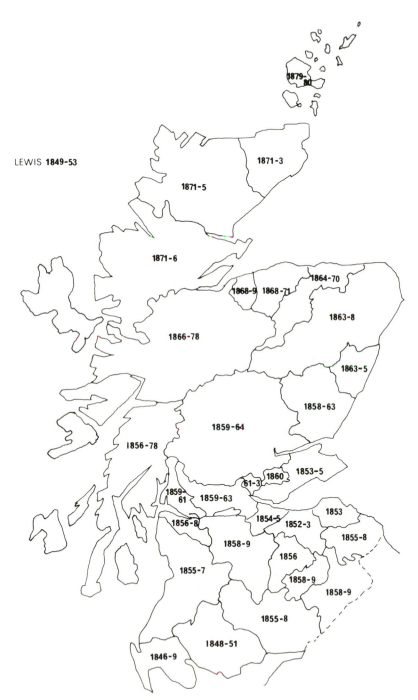

Fig 110. Survey dates, first edition Ordnance Survey of Scotland

outer guide vanes. The first production model was built in Glasgow and installed in a linen-beating mill in County Antrim in 1852. Thereafter, Vortex turbines were manufactured under licence by a number of firms, principal amongst which was Messrs. Williamson Bros. of Kendal.[14] From 1856 Callon and Girard (both of France) designed impulse turbines which were manufactured under licence in Britain.[15] With the exception of the Whitelaw turbines, it is far from easy to judge the extent to which these early turbines were made use of in Scotland. A turbine installed at Brooklinn Mill, Blairgowrie was reputed to have been the first in Scotland (excluding Whitelaw turbines) and Carron Works is known to have had a turbine in its engineering shop by 1869,[16] but evidence of more widespread use comes only after 1870, when Scottish firms such as John Turnbull & Co. and Messrs. Carrick & Ritchie produced large numbers of turbines: one of the latter's catalogues (c.1895) lists one hundred and sixty-nine turbines sold in Scotland, of which the greatest number, some sixty-seven, were for generating electricity.[17] By that time the availability of efficient turbines was such that new water-powered installations almost invariably made use of them, though water wheels were still being constructed to replace existing ones.

In following the development of the water turbine, it has been necessary to stray beyond the confines of our period, but from looking briefly at the late 19th century it is apparent that all was not lost for water power. On the contrary, it was about to undergo a renaissance which would give it a significant, if subordinate, place in industry. Furthermore, it is evident that, in Scotland at least, continuity was never quite broken: by the time some of the last great water wheels were being installed, during the 1860s, turbines of one kind or another had already been in use for twenty or thirty years.

The remainder of this chapter considers the fate of mills in Scotland between 1830 and 1870. For convenience, these have been grouped into three major categories: agricultural, grain and forestry mills; textile and paper mills; and mineral-exploiting mills. Ironically, the first comprehensive cartographic coverage of water mill distribution comes only with the surveying, between 1846 and 1878, of the first Ordnance Survey maps, at a time when they were already in decline. These maps have been extensively used in compiling distribution maps for each type of mill, and in view of the long period over which the survey was carried out, details of survey dates are given in Figure 110.

Agricultural, Grain & Forestry Mills

Grain Mills

Long before 1830 the number of grain mills had begun to decline, and the further reduction in numbers during the next forty years was no more than an extension of an existing trend. With so large a stock of existing mills, it is not surprising to find so few mills being built. On the other hand rebuilding was common enough, not only in the richer agricultural districts such as the Merse and East Lothian, but also in poorer districts, such as the far north, where coal for steam engines was not available locally, where urban markets were some distance away and where the process of agricultural Improvement came relatively late.[18] In the absence of thirlage, falling rural and rising urban populations, a much improved transport network and the rise of the grain merchant all favoured a move towards market-orientated urban grain mills at the expense of their rural counterparts.

Notwithstanding this decline, the first Ordnance Survey maps still show some 2,300 working corn, barley and flour mills in Scotland, the greatest number being in east-central Scotland from Fife to Aberdeenshire. By no means all the grain mills given up between 1830 and 1870 were left to decay, but were adapted for use in rural industries which were still expanding, such as saw-milling and bone-milling.

Farm Mills

Threshing mills arrived relatively late on the scene, and it is almost certain that their diffusion — outwards to more remote districts and downwards to farmers of lesser means — was still going on in the mid-19th century. In those places where arable farms were large and coal was available cheaply, water power may have lost a little ground to steam, although from the evidence of East Lothian, where steam power had established itself at an early date, it can be shown that, up to the early 1850s at least, the number of water-powered mills continued to increase at the expense of those powered by horses:

Power	*No. of Machines c.1839*[19]	*No. 1853*[20]
Steam	c.80	158
Wind	7	—
Water	30	81
Horse	269	107
Total	386	346

The slight fall in numbers may be due to farm amalgamation.[21] The first Ordnance Survey maps show something like 4,300 water-powered threshing mills, with the strongest concentrations on cultivated upland margins where grain was produced in quantities large enough to justify the use of water power and where suitable falls of water were readily available.

Distilleries

We are particularly fortunate in having two good sources of information on distilleries, though both lie slightly outwith our period. In 1870 concern over river pollution in Scotland prompted the Government to commission a report on the matter, in connection with which 2,534 questionnaires were sent out, asking manufacturers in a wide range of industries to provide details of the number of their employees, the rateable value of their premises, the quantity of each raw material used and of finished product turned out, and the amount of steam and water power available to them. Had all the questionnaires been returned, it would have represented a remarkable record of industry in Scotland, but in all only 393 came back, and these were in turn published in 1872.[22] Information for distilleries is better than for most industries and, used in conjunction with a second source, Alfred Barnard's *Whisky Distilleries of the United Kingdom*, gives a good coverage. Barnard's survey of one hundred and twenty-nine Scottish distilleries was carried out in the 1880s, but has the redeeming feature of generally giving dates of foundation or rebuilding and some indication of whether water and/or steam power were used. Using both sources together, it is possible to draw several conclusions about the distribution, chronology and scale of distilleries in Scotland and their utilisation of water power at the end of the period.

Barnard gives dates for one hundred and twelve of the one hundred and twenty-nine distilleries visited, but as seventeen of these date from after 1870, only ninety-five are of interest here. Of these, only twenty-five had been established between 1830 and 1870, the vast majority dating from the 1820s but some from as far back as the 1770s and '80s (Figure 111). Of the twenty-five, the majority dated from the 1830s or '40s; very few distilleries were built during the 1850s or '60s, though Barnard's evidence points to a revitalisation of the industry in the 1870s and '80s, with much new building and rebuilding. Unfortunately it cannot be ascertained how many distilleries had gone out of production between 1830 and 1870, nor from when they dated.

On the basis of the two surveys, four distilling districts can be identified (Figure 112), each with fairly clear-cut characteristics of scale and power use:

1. *The Eastern Highlands* from Crieff, north-eastwards to Buchan, across to Moray and the Moray Firth lowlands and north-eastwards again to Caithness and Orkney, with concentrations in Strathspey below Grantown, and, to a lesser extent, in Strathtay and Glengarry.
2. *The Western Highlands and Islands* from Kintyre to Fort William and including the Inner Hebrides northwards to Skye, with concentration in Campbeltown and Islay.
3. *The Central Lowlands* with concentrations in the Glasgow area and the upper half of the Forth Estuary.
4. *Dumfries and Galloway* with no significant concentrations.

Although the characteristics of each group differ, 1 and 2 can be grouped together as Highland distilleries and 3 and 4 as Lowland ones. With regard to the scale and type of power used, area 1 was still dominated by water power, with twenty-seven distilleries still exclusively dependent on it, three using both water and steam power and only four exclusively steam-powered, two of these latter being in the city of Aberdeen. The 1870 enquiry shows a power range of

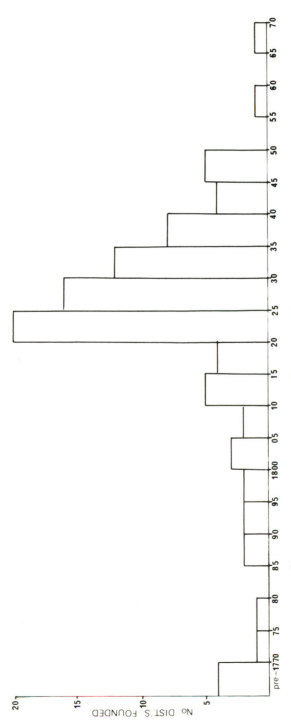

Fig 111. Foundation dates of Scottish distilleries working in 1886. *Barnard, 1887*

33

Fig 112. Distribution of water-powered distilleries, *circa* 1886. *Barnard, 1887*

four to fourteen horse power for water and steam power alike, a level at which the former could compete with the latter quite readily.

In area 2, the level of power used is about the same, but the ratio of water to steam is quite different, principally on account of the dominant position of Campbeltown where, of eighteen distilleries, not one used water power. Islay, which had the only other significant concentration of distilleries, had three powered by steam, while elsewhere in the Western Highlands and Islands area a combination of water and steam power was used. A total of thirty-three distilleries is recorded for the area, of which only six are known to have been exclusively water-powered, three using both water and steam power and sixteen using steam power only.

In the third area one finds quite a different type of distillery, for although some are of the same scale as those found in the Highlands and Islands, there were others principally in urban areas, which were of much greater extent. The inability of water to respond to increased demands is best illustrated by Carsebridge Distillery, Clackmannanshire where, of one hundred and thirty-three horse power used in 1870, only three came from water power, though evidence from Cameron Bridge, Fife, where fifty horse power came in equal proportions from water and steam, and Kirkliston, West Lothian, where thirty of the sixty-six horse power used came from water power, shows that some flexibility was possible on more favoured sites. In all, thirty-one distilleries are recorded for the area, of which only three were exclusively water-powered, seven used both water and steam power and twenty-one used steam power only.

In the fourth area distilling was of relatively minor significance, with only four sites recorded, all exclusively water-powered except for one at Langholm which used both water and steam power. Nevertheless, the scale of power utilisation is more in line with that of the Central Lowlands than the Highlands: Bladnoch Distillery had the use of twenty horse power in 1870, and one of the two distilleries at Langholm had an overshot wheel twenty feet in diameter in the 1880s.

In the case of distilleries it has been found necessary to dwell on the subject at greater length than the number of sites alone would justify. However, the excellent nature of the sources available brings out several useful points which may be extended to the utilisation of water power in general.

Firstly, it is apparent that water power was still being used as late as 1870 in new and reconstructed distilleries, despite increasing mechanisation. The Aberlour-Glenlivet Distillery, Banffshire, rebuilt in 1880, used only water power for grinding, mashing, elevating, steering and pumping.[23]

Secondly, and despite the prestige of Highland whisky, particularly that from Speyside, the importance and scale of urban distilleries was on the increase, much as in other industries. Distilleries in Campbeltown, having the threefold advantage of being in a town, being in the Highlands, and having ready access to Glasgow by steamer, flourished: five new distilleries were built between 1830 and 1870, bringing the total there to eighteen. The town also illustrates how the tendency of an industry to concentrate in a small area

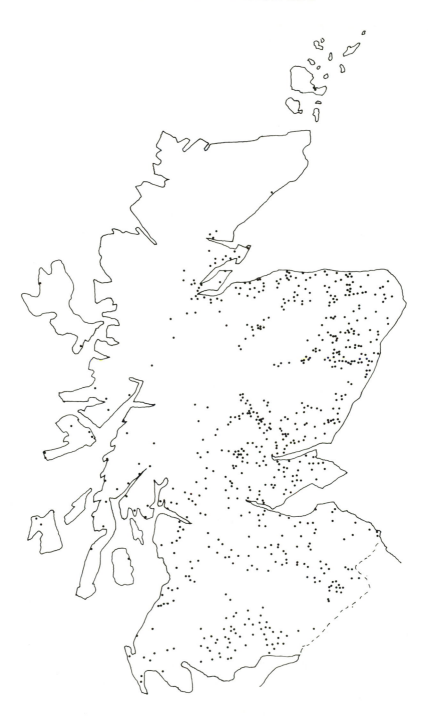

Fig 113. Distribution of water-powered saw mills *circa* 1846-80. *OS*

meant that steam power was not so much profitable as necessary, though the availability of local coal may have influenced this decision. The urban distilleries of Central Scotland show a need to use steam power, born not so much of concentration as of competition for water power from other industries and of scale. Doubtless this last consideration also applied to most distilleries using steam power in other districts.

Before moving on, it should be noted that by the period 1830-70 brewing in rural areas, as opposed to towns and cities, was no longer an industry of any significance. No instances have been found of water power being used.

Saw Mills

In Chapter 26 it was stated that estate sawmills, using the product of plantations, were just beginning to appear in significant numbers by 1830. The New Statistical Account contains references to about eighty saw mills, many of which were newly established. While this cannot be taken as a comprehensive assessment of the number of saw mills, growth certainly continued thereafter, for by the time the first Ordnance Survey maps were surveyed, there were about seven hundred water-powered saw mills in Scotland (Figure 113). The Scots portable mill, a form of mobile steam saw mill, came into use about 1860,[24] but after 1870 the use of turbines provided a further boost for the use of water power.

Urban saw mills continued to grow in importance, using steam power and imported timber; the city saw mills, Glasgow (1849), situated at Port Dundas on the Forth & Clyde Canal, were well placed to receive timber from the Baltic and the New World, and to distribute it to secondary timber industries and other users in the Glasgow area.[25] Not all the urban saw mills were steam-powered: two in the Falkirk area, for example, were water-powered, occupying former corn mill premises.[26]

Rural saw mills also prospered, with new or growing markets in railways (sleepers) and mining (pit props), which the by now more mature plantations were able to provide for. Furthermore, the rural end of the industry had certain characteristics which assisted its growth: the raw material was widely scattered and under the control of the landowner; despite the emergence of new markets further afield, local demand was still enough in itself to support a small, easily financed mill. Having control of water power, a locally available raw material and the means of capitalising on it at no great cost, a landowner might readily choose to build a water-powered saw mill, except in those areas where ample coal, rail transport or, exceptionally, water power too weak and mature plantations too large made steam power a more attractive option. In some industries the scale of production and the extent of mechanisation left no choice but to use steam power. In the case of Scottish home-grown timber, the option of using water power was still open, and it was this option which was most commonly taken. Above and beyond the obvious consideration of the location of woodland, the distribution of saw mills shows a preference for

Fig 114. Distribution of water-powered wood-turning mills, *circa* 1846-80. OS

areas of medium-quality land, with the greatest concentration of mills in the Inverness-Aberdeen-Perth area and, to a lesser extent, in Galloway and east-central Scotland. These centres were also well removed from coalfields and from major centres of population. By contrast, there were hardly any saw mills in the Northern and Western Highlands, where land was exposed, of poor quality, and with few mature plantations. In the Central Lowlands, too, there were relatively few mills, possibly on account of the generally higher quality of the land which could be more profitably used in agriculture; this area was also within easier reach of urban saw mills and of coal for steam engines.

Not all of the saw mills in rural Scotland were operated by estate owners. By the 1840s it was already customary in some areas for circular saws to be incorporated in farm mills, and the trade of timber merchant was emerging. The New Statistical Account for Kirkmichael parish, Ayrshire refers to a saw mill built by a local man, allowing plantations on several estates, each too small to support its own mill, to be exploited.[27] A few mills took up specialised work, such as producing spindles and bobbins for the textile industry (Figure 114). The provision of saw-milling equipment did not necessarily involve the construction of a new mill: redundant corn or lint mills might be adapted or machinery might be incorporated into a mill still engaged in some other activity.

Farina Mills

In the face of a general decline in the significance of water power, it is perhaps surprising to find three new applications appearing between 1830 and 1870, namely the milling of farina, the milling of bones, and the manufacture of drainage tiles. Although none of these appeared in any great numbers, their close associations with agriculture predisposed them towards a rural situation and thereby the use of water power.

Farina mills, which were employed in making potato starch for textile finishing, and, to a lesser extent, for bakers,[28] began to appear in the 1830s, although the industry dates back to at least the 1780s.[29] Predictably, their distribution corresponds to that of potato-growing districts (Figure 115), with concentrations in north-east Perthshire, where the proximity of the linen industry was an additional consideration, and in south Ayrshire/Wigtownshire/west Kirkcudbrightshire. In the coastal towns, from Montrose down to Perth, steam power was used, but elsewhere mills generally relied on water power. The largest mills could use up to four thousand tons of potatoes, four tons of lime and a ton of hydrochloric acid per annum,[30] but even the smaller mills could make a significant contribution to the local economy: a mill at Tillimet (Perthshire) was said to be the market for potatoes grown in the Dunkeld area.[31] A typical mill might employ six workers.

In west-central Scotland quite different circumstances prevailed. By 1870 a group of steam-powered starch works in the Paisley area, possibly attracted initially by the textile-finishing industry, were using several thousand tons of imported maize, sago and rice: Brown and Polson's works employed two hundred workers, consumed four thousand tons of maize, and had one hundred horse power installed steam power.[32]

In all, there were probably about thirty water-powered farina mills at work between 1830 and 1870. As with saw mills, existing mill buildings might be adapted (a former shot mill at Creetown, Kirkcudbrightshire) or added to (a

Fig 115. Distribution of bone and farina mills, *circa* 1846-80. OS

corn and flour mill at Coupar Grange, Perthshire).[33] One of the few mills for
which more than a minimal amount of information has survived was that at
Tongland, Kirkcudbrightshire, on which John Gillone, tacksman of the
fisheries and flour mill, started work in May 1845. The mill which Gillone
built was quite substantial for its type. The River Dee at that point provided a
good command of water power, and already drove a flour mill and saw mill,
and had at one time driven a paper mill too. By April 1846 the works,

comprising tub house, stoves and kiln, mill and weigh house, covering in all four thousand nine hundred square feet, had been completed at a cost of £1,500, and efforts were made to secure for Gillone a feu of the sites.[34]

Bone Mills

Bone meal fertiliser, a source of phosphates, was used in Scotland from the 1820s onwards. In 1828 a steam-powered bone mill in Dundee was still sufficiently novel for the Highland and Agricultural Society to carry a report on it in its *Transactions*. Between 1830 and 1870 bone mills were set up at a number of sites in Scotland, principally in Galloway and along the eastern Lowlands from Berwickshire to Moray (Figure 114). The bones used were imported from Prussia, Russia and the Mediterranean; a mill in Inveresk parish, Midlothian imported one thousand two hundred tons per annum from these sources.[35] In a second source, whale jawbones, use was made of a by-product from an important east-coast industry, although these were considered to be inferior to the bones of terrestrial mammals. The first bone mill in mid-Aberdeenshire was built by Mr. Hutchison of Cairngall, who was able to use whale jawbones brought to Peterhead in his own ship.[36]

Bone mills could be quite a lucrative business: between 1840 and 1847 the bone mill at Gordon Castle, Aberdeenshire made a profit of £778 2s 2d on an initial outlay of £730 5s 1d.[37] A farmer in Ayton parish, Berwickshire, who ground one hundred and sixty tons of bones per annum, mostly from Hamburg, made the same profit in a single year during the early 1830s.[38]

Most of the mills around the Firth of Forth were steam-powered, but elsewhere water power was generally used. As with saw mills and farina mills, it was not unusual for bone-milling to share premises with other users: in Farnell parish, Angus a saw mill was occasionally used to cut whale jawbones for manure; at Invermessan, Wigtownshire the mill also carded wool, and at Portsoy, Banffshire a bone threshing and saw mill in the town centre was driven by a single water wheel.[39]

The Tweeddale Tile Machine

During the late 18th and early 19th centuries a considerable amount of land drainage had been carried out, initially with stone drains and latterly with clay tile drains. Handmade tiles could only be produced slowly, and attention eventually turned to a means of mechanising production. In 1830, or thereabouts, James Murray, manager of the Garnock Coal Company, tried to produce a machine which could both amalgamate the clay (as in a pug mill) and turn out a fully formed tile,[40] but he was unable to find a means of removing stones from the clay.

Within a few years the problem had caught the attention of the Marquis of Tweeddale, a noted East Lothian Improver:

> His frequent opportunities of observing the tile-moulders at work in his own immediate neighbourhood, induced him to think of something that might facilitate their manufacture. Three men were then generally employed in what is technically called *pacing* for the moulder — that is, in forming oblong sheets to suit the size of the mould. It was with the view of making these oblong pieces of clay only that the inventor conceived the idea of rolling them out; but when he saw that the first attempt was successful, he immediately conjectured that the same machine would turn out a complete web of clay, and at the same time, give the necessary bend of a drain tile — thus at once producing them in a perfect form.[41]

In July 1834 Mr. Hay of Newton was approached for permission to use clay from his land, with an offer to hand over the tile works to him after three or four years, by way of payment. By November 1835 the first tiles had been produced; in the opinion of Thomas Struthey of Blackness tile works, it represented 'quite an original idea in the art of tile making'. Success prompted moves towards diversification, and in December 1835 James Ritchie, tile maker at Musselburgh, sent details of the formula for glazing tiles.[42]

In August 1836 the machine, in model form, had its first public showing at the Highland & Agricultural Society's Perth Show,[43] and on 9th December, 1836 the first of two patents[44] was taken out on 'Making tiles for draining, also house-tiles, flat roofing tiles and bricks'.

A water-powered tile machine, with kiln, was set up in the grounds of Yester House, East Lothian, and 270,000 tiles and soles were manufactured during the 1837 season. Early in 1838, a number of modifications were made: the kiln was rebuilt, a new water wheel installed and a railway constructed to carry tiles from the machine to the kiln. By this time machines had also been set up at Ballencrieff and East Fenton, East Lothian, which, despite installation costs, had led to a 10s per thousand reduction in the cost of tiles. Notwithstanding this, the Tweeddale machine was held in low regard in the county, and it may well have been this which persuaded Tweeddale to look further afield by leasing the patent to two Englishmen, Messrs. Birnie & Stephens. By the end of 1838 no licences had been sold by them, but early in 1839 a customer was showing interest in the machine for his Hampshire estate and another for a works in Jersey.[45] Business seems to have picked up: licence No. 55 was granted to the Earl of Dalhousie in May 1839 for two brick machines and four tile machines at Dalhousie Castle, Midlothian, and Colstoun, East Lothian. Dalhousie was to pay 3s per thousand drain tiles made (with no charge on soles), 2s per thousand flat (roofing) tiles and 1s-3s per thousand bricks. For their part, the lessees of the patent agreed not to grant any licences for tiles to anyone within five miles of Dalhousie Castle, save James Howden of Smeaton, or any licence for bricks in the Lothians, Stirlingshire and Fife without Dalhousie's permission.[46] Unfortunately it has not been possible to determine whether these machines used water power.

By the 1850s a proliferation of tile and pipe machines had come into use, many of them plagiarising features of the Tweeddale machine.[47] As for its capabilities, estimates varied: in 1839 it was claimed that, with prepared clay, one man and two boys could make twelve thousand tiles in a ten-hour day,[48] but by 1853 this had been revised to 6-8,000 tiles made by one man and four boys.[49]

The first Ordnance Survey maps show a number of other brick and tile works where water power may have been used: Millands (Auchterarder, Perthshire), Haining (Selkirk), Tods Mill (Bo'ness, West Lothian) and Wards (Gartocharn, Dunbartonshire) are all likely candidates. In the absence of further documentation, the question might be resolved by fieldwork.

Textile and Paper Mills

Paper Mills

For much of its history, the location of the paper industry was influenced by two contrasting though not conflicting requirements: on the one hand it had to have access to its basic raw material, rags, which came from towns or were imported through coastal towns, and to its markets which, like its sources of raw materials, were primarily urban. On the other hand, water power and clean process water were also required, but were more readily available in rural areas. From its first appearance in Scotland, the industry was able to resolve the contradiction by settling within a few miles of towns and cities, and it is no accident that the majority of mills established by 1830 lay within easy reach of Edinburgh, Glasgow and Aberdeen, with most of the remaining mills scattered in accordance with the location of lesser population centres. Despite improvements in the sources of raw materials, the availability of power and the effectiveness of the transport network, the period 1830-70 brought little change in distribution, apart from the decline of more marginal mills, a process already underway before 1830 (Figure 116).

The first steam engines had been installed in paper mills during the 1800s (Chapter 22, page 359), and in an age of steam power the paper industry was fortunate in that its principal manufacturing districts were within easy reach of coal — from the immediate area in the case of Midlothian, Glasgow and Fife, or carried by sea in the case of Aberdeenshire and east Berwickshire. However, this did not precipitate a wholesale move to steam power immediately after 1830.

Of the seventeen or so mills founded between 1830 and 1870, at least six were still using water power in 1870, and it is possible that a further six used it during part of the period. The Franks Report (1843) showed a steam to water ratio of only 1:1.4.[50] The 1870 River Pollution Report gives details of the use of power among forty of the fifty-seven mills known to have been working. Whilst only four — Peggy's, Cathcart, Crook of Devon and Dalbeattie —

Fig 116. Distribution of water-powered paper mills, *circa* 1846-80. OS

were exclusively water-powered, a further twenty-three used water power for part of their requirements — generally only about thirty to fifty horse power out of a total of perhaps one to three hundred horse power, but a massive five hundred horse power at Stoneywood/Woodside, Aberdeen. The 1872 Factory Returns show water power contributing little more than one quarter of the industry's total power requirements (2,187 horse power out of a total of 8,144 horse power) — quite an abrupt change from the situation in 1843.

The paper industry had already undergone a revolution in its technology without resorting to the use of steam power on any great scale.[51] What seems to have happened between 1843 and 1872 was a revolution in raw materials. The greater level of output made possible by the use of the paper machine obviously put further pressure on the rag supply. According to Bremner (1869), 'the demand for paper has always threatened to exceed the supply of rags', and the abolition of paper duty in 1861 removed a further barrier.[52] By 1857 more than two hundred patents had been taken out on rag substitutes, including bracken (1854) and stone (1856), but it was in esparto grass that the industry's salvation lay. To some extent its capabilities had been known since 1839; from about 1858 Eynsham Paper Mills (Oxford) were producing paper from esparto alone, but not until the results were shown at the 1862 Exhibition was its value fully appreciated.[53]

Papermakers were quick to take up the new material: Bremner states that by the late 1860s esparto supplied all the newsprint used in Britain and was extensively used in the production of other types of paper.[54] This is entirely borne out by evidence from Scottish mills: by 1870 the forty mills enumerated by the River Pollution Report were using over 44,000 tons of esparto, compared with just over 18,000 tons of rags and less than 2,000 tons of other materials. With few exceptions, only those mills producing cartridge and wrapping paper still relied exclusively on traditional raw materials; seven mills had gone over entirely to esparto. Between 1825 and 1860 output per mill had already been rising steadily;[55] for a continued dependence on water power, the implications of so suddenly and abundantly available a raw material must have been profound, all the more so with the abolition of duty. Without further research it is impossible to say whether esparto supplanted rags or simply supplemented them as a raw material. In either case a rapid increase in output seems probable, a development which could account for a greatly accentuated use of steam power.

The Woollen Industry

For the Scottish woollen industry, the period 1830-1870 was an important one of consolidation and growth. Up to the late 1820s its products were still the greys, blues and other traditional cloths on which the mechanised industry had grown up, but thereafter the principal manufacturing districts developed new lines of their own which helped to ensure their continued prosperity up to 1870. The Borders took to making 'Tweeds' (Chapter 19, page 289), while the Hillfoots went over to tartans and shawls. Other districts followed. In the west, notably in Ayrshire and later Glasgow, carpetmaking assumed great importance and worsted manufacture, though never comparable with wool in Scotland, developed in the west, in central Scotland and in Aberdeenshire. In contrast to this heightened activity in the main centres, the widely dispersed manufacture of traditional cloths, often for local use only, fell into decline, although a considerable number of small carding and (perhaps also) spinning

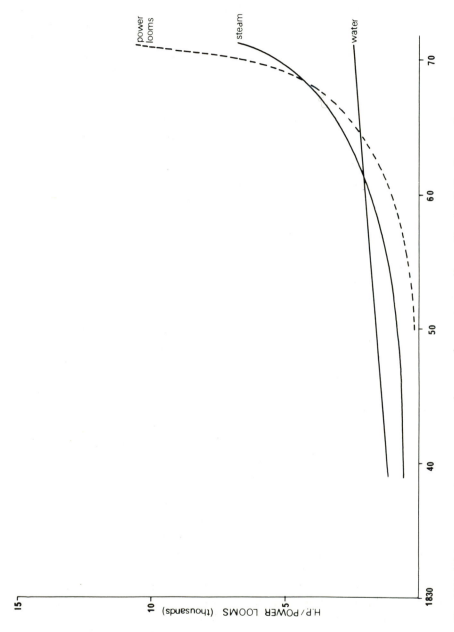

Fig 117. Water power, steam power and power looms in woollen mills, 1838-71. *Factory Returns*

mills in the Highlands, dating from the early 19th century, stayed in production.

The industry also underwent further mechanisation. In addition to the slubbing and carding already used, a third carding became customary. During the early 1830s a Hawick millwright, John Melrose, produced a 'piecing machine' which did away with the child labour formerly employed in piecing together slivers from carding machines and in feeding these into the slubbing billy. The piecing machine was in turn superseded by the condenser, a machine of American origin (but with strong Borders connections), first patented in Scotland in 1842 and widely used by the 1860s. From the late 1860s semi-automatic spinning mules were replaced by self-acting mules.[56] However, the most significant development by far was the rise of power loom weaving.

Power looms had been available before 1830, but few had been installed by that date; by 1850 there were still only 247 in use, but during the 1850s rising wages among handloom weavers created a further incentive to install power looms;[57] by 1856[58] there were 665, and, by 1861,[59] 1,303. During the next decade [60] numbers rose dramatically (Figure 117). In 1850, only 17 out of a total of 182 woollen mills had power looms; by 1871 they were to be found in 140 of Scotland's 218 mills, of which 43 were employed solely in weaving. At the same time as power looms were being installed, principally in the established manufacturing districts, the range of mechanised processes was extended at outlying mills. Inverness-shire, Ross-shire and Moray turn up for the first time in the 1850 Returns,[61] Sutherland and Banffshire in those for 1867, and Caithness and Argyll in those for 1871. However, it should be stressed that in this context the Factory Returns need to be treated with some caution; the omission of these counties from earlier Returns might not necessarily stem from the total absence of integrated mills before these dates.

The additional demands for power which stemmed from increased capacity and an extension of the range of mechanical processes were bound to be reflected in the relative importance of water and steam power. Figures from the Factory Returns bear this out (Figure 117). Water power continued to grow for some time after 1830, actually outstripping growth in steam power between 1838 and 1850. However, a meteoric rise in the use of steam power is noticeable in the 1867 Returns, rising even more steeply to 1871. Of the 9,305 horse power available to woollen mills by that date, only 2,476 horse power came from water power. Looked at on a regional basis, the picture becomes more complex, with the Borders, the Lothians, north-eastern Scotland and the Highlands making a greater and more sustained use of water relative to steam power than did central and south-western Scotland (Figure 118). In the Borders, the best water-power sites at Galashiels and Hawick had already been taken up, but there was still ample room for expansion in the upper reaches of the Tweed and its tributaries. On Ettrick Water at Selkirk, Dunsdale, Ettrick and Forest Mills, all using water power, were developed during the 1830s.[62] In 1839 there was still only one integrated woollen mill in Peeblesshire, Caerlee Mill at Inverleithen. Below this another mill, Leithen Mills, was built about

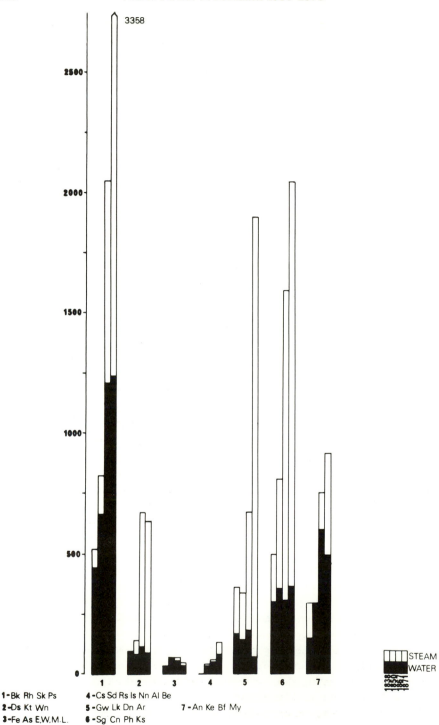

Fig 118. Water and steam power in woollen mills, 1838-71. *Factory Returns*

1 - Bk Rh Sk Ps   4 - Cs Sd Rs Is Nn Al Be
2 - Ds Kt Wn   5 - Gw Lk Dn Ar   7 - An Ke Bf My
3 - Fe As E.W.M.L.   6 - Sg Cn Ph Ks

1845, and a third, St. Ronans Mill, about 1847. Both were initially water-powered and were first employed in spinning only. A fourth mill below St. Ronan's was established at about the same time.[63] On the Tweed itself two large water-powered mills were built at the hamlet of Walkerburn: Tweedvale Mills in 1856 and Tweedholm Mill in 1860.[64] As a result of mill development, Walkerburn rose from consisting of a few houses to becoming a prosperous village. In the 1920s the Walkerburn mills were the subject of an important water-power project which included turbines, pump storage and a Pelton wheel.[65] Further growth took place in Galashiels and Hawick, but even in 1850 steam power in the counties of Berwickshire, Roxburghshire, Peeblesshire and Selkirkshire still provided less than 20% of the power used by woollen mills: by 1867 steam power's share had risen to nearly 60%. Gulvin, who has been able to consider the matter in much greater depth than is possible here, concludes that 'it was the advent of power weaving . . . that drove the tweed manufacturer to the use of steam power; until then it had possessed no real attraction for him'.[66] Generally speaking, urban mills were more likely to use steam power than those in rural districts, as were the mills in those places where the industry was more concentrated and more highly developed. Thus steam power dominated urban centres from Inverness and Aberdeen in the north to Dumfries in the south, while in the north-east and the Highlands, where there was a preponderance of small rural mills, water power retained a relatively greater importance.

To summarise: although the contribution made by water power continued to grow throughout the period 1830-70, the rapid introduction of power-loom weaving from 1850 onwards pushed power requirements far beyond what water power could provide. The industry's need for steam power was further accentuated by the increasing scale of individual mills and by concentration in a few favoured areas. In the Borders, some upriver expansion provided extra water-powered spinning capacity, but the well-established infrastructure of Galashiels, Hawick and, later, Selkirk (where steam power had to be used), attracted additional mills, despite the distance from coal and from sources of imported wool. In the Hillfoots only a little water power was available, but the industry's momentum and its proximity to coal helped to maintain a largely steam-powered industry in the area. Glasgow's centripetal force, which drew so many industries to the city, helped attract several weaving mills.

Without much extra research it cannot be determined whether woollen mills were attracted to the larger burghs because steam power was more readily accessible there or whether they were drawn to the burghs by other considerations, such as labour supply, with the use of steam power counting as a cost rather than a benefit. At the rural end of the industry, and in smaller burghs with few mills, water power continued to play a dominant role. Here too a number of mills continued to work on carding and fulling, functions which in more industrialised and urbanised districts had been incorporated into 'integrated' mills long before. Those water-powered woollen mills appearing on the first Ordnance Survey maps are shown in Figure 119.

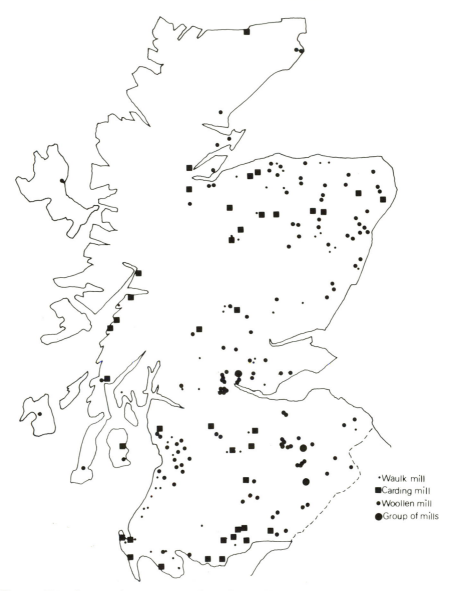

Fig 119. Distribution of water-powered woollen mills, *circa* 1846-80. OS

The Linen Industry

By 1830 the cultivation of flax in Scotland was already well into decline. In the first three decades of the century lint mills were still being built, but in ever smaller numbers and in only a few districts (Chapter 15, page 194). After 1830 there were very few new mills indeed, but in the Bathgate-Airdrie-Falkirk area, and in the valleys of Highland Perthshire, both areas of active mill-building

Fig 120. Distribution of water-powered lint mills, *circa* 1846-80. *OS*

during the early 19th century, a number of mills survived until the 1850s and
'60s (Figure 120). In 1851, at a time of depressed grain prices, Peter Reid,
proprietor of the *John O'Groats Journal*, tried to revive flax cultivation in
Caithness:

> Mr. Reid erected at Wick a mill for dressing flax by Schenck's process, and with
> the aid of the Caithness Agricultural Society, got a number of farmers to devote an

acre or two of ground to raising flax. He furnished the seed, paid a rent for the ground, and gave prizes to those who produced the heaviest crop per acre. In Aberdeenshire, Fifeshire and Lanarkshire, mills similar to Mr. Reid's were built and inducements were offered to farmers to undertake the cultivation of flax, and for a time it was thought that matters would turn out advantageously for all concerned. The hopes which had been raised were not realised, however, for in the course of a year or two the price of grain rose, and the farmers refused to have anything to do with flax which they considered a troublesome crop, and not so remunerative as they had expected.[67]

Practically all of the flax used by Scottish flax-spinning mills came from abroad; eventually the woollen industry had taken to importing wool, but the home clip could still find a market and could be processed by carding mills. In the linen industry, however, the cultivation and processing of Scottish-grown flax had already come close to extinction, and the ties between agriculture and industry, still evident in parts of the woollen industry, had been severed.

Ever since the first mechanisation of flax-spinning, yarn and thread mills had been firmly rooted in east-central Scotland; little happened to change this situation between 1830 and 1870. Initially the coarse nature of the region's product had made mechanisation easier. A large number of weavers were already employed in working up handspun yarn, and once spinning had been mechanised, their ranks were swollen with redundant hand-spinners. As the woollen and cotton industries had only taken on in a small way on the margins of the region, there was little competition for labour. From the point of view of imports, east-central Scotland could hardly have been better placed, with ready access by sea to the flax-growing districts of eastern Europe.

Latterly, a small group of mills developed in the north Ayrshire/Renfrewshire/Glasgow area, but with this exception all the flax-spinning mills in production between 1830 and 1870 were in east-central Scotland.

In its application to flax-spinning, the steam engine made an early, if fitful, start. In 1792-3 Messrs. Fairweather and Marr started a mill in Chapelshade, Dundee, with a ten horse power engine, and despite its failure further attempts had been made by the end of the century.[68] By 1810 steam power had also been tried at Kirkcaldy and Arbroath.[69] However, in places better endowed with water power, steam power remained a second choice. The early 1820s brought a boom in mill-building, and with wet-spinning now available, and the steam engine more widely used, the — in other respects — favoured position of Kirkcaldy, Arbroath and — particularly — Dundee attracted most of the new mills. Despite a number of setbacks, the number of mills in each town and their relative importance within the industry continued to grow, so that by 1839 Dundee's 46 steam-powered mills were already using 1,333 horse power, while the 18 at Arbroath and the 10 at Kirkcaldy used 332 and 139 horse power respectively. Together they accounted for about forty per cent of the mills and of the power used in Scotland.[70]

Besides additions to steam-powered spinning capacity, two further developments helped further to strengthen the position of the coastal towns. As in the woollen industry, the mechanisation of weaving required a major addition to the power already employed in preparing and spinning, an addition which could not be met from the already fully utilised water power. Furthermore, by the 1830s Dundee was already established as the hub of the industry, and the advantages which had drawn the industry to this and other coastal towns also applied to power-loom weaving. Experiments in power-loom weaving were carried out at Dundee in 1821, but not until 1836 was the first successful works built there. By 1850 there were 2,529 power looms in Scottish linen mills, 12,985 in 1867, and 17,419 in 1871. Almost all of these were steam-powered.

A new fibre, jute, was being spun with flax and tow by the early 1830s and by itself by 1835. By the mid-1850s more jute was being imported into Dundee than flax, hemp and tow, though its manufacture did not spread beyond the two principal centres of Dundee and Kirkcaldy. The additional capacity required to process jute could only be obtained by using more steam power, much as was the case with the introduction of esparto to the paper industry.

The areas with the best water power. tended to be away from the main coastal centres, and by 1830 groups of mills had been established on the North Esk (Angus), the Lunan, Ericht and Almond (Perthshire), and the Eden and the Leven (Fife). On the Almond and Dighty, spinning gave way to a greater specialisation in finishing, on the Dighty for mills in Dundee and on the Almond for mills in West Fife and further afield. Lunan Water, the least powerful of the rivers, declined in significance, but the North Esk, Leven and, above all, the Ericht, continued to make use of water power between 1830 and 1870. In 1839 the Eden and its tributaries carried thirteen flax-spinning mills with an installed water power of one hundred and sixty-two horse power and sixty-eight of steam. Several of these mills continued to use water power for some time thereafter: Cupar spinning mill was still working in 1867, Russel Mill had a fifty horse power water wheel until 1890, when a turbine was installed, and Lydox Mill was still using water power in 1900, when it was burnt out.[71] On Ceres Burn, a tributary of the Eden, the third and largest of a group of flax-spinning mills was constructed in 1839; in 1864 one hundred horse power was available from the burn during winter, supplemented in summer by seventy to eighty horse power from steam engines.[72]

On the Leven, fourteen generally more powerful mills had an installed water power of three hundred and thirty-nine horse power in 1839 with only fifty-eight horse power from steam. Thanks to the huge natural reservoir of Loch Leven, and the water management scheme completed in the 1830s (Chapter 28, p. 488), the Levenside mills could rely on a steadier, stronger flow than could those on the Eden, although since they were on the Fife coalfield, additional steam power could be obtained more economically. In 1864 Kirkland Works, the largest mill on the river, derived seventy-five horse power from the Leven and an equal power from steam;[73] at least eight other mills in the district were still obtaining some of their power from water.[74] In 1839 the Eden and Leven

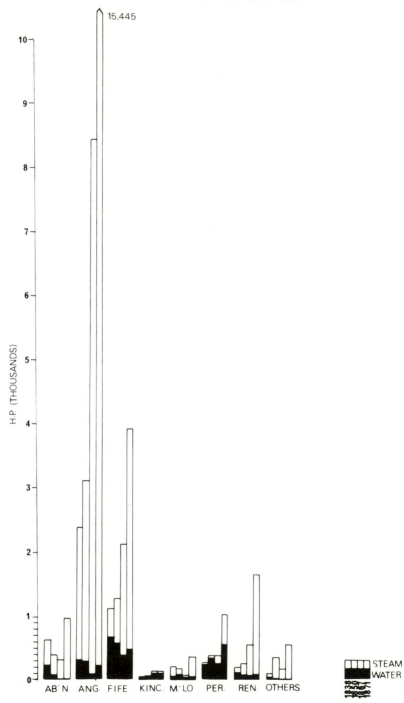

Fig 121. Water power and steam power in flax-spinning mills, 1838-71. *Factory Returns*

mills had accounted for all but 30 of the 531 horse power derived from water power in Fife (Figure 121). At this time more power was being obtained from water than from steam, though the latter's rapid subsequent growth left water power behind soon afterwards.

In Perthshire, despite an increase in the use of steam power, it had still not surpassed water power by 1871. In the Perth area flax-spinning mills had been built at Cromwellpark (1834), Logiealmond (c.1835), Pitcairn (1837) and at three sites in Perth itself (1833-38); the three Perth mills soon failed,[75] and most of the later growth in the use of water power was accounted for by developments on the Ericht at Blairgowrie and Rattray. Here there had already been eleven mills by 1839, with a combined water power of one hundred and ninety-eight horse power. The latest of these, Ashbank, had only been built about 1836. Westfield Mill, with sixty-five horse power, was established in the mid-19th century, and Ericht Mills were rebuilt in 1867 with fifty horse power. Only in this last case was steam power used, to the extent of thirty horse power, in driving power looms.[76] Reference has already been made to the large and very powerful wheels installed on the Ericht in the 1860s and '70s, and no more need be said here. The eleven mills enumerated by Warden (1864) had a combined water power of two hundred and eighty-nine horse power.[77] Significantly, Perthshire was the only county to use water power to any extent in power-loom weaving. By contrast, in Angus — the heart of the power-loom weaving industry — water power in spinning declined and was hardly used at all in power-loom weaving.

On a national basis, the difference between the 1,495½ horse power which water power produced in 1839 and the 1,380 horse power of 1871 shows little absolute decline, and from the preceding examples it is evident that in some areas its use continued to grow. However, its decline relative to steam was quite pronounced. Already by 1839 the mills of Dundee had almost as much capacity in steam power as had the entire Scottish industry in water power, and further developments, notably the introduction of power-loom weaving and the substitution of jute for flax, emphasised the lead held by steam power in Dundee and its smaller counterparts, Arbroath, Kirkcaldy and Montrose. In 1839 the ratio of water power to steam power had been 5:11, but by 1871, including hemp and jute mills, it had increased to 1:22 (Figure 122). The distribution of water-powered flax mills on the first Ordnance Survey maps is shown in Figure 123.

Finishing processes were less readily moved to urban centres. Certainly at Dundee, separate calendering works developed, away from the bleachworks, but notwithstanding the availability of chemical bleaching processes, locations determined originally by water power continued to be occupied, and water power to be used. As late as 1871 the fifty-five bleachworks in east-central Scotland still derived 684 horse power from water power, but only 583 horse power from steam.[78] With the exception of Dollarfield, Clackmannanshire,

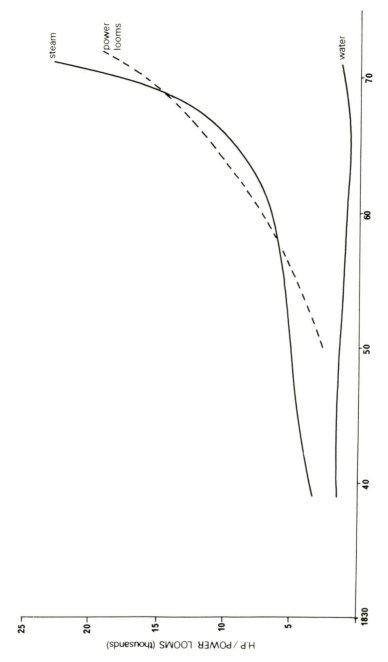

Fig 122. Water power, steam power and power looms in flax mills, 1838-71. *Factory Returns*

Fig 123. Distribution of water-powered flax-spinning mills, *circa* 1846-80. *OS*

where Dunfermline table linen was bleached, the distribution of linen bleachworks had contracted, to fit fairly closely that of mechanised spinning and weaving; in some cases, as at Craigo and Logie in Angus, bleaching and spinning were carried out in the same factory complex.[79]

Within the linen manufacturing region there were significant variations in the relative importance of water and steam power (Figure 121). In each of the three major counties, water-powered bleachworks were concentrated in a

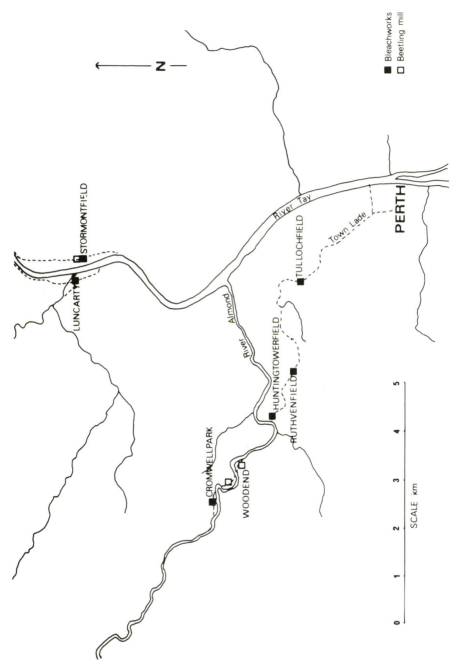

Fig 124. Bleachworks and beetling mills in the Perth area, *circa* 1860. OS

single area: on the Leven in Fife, the Dighty in Angus and the lower reaches of the Almond and Tay in Perthshire (Figure 124). The last-mentioned area achieved particular prominence, with an influence which extended far beyond east-central Scotland. Ruthvenfield and Tulloch field had temporarily gone over to printing when the influence of cotton had extended this far north, but latterly they reverted to bleaching.[80] Stormontfield and Cromwellpark were still active in 1864. During the preceding ten years Huntingtower, the most important site within the group, was completely rebuilt with thirty-eight sets of beetles, twelve pairs of wash stocks and two calenders, all driven by water power, of which ninety to one hundred horse power was available.[81]

The Cotton Industry

Cotton, the youngest of Scotland's three major textile industries, had swept across the country during the 1780s and '90s but by 1830 it had pulled back to west-central Scotland, leaving behind only a few, generally large, water-powered mills. Glasgow had achieved a position comparable with, but even more dominant than that of, Dundee in the linen industry: of 198 cotton mills enumerated in 1839, no fewer than 102 were in Glasgow itself, accounting for 3,395 horse power out of 5,612 horse power derived from steam power in Scottish cotton mills. Two minor centres, Paisley, with fourteen mills, and Johnstone, with sixteen, accounted for a further 649 horse power, only 56 horse power of which, at Johnstone, was obtained from water power. A further 66 mills, concentrated in Renfrewshire, but scattered from Aberdeen to Kirkcud-brightshire, accounted for the remaining 1,568 horse power in steam and 2,672 horse power in water power.[82]

Although cotton was the last of the three major Scottish textile industries to appear, it was the first to undergo each phase of mechanisation, including power-loom weaving. Cartwright's power loom, patented in 1785, had reached Glasgow by 1793, where two machines were powered by a Newfoundland dog.[83] Further refinements in its design, notably by Horrocks between 1803 and 1810,[84] helped to bring the power loom into much wider use and at an earlier stage in the cotton industry than in either linen or wool. One significant by-product of this early mechanisation of weaving was that it was already underway before water power had been developed to its full potential, and its early users included water-powered mills such as Catrine in Ayrshire.[85]

By 1850 there were already 23,564 power looms in use, and in almost all of the counties in which they were to be found, water power was being applied, to a greater or lesser extent, in driving them.[86]

When the Crimean War had threatened supplies of flax, the linen industry had been cushioned to some extent by the availability of an alternative fibre, jute, and its gradually more extensive use thereafter helped to ensure that the industry continued to grow up to and beyond 1870. In the cotton industry, notwithstanding alternative sources of raw cotton in the east, there was no comparable way out when the American Civil War disrupted supplies in the

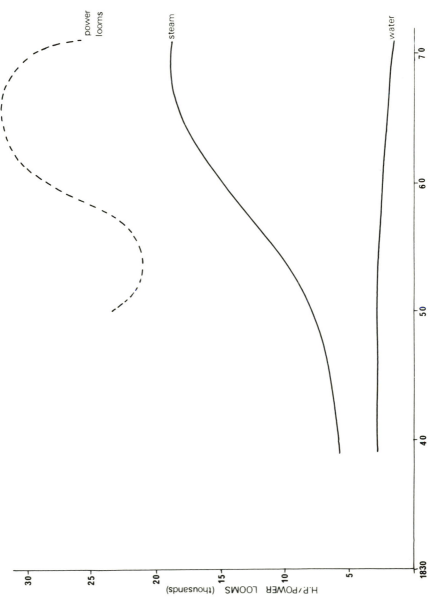

Fig 125. Water power, steam power and power looms in cotton mills, 1838-71. *Factory Returns*

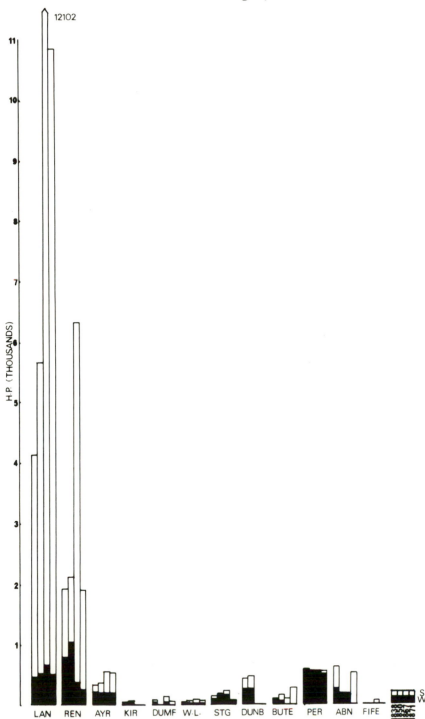

Fig 126. Water power and steam power in cotton mills, 1838-71. *Factory Returns*

1860s. In any case, the industry had already begun to decline. Since 1830, west-central Scotland had been moving towards an economy based on iron working, although as a user of male rather than female labour it was not in direct competition with the cotton industry. MacIntyre (1901) attached much importance to the 1857 financial crisis and a subsequent failure to invest in modern machinery in the face of ever keener competition from Lancashire.[87] The total number of mills fell from 198 in 1839 to a mere 98 in 1871, although between 1850 and 1867 the amount of steam power used rose sharply and the number of power looms also increased. Between 1867 and 1871 the use of steam power showed only a very slight increase and the number of power looms a marked decrease (Figure 125).

In 1839 water power still accounted for nearly one third of the power used by Scottish cotton mills. Between 1839 and 1850 it rose slightly, but at nothing like the rate of growth achieved by steam power; thereafter it fell back sharply.

The extent to which water power was used varied considerably from place to place. Generally speaking, the very large mills, with good water supplies — Stanley, Deanston, Catrine, New Lanark and Blantyre — fared better than their smaller counterparts. Thus the use of water power in the counties of Perth, Ayr and Lanark remained fairly constant (Figure 126). In Aberdeenshire, where cotton spinning was restricted to the vicinity of the city of Aberdeen, water power still made a significant contribution in 1839, but by 1850 the industry was exclusively steam-powered. At the opposite end of the country, Kirkcudbrightshire's only surviving cotton works, at Gatehouse, remained exclusively water-powered but had gone out of use by 1867. The only other water-powered mill in the south-west, at Annan, maintained its thirty or so horse power, but already supplemented by a further thirty horse power in steam power by 1839 and sixty horse power by 1867. In each of the counties of Bute, West Lothian and Dunbartonshire, cotton mills were already confined to a single locality (Rothesay, Blackburn and Duntocher) by 1839, each using both water and steam power. Of the three mills in Stirlingshire in 1839, only Culcreuch, with forty horse power, was still exclusively water-powered, yet growth in water power continued, surpassing steam in 1867 and only thereafter slumping in line with the general decline in the cotton industry.

If Glasgow was the home of the steam-powered cotton industry, then Renfrewshire was, for the first half of the 19th century, the home of the water-powered industry. The district's development has already been the subject of detailed consideration (Chapter 20, p. 331); the eventual decline of water power, while not taking place until after 1850, was nevertheless rapid, falling to a mere third of its 1850 level during the next seventeen years, while the power obtained from steam rose sixfold. By 1871 the Renfrewshire cotton industry was well into decline.

In finishing processes — bleaching and printing — water power continued to be used in most districts but failed to keep pace with growth, so that by 1871 it contributed only one-sixth of the power used in bleaching and less than one

Fig 127. Distribution of water-powered cotton mills, *circa* 1846-80. OS

twentieth of that used in printing (Table 12). The distribution of water-powered cotton mills on the first Ordnance Survey maps is shown in Figure 127.

Seen as a whole, the Scottish textile industries maintained their long-standing association with water power for much of the 19th century. However, the spread of power-loom weaving, increases in scale of unit, and a tendency to concentrate in urban centres called for power on a scale which water power was incapable of providing, and which only steam power, with its infinite capacity for growth, could satisfy. Significantly, it was in the woollen industry, where links with rural Scotland remained strongest and power-loom weaving arrived latest, that water power managed to sustain its contribution longest.

Table 12

Water and Steam Power in Printworks, 1870

County	No. of Works	H.P. Steam	H.P. Water
Ayrshire	3	32	—
Dunbartonshire	4	751	82
Lanarkshire	6	1102	50
Renfrewshire	6	3255	94
Stirlingshire	5	897	76
	24	6037	302

Water and Steam Power in Bleaching and Dyeing Works, 1870

County	No. of Works	H.P. Steam	H.P. Water
Aberdeenshire	2	53	—
Clackmannanshire	1	—	25
Dunbartonshire*	2	50	12
Fife	16	131	38
Forfarshire	22	266	135
Lanarkshire*	14	456	75
Midlothian	1	2	—
Perthshire	13	131	486
Renfrewshire*	23	1189	126
Stirlingshire*	5	100	150
	99	2378	1047

* Predominantly cotton. Others predominantly linen.

Minerals

During the quarter-millennium up to 1830, water power had built up an impressive range of applications in connection with mining and quarrying, smelting, forging, founding and the preparation of inorganic raw materials for potteries and other industries. How did it fare during the forty years thereafter?

Something has already been said of the revival in the use of water power in lead-mining after 1830 (Chapter 24, p. 408). In 1861 the Leadhills mines were let to a Scottish company headed by William Muir, from Leith, under the title

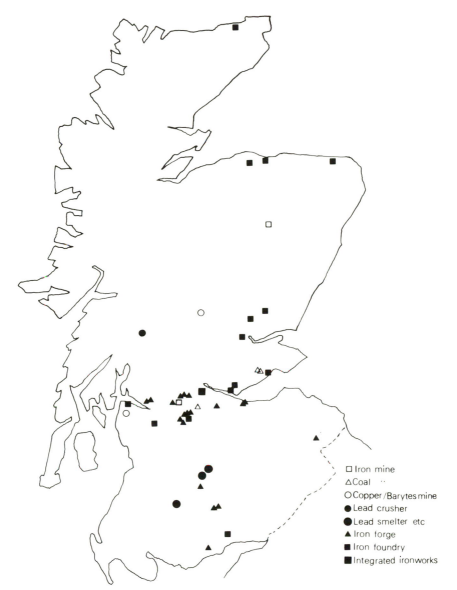

Fig 128. Distribution of water-powered mining and metal working sites, *circa* 1846-80. *OS*

of the Leadhills Mining Company. At that time both steam and water power were being used, but by means of an extensive system of reservoirs and lades the company was able to give up steam power completely:

> For working these mines water power alone is now employed, and at present [1864] there are 4 hydraulic engines for pumping, 1 hydraulic engine and 4 water wheels for drawing work, 1 water wheel for crushing and dressing the ores and 1

ditto for driving the blast at the smelting works — the united horse power of which is upward of 550. One of these hydraulic engines, recently erected, is the largest in Scotland . . . and when double acting is equal to 139 horses. Other two of these powerful engines will shortly be erected.[88]

The iron industry, with quite different requirements and a distribution centred on the coal and iron of north Lanarkshire, was already predominantly steam-powered by 1830, and its rapid growth thereafter was entirely powered by steam. At Carron, the last of the water-powered Lowland works, a ninety horse power steam engine was installed in the 1830s to provide the blast.[89] According to Bremner, a beam engine provided all the blast, yet the 1871 Factory Returns indicate that water power to the extent of 165 horse power was still being used by one of the two Stirlingshire iron works, which could only have been Carron.[90] In the 1850s water power was still being used at Carron to grind fireclay, bore cylinders, and grind and polish cast metal,[91] and in 1868 a water turbine provided power for the engineering workshop.[92] Bonawe, the last of the charcoal ironworks, only closed down in 1874 (Chapter 25, p. 427).

Though all but excluded from iron smelting, water power still found a use in a number of smaller units such as foundries and forges. The first Ordnance Survey maps show several (Figure 128), some of which, in the Monklands district, dated from the period 1840-60.[93] The 1871 Factory Returns show that water power was still being used in a small way to power foundries and machine shops in Kilmarnock, Kirkcudbrightshire, Moray, Fife and Perthshire, and to the extent of 148 horse power in Greenock.[94] A rather enigmatic mill at Tomintoul mines, which appears on the first Ordnance Survey maps, was probably used in ore-crushing and may date from the period after 1830.[95]

In coalmining, water power had been all but given up by 1830; only three working water engines appear on the first Ordnance Survey maps, two at Balbirnie (Fife) and one at Slamannan (Stirlingshire).

Minor Users of Water Power

Most of the minor users of water power have already been given as much attention as their numbers merit and in some cases pursued beyond 1830.

The extension of the Factory Acts, to cover workshops under the 1867 Workshops Regulation Act, brings to light a number of very small and, in some cases, unexpected users of water power: letterpress printing at Dundee, Perth and in Lanarkshire and Stirlingshire, bookbinding in Edinburgh, glass-making and furniture making at Perth.[96]

One of the few new industries to take up water power between 1830 and 1870 was the quarrying and dressing of paving stones in Angus and Caithness. In Angus steam power was extensively applied at Leysmill and Carmyllie, but at Myrestone a water mill was used, probably to drive a planing machine and a ridge-stone machine.[97] Although stone had been exported from Caithness since at least the 1790s, it was not until about 1825 that James Traill of Rattar sent the first consignment of flagstones from Castleton. Subsequently he enlarged the harbour, constructed a waggonway to the quarries and built the village of Castleton to house workers.[98] In 1869 the Castleton works was using a combination of water and steam power to drive sawing and polishing machinery.[99] Cartographic evidence suggests that water power was also being used to saw flags at the Spital quarries (GR ND172541) in the early 1870s.[100]

It is also worth noting that the drainage of flagstone quarries was the last industrial use to which wind power was applied to any extent.

NOTES

1. For a complete list of Scottish railways, see Glasgow Museums & Art Galleries, *Scottish Railway Locomotives*, Glasgow, 1967, Appendix 1, 32-48.

2. Corrins, R. D., 'The Great Hot-Blast Affair', *IA* VII (1970), 233-263.

3. Fairbairn, Sir W., *Treatise on Mills & Millwork*, 2 vols., 4th Edition, London, 1878; Glynn, J., *Power of Water*, 5th Edition, London, 1875.

4. Wilson, J. M. (ed.), *The Imperial Gazetteer of Scotland*, 2 vols., Edinburgh, London & Dublin, n.d. (c.1875), II, 16-17.

5. Hume, J. R., *The Industrial Archaeology of Scotland*, 2 vols., London, 1976-7, II, 257-8.

6. Allen, J., in Singer, C. J., Holmyard, E. J., Hall, A. R. & Williams, T. I. (eds.), *A History of Technology*, 5 vols., Oxford, 1956-9, V, 528.

7. *Ibid.*, V, 528.

8. Thomas, J., *The North British Railway*, Vol. 1, Newton Abbot, 1969, 204; McNeil, I., *Hydraulic Power*, London, 1972, 62.

9. Allan, *op. cit.*, 535.

10. For a more detailed account, see Wilson, P. N., 'Early Water Turbines in the United Kingdom', *TNS* XXXI (1957-9).

11. *Ibid.*, 223.

12. Trade Catalogue, Whitelaw & Stirrat, c. 1843. I am indebted to Ian Gibson, Keeper of Technology, Lancashire Museums, for bringing this material to my attention.

13. Allen, *op. cit.*, 529-31.

14. Gribbon, H. D., *The History of Water Power in Ulster*, Newton Abbot, 1969, 32.

15. Allen, *op. cit.*, 531-2.

16. Butt, J., *Industrial Archaeology of Scotland*, Newton Abbot, 1967, 63; Bremner, D., *The Industries of Scotland* (1869), Newton Abbot, 1969, 43.

17. Trade Catalogue, Carrick & Ritchie, c.1895.

18. For examples, see Butt, *op. cit.*, and Hume, *op. cit.*

19. *NSA* II, 374, General Remarks, East Lothian.

20. Wilson, J. M., *op. cit.*, II, 34.

21. For details of farm amalgamations in the eastern half of the county, see Shaw, J. P., The making of the Landscape: The Eastern Parishes of East Lothian, 1700-1971, MA (Hons) Geography Dissertation, University of Edinburgh, 1971.

22. *PP* 1872, XXXIV, River Pollution Commission (Scotland).

23. Barnard, A., *The Whisky Distilleries of the United Kingdom* (1886), Newton Abbot, 1969, 200.

24. Anderson, M. L., *A History of Scottish Forestry*, 2 vols., London, 1967, II, 320.

25. Hume, J. R., *The Industrial Archaeology of Glasgow*, Glasgow, 1974, 90.

26. *NSA* VIII, Falkirk, Stirlingshire, 19.

27. *NSA* V, Kirkmichael, Ayrshire, 508.

28. *NSA* II, 230, Spott, East Lothian.

29. SRO NG1/1/24 17/12/84.

30. *PP* 1872 XXXIV, 89, River Pollution Commission (Scotland).

31. *NSA* X, 998, Dunkeld & Dowally, Perthshire.

32. *PP* 1872, XXXIV, 162-3.

33. *NSA* IV, 341, Kirkmabreck, Kirkcudbrightshire; *NSA* X, 1195, Bendochy, Perthshire: potato mill built 1840 by Mr. Archer; *OS* 1st Edition, 6″/mile: Corn, flour & farina mill.

34. SRO GD10/1536: Copy Correspondence as to Feu Charter to John Gillone of Farina Mill at Tongland; SRO RHP 8813.

35. *NSA* I, 292, Inveresk, Midlothian.

36. *NSA* XI, 111, Farnell, Angus; *NSA* XII, 865, Longside, Aberdeenshire.

37. SRO GD44/49/28.

38. *NSA* II, 141, Ayton, Berwickshire.

39. *NSA* XIII, 191, Fordyce, Banffshire.

40. Boyle, R., 'On Drainage and Pipe Machines', *TH&AS* New Series (1853-5), 40.

41. *Ibid.*, 41.

42. NLS Acc. 4862/28/f.1.

43. *TH&AS* XII (1839), 50.

44. Woodcroft, B., *Alphabetical Index of Patentees of Inventions* (Facsimile Edition), London, 1969, Nos. 7253, 7757.

45. NLS Acc.4862/28.

46. SRO GD45/17/1211.

47. Boyle, *op. cit.*

48. *TH&AS* XII (1839), 54.

49. Boyle, *op. cit.*, 42.

50. Thomson, A. G., *The Paper Industry in Scotland*, Edinburgh, 1974, 159.

51. *Ibid.*, 161.

52. Bremner, *op. cit.*, 325, 328.

53. *Ibid.*, 324.

54. *Ibid.*

55. Thomson, *op. cit.*, Figure 15, p.183.

56. Gulvin, C., *The Tweedmakers*, Newton Abbot, 1973, 101-2.

57. *Ibid.*, 103; *PP* 1850, LXII, 13, Factory Returns.

58. *PP* LX, 288, Factory Returns (1862).

59. *Ibid.*, 288.

60. *PP* 1871, LXII, 49-51.

61. *PP* 1850, XLII, 13.

62. Craig-Brown, T., *History of Selkirkshire*, 2 vols., Edinburgh, 1886, 180-1.

63. Buchan, J. W., *A History of Peeblesshire*, 3 vols., Glasgow, 1925, 219.

64. *Ibid.*, 220.

65. Anon: *Wonders of World Engineering*, 2 vols., London, n.d. (c. 1930), II, 1489-91.

66. Gulvin, *op. cit.*, 97.

67. Bremner, *op. cit.*, 225.

68. Warden, A. J., *The Linen Industry, Ancient & Modern*, London, 1864, 588-9.

69. *Ibid.*, 544, 565.

70. *PP* 1839, XLII, 330-332, Factory Returns.

71. Jespersen, A., 'Watermills on the River Eden', *PSAS* XCVII (1963-4), 242-3.

72. Warden, *op. cit.*, 507.

73. *Ibid.*, 536.

74. *Ibid.*, 516, 520, 533.

75. Turner, W. H. K., 'The Textile Industry of Perth & District', *TIBG* XXIII (1957), 127.

76. Warden, *op. cit.*, 654.

77. *Ibid.*, 654.

78. *PP* 1871, LXII, 56, Factory Returns.

79. Warden, *op. cit.*, 518.

80. Turner, *op. cit.*, 131.

81. Warden, *op. cit.*, 529-30.

82. *PP* 1839, XLII, 306-322, Factory Returns.

83. MacIntyre, R., 'Textile Industries', in McLean, A. (ed.), *Local Industries of Glasgow and the West of Scotland* (British Association Handbook), Glasgow, 1901, 142.

84. Bremner, *op. cit.*, 278.

85. MacIntyre, *op. cit.*, 143.

86. *PP* 1850, XLII, 12, Factory Returns.

87. MacIntyre, *op. cit.*, 144-5.

88. Murray, A., *The Upper Ward of Lanarkshire*, 3 vols., Glasgow, 1864, III, 46-8.

89. Bremner, *op. cit.*, 43.

90. *Ibid.*, 43; *PP* 1871, LXII, 58, Factory Returns.

91. Wilson, J. M., *op. cit.*, I, 253.

92. Bremner, *op. cit.*, 43.

93. Butt, *op. cit.*, 114.

94. *PP* 1871, XLII, 58-9, 174, 175, 180, 184, 227.

95. *OS* 1st Edition, 6"/mile; Hume, *op. cit.* (1976-7), II, 182, Plate 26.

96. *PP* 1871, XLII, 174, 181, 189, 238-9, 239.

97. Bremner, *op. cit.*, 417.

98. Omand, D. (ed.), *The Caithness Book*, Inverness, 1972, 202.

99. Bremner, *op. cit.*, 423.

100. *OS* 1st Edition 6"/mile.

30

Conclusion

In attempting to make a brief summary of so broad a subject as the utilisation of water power in Scotland over a period so long as that between 1550 and 1870, a subject-by-subject approach would be impracticable and would only duplicate much of what has already been said under individual chapter headings. A more useful approach is to identify general trends, each applicable to several types of mill, following the same sequence of major headings as has been used in preceding chapters.

Technology

In the history of technology, water power occupies an intermediate position, along with wind power, between manual and animal power on the one hand and, on the other, the use of fossil fuels to produce mechanical and electrical power. The use of each source of power has implications for the scale of industrial production and the level of industrial development; historically, no one source has been used to the exclusion of all others: fossil fuels had been applied to driving steam engines long before water power reached its zenith, water power itself is still not quite extinct, and certain processes continue to be performed manually to the present day. In some cases, where mechanisation came late, the intermediate phase was omitted: land transport, for obvious reasons, is one such case, and the same was nearly true of weaving (see, however, Chapter 27, p. 475 [Closeburn Limeworks]).

In the Scottish context, our period starts at a point when water power had already been in use for several centuries, but only in connection with two processes, grain-milling and cloth-fulling. From the late 16th century onwards it found new applications in a vast array of industrial processes, continuing to do so throughout the 16th and 17th centuries and well into the 19th, long after the advent of the steam engine. Of the two forms of water mill found in Scotland — those with horizontal and those with vertical wheels — both were used throughout the period, but the former was almost exclusively confined to grain-milling, initially over the entire Highlands and Islands of Scotland, but latterly only on the extreme northern and western fringes. As for its origins, no firm conclusions can be reached until much more archaeological field work has been carried out. Wind power was never used to any great extent in Scotland.

The development of water power after 1550 was based on modifications to the vertical mill. By 1730, in addition to the rotary motion used in meal mills since at least the 12th century, water mill machinery had been adapted to produce an intermittent rising and falling movement — as in the waulk mill and various stamping mills — by means of cams, and a reciprocating movement — as in frame-saw mills and water engines — by means of cranks. This latter technique was eventually employed in reverse to produce rotary motion from the reciprocating action of the steam engine. Once these three techniques had been mastered, they could be used in conjunction with any number of machines, as and when these became available.

The changing sources from which new uses for water power came to Scotland reflect her changing political and economic ties with the rest of Europe and her relative level of economic development. Prior to the Union of the Parliaments most new techniques, such as papermaking, mine drainage and probably saw-milling, came from Continental Europe — Germany, France and, particularly, the Low Countries. The contribution made by England was as yet only small, and that of Scotland itself negligible. Following the Union, Flemish influences continued to play their part, notably in the linen industry, but a greater use of inventions originating in England reflected that country's rise as an industrial nation and the closer links between her and Scotland. This is particularly marked from the mid- to late 18th century, in the iron and textile industries, those traditionally associated with the Industrial Revolution. Scotland's own improving economic position, in absolute terms and relative to that of her competitors, is reflected in the introduction of new techniques from indigenous sources, the best-known example being the threshing machine. Scotland's rise as an industrial nation is also apparent from the shorter time in which innovations reached the country. It took several centuries for papermaking to arrive from mainland Europe (in 1590) and perhaps one hundred years for water-powered pumps (1595), but only a few years for cotton-spinning machinery (1778), and just one for flax-spinning machines (1789). By the late 18th century Scotland was exporting, as well as importing, new technologies. Although a continuous process of innovation was sustained throughout the rest of the period, those industries in which Scotland excelled after 1830, such as heavy engineering and metallurgy, were users of steam rather than water power, so that from then onwards few of the innovations in water-powered industries, such as grain processing and textile manufacture, were of Scottish origin.

Whilst poorly designed mills with only an intermittent water supply might have sufficed for the limited demands of customers who had little choice but to use a particular mill, several developments during the 18th and 19th centuries created incentives to improve the efficiency of water power. Firstly, the uses to which water power was put now extended into industries producing for a free market, in which customers could make use of facilities elsewhere, and in which a stoppage arising from shortage of water was not merely a source of inconvenience as with, say, a rural meal mill, but also the cause behind a loss of profitability. In these circumstances all efforts were made to maximise production, to the extent of introducing round-the-clock working; in certain industries, such as iron-smelting, continuous production was not only desirable but necessary if plant was to be maintained. Steam power, using an abundant fuel rather than a variable, often inadequate, water supply, had obvious advantages in this respect. Secondly, the scale of individual units, and the range of mechanised processes within any one industry, grew so as to put pressure on available water power. Thirdly, the more favourable resource endowment of certain areas led to the concentration of particular industries, with a consequent pressure on water power, in some areas and under-utilisation in others. Finally, as has already been suggested, steam power eventually came to dominate manufacturing industry, dictating the pace and scale of production and, through its greater locational freedom, making use of those sites best favoured by other circumstances.

That water power was still considered to be a viable alternative is evident from the considerable amount of effort which went into improving it, starting in the mid-18th century with Smeaton's *Experimental Enquiry* and continuing through Smeaton's own work and that of Rennie, Fairbairn and many lesser known engineers and millwrights, well into the 19th century. Scotland already had climatic, topographic and drainage characteristics which favoured the use of water power; by improvements in the efficiency with which it was used, and by the construction of upland storage reservoirs, it was possible for water power to expand and to keep pace with steam power well into the 19th century. Of long-term significance, but largely outwith the current terms of reference, was the introduction of the water turbine.

Sources of Finance

In the poor and underdeveloped Scotland of the late 16th century, there was little prospect of raising capital for industrial investment from sources within the country, except from the larger landowners, whose estates yielded surplus funds, the Crown, which had not only land but also control of taxation, and a few goldsmiths and other parties who, through their dealings with the Crown, had access to sufficient capital. For most of the lesser landowners, investment was restricted to the establishment of corn, waulk and occasionally saw mills, mills which could provide them with an income by exploiting the resources of their estates.

Thus, the beginnings of industrial development were largely financed by funds which originated, in one sense or another, outside Scotland. During the 16th century the mining of non-ferrous ores was dominated by Flemings and Germans; the earliest Scottish paper mills drew their inspiration from the same source, and the earliest woollen manufactories, such as that in Glasgow, owed much to English initiatives. In a less obvious sense the landowners whose collieries fed, *inter alia*, the salt industry depended on the Dutch market for the funds required to build and maintain their water engines. Despite this dependence on foreign capital, the state made repeated efforts to bring industry under Scottish control, restricting the exploitation for export of natural resources and attempting to encourage manufacturing industry. Most of these efforts ended in failure. By the late 17th century there was a noticeable increase in Scottish initiatives, but the difficult times which followed the Union of 1707 brought a relapse which was all the more marked on account of widespread English investment in mining, metalworking, sawmilling and other industries.

By the 1730s there were signs of a revival. Firstly, the larger and more enlightened landowners, then their smaller counterparts, began to look for ways to generate more income and employment from their estates, notably in building lint mills, but also in a wide range of small-scale water-powered industries. By the last quarter of the 18th century, initiative had also passed to tenants and artisans whose activities gave them an interest in developing water mills of one kind or another. Some of the larger landowners moved into other, more risky activities, such as lead-mining, but for the most part they were content to leave these more heavily capitalised, less predictable processes to others. As the necessary scale of investment increased and raw materials came to be drawn from further afield, landowners gradually lost interest in industry, so that by the mid-19th century their attentions were confined to those sectors directly associated with farming or forestry.

The generally favourable disposition of landowners towards rural industry also helped encourage other parties to invest in water mills. In many cases these were people who already had indirect interests in industries using water power: stationers and publishers in the case of paper mills, waulkers in the case of wool-spinning mills, linen manufacturers and merchants in the case of bleachfields and flax-spinning mills, cotton manufacturers in the case of printfields, and bar-iron manufacturers in the case of iron works. These are but a few examples of many instances in which those with established interests in manufacturing or distributing a particular commodity extended their interests by investing back into the water-powered processes of their respective industries. In a few industries, notably in cotton-spinning, the attractions were sufficiently strong to bring investment from other parties, with no established interests in the industry in question. In the long term, however, the greater entrepreneurial skill of merchants and manufacturers, their readier access to capital and their existing control of sectors of a particular industry ensured that, by the early 19th century, they had control of almost all new industrial investment.

The role of the state during the period 1730-1830 accords very closely with that of the more enlightened landowners. On the one hand the Board of Trustees for Manufactures, the principal agents of state involvement, was prepared to lay out funds on developing small-scale mills, particularly if none of a particular type had been established yet in that area, and if benefits would accrue to the rural community. However, when it came to supporting cotton or flax-spinning mills, its help was not forthcoming. It is interesting to note that wool-spinning mills, which used Scottish raw materials and which were initially fairly small-scale, continued to enjoy the Board's support right up to the 1830s. During the early 19th century the Board was at loggerheads with the owners of flax-spinning mills and, in line with more general trends, it was the latter who eventually won the day. From the 1830s onwards manufacturers found themselves subject to state involvement of another kind, in the shape of the Factory Commission.

Distribution and Chronology

At the start of our period, the earliest, and for a long time the only, user of water power, the meal mill, had already come into general use in Scotland except in the far north and west, where querns were adequate enough to meet the needs of the population. References to mills between 1550 and 1730 indicate very large numbers, with particularly high densities in Lowland districts but with very few indeed at elevations of more than 750 feet. Their high frequency and widespread dispersion reflect their limited capacity, the lack of local, regional and agricultural specialisation and the restrictions imposed by thirlage on the disposal of grain.

Between 1550 and 1730 waulk mills, with already a history of several hundred years, are known to have existed at about three hundred localities throughout Lowland Scotland and in the more accessible parts of the Highlands, with additional mills still being built during that period. A few other processes, such as saw-milling, lead-smelting and coalmining, began to use water power for the first time between 1550 and 1730, their location being determined by that of their raw materials. In the case of papermaking, location near to urban communities ensured a proximity to both raw materials and markets.

Between 1730 and 1830 the number of grain mills fell in response to the decay of thirlage, the abandonment of some marginal cultivation and the increased capacity of individual mills, but water power came to be used in other grain processing activities such as flour and pot barley milling, threshing and distilling, the distribution of each starting in the Central Lowlands and extending through time to most districts. Threshing mills in particular achieved a rapid growth and dispersion which ensured that by 1830 they were probably the commonest and most widely distributed type of mill in Scotland.

During the same period the range of processes using water power underwent an unprecedented expansion: in most cases an initial phase of expansion was followed by one of contraction until, in some cases, mills of a particular type were confined to only one or two districts. The best instance of this is probably the lint mill: almost unknown in 1730, by the end of the 18th century it had spread to most of the arable districts of Scotland, only to contract again with the decline of flax cultivation, until by 1830 it was confined to a few areas of generally poorer-quality land. In other cases, such as cotton-spinning and papermaking, it was the established skills or the other attributes of a particular district which concentrated an industry there: flax-spinning, which first used water power in the late 1780s, never developed to much extent outwith east-central Scotland.

Certain industries working with bulky or heavy raw materials remained in close proximity to these: lead-smelting and saw-milling exemplify this well, although improvements in communications reduced the necessity of doing so. Where materials of this nature were imported, as with Highland iron works or urban saw mills, seaboard locations were preferred. Changes from home-produced to imported raw materials tended to reduce the attractiveness of water power and to enhance that of steam.

Besides considerations of raw materials and markets, the availability of a labour force became more crucial as the period progressed. Grain mills, lint mills and other small-scale units closely related to agriculture had very limited labour requirements, some of which could be met on a seasonal basis. However, problems arose with larger units such as textile-spinning mills in which several hundred workers might be required to work day in day out at any one site. To some extent the problem was eased by the declining labour requirements of agriculture, and the provision of on-site workers' housing, but once steam power became a viable alternative, the ready availability of labour was a potent force in drawing industry to the larger, established centres of population.

No reference has yet been made to the availability of water power itself as a factor in determining the distribution of mills. Certainly there were a few cases, such as New Lanark, Deanston and Stanley, where the presence of exceptionally powerful falls did attract mills; larger mills in general may have been restricted to the more substantial rivers, but in Scotland the availability of such rivers was sufficiently general to allow other considerations to outweigh water power itself in determining the overall distribution of sites. Where only a small amount of power was required, the availability of water power was of even less significance, for not only were adequate streams widely available, but also, on the most localised level, those establishing mills were usually prepared to make artificial water courses of a mile or more in length to enable them to install, say, a threshing mill in a farmstead, rather than locate the mill at a less convenient point on the stream itself.

By 1730, in a few industries, water power was already playing a significant part in the economic development of Scotland, reducing the need for imports and increasing the value of exports by processing indigenous raw materials within, rather than outside, the country. Between 1730 and 1830 water power came into its own, providing the motive force for new and newly mechanised industries, paralleling the overall industrial development of Scotland and making a far greater contribution than did steam power. The latter's subsequent prominence has tended to overshadow the importance of water power during the long period of accelerating economic growth before the mid-19th century. The concept of an Industrial Revolution assignable to a particular period may be less tenable that it once was, but if the timing of the Classical Industrial Revolution is to be tied down, then it must be to the late 18th and early 19th centuries, within the hundred years which has rightly been named the Age of Water Power.

The decline of water power in the face of large-scale, urban-based, steam-powered production has always been assumed rather than proven. In relative terms there certainly was a decline, but the available evidence suggests that the amount of power derived from water continued to grow until at least the middle of the 19th century. However, its rate of growth had become so slow, and that of steam power so rapid, that the latter's dominance was unquestionable. The potential of water power in Scotland was never fully realised, except in a few localities favoured by other attributes. The end of the Age of Water Power came about not so much on account of any inherent weakness as through changes in the scale of industrial units, in work patterns, population distributions and economic goals. Once the object of manufacturing changed from providing for basic, fairly stable requirements to one of producing as much as possible, in ever larger volumes, the stage was already set for the decline of water power. In the few instances where the volume of work has been small and consistent, water mills have continued to function to the present day, notably in grain- and saw-milling; furthermore, the advent of the turbine has brought a renewed viability to water power since 1870.

In an age which has started to question the sustainability of perpetual economic and urban growth, to recognise the alienation caused by unfulfilling work or technologically engendered unemployment, and to foresee the potential exhaustion of fossil fuels, Small is once more Beautiful. In such an age water power may yet find its place again.

Glossary

Abstraction:	In grain milling, the failure to take grain to that mill to which it is bound by *thirlage*.
Apron:	The area around the *bedstone*, into which the *mill eye* is set.
Ark:	1—The bin into which the meal passes from the *mill eye*.
	2—The *outer head*, i.e. the low wall onto which is fixed the gudgeon which takes the outer end of the *axle tree*.
Arms:	The spokes of a wheel, usually those of the water wheel, but also used for those of *cog wheels*.
Ashlar:	Roughly squared-off stone.
Augerem:	A dish containing 6 lbs Dutch weight meal which was used to measure the miller's and mill servants' share of the meal.
Awes/Yaaves/Havs:	The paddles of a water wheel (also — the sails or shaft of a windmill) (cf. *Starts*).
Awn:	The spike or beard on a grain of barley.
Axle tree:	The horizontal shaft on which the water wheel and *pit wheel* turn.
Axtree bond:	Thin metal ring on the *axle tree*, possibly at its end, to prevent excessive wear against the bearing of the *head stock*.
Back water:	The water of a mill *lade*, which is gorged up by ice, or by the swelling of the river below, so that it cannot get away from the mill, and thereby slows or stops the water wheel.
Bannock:	A small quantity of meal, of oats, barley or pease (enough to make a bannock), due to the servants of a mill by those grinding their corn in it or thirled to it.
Baxter:	Baker.
Beaterman:	In papermaking by hand, the person who supervised the mortar and pestle engine(s) in which rags were pulped.
Bedstone:	The lower, i.e. stationary, millstone. Also known as the *understone*.
Bere:	A four-rowed barley, once widely grown in Scotland.
Bevel wheel:	A wheel with gearing cut at an angle.
Bitch:	The small sack into which the *mill mooter* passes.
Black mill:	Anglicised form of Mhuilinn Dhu, a Gaelic term for the simple mills which were common in the Outer Hebrides and which had horizontal water wheels, on the same axis as the millstones (cf. *Shetland mill*).
Bob gin:	A water-powered pump worked via cranks and oscillating beams.
Boll:	A unit of grain volume measurement. In avoirdupois equivalents, a boll of oatmeal weighed approximately 140 lbs.

Bolster:	Bearing for a wheel shaft, generally the *axle tree*. *Inside bolster:* the *bolster* attached to the *head stock* at the inner end of the *axle tree*. *Outer bolster:* the *bolster* attached to the *ark*, or *head stock*, at the outer end of the *axle tree*. *Bolster head* (Shetland): a wooden beam along the back wall of the super-structure of a water mill, serving as a support for the inner-most end of the *ground sile*, into which the axle of the mill is fitted. Also used as the actual joint of the two beams.
Boulting:	The separation of coarse particles from flour after milling.
Brayer:	The hinged *bridge tree*, raised or depressed by a screw nut or *mill hand*, whereby *tentering*, or controlling, the stones was achieved.
Bridge tree:	Cross-beam which supports the lower end of the spindle.
Bridge:	Curved bar for supporting the upper millstone on the spindle. Also known as *rind*.
Buckets:	The compartments on the circumference of a water wheel, consisting of paddles enclosed at their sides by the shroud, the base of the buckets being referred to as the *sole*. *Ventilated buckets:* buckets designed to allow the escape of air from beneath or behind the incoming water. This was effected by leaving a space between the *sole board* and the underside of the bucket 'above' it.
Buddle:	In mining, a rotating water vessel for separating ore from lighter particles.
Calender:	A roller press for finishing cloth.
Carry/Caul/Cauld:	A weir or dam which diverts water from the supplying stream into the *lade*.
Caseys:	Streets with a hard, often cobbled surface.
Cautioners:	Guarantors.
Circles:	The circular rims of the water wheel, onto which the paddles are fixed.
Clap/Clapper:	Device attached to, or contacting, the *shoe*, which through contact with the moving *runner stone* causes the *shoe* to jump, and thereby to continuously release more grain from the *hopper* into the *eye* of the millstone. Generally it has been replaced by a *damsel*.
Clasp arm:	A type of water wheel construction in which the axle is squared off and braced by arms fixed in a cross shape.
Click mill:	See *Shetland mill*.
Cloose:	Sluice or sluice-gate.
Coalheuch:	Coalmine, particularly the surface buildings.
Cog:	1—A measure used in some mills (north Scotland), containing the fourth part of a peck.
	2—Removable wooden tooth of a gear wheel.
Cog hole:	The undercroft of a mill, in which the pit wheel, often referred to as the *cog wheel*, is situated.
Cog wheel:	Gear wheel with wooden teeth, generally the pit wheel in Scottish contexts, but also used as *spur wheels*.

Coom:	The dust which comes off the grain when first passed through the process of *shilling*.
Coucher:	In hand papermaking, the person who turns out pieces of paper from the frame onto sheets of felt to be pressed dry.
Cradle:	The frame which supports the *hopper*.
Crib:	See *Hoops*.
Cross-tree:	(Shetland). A horizontal bar which steadies the *lightening tree* at half its height, and which prevents side thrust. Also known as the *guy tree*.
Crown wheel:	Gear wheel situated at the top of the main shaft, which drives the ancillary machinery of the mill. According to Gray, a crown wheel is a gear wheel, toothed on the upper side, like a crown.
Croy:	A mound or quay projecting into a river to break the force of the stream, and to protect the adjacent ground from encroachment.
Crub:	See *Hoops*.
Dam dyke:	The retaining wall of a dam or reservoir.
Dam eye:	The outlet from a mill dam.
Dam head:	Weir to divert water into a mill lade. Body of water confined by such a dam.
Damsel:	Metal extension of the spindle, flanges on which jog the *shoe* and thus maintain the flow of grain from the hopper.
Day level:	In mining, a subterranean passage for draining off water.
Divot:	Piece of cut turf.
Draughts (Mill):	(Mill) *lade*.
Drawboard:	A primitive type of sluice in the form of a gate-like board, hinged at one side, which by manipulation with a *drawtree* can be pushed across either entry to the channel passing the wheel or the overflow channel.
Drawtree:	Lever attached to the *drawboard*, and passing through the mill wall, whereby the *drawboard* could be adjusted.
Dry multure:	See *Multure*.
Eye:	The hole in the centre of the *runner stone*, through which grain is admitted for grinding. Not to be confused with the *mill eye*.
Face wheel:	Gear wheel with the cogs set on the face or side.
Failzie:	Fine payable on failure to carry out a legal commitment.
Fanners:	Winnowing machine.
Feathers:	(Shetland). The blades of a horizontal mill wheel or *tirl*.
Feeder:	*Damsel*.
Fence:	Grill for preventing floating material from becoming entangled with the water wheel.
Firlot:	Unit of volume, equal to .25 boll or 4 pecks. The Linlithgow wheat firlot equalled, almost exactly, the Imperial bushel, but the barley firlot was just under half this size.
Float boards:	The blades or paddles of a water wheel.
Flude shutters:	Sluice gates.

Gang water:	Water diverted from a stream but not collected in a *gather dam* for use in driving a water wheel.
Gather dam:	Dam which collects water from the drainage of the subsoil, from rain and from minor streams, as opposed to a dam which diverts part of a flowing stream without storage.
Gault:	See *Mill gault.*
Gin:	In mining, a horse- or water-powered machine for raising coal or water.
Graith:	The buildings and machinery of a mill, the former being referred to as the *lying graith* and the latter as the *going* or *running graith.*
Grist:	To dress stones for the purpose of grinding meal.
Grit:	Kernels of oats after shells removed.
Grop:	To grind corn coarsely.
Grot/Groot/Grud:	Coarse-grained stone suitable for making millstones.
Ground sile:	(Shetland). The bearing which supports the *tirl* spindle.
Grutte:	(Shetland). A bush of wood or cork in the bedstone which acts as a bearing or steady.
Guy-tree:	See *Cross-tree.*
Happer:	See *Hopper.*
Harp:	A hand sieve.
Heads:	The projecting points of a millstone face which stand out more prominently than others which have been worn down.
Head stock:	The support for the inner and outer end of the *axle tree. Inner head stock:* the head stock which supports the inner end of the *axle tree. Outer head stock/water head stock:* the support for the outer end of the *axle tree,* usually part of the outside wall of the *lade* adjacent to the wheel.
Hem:	The *skirt* or outer edge of a millstone.
Heritor:	An owner of heritable property.
Hoops:	The circular wooden casing which fits closely around the millstones to prevent the spilling out of meal onto the floor *(stool)* of the mill. Also known as *Krubs* and *Cribs.*
Hopper:	A wooden box in the form of an inverted pyramid, in which grain is held for release through the attached *shoe* into the *eye* of the *runner stone.*
Horse gin:	See *Gin.*
Husbandland:	A tenant's holding, equal to about 26 Scots acres (1 Scots acre = 1.26 English acres), though sometimes used to express a proportion of a township rather than an exact acreage.
Inlay:	To divert water to a mill.
Inlayer/Inlair:	Channel carrying water to a mill wheel. A small dam leading into such a channel.
Inner wheel:	The *Pit wheel.*
Insucken:	See *Sucken.*
Intown multure:	See *Multure.*
Intown suckener:	See *Suckeners.*
Kainfowl:	A fowl, payable at Christmas time by tenants to landowners.
Keir:	A boiler used in bleaching yarn or cloth.

Kil/Kill:	Scottish, Kiln. *Kilnace/Kilnlaece:* main beam supporting the drying floor of a kiln. *Kilnark:* large chest or receptacle for storing or holding the dried grain. *Kilnbarn:* storehouse for grain adjoining the kiln. *Kiln bedding:* packed straw on the drying floor of a kiln, over which grain was spread. *Kiln breist:* arch over entrance to kiln. *Kiln cast:* quantity of grain taken to the mill at one time to be ground into meal for household use. Generally enough for four bolls. *Kiln eye:* open space in front of kiln fireplace. Also known as *kiln heugh* and *kiln ring*. *Kiln fud(die):* aperture by which fuel put into the kiln fire. *Kiln head:* roof of *kiln pot* forming the floor of the drying chamber. *Kiln heugh:* see *Kiln eye*. *Kiln ingle:* kiln fire. *Kiln kebbar:* one of the beams or joists supporting the drying floor. *Kiln mathie:* space at back of kiln, below the drying loft. *Kiln meat:* under miller's share of the husked grain. *Kiln pot:* heating chamber under a corn kiln. *Kiln rib:* one of the small moveable wooden bars laid across the kiln joists to support the bed of straw on the drying floor. *Kiln ring:* see *Kiln eye*.
Kluse:	(Shetland). Sluice.
Knaveship:	A small proportion of the grain ground at the mill which was the perquisite of the under miller or miller's servant.
Krub:	See *Hoops*.
Laddle Mill:	Mill with a horizontal water wheel.
Lade/Ledd/Lead:	Channel leading water to the water wheel (and back to the natural course).
Lag:	The setting of millstones so that they are spaced out correctly for a particular type of work. Hence bere-lag, oat-lag etc.
Lair:	To settle a millstone into position.
Lantern wheel:	See *Trindle*.
Lapping:	Folding.
Lever, Leverer:	In hand papermaking, the person who operates the drying press.
Level:	See *Day level*.
Lewder:	(Shetland). The floor supporting the nether millstone. References to lowder planks from elsewhere in Scotland, which may have the same meaning.
Lichens (Mill):	1—The levers in the pit of the mill which adjust the millstone.
	2—The entry into the space where the *inner wheel* turns.
Lichten:	To raise or lower the *runner stone*.
Liftin tree:	Wooden lever for raising or lowering a millstone to control the fineness of grinding.
Lightening tree:	(Shetland). As *Liftin tree*.
Lint:	Flax.
Lippie:	Unit of volume measurement equal to .25 peck.
Lith:	(Shetland). Check or notch on the underside of the upper millstone, into which the *sile* is fitted to transmit the motion from the water wheel.
Louther tree/letter tree:	See *Liftin tree*.

Lying stone:	See *Bedstone.*
Lying graith:	See *Graith.*
Maitin pin:	Pin in the *hopper* of a mill which regulates the supply of grain to the *eye* of the millstone.
Mash tun:	The vessel in which malted barley and boiling water are infused during brewing.
Mask:	A brew of ale or beer; the amount produced by one filling of the *mash tun.*
Maul:	A heavy wooden hammer.
Melder:	1—The corn put through the mill at one time.
	2—Oatmeal ground for hinds and shepherds at the beginning of winter, which served them for porridge and oatmeal during most of the year.
Mell:	1—Mallet-shaped block of wood used to prop millstones while being dressed.
	2—To put a quantity of corn through the mill at one time.
Merk:	Unit of currency, equal to 13/4d Scots, approximately 1/1½d (5½p) Sterling.
Metts:	Measures of weight.
Mill dozen:	The thirteenth peck of grain milled, payable to the mill owner.
Mill dust:	Light fibrous dark brown dust which separates from the oats during the mealing process.
Mill eye:	The hole or shute by which the meal passes from the stones into the meal bin.
Mill gault:	Young pig or castrated boar paid to a miller by the tenants of an estate as part of his perquisites.
Mill hand:	A lever attached to the cross supports at either end of the *bridge tree,* by which the latter, and hence the stones, can be adjusted.
Mill heave:	Vessel for measuring the shelled grain in a mill.
Mill lichens:	See *Lichens.*
Mill mooter:	The miller's share of the meal, collected in a sack *(bitch)* through a small hole in the spout from the stones.
Mill peck:	A peck measure used by millers for measuring the shelled grain which was their due.
Mill pot:	The section of the mill *lade* which lies below the water wheel.
Mill pound:	Mill dam.
Mill race:	*Lade,* particularly the section above the water wheel.
Mill spout:	Fall of water used to drive a mill.
Mill steep:	Lever used to adjust the distance between the upper and lower stones.
Mill timmer:	Stout beam used as a support or prop in a mill.
Miln, Milne, Mylne:	Scottish, mill.
Multure:	The duty, consisting of a proportion of the grain ground, exacted by the proprietor or tenant *(Multurer)* of a mill on all corn ground there. *(Abstracted) multure:* multure payable on grain taken without authorisation to a mill other than that to which the multure was due.
Multure cap:	A wooden measure used by the miller for taking his *multure.*

Multure chest:	Large box for storing grain or meal collected as *multure.*
Multure court:	A court held to settle disputes arising from the payment of the miller's dues.
Multure (Dry):	Sum of money, or quantity of corn, paid to a mill by those whose lands are under *thirlage* of growing corn, in exchange for the freedom to go to a market with the rest of their corn.
Multure (Intown):	The rate of *multure* payable by those within the thirl of a certain mill. See *Thirlage.*
Multure (Outertown):	The *multure* payable by those outwith the thirl if they grind at a mill to which they are not thirled.
Multure pock:	Sack into which *multure* put.
Multure rent:	Total amount of *multure* payable to an estate mill.
Multure shilling:	Proportion of oat husks or *shilling* appropriated by the miller as his due.
Neck:	The part of the millstone around the central hole or *eye.*
Outer head:	See *Head stock.*
Outer wheel:	The water wheel.
Outsucken:	See *Sucken.*
Peck:	Unit of volume, equal to 4 lippies or .25 *firlot.*
Pen stock:	Device for controlling flow of water from the *pen trough.*
Pen trough:	Trough which delivers water onto the wheel.
Pit wheel:	Gear wheel situated on the *axle tree,* in the *cog hole* or cog pit which, through engaging with the *rungs* of a *trundle,* or the teeth of a *wallower,* transfers the drive from the horizontal plane of the *axle tree* to the vertical one of the *stone spindle,* or of the main shaft respectively. Traditionally it had wooden pegs or *cogs.*
Plash boards:	The sections of wood fitted onto the circumference of a breast shot water wheel, at right angles to the paddles or *float boards.*
Plummer block:	Iron casting with cylindrical hole through the middle, within which is a journal, usually of brass. Plummer blocks were used, for example, to take the end of an *axle tree.*
Pockmen:	Men employed by the miller to go round collecting batches or pocks of corn to be ground.
Pot:	1—Pestle.
	2—Gudgeon which houses the lower end of the spindle. Like the journal of the *plummer block,* it is usually brass.
Reed:	The inner fibres of plant stems, especially flax.
Rimmer:	A hoop or band, generally of iron, fastened round the *runner stone* to prevent it from bursting.
Rind:	The outer skin of plant stems, especially flax.
Rind/Rhynd/Rynd:	Metal *bridge* fitting onto the top of the spindle. The *runner stone* is balanced, and turns upon it. Two, three or four projections fit into similarly shaped holes in the *runner stone.*
Ring:	Meal which in grinding has fallen into the space between the millstones and the casing (*Hoops, krub* etc.) surrounding it. Regarded as the miller's perquisite. Compound forms: ring bear, ring corn, ring malt. *To ring the mill:* to provide the first

	grain for a mill to grind after the millstones have been picked. To collect the meal which has fallen into the *ring*.
Road:	To dress a millstone — to cut *roads* or grooves in it.
Rounds:	The staves which connect the two circular boards of the *trundle*.
Roup:	Public sale by auction.
Row, Rowhead:	Convex curved part of the mill *trough* which directs water from the mill *lade* onto the wheel.
Ruch:	The state of malt before grinding.
Rungs:	See *Rounds*.
Runner stone:	The upper (revolving) millstone.
Saugh:	Willow tree.
Sequels:	Pertinents.
Shetland mill:	Simple mill without gearing, the horizontal water wheel being situated at opposite ends of the spindle. In other respects the machinery is not dissimilar to that of some ordinary mills: it has a lever which adjusts the stones, a spindle, which rests on this, two horizontal stones, the upper one of which rests on a *rind*, and a system of delivery consisting of *hopper*, *shoe* and *clapper*. There are, however, no *hoops*, the meal simply discharging onto a slightly raised platform around the *understone*.
Shill:	To remove the adherent glumes (shells) or *shilling sids* and *coom* from the grain by passing it through widely spaced stones.
Shiller:	The pair of stones used to remove the outer shell from the grain. (In small mills which had only one pair of stones, it was usual to do the shilling and mealing with the same stones at different *lags*.)
Shillin/Shilling	1—The first grinding of meal.
	2—The grain after the shilling *sids* have been removed by shilling.
Shock loss:	The loss of impetus in moving water on coming into contact with the *bucket* of a water wheel.
Shoe:	The shute, connected to the hopper at its upper end, which feeds grain into the *eye* of the stones.
Shrouds:	The outer casing at the circumference of a water wheel, which encloses the paddles and *sole* to form *buckets*.
Sids/Seeds:	The glumes, or shells, of the grain. *(Shillin) sids:* the glumes removed in shilling. *(Meal) sids:* the remaining glumes, separated from the meal by sifting. The meal adhering to the meal sids is removed by steeping in water.
Sile:	(Shetland). The bearing which supports the *tirl* spindle.
Silver mail:	Rent payable in cash.
Skirt:	The outer edge of a millstone (see *Hem*).
Sluice:	Gate controlling the flow of water along a *lade* and onto a water wheel.
Sluice frame:	Housing for a sluice gate.

Sole board/sole plates:	The wooden boards or metal segments which make up the floor of the *buckets* in a water wheel.
Sole tree:	(Shetland). An underbalk, in the form of a lever, upon which the *tirl* spindle rests.
Spur wheel:	A cogged wheel on the main shaft which engages with the *stone nuts* to drive the *stone spindles.*
Starts:	The lengths of wood inserted in the rim of a water wheel to act as stays for the *floats* or *buckets* (see *Plash boards*).
Stone nuts:	Pinions on the *stone spindles* which engage with the *spur wheel.*
Stone pinion:	See *Stone nut.*
Stone spindle:	The vertical shaft which carries, and takes, the drive to the *runner stone.*
Stool/Stooling:	The platform or floor on which the millstones are situated.
Sucken:	The area astricted to a particular mill (see *Thirlage*).
Suckeners:	Those to whom the grain product of the *sucken* belongs. *In-sucken:* lands within the *sucken* or thirl. *Out-sucken:* lands outwith the *sucken* or thirl. (Both used particularly in connection with *multure.* See *Multure (Intown)* and *Multure (Outertown).*) *Intown suckeners:* those whose grain is within the thirl of a particular mill.
Swingle:	In flax processing, to soften fibres by beating (scutch).
Tack:	Lease.
Tentering:	Of millstones, adjustment of the gap between upper and lower stones to produce coarser or finer meal.
Thirlage:	The system whereby persons *(suckeners)* cultivating certain lands were obliged to take their corn to a particular mill for grinding, and to pay *multure* at rates varying from one tenth to one fortieth of the product of their grain, a rate generally higher than that paid by those outwith the thirl. Besides this payment and those of *bannock* and *knaveship,* those within the thirl were often required to clean out the mill lades, and provide materials, including millstones. In some extreme cases they were even expected to mill the grain themselves, the miller doing little else than regulate the flow of water to the wheel. On the other hand, the miller was required in most cases to give good service, and often to take care of the whole operation from collecting the grain from the *sucken* to delivering the meal. If the machinery of the mill was not in a good enough condition, the *suckeners* could, in theory at least, either take their corns elsewhere or demand that a mutually chosen arbiter be appointed to declare whether or not the mill was, in fact, sufficient, his findings being binding on both parties. *Types of Thirlage: Thirlage of Grindable Grain:* applies only to oats and barley required by the *sucken* for food (Grana Crescentia). *Thirlage of Growing Corn:* applies to all the corn from the servient lands, excepting only seed and horse corn. *Thirlage of Invecta et Illata:* urban thirlage. All corn, whether produced or bought for con-

	sumption within the boundaries of the thirl, must be taken to the mill and manufactured there. Found at one time in most Scottish burghs. In the case of Royal Burghs the mill generally belonged to the Incorporation; in Burghs of Barony the mill was generally the property of the superior.
Tirl:	(Shetland). The horizontal water wheel.
Trindle/Trinle/Trundle:	A *lantern wheel*, that is to say one with two discs connected by staves or *rounds* set into discs, near to their circumference.
Trinle boards:	The discs of a *trinle*.
Trinle rings:	The rounds of a *trinle*.
Trough/Trow/Trowse:	Conduit which carried water onto the wheel. In England the term refers to a wood or metal channel, but in Scotland it is used much more loosely.
Trough:	Sometimes used of the vessel which collects the meal after it has left the stones. Also appears as stone-trough.
Trundle:	See *Trindle*.
Trundle head:	English term for *trinle*.
Understone:	(Shetland). The *bedstone*.
Unlaw:	A fine for breaking the law.
Vatman:	In hand papermaking, the person who immerses the frame in a vat of fibres, suspended in water, and passes it on to the *coucher*.
Visitor:	An official post in a craft guild.
Wads:	See *Road*.
Wallower:	Small toothed wheel on the main upright shaft in gear with the *pit wheel*.
Wand:	Stout wooden beam.
Water axle:	See *Axle tree*.
Water engine:	In mining, a water-powered pumping engine.
Water gang:	*Lade*, especially that section above the water wheel.
Water gate:	Sluice gate.
Water shaft:	See *Axle tree*.
Water wall:	The wall of the mill which faces onto the *lade*.
Wedder:	Gelded ram.
Wipers:	The blades of a scutching machine.
Wool fells:	Fleeces of wool, attached to the sheep's skin.

Bibliography

Manuscript Sources

1. *Scottish Record Office*

CS96   (Formerly RH15) Court of Session Productions
CS96/48   Terrence Dougan, Bleacher, Ford   1766-70
141   Alexander Duncan, Millwright, Cromarty   1829-30
149   Glasgow & Verreville Pottery Co.   1838-39
203   Balgonie Iron Co.   1812
207-9   Beauly Distillery Co.
257   Crosslee Cotton Spinning Co., Houston   1803
395   Macfarlane, Malcolm, Cotton Spinner, Busby   1813-15
393   Verreville Pottery Co.   1833-36
419   James Smith, Flax Spinner, Strathmartin   1822-23
455   John Amory, Distiller, Denny   1820-21
695   James Cleghorn, Paper Maker, Kinleith   1827
731   William Ainslie, Brewer, Clock Mill, Duns
742   Alexander Gibson, Manufacturer, Kilmarnock   1815-23
764   Robert Kilgour & Son, Manufacturers, Aberdeenshire   1828-32
767   James Laird, Millspinner, Murthill, Forfar   1817-19
785   Robert Scott, Manufacturer and Flax Spinner, Cupar   1826-37
791   Scott, J. and Taylor, P., Flax Spinners and Bleachers, Kirkforthar, Fife   1831
803   John White & Son, Paper Makers, Eskhill and Brewers, Haughhead 1814-17
807   Hamilton Watson, Earthenware Manufacturer, Prestonpans   1838
813   John Paple, Surgeon and Manufacturer, Gatehouse   1795-96
817   David Russel, Founder, Leven   1817-18
831   John Bathgate, Skinner, Bellsmills   1813-19
822   William Roberts and William Crawford, Paper Makers, Kinleith 1825-28
853   John Thomson & Son, Carpet Makers, Kilmarnock   1828-31
1042   Robert Smith, Bleacher, Renfrewshire   1826
1057   Thomas Wright, Flax Spinner, Leslie   1808-20
1303   Matthew Hope, Cotton Spinner, Newton Stewart   1796-1810
1306-9   Adam Rennie, Miller, Grahamstoun   1803-07
1676-8   John Kerr, Millwright, Yetholm
1797   Nisbet, Macniven & Co., Paper Makers, Edinburgh   1790-96
2013-4   Leadhills Mining Co.   1839-41
2053   Dumbreck, John, Gunpowder Manufacturer and W.S., Edinburgh 1835-38

51   Melville Castle Muniments
52   Forbes Papers
53   Harwood Writs
54   Murray of Ochtertyre Muniments
56   Rollo Charters
57   Mss Presented by Messrs Burnett & Reid
58   Carron Company Records
59   Wilkie of Foulden Muniments
60   Bennan & Finnarts Writs
61   Macfarlane of Ballancleroch Muniments
62   Pittenweem Writs
63   Bell-Brander Muniments
64   Campbell of Jura Papers
65   Carlops & Abbotskerse Muniments
66   Boswell of Balmuto Writs
67   Gordon of Cairness Muniments
68   Lintrose Writs
70   Scott of Brotherton Muniments
71   Munro of Allan Muniments
72   Hay of Park Papers
73   Hay of Belton Muniments
74   Burnett of Powis Muniments
75   Dundas of Dundas Papers
76   Henderson Muniments
77   Fergusson of Craigendarroch Manuscripts
78   Hunter of Barjarg Muniments
79   King James VI Hospital, Perth
80   Macpherson of Cluny Papers
81   Mss Presented by Lindsay, Duncan & Black W.S.
82   Makgill Charters
83   Bamff Charters & Papers
84   Reay Papers
85   Naismith Writs
86   Fraser Charters
88   Mackay Collection
89   Skirling Writs
90   Yule Collection
91   Pitreavie Muniments
92   MacDonald of Sands Muniments
94   Lordship of Urquhart Papers
96   Mey Papers
97   Duntreath Muniments
98   Douglas Collection
100 W. Moir Bryce Charters
101 Wigtown Charters
102 Hunter of Hunterston Papers
103 Society of Antiquaries
104 Scott of Raeburn Muniments
105 Fetteresso Papers

107   Callendar of Pitcaple Charters
109   Bargany Papers
110   Hamilton-Dalrymple of North Berwick Muniments
111   Curle Collection
112   Breadalbane Letters
113   Innes of Stow Papers
114   Rutherford of Edgerston Muniments
115   Burnett Stuart Collection
116   Campbell of Duntroon Muniments
117   Cathcart of Carleton & Killochan Muniments
118   Shieldhall Writs
119   Torphichen Writs
120   Lawson of Cairnmuir Papers
121   Murthly Castle Muniments
123   Erskine of Dun Muniments
124   Mar & Kellie Muniments
125   Rose of Kilravock Muniments
126   Balfour/Melville Manuscripts
128   Fraser Mackintosh Collection
129   Balnagowan Castle Manuscripts
130   Earl of Northesk Papers
132   Robertson of Lude Manuscripts
135   Stair Muniments
137   Scrymgeour-Wedderburn Muniments
141   Logan Charters
142   Hamilton of Pinmore Papers
146   Robertson of Kindeace Papers
148   Craigans Writs
150   Motton Papers
152   Hamilton Bruce Papers
154   Agnew of Lochnaw Muniments
156   Elphinstone Muniments
157   Scott of Harden
158   Hume of Marchmont
159   Ross of Cromarty Manuscripts
161   Buchanan of Leny Muniments
163   Auchincloich Estate Papers
166   Burnet of Barns Papers
167   Blair of Blair Muniments
170   Campbell of Barcaldine Muniments
171   Forbes of Callendar
173   Marquis of Zetland — Kerse Estate Manuscripts
175   Erroll Charters
176   Mackintosh Muniments
180   Cathcart of Genoch & Knockdolian Manuscripts
185   Abercromby of Forglen
186   Leith Ross Muniments
188   Guthrie of Guthrie Manuscripts
198   Haldane of Gleneagles

201	Clanranald Papers
205	Ogilvy of Inverquharity
214	Professor Hannay's Papers
215	Beveridge Papers
217	Scarth of Breckness Muniments
219	Murray of Murraythwaite
221	Lord MacDonald Manuscripts
224	Buccleuch Muniments
225	Leith Hall Muniments
228	Findlay of Carnel Muniments
231	Craigengillan Muniments
233	Dundonald Muniments
237	Messrs Tods, Murray & Jamieson W.S.
240	Bruce & Kerr W.S.
241	Thomson & Baxter W.S.
242	Shepherd & Wedderburn W.S.
244	Skene, Edwards & Garson W.S.
245	MacKenzie Innes & Logan W.S.
246	Hope Todd & Kirk W.S.
247	Messrs John C. Brodie W.S.
248	Seaforth Muniments
250	Sempill of Craigievar Muniments
253	D. & J. H. Campbell W.S.
254	Lindsay of Dowhill Papers
255	Haldane, Brown & Co., C.A.
258	Row-Fogo Manuscripts
259	Scott of Ancrum Manuscripts
260	Miscellaneous Records of D. McIntosh, Solicitor, Dumbarton
263	Heddle Manuscripts Relating to Orkney
266	Messrs Pearson, Robertson & Maconochie, W.S.
267	Home of Wedderburn Manuscripts
275	Ardgaty Writs
276	Melrose (Hawick) Ltd.
277	Merchant Company of Edinburgh
279	Comrie Papers
280	Sinclair of Dunbeath Papers
288	Balfour of Balbirnie Muniments
345	Grant of Monymusk Muniments
NG 1 *et seq*	Records of the Board of Trustees for Fisheries, Manufactures and Improvements
RH 15	Miscellaneous Bundles
RHP	Register House Plans
SCP	Sheriff Court Plans

2. *National Library of Scotland*

NLS Acc.	Accessions
NLS Acc. 2933	Saltoun Papers
4862	Yester Papers
5111	John Rennie

	5381	John Rennie
NLS Mss.		Manuscripts
NLS Mss.	29	Strontian Lead Mines
	1913	Scots White Paper Company
	5844-64	Stevenson Plans

3. *Signet Library*

OSP   Old Court of Session Papers (Index at SRO)

4. *Hopetoun House*

Hopetoun Lead Mining Papers (Now at SRO) (Index by T. C. Smout at NLS)

Parliamentary and State Papers

1. *Scotland* (pre-1707)

The Acts of the Parliaments of Scotland (1124-1707), 12 vols., London, 1848-75

Inquisitionum ad Capellam Domini Regis Retournam Abreviato, 3 vols., Edinburgh, 1811-16

Registrum Magni Sigilli Regnum Scotorum, 16 vols. (1545-1691), Edinburgh, 1877-1970

Registrum Secreti Signilli Regnum Scotorum, 11 vols. (1306-1668), Edinburgh, 1886-1914

2. *Great Britain* (post-1707)

1831-2	XLII	Boundary Reports, Scotland
1832	XV	Labour of Children in Factories
1834	XIX, XX	Factory Commission
1835	V	Municipal Corporations, Scotland
1839	XLII	Factory Returns
1843	LVI	Factory Returns
1850	XLII	Factory Returns
1852	LI	Paper Mills in Scotland
1854-5	XVIII	Bleaching Works
1862	LX	Factory Returns
1867-8	LXIV	Factory Returns
1871	LXII	Factory Returns
1872	XXXIV	River Pollution Commission, Scotland

Directories and Gazetteers

Barbieri, M., *Descriptive & Historical Gazetteer of Fife, Kinross & Clackmannan,* Edinburgh, 1857

Davidson, W., *The Edinburgh Directory 1773-4,* Facsimile Edition, Edinburgh, 1889

Hutcheson's Greenock Register, Directory & General Advertiser for 1845-6, Greenock, 1845

Wilson, J. M. (ed.), *The Imperial Gazetteer of Scotland,* 2 vols., Edinburgh, London & Dublin, n.d. (c.1875)

Trade Catalogues

| Whitelaw & Stirrat | c.1843 | (Lancashire Museums) |
| Carrick & Ritchie | c.1895 | (Glasgow Museums) |

Theses

Devine, T. M., Glasgow Merchants and Colonial Trade 1770-1815, Strathclyde University PhD, 1972

Durie, A. J., The Scottish Linen Industry 1707-1775, with Particular Reference to the Early History of the British Linen Company, Edinburgh University PhD, 1973

Lindsay, J. M., The Use of Woodland in Argyllshire and Perthshire between 1650 and 1850, Edinburgh University PhD, 1974

Marshall, J. S., A Social & Economic History of Leith in the Eighteenth Century, Edinburgh University PhD, 1969

Whyte, I. D., Agrarian Change in Lowland Scotland in the Seventeenth Century, Edinburgh University PhD, 1974

Wood, J. D., The Geography of the Nithsdale-Annandale Region, 1813-16, Edinburgh University PhD, 1962

Newspapers & Periodicals

Caledonian Mercury 1775, 1793
Edinburgh Advertiser 1780
Glasgow Advertiser & Evening Intelligencer 1789, 1790
Farmers' Magazine
Scots Magazine

Maps

Ainslie, J.	Selkirkshire	1772
Ainslie, J.	Fife	1775
Ainslie, J.	Wigtownshire	1782
Ainslie, J.	Angus	1794
Ainslie, J.	Renfrewshire	1796
Ainslie, J.	Kirkcudbrightshire	1797
Armstrong, M.	Berwickshire	1771
Armstrong, M.	Ayrshire	1773
Armstrong, M.	Peeblesshire	1775
Armstrong, M.	Lothians	1777
Blackadder, J.	Berwickshire	1797
Blaeu	(Atlas of) Scotland	17th Century
Edgar, W.	Stirlingshire	1777
Edgar, W.	Peeblesshire	1741
Forrest, W.	East Lothian	1799
Forrest, W.	Lanarkshire	1813
Forrest, W.	West Lothian	1818
Garden, W.	Kincardineshire	1797
Grassom, J.	Stirlingshire	1817
Johnson, W.	Ayrshire	1828
Knox, J.	Midlothian	1812

Laurie, J.	Midlothian	1766
Robertson, J.	Aberdeenshire, Banffshire & Kincardineshire	1822
Ross, C.	Dunbartonshire	1777
Roy, General	Scotland	c.1746-50 (Copy at NLS Map room)
Sharp, Greenwood & Fowler	East Lothian	1825
Sharp, Greenwood & Fowler	Berwickshire	1825-26
Sharp, Greenwood & Fowler	Fife	1828
Stobie, J.	Roxburghshire	1770
Stobie, J.	Perthshire	1783
Thomson, J.	Peeblesshire	1821
Wood, J.	Dunbartonshire	1825
Wood, J.	Town Atlas of Scotland	c.1825
Ordnance Survey	First Edition 6″/mile Scotland	c.1846-82

Articles

Beckles, N. I., 'Textiles & Port Growth in Dundee', *SGM* LXXXIV, 1968

Bowman, A. I., 'Culross Colliery: A Sixteenth Century Mine', *IA* VII, 4 (1970)

Bowman, G., 'John Smeaton — Consulting Engineer', in Selmer, E. G. (ed.), *Engineering Heritage*, Vol. 2, London, 1966

Boyle, R., 'On Drain-tile and Pipe Machines', *TH&AS*, New Series, 1833-35

Broun-Lindsay, Lady (ed.), 'The Barony Court of Colstoun: Extracts from its Records', *TELA&FNS*, II, 1930-31

Burne, E. L., 'On Mills. Thomas Telford, 1796', *TNS*, XVII, 1936-37

Butt, J., 'The Industrial Archaeology of Gatehouse-of-Fleet', *IA*, III, 1966

Butt, J., 'Glenbuck Ironworks', *AAC*, 2nd Series, VIII, 1967-69

Butt, J., 'Valuation of Scottish Cotton Mills by Sun Fire Office, 1795', *EcHR*, 2nd Series, XXIII, 1970

Campbell, R. H., 'The Industrial Revolution & the Scottish Countryside', *TGAS*, XV, 1960

Campbell, R. H., 'The Iron Industry in Ayrshire', *AAC*, 2nd Series, VII, 1961-62

Carmichael, J., 'An Account of the Principal Limestone Quarries of Scotland', *TH&AS*, New Series, XI, 1838

Carmichael, J., 'An Account of the Principal Marble, Slate, Sandstone and Greenstone Quarries in Scotland', *TH&AS*, New Series, XI, 1838

Cartwright, J. N., 'The Meikle Threshing Mill at Beltondod', *TELA&FNS*, XI, 1968

Carus-Wilson, E. M., 'An Industrial Revolution in the Thirteenth Century', *EcHR*, XI-XII, 1941-43

Clouston, J. S., 'The Old Orkney Mills', *Proceedings of the Orkney Antiquarian Society*, III, 1925

Corrins, R. D., 'The Great Hot-Blast Affair', *IA*, VII, 1970

Cunningham, J. H., 'Geonostical Description of the Stewartry of Kirkcudbrightshire', *TH&AS*, New Series, VIII, 1843

Curwen, E. C., 'The Problem of Early Water-mills', *Antiquity*, XVIII (1944)

Dickinson, H. W. & Straker, E., 'The Shetland Watermill', *TNS*, XIII, 1932-34

Dickson, J., 'Some Account of the Orkney Islands', *TH&AS*, New Series, VII, 1841

Donnachie, I. L., 'Scottish Windmills — an Outline and Inventory', *PSAS*, XCVII, 1964-66

Donnachie, I. L., 'Monksmill, New Abbey, Kirkcudbrightshire', *IA*, VIII, 1971

Ferrier, J., 'The Water Cuts of Robert Thom', *TGAS*, New Series, XV, 1966

Forsyth, C., 'On the Mines, Minerals & Geology of West Lothian', *TH&AS*, 3rd Series, II, 1845-47

Gauldie, E., 'Water Powered Beetling Machines', *TNS*, XXX, 1966-67

Gauldie, E., 'Mechanical Aids to Linen Bleaching in Scotland', *Textile History*, I, 1969

Goudie, G., 'The Horizontal Watermills of Shetland', *PSAS*, XX, 1885-86

Graham, A., 'Morison's Haven', *PSAS*, XCV, 1961-62

Gunn, C. B. (ed.), 'Records of the Baron Court of Stitchill, 1655-1807', *SHS*, L, 1905

Harvey, W. S., 'Lead Mining in 1768: Old Records of A Scottish Mining Company', *IA*, VII, 1970

Harvey, W. S. & Downs-Rose, G., 'Water Bucket Pumps and the Wanlockhead Engine', *IA*, X, 1973

Hume, J. R., 'Mills of the River Ayr', *AAC*, 2nd Series, VIII, 1967-69

Jespersen, A., 'Watermills on the River Eden', *PSAS*, XCVII, 1963-64

Lenman, B., Lythe, C. & Gauldie, E., 'Dundee and its Textile Industry, 1850-1914', *AHS*, XIV, 1969

Lindsay, J. M., 'The Commercial Use of Highland Woodland, 1750-1870: A Reconsideration', *SGM*, XCII, 1976

MacAdam, W. I., 'Notes on the Ancient Iron Industry of Scotland', *PSAS*, XXI, 1886-87

McClain, N. E., 'Scottish Lintmills, 1729-70', *Textile History*, I, 1970

McCutcheon, W. A., 'Water Power in the North of Ireland', *TNS*, XXXIX, 1966-67

Martine, T. C., 'Old Haddington', *TELA&FNS*, XII, 1970

Marwick, W. H., 'The Cotton Industry and the Industrial Revolution in Scotland', *SHR*, XXI, 1924

Marwick, W. H., 'Bibliographies of Scottish Economic History', *EcHR*, V, 1935; 2nd Series, II, 1952; 2nd Series, XVI, 1963

Mitchell, G. M., 'English and Scottish Cotton Industries', *SHR*, XXII, 1925

Mitchison, R., 'Movement of Scottish Corn Prices in the Seventeenth and Eighteenth Centuries', *EcHR*, 2nd Series, XVIII, 1965

Oliver, J. E., 'Framework Knitting in Scotland, 1682-1770', *THAS*, 1969

Paterson, J., 'Account of the Island of Arran', *TH&AS*, 2nd Series, XI, 1838

Russell, J., 'Millstones in Wind and Water Mills', *TNS*, XXIV, 1943-44

Scott, E. K., 'Early Cloth Fulling & Its Machinery', *TNS*, XII, 1931-32

Stephen, W. M., 'Two Flint Mills Near Kirkcaldy', *IA*, III, 1966

Stowers, A., 'Observations on the History of Water Power', *TNS*, XXX, 1955-57

Thomson, G., 'The Dalnotter Iron Company', *SHR*, XXXV, 1956

Turner, W. H. K., 'Some Eighteenth Century Developments in the Textile Region of East Central Scotland', *SGM*, LXIX, 1953

Turner, W. H. K., 'The Textile Industry of Perth and District', *TIBG*, XXIII, 1957

Turner, W. H. K., 'Significance of Water Power in Industrial Locations: some Perthshire Examples', *SGM*, LXXIV, 1958

Turner, W. H. K., 'Wool Textile Manufacture in Scotland: an Historical Geography', *SGM*, LXXX, 1964

Wailes, R., 'Tidal Mills in Great Britain', *Engineering*, CXLVI, 1938

Wailes, R., 'Water-Driven Mills for Grinding Stone', *TNS*, XXX, 1966-67

Wallace, J., 'An Account of the Method of Calcining Limestone in Some of the Limestone Quarries of Scotland', *TH&AS*, XI, 1838

Waterston, R., 'Early Paper Making near Edinburgh', *BOEC*, XXV, 1945

Waterston, R., 'Further Notes on Paper Making near Edinburgh', *BOEC*, XXVII, 1949

Watson, D. M., 'The Early Manufacturers of Hawick', *THAS*, 1868, 1873

Wilson, P. N., 'Water Power and the Industrial Revolution', *Water Power*, August 1954

Wilson, P. N., 'Early Water Turbines in the United Kingdom', *TNS*, XXXI, 1957-59

Wilson, P. N., 'The Waterwheels of John Smeaton', *TNS*, XXX, 1955-57

Wilson, P. N., 'Water-Driven Prime Movers', in *Engineering Heritage*, Vol. 1, London, 1963

Books

Accum, F., *Treatise on the Art of Brewing*, London, 1820

Adam, R. J. (ed.), 'Sutherland Estate Management 1802-16', *SHS*, 4th Series, XIII-IX, 1972

Adams, I. H., *Descriptive List of Plans in the Scottish Record Office*, 3 vols., HMSO 1966, 1970, 1974

Adams, J., *Lunan Water*, Arbroath, 1923

Agricola (Hoover, H. C. & Hoover, L. H., eds.), *De Re Metallica* (1556), New York, 1950

Aiton, W., *General View of the Agriculture of the County of Ayr*, Glasgow, 1811

Allan, A., *History of Channelkirk*, Edinburgh, 1900

Allan, J. R. (ed.), *Crombies of Grandholm & Cothal*, Aberdeen, 1960

Anderson, J., *General View of the Agriculture of the County of Aberdeen*, Edinburgh, 1794

Anderson, M. L., *A History of Scottish Forestry*, 2 vols., London, 1967

Anon., *Carron Company*, 1959

Anon., *Henry Ballantyne & Son, Walkerburn*, London, 1929

Anon., *Paper Mills in Scotland*, Edinburgh & Glasgow, 1832

Armytage, W. H. G., *A Social History of Engineering*, London, 1961

Ashton, T. S., *Iron & Steel in the Industrial Revolution*, Manchester, 1924

Ashton, T. S. & Sykes, J., *The Coal Industry of the Eighteenth Century*, Manchester, 1929

Atkinson, S., *The Discoverie and Historie of the Gold Mynes in Scotland* (1619), Bannatyne Club, Edinburgh, 1825

Baird, W., *Annals of Duddingston & Portobello*, Edinburgh, 1898

Bald, R., *A General View of the Coal Trade in Scotland*, Edinburgh, 1808

Barnard, A., *The Whisky Distilleries of the United Kingdom* (1887), Newton Abbot, 1969

Barron, D. G., 'The Court Book of the Barony of Urie in Kincardineshire, 1604-1747', *SHS*, XII, 1892

Barty, A. B., *The History of Dunblane*, Stirling, 1944

Bayne, J. F., *Dunlop Parish*, Edinburgh, 1935

Beath, D., *Reminiscences of Leslie & Neighbourhood*, Kirkcaldy, 1912

Bell, R., *A Dictionary of the Law of Scotland*, 3rd Edition, Edinburgh, 1826

Bell, S. S., *Dictionary of the Decisions of the Court of Session from November 1808 to November 1833*, 2 vols., Edinburgh, 1842

Bennett, R. & Elton, J., *The History of Corn Milling*, 2 vols., Liverpool, 1898-99 and 4 vols., New York, n.d.

Berry, J. C., *Cameron Bridge Fifty Years Ago* (Distillers Co.), 1927

Beveridge, E., *North Uist*, Edinburgh, 1911

Biringuccio, V., *De la Pirotechnia*, Venice, 1540

Black, D. D., *The History of Brechin to 1864*, 2nd Edition, Edinburgh, 1867

Blair, M., *The Paisley Thread Industry*, Paisley, 1907

Boucher, C. T. G., *John Rennie 1761-1821. The Life of a Great Engineer*, Manchester, 1963

Bremner, D., *The Industries of Scotland* (1869), Newton Abbot, 1969

Brown, J., *The History of Sanquhar*, Dumfries, 1891

Brown, R., *The History of Paisley*, 2 vols., Paisley, 1886

Buchan, J. W., *A History of Peeblesshire*, 3 vols., Glasgow, 1925

Buchanan, R., *On Millwork*, 2nd Edition, 2 vols., London, 1823

Burleigh, J., *Ednam & Its Indwellers*, Glasgow, 1912

Butt, J., *Industrial Archaeology of Scotland*, Newton Abbot, 1967

Butt, J. & Ward, J. T. (eds.), *Scottish Themes. Essays in Honour of Professor S. G. E. Lythe*, Edinburgh, 1976

Cadell, P., *The Iron Mills at Cramond*, Edinburgh, 1973

Cameron, J., *Parishes of Campsie*, Kirkintilloch, 1892

Campbell, R. H., *Carron Company*, Edinburgh, 1961

Campbell, R. H., *Scotland Since 1707*, Oxford, 1965

Carew, R., *Survey of Cornwall*, London, 1602

Carvel, J. L., *One Hundred Years in Coal. The History of the Alloa Coal Company*, Edinburgh, 1944

Chalmers, G., *Caledonia*, 4 vols., London, 1810

Chalmers, P., *Historical and Statistical Account of Dunfermline*, Edinburgh & London, 1844

Chambers, R., *Domestic Annals of Scotland from the Renaissance to the Rebellion, 1745*, 3rd Edition, 3 vols., Edinburgh, 1874

Chapman, S. D., *The Cotton Industry and the Industrial Revolution*, London, 1972

Charles, B. H., *Pottery and Porcelain. A Dictionary of Terms*, Newton Abbot, 1974

Cleland, J., *The Annals of Glasgow*, 2 vols., Glasgow, 1816

Clow, A. & Clow, N. L., *The Chemical Revolution: a Contribution to Social Technology*, London, 1952

Cochrane, A., *Description of the Estate of Culross*, Edinburgh, 1793

Cochran-Patrick, R. W., *Early Records Relating to Mining in Scotland*, Edinburgh, 1878

Cochran-Patrick, R. W., *Mediaeval Scotland*, Glasgow, 1892

Coleman, D. C., *The British Paper Industry 1495-1860. A Study of Industrial Growth*, Oxford, 1958

Cormack, A. A., *Our Ancient and Honourable Craft*, Aberdeen, 1933

Cowper, A. S., *Linen in the Highlands, 1753-1762*, Edinburgh, 1969

Craig, R. & Sons, *A Century of Paper Making, 1820-1920*, Edinburgh, 1920

Craig-Brown, T., *History of Selkirkshire*, 2 vols., Edinburgh, 1886

Crawford, G. (revised Semple, W.), *The History of Renfrewshire*, Paisley, 1782

Cruden, S. H., *Click Mill, Orkney*, HMSO, London, 1949

Cunningham, A. S., *Mining in the Kingdom of Fife*, Leven, 1907

Cunningham, A. S., *Upper Largo, Lower Largo, Lundin Links and Newburn*, Leven, 1907

Cunningham, A. S., *Mining in Mid and East Lothian*, Edinburgh, 1925

Dalyell, Sir J. & Beveridge, J. (eds.), 'Binns Papers', *SRS*, LXX, Edinburgh, 1938

Devine, T. M., *The Tobacco Lords*, Edinburgh, 1975

Dickinson, H. W., *A Short History of the Steam Engine*, Cambridge, 1938

Dickinson, W. C. & Donaldson, G., *A Source Book of Scottish History*, Vol. 3 (1567-1707), Edinburgh, 1954

Dick-Lauder, Sir T., *An Account of the Great Floods of August 1829, in the Province of Moray and Adjoining District*, Edinburgh, 1830

Dickson, J., *Crichton Past and Present*, Edinburgh, 1911

Diderot, D., *L'Encyclopédiè, ou Dictionnaire Raisonné des Sciences, des Arts et des Métiers*, Paris, 1751-72

Dixon, J. H., *Gairloch*, Glasgow, 1886

Dobson, T., *Reminiscences of Innerleithen and Traquair*, Innerleithen, 1896

Donnachie, I. L., *Industrial Archaeology of Galloway*, Newton Abbot, 1971

Donnachie, Ian, *A History of the Brewing Industry in Scotland*, Edinburgh, 1979.

Douglas, G., *A History of the Border Counties*, Edinburgh & London, 1899

Duckham, B. F., *A History of the Scottish Coal Industry*, Vol. 1 (1700-1815), Newton Abbot, 1970

Dunnet, H., *Invera'an, A Strathspey Parish*, Paisley, 1919

Durie, Alastair J., *The Scottish Linen Industry in the Eighteenth Century*, Edinburgh, 1979

Dussause, H., *A New and Complete Treatise on the Arts of Tanning, Currying & Leather-Dressing*, London & Philadelphia, 1865

East Lothian County Planning Department, *East Lothian Water Mills*, Haddington, 1970

English, W., *The Textile Industry*, London, 1969

Fairbairn, Sir W., *Treatise on Mills and Millwork*, 2 vols., 4th Edition, London, 1878

Farey, J., *A Treatise on the Steam Engine*, London, 1827

Fell, A., *The Early Iron Industry of Furness & District*, Ulverston, 1908

Fenton, A., *Scottish Country Life*, Edinburgh, 1976

Findlater, C., *General View of the Agriculture of Peeblesshire*, Edinburgh, 1802

Fleming, J. A., *Scottish Pottery*, Glasgow, 1923

Flinn, M. W., *Origins of the Industrial Revolution*, London, 1966

Forsyth, R., *The Beauties of Scotland*, 5 vols., Edinburgh, 1806

Fraser, A., *Lochfyneside*, Edinburgh, 1971

Gale, W. K. V., *The British Iron & Steel Industry*, Newton Abbot, 1967

Gauldie, E. (ed.), 'The Dundee Textile Industry, 1790-1885', *SHS*, 4th Series, IV, 1969

Gauldie, Enid, *The Scottish Country Miller, 1700-1900*, Edinburgh, 1981

Geddie, J., *The Water of Leith from Source to Sea*, Edinburgh, 1896.

Gibson, R. (Gibson, T. (ed.)), *An Old Berwickshire Town*, Edinburgh, 1905

Gibson, W., *Reminiscences of Dollar, Tillicoultry and Other Districts Adjoining the Ochils*, Edinburgh, 1883

Gilbert, K. R., *The Portsmouth Block-Making Machinery*, London, 1965

Gillespie, J. H., *Dundonald*, 2 vols., Glasgow, 1939

Gillies, W. A., *In Famed Breadalbane*, Perth, 1938

Glynn, J., *Power of Water*, 5th Edition, London, 1875

Gordon, T. C., *A Short History of Alloa*, Alloa, 1937

Gordon, T. C., *The History of Clackmannan*, Glasgow, 1937

Graham, P., *General View of the Agriculture of Stirlingshire*, Edinburgh, 1812

Grant, E. (Lady Strachey), *Reminiscences of a Highland Lady*, Revised Edition, London, 1960

Gray, A., *The Experienced Millwright*, London, 1806

Gray, A., *A Treatise on Spinning Machinery*, Edinburgh, 1819

Gray, W. F. & Jamieson, J. H., *A Short History of Haddington*, Edinburgh, 1944

Greenshield, J. B., *Annals of Lesmahagow*, Edinburgh, 1864

Grewar, D., *The Story of Glenisla*, Aberdeen, 1926

Gribbon, H. B., *The History of Water-Power in Ulster*, Newton Abbot, 1969

Grieve, S., *The Book of Colonsay & Oronsay*, 2 vols., Edinburgh, 1923

Grossart, W., *Historical Notes on the Parish of Shotts*, Glasgow, 1880

Gulvin, C., *The Tweedmakers*, Newton Abbot, 1973

Hall, R., *The History of Galashiels*, Galashiels, 1898

Hamilton, H., *The Industrial Revolution in Scotland*, Oxford, 1932

Hamilton, H. (ed.), 'Selections from the Monymusk Papers 1713-55', *SHS*, 3rd Series, XXXIX, 1945

Hamilton, H., *An Economic History of Scotland in the Eighteenth Century*, Oxford, 1963

Handley, J. E., *Scottish Farming in the Eighteenth Century*, London, 1953

Handley, J. E., *The Agricultural Revolution in Scotland*, Glasgow, 1963

Hartwell, R. M., *The Industrial Revolution and Economic Growth*, London, 1971

Harvey, C. C. H. & MacLeod, J., 'Calendar of Writs preserved at Yester House, 1166-1625', *SRS*, LV, 1930

Hay, G., *History of Arbroath*, Arbroath, 1876

Hay, J., *The Sound of the Mill*, Liverpool, 1924

Headrick, J., *General View of the Isle of Arran*, Edinburgh, 1807

Headrick, J., *General View of the Agriculture of Forfarshire*, Edinburgh, 1813

Henderson, E., *The Annals of Dunfermline*, Glasgow, 1879

Henderson, J., *General View of the Agriculture of Sutherland*, London, 1812

Hills, R. L., *Power in the Industrial Revolution*, Manchester, 1970

Home, H. (Lord Kames), *Progress of Flax Husbandry in Scotland*, Edinburgh, 1766

Hume, D., *Decisions of the Court of Session* (1781-1822), Edinburgh & London, 1839

Hume, J. R., *Industrial Archaeology of Glasgow*, Glasgow, 1974

Hume, J. R., *Industrial Archaeology of Scotland*, 2 vols., London, 1976-77

Hume-Brown, P., *Scotland in the Time of Queen Mary*, London, 1904

Huntly, Charles, Marquis of, 'Records of Aboyne', *New Spalding Club*, 1894

Hutchison, J. M., *Notes on the Sugar Industry of the United Kingdom*, Glasgow, 1901

Irons, J. C., *Leith & Its Antiquities*, 2 vols., Edinburgh, n.d.

Irving, J., *History of Dunbartonshire*, 3 vols., 1919-24

Jamieson, A., *A Dictionary of Mechanical Science*, 2 vols., London, 1827

Jenkins, J. G. (ed.), *The Wool Textile Industry in Great Britain*, London, 1972

Jespersen, A., *Gearing in Watermills in Western Europe*, Virum (Denmark), 1953

Jewitt, L., *The Ceramic Art of Great Britain*, 2 vols., London, 1878

Keith, G. S., *A General View of the Agriculture of Aberdeenshire*, Aberdeen, 1811

Kemp, D. W., *Notes on Early Iron Smelting in Sutherland*, Edinburgh, 1887

Kennedy, W., *Annals of Aberdeen*, 2 vols, London, 1818

Kerr, R., *General View of the Agriculture of the County of Berwick*, London, 1809

Kettleby, C. D. M., *Tullis Russel, 1809-1959*, Markinch, 1967

Lamont, Sir N. (ed.), 'An Inventory of Lamont Papers 1231-1897', SRS, LIV, Edinburgh, 1914

Leach, B., *A Potter's Book*, London, 1967

Leslie, W., *General View of the Agriculture of the Counties of Moray & Nairn*, London, 1811

Lewis, S., *Topographical Dictionary of Scotland*, 2 vols., London, 1846

Lindsay, I. G. & Cosh, M., *Inveraray & the Dukes of Argyll*, Edinburgh, 1973

Livingston, P. K., *Flax and Linen in Fife through the Centuries*, Kirkcaldy, 1952

Loch, D., *A Tour through Most of the Trading Towns and Villages of Scotland*, Edinburgh, 1778

Loch, J., *An Account of Improvements on the Estates of the Marquis of Stafford*, London, 1820

Lord, J., *Capital and Steam Power, 1750-1800*, 2nd Edition, London, 1966

Lothian, J., *Alloa and its Environs*, Alloa, 1871

Loudon, J. C., *Encyclopaedia of Agriculture*, London, 1825

Low, D., *Report on Marchmont Estate*, Printed Privately, 1819

Low D., *On Landed Property and the Economy of Estates*, London, 1844

Lythe, S. G. E., *The Economy of Scotland in its European Setting, 1550-1625*, Edinburgh, 1960

Lythe, S. G. E. & Butt, J., *An Economic History of Scotland, 1100-1939*, London, 1975

MacAdam, J. H., *The Baxter Books of St. Andrews*, Leith, 1903

MacArthur, J., *New Monkland Parish*, Glasgow, 1890

McArthur, M. (ed.), 'Survey of Lochtayside 1769', SHS, XXVII, 1936

Macarthur, W. F., *History of Port Glasgow*, Glasgow, 1932

McCall, H. B., *The History & Antiquities of the Parish of Mid-Calder*, Edinburgh, 1894

Macdonald, J. A. R., *A History of Blairgowrie*, Blairgowrie, 1899

McDowall, J., *History of Dumfries*, Edinburgh, 1867

MacGill, W., *Old Ross-shire and Scotland*, Inverness, 1909

McInnes, C. T. (ed.), 'Calendar of Writs of Munro of Fowlis, 1299-1823', SRS, LXXI, 1940

MacJannet, A. F., *Royal Burgh of Irvine*, Glasgow, 1938

Mackay, W., *Urquhart & Glenmoriston*, Inverness, 1893

McKechnie, K., *A Border Woollen Town in the Industrial Revolution*, London, 1968

MacKenzie, R. D., *Kilbarchan, A Parish History*, Paisley, 1902

MacKenzie, W. C., *Andrew Fletcher of Saltoun*, Edinburgh, 1935

McKerral, A., *Kintyre in the Seventeenth Century*, Edinburgh, 1948

McKinnon, J., *The Social & Industrial History of Scotland from the Union to the Present Day*, London, 1921

McLean, A. (ed.), *The Local Industries of Glasgow and the West of Scotland* (B.A. Handbook), Glasgow, 1901

MacLeod, D., *Dumbarton and the Vale of Leven*, Dumbarton, 1884

MacLeod, D., *Clyde District of Dunbartonshire*, Dumbarton, 1886

McNeil, I., *Hydraulic Power*, London, 1972

NcNeil, P., *Prestonpans & Vicinity*, Tranent, 1911

Mactavish, D. C., *Inveraray Papers*, Oban, 1939

McVeigh, Patrick, *Scottish East Coast Potteries, 1750-1840*, Edinburgh, 1979

Mackie, A. D., *An Industrial History of Edinburgh*, Glasgow, 1963

Maitland, W., *History of Edinburgh*, Edinburgh, 1753

Martine, J., *Reminiscences of Fourteen Parishes of Haddingtonshire*, Haddington, 1894

Martine, J., *Reminiscences & Notices of Ten Parishes of the County of Haddington*, Haddington, 1894

Maxwell, R., *Select Transactions of the Honourable Society of Improvers in the Knowledge of Agriculture in Scotland*, Edinburgh, 1743

Metcalf, W. M., *A History of the County of Renfrew from the Earliest Times*, Paisley, 1905

Metcalfe, W. M., *A History of Paisley, 600-1908*, Paisley, 1909

Miller, A. H. (ed.), 'A Selection of Scottish Forfeited Estates Papers, 1715, 1745', *SHS*, LVII, 1909

Miller, J., *The Lamp of Lothian or the History of Haddington*, Haddington, 1844

Miller, J., *History of Dunbar*, Dunbar, 1859

Mitchell, Sir A. (ed.), 'Macfarlane's Geographical Collections', *SHS*, LI, 1906; LII, 1907; LIII, 1908

Mitchell, Sir A. & Cash, C. G., *A Contribution to the Bibliography of Scottish Topography*, Edinburgh, 1917

Mollyson, C. A., *The Parish of Fordoun*, Aberdeen, 1893

Monteath, R., *The Forester's Guide & Profitable Planter*, Edinburgh, 1824

Morgan, P., *Annals of Woodside & Newhills*, Aberdeen, 1886

Morrison, W. M., *Dictionary of Decisions of the Court of Session*, 36 vols., Edinburgh, 1811

Murdoch, A., *Ochiltree. Its History and Reminiscences*, Paisley, 1921

Murray, A., *The True Interest of Great Britain, Ireland and Our Plantations*, London, 1740

Murray, A., *The Upper Ward of Lanarkshire*, 3 vols., Glasgow, 1864

Murray, D., *The York Buildings Company. A Chapter in Scotch History*, Glasgow, 1883

Murray, J., *Kilmalcolm*, Paisley, 1898

Musson, E. A. & Robinson, E., *Science and Technology in the Industrial Revolution*, Manchester, 1969

Naismith, J., *Thoughts on the Various Objects of Industry Pursued in Scotland*, Edinburgh, 1790

National Coal Board, *A Short History of the Scottish Coal-Mining Industry*, 1958

Nef, J. U., *The Rise of the British Coal Industry*, 2 vols., London, 1932

Newcomen Society, 'Catalogue of Civil & Mechanical Engineering Designs, 1741-92, of John Smeaton, FRS', *Newcomen Society Extra Publications* No. 5, 1950

New Statistical Account of Scotland, Collected Edition, 15 vols., Edinburgh, 1845

Omand, D. (ed.), *The Caithness Book*, Inverness, 1972

Pelham, R. A., *Fulling Mills*, SPAB 1958

Pennant, T., *A Tour in Scotland, 1769*, 2nd Edition, London, 1772

Phillips, J. A. & Darlington, J., *Records of Mining & Metallurgy*, London, 1857

Pococke, R., 'Tours in Scotland, 1747, 1750, 1760', *SHS*, I, 1887

Porteous, A., *History of Crieff*, Edinburgh, 1912

Porteous, J. M., *God's Treasure House in Scotland*, London, 1876

Pride, D., *A History of the Parish of Neilston*, Paisley, 1910

Purves, Sir W., *Revenue of the Scottish Crown, 1681*, Edinburgh & London, 1897

Raistrick, A. & Jennings, B., *Lead Mining in the Pennines*, London, 1965

Reid, J. E., *History of the County of Bute*, Glasgow, 1864

Reid, R. C. (ed.), *The Records of the Western Marches*, Vol. 1, Dumfries, 1915

Reynolds, J., *Windmills and Water Mills*, Newton Abbot, 1970

Robertson, G., *A General View of the Agriculture of Kincardineshire*, London, 1813

Robertson, J., *General View of the Agriculture of Southern Perthshire*, London, 1794

Robertson, J., *General View of the Agriculture of Inverness-shire*, London, 1808

Robinson, E. & Musson, A. E., *James Watt and the Steam Engine*, London, 1969

Rolt, L. T. C., *Tools for the Job*, London, 1968

Romanes, C. S. (ed.), 'Selections from the Records of the Regality of Melrose', *SHS*, 2nd Series, VI (1605-61), 1914; VII (1662-76), 1915

Salmon, T. J., *Bo'ness and District, c.1550-1850*, Edinburgh, 1913

Scott, W. R., *Joint-Stock Companies to 1700*, 3 vols., Cambridge, 1910-12

Scott, W. R. (ed.), 'Newmills Cloth Manufactory, 1681-1703', *SHS*, XLVI, 1905

Scottish Women's Rural Institute, *Auchenblae*, Edinburgh, 1967

Shearar, A., *Extracts from the Burgh Records of Dunfermline*, Dunfermline, 1951

Shirley, G. W., *The Growth of a Scottish Burgh*, Dumfries, 1915

Shorter, A. H., *Paper-Making in the British Isles*, Newton Abbot, 1971

Sibbald, Sir R., *History of Fife and Kinross* (1710), Edinburgh, 1803

Sinclair, G., *The Hydrostaticks*, Edinburgh, 1672

Sinclair, Sir J. (ed.), *The (Old) Statistical Account of Scotland*, 21 vols., Edinburgh, 1791-99

Sinclair, Sir J., *An Account of the Systems of Husbandry of Scotland*, 2 vols., Edinburgh, 1813

Sinclair, Sir J., *General Report of the Agricultural State and Political Circumstances of Scotland*, 3 vols., and Appendix, 2 vols., Edinburgh, 1814

Singer, C., Holmyard, E. J., Hall, A. R. & Williams, T. I. (eds.), *A History of Technology*, 5 vols., Oxford, 1956-9

Singer, W., *General View of the Agriculture of the County of Dumfries*, Edinburgh, 1812

(Smeaton, J.), *Reports of the Late John Smeaton*, 3 vols., London, 1812

Smiles, S., *Lives of the Engineers*, 5 vols., London, 1874

Smith, G. G., *The Book of Islay*, Glasgow, 1895

Smith, J., *General View of the Agriculture of Argyll*, London, 1805

Smith, J. G., *The Parish of Strathblane*, Glasgow, 1886

Smith, R. M., *History of Greenock*, Greenock, 1921

Smith, S., *General View of the Agriculture of Galloway*, London, 1813

Smout, T. C., 'Lead Mining in Scotland, 1650-1850', in Payne, P. L. (ed.), *Studies in Scottish Business History*, London, 1967

Smout, T. C., *A History of the Scottish People, 1560-1830*, London, 1969

Somerville, R., *General View of the Agriculture of East Lothian*, London, 1805

Souter, D., *General View of the Agriculture of the County of Banff*, Edinburgh, 1812

Southey, R., *Journal of a Tour in Scotland, 1819*, Facsimile Edition, Edinburgh, 1972

Steven, H. J., *Sorn Parish. Its History and Associations*, Glasgow, 1898

Stewart, A., *A Highland Parish or the History of Fortingall*, Glasgow, 1928

Stewart, J., *List of Pollable People in the Shire of Aberdeen, 1696*, 2 vols., Aberdeen, 1844

Stewart, W., *Brewing & Distillation*, Edinburgh, 1849

Strada, O., *Kunstliche Abriss, aller handt Wasserkunsten*, Basel, 1618

Svedenstierna, E. T. (translated Dellow, E. L.), *Svedenstierna's Tour of Great Britain, 1802-3*, Newton Abbot, 1973.

Taylor, C., *The Levern Delineated*, Glasgow, 1831

Taylor, F. S., *A History of Industrial Chemistry*, London, 1957

Thomson, A., *Lauder & Lauderdale*, Galashiels, n.d. (c.1902)

Thomson, A., *Coldingham Parish & Priory*, Galashiels, 1908

Thomson, A. G., *The Paper Industry in Scotland*, Edinburgh, 1974

Thomson, J., *General View of the Agriculture of Fife*, Edinburgh, 1800

Towner, D., *Creamware*, London, 1978

Trotter, J. F. (ed.), *The Book of Buchan*, Peterhead, 1910

Trotter, J., *General View of the Agriculture of Linlithgowshire*, Edinburgh, 1794

Trotter, J., *General View of the Agriculture of Linlithgowshire*, Edinburgh, 1811

Turner, G., *The Ancient Iron Industry of Stirlingshire and Neighbourhood*, Stirling, 1919

Ure, A., *The Cotton Manufacture of Great Britain*, 2 vols., London, 1836

Ure, D., *The History of Rutherglen & East Kilbride*, Glasgow, 1793

Vincent, C. W. (ed.), *Chemistry as Applied to the Arts and Manufactures*, 8 vols., London, n.d. (c.1875-80)

Wailes, R., *Tide Mills*, SPAB Pt. 1 1956, Pt. 2 1957

Warden, A. J., *The Linen Trade Ancient & Modern*, London, 1864

Warwick, J., *History of Old Cumnock*, Paisley, 1899

Webster, J. M., *History of Carnock*, Dunfermline, 1912

Weir, D., *History of the Town of Greenock*, Greenock, 1829

Whitehead, W. Y., *History of Ormiston*, Haddington, 1937

Whyte, A. & MacFarlane, D., *General View of the Agriculture of Dunbartonshire*, Glasgow, 1811

Wight, A., *Present State of Husbandry in Scotland*, 4 vols., Edinburgh, 1778-84

Wilson, G. V., *Special Report on the Mineral Resources of Great Britain*, Vol. XVIII, *Lead, Zinc, Copper & Nickel Ores of Scotland*, Edinburgh, 1921

Wilson, J., *General View of the Agriculture of Renfrewshire*, Paisley, 1812

Wilson, J. J., *The Annals of Penicuik*, Edinburgh, 1891

Wilson, P. N., *Watermills: an Introduction*, SPAB 1956

Wilson, R., *A Sketch of the History of Hawick*, Hawick, 1825

Woodcroft, B., *Alphabetical Index of Patentees of Inventions*, Facsimile Edition, London, 1969

Young, A., *History of Burntisland*, Kirkcaldy, 1913

Youngson, A. W., *Remarks on Blairadam Estate*, 6 vols., Printed Privately, 1834

Miscellaneous Publications

Dictionary of the Older Scottish Tongue, Edinburgh, 1937 *et seq*

'The Justiciary Records of Argyll & the Isles 1664-1742', Stair Society, XXV

'Reports on the State of Certain Parishes in Scotland 1627', Maitland Club, XXXIV (1835)

RCAHMS, Argyll, Vol. 2, *Lorn*, Edinburgh, 1975

SBRS, 'Extracts from the Records of the Burgh of Aberdeen', III (1643-1747), Edinburgh, 1872

SBRS, 'Extracts from the Records of the Burgh of Edinburgh':

II	(1528-57)	Edinburgh, 1871
III	(1557-71)	Edinburgh, 1875
IV	(1573-89)	Edinburgh, 1882

V	(1589-1603)	Edinburgh, 1927
VI	(1604-26)	Edinburgh, 1931
VII	(1626-41)	Edinburgh, 1936
VIII	(1642-55)	Edinburgh, 1938
IX	(1655-65)	Edinburgh, 1940
X	(1665-80)	Edinburgh, 1950
XI	(1681-89)	Edinburgh, 1954
XII	(1689-1701)	Edinburgh, 1962

SBRS, 'Extracts from the Records of the Burgh of Glasgow':

I	(1573-1642)	Glasgow, 1876
II	(1630-62)	Glasgow, 1881
III	(1663-90)	Glasgow, 1905
IV	(1691-1717)	Glasgow, 1908
V	(1718-38)	Glasgow, 1909
VI	(1739-59)	Glasgow, 1911
VII	(1760-80)	Glasgow, 1912
VIII	(1781-95)	Glasgow, 1913
IX	(1796-1808)	Glasgow, 1914
X	(1809-22)	Glasgow, 1915
XI	(1823-33)	Glasgow, 1916

SBRS, 'Extracts from the Records of the Burgh of Lanark' (1150-1722), Glasgow, 1893.

SBRS, 'Charters & Documents Relating to the Burgh of Peebles' (1165-1710), Edinburgh, 1872

SBRS, 'Extracts from the Records of the Burgh of Peebles' (1652-1714), Glasgow, 1910

SBRS, 'Extracts from the Records of the Royal Burgh of Stirling' (1519-1666), Glasgow, 1887; (1667-1752), Glasgow, 1889

The Scottish National Dictionary, 10 vols., Edinburgh, 1929-76

'Synod of Fife, 1611-87', Abbotsford Club, 1837

Index

The abbreviations following placenames refer to pre-1975 counties and cities, and to countries other than Scotland, as follows:

ABD	Aberdeen	IRL	Ireland
ABER	Aberdeen City	KCB	Kirkcudbright
ANG	Angus	KCD	Kincardine
ARG	Argyll	KNR	Kinross
AYR	Ayr	LAN	Lanark
BNF	Banff	MLO	Midlothian
BTE	Bute	MOR	Moray
BWK	Berwick	NAI	Nairn
CAI	Caithness	ORK	Orkney
CLA	Clackmannan	PEB	Peebles
DNB	Dunbarton	PER	Perth
DMF	Dumfries	RNF	Renfrew
DUND	Dundee	ROS	Ross
EDIN	Edinburgh	ROX	Roxburgh
ELO	East Lothian	SHE	Shetland
ENG	England	SLK	Selkirk
FIF	Fife	STL	Stirling
GAL	Galloway	SUT	Sutherland
GLAS	Glasgow	WAL	Wales
HEB	Hebrides	WIG	Wigtown
INV	Inverness	WLO	West Lothian

Numbers in *italics* refer to figures.

Strontian ARG 396, 400, 401, 404, 405, 407
Strowan, Kirkton of PER 270
Struan estate PER 454
Struthey, Thomas 510
Sugar works:
 Greenock RNF 470, 485, Table 11
Sunderland ENG 449
Surgeons 325
Surtees, John 424
Sutherland 159, 160
Sutherland, Duke of 160
Sutherland, William 293
Swellhead KCD 163
Swiss 343

Tain ROS 175
Tait, John 54
TANNING *see* LEATHER WORKING
Tarbolton AYR 482
Tartreven WLO *see* Hilderston
Tarves ABD 160
Tasker, Young & Co. 470, 485
Tay, River 95, 345, 527
Taylor, Walter 441
Taymouth Castle PER 119
Team Ironworks ENG 423
TECHNOLOGY:
 108-11, 533-44
 Gearing 108-9
 Sluices 110
 Water bucket pumps 393
 Water pressure engines 393, 408, 495,
  538-40
  Sites:
   Granton EDIN 495
   Leadhills LAN 533-4
 Water turbines 495-8, 505, 517, 534, 544
  Fourneyron 495
  Pelton wheel 517
  Ponselet wheels 495, 496
  Scotch turbines 496
  Vortex 496-8
  Sites:
   Brooklinn Mill PER 498
   Carron Ironworks STL 436, 498, 534
   Greenock REN 485
 Water wheels 12, 5, 109-11
  Horizontal 1-11
   Sites:
    Black Mill of Clocheran PER 8
    Caithness 6
    Dalswinton DMF 2
    Howmuir ANG 156
    Kinlochbervie SUT 7
    Kintyre ARG 7-8
    Kirkomy SUT 6-7
    Lewis 5

Mill of Ednaughtie ANG 8-9
Mill of Foyell PER 9
Mull 5
Orkney 5
Shetland 2-3, 6
Tara IRL 2
Taransay 5
Vertical 11
See also MILLWRIGHTS and main
 headings: Technology
Teith, River PER 165
Telfer, Alexander 395, 398, 404
Telfer, William 395, 404
Telfort, William 446
Terrand, Richardson 409
Terreoch AYR 430
Thom, Robert 482
Thomson, Alexander 379
Thomson Brothers 495
Thomson, David 289
Thomson, James 496
Thomson, John 157
Thomson, Thomas 424
Thomson, William 283, 289
Thomson, William junior 289
Thomson, W. & D. 283
Thornliebank RNF 334, 343
Thorntonloch ELO 87
Thread-makers 236, 253
THREAD MILLS:
 351-3, 520
 Beating 352-3
  Sites:
   Dighty Water ANG 353
   Greenburn ABD 353
   Lethan (Dunnichen) ANG 353
   Lundie ANG 353
   Mill of Craigo ANG 353
   Mill of Logie ANG 353
   Monifieth ANG 353
   St Vigeans ANG 353
 Twisting 351-3
  Sites:
   Bonnington Mills EDIN 353
   Dalquhurn DNB 353
   Dumfries 353
   Elgin MOR 353
   Kirkoswald AYR 353
   Pencaitland ELO 353
   Pettyvaich BNF 353
   Strathmiglo FIF 353
THRESHING:
 Hand 155, 161
 Mill 102, 103-4, 106, 109, 155-62, 429,
  499, 542
 Benefits 161-2
 Development 155-9
 Diffusion 159-60
 Sources of power 160-1